THE WORKS

OF

RUFUS CHOATE

WITH A

MEMOIR OF HIS LIFE.

BY

SAMUEL GILMAN BROWN,

PROFESSOR IN DARTMOUTH COLLEGE.

Ἐν μύρτου κλαδὶ τὸ ξίφος ἐφόρει.

IN TWO VOLUMES.

VOL. II.

BOSTON:

LITTLE, BROWN AND COMPANY.

1862.

RIVERSIDE, CAMBRIDGE:
PRINTED BY H. O. HOUGHTON

CONTENTS OF VOLUME II.

SPEECHES IN THE SENATE OF THE UNITED STATES.

MISCELLANEOUS SPEECHES.

APPENDIX.

ERRATA FOR VOL. II.

Page 469, 10th line from bottom, *read* Corcyra for Epidamnus.
Page 470, 10th line from bottom, just before the figure 3, a sentence is omitted, viz: "They were willing also to refer the case to the oracle at Delphi."
Page 480, 6th line from top, *read* one thousand for ten thousand.

SPEECHES

IN THE

SENATE OF THE UNITED STATES.

SPEECH

IN THE CASE OF ALEXANDER McLEOD.[1]

DELIVERED IN THE SENATE OF THE UNITED STATES, FRIDAY, JUNE 11, 1841.

[The business before the Senate being the motion of Mr. Rives to refer so much of the President's Message as relates to our foreign affairs to the Committee on Foreign Affairs, Mr. Choate spoke as follows:]

I REGRET to be obliged to consume a moment of the crowded time of the senate in a discussion which can produce no practical results. But as the subject has been forced upon the friends of the Secretary of State and of the Administration, it possesses a good deal of interest intrinsically, and, therefore, holding a place upon the Committee of Foreign Relations, to whom it perhaps appropriately belongs, I venture to submit a few thoughts upon it less maturely considered than I could wish. I fear I can add little to the splendid and masterly speech of the Senator from Virginia. [Mr. Rives.]

I confess that when I read, a few days since, the letter of the Secretary of State to Mr. Fox, on which the Senator from Pennsylvania [Mr. Buchanan] has commented, it seemed to me written with much ability, and that it ought to and would satisfy the judgment and feelings of the whole American people. The views it presented I thought sound, clear, and some of them new; the manner, not an unimportant consideration, good; frank, decided, not rude, not boisterous, not timid; and the whole tone, temper, and spirit elevated, national, American; worthy of the man, the cause, and the country. The objections taken to it in this debate seemed to me to be its essential

[1] A brief account of this case will be found in Vol. I. p. 49.

merits. By concealing just what he did, and by denying just what he did, he had gone far, I thought, to withdraw this controversy about The Caroline from the false position it rested upon, and to place it on such grounds that it may be adjusted with ease and honor, or, if we must fight, that we may carry into battle the approbation of our own consciences, and the supports of a just pride.

So the letter struck my mind. Other gentlemen, or, at least, one other, regard it differently. And, in the first place, a doubt is intimated by the distinguished Senator from Pennsylvania, whether the concession of the Secretary, that a person in the asserted predicament of McLeod is entitled to immunity, assumes an accurate proposition of international law. He argues that it does not; and he holds the opinion that we may well enough hang that person for robbery and murder; that we may do this in entire conformity with the received ameliorated codes of international law of the nineteenth century, and without justly bringing on ourselves a murmur of disapprobation from any of the families of man, or any individual of any family. Sir, let us pause for a moment on this great question of nations.

What is the concession of the Secretary of State? Why, only and exactly this: that a soldier or sailor — *de facto* such — actually engaged in a military or naval enterprise of force, under the authority, in obedience to the command, of his government, and keeping himself within the scope of that authority, is not guilty, as the law of nations is administered to-day, of a crime against the municipal code of the country upon which he thus helps to carry on war; that he is not punishable as for such crime by that country; and that the responsibility rests upon his own government alone to answer, as nations answer for their crimes to their equals. That is the concession. He does not deal at all with the case of a soldier straggling away from his colors to commit a solitary and separate murder. He does not deal with a case of alleged excess of authority. He supposes him to obey the precise directions of his government, and, so doing, he declares him clothed with a personal immunity.

It has been said in some of the discussions of this subject, although not here, that McLeod left The Caroline after the whole object of the enterprise had been accomplished, and committed an unnecessary and distinct and malicious murder on shore. I can only say to this that no such fact forms any part of the basis of the opinion of the Secretary. He had either never heard of it, or he disbelieved it, or he assumed that the courts of law, or the Attorney-General, would allow its proper influence to a discriminating circumstance so important.

If you turn to the fourth page of his letter, you may see that the murder for which he supposes McLeod is indicted was " a murder alleged to have been committed in the attack ; " forming an inseparable, very painful part of the entire military violence exerted to capture and destroy the vessel, and not succeeding it. For the purposes of the concession, he takes for true the express declaration of Mr. Fox, " that the transaction, on account of which Mr. McLeod has been arrested and is to be put on his trial," including the homicide as an unavoidable incident in it, " was a public transaction " conducted by her Majesty's Government.

Such is the concession. I have the honor to submit, first, that the concession is right, in point of international law; and then, that it was the duty of the Secretary of State to make it, and of the government to act upon it, exactly as it was made and acted upon.

In entering on this investigation, then, you observe that, to a certain distance, we proceed on all sides of the senate harmoniously together. Thus, it is admitted by the Senator from Pennsylvania, and by everybody, that persons taken fighting, or for having fought, in the battles of an open, general, regularly declared war, are not responsible as for crime committed by the act of fighting against the country which they devastate and wrap in mourning and blood. They become technically prisoners of war. As such, on a principle of policy, as a mode of prosecuting war, they are subjected to restraint, imprisoned, held to ransom, exchanged, and otherwise disposed of, with more or less indulgence and humanity, according to circumstances. But criminals, robbers, murderers, by the act of fighting, although the act involved the destruction of property and life, they are not by the theory or practice of any civilized race of men.

Thus far we proceed together. On this admitted principle we all stand, and from this we all take our departure. The truth is, the nations have agreed, and that agreement makes the law of nations, that it is a duty and a virtue in the individual citizen — his first duty, his highest virtue — to be obedient to his own government. They have agreed to regard him, as our Decatur, the elder Decatur, said of his children, as the property of his country. Whithersoever he goes, whatsoever he does, wheresoever he lies down, slain in battle in obedience to her sacred and parental command, it is, as the general rule, not imputed to him for crime at all. His nation, the collective natural person, must answer it on the high places of the world, and to the whole extent of the undefinable responsibilities of war.

If, therefore, McLeod had been a member of one of those bodies of troops which, during the last war, occasionally passed our line of boundary, burning our dwellings and killing our people, and had been taken even at the time, and with the red hand, he could not have been declared guilty of a crime against any law of a State or of the Union.

Setting out from this admitted principle, the real question is, whether the special circumstances, under which McLeod's government sent him forth to this midnight work of strife and blood, withdraw him from the protection of the principle of individual immunity with which humanity and wisdom have relieved and adorned the law of nations? What were those special circumstances? Exactly these. He was a soldier or sailor, *de facto*, for the time, for the act, in a military and naval expedition of force, planned and sent abroad by his own legitimate government, having the right to exact his service to the last drop of his blood,—sent abroad not to plunder, but, as it represented to him when it called him out of his bed, and disclosed its purpose, to do an act for the defence of the country he lived in against invasion. This expedition was a single act, not preceded nor followed by any other; it was preceded by no declaration of war, and, as this government alleges, it was unjustifiable. Such were the circumstances; and the question is, Do they withdraw him from the principle of personal responsibility?

Let me say, then, first, that in proceeding to determine

whether that principle shall or shall not be applied to a given special case arising in the ever-varying developments of things, the inclination of civilized States will be, and ought to be, to take the principle largely and liberally in favor of individual immunity, and of exclusive national responsibility. Every motive which operated to introduce the principle into the law of nations at first is a motive to an enlarged and benignant construction and application of it to-day. Its adoption originally marked a vast advance on the ferocious systems of what we call natural society. It was a grand triumph of reason as well as of humanity. Policy and wisdom carried the world up to it, as well as right feeling. It was resorted to to relieve war of its horrors while it lasted; to make it easier to go back to peace, which is the true condition of man; to ameliorate the stern lot of the millions whom, in one age and in one country and another, force or patriotism crowds into the ranks of their country; and to lift up war itself from a vulgar and dreary business of general butchery, to a service of glory, in which great souls may engage without degradation and without deterioration. These were the motives in which the principle was made part at first of the law of nations; and every one of them is a motive to give it the most expanded application in the light of this better day. Sir, it is one of the brightest glories of civilization. Do not cause it to be dimmed by a penurious and reluctant interpretation and application. To do so would be to misconceive the direction in which the world is moving. I do not know when wars shall wholly cease; but I believe, I trust, that as the world comes nearer to that time, it will regard war more and more every day as an enormous evil, if a necessary evil, and will desire to relieve it more and more every day by the offices of Christian and of chivalrous forbearance towards individual actors, — struck down, unarmed, and unresisting.

Giving, then, to the law of personal immunity that enlarged effect which the time and the country demand, let us attend to the special circumstances, one by one, which mark the case of McLeod, and see if they do or do not leave him the protection which is thrown round the captive of open, regular war.

In the first place, observe that the expedition on which he went out was an expedition of war. It was not an expedition to rob the mail, or to rob a hen-roost, or to throw an assassin or spy into an enemy's camp, by which happy analogies we have had it illustrated. It was an enterprise of war, undertaken under the iron responsibilities, surrounded by the iron rights of war. Its exact legal denomination is "*informal, insolemn hostility*." Let us call things by their right names, and hold England and hold ourselves up consistently to this view of the transaction. Look at it. There was a forcible temporary occupation of our territory by an armed foreign body, acting in organization, sent across by a foreign government as a government, — not for plunder, but as an alleged grave measure of state policy, — for the alleged defence of its own soil and its own law against revolutionary invaders from without. What sort of act is that, Sir? The mover is a government; the inducement a high reason of state; the instruments and the effects such as ordinarily do the work, and mark the giant tread of war. Armed men violently assail a vessel moored on our waters, owned by our citizens, — reposing, as we allege, beneath the protection — not forfeited — of the folds of our flag. It is the cry of brief but actual battle, which rises above the murmur of that onward, unreturning stream. The peace of our territory was disturbed; its sanctity was violated; the charmed life of an American citizen was taken in fight; the property of an American citizen — itself part of the general wealth of the community — was destroyed. This, Sir, in the language of the publicists, is "informal hostility" against the United States; and the responsibility of England, who ordered it to be committed, and the immunity of the soldiers who enforced the order with the bayonet and cutlass, result, of course, according to the principle on which, as I have said, we all take our stand, and in which all publicists agree. I do not say that by this act England intended to begin a war on the United States, or to impair our strength, diminish our treasure, or insult our flag as a nation. Certainly not. But the act which she does is to invade our territory forcibly and unlawfully for the purpose of reaching and destroying the property of one of our citizens, which she had no right so to reach and so to destroy, and to effect that purpose by military violence and by shedding innocent blood in battle. And this act is hostility against us because our rights are outraged, — and they are outraged by the methods and the processes and according to the forms of war; and because every nation and every man must be holden to intend the acts which he does and their necessary consequences. How do you distinguish this proceeding from the attack on Copenhagen in 1808, to which the Senator from Virginia alluded last evening? What was that transaction? England, cherishing no hostile feeling against Denmark, (for Denmark, like herself, was actually in arms against the Emperor of the French,) conceived a fear that that ancient, gallant, but not very powerful nation might fall before him; in which case her sixteen ships-of-war would become his, — a formidable accession to the strength by which he was urging forward his aim of universal dominion. Thereupon she sent Admiral Gambier to Copenhagen, bombarded it, killed and wounded above a thousand persons, and carried off the whole Danish fleet. That is, she forcibly invades the Danish territory for the purpose of possessing herself of divers ships, of which, as against Denmark, she had no right to take possession, — not for the purpose of weakening or insulting her, but to prevent their becoming, in other hands, the instruments of annoyance against herself. So here. She invades our territory with military force for the purpose of possessing herself of a vessel, of which, as against us, she had no right thus to take possession, — not to weaken or insult us, but to prevent its being, in other hands, the instrument of annoyance against herself. The cases are alike cases of informal war against the nation whose national rights are invaded. In the affair of Copenhagen, the object of the invasion was the capture of Danish government ships. If, instead of that, it had been Danish merchant ships, — lest their cargoes might go to fill the coffers of France, or to transport French munitions of war, — would the act have been at all the less an act of hostility against Denmark? Nay, if Denmark had been neutral, and the object had been to cut out a French ship which had fled to Copenhagen for shelter, it would still have been a hostile aggression against Denmark herself. The attack upon Copenhagen was upon a grander scale than that upon The Caroline, — more ships, more men, greater names, a more picturesque arrangement of the spectacle of war. But the essential character, the legal name, the legal conse quences — national and personal — were the same. Sir, if one government trespasses on the rights of another by the employment of warlike instruments, it is, to the extent of the trespass, war on the injured nation.

But I advance to a second and far more important circumstance. The expedition in which he served was the act of a government competent to compel him to serve. Independent of or prior to any knowledge or approval of the act by the mother-country, it was so. I wholly reject the suggestion that this daring enterprise was at first an unauthorized proceeding of individuals, and that it subsequently became the act of a government by ratification. From beginning to end it was the work of a government, and of a government having the right to exact McLeod's obedience to the last drop of his blood. Who planned and conducted the attack? The Colonial authorities. Such is, for substance, the explicit declaration of Mr. Fox. Such is the legal conclusion from the facts stated by Sir Francis Head in his despatch of the twentieth of January, 1838. Sir, the matter stands exactly thus: The Colonial authorities specially empowered Colonel McNab to defend her Majesty's territories, and to defend her Majesty's subjects. Such is the concurrent statement of Mr. Fox and Sir Francis Head. For this purpose they expressly empowered him to adopt all needful defensive measures; and they thereby clothed him, by inevitable implication, with the discretionary power of judging what measures were needful. In the exercise of that discretion, he judged this measure to be needful, and he adopted it. Now, for the protection of the soldiers by whom it was achieved, it is precisely as if the Colonial authorities had directly and in terms planned and commanded it. Colonel McNab, for this purpose, conclusively represented them. How could a common soldier pronounce or conjecture that the judgment of the official representative was erroneous? Sir, he had the right, and was bound to assume it to be the judgment of the Colonial authorities. And who were they? Why, as between them and McLeod, and for the purposes of this question of individual immunity as between McLeod and ourselves, they were his rightful and only government. Nice questions may be moved on the competency of a Colonial government, from its subordinate relations to the imperial head, to set on foot an enterprise of war. But it is everywhere conceded that such a government may undertake defensive war. The mother-country, by the act of establishing it, clothes it with the power, and imposes on it the duty of defending itself; and it clothes it also with the power of judging for itself, in the first instance, how that duty shall be done. When, therefore, it resolves that a particular measure of war is necessary for its defence, and that the crisis requires a blow to be struck at once, and without waiting for advice from the paramount power at home, it may call the whole Colonial population to arms by day or night; and obedience to such a call is as rightful as unavoidable, and as effective for individual immunity as the obedience of a conscript or an impressed seaman. Such was this case. Was McLeod to say that the Colonial authorities misjudged on the question of necessity? They told him the defence of the territory and of the constitution of Upper Canada required this act. Did he know better? Did he command a wider horizon of view? Could he be sure he had all the elements of a sounder opinion? Consider that to the Colonial residents the Colonial government is everything. It is all of majesty, of monarchy, of aristocracy that he ever sees in his life. To that all his duties appear to be owing; and consider, too, that the spirit of this grand principle of individual responsibility is, that *bonâ fide* obedience to his actual and lawful government on a requisition of warlike service shall never be reckoned a crime in any man.

You have before you, then, the case of a government commanding a subject who was bound to obey, to shoulder his musket for the defence of his country. It is true, the Senator from Pennsylvania tells us that McLeod was a volunteer. But he deduces no legal conclusion from the fact; undoubtedly because he remembers that, by the admitted doctrine of international law, no distinction is recognized between volunteer and any other soldiers. He will remember that Vattel, at page 401, is a direct authority for this. In the reason of the case there can be no distinction. The regularly enlisted soldier engages voluntarily at first for a longer term, and for all service; the volunteer engages for a shorter term, and for a special service. But both alike go forth to execute an authoritative public will, and both stand, therefore, on the same plane of immunity and hazard. Consider, Sir, what a great concern of all nations it is, — and of ours more than all others, — to hold a rule of international law on this subject that shall make their inhabitants willing and ready to leap to arms, at half a moment's warning, at the midnight cry of their country.

You have, then, I repeat, the case of a government commanding a subject to go forth to an enterprise of war. Why is he not, then, within the terms and spirit of the great principle of immunity which we all agree surrounds the soldier of a formal and public war? What are the peculiarities that distinguish this particular service from the general trade of war? Why, Sir, they are said to be these: that it was a single act of hostility, not preceded nor followed by any other, not preceded by a declaration, and wholly unjust. This is all true, but for the objects of this inquiry it is wholly immaterial. Sir, publicists and the practice of nations recognize various modes, kinds, and degrees of hostility. War is not always general or "perfect," nor is it always preceded by a declaration. It sometimes begins and ends with one single crushing blow. Such was the attack on Copenhagen in 1801, and that in 1808. It may be limited to one single act of reprisals, by a single individual, under a license communicated to him alone. A foreign power has seized his ship, and his own government gives him letters of marque to help himself to another. In point of fact, too, war often begins without any declaration at all, at home or abroad. The bolt outruns the flash. Modern history is full of such instances; but I spare you the rehearsal of them. Now, Sir, what I would say, is, that for the purposes of immunity to the soldier and sailor, all these modes, kinds, and degrees of war, come exactly to the same thing. They are all, and all alike, modes of governmental action, involving only governmental responsibility. In many things they certainly differ one from another. Some of them are more chivalrous, more magnanimous, more conformable with a strict and punctilious proceeding, and a technical law of war, than others.

Some of them afford less ground of complaint to the government assailed than others. But, for the purpose of personal irresponsibility, they are all one and the same thing. In reason it must be so. Consider that a leading object of this principle of immunity is the protection of the unfriended instruments of ambition or patriotism who furnish the rank and file of war. It is to protect the common soldier. And what an unavailing, uncertain, ensnaring thing it would prove for him, if his title to it depended on such shades of diversity as these! How does he know whether the war, to which you hurry him away from all that is dearest to him in the world, is just or unjust? How does he know by what heralds of declaration it has been preceded? How does he know whether the desperate midnight enterprise, for which you have called him up from sleep, is to be a single enterprise, or whether it is designed to kindle the fires of a war that shall encircle the world? Sir, he knows only that his own government, in obedience to which he was bred, that the land of his birth, — that the land of his fathers' graves, bids him go forth; and that, if he shrinks for a moment from his post when the storm of battle rages highest, he dies by the hands of his officers; and he goes forth relying on the armed but manly justice of civilized war.

And so are all the authorities. The Senator from Virginia recited them so copiously to you last evening, that I shall spare you the repetition, and content myself with a reference or two. The Senator from Pennsylvania and the Secretary of State tell you that the attack on The Caroline was unjust. But look into Vattel, on pages 380 and 383, and Rutherforth, second volume, page 546, and you find that they concur that the injustice of the war does not affect the soldier's title to immunity. If it did, the nations would at once return to the murder of prisoners, for was there ever a war in which each belligerent did not think his antagonist in the wrong?

But you say this was only a single act of hostility, breaking out in a time of general peace, unannounced by any declaration. So it was. But Rutherforth expressly declares, that this does not withdraw it from the law of immunity. I read at large the passage from page 548 of his second volume, and commend it to the meditations of the Senator from Pennsylvania. "This external lawfulness, in respect of the members of a civil society, extends to public wars of the imperfect sort, to reprisals, or to other acts of hostility."

Such is the doctrine of this publicist, vindicated and illustrated by a masterly train of reasoning; approved by the heart and judgment of universal civilized man. Against this authority there cannot be placed one solitary act of a Christian nation for the last five hundred years, nor one word of any writer who undertakes to record the existing systems of international law. What is the nation now on earth, or descended into the graves of empire — where is the modern Christian nation that has shed the blood of a prisoner because the war to which his government detached him was informal, insolemn, unannounced by a declaration, beginning and ending with one single act? Call up the nation, if such there is or has been, and let it answer to the outraged spirit of law? Did Denmark claim the right to do such an atrocity — humbled and exasperated by the repeated bombardments of her capital — did that ancient and gallant race ever dream of avenging the defeats of the castle by the triumphs of the gallows? Did Spain, the most formal, the most punctilious of governments, and adhering the most tenaciously to the slow and prescriptive solemnities and technicalities of the old fashions of war — did Spain dream of it when, in 1804, England, in a time of peace, intercepted her treasure-ships returning from America, and captured or destroyed them?

Nor can you find, as I have said, a word in any approved expounder of the actual law of nations, to oppose to the text of Rutherforth. Dicta of Grotius seem to conflict with it. But they only seem to conflict with it. Even these the Senator from Pennsylvania has not availed himself of, because he knows that Grotius, admirable for his genius, his studies, his most enlarged and excellent spirit, lived too early to witness the full development of his own grand principles and the accomplishment of his own philanthropic wishes. The existing law of nations has been slowly built up since his time, and to learn it we must have recourse to writers far his inferiors in capacity and learning, but fortunate in being able to record the ameliorated theory and practice of a better day than his. From no one of these can you cite anything in opposition to the authority I have relied on. The Senator from Pennsylvania thought he had discovered some such doctrine as he needs in the 75th section of book 2d, chapter 6th, of Vattel. But the Senator from Virginia was entirely accurate in his observation upon this passage; that it plainly refers to the case of an individual acting without authority from his government, and to nothing else. And then, in support of the position of Rutherforth, I may remind you that, as the law of nations is holden now, no war requires to be preceded by a declaration. (Martens, 274; 2 Wheaton's Laws of Nations, 12; 1 Kent's Commentaries, 54, 2d edition.) Defensive war never required it, according to any theory. (Vattel, 317.) But it was defensive war to which McLeod's government assured him that he was summoned forth. The want of declaration, therefore, cannot affect him, unless we are guilty of the indecent and ludicrous barbarity of requiring him to judge better than his government on the necessity of resorting to a particular measure of armed resistance to a threatened invasion.

I submit, then, Sir, that McLeod is not responsible as for crime against the municipal law of New York or of this Union by participating in this act of English national wrong. Criminal in England, in him it was no crime. Let me add that if, in thoughtlessness or anger, we had stooped to shed his blood, it would have impressed a stain on the radiant flag of our pride and love which a hundred victories, aye, a hundred years of victory, would not wipe away.

The concession of the Secretary of State was right, then, in point of international law. But the Senator from Pennsylvania thinks he ought not to have made it, right or wrong. I submit, then, in the second place, that he ought to have made it, and the government to have acted on it, exactly as it was made and acted on.

What was the duty of the Secretary of State on the 12th of March last, when McLeod, guilty of no manner of crime against the law of New York by participation in the attack on The Caroline, had been indicted, imprisoned, and ordered for trial to be had on the 22d of March, as for such crime, under circumstances justifying a reasonable anxiety, lest he might fall a victim to a natural and a tremendous popular excitement; and when her Majesty's minister came forward, announced the doctrine of international law,—which we all know to be just,—

and demanded that McLeod should be holden entitled to immunity under it? What was the Secretary of State to do? Should he have wrapped his diplomatic mantle about him and have answered, "Sir, I do not know about your doctrine of international law; the American government is not advised exactly whether it may hang prisoners of war or not. Besides, it happens to have nothing at all to do with the matter; McLeod is in the hands of the State of New York, a great and patriotic State, Mr. Minister, giving forty odd electoral votes; she will do what is right; if she hangs him, why then we shall know that he deserved it; and if she does not, so much the better for himself"? Should he really, so saying, have bowed the minister out, and have retreated into an Epicurean heaven of indifference and non-committal, until he and you were startled by the thunder of an enemy's cannon,—a music I acknowledge at which a brave nation has no great objection at any moment to wake up? No, Sir, I submit on the contrary, that the duty of our government was perfectly clear; to avow its acknowledgment of the doctrine of international law advanced by the minister; to declare its purpose to do what it constitutionally might to secure McLeod the benefit of it; to do it, and then, having removed this disastrous interlocutory controversy out of the way, to demand satisfaction at once of England for the burning of The Caroline, as that language is understood among nations of the first class. To simplify the matter somewhat, suppose that McLeod had at that moment been in our jail, in our courts, instead of those of New York, then, I repeat, it was most palpably our duty to have conceded the proposition of law; to have expressed our assurance that the courts would acquit him of the accusation of crime against our municipal codes, and even that the Attorney-General representing the government would enter a *nolle prosequi*, thus committing him to the disposal of the Executive as a prisoner, or a *quasi* prisoner of war, or whatever else his legal character might be; and then and thus having washed our hands clean, and set ourselves right before God and man, to call this island-mistress of a thousand ships-of-war to instant account.

That this was the duty of our government, is too plain to be debated. Was it not its duty to cause this nation to keep the law of nations? Was it not its duty to be just? And was not this bare justice to McLeod, to England, to the universal spirit of humanity? Was it not its duty to preserve peace, if it might be had with honor, and, if war must come, to secure us one in which a Christian people might draw its sword? Now, Sir, the difficulty was, that, on the twelfth of March, we were in an eminently false position. With ample materials of the highest tone of complaint, perhaps even of reprisals or war against England, for her conduct towards us, here she was holding us up before all the world, for a little piece of our own conduct, in which we were, or were apparently, just about to be entirely in the wrong. With the burning of The Caroline, with the groundless yet pertinacious grasp of our territory in the north-east, with the repeated seizures and searches of our ships at sea to complain of and go to war about,—if a wise and moral people had a taste for such entertainment,—we were actually just about compelling England to declare war on us for hanging one of her soldiers because he did not run away from his colors? Why, Sir, this was not a position for men of sense to stand on long enough for her Majesty's minister to pull off his hat. Policy, honor, justice, honesty, humanity all required us to quit it in an instant. Why give England such a perilous advantage as to make up a false issue like this? Why unite all her classes, and every man in every class, in what they must think a holy war? Why alienate the sympathies of the world by such a thing? Why commit a blunder as well as a crime? Why forget that he is trebly armed that has his quarrel just? Why shock and shame the pride of America by turning away from England to strike down McLeod? Sir, if you speak of blows, I believe the people of this country would choose to be seen aiming full at the front of the proud and giant master, rather than dragging the servant, unarmed, unfriended, and handcuffed, to the gallows. They feel that no laurels are to be won in such a field by a nation of gallant men, of men of honor, and of Christians. They will seek those laurels rather where they do naturally grow, far up on the "perilous edge of battle when it rages." Sir, I was just now told that the late Chief Magistrate observed to a friend, some time during that fleeting month of his administration, that in a just cause, if congress would give him men and money, he had no objection to going into a war with England;

2*

but that he could not bring himself to buckle on his armor and take the field against Alexander McLeod. I can appreciate the disinclination of the kind, brave, and just old man to such a service.

I repeat, then, Sir, that if, on the twelfth of March, McLeod had been awaiting trial in the courts of the United States, we ought to have replied to the demand of her Majesty's minister thus: We admit your proposition of international law; we are not quite so rude and recent among the nations as not to know the elements or the code that knits the families of the earth together. From this accusation of municipal offence your subject is safe. And now will you in your turn inform us (for three years we have waited in vain to know), on what pretence her Majesty's forces, at the dead hour of night, crossed the inviolate line of our boundary, invaded our soil, dishonored our flag, wasted the property and shed the blood of American citizens?

It happened, however, that at the time when this demand was made, McLeod was awaiting his trial in the courts of New York. He was in a New York prison, under New York process; and the distinguished Senator from Pennsylvania insists that for this cause, at least, the government should have done nothing, and said nothing to the demand, but just have directed Mr. Fox to tell his story and carry his law to New York. We should have made no concessions of the legal principle; we should not have dared to communicate to the Executive of that State the official evidence of the claim and of the doctrine of England, and our own opinion of it; we should not have lifted a finger; we should have stood speechless, unconscious, innocent, and dignified, to see England, New York, and McLeod settle this little concern of national law, peace, war, life, and death among themselves.

Sir, the position McLeod stood in to that great and admirable State, undoubtedly limited the rights, and embarrassed the action of the General Government. But, because we could not do all that we would, were we not to do the little that we could? Were we to do nothing? Whom have we offended? The State of New York? How? By desiring to secure to this prisoner, to whose fate interests so large and so precious were attached, a fair trial? Sir, I cannot believe it. New

York was proceeding against him in the ordinary course of the administration of criminal law. To recognize her jurisdiction over him, which in the amplest manner this government did, and then to wish for him just what New York wished for him, that first of social privileges, a fair trial; was there in this anything to affront her pride of character? Anything to ruffle a feather in the plume of her acknowledged prerogative?

But we sought to operate on the government of that State by communicating our opinion on the points of international law, and in effect advising it what course to pursue. Well, Sir, does the conveyance of advice imply disrespect towards the object of it, or a distrust of his integrity or his capacity? Does it prove anything more than that you feel a deep solicitude that, in a great crisis of his fortunes and yours, he shall, for his sake and yours, make no mistake? Sir, here was a State with the physical power of engaging you in a national war. If hostilities followed the execution of McLeod, it would not have been a war on New York alone, but on Louisiana, on South Carolina, on Maryland, on Massachusetts. If they should be more immediately aimed at her, your valor and your treasure must have united with hers for her defence. A State, then, might plunge you in a general war; and yet, under the Constitution, no State has the legal and direct right to make a war for you or for herself. She has no right to terminate it by treaty, after it has begun. That great prerogative is yours alone. Those transcendent imperial powers, by which and through which we are known to the nations, are your powers. And now, is it possible that a State, prohibited by the Constitution from making war, from making treaties, may consummate an act for which we must answer with our best blood, on the field and on the deck; and yet that this government, clothed by the Constitution with all these great trusts, charged with the conservation of peace, with the conduct, expenditures, and hazards of war,—this government, whose flag alone it is that waves over the universal American family, wheresoever a member of it wanders, on land or sea—that we cannot respectfully approach any State with the communications of advisory suggestion, and deliberate with her on a subject of great novelty, difficulty, and importance? I have no great opinion of such transcendentalism of delicacy as this — good for winning electoral votes, possibly, but unfitting a man, or a government, for manly and useful action. Sir, New York is ably represented here, by gentlemen of both political parties, and they can answer for her; but I believe she will laugh to scorn the suggestions we hear of out of doors, that any disrespect has been shown or felt for her government or her people, for her judicial learning, or for the temper, feelings, and views of any portion of her widespread community.

In judging on this part of the subject, in this inquiry how far this government has exceeded its powers, invaded State rights, or betrayed indecorous anxiety and haste to save this person from the gallows, I ask you to take one thing into your consideration. Sir, it is no answer at all to England to say, this is the affair of New York. She knows nothing even of that magnificent Empire State as a separate State. We do not allow her to know anything of any State, by our Federal Constitution, in that capacity. We do not allow her to have diplomatic access to any. To attempt to make a treaty with any, would be clear ground of war. We inform her that, by our federal Constitution, the foreign relations of New York are reposited here; and if she has any cause of complaint against her, she will please to leave her card at our door. England, of course, all the nations, must hold us to this; and if any State affords her ground of war, it is against us that we ourselves direct her to turn her steel. At the same time therefore, that our federal relations to New York hindered us from doing much, our obligation on the laws of nations to England to do everything was not in the least degree lessened by them. The clear course of the government, therefore, was to do what it did, — to apprise that patriotic and noble State of our opinions on the justice of the demand of England; to do what we decorously could to avert so senseless and fatal an act as the execution of the prisoner; to have his case fairly tried, and, if needful, to have his case brought into the national tribunals; to explain to England why we could go no farther, and then abide the result. Anything, everything were better than a war on such a ground, that no man could hear of a defeat or a victory without tears of bitterest humiliation for America.

Mr. President, I have one duty here to perform, not so much to the Secretary of State as to my own feelings; and then I shall have done. I have said that it was the business of the government, after, as far as was practicable, clearing itself of fault in the matter of McLeod, to demand satisfaction, withholden and slept upon by England under the last Administration for three years, for the destruction of The Caroline. Gentlemen will do the Secretary of State the justice to remember that far the larger part of the letter to Mr. Fox is devoted to the performance of what he must have felt, as we feel it to be, his most agreeable duty. They will concede, too, that this part of his work is eminently well done. I should but degrade the seat which I hold in this high place by public adulation of any man, even of him. That he is my strong and constant friend would be no apology at all. Yet I will say that the ability and spirit with which this paper is written will give it a high place among the ablest diplomatic compositions, which enrich the archives of even the Department of State. He has vindicated the government of his country under all administrations, making no narrow, unnational discriminations between them, from every shadow of blame in reference to the Canadian border troubles; has proved that, so far from permitting or conniving at any participation in them by our people, we have set an example to the world; we have been the first nation in the world to prohibit our citizens from making any form of war on a country with whose government our own government was at peace; has proved that England had no right to make so rash and fatal an invasion on this. Sir, with this letter unrecalled, I think no English minister will tell us again, at the end of three more years, that he understood our claim for satisfaction had been withdrawn.

That this argument is ably conducted you all admit. But the course of the distinguished Senator's observations makes it more immediately due to Mr. Webster, to remind you that the argument is so conducted as not only to inform the public judgment about this wrong, but to excite just sensibilities in relation to it. It is so conducted as not only to enlighten the understanding, but to lift up the spirit of the country. He has not stooped to pick up and bluster about what is called the language of threat, but he has met the whole claim and the whole case of England with a composed and firm dignity, and with a manly decision; in the temper of a statesman, he holds the peace and glory of his country in his hands.

The Senator from Virginia [Mr. Rives] last evening read to us a portion of this paper. Let me enable its distinguished author, now no more among you, again, though absent from this scene of his long and splendid series of patriotic service, to speak for himself.

"Under these circumstances, and under those immediately connected with the transaction itself, it will be for her Majesty's government to show upon what state of facts, and what rules of national law, the destruction of The Caroline is to be defended. It will be for that government to show a necessity of self-defence, instant, overwhelming, leaving no choice of means and no moment for deliberation. It will be for it to show, also, that the local authorities of Canada, even supposing the necessity of the moment authorized them to enter the territories of the United States at all, did nothing unreasonable or excessive; since the act, justified by the necessity of self-defence, must be limited by that necessity, and keep clearly within it.

"It must be shown that admonition or remonstrance to the persons on board The Caroline, was impracticable, or would have been unavailing; it must be shown that daylight could not be waited for, that there could be no attempt at discrimination between the innocent and the guilty; that it would not have been enough to seize and detain the vessel; but that there was a necessity, present and inevitable, for attacking her in the darkness of the night, while moored to the shore, and while unarmed men were asleep on board, killing some and wounding others, and then drawing her into the current, above the cataract, setting her on fire, and, careless to know whether there might not be in her the innocent with the guilty, or the living with the dead, committing her to a fate which fills the imagination with terror. A necessity for all this, the government of the United States cannot believe to have existed."

To these hands, for one, I am willing to intrust the rights and the fame of my country.

Mr. President, I concur entirely with both the Senators

who have preceded me that there need be felt no apprehension of a war with England. Like them, I neither expect nor desire it. Heaven forbid! I know of nothing between the governments that ought not to be and may not be easily and honorably composed. But whatever may befall, I claim it as the praise of this administration, that it has had the manliness to seek peace by justice; and that if war shall come, it has done all that man can do to enable us so to go into it that we may have the approval of our own consciences, self-respect, the moral judgments of the world, and may I not add, the God of our fathers with us in the conflict.

SPEECH ON THE BILL TO PROVIDE FURTHER REMEDIAL JUSTICE IN THE COURTS OF THE UNITED STATES, BY AN EXTENSION OF THEIR POWERS.[1]

DELIVERED IN THE SENATE OF THE UNITED STATES, MAY 10, 1842.

I CONCUR with the Senator from Pennsylvania [Mr. Buchanan] in regarding this as an important bill. All legislation is so which involves a question of the Constitution; but this, which no doubt approaches, although it does not touch, the impassable line that separates State and national jurisdiction, and which has for its object to secure the national peace and honor, by retaining the conduct of our foreign intercourse in the nation's hands, possesses a peculiar importance. It was for this reason that I expressed a desire last evening to trespass for a short time on your indulgence.

I have nothing to say to any part of the bill except that which gives qualified jurisdiction to the national courts in cases arising upon the laws of nations, and affecting the subjects of foreign governments domiciled abroad. All the rest of the bill, in so far as any constitutional principle is involved, is as old as the judiciary act; as old as the Constitution. Always we have exercised a superintending appellate control over the criminal jurisdiction of the States, after judgment, in cases arising under the Constitution, the laws, or the treaties of the United States. Always we have asserted the great conservative principle, that the determinations of the national courts in these cases are the supreme law; and that those courts are our tribunals of the last resort. This great principle we have

[1] The object of this bill was to meet such cases as that of McLeod; and to prevent a conflict of authority between any of the States and the United States. It passed, with some amendments, July 7, 1842.

held fast in the worst of times, and at all times; under all administrations; whatever party was uppermost; with the approbation of the people, of the States, and, I was happy yesterday to hear, of the Senator from Pennsylvania. Permit me to say, Sir, that when we shall be driven or seduced to let go our hold on this, we are lost indeed. The only novelty in this part of the bill is a change of the stage of the cause, in which the controlling interposition of the national courts is to be put forth; but, in point of jurisdictional principle, there is nothing new, and nothing to be defended. To much the larger part of the Senator's speech, therefore, I attempt no reply.

Addressing myself, then, to that provision of the bill which gives to the national tribunals qualified jurisdiction of criminal causes, commenced in State courts and under State authority, against foreigners, the subjects of a foreign government, and domiciled abroad, who defend themselves upon the laws of nations, I submit that you have the constitutional power to pass it, and that it is in a high degree expedient to do so.

You have the constitutional power. The cases to which this provision applies are either, in the language of the second section of the third article of the Constitution, "cases arising under the Constitution and the laws of the United States;" or they are "controversies between a State and foreign citizens or subjects;" or they are both; and either way, to the extent contemplated by the bill, you may commit them to the national judiciary.

I say to the extent contemplated by the bill; and that is a very limited extent. The national tribunals interpose so far only as to determine whether the laws of nations entitle the prisoner to his discharge. If they do, he is discharged; if not, whatever the evidence or the deficiency of evidence against him, he is remanded to the court of the State for general trial. The jurisdiction given by this provision of the bill, therefore, is of a single point, the relevancy and the sufficiency of the laws of nations to rescue the party and the act from the operation of the mere municipal and local law.

Before advancing to the inquiry, by what precise clause and denomination this jurisdiction is communicated, permit me to premise a preliminary and preparatory suggestion; and that is, that one of the grand objects, which we certainly know that the framers of the Constitution had in view in the construction of the judicial department, as well as throughout the whole of their vast work, was such, and some of the acknowledged powers of the national judiciary are such, as to afford a moral certainty, *a priori*, that this particular and limited jurisdiction over prosecutions begun in the State courts against foreigners domiciled and owing allegiance abroad, and pleading the laws of nations in their defence, must, under some clause, and by some denomination or other, be found to be also given. The Constitution gives so much jurisdiction, and on such policy, to the national courts, that it must have given this too. It goes so far, on such reason, that it must, as a systematic organization of government, resting upon any principle at all, be found to go the whole length of this bill. Why, Sir, advert to this single consideration: If the State of New York, or any other State, or any citizen of any State, has the most frivolous civil lawsuit with a subject of England resident in Canada, the Constitution gives the trial of it to the federal courts. If the owner of The Caroline, for example, should bring his action of trover against the persons who carried off and burned her; or if the State itself, happening to be the proprietor of the wharf where she lay, should sue them in trespass *quare clausum fregit*, for breaking and entering its close, and subverting the soil, by the Constitution the case may be brought into your tribunals. These suits, out of all manner of doubt, and by the admission of everybody, are "controversies between a State, or its citizens, and foreign citizens or subjects;" to which we know the national judicial power, by the express terms of the Constitution, is extended.

And now, sir, do you think that, when we come more critically to analyze the article by which the judicial department is constructed, we shall find that the Constitution has done so capricious, inconsistent, not to say incomprehensible and absurd a thing, as to have given, with so much solicitude, to your courts, jurisdiction over such disputes as these, and yet to have overlooked altogether the weightier matters of this bill? Why, what is the policy on which you have, and may assert, jurisdiction of these small civil suits against aliens? Confessedly and notoriously this only: to preserve, undisturbed, harmonious intercourse with the rest of the world. Presuming, not that the State courts, or the State judges, are cannibals, as the Senator from Pennsylvania arraigns this bill for presuming them to be — not so — but presuming, whether right or wrong I do not say, that they, by possibility, may be somewhat less certain to be impartial in a case where their own States, or their own neighbors, are parties on one side, and a desolate stranger on the other; presuming that they may be more exposed, somewhat, to be disturbed and darkened by sympathy with local passion and excitation, with the pride, and anger, and short-lived and circumscribed emotions that convulse a State, without sending a pulsation beyond its borders, as a smaller water may be moved through all its depths and extent by a breeze which the main sea will not feel; presuming that they may be, by possibility, less profoundly impressed with the responsibilities attendant upon bringing on, by a judicial decision, a war which their State would not have to sustain, and which the nation would; proceeding upon the obvious principle of common sense and common justice, that the government which must answer, by its treasure and its blood, for a verdict or a judgment, ought to have the right to give the verdict and render the judgment — upon this policy and on these reasons it was that the Constitution has withdrawn, has enabled Congress to withdraw, from the State courts and give to yours the ultimate determination of this kind of case against this kind of party. Although no foreign government has anything to do with the matter, nor any domestic government, State or national, has anything to do with it; although the decision may depend wholly upon the local law of the State, and involve no immediate consequence beyond the payment of an inconsiderable execution, yet, for the sake of preserving the public peace, and because the denial of civil justice to a subject of a foreign nation may possibly bring on collision with that nation, with a wise and decisive forecast, it has given this unquestionable expansion to your judicial power. And now, I repeat it, can the Constitution, after all this, have done so fitful, capricious, timid, and inconsistent a thing as to leave a question on the life of a man — the life of a soldier, coming into your territory by the command, and to do the will of his sovereign; in a case where a foreign government is the real *actor* on one side, and your own national government the recipient of wrong on the other — a case which is to be decided, not by the smaller reason of local law, but by the code which governs the nations, and where the inevitable consequences of conviction and execution will be, not the payment of a trifling sum of money, but a war, which may encircle and shake the globe — to leave such a question as this, exclusively or concurrently, to those very tribunals which it authorizes you to prevent from rendering a judgment against a foreigner on a fifty-dollar promissory note? Is this great device of wisdom and policy, the Constitution, so little systematic and consistent; so untrue to itself; such a jumble of incongruities, and of the discordant seminal principles of ill-assorted things as this comes to?

I say then, Sir, that the Constitution has gone so far in its grant of federal jurisdiction, and upon such policy, that there is a sound, not to say an irresistible presumption, *a priori*, that we shall find, in some clause, a grant of the jurisdiction asserted by this bill.

I attach, Mr. President, so much importance to this preliminary consideration that one great object in the view of the framers of the Constitution, in the organization of the judicial department as well as of the entire scheme of national government, and in the conception of the Union itself, was to clothe this government with the means of preserving national peace, by holding in its hands the determination of all judicial questions affecting its foreign relations as a government to other governments; it affords such a valuable general principle by which to interpret the particular clauses of the instrument, and answers in advance so much of the argument of the Senator from Pennsylvania, that, before proceeding to an inspection of these clauses, I beg to dwell a little longer on it. Go back to the birth-time of the Constitution, and ask its authors what they expected of its judicial department. The Senator from Pennsylvania inquires if our fathers dreamed of such a grant of federal jurisdiction as this? Sir, what they dreamed of I know not; that was not a race or an age of dreaming men; but of heroical sentiments; far, large, and practical aims; profound thoughts, and great deeds; and what they thought, and what they did, we do know, and may usefully meditate.

Let me read first a passage from "The Federalist;" the same which was read, I believe, by the Senator from Georgia [Mr. Berrien] in his able opening exposition and defence of the bill; but it will bear repetition:

"It seems scarcely to admit of controversy, that the judiciary authority of the Union ought to extend to these several descriptions of cases:" — "4th. To all those which involve the PEACE of the CONFEDERACY, whether they relate to the intercourse between the United States and foreign nations, or to that between the States themselves; 5th. To all those which originate on the high seas, and are of admiralty or maritime jurisdiction; and, lastly, to all those in which the State tribunals cannot be supposed to be impartial and unbiassed." "The fourth point rests on this plain proposition, that the peace of the WHOLE ought not to be left at the disposal of a PART. The Union will undoubtedly be answerable to foreign Powers for the conduct of its members; and the responsibility for an injury ought ever to be accompanied with the faculty of preventing it. As the denial or perversion of justice by the sentences of courts is with reason classed among the just causes of war, it will follow that the federal judiciary ought to have cognizance of all causes in which the citizens of other countries are concerned. This is not the less essential to the preservation of the public faith than to the security of the public tranquillity. A distinction may perhaps be imagined, between cases arising upon treaties and the laws of nations, and those which may stand merely on the footing of the municipal law. The former kind may be supposed proper for the federal jurisdiction; the latter for that of the States. But it is at least problematical, whether an unjust sentence against a foreigner, when the subject of controversy was wholly relative to the *lex loci*, would not, if unredressed, be an aggression upon his sovereign, as well as one which violated the stipulations of a treaty, or the general law of nations. And a still greater objection to the distinction would result from the immense difficulty, if not impossibility, of a practical discrimination between the cases of one complexion and those of the other. So great a proportion of the controversies in which foreigners are parties involves national questions, that it is by far most safe and most expedient to refer all those in which they are concerned to the national tribunals." — *Federalist*, No. 80.

I have not been deterred from presenting this evidence of the objects for which the judicial department was constructed, by the imputation of centralism, or consolidationism, or federalism, so liberally heaped upon this bill, and its policy and its aims, by the Senator from Pennsylvania. Upon the value of this great contemporaneous commentary, as evidence of the contents of the Constitution, I have not supposed there were two opinions. In the history of controversy, in the history of political literature, and of all literature, I know of no writing whatever which was given to the world under circumstances affording so high a degree of security that it truly exposed the contents of another writing, as the circumstances, under which "The Federalist" appeared, afford that it truly exposes the contents of the Constitution. Two of its writers, and these the writers of this number, and of almost all of the entire work, were members of the convention. All three possessed extraordinary ability and uprightness; they would not misstate, and could not misunderstand, the Constitution; and they knew that they addressed a community whose utmost intelligence was at the moment all concentrated, with an intensity of interest which we can scarcely conceive, upon the study of its meaning. Especially were they under no temptation to *overstate* the powers of the new government. They wrote to urge its adoption upon an anxious and distrustful people, who desired union, to be sure, and commerce, and manufactures, and all social prosperity, but whose passion was liberty; and whose more habitual and more ardent affections were towards the States. They wrote to allay fears of its extent; to diminish the sense of the change it wrought; to bring down the exaggerated features, which timidity or design had sketched, to the dimensions of actual existence. The only temptation they in fact were exposed to was to *understate* its powers, and especially the judicial power, of which the old confederation had possessed next to none. Where, then, as a general remark, the writers of "The Federalist" *admit* a power or a principle in the Constitution, you may be sure it is there. Let me fortify the opinion I have thus given by the authoritative words of our great judicial expounder of the Constitution: —

"The opinion of 'The Federalist' has always been considered as of great authority. It is a complete commentary on our Constitution, and is appealed to by all parties, in the questions to which that instrument has given birth. Its intrinsic merit entitles it to this high rank; and the part two of its authors performed in framing the Constitution put it very much in their power to explain the views with which it was framed. These essays, having been published while the Constitution was before the nation for adoption or rejection, and having been written in answer to objections, founded entirely on the extent of its powers, and on its diminution of State sovereignty, are entitled to the more consideration where they frankly avow that the power objected to is given, and defend it." — *Chief Justice Marshall, in Cohen* v. *Virginia*, 6 Wheaton, 413.

Hear the avowal of Mr. Madison upon this subject, in the Virginia convention, during the discussion on the adoption of the Constitution, in the face of an opposition "before which the eyes of eagles would have blenched:"—

"The general policy of that clause (the 1st and 2d sections of the 3d article on the judicial power) is to prevent all occasions of having disputes with foreign powers, to prevent disputes between different States, and remedy partial decisions. I believe this to be wise and salutary."—2 *Elliot's Debates*, 389.

And General Randolph, in the same convention (p. 418), said, speaking of the national judiciary:—

"Its next object is to perpetuate harmony between us and foreign Powers. The general government, having the superintendency of the general safety, ought to be the judges how the United States can be most effectually secured and guarded against controversies with foreign nations. I presume, therefore, that treaties, and cases affecting ambassadors, other public ministers, and consuls, *and all those concerning foreigners*, will not be considered as improper subjects for a federal judiciary. Harmony between the States is no less necessary than harmony between foreign States and the United States. Disputes between them ought, therefore, to be decided by the federal judiciary."

Let me ask you to go a little farther back, and trace the history of the construction of the judicial department in the convention which framed the Constitution. See there how solicitously, and to what extent, the grand function of preserving the national peace was meant to be bestowed on it, and consider what rule of construction of its particular clauses this fact suggests. The Virginia plan of a Constitution was introduced, as Senators remember, by Mr. Randolph, on the twenty-ninth of May, in fifteen resolutions. How this proposed to frame the judicial power, I will remind you in a moment. It was held under discussion until the fifteenth of June, when the Jersey plan, as it was called, was introduced by Mr. Patterson, in eleven resolutions. This was the plan of the State-rights party in the convention; of those who advocated the closest practicable adherence to the articles of confederation; the political ancestry of the State-rights sect of this day. And how did this construct the judicial department of the amended but still inadequate system of federal government which it designed? Mark the terms of the last branch of the fifth resolution:—

"*Resolved*, That the judiciary so established shall have authority to hear and determine, in the first instance, on all impeachments of federal officers, and, by way of appeal, in the dernier resort, in all cases touching the rights of ambassadors; of all cases of captures from an enemy; in all cases of piracies and felonies on the high seas; in all cases in which foreigners may be interested." — 2 *Madison Papers*, 865–6.

These resolutions having been rejected, for the general reason that they did not frame a sufficiently strong and a sufficiently national government, the convention resumed the examination of the Virginia plan; and, on the twenty-sixth of July, the grand general principle, on which the judicial power was to be erected, was finally adopted. Observe the comprehensive and energetic terms of that well-considered principle: —

"*Resolved*, That the jurisdiction of the national judiciary shall extend to cases arising under laws passed by the general legislature, *and to such other questions as involve the national honor and harmony*." — 2 *Madison Papers*, 1284.

It was on that day referred, together with other resolutions, which had also been adopted as the basis, in part, of the new Constitution, to a "committee of detail," for the purpose of being expanded and carried out into the necessary particular enumeration, and cast into technical expression; and that committee, on the sixth of August, reported this second section of the article of judicial power, substantially in the form in which it stands in the Constitution.

Pause now, for a moment, on these facts, and see if they do not prove, *a priori*, that the jurisdiction given by this bill must be found to be authorized by some part of the Constitution. You observe that all opinions in the convention concurred in the general principle, that the judicial department ought to be so constructed as to secure harmony of intercourse with the nations of the world. So much is certain; and how was this to be done? Precisely by intrusting all cases affecting that intercourse to the national tribunals. The State-rights party, as you have seen, would have committed to those tribunals "all cases affecting foreigners," in so many words; all cases — criminal, of course, as well as civil. Rejecting the plan of that party, for its incompleteness and inadequacy, do you believe that the majority of the convention meant to give to their own judiciary a narrower and feebler jurisdiction? Did they mean to do less than even their anti-national opponents were willing to do? The principle which they adopted, as I have shown, was, that it should have cognizance of "all questions involving national peace and harmony." Now, when you advance to the construction of the detailed enumeration of the particular cases of jurisdiction into which this principle is expanded, and in which it is embodied in the Constitution, must you not so interpret that enumeration, if the letter of the language will allow you to do so, as to completely satisfy and exhaust the general principle itself? Must you not, are you not bound to so interpret it, to the limit of the letter, as to embrace all judicial cases and questions *involving national peace and harmony?* Did not the committee of detail frame this enumeration, did not the convention receive and adopt it, expressly and exactly, as embodying, expanding, and executing the whole of the great principle which had been resolved upon? Did not everybody understand that, under one or another, or all, of the cases and controversies enumerated, were comprehended all questions whatever of a judicial nature, affecting the national peace? Why, look again at the facts. The general principle was adopted, and sent to the committee of detail on the twenty-sixth of July, as I have said. The business of that committee was, not to narrow, enlarge, or change the principle, but to *express* it, perfectly and technically. The convention never afterwards narrowed or changed their own principle. They adjourned on that same day to await the report of the committee; and they accepted that report on the sixth of August, as their own principle, given back to them, in form and substance, neither less nor larger, nor other than when they committed it, except that it was drawn out into the requisite particularity of detail. Are we not bound, then, if the language will admit it — are we not bound to put such construction on these clauses granting judicial power as to give full effect to what we know was the meaning of the convention? Do you not defraud what you know was the principle intended to be embodied here, if you adopt an interpretation which will withdraw a large class of questions, or any questions, involving national peace and harmony, from the national judiciary? To your honor, to your integrity, I appeal, not less than to your intelligence, completely and in good faith, to execute the Constitution, which is the record of the people's will, when you cannot fail to see you have discovered its meaning.

If, then, Sir, the cases comprehended in this bill — cases of State prosecutions against subjects of foreign governments domiciled abroad — for acts done in the foreign character, under an order of the foreign government, and within the immunity of the laws of nations — if such cases as McLeod's, for example, do constitute a question involving the national peace and harmony, you are prepared to find them, by a diligent and a conscientious interpretation, under some clause or other of the article creating the judicial power, committed to the national judiciary. We must find them there, or the Constitution is untrue to its own ascertained principles, and inconsistent with its own expressed provisions.

Well, do not such cases directly involve the national peace? That of McLeod, for instance, did it not? Why, Sir, the Constitution deems that the execution of a five hundred dollar judgment against the foreign acceptor of a bill of exchange may involve the national peace; and therefore it sends the trial to the national courts. In your consciences, do you not think that the same Constitution deems the sentence of death and the infliction of death on a foreign soldier, for obeying the order of his sovereign, and who pleads that order, — the responsibility of his government and the benignity and manliness of the laws of nations for his life, — to be at least equally likely to involve national peace?

I have thus far, Mr. President, attempted no more than to raise a presumption, — *a priori*, — that under some clause or other of the article establishing the judicial power, this jurisdiction over State prosecutions of foreigners resident abroad, and depending on the laws of nations, will be found to be communicated. Let me now approach the question, under which clause it is communicated. The whole grant reads thus: —

"The judicial power shall extend to all cases, in law and equity, arising under this Constitution, the laws of the United States, and treaties made, or which shall be made, under their authority; to all cases affecting ambassadors, other public ministers, and consuls; to all cases of admiralty and maritime jurisdiction; to controversies to which the United States shall be a party; to controversies between two or more States, between a State and citizens of another State, between citizens of different States, between citizens of the same State claiming lands under grants of different States, and between a State, or the citizens thereof, and foreign States, citizens, or subjects." — *Constitution, art.* 3, *sect.* 2, *cl.* 1.

It would seem a pretty fair deduction from the grand general principle of policy on which I have been insisting, that the designation "controversies between a State and foreign States, citizens, or subjects," should include criminal accusations by a State against a foreign subject, who pleads the laws of nations and the orders of his government. Civil suits by a State against aliens are triable in the national courts for the preservation of the national peace. Why should not criminal charges also between the same parties be so tried on the same policy? And if so, — unless the preceding description of "cases arising under the Constitution, laws, and treaties of the United States" embraces and provides for them, — why do they not fall under the denomination of *controversies?*

I concur, however, with the able and judicious chairman of the judiciary committee, [Mr. Berrien,] in not placing the bill upon that ground. I think, with him, it may be placed on far other and far clearer ground. Indeed, it is framed avowedly with reference to another principle of jurisdiction. At the same time that I say this, I beg to add that I do not mean to concede that the cases which are embraced in it are not controversies between a State and a foreign State or subject, within the very letter and the acknowledged spirit of this grant. Upon this point I neither affirm nor deny. I do not concede that "controversies" do not include criminal cases; because I would do nothing to weaken or bring into question any power of this government; and because even the hasty and inconsiderate concessions of debate may help, silently and irrecoverably, to change the Constitution. Doubtful, on the contrary, at least, it seems to me to be, whether criminal cases are not *controversies*, and were not meant to be comprehended in that term. Let me intimate the grounds of this suggestion very briefly, without pausing to attempt to enforce them. It is settled, and is admitted, that the term *cases*, in this part of the Constitution, "all cases arising under the Constitution, laws, and treaties of the United States," includes cases of a criminal as well as civil nature; but it is supposed that the term "controversies" includes those of a civil nature only. There is, I know, an *obiter dictum* to this effect, of Mr. Justice Iredell, in the early and celebrated case of Chisholm *v.* State of Georgia, (2 Dall. 419.) Mr. Tucker intimates the same thing in a passage of his appendix to Blackstone's Commentaries, (1 Tucker's Black. Com. app. 420, 421;) and Mr. Justice Story silently records these opinions in a note, (3 Story's Com. on Constitution, 536,) without any expression of assent, however, to which his name would have lent an authority so commanding. Besides this, I find nothing on that side of the question.

Now, the word *controversy*, in its popular or its professional use, does not, I think, apply exclusively to civil disputes. It seems rather to have a wider and more flexible signification than the word *case*, which certainly includes criminal accusations. Judicial controversies are disputes, disagreements, differences between parties, respecting their legal rights and wrongs, wherein one controverts what the other alleges, and which are put in a form for judicial determination. These are judicial controversies. And does not an accusation of a State against a foreign subject, for an act done within its borders, which he asserts an authority to do under the laws of nations and the commands of his sovereign, come exactly within the terms of the definition? Is it the less truly a controversy because it relates to crime, or because one of the parties is a State and the other a man, — both standing, however, on the same plane of privilege in a court of law? Let me, without indecorum, remind you that the dictionaries — in illustration of one of the meanings of the word — refer to two verses in our translation of the Bible, — a book which, more truly than Chaucer's poetry, may be called a "well of English undefiled;" and that in one of these it denotes a legal prosecution for crime, — the parties to which are the righteous and the wicked, — and which terminates in punishment by stripes; while in the other, in a still more awful sense, the Supreme Being is declared to have "a controversy with the nations."

Certain it is, I think, that, if the Constitution had intended by the term *cases* to include civil and criminal proceedings, and by the term *controversies* civil proceedings only, it would have employed some qualifying and explanatory epithet or expression to convey that limitation of the sense. There is no such broad and recognized difference of signification between the words, standing alone, as to warrant the belief that the Constitution, distinguished always for its perspicuous, simple, and popular phraseology, could have expected or intended that they would be understood in so fine, far-sought, and yet so momentous a diversity of signification. This would be more like and more worthy the compilers of synonymes than the framers of a fundamental law, to be read by a whole people. The judiciary act, passed in 1789, carefully says, "controversies of *a civil nature*," where it means *civil causes*, acknowledging and feeling that the constitutional term *controversies*, standing alone, included a great deal more.

The truth seems, in short, to be, that, in their ordinary and their professional use, the words *cases* and *controversies* are coextensive, but that we employ *case* when we refer to the *subject* of the dispute, *controversies* when we refer to the parties. We speak of a painful controversy between a husband and wife and their friends, on a libel for a divorce; but we speak of a new case on the statute of frauds, or on the doctrine of presumption. And the Constitution adopts this general habit of our ordinary language in the clause which confers jurisdiction. But the very next clause, which distributes jurisdiction into original and appellate, is in these words: —

"2. *In all cases* affecting ambassadors, other public ministers, and consuls, and those in which a State shall be a party, the Supreme Court shall have original jurisdiction. *In all the other cases before* mentioned, the Supreme Court shall have appellate jurisdiction, both as to law and fact, with such exceptions, and under such regulations, as the Congress shall make."

And here, you observe, the word *cases* is used to include all which, in the preceding clause, had been denominated both *cases and controversies*.

I propound it as a doubt, therefore, whether — when you consider the ordinary import of the term itself; that it is used here without limitation or qualification; that the word cases, (with which this word certainly does not, in general speech, stand in any well-known contrast of sense,) in this same clause, includes criminal and civil suits; that the same reason of policy which assigns civil controversies to the national tribunals would, with far more urgency, assign to them criminal controversies also; — I suggest a doubt, upon these considerations, whether the term does not cover the whole ground of this part of the bill. Certain it is, that, unless this description of prosecutions are within the preceding clause, "cases arising under the Constitution, laws, and treaties of the United States," they must be holden to be controversies between a State and foreigners, and thus, *quacunque viâ datâ*, cognizable in the national tribunal.

But, Mr. President, on this question, listen to a witness of the age of the Constitution; listen to the "genuine information delivered to the legislature of the State of Maryland, relative to the proceedings of the general convention held at Philadelphia in 1787, by Luther Martin, Esq., Attorney-General of Maryland, and one of the delegates in the said convention." Mr. Martin, just returned from the convention, of which he had been an energetic member, in the presence of one or more of his colleagues in that body, in the presence of the house of delegates of Maryland, to which he was making an elaborate report of the deliberations and proceedings which had resulted in the Constitution, and an elaborate analysis of the Constitution itself, then and there employs this language: —

> "The inquiry concerning and trial of every offence against and breach of the laws of congress are also *confined* to its courts. *The same courts, also, have the sole right to inquire concerning and try, every offence, from the lowest to the highest, committed by the citizens of any other State, or of a foreign nation, against the laws of this State, within its territory.* And in *all these cases,* the decision may be ultimately brought before the supreme tribunal, since the *appellate jurisdiction* extends to *criminal* as well as to civil cases." — *Yates's Minutes of the Federal Convention of* 1787. 4 *Elliot's Debates,* p. 46.

He, then, certainly believed that "*controversies*" embraced *criminal* controversies. I know he opposed and dreaded the Constitution. I even admire, although I wonder at and disapprove, the solemn earnestness and energy of thought and expression with which he cautions the delegates of Maryland to dash to the earth the cup of poison which the convention had commended to their lips. But he was then a man, as I have always heard, of a most powerful and penetrating understanding; trained by all the learning and by the long exercise of his profession, and of perfect integrity and honor. That he rightly comprehended the objects and the provisions of the judicial power would seem, in the highest degree, probable; that he would venture, the highest law-officer of Maryland, at the head of his profession, fresh from the sittings of the convention, in presence of his colleagues, in presence of the legislature, to misstate these objects and provisions, I do not believe. Certainly you cannot produce a particle of contemporaneous testimony in opposition to this, to be compared a moment with it for pertinence and for strength.

I understand Governor Randolph, speaking in the Virginia convention, to express the same opinion in other language.

"I presume, therefore, that treaties and cases affecting ambassadors and other public ministers, and consuls, *and all those concerning foreigners*, will not be considered as improper subjects for a federal judiciary." — 2 *Elliot's Debates*, p. 418.

To this construction I know there are grave objections. I feel and admit their force. As I do not place my main reliance, nor much reliance, upon it in support of the bill, I shall detain you upon them but a few moments.

It is said that the withdrawal from the States of the trial of crimes is a more extensive and more formidable invasion of the sovereignty of the States than the withdrawal of the trial of civil suits, and that this suggests a reason for so restraining the meaning of *controversies* as to exclude trials of crimes and include trials of contracts.

I answer, first, that the general principle settled by the convention warrants no such discrimination in favor of State sovereignty, or for any other reason, between civil and criminal litigation. That principle, you have seen, is, that your judicial power shall extend to all questions involving national peace and harmony. All questions; not part; not half; not those only *quæ frequentius accidunt;* not those by the trial of which you will least invade State sovereignty; but all. The object of the resolution adopting the principle was *national harmony*, not *State sovereignty*. That State sovereignty was to be invaded and restrained, was a thing determined on. It was just what the convention were engaged in doing; just what the people were engaged in doing, through and by the convention. They were reducing the sovereignty of the States to establish yours. They were borrowing from these dispersed, lesser, and golden urns,—or rather from the great primal source, the people,—light and fire for a central sun. Have you, then, any insuperable difficulty in supposing, when you find them adopting this principle of policy upon the subject of national jurisdiction, that, to the whole extent of the principle, they meant to abridge the original sovereignty of the States? Show me that criminal trials do not involve national peace, and you take them out of its operation. But if you cannot do this, then, whether more or less essential to State sovereignty, the principle transfers them to this government.

Let me add, Sir,—although the argument of the honorable chairman of the committee upon this subject left little more to be desired,—that I know of nothing in reason, or in the Constitution, to warrant the imagination that you invade the sovereignty of the States any more, when you take from them the trial of crimes, than when you take from them the trial of contracts. Gentlemen, with great serenity, allow the federal jurisdiction over a suit by a citizen against an alien, on a five hundred dollar bill of exchange payable here, depending wholly on the law of the State; but the trial for his life, of a foreign soldier, wearing the uniform, receiving the pay, obeying the command of his sovereign, and cloven down and captured in his actual service; who claims the protection of the ancient and universal law of the Christian world; whose cause is his country's cause; whose security his country guarantees; whose blood his country must avenge, or be a by-word and a hissing among the nations—such, so grand, so solemn and so eventful a State prosecution, they say you cannot try, even on the single point contemplated by the bill, because it would be to invade the sovereignty of the States. Pray, Sir, is it not just as much invaded in one case as in the other? Is it not just as much an act, or an attribute of sovereignty, as grand, as beneficent, as beautiful, to sit in the great halls of national civil justice, with eyes averted, the golden scales suspended aloft, and administer that justice "freely and without price, completely and without any denial, promptly and without delay, conformably to the laws," as it is to punish crime? Is it only when a State is in anger; is it only when she is avenging a wrong directly to herself, that she is a sovereign, and acting as a sovereign? By what tests, by what well-compounded instrumentality do you undertake thus to distinguish between one ray, or one beam and another of all those which blend and blaze in the wide rainbow arch of sovereign power?

The Senator from Georgia, however, suggested what I deem a much more formidable objection to this interpretation of the word *controversies*, and that is the startling extent of the consequences which would flow from it. It might follow, in the strong language of Luther Martin, which I have just read to you, "that the national courts have the *sole* right to inquire concerning, and try, every offence, from the lowest to the highest, committed by the citizens of any other State, or of a foreign nation, against the laws of this State within its territory."

I recognize the force of the objection. But is it certain that the Constitution did not, however, mean to commit even this power to a sound legislative discretion? The Constitution, designed to create a national commonwealth which should be immortal, and looking forward to those possible varieties of untried national being through which it might pass, to enable you to preserve peace with foreign governments, and peace among yourselves, bestows upon you perhaps the power to clothe your courts with even this expansion of jurisdiction. But it does not command you to exert it at once, or to exert it at all. It intrusts it to your discretion. Observe the change of language in these successive clauses of this article. "The judicial power shall extend to *all* cases arising under the Constitution, laws, or treaties of the United States;" but it shall extend "*to controversies* between the enumerated parties;" not saying *all*, significantly, perhaps, dropping that word; thus leaving you the power to extend it to all, or to part, and to draw your line of jurisdiction where and how you please. I adopt this conjecture from the opinion of Mr. Justice Story in the case of Martin *v.* Hunter's lessee, (Wheat. 335–6.)

In the exercise of this discretion accordingly, the judiciary act gives jurisdiction to the national tribunals of such civil suits only against aliens as ascend to a certain degree of importance. Is there any more difficulty in the exercise of the same discretion, in extending the jurisdiction of the same tribunals over criminal prosecutions by the States to the cases, and for the purpose, contemplated by this bill? Is there any difficulty in cases where a foreigner, accused of crime, admits or postpones the denial of the facts, and interposes a special claim of immunity, founded on the law of nations, in permitting the national courts to pronounce solely upon that single preliminary or collateral claim of immunity? The general case they scarcely may be said to try at all. They do not assume to interpret and administer the criminal, municipal law of a State. They only inquire and decide, whether that law is not, under the particular circumstances, superseded, displaced, overridden, by the universal code of civilization. To the extent of that inquiry and that decision, the *case* becomes a *controversy* on a collateral, or rather a special, matter; and, to that extent, the jurisdiction of the national tribunals might seem to be safe, salutary, and within this clause of the Constitution. So far only, be it observed, does the bill assume to go.

It has been suggested, as another objection to this interpretation of the word *controversies*, that it would give to the general government, to some extent, the administration of the criminal jurisprudence of the States; that this involves a solecism, and a dangerous solecism, too; that the government which tries must necessarily have the power to pardon; and, of course, the President would become armed with the power of taking from the States their means of punishing crimes against their own laws. Confusion and collision, it is argued, must inevitably be the consequence.

I agree, undoubtedly, Sir, that this consideration is of weight to induce a sparing, and unfrequent and qualified exercise of this jurisdiction, *ratione personarum*. Limited, however, to a mere inquiry how far the laws of nations withdraw the foreigner, in the particular case, from the condition of general liability to the local criminal code, I see nothing so very formidable in the jurisdiction. Certainly, it carries to the national executive no power to pardon. This is a jurisdiction, so far as this clause is concerned, founded on the character of the parties, not on the nature of the cause. It is a jurisdiction given by the Constitution to the judiciary only. It is a jurisdiction to that department to try, to acquit, or convict and sentence, according to a prescribed law.

The power of pardon is a strict executive power; is totally unaffected by this grant of judicial power, and remains unimpaired, uncontrolled, in the executive of the State. The jurisdiction which is founded on the nature of the cause, rests, I need not say, on different principles altogether; and to cases within those principles the national executive may hold a very different relation.

But I am glad to arrive, at last, at the true ground on which your constitutional competence to pass this bill is to be asserted. The cases embraced in it are, all of them, cases "arising under the Constitution and laws of the United States," and therefore expressly within the national judicial power. They are such, for the general reason that they involve, accomplish, and depend on the interpretation and administration of certain constitutional powers and duties, and certain laws of this government.

The bill before you is, in form, a bill to give jurisdiction, in a certain mode, of a certain description of cases, to the national courts. Like every other bill, however, which assumes to give jurisdiction, it assumes to do, and it does, another thing also. It does two things: It first adopts, or makes a law to be administered, and then it designates a tribunal to administer it; it first makes a law, and then it makes a court; it first adopts the law of nations as the law to be administered, and then commits the administration of that law to the national judiciary.

I think, Sir, it will facilitate the investigation in which we are engaged, to separate these two objects of the bill, and to take them up one at a time. Let us look at it then, first, as a bill *making law*, and then as a bill *conferring jurisdiction.*

In the first place, then, as a law-making bill. What does it do; and is it, in that view of it, constitutional?

Well, then, Sir, the bill, in this aspect, does, by inevitable implication, exactly this: It declares, in effect, and by inevitable implication, that, whereas, in the intercourse of independent commonwealths, there are cases in which the rights and liabilities of subjects of one government, domiciled abroad, for acts done within the territory of another, depend, according to the laws of nations, *upon the laws of nations*, administered by the injured government, and overriding and displacing the mere municipal and local code; that, therefore, in such cases, the laws of nations shall be applied, shall form the rule of determination, and shall relieve from restraint the alien imprisoned in violation of them. This, I think, is exactly the effect of the bill, as a bill making a law to be administered. If, by the laws of nations, as understood and observed among independent, Christian, and civilized commonwealths, there are cases where the liabilities of the citizens of one commonwealth, and resident there, for acts done in the country of another, depend on, and ought to be tried by, the laws of nations, then, in such cases, judicially ascertained to exist, the laws of nations shall be the code of trial; and the courts of the injured commonwealth shall interpret and administer that code accordingly, to the extent of affording relief from restraint. The bill recites and enacts all this by implication. It does so by directing the discharge of the party, if, by the law of nations, the courts find him entitled to discharge. What the cases are in which the law of nations thus interposes itself; what are the cases in which it rescues the party from the mere municipal law, it does not attempt to define. But where the judicial power declares the case to exist, according to the law of nations, that law is to govern that case.

And now the question is, whether it is competent to congress thus to adopt and to provide for the administration of the law of nations, as part of the law of the United States, in cases affecting the security of foreigners domiciled abroad, and through them affecting our foreign relations and foreign intercourse? I submit, then, Sir, that this is clearly within your constitutional competence.

I deduce your authority, *first*, from a general view of the powers bestowed by the Constitution, and, *secondly*, from certain particular provisions.

In the first place, congress is expressly authorized "to make all laws which shall be necessary and proper for carrying into execution the foregoing powers, and all other powers vested by this Constitution in the government of the United States, or in any department or officer thereof." (Constitution, art. 1, sec. 8, clause 17.)

You may make, then, all laws necessary and proper for executing all the powers vested in the general government, and performing all the duties imposed on it by the Constitution. But the adoption and administration of the laws of nations, to the extent of the cases in this bill, is a necessary and proper means of executing certain of those powers, and performing certain of those duties, and, therefore, you may so far adopt them and provide for their administration. Such, in other words, in the same words rather, are your powers,—such your duties under the Constitution, that the adoption and administration of the law of nations is proper, necessary, indispensable, to enable you to execute and perform them.

I say nothing, in aid of my argument, of the "common defence and general welfare." I do not attempt, and I did not understand the Senator from Georgia to attempt, to deduce any power at all from that language, so broad, but so vague, and of such uncertain and disputed signification. But, finding an express authority, carefully and clearly conveyed, to do what is necessary and proper to be done for the purpose of executing the Constitution, I hope that a sober and free inquiry, whether the adoption and administration of part of the laws of nations are a necessary means to that end, may not very rapidly accelerate the fulfilment of the prophecy, which the Senator from Pennsylvania has found in the Foreign Quarterly Review, that our institutions, so instinct throughout with fervid, passionate, and inextinguishable liberty, are soon to merge in centralization and monarchy.

Let this proposition, then, be examined. It is admitted by everybody that the Constitution holds out the Union under the general government, for all purposes of foreign intercourse, for all foreign relations, as THE NATION. It makes, and it proclaims it such. It bestows on it all the powers of foreign public intercourse known to our system,—belligerent, pacific, diplomatic, commercial. It intrusts to its control and administration all the modes by which one nation, as such, can communicate with another nation, as such. A State cannot go to war, nor make a peace, nor send nor receive ministers, nor regulate the terms on which it will trade with a single spot on the globe beyond its own borders. In all these respects, for all these purposes, for everything beyond its own borders, States are no more, no other, than individual, natural persons, component atoms of the great unit mass. "If," says Mr.

Madison, in the forty-second number of "The Federalist," "we are to be one nation in any respect, it clearly ought to be in respect to other nations." And one nation we certainly are, *e pluribus unum*, for some purposes.

"That the United States form, for many and for most important purposes, a single nation, has not yet been denied. In war we are one people; in making peace we are one people; in all commercial regulations we are one and the same people; in many other respects, the American people are one; and the government, which is alone capable of controlling and managing their interests in all these respects, is the government of the Union. It is their government, and, in that character, they have no other. America has chosen to be, in many respects, and to many purposes, a nation; and for all these purposes her government is complete; to all these objects it is competent. The people have declared that, in the exercise of all powers given for these objects, it is supreme. It can, then, in effecting these objects, legitimately control all individuals or governments within the American territory. The constitution and laws of a State, so far as they are repugnant to the Constitution and laws of the United States, are absolutely void. These States are constituent parts of the United States. They are members of one great empire — for some purposes sovereign, for some purposes subordinate." — *Opinion of Chief Justice Marshall in Cohens* v. *Virginia.*

In Holmes *v.* Jennison, 14 Peters, 570, Chief Justice Taney says, —

"All the powers which relate to our foreign intercourse are confided to the general government. Everything that concerns our foreign relations, *and that may be used to preserve peace* or to wage war, has been committed to the hands of the federal government."

In holding you out as the nation, in making you the nation, the Constitution makes you alone responsible to the complaint, well or ill founded, of every other nation in the world. It makes you responsible, and it makes the States irresponsible. It withdraws the States, and it withdraws the people from view, and incloses and shelters them within one common and wide sweep of city wall. It does not allow a State, as such, so much as to be spoken to, in anger or in kindness, by a foreign nation, as such. Not even a blow, not even a shot, can reach a State. Whatever it is aimed at, by the theory of our system, it strikes, alight where it will, your giant form alone. The duty of avoiding war, by doing justice, or by displaying spirit; the whole vast cost of maintaining it when it comes; the duty and the cost of closing or of preventing it by negotiation; all are devolved directly and solely on you. Your position would not, in these particulars, be varied a jot that I can see, if the States were melted down into a single people, and their constitutions, their partial sovereignty, their lines of boundary, and their very names, had perished, like the architecture, the polity, and all the glories of a primitive and forgotten civilization. There is a sense, no doubt, in which it may be the duty of every citizen and every State to assist in preserving the national peace, but all which the nation, as such, can do to that end, is your business and your duty alone.

In thus erecting you into the nation, and setting you, not the States, on the high places of responsibility, the Constitution subjects you, subjects the Union, the general government, to the general law of nations, in so far as that law applies to your intercourse with and relation to the rest of the world. It subjects you to it in a totally different sense from that in which the States are subject to it. It places you in a position, it clothes you with powers, it imposes on you duties, which make it your peculiar, national, imperial duty to the Constitution and under the Constitution to observe and administer that law to that extent. I regard the Constitution as declaring, by inevitable implication, as intelligibly and as peremptorily as if it were written in it, that the laws of nations, in so far as they apply to and regulate intercourse with foreigners and foreign governments, are, or may be made by the legislature, obligatory on and in the United States, exactly as they are on and in the other Christian and civilized nations of the world.

The Constitution declares this in and by the mere act of bringing you into the circle of independent, Christian, and civilized nations. It is *the condition* of such national existence to be under that code. You cannot be a nation at all, and yet be so great as to be exempted from the power, or so little as not to feel the care, of that law "whose seat is the bosom of God, whose voice is the harmony of the world." If I may vary the fine and strong thought of Cicero, to escape from it, you must fly from yourselves, and spurn even your own national nature. You may cease to be a nation; you may break the golden, unseen band of the constellation in which we move along, and shoot apart, separate, wandering stars, into the infinite abyss; you may throw down the radiant ensign, and descend from the everlasting and glittering summits of your freedom and your power; but while you exist as now you do, the only nation of our system known to the other nations, you are under, you must obey, and you may claim upon, the common code of all civilized and Christian commonwealths.

And not so only, Sir; but the Constitution everywhere assumes and sends you to that law as your law. You may make war, it tells you; but the causes of war, the law of war, the conduct of war, its iron rights, the rights and duties of neutrality—where are you taught these things, where are you prescribed these things, but by this venerable and universal jurisprudence? You may negotiate, and what is that but the bringing up of national controversies to this standard and exponent of the *jura gentium?* You may make treaties, and where do you find the learning of treaties? You are to "establish justice," and what is its *measure* but this? You may regulate commerce; but the grand, controlling, and elementary principles of the international intercourse, even of trade, are they not to be found here, and here alone? You may define and punish offences against the law of nations; and is it not then your law,—yours for interpretation,—yours for enforcement? You are an independent nation; and are not the principles of national independence a leading title of international law?

Accordingly, Mr. President, from the first national breath we drew, we have assumed that we were subject, to the extent I have defined, to the laws of nations. Every minister we have sent or received, every demand of justice we have made or had made on us, every diplomatic act, every peace, every war, innumerable executive and judicial and legislative determinations, have assumed and recognized it. I do, indeed, understand the Senator from Pennsylvania himself, as conceding the position as fully as I have urged it.

And now, Sir, the question is narrowed to this: since the Constitution makes you a nation, the only nation for intercourse with the world known to our system; since it makes you alone responsible to the call of the world; since it devolves on you alone the duty of preserving honorable peace and of securing just war, so far as any such national duty exists on any body; since it subjects you to the general law of nations, and imposes on you, as a nation, the duty of obedience to it, does it not clothe you with the power to provide for the administration of that law? Is not this a necessary and proper means to execute a clear power, and to perform a clear duty? When the Constitution placed you in such a position that it became your duty to other nations to observe the laws of nations, did it not mean to make it your duty also to the Constitution itself, and to the people, or to the States by whom and for whom it was framed, to observe those laws? And, if so, did it not give you the power to perform the duty which it thus imposed? When it made you alone responsible *for the breach*, did it refuse you the ability to secure *the observance?* When it forever relieved the States from *responsibility* for the violation of that law, and transferred it to you, did it still continue to them the uncontrollable *power of violation at your expense?* "Ought not," in the terse and sententious expression of "The Federalist," "the responsibility for an injury to be accompanied with the faculty of preventing it?"

In a more general view, Sir, is there one single duty more clearly yours, under the Constitution, than that of maintaining just and honorable peace? Is it not your duty to other nations, as one of the vast family of nations, and to the people and the States of this nation? In subjecting you to the responsibilities and burdens of war; in submitting to your control all the modes and forms in which this nation can possibly have intercourse with any other nation; in clothing you exclusively with the power of negotiation and of commercial regulation; in depriving the States of all the known instrumentality of cultivating national peace, does not the Constitution put it out of all doubt that it imposes this duty on you? And, if so, has it not given you the ordinary, indispensable, national means of performing the duty? And is not the observance of the laws of nations among those means? Can you not constitutionally preserve peace, by obeying the law to which the Constitution has subjected you? Can you not preserve peace, by performing the duties to others which the Constitution exacts of you? Has the Constitution brought you into a world of war, and yet given you no power to be at peace, and no power to attract to yourselves the regard and sympathy of man, by just sentiments and just conduct? Has it set you upon the seat, and put into your hands the reins of the chariot of the sun, and yet given you no power to keep the safe and open highway of heaven, — shunning the serpent constellation on the one hand, and the altar on the other?

I submit, then, Sir, that the case stands thus clear and simple. You may pass all laws necessary and proper to execute any constitutional power, or perform any constitutional duty of the general government. Among those powers and duties is that of preserving peace, by observing international law. Then you have the power to secure that observance, and of course the power to pass this part of this bill, adopting and executing it so far as it regulates foreign intercourse.

The Senator from Pennsylvania has told you, indeed, that the States are bound to observe the laws of nations; and therefore, of course, that you have not the power to pass a law, of your own, like this bill, providing for their adoption and administration. But is this so? In the first place, supposing the States are thus bound; it does not prove that you have not the power for which I am contending. So are the States bound to obey the Constitution, and the treaties, and the laws of the United States; but have you, therefore, not the power to provide, by your own direct act, for their administration and their execution? Do you, or need you, refer it to the good pleasure of the States, whether the Constitution, laws, and treaties are observed or not? Does their duty of obedience take away *your power of administration?*

But how far or to what useful purpose in argument is it true at all, that the States are bound to obey the laws of nations? There is a loose and inadequate sense, no doubt, in which the States, and every individual member of every State, and of every civilized commonwealth, may be said to be so bound. But are they bound as you are; in the same sense; to the same extent; under the same responsibilities; with the same consequences? No indeed, Sir. Can they answer for a violation of them by war? No. Can they compensate for such violation by treaty? No. Can they unite with other nations in defining their principles; declaring the rights secured; and the wrongs forbidden by them; in varying and accommodating them from age to age so as to keep pace with the ebb and flow of human affairs; and the general, though slow and interrupted, advancement of civilization? No. Are they bound by them in any other sense than every merchant and every sailor in the world is bound by them? Is not the law of nations a law *for* nations? Are not its subjects independent commonwealths? Is not the absolute equality of all the nations to whom it extends its very *first principle?* May you not just as well say that the States are bound to preserve national peace? So in one sense they are; so are we all. But is there not a peculiar and constitutional sense in which that is the duty of this government alone?

I cannot think, then, Sir, that the reasoning on which I have deduced your power to provide for adopting and administering the laws of nations, from your general constitutional powers and duties, is answered by this position of the learned and honorable Senator.

Let me say, before leaving this branch of the discussion, that the writers of "The Federalist," in the passage from the eightieth number of that work which I just now read, assume it as clear and conceded by the opponents of the Constitution, that causes, in which citizens of other countries are concerned, and which arise upon the laws of nations, will be cognizable by the national judiciary. They do not, therefore, discuss that proposition at all, but, taking it for granted, proceed to argue that all causes affecting foreigners, although not arising upon the laws of nations, should be committed to the same judiciary.

But see now if the power may not be deduced from specific provisions of the Constitution. I have remarked that, everywhere, in numerous provisions, the Constitution assumes that you observe the laws of nations. In making war, concluding peace, in trade, in negotiation, in all your intercourse with the world, it supposes it. But look a little more nearly. There is the treaty-making power. The general government, the executive of that government, may make treaties, and, when made, they are supreme law; displacing and overriding the State law wherever it stands in their way; and they are expressly committed to the administration, exclusively so, in the last resort, of the national courts. Now, without attempting to define the exact and whole extent of this power, and to enumerate all things that it can do, and that it cannot, I submit to you that it is perfectly clear that it enables the executive of this government to do, by a treaty, exactly what we seek to do by the law-making part of this bill; that is, to engage the faith and honor of this nation, that, in all cases in which, by the laws of nations, the rights and liabilities of foreigners, subjects of other governments, domiciled abroad, depend not on the municipal law, but on the laws of nations, mitigating and superseding it, that those laws shall form the code of trial. Does any senator deny the power of the executive to make such a treaty? Is there a particle of doubt that the treaty might even be made to go farther, and define the cases which the laws of nations should govern, dealing with just such cases as McLeod's, for example, and formally, and in terms, declaring, not only that such a case should be governed by the laws of nations, but that, by that code, he ought to be released; thus not only applying, but declaring the law? I should hardly be excused for debating this proposition, or citing an authority for it. In the case of Holmes *v.* Jennison, in 14 Pet. S. J. C. U. S. 569, the chief justice observes, "The power to make treaties is given by the Constitution in general terms without any description of the objects intended to be embraced by it; and consequently it was designed to include all those subjects which, in the ordinary intercourse of nations, have usually been made subjects of negotiation and treaty, which are consistent with the nature of our institutions and the distributions of powers between the general and State governments. Without attempting to define the exact limits of the treaty-making power, or to enumerate the subjects intended to be included in it, it may safely be assumed that the recognition and enforcement of the principles of public law, being one of the ordinary subjects of treaties, were necessarily included in the power conferred on the general government." And Mr. Justice Barber, dissenting from the chief justice, and those learned members of the bench who concurred with him, on the general question in the case, however, distinctly admits "that *as, by the usage of nations* as well as by the practice of the United States, the surrender of fugitives is deemed to be a proper subject of a treaty; that, therefore, it is competent to the president and senate to make treaties in relation to that subject" — thus extending the treaty-making power to the limit of known and ordinary national usage. (S. C. p. 589.)

Everything, then, which this bill seeks to do, the general government might do by treaty. So much is certain. I do not say that it follows that you can therefore do the same thing by a law. That depends not on the comparative powers of the State and national governments, but on the distribution of federal power itself among the departments. But the State-right argument against the bill is forever silenced by this consideration. How can it be pretended, as we have heard it urged, that it plunders the States of that poor, shrunken residue of sovereignty which the Constitution secured to them; that it wrests an inalienable as well as a favorite jurisdiction out of their hands; robbing them of their proud and cherished privilege of vindicating the supremacy of their own criminal law, when, beyond a shadow of doubt, there is a department of the general government that can rightfully do the whole work of the bill in a moment?

Into the question, whether we may not do by law what the executive could do by treaty, I do not propose to enter. The subject is discussed somewhat by Mr. Madison, in the papers under the signature of Helvidius, in reply to Pacificus, by General Hamilton; and was very elaborately debated by the House of Representatives in 1815, on a bill to carry into effect a commercial convention with Great Britain. My general opinion is, that within our own territory, in so far as direct action on our own citizens and others within it is involved, we may do all things, for the preservation of national peace, *by law*, that we could do by *treaty*. If, with a view to the preservation of peace, we can incorporate the laws of nations into the laws of the United States for the government of our own territory *by treaty*, then, with a view to the same end, we can do it *by law*. The treaty-making function can only be exerted to execute some power or perform some duty of the Constitution; and the law-making function, *infra territorially*, can be exerted for such purpose, and with similar efficacy.

But there is another provision of the Constitution which seems to put an end to this question. Congress is expressly authorized "to define and punish offences against the laws of nations." Pause for a moment on this, and see how much more power it gives you than you attempt to exert in this bill. The single question we are discussing is, whether we have not the constitutional power to adopt and execute the laws of nations, — as and for our own law, — in so far as they protect foreigners, under special circumstances, from imprisonment in violation of them, by the municipal law of a State, for acts done within our territory. This bill, to that extent, adopts those laws, treats such imprisonment as an offence against them, and relieves from it accordingly.

Now, I have to say that this provision seems to me forever to settle the question. It commits to Congress the exclusive and the entire administration of the whole law of nations as a criminal code, in just so many words. It authorizes you to pass a statute which shall formally declare the laws of nations to be the law of the United States, and shall formally prohibit all offences against them, which shall enumerate and classify and define every one of those offences; shall relieve and protect the person, or the right against which the offence is committed, and shall punish the offender. Against the provisions of such a statute, of course, no law of a State, and no judicial decision of a State could be set up. It becomes, by express terms of the Constitution, supreme law. If an act, by whomsoever done or authorized, is an offence against the law of nations, you may prohibit it. Whether an act be such offence or not depends, not on the perhaps conflicting definitions of twenty-six States, but on your definition. How it shall be relieved against; how it shall be punished; whether it shall be relieved against or punished at all, depends not upon the perhaps conflicting wills of twenty-six States, but on your will. If a doubt is moved whether you have not declared an act to be an offence against the laws of nations which was no such offence, thus usurping upon the municipal jurisprudence and legislation of a State, this, like every other judicial question on the validity of a law of the United States, must be determined by the national judiciary.

Such is the palpable extent and sense of this provision. See, then, in the first place, how completely it answers the argument, that the general government is bound to presume that the States will execute the laws of nations, and to rely upon them for it accordingly; that their relations to these laws are the same with yours; and that though responsible for their violation, you have no adequate and supreme power to secure their observance. Sir, this provision was inserted, in part, to enable you to prevent those violations of these laws by everybody, States and persons, which might give just offence to the rest of the world. Speaking of this very subject, Mr. Madison says, in a paper of "The Federalist," which I have before referred to — the forty-second number — "these articles" (the articles of confederation) "contain no provision for the case of offences against the laws of nations, *and consequently leave it in the power of any indiscreet member to embroil the confederacy with foreign nations.*" It was inserted to enable you to preserve peace by keeping the law to which as a nation the Constitution had subjected you, and for whose just and uniform administration the world was authorized to hold you to answer.

But I would have you remark a little more particularly how fully this provision authorizes you to do all, and a great deal more than all, which is attempted by this bill. You might, as I have said, enumerate the cases, in which the imprisonment, under the authority of a State, of a foreign subject, domiciled abroad and pleading the laws of nations, would be an offence against those laws; and you might provide *both for punishing and for relieving from* that imprisonment. You might, for instance, deal with such a transaction as that of the burning of The Caroline. You might declare it an offence against the laws of nations; but the individual actors in the business — the soldier, the sailor, whose government set him the inglorious and perilous task of midnight war — these actors you might declare to be clothed with perfect immunity by that same manly and just code; and that therefore to imprison them, as for a breach of municipal law, was itself an offence against that code for which you might relieve and for which you might punish. All this you might do, because all this is but a defining and punishing of offences against the law of nations, which is one of your enumerated powers. If it were doubted whether such an imprisonment were properly declared, in the cases specified, to be an offence against these laws, the national judiciary is appointed by the Constitution the tribunal to resolve the doubt.

Now, Sir, how far within these limits of your undoubted

power is the whole action of this bill! Instead of enumerating the cases in which the imprisonment of a foreigner by the authority of a State is an offence against the laws of nations, you refer it at once to the judicial power to ascertain whether a given case, judicially presented, is such an one or not. Instead of providing for punishing, as well as for relieving from such imprisonment, you, with a wise abstemiousness, provide for relieving from it only. And will anybody say that the proposed law is void, because it does not go far enough? Does not the Constitution commit it to a sound legislative discretion to determine whether you shall define an offence, or whether you shall adopt the definition of the laws of nations, and refer it to the judicial power to collect and pronounce that definition? By the ninth section of the judiciary act, concurrent jurisdiction is committed to the district courts "of all causes where an alien sues for a tort only in violation of the law of nations." Is this void, because, instead of enumerating and defining those torts, the courts are authorized to pronounce, by recurrence to that law, whether in a given case such an one has been committed? The act of congress of 1819, v. 6, p. 489, sec. 5, enacts that if any person shall on the high seas commit the crime of piracy, *as defined by the law of nations*, he shall suffer death; and yet it was holden in the case of The United States *v.* Smith, (5 Wheaton, 153,) that this was a constitutional exercise of the power of congress to define and punish piracy.

Is it not intrusted also to a sound legislative discretion to say whether it will do more than relieve the foreign subject from the illegal punishment? Is there any compulsory duty to go further and incur the odium of punishing the native offender also? Is there any obligation on you to do all in one bill? You might as well say the judiciary act is void, because it does not exhaust the whole constitutional grant of federal jurisdiction.

I cannot doubt, then, Mr. President, on a view of the general structure, objects, and powers of the Constitution, and on a narrower inspection of its particular provisions, that you may constitutionally pass this bill so far as it is a law-making bill. You may adopt and provide for an administration of the laws of nations, so far as they exempt and relieve foreign subjects, domiciled abroad, from the imprisonment or other punishment, inflicted under municipal law, in violation of their principles and their policy.

The next question is, whether jurisdiction of cases under this bill — the judicial administration and execution of the bill — may be given to the national courts?

Sir, I suppose this to be no question at all.

In the first place, cases under this bill — cases under the laws of nations, as adopted by this bill — become instantly cases arising, in the very terms of the Constitution, "under a law of the United States," to which your judicial power is expressly extended. They arise *under this very statute.* This statute, this formal act of your legislative power, makes, by adoption, the law which tries them. I subject you to this dilemma. If the Constitution, by direct operation, makes the laws of nations your law, then these cases arise under the Constitution. If by this statute they are made such, then the cases arise under a law of the United States; and either way are unquestionably within your judicial power.

Certainly these cases do not the less strictly and the less properly arise under a law of the United States, that you adopt the laws of nations by a general reference and a general denomination. If you assumed, by this statute, to codify that venerable and ample jurisprudence, to define and classify the offences which it prohibits, and to anticipate and provide for all the cases in which it may interpose to control the narrow technicalities, and unyielding, conventional, and arbitrary rules of municipal law, then all would admit, I suppose, that the very cases contemplated in the bill, as now it is framed, would arise under a law of the United States, and go constitutionally to the national judiciary. But it obviously comes exactly to the same thing, when you incorporate the international law into your own by general reference. So you did by the fifth section of the act of congress of 1819, which I have just read to you; and yet, an indictment on that section, is it not upon, and should it not conclude against the form of, the statute of the United States?

Since, then, Sir, in a trial under this act, the defendant sets up a right, privilege, or exemption, secured him by a statute of congress, within the words of the Constitution, and the exposition of its meaning by the twenty-fifth section of the judiciary act, the case arises under a law of the United States, and your jurisdiction is perfect.

But in a more general view, Sir, this statute is a declaration, by the legislative power of this government, constitutionally put forth, that the laws of nations, to a certain extent, shall be administered in the United States. It follows, as a matter of course, under our system, that the national tribunals are to execute that declaration, and, in the last resort, to do so exclusively.

Is it not, as Chief Justice Marshall, in the case of Cohens *v.* The State of Virginia, pronounced it, as every elementary writer on government has pronounced it, an *axiom*, that the judicial power, in so far as judicial questions, *judicial cases*, can arise, is coextensive with the legislative power? Is it not an axiom, that the administrative and executive power is coextensive with the law-making power? The government which can will, which can decree, can it not enforce? Does not the Constitution embody and announce this great principle, when, departing from and ascending above the timidity and the imbecility of the old Confederation, it declares that "the judicial power shall extend to all cases in law and equity arising under the Constitution, the laws, and treaties of the United States;" and "that this Constitution, and the laws of the United States which shall be made in pursuance thereof, and all treaties made under the authority of the United States, shall be the supreme law of the land"? The Senator from Pennsylvania admits that the judiciary act is constitutional; and does not that act proceed on and execute this exact principle? Can you imagine a case in which it was more important that the Constitution should not have left it to the States to execute your legislative will, to refuse to execute it at all, to misconstrue it, to construe it diversely, than it is in these very cases in this bill? You see, I think I have shown, that the Constitution, on a large, obvious, unavoidable policy, to enable you to preserve peace, by performing your national duties, and rightly ordering your national life, has authorized you, by legislation, to adopt the laws of nations, and to declare that they shall be administered. And now, having gone so far, do you think it stops short and withholds from your own judiciary the power to execute that declaration? Does not every consideration which dictated the intrusting of this power to the national legislature demand that the national judiciary, in its sphere and mode, should have it too? Why, Sir, you have seen that it was especially held in view in the construction of the judicial department, that it should be armed with the means of executing the precise policy of this bill, — the preservation of the national harmony. And, after all that, can you imagine that the Constitution is so incongruous and unintelligible and poor a mimicry of government, as to clothe you, for reasons of peace and justice, with power to adopt a code of laws, the boast, the glory of which is, that it is not one thing at Rome and another at Athens; one thing to-day, and another to-morrow; but that it reaches to the farthest verge of civilization; the same everywhere and always; the guardian of the sailor's midnight sleep; the sovereign of the king on his throne; and yet, leave it to six-and-twenty States to change it into six-and-twenty conflicting codes, or to annul it altogether? Sir, the thing is so absurd, that I lose the practical in the intellectual contemplation. It is not so much a bad government as an impossible idea. There is such a "reconciliation of antipathies" in it; such boastful and large pretensions, and such insignificant performance; such an exaction of obligation, with such denial of free-will; it so mocks you with such a semblance of power, without a particle of the reality, that the understanding does not so truly refuse to believe, as admit its inability to comprehend. The serene writers of "The Federalist" pronounce such a thing "a hydra in government," and I confess I do not think it too far-sought or too harsh an illustration.

But, Mr. President, to those of us who admit that the judiciary act is constitutional, and who receive the decisions of the supreme national court as the law of the land, these general reasonings are superfluous, or worse. If the law-making portion of this bill is constitutional, the jurisdiction of the national judiciary follows of course. The acquiescence of fifty years, of every administration, every party, the refusal of congress to repeal the judiciary act, repeated and masterly judgments of the courts, concur to declare that, in the public opinion of America, this branch of this question is wholly at rest.

One word only, therefore, upon an objection or two of the honorable Senator, not yet particularly adverted to, and I relieve your attention.

It has been said that, even if the Constitution or this bill makes the laws of nations the law of the United States, the State courts may be relied on to administer them; because the laws of the United States are the laws of the separate States also. But is not the Constitution, are not the treaties, is not every law of the United States, the supreme law of the States; and yet, does not the Constitution expressly extend your judicial power to all of them?

The Senator has said, too, that to give this jurisdiction to the national courts is to interpolate, after the words of the Constitution, "the judicial power shall extend to all cases arising under this Constitution, the laws of the United States, and treaties made under their authority," these words, "and the laws of nations;" and that is to change the Constitution. By no means, Sir. That would indeed be to change the Constitution; for, undoubtedly, not every case arising under the laws of nations is within your jurisdiction. Such there are, many such, between citizens of the same State, on policies of insurance, for example; cases turning wholly on the application of that code to breaches of blockade, neutral conduct and liabilities, the character and the consequences of illicit trade, and the like. But it is not of such cases, between such parties, that you can give jurisdiction to the national tribunals. It is of such only as, in their prosecution or their defence, involve, depend on, and accomplish, some power conferred, or some duty imposed, by the Constitution. The portion of the great and entire international code which you can adopt, and can administer, is that which regulates our intercourse with, and our duties toward, other nations, their subjects and their governments. That portion only you adopt and administer by this bill. You do this as a means of exerting some power conferred, or performing some duty imposed, by the Constitution. You do it in execution of the Constitution. All the cases which arise, under this part of this bill, are cases under the laws of nations, indeed, in one sense; but, in a true, large, and ultimate sense, they are cases under the Constitution, too, and a law of the United States "made in pursuance thereof."

In truth, the title, right, privilege, or exemption, supposed by this bill to be set up and claimed under the laws of nations, is really set up or claimed under the Constitution, and a constitutional statute; and I have no doubt at all, that, within the twenty-fifth section of the Judiciary Act, a decision against such claim or exemption, in the highest court of a State, could now be removed by writ of error to the Supreme National Court. There is no enlargement, then, and no change of the judicial power of the Constitution by this bill. We interpolate nothing. We just make a constitutional statute, adopting a part of the law of nations, and then, within the precise words, and the necessary and obvious spirit of the Constitution, we give to your tribunals the cases arising under it.

The bill under consideration provides for the interposition of the national courts by *habeas corpus*, where the foreign subject is imprisoned for acts done "under any alleged right, title, authority, privilege, protection, or exemption, set up or claimed under the law of nations, *or under the commission or order or sanction of any foreign State or sovereignty, or under color thereof.*" The description of cases last mentioned in this enumeration, — cases arising *under the commission, order, or sanction of any foreign State or sovereignty*, — arise, like the former, under the laws of nations. They are only one class, or one illustration, of cases so arising. The effect which is to be allowed to such commission, order, or sanction, for the protection and defence of a foreigner imprisoned under the authority of the State courts, depends on that code alone; and perhaps there was no urgent necessity, in the construction of this bill, to single out these, for enumeration, rather than any other cases to which that code applies, and over which, of course, this jurisdiction should be extended. And yet it may have been proper to do so, because, more almost than any other, they exemplify the grounds and the importance of a national, legislative, and judicial control, to the extent proposed by the bill. Take the case of The Caroline and of McLeod, for an instance, and see how conclusively it refutes that large State-rights doctrine which has been contended for here, and now, as well as elsewhere, and formerly — the doctrine of a right in the States, as against the general government, to try, in their own courts, and under their own laws, the individual actors in such a transaction, and overruling the plea of the laws of nations, to execute them for murder against the form of the statute of the State. Sir, without repeating any of the general reasoning, on which I have detained you too long already, and without troubling you further on the particular character of this bill, I submit that a State right to this extent cannot be maintained for a moment.

Of your general jurisdiction over such a transaction, your jurisdiction to some extent, and for some purposes, there is of course no doubt. That it was an entry upon our territory by the government of Great Britain; that it was a wrongful entry upon a neutral territory; that this constitutes an offence by a nation against a nation, against the Union under the general government, against this nation; that it was attended and was consummated by the instrumentality of war, — by organized, armed men, by the application of military force, by terror, and by the shedding of blood — all this we all admit and all assert, the former Secretary of State as well as the present, the last administration as well as this, all who have debated the American side of the question, in and out of congress, from the burning of The Caroline to this hour. And this we assert, on the most satisfactory evidence for the facts, and the most conclusive and most venerable authority for the law.

It follows, of course, that of this transaction, as a national wrong against this nation, the general government has a general jurisdiction to some extent and for some purposes. This also we all admit. In the exercise of that acknowledged and undoubted jurisdiction, Mr. Forsyth, Mr. Stevenson, and Mr. Webster, have successively complained of it, and demanded redress. In the exercise of that jurisdiction, negotiations are at this moment pending between the two national governments, with the acquiescence of everybody. The actor being a nation; the recipient of the wrong a nation; the means of redress and of adjustment, reprisals, declared war, negotiation, being all national, and such as you alone can employ, this general jurisdiction for the purposes of diplomacy is conceded as a thing of course.

Observe, too, under another view, how comprehensive and how controlling is your general legislative, as well as diplomatic jurisdiction, over such transactions. You do not doubt that congress may pass a law declaring that prisoners taken during an actual war within a State shall be deemed subject to the laws of nations, shall be placed in the custody of the executive officers of the United States, and that the President may provide for their safe-keeping, support, and exchange. Such, in effect, was the legislation of congress in 1812, by the acts of June 26, sec. 7, and July 6. You deduce your power to do this from the powers to declare war and to conclude peace, both belonging to the general government, the first to you and the other to the executive.

Well, Sir, have you not just as much power to declare that such acts as the burning of The Caroline are acts of war, *unlawful, informal, insolemn*, but acts of war; that they are acts of war by the government of Great Britain upon the United States; that, as such, the laws of nations become applicable to them; and that the liabilities and immunities of the individual actors in particular must be determined by that code? Much edifying discussion there has been, in and out of congress, much expenditure of learning and logic, to show that a State court of justice could not recognize that transaction as an act of war. But has anybody denied *that congress might declare it and all similar transactions to be acts of war?* Pray, Sir, has not this government, and has not that branch of this government to which it belongs to declare war, the power to declare what, in the judgment of this nation, is the true character of a particular wrong done by another nation to this? Has not the legislature, which may declare that a particular act of a foreign government justifies and requires an open war, the right to pronounce that the particular act itself *assumed the nature and the guilt of war, and was war while it continued, as far as it extended, and in what it did?* I believe nobody will doubt this. Then you may pass a law to-day declaring that exactly such enterprises as that against The Caroline are and shall be deemed and taken to be acts of war, unlawful, informal, insolemn, by the government which perpetrates them against the United States. You may, therefore, as you did in 1812, declare that the individual actors, if taken, shall be prisoners of war, subjected to the laws of nations, held in custody by the general government, and exchanged by the executive.

Well, now, Sir, setting out with this incontestable, general, diplomatic, and legislative jurisdiction, and these plain powers of this government over such transactions, is it not perfectly palpable that you cannot stop short of the conclusion that you have a general jurisdiction over all parts of them, including the case of the individual actors, which is repugnant altogether and fatal to the claim of State power, which I am now examining? The truth seems to be that these transactions, and such as these, are entire transactions. They are in their nature, and from the necessity of the case, indivisible. They are wholly within the domain of national diplomacy, for example, as against the State claim of jurisdiction, or they are not within it at all. You admit that this government may adjust the transaction, as a governmental act of England, by negotiation. Under its power to make treaties, to conclude peace, to regulate foreign intercourse, you admit that it may and must do this. But if it can do this, it can adjust the case of the individual actors, too. Nobody can so much as conceive a theory of the extent and nature of your treaty-making functions, according to which they should include one of these powers and not include the other. Why, Sir, one of the powers would be totally useless without the other. Can you amicably and honorably adjust the controversy with the government which commanded, while you declare your purpose, or a State declares its purpose, to hang the servant who obeyed? Will the foreign nation settle for itself, and leave its soldiers to be punished for murder? To render the treaty-making capacity of the slightest value, then, it must cover the whole of the ground. And so it must in every possible view. By immemorial usage it is the means, it is the agent, by which to adjust the case of such of the subjects of one nation as become implicated in its foreign relations, and obnoxious to the complaints of another nation. Then you may wield it for that purpose and to that extent. By the universal understanding of the world, according to all acknowledged principles of international law, in the nature of things, in reason, in justice, the case of a nation which does a wrong to another through the instrumentality of its servants, and the case of the servants themselves, the national and the individual offence and responsibility fall within the cognizance of one and the same code; constitute one complex but inseparable consideration; must be all adjusted together or all kept open together. In truth, although it is not necessary for this discussion to go so far, the fact that as, in such a transaction as this, it is a nation which has entered your territory and perpetrated the act you complain of; that a foreign nation has wielded an individual instrument to assail this nation—this fact impresses instantly on the whole affair a mere and pure national character, subjects it to national control, and merges, annihilates, and excludes all subordinate constituents and all subordinate and individual agency of crime. Certainly, at least, it commits *to one and the same jurisdiction* the disposition and adjustment of the public act, and of all such constituents and all such agency. The conclusion is unavoidable, therefore, that the State right here asserted cannot be set up against the powers of the general government. As against them it has no existence.

You arrive at the same conclusion by a consideration of the legislative power of this government over this kind of transaction, of which I have just spoken. If, by a legislative declaration that the invasion of our territory by force and by armed men, the burning of The Caroline, and the destruction of life, was an act of war, and that similar enterprises are acts of war, you confessedly subject the actors in these transactions to the control of the national government alone; and if you may make such a declaration, then what becomes of an asserted, inalienable, constitutional State right to try and to hang such actors as for a pure municipal offence? Sir, it has no existence; and the only question which is open at all is, whether you may exert your own acknowledged power in the particular mode proposed by the bill. The question is not whether you invade any State right and transcend any power of the general government by doing so, but whether you exercise your constitutional power in a constitutional way. That question I have already too much at large attempted to answer.

I have left myself neither time nor strength to say much upon the expediency of passing this law. It has been very earnestly maintained by the Senator from Pennsylvania that, even if you have the constitutional power to interpose your appellate and supervising jurisdiction in this class of cases, after judgment in the State courts, you have no constitutional power to do it before judgment; and that, even if it were expedient so to interpose after judgment, it is not expedient to do so before.

Let me say, Sir, in the first place, that, if you have power to interpose after judgment, you have power to do so before. If you can reverse a judgment, you can anticipate its rendition. If, within the Constitution, your judicial power extends to these cases or these controversies, whether you take hold of the case or of the controversy in one stage or another, is totally immaterial. The single question submitted to the national tribunals — the question, whether, under the statute adopting the laws of nations, the prisoner is entitled to the immunity or exemption he claims — may as well be extracted from the entire case, and presented and decided in those tribunals before any judgment in the State court, as it can be revised afterwards, on writ of error. Either way they pass on no other question. Either way they do not administer the criminal law of a State. In one case as much as in the other, and no more, do they interfere with the State judicial power.

And this, Sir, I understand to be the opinion of the Supreme Court in Martin *v.* Hunter's lessee, 1 Wheaton, 304. In the very masterly judgment pronounced by Mr. Justice Story for the court, he says, (commenting on the power of removing causes from State to the national courts before judgment, page 349): "The existence of this power of removal is familiar, in courts acting according to the course of the common law, in criminal as well as civil cases, and it is exercised before as well as after judgment. But this is always deemed, in both cases, an exercise of appellate and not of original jurisdiction. If, then, the right of removal be included in the appellate jurisdiction, it is only because it is one mode of exercising that power, and, as congress is not limited by the Constitution to any particular mode or time of exercising it, it may authorize a removal before or after judgment. The time, the process, and the manner, must be subject to its absolute legislative control." The honorable Senator interprets this opinion differently, and relies, first, on a passage in it on page 592 of the third volume of the condensed reports, from which he reads. But that passage applies only to a case where congress has made no law for the removal of the cause before judgment, and does not touch the question of your power to make such a law. His other citation, from page 597, is equally inapplicable. It asserts nothing, and it says nothing, of your power to remove the cause; but intimates an apprehension only that the removal would be unavailing, without an attendant power to act on the State tribunal itself. But, as Mr. Justice Johnson observes, and as this bill supposes, the removal by *habeas corpus* supplies all that is needed to make a plain power an effectual one.

Hear Mr. Justice Johnson in the same case, page 379:

"This method," (he is speaking of the removal of causes from the State courts to the national, before judgment, as contrasted with the reversal of the judgments of the State courts by writs of error,) "this method, so much more unlikely to affect official delicacy than that which is resorted to in the other class of cases, might, perhaps, have been more happily applied to all the cases which the legislature thought it advisable to remove from the State courts."

And, in another passage, that learned judge seems to anticipate and advise the very process provided by this bill, page 381:

"With this view, by means of laws avoiding judgments obtained in the State courts, in cases over which congress has, constitutionally, assumed jurisdiction, and inflicting penalties on parties who shall contumaciously persist in infringing the constitutional rights of others, *under a liberal extension of the writ of injunction and the habeas corpus ad subjiciendum*, I flatter myself that the full extent of the constitutional revising power may be secured to the United States, and the benefits of it to the individual, without ever resorting to compulsory or restrictive process upon the State tribunals."

The honorable Senator objects, too, that a removal of the cause, before judgment, to the district court, and thence to the circuit court by appeal, and thence, by a second appeal, to the supreme court, results in giving to the supreme court original jurisdiction in a case where, by the Constitution, it can take appellate jurisdiction only. This seems to me not very intelligible, or, if intelligible, not at all sound. Certainly all the jurisdiction which the supreme court obtains by this bill is appellate in the strictest sense. The cause is removed first to the district court, and there tried once on its merits. It goes thence, by appeal, to the circuit court, and is there tried on its merits again. It passes, at last, to the supreme court, where it is finally and fully tried on its merits again; and yet, obtaining the cause through this series of appeals, the supreme court is supposed to exercise original, not appellate, jurisdiction. True, the State court did not try the cause, and, if the bill removed it *per saltum*, by the writ of liberty, from that to the supreme court, it might be objected that it communicated original jurisdiction to the supreme court. But it does no such thing. Surely it is not meant to be said that the jurisdiction which it does give to the supreme court is not appellate, because the appeal is from a federal court, and not, directly or indirectly, from a State court? Appellate jurisdiction is that which is exercised by a court over causes submitted to it by appeal from another court. This is all it means in this part of the Constitution. This is exactly the jurisdiction given in this bill to the supreme court. To say that, because you cannot remove the cause at once, before judgment, by *habeas corpus*, to the supreme court, you cannot do it indirectly, mediately, through the district and circuit courts, after successive trials there, is to say that you cannot give appellate, because you cannot give original jurisdiction. If no more is meant, however, to be said, than that the State court must try the cause to judgment before it can be removed at all, why this, of course, assumes the precise proposition to be proved.

I submit, too, Sir, that if it be expedient to review judgments of the State courts in this description of cases, it is expedient to interpose before they are rendered. The honorable Senator vehemently contends that it is odious and offensive to the States not to wait till judgment, humiliating to their pride, exasperating to their feelings,—the last and unkindest cut of all, to their dimmed, affronted, and diminished sovereignty. Sir, mark the change of time and opinion. Within five minutes he has interrupted me to remind you that the counsel in Martin *v.* Hunter's lessee, contended that, as matter of policy, to disarm the controlling jurisdiction of your courts, as far as might be, of its harsher and more offensive aspects and operation, it ought to be exerted in the earliest practicable stage of the proceeding below. Such was Mr. Justice Johnson's opinion in the same case. Such, I own, is mine. In the beginning of these prosecutions, little or no interest may be felt by anybody. The private prosecutor, the court, the law-officer of the State, and the counsel of the prisoner, alone, know or care much about the matter; and a preliminary and single issue of law, or fact, or both, to settle the question of the claim of exemption from the criminal jurisprudence of the State, may be framed, and submitted, and even decided quietly, and without excitement. But let the cause go forward in the court of the State; let the jury try it; let the bar discuss it before the assembled country; let the press, and let party lay hold on it; let a foreign government begin to take the matter up; enlist the pride and the sense of character of the bench, and the whole State, by an elaborate judgment, fully committing their judicial reputation against the exemption claimed; and then the interposition of the national tribunals becomes, indeed, an odious and perilous enterprise.

Besides, Sir, in determining upon the stage in which you are to interpose, if you will interpose at all, you will not lose sight of the consideration, that the object of your interposition, the ground on which you are authorized to interpose at all, is the preservation of the national peace. A leading question would be, therefore, whether the earliest will not be the most effectual interposition for the great object in view? Is it not so, that the sooner the prisoner is in the hands and within the control of the government, to which his country looks for his deliverance,—the government which must insure his acquittal, or answer for his condemnation,—the better for all parties?

But the honorable Senator is against your jurisdiction in all forms and in all stages. Sir, I cannot concur with him. I would assert the jurisdiction, on the contrary, on the same grand, general reason, for which it was given to you. It was given as a means of enabling you to preserve honorable peace, or to secure the next best thing, a just war, a war into which we may carry the sympathies and the praise and the assistance of the world. Accept and exert it for these great ends. Do not be deterred from doing so, and from doing so now, by what the honorable Senator so many times repeated to you, that negotiations are pending with England; that she has insulted and menaced you, and withheld reparation, and withheld apology; and that, therefore, the passage of the bill, at this moment, would be an unmanly and unseasonable courtesy or concession to her. How much England knows or cares about the passage of this bill; what new reason it may afford to the Foreign Quarterly Review for predicting the approach of his monarchical millennium in America, we need not, I believe, no one here, need know or care. But does it mark unmanly fear of England, an unmanly haste to propitiate her good-will, because I would commit the quiet and the glory of my country to you? Where should the peace of the nation repose, but beneath the folds of the nation's flag? Do not fear, either, that you are about to undervalue the learning, abilities, and integrity of the State tribunals. Sir, my whole life has been a constant experience of their learning, abilities, and integrity; but I do not conceive that I distrust or disparage them, when I have the honor to agree with the Constitution itself, that yours are the hands to hold the mighty issues of peace and war.

Mr. President, how strikingly all things, and every passing hour, illustrate the wisdom of those great men who looked to the Union, the Union under a general government, for the preservation of peace, at home and abroad, between us and the world, among the States, and in each State. Turn your eyes eastward and northward, and see how this vast, but restrained and parental, central power holds at rest a thousand spirits, a thousand elements of strife! There is Maine. How long would it be, if she were independent, before her hardy and gallant children would pour themselves over the disputed territory, like the flakes of her own snow-storms? How long, if New York were so, before that tumultuous frontier would blaze with ten thousand "bale fires"? Our own beautiful and beloved Rhode Island herself, with which the Senator rebukes you for interfering, is it not happy even for her, that her star, instead of shining alone and apart in the sky, blends its light with so many kindred rays, whose influence may save it from shooting madly from its sphere?

The aspect which our united America turns upon foreign nations, the aspect which the Constitution designs she shall turn on them, the guardian of our honor, the guardian of our peace, is, after all, her grandest and her fairest aspect. We have a right to be proud when we look on that. Happy and free empress mother of States themselves free, unagitated by the passions, unmoved by the dissensions of any one of them, she watches the rights and fame of all, and reposing, secure and serene, among the mountain summits of her freedom, she holds in one hand the fair olive branch of peace, and in the other the thunderbolt and meteor flag of reluctant and rightful war. There may she sit forever,—the stars of union upon her brow, the rock of independence beneath her feet!

Mr. President, it is because this bill seems to me well calculated to accomplish one of the chief original ends of the Constitution that it has my hearty support.

SPEECH ON THE POWER AND DUTY OF CONGRESS TO CONTINUE THE POLICY OF PROTECTING AMERICAN LABOR.

DELIVERED IN THE SENATE OF THE UNITED STATES, MARCH 14, 1842.

[THE resolutions of Mr. CLAY being under consideration, one of which was in the following terms:

"*Resolved*, That, in the adjustment of a tariff to raise an amount of twenty-six millions of revenue, the principles of the Compromise Act generally should be adhered to, and that especially a maximum rate of ad valorem duties should be established, from which there ought to be as little departure as possible," Mr. Choate spoke as follows:]

MR. PRESIDENT, —

I HAD wished to say something on one branch of one of the subjects to which the resolutions extend; I mean that of the readjustment of the tariff, as it may affect domestic industry. In my view, it is the great subject of the session and of the day. I agree with the Pennsylvania memorialists, whose petition has just been read, that the subject of the currency — difficult, delicate, and important as it is, and creditable as it will be to my friend from New York, [Mr. Tallmadge,] and useful to the country to adjust it — bears no comparison, in point of importance, with this. We are coming, whether we will or not, by the progress of the Compromise Act, to an era in the history of the national industry and the national prosperity. We have it in our power to mark this era by the commission of a stupendous mistake, or by the realization of a splendid felicity and wisdom of policy. This very tariff which we are about to construct may, on the one hand, paralyze American labor, drive it from many of its best fields of employment, arrest the development of our resources of growth and wealth, and even the development of the mind and genius of America, our main resource, turning back the current of our national fortunes for an age; or it may, on the other hand, communicate an impulse, that shall be felt after we are in our graves, to that harmonized agricultural, manufacturing, and commercial industry, which alone can fill the measure of this or of any country's glory.

Under this impression of the importance of the subject, I have wished to take part in the discussion of it. In the present stage, however, of this business of arranging the tariff in the two houses of congress, — with no bill before us, with no report of either of the committees on manufactures, although we have had a very able speech from the chairman of our own committee, [Mr. Simmons,] unaided to any considerable and useful extent by the voice of the country, which, if I do not misunderstand the country, will come up, peremptory and unequivocal, the moment you have a bill reported, and before, if that is delayed much longer, — I do not think it expedient, or even practicable, to go far into the consideration of details. I mean to abstain from them altogether at this time. I move no question now about the amount of annual revenue which you will require for the wants of government, nor whether you should raise it from duties on imports alone, or partly from the proceeds of the public lands. I have nothing now to say about specific duties or ad valorem duties, horizontal or discriminating tariffs, home valuation or foreign valuation. The actual state of information before us, in parliamentary and authentic form, is not such as to make it worth while to anticipate that kind of discussion. But there is one preliminary and general principle upon which I shall consider myself obliged to stand; by which I shall consider myself obliged to try every question of detail that shall present itself; and which it may be as fair and proper to announce at this moment as at any other; and that is, that congress has the constitutional power so to provide for the collection of the necessary revenues of government as to afford reasonable and adequate protection to the whole labor of the country, agricultural, navigating, mechanical, and manufacturing, and *ought to afford that protection.* This general principle I shall take with me through all this investigation; and it is the only one which it is necessary now to declare. I mean by this to say, that I shall enter on this business of the tariff with no unalterable predetermination as to the precise mode of effecting the grand object in view; although I certainly hold a very confident opinion that discriminating and specific duties will be found indispensable. But this I am ready to avow: that the protection of American labor, on all its fields and in all its forms, is to be kept constantly and anxiously in view in all our arrangements; that you have the constitutional power to secure that protection; and that you are bound to do so, regardless of everything and everybody but the Constitution, justice, and a true and large American policy.

There can be no doubt then, it would seem, in the first place, on the constitutional power of congress, in the assessment of duties of revenue, so to discriminate among objects of duty as to bring to life and to keep alive the whole multiform, agricultural, manufacturing, and commercial industry of the country. To state the immediate proposition which I mean to examine more precisely: You are about determining to raise a certain annual amount of revenue, — twenty-six millions of dollars, if you please. The wants of government require at least so much, whatever becomes of the land bill. The amount is fixed by reference to those wants. Now, without intending by any means to concede that this is the extent of your constitutional power, — for certainly, in my judgment, it goes a great deal further, — what I would say is, that, in assessing the duties which are to yield the amount thus determined on, you may discriminate for the protection of labor. You may admit some articles free, and just as many of them as you please, without any regard to the enumeration in the Compromise Act. You may prohibit the importation of others. You may admit some under specific, and some under ad valorem duties, — some under a low rate, and some under a high one, — some under a foreign valuation, others under a valuation at home, — and others, or all, under that legislative preëstablishment of value which the Senator from Rhode Island [Mr. Simmons] proposes to substitute for fraudulent or mistaken estimates of actual and changeable value made abroad or at home. All this you may do; these varieties of proceeding you may choose between, with intent to bring out and sustain the domestic labor of America against the capital, the necessities, or the policy of foreigners, whether individuals or governments. Upon the words of the Constitution, if it were an open question to-day, this is clear. The history of the origin, construction, and adoption of that instrument demonstrates it. And, then, there is a weight of opinion, and a series of practical interpretation, which should put the matter forever at rest.

Mr. President, the senate would hardly excuse me for assuming to offer a formal and laborious argument as an original one, in proof of this matter. Delicacy, honor, and good sense would forbid such an attempt to appropriate borrowed plumes. No man's ability or research could clothe the subject with any useful novelty; how much less can mine! I desire, therefore, only to recall to your mind the general nature and main points of an argument already and long ago familiar to you. And even this I should not venture on, if the state of opinion in the country and in congress did not appear to render such a discussion seasonable and useful. Sir, the tendency of the time is to regard this protecting power as stricken out of the Constitution. I have even heard judicious men speak of it as an *exploded* thing. We reason, some reason — certainly not the honorable mover of these resolutions — but some reason as if it had been agreed somewhere, at some time, and by somebody or another, that the power should never again be asserted, or never again be exercised. They would persuade you that the people, nine years ago, to secure to themselves the peaceable enjoyment of their rights for nine years longer, had stipulated that, at the end of the time, they would surrender the principle of constitutional protection forever. For a fleeting term of possession, — nothing in the life of a nation; nothing in the life of a man, — they agreed to squander away the inheritance itself!

Now, Sir, without pausing to inquire into the origin of this opinion, without pausing to inquire how far it may be attributable to the silent influence of the Compromise Act in unsettling the tone of the public mind, still less to debate the merits of that celebrated arrangement, or to judge between the sagacity, patriotism, and firmness of those who suggested and those who opposed it, I think it may not be unseasonable to ascend from that act to the contemplation of first principles. Let us turn from the stormy passions, and unconstitutional organizations, and extorted expedients of 1833, and breathe the pure and invigorating air of 1789! Let us see what our fathers framed the government for, and what they expected of it.

I find your authority then, Sir, to pass laws of protection, where the calm and capacious intelligence of Mr. Madison found it in 1789, in 1810, and 1828. That great man, among our greatest of the dead or the living; who had helped so much to frame the Constitution and procure its adoption, defending and expounding it with his tongue and pen to his own Virginia, and to the whole country; who had weighed, aye, Sir, and helped to coin and stamp, every word in it; and who knew the evils, the wants, the hopes, the opinions in which it had its origin, as well as any man ever knew why he removed from an old house to a new one; Mr. Madison, in 1789 sustaining in congress that celebrated law laying impost duties for the support of government, the discharge of the public debt, and the encouragement and protection of manufactures, in 1810, in a message to congress, and in 1828, in his letter to Mr. Cabell, — at the beginning, in the midst, and at the close of his career; first when his faculties were at their best, his memory of events recent, his ambition high; again with the utmost weight of his official responsibilities upon him; and again in old age, when his passions were calmed, the measure of his fame full, and he looked round upon the widespread tribes of the people whom he had served, and who had honored him so long, and upon their diversities of interest and of sentiment with a parental and patriarchal eye, — he found your authority always in the Constitution, and he found it in your "power to regulate commerce with foreign nations, among the several States, and with the Indian tribes." Let me read a passage from his speech in congress in 1789, upon Mr. Fitzsimons's proposition to combine the objects of protection and revenue in the bill laying duties on imports: —

"The States that are most advanced in population, and ripe for manufactures, ought to have their particular interests attended to in some degree. While these States retained the power of making regulations of trade, they had the power to protect and cherish such institutions. By adopting the present Constitution, they have thrown the exercise of this power into other hands; they must have done this with an expectation that those interests would not be neglected here." — *James Madison, Gales and Seaton's Debates, old series,* vol. i. p. 116.

In his message of the fifth of December, 1810, after adverting to a "highly interesting extension of useful manufactures, the combined product of professional occupations and of household industry," he observes, "how far it may be expedient to guard the infancy of this improvement in the distribution of labor, by *regulations of the commercial tariff*, is a subject which cannot fail to suggest itself to your patriotic reflections." His letter to Mr. Cabell, written in September, 1828, in which he defines his opinions upon the power more precisely, and produces a very strong argument in support of them, is known to everybody. "The question is," he says, "whether, under the Constitution of the United States, 'the power to regulate trade with foreign nations,' as a distinct and substantive item in the enumerated powers, embraces the object of encouraging, by duties, restrictions, and prohibitions, the manufactures and products of the country? And the affirmative must be inferred from the following considerations;" which he proceeds to unfold and urge with that force of persuasive reason for which he was so remarkable.

I derive, then, your power to arrange duties, for the purpose of protection, from your power to regulate commerce. The "Congress shall have power to regulate commerce with foreign nations, and among the several States, and with the Indian tribes." What does this language mean? *How, and by what means,* does the Constitution authorize you to regulate commerce, and *for what ends* to regulate it? The answer is, it authorizes you to regulate it, among other means, by the imposition of discriminating duties, or prohibitory duties on imports of foreign manufactures, or other articles, for the purpose, among other purposes, of encouraging domestic manufactures, and any and every other form of domestic industry.

The presumption, certainly, in the first instance is, that these words of the Constitution mean to communicate the power to pass any law, to do any act, for any purpose, which, in the general and political language of the country in 1787, was deemed and called an ordinary and usual governmental commercial regulation. You may regulate commerce. Then you may do it by any and all such means, and for any and all such ends, as formed at that time the known and usual means and ends by and for which governments habitually regulated commerce. If you cannot do it by all such means, and for all such ends, you cannot by any, nor for any. All the known and usual modes, and all the known and usual ends, are committed to you; or none are so. This is the first and legal import, *primâ facie*, of so general a grant. The presumption in the first instance is, that this language was used in the sense which it was generally understood to bear when asserted of or applied to other governments in other writings, or in the current speech of the age of the Constitution. If, in the contemporaneous written and spoken vocabulary, a "commercial regulation" comprised and meant a certain act, or certain classes of acts, a certain act for a certain purpose; if a law of England, or of one of the States, laying duties on imports for the encouragement of domestic labor, mechanical, manufacturing, navigating, or agricultural, was, in that vocabulary, held and called a common commercial regulation; one of the recognized and familiar exercises of the power to regulate commerce; the presumption is, that the words here mean what they meant everywhere else. If you can control this presumption by inspection of other parts of the Constitution, or of its general structure, or by other legitimate evidence, do so; but the burden will be on you. It was upon this presumption that the discussion in this body, the other day, upon the bankrupt law proceeded. To determine the nature and limits of your power to pass such a law, you inquired what bankruptcy meant, and what laws upon the subject of bankruptcy were, in the legal language of the time? The senators from Delaware, [Mr. Bayard,] and from Missouri, [Mr. Benton,] who debated this subject so ably, in opposition to the bill, did not argue that, from the nature of this government, the phrase "laws upon the subject of bankruptcy" must be supposed to mean less or more than the same phrase anywhere else. They treated it as a question on the meaning of language; and, assuming that the words in the Constitution meant what the same words meant elsewhere, they sought that meaning in the contemporaneous, popular, and technical vocabulary of the States, and of England. Just so here. To determine the nature and limits of this power to regulate commerce, to determine whether it enables you to construct a protecting tariff, inquire whether in the political and popular vocabulary of 1787 such a tariff was an ordinary form and kind of commercial regulation. If it were, the doubt is resolved.

And now is it not indisputable that, at that day, what we now call a discriminating tariff for protection was universally known and described as one familiar and recognized kind of commercial regulation? and that a power of government to regulate commerce was universally understood to include the power to make such a tariff? Sir, nothing is more certain. Nothing is more certain than that, by a concurrence of extraordinary circumstances, the expressions, *commercial regulations, regulations of trade, the power to regulate commerce, the power to regulate trade*, and the like, had acquired, in the political and popular language of the day, a definite and uniform sense; and that, according to that sense, a protecting tariff was a form of commercial regulation, and the power to regulate commerce included the power to construct such a tariff.

Go back, for a moment, in the first place, to the close of the war in 1783, and inquire what this language meant then. No other words, or combination of words, had so settled, so precise, and so notorious a signification. You remember how this came to pass. The discussions and the events of the twenty years before had given them currency, and fixed their meaning. They had been burned and graven, as it were, into the memory of America. The disputes of England and her colonies, which brought on the Revolution, had turned on the extent of her power over them. She asserted in 1764 an enlarged and a menacing extent of claim; a claim not only to regulate their trade, but to lay internal and external taxes, and to bind them in all cases whatsoever. They admitted the right to regulate trade; they admitted the right to do it by the imposition of duties on imports into the colonies, and on their imports into England; they admitted the right to do it for the purpose of developing and sustaining the manufacturing, mechanical, and navigating industry of the mother-country; but they denied the right, for the first time asserted in the Stamp

Act, to lay internal taxes. She asserted both rights; and from this conflict of the exactions of dominion and the resistance of liberty, arose the discussions which preceded the war, and the war itself. Now, what I ask you particularly to remark is, that, in all the stages and in all the forms of this controversy; a controversy extending over twenty years; a controversy which addressed the reason and exasperated the feelings of all America, and made everybody familiar with its topics and its vocabulary, — *all the disputants on both sides agreed exactly on the nature of a commercial regulation, and of the acts which might be done under the power to make such a regulation.* Grenville, Lord North, Lord Chatham, and Burke, in England; and in the colonies, John Dickinson the Pennsylvania farmer, Benjamin Franklin the Boston mechanic, John Adams the Massachusetts lawyer, whose energy and eloquence brought up a hesitating congress to the Declaration of Independence, Sewall, the champion of parliament and the crown, Jefferson, who first denied the right of England to exert either of the powers she claimed — these and a hundred others, some of whose names we know, while some have perished — *stant nominum umbræ!* — all who took part for you or against you in that, your "agony of glory," concur in this. All of them agreed that the long series of legislation by which England had laid duties on imports of the colonies, for the purpose of bringing out and sustaining her domestic industry of all kinds, were regulations of trade; all of them agreed that, if she had power to regulate the trade of the colonies, her protecting tariffs were clearly within the exercise of the power; and all of them at first, and most of them, even on the American side, down nearly to the Declaration of Independence, conceded to her that precise power. Taking their stand upon the nature of this power, and of the acts it authorized, those who sustained the claim of England argued that her right to lay internal taxes followed of course, while those who espoused the cause of liberty denied that it followed at all; but upon the nature of that power, and of the acts it authorized, if it existed, there was no diversity of opinion, and there was nearly a unanimous concession that it did exist. Every speech, every address, every public act, every essay, every pamphlet, all the written remains of that anxious and momentous controversy, which employed so many eloquent tongues and pens, and went, at last, to the arbitrament of war, prove this. It is wholly indisputable that if, in the year 1783, it were written or said that England, before the Revolution, and the States after it, had the power to regulate the trade of America, the writer or speaker meant to declare that England first, and subsequently the States, had the power, among other things, *to tax imports in order to protect manufactures, the arts, navigation, and agriculture; and that he was understood to mean so by all England and all America.*

Mr. President, I could not exhibit in a day all the evidence of this which breaks forth from every page of our Revolutionary and ante-Revolutionary political literature. You know how considerable a body of writing it is. It is familiar to the earlier and the maturer studies of senators. You have not been inattentive to a class of compositions, some of which the masculine taste of Chatham did not refuse to rank with the best political writings of the master States of antiquity.

Let me read a few selections, however, in proof and illustration of the currency and the meaning of this language prior and down to 1783. Some of them, I know, have been accumulated and arranged for this purpose by others; and, indeed, the *principle* of this whole mode of argument, and the nature of the investigations by which it should be conducted, are suggested by Mr. Madison's letter. But I have not thought it proper to omit any for this reason; and some of them, I think, have not been adverted to at all.

In an anonymous pamphlet, published as early as August, 1765, entitled "Considerations on the propriety of imposing taxes in the British colonies, for the purpose of raising a revenue, by act of Parliament," of which I know only that it was one of the numerous and effective contributions of Virginia to the cause of colonial liberty, the writer, (page 33,) says: —

"It appears to me that there is a clear and necessary distinction between an act imposing a tax for *the single purpose of revenue*, and those acts which have been made *for the regulation of trade*, and have produced some revenue *in consequence of their effect* and operation as *regulations of trade*." And again, (page 34): "It is a common, and frequently the most proper method, to regulate trade by duties on imports and exports. The authority of the mother-country to regulate the trade of the colonies being unquestionable, what regulations are the most proper are to be of course submitted to the determination of the Parliament; and, if an *incidental revenue* should be produced by such regulations, these are not, therefore, unwarrantable."

I ought to have reminded you that before this, in 1761, even James Otis, in that great argument upon the subject of writs of assistance which breathed (I may use the vivid expression of John Adams) "the breath of life into America," admitted, upon the ground of *necessity*, the power of England to pass her whole series of acts of trade "as regulations of commerce," while he utterly denied their validity as laws of revenue. Let me refer you to the glowing and remarkable analysis of that argument, contained in the letters of Mr. Adams to Mr. Tudor, written in 1818.

In October, 1765, the first congress of the colonies assembled at New York to confer on the means of preserving the liberties of America, menaced by that new system of imperial policy of which the Stamp Act was the most palpable, most alarming, but not the only manifestation. Of the proceedings of this congress we know little. Tradition has preserved something of the impression which the genius and eloquence of James Otis, and his profound knowledge of the interests, and his deep comprehension of the rights and unappeasable resentment for the wrongs of the colonies, produced on the assembly; but his words of fire are perished forever. There survive, however, of the labors of that body, a general declaration of rights, an address to the king, a petition to each house of parliament, and a report of a committee on the subject of the colonial rights. I read you a sentence from the address to the king, which is repeated, almost in the very same words, in the report of the committee. You may find it in Pitkins's "Civil and Political History," first volume, pages 185 and 453.

"It is also humbly submitted whether there be not a material distinction, in reason and sound policy at least, between the necessary exercises of parliamentary jurisdiction in general acts, for the amendment of the common law, *and the regulation of trade and commerce* through the whole empire, and the exercise of that jurisdiction by *imposing taxes on the colonies.*"

In February, 1766, Dr. Franklin underwent his celebrated

examination "before an august assembly," as the colonial writers of the day called the house of commons; and to the question "was it an opinion of America, before 1763, that parliament had no right to lay duties and taxes there?" he answered, "I never heard an objection to the right to lay duties to regulate commerce." See how fully this is confirmed by John Dickinson, in the second of the "Farmer's Letters," written in 1767: —

"The Parliament," he observes, (page 4,) "unquestionably possesses a legal authority to regulate the trade of Great Britain and all her colonies. Such an authority is essential to the relation of a mother-country and her colonies, and necessary for the common good of all."

He then adverts to the legislation of England for the colonies before the Stamp Act, makes extracts from the several statutes, beginning with 12 Car. II., and then adds: —

"All before the Stamp Act are calculated to regulate trade, although many of them imposed duties on it." "Great Britain," he proceeds in the same letter, (page 9,) "has prohibited the manufacturing iron and steel in these colonies without any objection being made to her right of doing it. The like right she must have to prohibit any other manufacture among us. Our great advocate, Mr. Pitt, in his speeches on the debate concerning the repeal of the *Stamp Act*, acknowledged that *Great Britain* could restrain our manufactures. His words are these: 'This kingdom, as the supreme governing and legislative power, has *always* bound the colonies by her regulations and *restrictions* in trade, in navigation, in *manufactures* — in everything, *except that of taking their money out of their pockets without their consent.*' Again he says: 'We may bind their trade, *confine their manufactures*, and exercise every power whatever, except that of taking their money out of their pockets without their consent.'" "External impositions, (this is Mr. Dickinson's language, letter 4, page 17,) *for the regulation of our trade*, do not grant to his Majesty the property of his colonies."

"There is a plain distinction," Lord Chatham had said the year before, in one of those glorious efforts of his eloquence which so much endeared him to our fathers, and stirred their hearts like the sound of a trumpet — "there is a plain distinction between taxes levied for the purpose of raising a revenue and duties imposed *for the regulation of trade*, although some revenue might arise from the latter." We may regulate trade, — such was his argument, — we may regulate it by the imposition of duties; we may do it for the purpose of giving direction and development to the whole industry of the empire. But we cannot levy an internal tax for revenue.

Burke, whose long series of exertions for the rights of the colonies do him as much honor as the marvellous affluence of his genius, proceeds everywhere upon the same distinction, and uses everywhere the same language. "Without idolizing the trade laws," he says, in his speech on conciliation with America in 1775, "I am sure they are still, in many ways, of great use to us. But my perfect conviction of this does not help me in the least to discern how the revenue laws form any security whatsoever to the *commercial regulations*, or that these *commercial regulations* are the true ground of quarrel." And the year before, in his speech on American taxation: "This is certainly true, that no act avowedly for the purpose of revenue, and with the ordinary title and recital, taken together, is found in the statute book till the year 1764. All before this period *stood on commercial regulation and restraint.*"

Nearly at the same time the congress which declared our independence, in a grave and lofty paper, in which they claimed for the colonies "the free and exclusive power in all cases of taxation and internal policy," avowed nevertheless, —

> "That, from the necessity of the case, we cheerfully consent to the operation of such acts of the British Parliament as are *bonâ fide* restrained to the *regulation of commerce* for the purpose of securing the commercial advantages of the whole empire to the mother-country, and the commercial benefits of its respected members, excluding every idea of taxation for raising a revenue on the subjects of America without their consent."

In 1774 and 1775, John Adams, in a series of papers, under the signature of Novanglus, vindicated the cause of American liberty against the king's attorney-general, Sewall, with a vigor and ability which gave assurance of the future champion of independence. These papers and those of his antagonist discussed all the points of controversy between England and her colonies, and reviewed the whole history of their original and their altered relations; and, exasperated and soured as the colonists had become, clearly and far as the eagle glance of the orator of independence already saw into the future, it is remarkable that then, even almost down to the battle of Lexington, this distinction was still recognized and respected and reasoned on.

"And from that time to this, (i. e. for more than a hundred years,) the general sense of the colonies has been, that the authority of parliament was confined to the regulation of trade, and did not extend to taxation or internal legislation." "Duties for regulating trade we paid because we thought it just," &c. "As for duties for a revenue, none were ever laid by parliament for that purpose until 1764, when, and ever since, its authority to do it has been constantly denied." — *Letters of Novanglus and Massachusettensis*, pp. 38, 39. *Feb.* 13*th*, 1775.

The ministry at length perceived the expediency of admitting the justice of a distinction with which England and America had become so familiar. In 1778 Lord North, aroused to the realities of his situation, and seeking to win the insurgent colonies from independence and from France, procured the passage of a bill which offered a compromise upon the precise basis for which they had so long contended. "It is expedient," such was the language of the bill, "to declare that the King and Parliament of Great Britain will not impose any duty or tax for the purpose of raising a revenue in the colonies, except only such duties as may be expedient to impose for the *regulation of commerce*." (St. 18, Geo. III.) But, in the phrase of Paine, "the charm had been broken," and the tardy offer of conciliation was unheard, or distrusted, or distasteful, amid the voice of battle, by the hoarded up resentments of a whole people, to the spirit of liberty and to the passion of glory.

And now, what kind of regulations were those which the colonies so long and so universally conceded to England the right to make? Sir, they were, among others, what, in the language of this day, we call discriminating and protecting tariffs. They were laws imposing duties on imports, as you see by the passages I have selected, and imposing them for the purpose of encouraging the navigation and trade, and developing the manufacturing capacity and labor, that had seated England on the throne of the commercial world. "One thing at least is certain," says Mr. Madison in his letter to Mr. Cabell, "that the main and admitted object of the parliamentary *regulations of trade with the colonies* was the encouragement of the *manufactures* in Great Britain." They were designed, among other objects, expressly to secure to the English manufacturer the *home* market and the colonial market *for his fabrics*, and the *colonial* supply of his *raw materials*, against the competition which might reduce the price of the former and enhance the price of the latter. Other and broader objects they pursued, undoubtedly; but, for the purposes of this discussion, I speak only of this. For the accomplishment of this object they restrained, by heavy duties or by direct prohibition, the importation of foreign manufactures into the colonies; they discouraged the colonial manufacturers themselves; and they obliged them to send, in English ships, to English markets, and to English markets alone, the raw material, which English genius was to transfigure and refine into shapes of beauty and usefulness, to enrich and swell her commerce with the world. Read the titles and objects of that long succession of laws, in the argument of James Otis, to which I have alluded, and his burning commentary on them, and you will well comprehend the extent and energy of English governmental regulation. Read particularly pages 213 and 294 of the letters of Novanglus and Massachusettensis, and Pitkins's "Political and Civil History of the United States," first volume, page 401. Read the celebrated preamble of the act of navigation itself: —

"In regard his Majesty's plantations beyond the seas are inhabited and peopled by his subjects of this his kingdom of *England, for the maintaining a greater correspondence and kindness between them*, and keeping them in a firmer dependence upon it, and rendering them yet more beneficial and advantageous unto it *in the further employment and increase of English shipping* and seamen, vent of *English woollens*, and other manufactures and commodities, *rendering the navigation to and from the same more safe and cheap*, and making this kingdom *a staple*, not only of the commodities of those plantations, but also of the commodities of other countries and places, *for the supplying of them;* and it being the *usage* of other nations to keep plantations trade to themselves," &c.

Upon the policy here so vigorously sketched, that whole series of regulations of trade reposed. They may all be summed up under the terms of this description; that they were a body of English law, designed by the regulation of the commerce of England and her colonies with each other, and the rest of the world, to develop, to its utmost capacity, the labor of the British empire, in all its forms, according to the discretion of the imperial parliament.

I hold it then, Sir, clear and indisputable, that, down to the close of the war with England in 1783, the phrase "commercial regulations," in the understanding of everybody, included discriminating protecting tariffs; and that when it was said that, before the Revolution, England had the power to regulate commerce, and that, after the declaration of independence, the States had it, it was meant, in the understanding of everybody, that she first, and then they, could make such tariffs. So much is certain.

And now, when you consider that the Constitution was made only four years later; that it was made by and for the generation which had gone through the war and the whole preparatory controversy; that many of those who shared in that controversy, and were most familiar with its topics and its terms, were still alive, in the Convention, or mingling with the people; the presumption undoubtedly is, that this language continued to bear the same sense down to the date of the Constitution, and that it means in that immortal production just what it means in all the other written and spoken speech of the day. But I do not leave this upon what I should have deemed a resistless presumption. To show you that such was the fact, that its meaning remained unaltered to 1787, and that it was inserted into the Constitution precisely *because that was its meaning*, I proceed now to lay before you another kind of evidence, and, as I think, a conclusive body of it.

It is not wholly unworthy of remark, that that which I may call the *colonial*, *controversial*, and *technical* use of this language, — that use of it which I have been illustrating, — was exactly in conformity with its literary, general, and popular use. Mr. Verplanck observes, in his letter to Colonel Drayton, that Adam Smith calls those restrictive tariffs to which he objects commercial regulations. This is true. He sets the system of free trade and that of commercial restraint in contrast; and that whole body of prohibitions, taxations, and general policy, designed to foster domestic labor, he assails under the name of "commercial regulations." And as his work was first published in 1779, it may be presumed, and indeed is known, to have begun to attract the notice of intelligent persons as early as the period immediately after the war, and thus to have contributed to diffuse, impress, and define the sense of the language we are considering.

It is a fact, which bears still more directly upon the point of inquiry to which I have arrived, that after the war several of the States imposed duties, more or less heavy, on imports of foreign manufactures, avowedly for the purpose of sustaining their own manufactures, and that these tariffs were commonly called, in the language of our politics between 1783 and 1789, *commercial regulations.* Massachusetts, New York, Pennsylvania, and I believe other States, had done this. "It is happy for the mechanics in America," (says a writer of Maryland, at some time between 1783 and 1787, "American Museum," first volume, page 215,) "that they have met with the protection and encouragement of government in several of the wisest States." I cannot resist the pleasure of referring to the act of the State of Pennsylvania on this subject, passed in 1785, and of marking the good sense and the forecast which it exemplifies. It recites that divers useful arts and manufactures had been gradually introduced into that State, which had been able, during the war, to supply in the hour of need weapons, ammunition, and clothing, without which the war could not have been carried on; and then proceeds in section two: —

> "And whereas, although the fabrics and manufactures of Europe and other foreign ports, imported into this country in times of peace, may be afforded at cheaper rates than they can be made here, yet good policy and a regard to the well-being of divers useful and industrious citizens, who were employed in the making of like goods in this State, demand of us that moderate duties be laid on certain fabrics and manufactures imported, which do not interfere with, and which (if no relief be given) will undermine and destroy, the useful manufactures of the like kind in this country."

A writer in the "American Museum," on American manufactures, to whom I will refer you more particularly before I have done, at some time before 1787, warmly commends the noble example of Massachusetts in this particular. (Am. Mus. first volume, page 23.) Now, these impositions of duties, for this purpose, by the States, all impositions of duties on imports of the States were called *commercial regulations* by our writers and speakers of the period after the Revolution and before the

Constitution. "While the States," said Mr. Madison in the debate in 1789, to which I have referred, "retained the power of making regulations of trade," (referring palpably to these legislative taxations on imports,) "they had the power to protect and cherish manufactures." They were denominated *commercial acts*, *trade laws*, and *regulations of commerce*, indifferently and universally, in the current language of the time. Tench Coxe, in an inquiry into the principle of a commercial system for the United States, written before the adoption of the Constitution, describes and complains of them under all those appellations. (Am. Mus., first volume, 444.) I suppose it out of all doubt that if, at that time, it had been written or said that the States had the power to regulate commerce, as very frequently in those very words it was written and said, everybody would have understood it to be meant that this included, as one of its commonest exemplifications and exertions, a power to make a protecting tariff. When that precise form of speech was then embodied into the Constitution, did it not mean the same thing?

But, to put this matter at rest, let me ask you to look a little more at large into that considerable body of writings which appeared in the States, between the peace of 1783 and the adoption of the Constitution, upon the subject of a new Constitution. A word first on their general character.

You know how soon after the war an opinion began to prevail that the country needed a stronger government. Suggested at first, like the Revolution itself, by the intelligence of the community, it spread fast and far; the events of every day gave it diffusion and strength; it possessed itself at last of the general mind, and the Constitution was the result. During the progress of this opinion, it produced a great deal of discussion. These writings, into which I wish you now to look, are the fruits of that discussion, and embody its topics and its language. Less known than the more lofty and classical controversial literature of the more glorious revolutionary and ante-revolutionary time, they are to us the most interesting and most instructive writings in the world. No man, I could almost say, can understand the Constitution without the study of them. No man can understand the nature of the new remedial law until he has meditated the disease which it was made to cure, in these vivid pictures of it. No man can understand the vocabulary of the Constitution until he has familiarized himself, in these writings, with the current vocabulary of the people, by whom and for whom it was composed. The defects of the old confederation; its utter insufficiency for our greatness and our glory; the evils which bore the people to the earth, and made their newly acquired independence a dreary and useless thing; the disordered condition of the currency; our exhausting system of trade; the action of conflicting and inadequate commercial regulations of the States; the excessive importations of foreign manufactures; the drain of specie; the stagnation of labor, oppressed and disheartened by a competition with all the pauper labor of all the world; the depression of agriculture, sympathizing with other labor by an eternal law; the need of a system of divided and diversified employments, which should leave no one over-crowded, should leave no man's faculties undeveloped and unexcited, which should give a market and a reward to all industry; the wants, sufferings, fears, wishes; the universal stimulation of mind and fermentation of opinions in which the Constitution had its birth — you find them all there, and you find them nowhere else.

Looking with some labor into a collection of part of these writings in the "American Museum," a work embodying the general spirit of the press from 1783 to 1787, I think I find conclusive evidence of this fact, to wit: that a confident and sagacious and salutary conviction came to be generally adopted; First. That one capital source of the evils which oppressed us was the importation of too many foreign manufactures, and the use of too few domestic manufactures; too much encouragement of the foreign laborer, and too little encouragement of our own; Secondly. That a new and more perfect union and a stronger government were required, among other ends, very much for the cure and prevention of this precise evil; and Thirdly. That, in order to effect this end, the new government must be clothed with this *specific power of regulating trade, whereby it could check the import of foreign manufactures*, by duties and prohibitions, and thus bring to life and keep alive domestic manufactures, and with them the entire labor of America. If this is so, it will prove at once, *first*, that this language retained the same signification in 1787 which it had borne in 1764; and, *next*, that it means in the Constitution just what it meant everywhere else, and was inserted there *because* it bore that meaning. Let me ask your attention, then, to some evidence and illustrations of the fact, to which I might add a thousand.

In the first volume of the collection I have referred to is an article on American manufactures. It is continued through three months of the "Museum," and was written in Maryland at some time after 1783, and before 1787. The proposition which the essayist maintains is, that manufactures ought immediately to be established in the United States. In support of this, he reasons forcibly and zealously, and with much maturity and breadth of view, considering the time when he wrote; presents a vivid exhibition of the uses of manufactures and of manufacturing industry; of the rank they hold in all civilized States; of the division of labor which they render practicable, and the influence of that division in stimulating all the faculties of men and nations, and in supplying to each faculty and each mind its favorite employment and adequate reward; and, above all, he urges the actual evils which were weighing the country down; its foreign debt; its ruinous consumption; its expensive tastes; its incomplete development of industry; its deficiency in the means of self-reliance and self-support and self-regulation, as a decisive argument for his purpose. He goes on then to inquire how manufactures may be introduced and sustained; and his scheme is, *a government which should have power to regulate trade, and in the exercise of that power should, among other expedients, impose duties on imports of articles coming in competition with the domestic labor.* "I am convinced," he says, (page 212,) "that to begin at this juncture the establishment of manufactures will be the only way to lay the foundation for the future glory, greatness, and independence of America." "Well, how, then," he asks, "shall we make the beginning?" "Free trade," he argues, "in our situation, adopting the sentiment of Montesquieu, 'must necessarily lead us to poverty.'" "A State whose balance of trade is always to its disadvantage cannot grow rich." We must have regulated trade, then. "But, we are told by some," he proceeds, "that trade will regulate itself."

Hear how he combats this proposition, and what is the precise *regulation of trade* which he urges upon the statesmen of America: —

"If trade will regulate itself, why do the wisest and most prosperous governments make laws in favor and support of their trade? Why does the British Parliament employ so much time and pains in regulating their trade, so as to render its advantages particularly useful to their own nation? Why so preposterous as to abide by and enforce their boasted navigation act? But so far is trade from regulating itself, that it continually needs the help of the legislation of every country, as a nursing father. If we Americans do not choose to regulate it, it will regulate us, till we have not a farthing left in our land. Trade, like a helpless infant, requires parental care, and to be well looked after; for, says the same excellent author: 'A country that constantly exports fewer manufactures or commodities than it receives will soon find the balance sinking; it will receive less and less, till, falling into extreme poverty, it will receive nothing at all.' The truth is, trade regulates or corrects itself just as everything else does that is left to itself. The manner the late war, for instance, would have corrected itself, had we supinely sat still and folded our arms together, would have been such a correction as I hope no person who makes use of this flimsy argument would wish to have taken place; *and unless we shortly regulate and correct the abuses of our trade by lopping off its useless branches and establishing manufactures*, we shall be corrected perhaps even to our very destruction."

"The mechanics," he continues, "hope the legislature will afford them that protection they are entitled to; for, as the present baleful *system of trade* and scarcity of cash occasion numbers of them to want employment, though they are able and ready to furnish many articles which are at present imported, and as many of their branches are fast declining, and some are likely to become totally extinct, they conceive *that duties ought to be laid on certain imported articles in* such a manner *as to place the American manufacturers on the same footing as the manufacturers* of Europe, and enable them to procure bread and support for their families." And then, in further explanation, he adds, "An excessive duty might be only an encouragement to the smuggler; on the other hand, let them be only so high as to enable the manufacturer to procure a decent subsistence for his family."

Mark two things in this argument and these extracts: *the advice to encourage domestic manufacture* by duties on foreign manufacture, *and the use of language* which calls such an impost, for such an object, *a regulation of trade.*

I should never have done, Sir, if I attempted to read all the proofs which I find in these papers, that the importance of establishing American manufactures seems, even then, to have been generally apprehended; and that a powerful and an immediate impulse was expected to be given to them, in some way, by the new Constitution. The concurrence of opinion upon that point is marvellous. It is still more marvellous, the maturity of the public judgment upon the nature and uses of manufacturing industry, and the very considerable extent to which that industry already had taken root, when you consider with what severity the austere and long dominion of England had pressed upon it; and how short and how unpropitious the time had been for the arts of peace to grow, after that dominion had passed away. But I must confine myself closely to selections which illustrate the meaning and objects of the constitutional phraseology. Let me, however, read a passage or two from a series of letters, by a North Carolinian, under the signature of Sylvius. I find them in the second volume of the "Museum," page 107, and they appeared in August, 1787. His cure, too, for the oppressive indebtment, depreciated currency, scarcity of money, exhausting importations, and, what he calls, luxurious appetites of the day, is the encouragement of American manufactures, and the substitution of a tax on imported manufactures for all other modes of taxation.

"The more I consider" (says he, page 108) "the progress of credit and the increase of wealth in foreign nations, the more fully I am convinced that paper-money must prove hurtful to this country; that we cannot be relieved from our debts except by promoting domestic manufactures; and that during the prevailing scarcity of money the burdens of the poor may be relieved by altering the mode of taxation."

Addressing himself to the second of these propositions, he adverts to the appalling enlargement of the foreign debt since the peace; to the fact that it has been contracted for clothing; clothing for the master; clothing for the slave; furniture; "saws, hammers, hoes, and axes, as if," says he, "the wolf had made war against our iron as well as our sheep;" Irish butter and beef, and British ale, porter, and cheese, "as if our country did not produce barley, hops, or black cattle;" hazle and oak sprouts under the name of "walking sticks;" luxuries of all denominations, swelling it in three years to six millions of dollars; and then exclaims, —

"Let us turn our attention to manufactures, and the staple of our country will soon rise to its proper value, for we have already glutted every foreign market. By this expedient, instead of using fictitious paper, we shall soon obtain hard money sufficient; instead of toiling in the field, and becoming poor, that we may enrich the manufacturers of other countries, we shall prosper by our own labor, and enrich our own citizens." "Every domestic manufacture is cheaper than a foreign one, for this plain reason: by the first, nothing is lost to the country — by the other, the whole value is lost; it is carried away, never to return. It is perfectly indifferent to this State or to the United States, what may be the price of domestic manufactures, because that price remains in the country."

He proceeds then to recommend a substitution of an excise on foreign manufactures sold in the State, for other modes of taxation; and, although I do not find here an illustration of the meaning of the words which I am investigating, you will be struck with the confidence with which he presses the grand elementary suggestion of a tax on foreign labor for the encouragement of home labor.

"All wise governments" (such is his argument, page 124) "have thought it their duty, on special occasions, to offer bounties for the encouragement of domestic manufactures; but an excise on foreign goods must operate as a bounty." "I have said that an excise is more favorable to the poor than a land or poll tax. I will venture an additional sentiment: there never was a government in which an excise could be of so much use as in the United States of America. In all other countries, taxes are considered as grievances. In the United States, an excise on foreign goods would not be a grievance: like medicine to a sick man, it would give us strength; it would close that wasteful drain by which our honor and our wealth are consumed. What, though money was not wanted — though we did not owe a florin to any foreign nation — though we had no domestic debt — and though the expenses of civil government could be supported for many years without a tax, still it may be questioned whether an excise would not be desirable. It would certainly be the best expedient for promoting domestic manufactures; and the condition in which we now live, our general dependence on a foreign country for arms and clothing, is dishonorable — it is extremely dangerous."

"It is the duty of the statesman either to check or to promote the several streams of commerce by taxes or bounties, so as to render them profitable to the nation. Thus it happened in Massachusetts. A tax of twenty-five per cent. was lately imposed on nails, and the poor of Taunton were immediately returned to life and vigor."

"If any man has doubts concerning the effect of large taxes on foreign manufactures, he should turn his eyes to the Eastern States. The mechanic is generally the first who perceives the effects of a pernicious commerce; for the support of his family depends on his daily labor." "Hence it is that the merchant may be profited by a particular branch of commerce, and may promote it diligently, while his country is sinking into a deadly consumption."

You have heard the early and the mature good sense of North

Carolina. Listen to a sentence or two from an essay, "on the advantages of trade and commerce," written at *Charleston* in South Carolina, in 1786, and consider what inferences it suggests upon the general subject of the public opinion of that eventful day. It is signed "*American*," and breathes the very spirit of commercial, political, and industrial union; of union for defence against the arts as well as the arms of the world. "There are but two ways to national wealth," (he begins,) "conquest and the encouraging of agriculture, manufactures, and commerce." This he illustrates historically. England at first was poor; "but as soon as the spirit of manufacturing raised its head, *and commerce was regulated by good laws*," (is it not palpable that he means the protecting tariff, behind which that intellectual industry has so splendidly developed itself?) "they rose superior to every obstacle." ("American Museum," second volume, pages 328 and 329).

"It is in vain" (he continues, page 330) "for any people to attempt to be rich, or have a sufficient circulating specie among them, whose imports exceed their exports; the hand of the manufacturer in a distant land seems to act upon gold and silver as the loadstone does on the needle."

Again, after adverting to a revenue of three millions and a half raised by England, and by monopolizing our trade, he proceeds (page 331): —

"A great part of this may be saved to these States by our becoming our own merchants and carriers; and a great part of the remaining sum may be saved in a few years by *encouraging* our own manufactors; and even this encouragement will be of service to our revenues — I mean laying a duty on our imports, and giving a small part in bounties to our own tradesmen."

By tradesmen he means mechanics. And to the suggestion to turn planters into manufacturers, he answers: —

"I by no means wish it. I only wish to encourage European tradesmen to come to reside here. I wish to see as much as possible exported, and as little imported. The planters that buy the manufactures of America stop so much money in this country, which must return again to the planters' hands as long as traders eat."

Duties of encouragement, let me observe in passing, he calls "restrictions on the British trade."

I must hurry away from the accumulations of proof before me, which bear on the general subject; the formation of associations to encourage manufactures, the resolutions of the patriotic society of Richmond, of the ladies of Halifax in North Carolina, and of Hartford in Connecticut, and of the legislature and executive of Massachusetts to effect this by individual and organized exertion, and all the other indications which break from the universal press of that stirring and anxious time, and which show you with how true an instinct the genius of America was turning itself to take hold on the golden key that opens the palace of national wealth and greatness; I must hurry from these to call your attention to some others more immediately applicable to the proposition which I am maintaining. Look, then, for a moment, into an address by a "Jerseyman," in November, 1787, to the citizens of New Jersey, on the new Constitution. Hear him, one of the people, appealing to the people with the open book in his hand, speaking the language of the people, — hear him on the clause which you are attempting to interpret: —

"The great advantages," ("Amer. Mus.," second volume, page 437.) "which would be the result of the adoption of the proposed Constitution, are almost innumerable. I will mention a few among the many. In the first place, the proper regulation of our commerce would be insured, — the imposts on all foreign merchandise imported into America would still effectually aid our continental treasury. This power has been heretofore held back by some States on narrow and mistaken principles. The amount of the duties since the peace would probably, by this time, have nearly paid our national debt. *By the proper regulation of our commerce* our own manufactures would be also much promoted and encouraged. Heavy duties would discourage the consumption of articles of foreign growth. This would induce us more to work up our raw materials, and prevent European manufacturers from dragging them from us, in order to bestow upon them their own labor and a high price before they are returned into our hands."

Just then, too, a Pennsylvania patriot, under the signature of "One of the People," was making a similar appeal to the intelligence of that great State on behalf of the new Constitution. And how does he interpret this grant of power?

"The people of Pennsylvania, in general, are composed of men of three occupations, — the farmer, the merchant, the mechanic. The interests of these three are intimately blended together. A government, then, which will be conducive to their happiness, and best promote their interest, is the government which these people should adopt. The Constitution now presented to them is such a one. Every person must long since have discovered the necessity of placing the exclusive power of regulating the commerce of America in the same body; without this it is impossible to regulate their trade. The same imposts, duties, and customs, must equally prevail over the whole, for no one State can carry into effect its impost laws. A neighboring State could always prevent it. *No State could effectually encourage its manufactories* — there can be no navigation act. Whence comes it that the trade of this State, which abounds with materials for ship-building, is carried on in foreign bottoms? Whence comes it that shoes, boots, made-up clothes, hats, nails, sheet-iron, hinges, and all other utensils of iron, are of British manufacture? Whence comes it that Spain can regulate our flour market? These evils proceed from a want of one supreme controlling power in these States. They will be all done away by adopting the present form of government. It will have energy and power *to regulate your trade and commerce* — to enforce the execution of your imposts, duties, and customs. Instead of the trade of this country being carried on in foreign bottoms, our ports will be crowded with our own ships, and we shall become the carriers of Europe. *Heavy duties will be laid on all foreign articles which can be manufactured in this country*, and bounties will be granted on the exportation of our commodities; *the manufactories of our country will flourish;* our mechanics will lift up their heads, and rise to opulence and wealth."

And a little after this, in July, 1788, I find a "Bostonian" (Am. Mus., 4th vol., 331st page) advising duties on English importations, under the name of regulations and restrictions of trade for the encouragement of our own manufactures.

"The ill policy of our *commercial arrangements* has served to impoverish us in our finances, by the enormous remittances of our currency, occasioned an almost general bankruptcy, and has had the pernicious tendency to discourage our enterprise in manufactures, and ruined many of those branches which, during the war, had arisen to a flourishing state." "Our trade with that nation has been the principal source of all our misfortunes. It has thrown a number of our best estates into the hands of British merchants, has occasioned a most rapid decrease of our medium, has ruined our manufactures, and will, if pursued, sap the foundation of the best government that ever can be established in America. The first object, therefore, of the federal government must be to restrain our connection with Great Britain, unless on terms of reciprocity. While they continue their duties and prohibitions, *we must lay similar restrictions and embarrassments on their trade, and prevent, by excessive duties, the redundance of their manufactures.*"

Some time in the year 1783 or 1784, there were published in a Virginia newspaper, "Reflections on the policy and necessity of encouraging the commerce of the citizens of the

United States," by St. George Tucker, of Petersburg. They are written with great vigor, good sense, and a true national spirit, and present a powerful argument for a discrimination in favor of American tonnage. Towards the close of the essay, (page 274 of the 2d vol. of the Am. Mus.,) he adverts to another subject, in the following terms: —

> "Before I conclude, let me call the attention of my reader for a moment to the debt due from America to the subjects of Great Britain, which I have heard estimated at four or five millions of pounds. This debt was accumulated from a balance in trade annually accruing to Great Britain from the causes hereinbefore pointed out. That trade must be destructive where such a balance continually arises against us. Surely it is proper to guard against such an event in future. This might be effected, in part, perhaps, by laying heavy duties, if not actual prohibitions, on the importation of such articles as are the produce of the United States. Is it not surprising, for example, that bar-iron, lead, saltpetre, leather, train-oil, tallow, candles, soap, malt-liquors, butter, beef, pork, and potatoes, should constitute a part of the annual imports from Europe to America?"

Did not this writer understand that legislation, for the purpose of turning the balance of trade in our favor, was a "regulation of trade"? and is not the protecting tariff which he recommends exactly an instance of such legislation?

I spare you, Sir, the infliction of more of these superfluous proofs. And yet the nature of the fact to be proved — that a whole people, a whole generation of our fathers, had in view, as one grand end and purpose of their new government, the acquisition of the means of restraining, by governmental action, the importation of foreign manufactures, for the encouragement of manufactures and of all labor at home, and desired and meant to do this by clothing the new government with this specific power of regulating commerce — required and justified a pretty wide collection and display of their opinions, sufferings, expectations, and vocabulary, from sources the most numerous and the most scattered.

And now, from the bosom of the people holding these opinions, oppressed by these incommodities, nourishing these hopes, determined on this relief, and speaking this language, arose the Constitution, — immortal, unchangeable! In fulfilment of these hopes, it embodied the great governmental instrumentality which had been determined on, in the exact language which more than twenty years had made familiar. I say, then, sir, that when the country called the convention together which formed the Constitution, it was the *general design* to confer the protecting power upon the new government; that the governmental power to regulate trade was generally understood to embrace the protecting power; and it was inserted in the Constitution exactly because that was its meaning.

Before proceeding further in the accumulation of evidence, *ab extra*, of the meaning and objects of this power to regulate commerce, let me pause to attend to some of the reasoning by which the proposition which I maintain has been encountered.

I do not think, then, Sir, that anybody will deny that, in the commercial, political, and general vocabulary of 1787, and of all the period back to 1764, a discriminating tariff, a tariff discriminating for the protection of domestic industry, was universally called a commercial regulation. Everybody will agree that, if at that time it had been written or spoken that England, the States, or any other government upon earth, had the power to make a commercial regulation or to regulate commerce, it would have been universally understood (such was the settled form of speech) to include the power to make a strict protecting tariff, and that such a tariff would have been one of the most ordinary and most familiar acts in exercise of such power of regulation. But then it will be said that it does not follow that the same language means, in this Constitution, when applied to and asserted of this government, what it meant everywhere else, when applied to or asserted of any other government in the world. England, the States, under the power to regulate commerce, could make a strict and technical protecting tariff: Congress, under the same power, or rather under the same exact form of expression, the same enunciation *in terms* of power, can do no such thing.

Sir, he who asserts this has the burden of proof heavily upon him. Independently altogether of the evidence which I have already presented, to show that the country looked directly to this power of regulating commerce as the precise power under and by which the new government was to tax or prohibit imports for the encouragement of manufactures; independently of that, when you admit, as you must, that, for more than twenty years before the Constitution was formed, this language was universally current in the Colonies and States; that it had acquired, by force of circumstances, an unusually precise, definite, and well-understood sense; that it had all that time been employed to designate or to include a certain known governmental function; that when applied to England, the States, and all other governments, it had, in the understanding of everybody, embraced a certain species and exercise of power for a certain purpose; — when you admit this, and then find it here in the Constitution of this government, employed to confer a power on it, must you not admit that the presumption is, that it is used in the sense which everybody had understood it so long to bear, when applied to other governments, — neither larger nor narrower; that it means to include the same well-known function, and not to exclude it; that it means to communicate the same extent and the same purpose of power, and not less, — the same in quantity, the same in object?

How is this conclusion evaded? I have heard it attempted thus: The powers given by the Constitution to this government are given *in trust*, to accomplish the specific and few *objects of the Constitution*. The promotion of manufactures is not one of the objects of the Constitution; the promotion of commerce is. The power to regulate commerce, therefore, is given in trust, for the accommodation and promotion of commerce, technically and strictly so called. This, for substance, is the argument of a very able writer in the "Southern Review" of August, 1830.

Now, Sir, waiving for a moment the direct proof *aliunde* which I have produced, and shall produce, to show the exact meaning of this grant of the power of commercial regulation, I answer, that it is true that the powers of the Constitution are given in trust for its objects; that the powers are given in trust for the objects of those powers. But then arises the question, what are the objects of this particular power? What are the purposes which it was inserted in the Constitution to accomplish? You beg the whole proposition in dispute, when you assert that it is no part of the objects of the Constitution to develop the productive capacities of the country, by protecting it from an unpropitious and deleterious foreign commerce, and securing it a beneficial one. The precise question is, if this is not in part the object of this very power? It strikes me, Sir, that our opponents on this general question assume, that because commerce is the subject on which the constitutional regulations are to operate, therefore the end and purpose for which these regulations must be made, is the direct and immediate advancement or enlargement of commerce itself, without regard to its qualities or its adverse or propitious influence on the nation by which or with which it is carried on. What else they mean when they say that this power is given with a view to "commerce as an end," I confess I do not know; but surely this is pure assumption, and will not bear a moment's examination. In the first place, they forget that the unlimited terms of the constitutional grant, explained and defined by the historical deduction which I have exhibited, authorize the making of some such regulations as conclusively demonstrate that the object and purpose of the grant is not solely and directly the enlargement of commerce as an end, without regard to the question, what are its imports, or what its exports, or what its influence on the interior labors and prosperity of the country; but rather the *promotion of national prosperity by means of a judiciously regulated commercial intercourse.* The grant is of power to regulate commerce. The grant is general; it is exclusive as well as general. It is a power to prescribe rules by which commerce shall be conducted; it is a power to make commercial regulations. Unless, then, the extent of this grant is limited by other clauses of the Constitution, or by other evidence of an intent to limit it; unless, in some such way, it be shown that there are some commercial regulations which the Constitution did not mean to authorize you to make, taking the grant by itself, and construing it by the law of grant, it communicates power to make all commercial regulations. It is not a power to make some, but all. It is not a power to do some of the things, to pass some of the laws, which are acts in exercise of a general power to regulate commerce, but to do them all. It extends to all, or it reaches not one. Well, among them, among the most common and best known regulations of commerce, the most common and best known acts in exercise of a power to regulate commerce, as we have seen, was a discriminating and protecting tariff; a law moulding commercial intercourse in such manner as to invite to the development of domestic labor. The grant, then, communicates a power to make such a regulation among others. It stands precisely as if the constitutional language had been, congress shall have power to prescribe rules for the regulations of commerce, and among them protecting tariffs. The analysis of the whole complete aggregate of things authorized, reveals this act as one of them. We take, then, by the legal necessary construction of the grant, the power to make a protecting tariff; and the nature of the power itself involves and discloses the object of the power, to wit, protection. The nature of the operation authorized to be performed *on* commerce, evinces that there is an end and purpose in the contemplation of the Constitution *beyond* commerce itself as an end; and that is the national prosperity.

But, in the next place, these reasoners seem to forget that commerce is, from its nature, and was regarded by the people of this country, at the time of the adoption of the Constitution, and by all governments, and all people then or ever in the world, a mere vast *means* of prosperity, or of decay, to a nation by whom or with whom it is carried on; and therefore that the Constitution, when it clothed you with the general power of regulating it, intended that you should do so with a view to the attainment of those ends, of which, in its nature, and in the opinions of nations, it is capable of being made the instrument. The framers of the Constitution meant to clothe you with the power of disarming it of all the evil and extracting from it all the good to which the wisdom of government is equal. They could not have intended to do anything so absurd as simply to authorize and require you to promote, enlarge, or advance commerce, *per se*, and in the abstract, without regard to its quality; to its adverse or its propitious influence upon the prosperity, the morality, the health, and the industry of the people; to the goods it brought home; to the goods it carried away; the national character of the tonnage it employed, and of the labor it rewarded. They did not look to commerce, but to *beneficial commerce*. They saw the distinction perfectly. They regarded it, as did the country universally, and as all nations in all ages have done, as an agent of large and varied influence, sometimes of good and sometimes of evil, according to its nature, and according to the regulations under which it was conducted. They knew, or they believed, that in one form, under one system of regulations, it might strengthen, adorn, and enrich a State; might seat it on the throne of the sea; might raise its merchants to be princes, yet not impoverish and not depress its mechanics and its farmers; might stimulate the thousand hands of its labor by multiplying its occupations, enhancing its rewards, relieving it from oppressive competitions with the redundant capital, matured skill, and pauperism of older nations; might swell its exports with the products of its own skill; might turn in on it the golden stream of the metals, and make it the workshop, as well as the warehouse, of the world: while, in another form, and under another system of regulations, it might impoverish and enfeeble it; drain it of its specie; overstock its agriculture, yet deprive it of a market; plunge it beneath an insupportable foreign debt; and restrain the division of its labor and the development of its genius. This is the exact view taken of commerce, by the whole American press, from 1783 to 1787.

Commerce, then, in its nature, and the understanding of all, is a means. When, therefore, the general power of regulating it is given to the national government, according to what principles, for the accomplishment of what objects, are you to exert it? Are you not to do it for those ends, and for all of them, which, by the general theory and practice of governments, it is adapted to attain? And is not the relief of domestic labor, from the oppressive competitions of an unrestrained foreign trade, among these ends?

Well, now, Sir, to answer this reasoning, it must be shown, by inspection of other parts of the Constitution, by an analysis of its general structure, or by evidence *ab extra*, that this grant of power is not so broad. It must be shown, in some such way, that there were some well-known and important commercial regulations, some acts familiarly and notoriously done by all governments, in exercise of the power to regulate, which were not intended to be granted by the terms of this most comprehensive and most unlimited grant. It must be shown, in some such way, that this pretty important exception ought to be engrafted on the grant: the congress shall have power to regulate trade with foreign nations, provided, however, *that it shall aim at nothing but free trade;* that it shall have no power to make any, or no power to make all those commercial regulations by which other governments always endeavored, and the United States of America, since the Revolution, have endeavored, to increase their own tonnage; to make their exports exceed their imports, to avoid a drain of their specie; to preserve a favorable balance of trade; and to draw forth their own capacities of labor and of wealth, and their own means of independence. But can you thus qualify the unalterable and the unlimited terms of the Constitution? How do you do it? You say you reason from other parts, and from the general structure of the instrument; and that no other part of it displays any solicitude for the encouragement of domestic industry, nor does anything to enable you to promote it. But what is that argument worth, even if the fact were so? Does it abridge the clear and broad terms of this particular grant? Because the Constitution clothes you with no other means of developing the industrial capacities of the country than a discreet, wise, and customary commercial system, do you infer, against its positive terms, that it could not have intended to give you even that means? Might it not give you that, and yet give you no other? Might it not go so far, and no farther? Might it not clothe you with that large and imperial power, without going on to authorize you to prescribe the forms of apprentices' indentures, and determine how many hours in a day the operatives in a woollen-mill shall be held to labor? From the nature of the case, is not the selection of powers to be conferred on the general government, from the whole field of sovereign power, in some measure arbitrary, — arbitrary in what is given, arbitrary in what is left? The line must be drawn somewhere. How it is drawn, in fact, is a matter of pure interpretation. You cannot put your finger upon a granted power, and say, If the framers of the Constitution meant to give this, logical and political consistency would have led them to give another; but that they have not given, and therefore they have not given this. Such reasoning substitutes the fancies of sophists for the text of the Constitution, and turns the guide of life into foolishness and a stumbling-block.

And what is there in the general structure of the Constitution, what is there in the nature of the government established by it, which renders it so improbable that the power of regulating commerce, for the development of native capacity and industry, should be given to it, that you must abridge, by supposition, an apparently express grant of that very power? I say, Sir, that the Constitution, in conferring this power on this government, has been true to itself; it has acted like itself; it has acted in conformity with its peculiar structure, and its grand aims. What is the power, after all? Nothing more and nothing less than a means of defending American industry against foreign instruments of annoyance. Foreign governments, or foreign subjects, pour in upon us importations of articles which make us poor, or make us idle, or make us diseased, or make us vicious. No government that ever stood one hundred years on the earth but had the power of defending itself against aggression so deleterious, although in form pacific. To which of the governments in our system, the State or the National, should the power belong? Reasoning on the nature of our system, and *a priori*, which should possess it? Should it not be that which possesses the treaty-making power, the war- and peace-making power, the power of regulating all foreign intercourse? Should the States retain it? Was not the Constitution framed in great measure, because they were totally unequal to its effective administration?

In a still larger view, Sir, of the offices and the powers of the national government, under the Constitution, you ought to have this power of protecting the labor of your country. The means, the ends, the principles of determination, pertain appropriately to the imperial and grand trust with which you are clothed. The means is the regulation of foreign intercourse, which all belongs to you. The ends are the independence and the happiness of America. The principles of determination are the most interesting phenomena of the social and political world, the truths of the first of practical sciences, the loftiest and most comprehensive sentiments and aspirations of statesmanship and patriotism. What is it that you do when you exercise this power? Why, Sir, you determine by what system of foreign intercourse our vast capacities of growth and wealth may best be developed; the unsightly but precious elemental material that sleeps beneath our soil be transfigured into forms of beauty and use; the children of labor in all their fields be trained through labor to competence, comfort, and consideration; "our agriculture be made to grow, and our commerce to expand;" the golden chain of union be strengthened; our vast destinies unfolded and fulfilled. This is what you do. And I say the means you work by, the ends you aim at, and the policy you proceed on, are just such as such a system as ours should commit to you.

But, Sir, to advance from these less certain reasonings to indisputable facts, which, indeed, I have partially anticipated. I hold it to be susceptible of as rigorous moral demonstration as any truth of history, first, that, before the Constitution was presented to them, the people of this country, generally, demanded a government which should have power to mould their whole foreign intercourse into the most beneficial form, and, among other things, should have power to mould it into such form as might bring out American labor, agricultural, mechanical, manufacturing, navigating, and commercial, into its completest development, and for that end to make discriminating tariffs; secondly, that when, at length, the doors of the convention were thrown open, and the Constitution, the object of so many hopes, of so much solicitude, was presented to their eager view, they believed that they found in it just the power they had looked for so long, and they adopted it in that confidence; thirdly, that every member of the convention itself supposed it to contain the power; and fourthly, that the new government, from its first organization, proceeded to execute it vigorously and usefully by a broad policy of protection openly avowed,—protection of agriculture, protection of navigation, protection of manufactures; and that, although particular exertions of the policy were vehemently resisted on grounds of expediency, and although other national legislation was denied to be authorized by the Constitution, the power to push this policy to the utmost limit of congressional discretion was never called in question for more than thirty, or certainly more than twenty years.

Sir, if this be so, and yet the Constitution contains no such power, vain is the search after moral truth; idle the attempt to embody the ideas of a people in the frame of their government, and in the language of their fundamental law. You were as wisely employed in writing them upon the clouds of the summer-evening western sky, in the dream of seeing them carried round the world in the train of the next day's sun.

Well, is it not so? I have shown you already that the country demanded, and expected beforehand, a government which should possess this power; that it had done so for years; that the events of every hour, from the peace to the rising of the convention, only increased the urgency of the demand, and the confidence of the expectation. I proceed to show, in the next place, that when at last the Constitution was given to the longing sight of the people, and they threw themselves upon it as a famished host upon miraculous bread, their faculties sharpened and prepared by so many years of discussions, and by the more instructive discipline of suffering, stimulated to read by hope and fear and jealousy and curiosity, then they thought they found in it this power. There it was, in the very language familiar to them from childhood; language associated, fast and imperishably, with the story of the long wrongs of England, the resistance of America, the great names of heroes and wise men, the living and the dead, with liberty and with glory.

See if the fact is not so, and then see how resistless it is as *evidence* that the power really was there. Look into the press of that day, — that day when men were great, and events were great, — look into the newspaper press, and tell me if you find, anywhere, a whisper of complaint of any deficiency *of power in this regard in the new Constitution.* You have heard, in the selections I have read, something of what the people *expected;* do you find, by looking farther into the same source of evidence, that they were *disappointed* in their expectations? Fears there were, sickly fears, patriotic fears, and loudly uttered, that the Constitution was too strong, — too strong for liberty. But who said that, in its protecting energy, it was too weak? Who complained that he did not find it clothed with the whole power of defence against other nations, — defence against their arms, their policy, their pernicious trade, their extorted and pauper labor? I can only say that I have found no trace of such an objection.

But see the affirmative evidence of a general belief that the Constitution did contain the power. Look at the long processions of the trades, where the whole mechanical and manufacturing industry of the country assembled to celebrate, as a jubilee, the establishment of a government by which their interests might at length hope to be cherished. Is it not as if the universal heart of the people was throbbing with the sudden acquisition of a second and a real independence? Hear the debates in the conventions of the States, deliberating upon the Constitution. In that of Massachusetts, one of its advocates, urging the importance of making the entire grant of power to congress which it contemplated, said: —

"Our manufactures are another great subject which has received no encouragement by national duties on foreign manufactures, and they never can by any authority in the old confederation. Besides this, the very face of our country leads to manufactures; our numerous falls of water, and places for mills, where paper, snuff, gunpowder, iron-works, and numerous other articles are prepared, — these will save us immense sums of money that would otherwise go to Europe. *The question is,* have these been encouraged? Has congress *been able,* by national laws, to prevent the importation of such foreign commodities as are made from such *raw materials* as we ourselves raise? It is alleged that the citizens of the United States have contracted debts within the last three years, with the subjects of Great Britain, for the amount of near six millions of dollars, and that consequently our lands are mortgaged for that sum. So Corsica was once mortgaged to the Genoese merchants for articles which her inhabitants did not want, or which they could have made themselves; and she was afterwards sold to a foreign power. If we wish to encourage our own manufactures, to preserve our own commerce, to raise the value of our lands, we must give congress the powers in question." — *Elliot's Debates,* vol. i., page 76.

And again: —

"Our agriculture has not been encouraged by the imposition of material duties on *rival* produce, nor can it be, so long as the several States may make contradictory laws." — Page 74.

And an opponent, Mr. Widgery, was annoyed by so much earnest repetition and enforcement of this very topic in favor of the new government. It is perfectly plain that he felt it to be the effective and decisive consideration by which the masses were moved. "All we hear is," he says, "that the merchant and farmer will flourish, and the mechanic and tradesman make their fortunes directly."

The debates of other States the most interested in this species of industry are imperfectly preserved; but nowhere, as Mr. Madison has well said, do you find a particle of evidence that a doubt on the power was entertained. "The general objects of the Union," said Mr. Davie, in the Convention of North Carolina, "are, 1st, to protect us against foreign invasion; 2d, to defend us against internal commotions and insurrections; 3d, to promote the commerce, agriculture, and manufactures of America." — *Elliot's Debates*, vol. iii. p. 31.

Read the memorials in which the mechanics and manufacturers of the large towns, immediately upon the organization of congress, invoked an exertion of this power; and see how confidently its existence is assumed, and its prompt and beneficial exercise relied on. Familiar as they are to you, familiar to everybody who has examined this question at all, they embody in such vivid and comprehensive expression the grand, popular want and conviction in which the Constitution had its birth, and its instantaneous and universal interpretation, that I venture to call your attention again to passages from three of them. They were all presented during the pending of the first revenue and protecting law of congress, and they contributed, I have no doubt, to determine its policy and to shape its details. Hear the "tradesmen and mechanics of Baltimore."

"Setting forth" (I use the condensed summary of the reporter) "that, since the close of the late war and the completion of the Revolution, they have observed with serious regret the manufacturing and the trading interest of the country rapidly declining, and the attempts of the State legislatures to remedy the evil failing of their object; that, in the present melancholy state of our country, the number of poor increasing for want of employment, foreign debts accumulating, houses and land depreciating in value, and trade and manufactures languishing and expiring, they look up to the supreme legislature of the United States as the guardians of the whole empire, and from their united wisdom and patriotism and ardent love of their country, expect to derive that aid and assistance which alone can dissipate their just apprehensions, and animate them with hopes of success in future, by imposing on all foreign articles which can be made in America, such duties as will give a just and decided preference to their labors, discountenancing that trade which tends so materially to injure them and impoverish their country, measures which, in their consequences, may also contribute to the discharge of the national debt and the due support of government; that they have annexed a list of such articles as are or can be manufactured amongst them, and humbly trust in the wisdom of the legislature to grant them, in common with the other mechanics and manufacturers of the United States, that relief which may appear proper."

This was followed in a week by another, of the "mechanics and manufacturers of the city of New York," which, having recited that their prospects of improving wealth had been blasted after the peace by a system of commercial usurpation; that trade had been loaded with foreign fetters; enterprise and industry discouraged; the development of the vast natural resources of the country restrained; agriculture without stimulus; and manufactures, the sister of commerce, participating in its distresses; that a profusion of foreign articles had deluged the country, presenting a delusive appearance of plenty, and deceiving the people into the mistake that excessive and deleterious importation was a flourishing trade, proceeds: —

"Wearied by their fruitless exertions, your petitioners have long looked forward with anxiety for the establishment of a government which would have power to check the growing evil, and extend a protecting hand to the interests of commerce and the arts. *Such a government is now established.* On the promulgation of the Constitution just now commencing its operations, your petitioners discovered in its principles the remedy which they had so long and so earnestly desired. To your honorable body the mechanics and manufacturers of New York look up with confidence, convinced that, as the united voice of America has furnished you with the means, so your knowledge of our common wants has given you the spirit, to unbind our fetters and rescue our country from disgrace and ruin."

Then came in the "tradesmen and manufacturers of the town of Boston," who say, —

"That on the revival of their mechanical arts and manufactures, now ruinously depressed, depend the wealth and prosperity of the Northern States; and that the citizens of these States conceive the object of their independence but half obtained, till these national purposes are established on a permanent and extensive basis by the legislation of the federal government."

And who in that assembly of men — many of whom sat in the convention which framed the Constitution, all of whom had partaken in the discussions which preceded its adoption — breathed a doubt on the competence of congress to receive such petitions as these, and to grant their prayer? "I conceive," (said the most eloquent of the eloquent, Mr. Ames) — "I conceive, Sir, that the present Constitution was dictated by commercial necessity more than any other cause. The want of an efficient government to secure the manufacturing interest, and to advance our commerce, was long seen by men of judgment, and pointed out by patriots solicitous to promote our general welfare." But I have more to say, before I have done, on the proceedings of that congress, and leave them for the present; in the mean time I submit to you that the proof is complete, that the people who adopted the Constitution universally, and without a doubt, believed that it embodied this power. It was for that they received it with one wide acclaim, with tears of exultation, with ceremonies of auspicious significance, befitting the dawn of our age of pacific and industrial glory. Even those who feared its imperial character and its other powers, who thought they saw the States attracted to its centre and absorbed by its rays, did not fear this power.

And now, Sir, I wonder if, after all, the people were deluded into this belief! I wonder if that heroic and energetic generation of our fathers, which had studied the controversies and had gone through the tasks of the Revolution; which had framed the Confederation, proved its weakness, proved its defects; which had been trained by a long and dreary experience of the insufficiency of a nominal independence to build up a diffused and massive and national prosperity, if the trade laws of foreign governments, the combinations of foreign capitalists, the necessities of foreign existence, are allowed to take from the native laborer his meal of meat, and from his children their school, and depress his standard of comfortable life; which had been trained by experience, by the discussions of its ablest minds, in an age of extraordinary mental activity, and yet of great morality, sobriety, and subordination, peculiarly favorable to the task, trained thus to the work of constructing a new government,—I wonder if such a generation were deceived, after all! I wonder if it was not living water, that which they supposed they saw gushing from the rock, and sparkling and swelling at their feet, but only a delusive imitation, struck out by the wand of an accursed enchantment! No, Sir; no man who believes that the people of this country were fit to govern themselves, fit to frame a Constitution, fit to judge on it, fit to administer it,—no such man can say that the belief, the popular belief in 1789, of the existence of this power, under all the circumstances, is not absolutely conclusive proof of its existence.

And then, in addition to this, how do you deal with the fact that all the framers of the Constitution themselves, as well as every public man alive in 1789, and the entire intelligence of the country, supposed they had inserted this power in it?

Did not those who made it know what they had done? Considering their eminent general character, their civil discretion, their preparation of much study, and yet more experience of arduous public affairs, for the task; their thorough acquaintance with the existing systems, State and national, and with the public mind and opinions of the day; the long, patient, and solitary labor which they bestowed on it; the immediate necessity imposed on them of explaining and defending it to the country — in view of this, if you find them unanimously concurring in ascribing this power to the instrument, is it not the transcendentalism of unbelief to doubt? Do we really think we are likely to understand their own work now, better than they did the day they finished it?

Well, Sir, you have satisfactory evidence that the members of the convention went, all of them, to their graves in the belief that the Constitution contained this power. Mr. Madison's opinion I have read. We have it on unquestionable authority that Mr. Gallatin has repeatedly said that, upon his entrance into political life in 1789, he found it to be the universal opinion of those who framed the Constitution and those who resisted its adoption, the opinion of all the statesmen of the day, that congress possessed the power to protect domestic industry by means of commercial regulations. Stronger proof to this point, indeed, you cannot desire than is afforded by the history of the first revenue and protection law of the federal government. Let me recall that history a little in detail. Considering how many members of that congress had sat in the convention; that all the members of the convention were still alive, and still observers of what was passing on the public stage; how anxiously the whole people, now divided into two great and already excited parties, and the several local regions of the country, developing already the antagonism of their policy, were looking on — in this view, the express affirmation by some, and the tacit universal concession by others, of this power, in every stage of the protracted and anxious debate which resulted in that law, ought to be conclusive on the question of its existence with every sound mind. But observe its history.

It was Mr. Madison who, on the ninth of April, introduced the subject of providing a revenue by imposts. And it is very material to remark that his original purpose was to pass a strict and temporary revenue law, and to pass it immediately, in order, as he said, to intercept the importations of the spring. Accordingly he took, as the basis of his measure, the propositions of the congress of the Confederation, of 1783. Those propositions imposed a general and uniform ad valorem duty on the whole mass of imported articles, except spirituous liquors, wines, sugars, teas, molasses, cocoa, and coffee, which were charged with higher and specific duties. This old scheme of imposts Mr. Madison proposed to adopt as the basis of the new law, engrafting on it only a tonnage duty discriminating in favor of American vessels. His purpose, therefore, you perceive, as I have said, was *revenue* purely, and not *a commercial regulation for protection.* Not one of the articles on which the specific and higher duties would have been laid, and were laid, under this old model scheme, were produced in the United States, except rum. The discrimination was for revenue, and the whole measure was for revenue. Indeed, Mr. Madison said, on introducing it, in so many words, —

"In pursuing this measure, I know that two points occur for our consideration. The first respects the general regulation of commerce, which, in my opinion, ought to be as free as the policy of the nations will admit. The second relates to revenue alone; and this is the point I mean more particularly to bring into the view of the committee. Not being at present possessed of sufficient materials for fully elucidating these points, and our situation admitting of no delay, I shall propose such articles of regulations only as are likely to occasion the least difficulty. The propositions made on this subject by congress in 1783, having received, generally, the approbation of the several States of the Union, in some form or other, seem well calculated to become the basis of the temporary system which I wish the committee to adopt. I am well aware that the changes which have taken place in many of the States, and in our public circumstances, since that period, will require, in some degree, a deviation from the scale of duties then affixed; nevertheless, for the sake of that expedition which is necessary in order to embrace the spring importations, I should recommend a general adherence to the plan."

And later in the debate he said, —

"It was my view to restrain the first essay on this subject principally to the object of revenue, and make this rather a temporary expedient than anything permanent." — *Gales & Seaton's Debates, old series*, vol. i. pp. 107, 115.

But what followed? The next day, Mr. Fitzsimons, of Pennsylvania, presented a suggestion which resulted in a total departure from Mr. Madison's plan, *and in the substitution for a pure and temporary revenue law of a permanent law*, which was at once and avowedly a *measure of revenue* and a *commercial regulation for the encouragement and protection of American agriculture, navigation, and manufactures;* at once an exercise of the power of taxing imports and the power to regulate trade; at once, in the terms of its own preamble, an act "for the support of government, the debt of the United States, and the encouragement and protection of manufactures." He began by saying,—

"I observe, Mr. Chairman, by what the gentlemen have said, who have spoken on the subject before you, that the proposed plan of revenue is viewed by them as a temporary system, to be continued only till proper materials are brought forward and arranged in more perfect form. I confess, Sir, that I carry my views on this subject much further; that I earnestly wish one which, in its operation, will be some way adequate to our present situation, as *it respects our agriculture, our manufactures, and our commerce;*" —

and concluded with a motion, that there be added to the few articles which Mr. Madison had proposed to subject to specific duties, and duties above the general average, *more than fifty others*, which should be also specifically and more highly taxed. Forty-five of these were of the class of articles produced or manufactured in the United States; they were articles coming in competition with almost the entire circle of American manufacturing and agricultural labor; and they were subsequently so increased as to surround that whole circle with a protecting tariff.

This proposition of Mr. Fitzsimons was made for the purpose of uniting the objects of protection and revenue. He avowed this to be his object. "Among the articles," said he, in introducing his motion, (page 111,) "which I would have specifically taxed, are *some* calculated to encourage the productions of our country, and protect our infant manufactures; besides others tending to operate as sumptuary restrictions upon articles which are often termed those of luxury." So he was understood by everybody. Mr. White, of Virginia, who followed him next in the debate, in opposition to his amendment, suggested that its consideration would consume too much time; "for," said he, (page 112,) "in order to charge specific articles of manufacture, so as to encourage our domestic ones, it will be necessary to examine the present state of each throughout the Union." Mr. Tucker, of South Carolina, following him in opposition, "considered the subject of very great importance, as it related to our agriculture, manufactures, and commerce," but advised a temporary, immediate arrangement. Upon this, Mr. Hartley, of Pennsylvania, submitted a brief, but very clear and very sound argument, directly in favor of the policy of protection. He differed from those who preferred a "limited and partial" measure "relating to revenue alone," and advised to place the whole "on as broad a bottom as at that time was practicable." He thought the argument of Mr. Tucker ought not to "discourage the committee from taking such measures as would tend to protect and promote our domestic manufactures." "The old world," he proceeded, "had long pursued the practice of giving great encouragement to the establishment of manufactures, by such partial duties on foreign imports as to give the home manufactures a considerable advantage in the price in market; and it was both politic and just that the general government should do the same thing. Our manufactures had arrived at that stage of advancement, that, according to the policy of every enlightened nation, they ought to receive the encouragement necessary to perfect them without oppressing the other parts of the community." In this posture of the debate, Mr. Madison again rose, and, in a speech of considerable elaborateness, declared, at length, that he thought Mr. Fitzsimons's proposition ought to be entertained. "Upon the whole," he said, concluding his observations, "as I think some of the propositions may be productive of revenue, and some may protect our domestic manufactures, though the latter subject ought not to be too confusedly blended with the former, I hope the committee will receive them, and let them lie over, in order that we may have time to consider how far they are consistent with justice and policy."

The motion of Mr. Fitzsimons was thereupon immediately

adopted; the bill was transformed into a measure of blended revenue and protection; other articles were subsequently added to the class of articles specifically taxed, or taxed by discrimination above the general ad valorem; the rates of duties were arranged; and, after a discussion of extraordinary interest, ability, excitement, and importance, running through three months, the first congress of the new Constitution — at its first session, its very first measure of general legislation, its first measure of any kind after having declared by law in what manner its members should swear to support the Constitution — passed an act to raise revenue; and also to fulfil to the whole, vast, young, and anxious family of American labor; to the agriculture of the South and West; to the fisheries and the navigation of the East; to the mechanical trades of the cities; to the manufacturing industry of the central, and all the States — to fulfil to all, to the cotton, indigo, and hemp grower; to the grain grower and grazier; to the builder of vessels and the fisherman; to the manufactures of leather, clothing, cordage, iron, glass, paper, wood — to fulfil to all something of the promise of the new government, and to extend to all some portion of the security and the stimulus of a real national independence. And now, pause for a moment, and appreciate the light which the history of that act sheds upon the constitutional opinions of that congress, and what inferences those opinions suggest regarding the true meaning of the Constitution.

Sir, the doctrine of the extreme South, I mean rather the extreme doctrine of the South, confined I hope to few, is, that you can impose duties for revenue only; that, in doing so, you may discriminate to be sure, but only for purposes and on principles of revenue as such, laying a low duty or a high one, a specific or an ad valorem, accordingly as one or the other will yield the most revenue at the least expense and with the most certainty. If such a scheme of duties unintentionally (for if you intended the result it avoids the whole) aids the manufacturer or mechanic, well and good; if not, let him take care of himself. This, they say, is *incidental protection*, and it is all the Constitution authorizes! But was this the doctrine of the first congress? I say, on the contrary, that, in its main structure and its substantial character, the act whose history I have detailed was an act for protection as the principal, and for revenue as the incident; that, although at first designed for revenue only, it was wholly reconstructed with another object as the leading object, not indeed inconsistent with revenue, rather in aid of it, intended to be in aid of it, but obtaining it, so far as *purpose* was concerned, incidentally; that, from the beginning to the end, the power of affording protection *directly, as an end, as a main purpose*, was assumed by everybody; and that it was that power which every member must have considered himself exerting, in more than three quarters of all the legislation which was finally embodied in the law. True undoubtedly it is, that all the revenue which the act in its final form could be made to yield was needed by the young government. True it is, therefore, that, in my judgment, this act is not a precedent for bringing, with a view to protection, more money into the treasury than you require for the wants of government. But for discrimination, with a view to protection; for admitting some things free, as materials of manufacture, some under specific duties and some under ad valorem, some under low duties and some under high, for the purpose of protection; for rejecting a measure, efficient and suitable as a revenue measure, precisely because it did not recognize and did not secure protection, and substituting one which did; for putting forward protection as a great object of national policy, of somewhat more consequence than the idle and childish symmetry of horizontal tariffs; for treating a protecting tariff itself as a commercial regulation, and to be referred to the power of regulating commerce — for *this* it is a precedent, and a precedent belonging to a better age, sanctioned by a higher authority than almost any other in our whole series of national legislation.

Observe, Sir, how the mere pursuit of revenue was made to yield to other considerations. Mr. Madison thought that, *for the purposes of revenue*, more was lost than gained by seeking to unite the other object.

"I presume," said he, "that however much we may be disposed to promote domestic manufactures, we ought to pay some regard to the present policy of obtaining revenue. It may be remarked, also, that, by *fixing on a temporary expedient for this purpose, we may gain more than we shall lose by suspending the consideration of the other subject* until we obtain further information of the state of our manufactures. We have at this time the strongest motives for turning our attention to the point I have mentioned. Every gentleman sees that the prospect of our harvest from the spring importations is daily vanishing; and if the committee delay levying and collecting an impost until a system of protecting duties shall be perfected, there will be no importations of any consequence on which the law is to operate, because by that time all the spring vessels will have arrived. Therefore, from a pursuit of this policy, *we shall suffer a loss* equal to the surplus which might be expected from a system of higher duties."

Yet that congress held the loss of duties on spring importations a trifle, in comparison with permanently and systematically sustaining the great interests of domestic labor. Observe, too, and this is a consideration of great importance, where you are inquiring after the *constitutional opinions* and the *quo animo* of legislators, that, in making the successive additions of protected articles, and in fixing the duties upon them, and throughout the whole attempt to recast the original bill, no man assigns revenue, but every man assigns *protection* as his motive and object. I have read the grounds on which Mr. Fitzsimons and Mr. Hartley pressed and carried the original motion. Subsequently, on motion of others, other articles were successively subjected to the specific and higher duty; and every one of them for the avowed object of protection, not one for the avowed object of revenue. Sir, the arguments for the steel, cordage, molasses, beef, hemp, and tonnage duties, are exactly the arguments of those who, in 1816, 1820, 1824, built up that later and more developed policy which you call the American system, an anticipation in effect of the substance and language of those great debates.

Let me remind you now how pregnant the fact is, that not a doubt was whispered on any side about the constitutional power of Congress to think and do so much for protection. The policy of many of the provisions of the bill was vehemently controverted. The cordage duty, the tonnage duty, the duties on molasses, beer, tallow-candles, steel, — of which Mr. Madison observes, "the object of selecting this must be solely the encouragement of the manufacture, and not revenue," (page 154,) — hemp, nails, coal, were successively, and some of them keenly resisted; they were urged on the sole ground of protection, yet no man whispered a suspicion on the power. I should more nearly express the fact, if I said that everybody committed himself in favor of the power. Virginia asked protection for her coal, and prohibition for her beef; and South Carolina "was willing to make sacrifices to encourage the manufacturing and maritime interests of the sister States," but asked protection *for hemp*, which, Mr. Burk said, "her low, strong, rice lands produced in abundance." To appreciate, to approach at all, the strength, significance, and universality of this fact, you must meditate the entire debate. But read at least Mr. Madison's principal speech, upon Mr. Fitzsimons's first proposition. I would rather look there for his constitutional opinions, undesignedly announced, silently assumed as matter incontrovertible, and conceded by all, running underneath and upholding the whole structure of his thoughts upon the general subject, than even to his letter in 1828, written after a controversy had arisen, and age, and intervening events and cares, might have worn the earlier impression in any degree away. Let me open to you the leading idea of that speech, and leave it to you to see for yourselves how he develops it. The proposition of Mr. Fitzsimons, then, he suggested, made it necessary to consider, not merely temporary expedients of revenue, but the principles of a commercial system. He had intended to regard revenue alone, but the proposition led to, and would result in, "the general regulation of commerce," (pages 107 and 116.) Observe, sir, the moment it was suggested to blend protection and revenue, he thought himself engaged in a general *regulation of commerce.*

What, then, he proceeded to inquire, are the true principles of a commercial system? The first and the general rule is, to have it *free*,— as free as possible. He supports this briefly and forcibly. But there are exceptions to the rule, he declares, and he proceeds to enumerate them. And what are they, in his judgment? The first embraces discriminating provisions for the protection and encouragement of American vessels; the second, duties on imports to sustain or to develop manufacturing industry; the third, sumptuary prohibitions which, however, in any form but sumptuary duties, he disapproves; the fourth, embargoes in time of war; the fifth, provisions for encouraging the production within the nation of all its military supplies; the sixth, duties for revenue.

These are exceptions, he argues, by which we may wisely restrict the general freedom of commerce. These exceptions we have the constitutional power to engraft upon our general law of free trade. We may restrain it to encourage American ships and other American manufactures, for the uses of peace or war; to check luxury; to withdraw our too adventurous commerce from the grasp of an enemy, and to supply a revenue for the wants of government. I commend to your own reflections this enunciation of the general principle of commercial regulations and of the exceptions to it; the affirmation which it involves of the constitutional power of protection; the separation of the protecting and of the revenue power from one another, and the enumeration of each as substantive and distinct; and his acquiescence in Mr. Fitzsimons's proposition to unite the exercise and the objects of both powers in one law, "although he (Mr. Madison) thought the two objects ought not to be too confusedly blended." I commend all this to you, who would know his opinions on this part of that greatest work of his own hands or of any man's, the federal Constitution.

I have said that no man then denied the power. Mr. Ames, I have reminded you, expressly affirmed it. No newspaper denied it. The usurpations, imaginary or real, of the two first administrations upon the Constitution, — their alleged usurpations, — brought into life the party of State rights and of Democracy; but through all that tremendous contest which ended in the revolution of 1801, no man accused them for having dared to protect the planter, the farmer, the fisherman, the mechanic of America. No one laid that sin to their charge. The system of practical protection — founded by the framers and in the age of the Constitution and of Washington — grew with the growth and strengthened with the strength of the nation. Every president, every congress, almost every public man, approved it. It went on widening its circuit, increasing its energy, and multiplying its beneficial effects, but never changing its nature or its aims for more than thirty years, when a subtle and a sectional metaphysics suddenly discerned that it was all a fraud on the Constitution.

It is one of the bad habits of politics which grow up under

written systems and limited systems of government to denounce what we think impolitic and oppressive legislation as unconstitutional legislation. The language is at first rhetorically and metaphorically used; excited feeling, producing inaccurate thought, contributes to give it currency; classes of States and parties weave it into their vocabulary, and it grows into an article of faith. I have not a doubt that such is the origin of this heresy.

Look, then, over the whole field of view which we have traversed. The terms of the Constitution, interpreted by the most indisputable and universal use of language of the time and country, expressly grant the power. For years the whole people — men of business, statesmen, speculatists, the masses, all — had demanded a Constitution which should contain the power under those precise terms; and they adopted it, in the belief, and in a substantial sense *for the reason*, that it satisfied that demand. The master-workmen by whom it was constructed, — the entire contemporary intelligence and statesmanship, — supposed it contained the power. With the very first breath it drew, the new government, in the age of Washington, Madison, Hamilton, Adams, and Jefferson, and with their approbation, entered upon its declared exercise; and for more than thirty years its existence was universally admitted.

I propose no more, Sir, than to suggest the general nature and main points of an argument familiar to the thoughts of senators. To my mind it is conclusive. Exercise the power or not, as you deem best for the good and glory of your country, but do not deny its existence, lest you accuse that energetic and heroic generation which gave us Independence and the Constitution, of delusion, fraud, and folly, such as never disgraced any age or race of men before.

I said, Mr. President, that congress had the power, and that it was their duty also to afford adequate protection in this exigency to the entire labor of the country. Something I could wish to add upon this great duty; but perhaps it may better be reserved until we have, as I earnestly hope we soon shall have, a practical measure before us. I trust even that it may be unnecessary to urge its performance on you at all. The mode, the degree in which it shall be performed, may disclose diversities of opinions. On this we shall stand in need of mutual forbearance and indulgence; but, on the solemn and peremptory character of the duty itself, how can we differ? Take counsel of the "ancient prudence;" survey the subject in the spirit of the congress of 1789; purify your minds of the suggestions of a transient expediency, and of a small and local jealousy, by recalling and meditating anew the grand objects for which you know the Constitution was framed; and we cannot differ.

If our trivial and timid manufacturing and mechanical arts, at the organization of the government, not much further out of ground than this premature green grass of the month of March, were not below the care of such a congress as the first, how much more worthy of yours is this diversified and yet sensitive industry, which sends its roots and branches everywhere, but which a storm or a frost would prostrate and kill in an hour! Is that vast circle of employments, which gives to more than 800,000 operatives the means of a comfortable and respectable life; in which nearly three hundred millions of capital are invested directly; which supplies one tenth of all our exports, more in value than the export of rice and tobacco together; feeds our coasting trade, a nation's best trade, or certainly our best; animates, in a hundred ways, the sister or the parent art of agriculture, by keeping up its prices, by turning away from its cultivation the crowds who would overstock it, and by opening to its great staples of cotton, rice, flour, meats, and wool, a market at home, steady, growing, sure; which policy, or unkindness, or the storms of war, cannot close — is that too inconsiderable in the mass of the national policy to deserve your regard? And yet, is that interest by the side of England anything more than an infant, which her statesmen and capitalists coolly talk of "stifling in the cradle," and which thrives and lives by your care alone? If forty years ago, when we had a continent to plant, and so few to do it, and with a whole ocean unoccupied, occupied only for war, inviting us to go forth and carry on the commerce of the world with scarcely a competitor, sound policy was thought to require the establishment of this industry, how much more now, when we have arrived at the period in the course of national advancement in which it should, in the process of things, begin to take root, and when the condition of all our other occupations so impressively urges us to make the most of this for the benefit of all? If the exhausting importations of foreign goods, the overwhelming accumulation of foreign debt, the drain of specie to pay the foreign creditor, the derangement of American currency, the transportation of American produce in foreign ships, the antagonist regulations of foreign policy, and the consequent depression of all employments, were reasons for making the Constitution, are not the same things a reason to-day for administering it in its whole energy? If so many successive presidents, congresses, administrations, have invited, aye, compelled the investment of so much capital in this industry, and connected the labors, hopes, the daily livelihood, the whole scheme of life of so many thousands, their own, their children's, inextricably with it, does it not impose the duty of steady, just, and parental protecting legislation on you? Did you really mean in 1833, when you framed the Compromise Act, that if, unexpectedly, American industry, or one single branch of it, could not live under its ultimate reduction, to let it perish? We told you then that it would endanger the whole system of domestic labor, and that some portions, and they the most precious, the most popular, the first in favor from the date of the government, — woollens, the production of wool, the manufactures of leather, paper, glass, sugar, iron, hats, wood, cotton printing, the whole cotton manufacture in the hands of moderate capitalists, — would be destroyed by it. You differed from us; but do you not mean to admit us to the proof, that our predictions were true? Your compromise does not prevent your replenishing the treasury of the government; shall it prevent your protecting the labor of the people? Will you suffer the country to lose in a year all that it has slowly gained in twenty? Will you squander away the skill which has been acquired; break up your machinery, or send it to the East Indies; close the door to a hundred useful occupations just as men have learned how to pursue them; put your whole scale of prices, — which the establishment of every manufacture at home has regularly reduced and steadied, — into the hands of the experimental capitalists of England, to lower and raise at their pleasure? No, Sir; no, Sir. You will hear the proofs and the discussion with patience; and you will decide with wisdom.

Let me say, Mr. President, in a spirit of the utmost respect to the opinions of senators, that, if there is any power of the Constitution, — I do not know that there is any, — which it might be prudent to suffer to slumber, and, as I have heard it expressed, *to die out*, it is not this. No, Sir. Desirous always, and determined to administer it moderately, discreetly, justly; throwing no burden of discrimination on the South which the North does not at least equally feel; keeping the aggregate amount which it shall yield to the treasury in subordination to the wants of government, efficiently and wisely administered; clothing it, if that is preferred, under the forms, the name, and the reality, of a measure of revenue with discriminations for protection, giving all up but the practical, sufficient, and sure protecting energy itself; — that I would never give up. No, Sir; the power which this whole country with one voice demanded to have inserted in the Constitution, and which they hailed as another Declaration of Independence; the power by which we are able to protect all our children of labor, on whatsoever fields they wipe the sweat from their brow; by which, as Washington foretold, we may hope to bind these States together, to run the race of freedom, power, enjoyment, and glory with the nations, and to afford the example of a people, now counted by millions, every one of whom has work to do, and good pay for his work; — this power must not be surrendered, must not sleep, till the Union flag shall be hauled down from the last masthead! That sight, I trust, neither we nor our children, to the thousandth generation, are doomed to see.

SPEECH ON THE QUESTION OF ANNULLING THE CONVENTION FOR THE COMMON OCCUPATION OF THE TERRITORY OF OREGON; AND IN REPLY TO MR. BUCHANAN.

DELIVERED IN THE SENATE OF THE UNITED STATES, MARCH 21, 1844.

[The third article of the Convention between the United States and Great Britain, signed October 20, 1818, is in these words: —

"It is agreed that any country that may be claimed by either party on the north-west coast of America, westward of the Stony Mountains, shall, together with its harbors, bays, and creeks, and the navigation of all rivers within the same, be free and open for the term of ten years from the date of the signature of the present Convention, to the vessels, citizens, and subjects of the two powers; it being well understood, that this agreement is not to be construed to the prejudice of any claim which either of the two high contracting parties may have to any part of the said country, nor shall it be taken to affect the claims of any other power or state to any part of the said country; the only object of the high contracting parties in that respect being to prevent disputes and differences among themselves."

The Convention between the same governments, signed August 6, 1827, is in these words: —

"Art. 1. All the provisions of the third article of the Convention concluded between the United States of America and His Majesty the King of the United Kingdom of Great Britain and Ireland, on the 20th of October, 1818, shall be, and they are hereby, further indefinitely extended and continued in force, in the same manner as if all the provisions of the said article were herein specifically recited.

"Art. 2. It shall be competent, however, to either of the contracting parties, in case either should think fit, at any time after the 20th of October, 1828, on giving due notice of twelve months to the other contracting party, to annul and abrogate this Convention; and it shall, in such case, be accordingly entirely annulled and abrogated, after the expiration of the said term of notice.

"Art. 3. Nothing contained in this Convention, or in the third article of the Convention of the 20th October, 1818, hereby continued in force, shall be construed to impair or in any manner affect the claims which either of the contracting parties may have to any part of the country westward of the Stony Mountains."

On the 8th of January, 1844, Mr. Semple, of Illinois, introduced into the Senate of the United States the following resolution: —

"*Resolved*, That the President of the United States be requested to give notice to the British Government that it is the desire of the Government of the United States to annul and abrogate the provisions of the third article of the Convention concluded between the Government of the United States of America and His Britannic Majesty the King of the United Kingdom of Great Britain and Ireland, on the 20th of October, 1818, and indefinitely continued by the Convention between the same parties, signed at London the 6th of August, 1827."

In opposition to this resolution, Mr. Choate addressed the Senate on the 22d of February, in reply to Mr. Atchison, of Missouri. The debate was continued by Messrs. Hannegan, Breese, and Buchanan, in favor of the resolution, and Messrs. Dayton, Miller, Archer, Crittenden, and Rives, against it; after which, this speech was delivered.]

Mr. President, —

It is not my purpose to discuss this subject, at large, over again. I have been once heard on it; and, with you all, I have a very strong desire to bring such a dangerous and unseasonable debate to a close. A few words in explanation and aid of what I said before, seem, however, to have been made necessary by the speeches of the advocates of the resolution.

I acknowledge an anxiety to define and restate plainly, briefly, and directly, the position which I actually assumed upon this business. Without supposing any intention to misrepresent, which can never exist here, sure I am that no human being could form any tolerable conjecture of its nature, limits, and grounds, from all the replies, solemn, fervid, and sarcastic, that have been made to it.

Sir, my view of this matter was, and is, simply and exactly this: not that we should now determine that we will never give the notice to annul the convention; for who can say that we may not be required to give it in six months ?—but that we should not give the notice *now*. Whether we shall ever give it, when and with what accompaniments of preparation, and of auxiliary action we shall do so, I said were matters very fit for a committee to consider, or for events to be allowed to develop. Possibly the course of events might render such notice forever unnecessary. There was nothing in the past or the present to indicate the contrary with certainty. Let us await then, I suggested, the admonitions of events, as they should be uttered from time to time, keeping always a sharp look-out on Oregon, which a noiseless and growing current of agricultural immigration was filling with hands and hearts the fittest to defend it. This was my view; that is to say, that the notice should not be given now. Towards that single point all that was urged was made to bear, and upon that all was meant to tell.

And this view met the whole question before us. What is that question? Not whether the notice shall be given now or never given at all. Not so. The alternative is not between now giving it, and never giving it; but between giving it now, and not giving it now. That is the single point of difference. Senators upon the other side would annul the convention to-day; we would not annul it to-day; and there we stop. The duties of to-morrow we can better discern and better perform by the lights of to-morrow.

It is palpable, Mr. President, upon this bare restatement of the question, that much which made the matter of the speech of the honorable Senator from Pennsylvania, [Mr. Buchanan,] much perhaps which I said myself, was not very immediately or decisively relevant; certainly not very necessary to a suitable determination of it. He may be right or he may be wrong in unfolding himself with so much emphasis against what he is pleased to call a poetical and a self-deceiving theory of policy; I may have been right, or may have been wrong in calculating so sanguinely on the unassisted enterprise and the restless nature of my countrymen; I may have been right, or may have been wrong in supposing that those mysterious tendencies and energies that have carried our people to the eastern base of the Rocky Mountains would not die away there, as summer-evening waves on the shore, but would carry them, with your aid or without it, to the great sea; the honorable Senator may or may not be right in predicting that Great Britain will develop some new motive and new form of resistance to our occupation of the Oregon, or that the Hudson's Bay Company will take up some new or some old habit of Indian butcheries to keep us out; you may think what you will on all this, and yet you have not settled nor very closely approached the question, whether the notice of abrogation shall now be given under the actual, special, temporary, and passing circumstances of the case and the hour.

Returning to that, the only question, I stand as I stood, upon one single, sufficient, and decisive reason against the notice; and that is, that it may by possibility produce an inauspicious effect upon the negotiation just now beginning or begun; and therefore, as you have maintained this convention for the peaceful and common occupation of the Oregon Territory for six-and-twenty years, under all administrations, in all aspects of facts, steadily and with great unanimity of opinion, as a part of your entire Oregon policy; as there is nothing whatever in the past or the present to disclose any necessity for annulling it, or any ground of reasonable expectation of benefit from doing so; as it has operated and is operating well for you to-day, — it ought not, on the eve of negotiation, to be abruptly and capriciously abrogated. Such an act may, by possibility, prevent a treaty. It may diminish the chances of a treaty. It cannot help negotiation, and it may embarrass and break it up. For this single reason, without another, I opposed and oppose the resolution.

And what does the honorable Senator from Pennsylvania say to this? Why, that the Senator from Massachusetts has declared that we have slept upon our rights for twenty-six years; and that therefore, while we are about it, we may as well have a little more sleep, a little more slumber, and a little more folding of the hands to sleep!

Now, Sir, let me respectfully tell the honorable Senator that this is not even a good caricature of my reasoning. It is quite idle, I know, to complain that an opponent does not restate the position which he assails in exactly the terms in which it was propounded; and yet I always thought it a pleasing and honorable thing which I have heard said of an eminent debater in the British house of commons, and also of a late accomplished member of the American legal profession, that they would reannounce the argument to which they were replying, better than its author had expressed it, before they proceeded to demolish it irreparably. But this, Sir, of the honorable Senator, tried by the rules of the noble art of logical and parliamentary caricature, is a bad one. I made no such assertion, and deduced no such inference. I said not one word of our having slept on our rights six-and-twenty years, or six-and-twenty minutes, if by sleeping on rights I am to understand the neglecting to assert and proclaim them. I was speaking of this convention for common occupation, and I said, and said only, and exactly, that upon this convention you had stood, all parties, all administrations, from 1818 to this hour, *as a part of your entire Oregon policy;* that you had done so with a knowledge of every fact which is now urged as a reason of annulling it; and that therefore to annul it now, when its practical operation is better for you than ever before it was, and when a negotiation is just beginning, (to carry you in good temper through which was one of the leading inducements to making and continuing it,) would be a capricious, unintelligible, and unwise proceeding. This is what I said. With sleeping on your rights I never taunted you. Everybody knows that we have not slept on them. Everybody knows that we have recorded them; announced them to Great Britain, and to the world; urged them in every diplomatic conversation we have had with that government since we knew there was a Columbia River; and that we made and renewed this very convention with an express protestation and provision that it should not impair nor change them. Sir, let me, the more completely to satisfy the honorable Senator of his misapprehension of the remark to which he excepted, do so unusual a thing as to read from "The Congressional Globe," a brief extract from a speech which I had the honor to make in this place at the last session: —

> "Always this question of the Oregon has borne exactly the same relation to all our questions with England that it bore last summer. Always it has been thought important enough to be discussed with other subjects, and never has it been quite matured for adjustment, and never thought quite so important as to hinder the adjustment of other questions which were matured. How many treaties have you made with England, — how much diplomatic conversation have you had with her since Captain Gray discovered and named the Columbia River? And yet, through the whole series — in 1807, 1814, 1816, 1818, and 1826, — in the administrations of both the last Presidents, always there has been one course and one result with this subject. It has been treated of; formal and informal communications have been held on it; it has been found to be unripe for settlement; and it has been found to be, or believed to be, not difficult enough, or not pressing enough, to delay or alter the settlement of riper and more pressing elements of contention."

Sir, while I hold this book open, let me digress a moment to correct another misapprehension into which the honorable

Senator inadvertently fell, not at all affecting, it is true, the immediate discussion. Eager as he was to show that the American government had never slept upon our rights, because this seemed to controvert a position I had never taken, he could not deny himself the pleasure of conjecturing that in 1842 the then Secretary of State had proposed the parallel of 49° north as the boundary; and this conjecture he founded wholly upon a sentence contained in the speech from which I have just been reading. The sentence is this: —

> "I desired chiefly to assure the Senator and the senate that the apprehension intimated by him, that a disclosure of these informal communications would disgrace the American Secretary, by showing that he had offered a boundary line south of the parallel of forty-nine, is totally unfounded. He would be glad to hear me say that I am authorized and desired to declare, that in no communication, formal or informal, was such an offer made, and that none such was ever meditated."

From this he infers that the degree of 49 was proposed. Certainly, Sir, his inference is wholly groundless. The facts are these. The Senator from Missouri, [Mr. Benton,] whom the senate with a general and sincere pleasure have seen resume his seat this morning, had at the last session made a speech, the main effort of which was to prove that Great Britain had no color of title, at least south of 49°. He did not, certainly, concede her title so far as 49°, but his argument was almost exclusively directed to a vindication of the American title up to that parallel; that is, to the whole valley of the Columbia River. In the course of his remarks he observed that our government had steadily refused to concede a particle of right to Great Britain south of 49°, but that he feared that a proposition had been made by the American negotiator of the treaty of 1842 to fall below that degree; and thereupon he used this language, which I read from "The Congressional Globe:" "And now if, after all this, any proposition has been made by our government to give up the north bank of the river, I for one shall not fail to brand such a proposition with the name of treason."

The object of his denunciation, the senate perceive, was a supposed proposition to run a line south of 49°. Of any proposition to adopt 49° itself, or any higher parallel, he was not thinking, and did not speak. Intending to participate in that discussion, I addressed a note to the Secretary of State, inquiring simply whether a proposition had been made to take a line south of the 49th degree? The answer was immediate, and to the precise question, that none such had been made or meditated. Not another syllable was said or written; and the writer of neither note, I may venture to say, intended to ask or answer anything but the precise question, or had any other subject in his mind at all. I well remember that when this was announced, in the terms which the honorable senator has read, the Senator from Missouri audibly expressed his satisfaction. Surely those terms, upon this explanation, cannot be thought to afford the slightest evidence that this government proposed the 49th degree for a boundary; and I have been recently assured, and from high authority, that such is not the fact.

Returning from this digression, Sir, and taking leave, once and for all, of the treaty of 1842, I may repeat that the assertion which I actually made in debate the other day was only, that we have continued this convention as a means of enabling us, in one mode or another, to secure and enforce those very rights in the Oregon Territory which we have always asserted. We have kept up the convention, not because we were asleep, but because we were awake. All the reasons now urged by senators for abrogating it we have known perfectly well, and long ago. In 1818, we made the convention. In 1827, we renewed it. In 1829, in February, just upon the accession of General Jackson, that celebrated letter of Messrs. Clark and Cass to the Senator from Missouri [Mr. Benton] was written, from which is derived the fact, thrice repeated, I believe, by the honorable Senator from Pennsylvania, that five hundred of our citizens, hunters, traders, and trappers, have been murdered by Indians among and on each side of the Rocky Mountains, and about the upper Missouri and Mississippi, and perhaps by the instigation of British traders. That letter was written then. This fact was made known to congress and the country then; yet you did not abrogate the convention. In 1838, the Hudson's Bay Company obtained a renewal of its charter for twenty years, the British government reserving, however, the right, as against the company, of colonizing the territory embraced by the charter; which is another of the honorable

Senator's reasons for abrogation. This was six years ago, in Mr. Van Buren's term; yet you did not abrogate it. In 1839, during the same administration, elaborate reports were made to congress from the department for Indian Affairs, upon the precise subject on which the Senator from Ohio [Mr. Allen] has called for and obtained information at this session, to wit: the practice of the British government and British companies to make presents to Indians residing within our territory, and their general Indian policy, its principles, and its workings. This whole subject was fully laid open before you then, and yet you did not abrogate the convention. Ten years ago, just as well as to-day, you knew that our hunters and trappers could not and did not contend successfully with the Hudson's Bay Company for the furs of the Oregon. Yet you did not abrogate it.

So true it is, Sir, that without a particle of evidence of one single new reason against the convention, — without producing one single fact not perfectly well known for years, — senators now, — *now*, just when, upon the proofs which I have laid and shall lay before you, it is conclusively evinced that the convention is operating in your favor in the Oregon far more energetically and far more palpably than ever before, multiplying your numbers, extending your influence, — now, too, just when for the first time you are able to sit down to a negotiation on this single subject, disembarrassed of all other elements of controversy, — this well-chosen moment is that which senators seize on to take the first step towards abrogation. I said the thing was incomprehensible and capricious; and I say so still.

So much in correction of the misapprehension of the honorable Senator.

Well, then, why would the honorable Senator give the notice of abrogation?

Sir, he tells you why. It is to induce Great Britain to make a good Oregon treaty. It is for the sake of influencing that government to do what it would not do without. If you do not give the notice, he will risk his life that she will not give you a good treaty. If you do, she will or she may. This is his exact and exquisite reason.

But, Sir, when we, wondering and incredulous, ask how

the notice is to exert so desirable an influence upon Great Britain, the honorable Senator seems to me to become far less explicit than could be wished, or than was to have been expected. What is the precise information which the notice is to give her? What is it to tell her that we mean to do? The honorable Senator does not say. I miss something here of his habitual directness and clearness of speech, and frankness of explanation. May I not even complain of this? True, we have no great difficulty in making out the ominous and energetic meaning of the notice. We make out well enough, upon the whole, that it is a declaration that unless within a year Great Britain yields a satisfactory treaty, we will at the end of that time assert by force the exclusive occupation of the contested region. This we see. But we have to make it out by argument and inference, and by putting this part of the speech of the honorable Senator with that part, and reasoning up from consequences to causes. Sir, I complain of this. Surely, surely in a matter of such transcendent importance, those who influence the public councils and hold the public fortunes in their hands owe the country the utmost possible frankness and truthfulness of dealing. This notice, in the opinion of all here, is to work a great change in your relations to one of the first Powers in the world; it is to modify a pending negotiation, on the course and issue of which many anxious hearts, many vast and delicate interests, are suspended; it may in its results leave you in all things worse than it found you: it may give you, for peace, a sword. Then, Sir, you owe to the people the most unreserved declaration of your opinion of its exact and entire meaning; of the exact extent and nature of the information which it conveys to Great Britain; of the degree, and the way in which it commits you; of how far and in what direction it engages your pride and honor to go, if it does not happen to produce the treaty which you expect. Sir, this business of war and peace is the people's business. All measures legislative in their nature, as you assume this to be, at all tending to endanger the state of peace, are for them to judge on, from the beginning to the end. Yes, Sir, this all is their business. It is the business of the farmer, preparing to scatter his seed with tears, and looking forward to the harvest when he may come bearing his sheaves with joy, his happy household unsevered around him; it is the business of the planter; it is the business of the merchant in his counting-room, projecting the enterprises that bind the nations together by a thousand ties; it is the business of the fisherman on the deck of his nigh night-foundered skiff; of the minister of the gospel, and of all good men; of the widowed mother with her sailor child, the only son of his mother, and she a widow, the stay and staff of her declining age, whom the stern call of a country in arms may summon to the deck on which his father has fallen; it is their business! and if we deal fairly and frankly with them, excellently well will they perform it!

Nevertheless, Sir, it must be admitted that senators tell us enough to enable us to interpret the whole language which the notice speaks to Great Britain. It is exactly this: give us the Oregon by a treaty, or in a year we will take it ourselves,—for the honorable Senator informs us that it is to apprise the British government "that we at last are in earnest." In earnest, indeed! Well, what may that mean? Does not the Senator himself insist upon it, that we have been continually asserting our rights, by diplomacy and otherwise, for six-and-twenty years; that we have never slept upon them an hour; that, in and out of congress, we have been "earnestly agitating" the question, and "earnestly urging" an adjustment of it? When he advises, therefore, to a new measure, which shall admonish England that we are indeed and at last in earnest, he means that it shall announce something more than continued assertion of title on paper,—more than the harmless and vain quart and tierce of diplomatic conflict; he means that it shall tell her we have talked enough, and written enough; we now mean to act. I arrive at the same conclusion by an analysis of other portions of the Senator's argument. Great Britain, he says, will make no treaty while she retains possession and enjoyment, as now she does, of all she wants. She has the whole country now; and what more should she desire, and how can she improve her case by a treaty? We must tell her, then, he urges, that she shall no longer continue to have all or anything that she desires; that the existing *status* must and shall be displaced; that the possession is to change hands, if she does not treat in a twelve-month. Certainly, this is reasonably clear, after all; and I wonder only, that what is so palpably meant should not have been more directly said.

Then, Sir, the proposition is to induce an unwilling government to give us what we seek, by notice publicly communicated, that if it is not given we will take it.

Now, Sir, on one point we shall all agree; and it is, that this mode of influencing the diplomacy of a foreign government, by announcing in advance what shall be the consequences of certain determinations which it may adopt, is a thing to be pretty delicately handled. It is a prescription to be given in minute quantities, very minute quantities indeed. Homœopathic doses I think they should be. The patient should scarcely know what he takes, and the matter should be altogether between him and his confidential physician. Skilfully administered, it may do good; clumsily done, it is many thousand times worse than nothing. I said, therefore, on a former occasion that, since this matter of intimating anticipated consequences to a government you treat with, is one of so much delicacy; since a blunder in regard to it might produce results which two nations, which the world, might have cause long and unavailingly to regret; since we hold in our hands, not sticks and straws, nor yet more precious yet perishable things, as silver and gold, but the lives of men, — our more than material interests, our glory, our history; I thought that, in this view, good sense and prudence prescribed that we should leave this suggestion of consequences to be employed in some way in which it might work all the good of which it is intrinsically capable, with as little as possible of the evil from which it can scarcely be kept wholly free. I advised, therefore, and now advise, that it be all intrusted to the American negotiator, the Secretary of State. Let him deal with it. Let him, if he thinks fit, according to the courtesies of a firm diplomacy, enable the British minister to see the whole ground before him. Sir, we know from the papers of this morning who is the American Secretary. We know him. I am willing to commit this matter, and all else which is involved in this negotiation of Oregon, to that rapid and decisive intellect, that iron nerve, and energetic will. In his hands, this delicate suggestion may be usefully administered. In ours, published as it is proposed to be by legislative resolution to the world;

discharged as from a battery upon the new minister as he comes ashore, how can it fail to be wholly mischievous?

Disregarding all such sublunary considerations as these, the honorable Senator from Pennsylvania thinks it of no importance how this medicine is given; for England, says he, has no right to complain; the very convention itself reserves the power to either party to annul it at will upon a twelvemonth's notice; and she has no right or title at all to the country of Oregon. Why should she complain, then, of our giving a notice we have a right to give, and of our driving her from a place where she has no right to be? Nay, he seemed to think, that when I intimated a suggestion that the proceeding might, by giving offence, destroy one chance, were it but one in ten thousand of our chances for a treaty, I manifested something like a sensitiveness for English honor and for the sake of England.

Now, Sir, all this is well enough for the smartness of debate; but it does not touch, nor begin to touch, the difficulty. The question is not whether Great Britain deserves to be threatened, or deserves to be whipped, but whether the menace or the fulfilment will or will not diminish your chances of obtaining a treaty? It is a treaty which you say you desire. It is a treaty which the Senator from Pennsylvania desires. It is a treaty he is prescribing for. With this in view, is it wise or foolish to begin by putting the other party into a passion? Whether would you rather treat with a good-natured or an angry government? You say the former, of course. Well, is not an unreasonable passion as bad to treat with as a reasonable one? Will not a threat, felt to be deserved, or actually deserved, place the threatened party in as unpropitious a mood and situation for sweet-tempered, courteous, and rational diplomacy, as a threat wholly undeserved? What is the operation of all menace? Why, it puts the object of it in a condition in which he cannot do what he would, and what he feels to be right, lest he be subjected to the imputation of acting from fear. The justice or injustice of the menace itself does not help or hurt the matter.

It is of no sort of consequence, therefore, whether Great Britain has a right to take offence or not. I mean that it is of no consequence to your objects and your interests. It is of you, not of her, that I am thinking; it is for you, for our constituents, for our country, for our peace, our honor, our fortunes, I am anxious, not hers; and it is that you may acquire what you seek and what you deserve, that I counsel you not to lessen your chances of a treaty by a menace — no, nor by any act or declaration which may by reasonable possibility be so interpreted. I hope I may caution my child not to rouse with his little whip a sleeping irritable animal, without being told that I care much about the dog, and little about my son. For your own objects, with a prudent and useful selfishness, avoid the appearance of this thing.

Sir, we must distinguish. If any other conceivable purpose was expected to be served by this notice than that of inducing Great Britain to give us a treaty, you would not so much regard its possible effect on her temper. You might give *the notice for its other objects, and for its other operation;* and you might say that you would not presume, or, in consideration of other benefits, that you could afford to disregard, unreasonable ill-nature. But you observe, that the honorable Senator from Pennsylvania urges the notice as a mode, and an indispensable mode, of getting a treaty. This is exactly and all the good it is to do. If it will not do that, if it is not certain that it will do that, if it may do more harm than good in that precise regard; if, reasonably or not, it may by possibility be misinterpreted, then, on the very principles upon which it is proposed, you will refuse to burn your fingers with it.

But the honorable Senator agrees that we should not menace. If this may probably and not wholly unreasonably be taken as a menace, then he agrees it is not to be given. Well, is it not one? Is it not certain that it would be so taken?

Sir, the learning of threats is not recondite nor difficult. I well remember a reading on the title, by the honorable Senator himself, in this chamber, at the extra session of 1841. It was in the debate on the McLeod case, as it was called. The British minister had demanded that person, then in a New York jail, to be given up; and he did it in these terms: "But be that as it may, her Majesty's government formally demand, on the grounds already stated, the immediate release of Mr. McLeod; and her Majesty's government entreat the

President of the United States to take into his most deliberate consideration the serious nature of the consequences which must ensue from a rejection of this demand."

This, Sir, was not the language of the parliament of Great Britain, speaking to us in the hearing of the whole world. It was a letter from a minister to a secretary; and it was thought, by some who participated in that debate, that it spoke apprehension more than menace; that it meant to shadow out beforehand a possible, uncontrollable, and unmanageable popular outbreak, of Whig, Radical, and Tory, which government must obey. Not so the honorable Senator. He said, "*What* consequences? *What* consequences? After the denunciations we had heard in the British parliament, and all that had occurred in the course of the previous correspondence, could anything have been intended but the serious nature of the consequences which must ensue from war with England? And here let me put a case. I am so unfortunate as to have a difference with a friend of mine. I will suppose it to be my friend from South Carolina, [Mr. Preston]. I know, if you please, even that I am in the wrong. My friend comes to me and demands an explanation, adding, at the same time, these words: If you do not grant the reparation demanded, I entreat you to consider the serious consequences which must ensue from your refusal. Certain I am there is not a single member of this senate, I might say not an intelligent man in the civilized world, who would not consider such language as a menace, which must be withdrawn or explained before any reparation could be made."

Now, Sir, try this case by such a standard and such an illustration. Great Britain claims a right to the joint and common occupation of the territory from 42° to 54° 40′. She is wholly in the wrong; yet she claims; she has recorded and urged her claim; we have had a great deal of diplomatic conversation about the matter; different lines, it is said, have been proposed, formally or informally; there is a sort of mixed, shifting, anomalous possession,—here for hunting, there for farming; here by British subjects, there by American; and elsewhere, or mingled together, by French, half-breeds, and Indians. To some intimation or other of our ministers in 1827, the British government declared that it did not mean to colonize; but that if a forcible effort were made to expel her subjects, they would be defended.

In this state of things precisely, we by the executive organ of government propose to Great Britain to settle the whole by treaty. You are all wrong, we said, but let us treat. Great Britain agrees to it. Informal communications pass and repass for a year or two; and at length a British minister arrives, — not a special minister, the Senator from Pennsylvania assures us, — a general minister, but with no other subject whatever of importance to attend to than this. This alone of our British elements of disquiet, this alone, or this mainly, is left.

The negotiation is ready to begin. And let me say that all this has proceeded thus far, with the fullest knowledge, and the most entire virtual acquiescence of the national legislature. You knew at the last session, you have known from the first day of this, perfectly well, that the governments were negotiating on this subject. The President told us so. The chairman of the committee on foreign affairs told you so. Yet you did not interpose. You passed no resolution forbidding negotiation, or sketching its course, or embodying an ultimatum. You have drawn no red lines or black lines, within or without which diplomacy shall not come. You have virtually consented that the whole subject of controversy be treated on, reserving yourselves to your great constitutional duty of ratifying or refusing to ratify what negotiation shall propose to you. But to negotiation you, the legislature, and the executive, agree. To this the Senator from Pennsylvania agrees.

Well, the negotiators are taking their seats at table; the maps are unrolled; (I hope there are no red lines this time, traced by king or sage); the publicists are doubled down in dogs ears, and all is ready. In this precise state of things, the legislature, which in matters of pending and legitimate negotiation has no more to do than the army or navy, puts its head out of the window, and, in a voice audible all over the world, ejaculates, "God speed your labors, messieurs negotiators; treat away; we are all for a treaty; we are deeply anxious to have a treaty; we are pining for peace, — but hark ye, of the British side of that table, if you do not give us the whole subject in dispute, or just as much of it as we desire to have, we mean to take it by force and main strength, in twelve months from this day." I say, Sir, that looking to time, place, circumstance, to the explanatory speeches and the whole case, this is the language. And I say, further, it is menace; and nothing but my sincere respect and regard for senators who propose and urge it prevents my saying, still further, that it is the most indecent, indecorous, unintelligible proceeding the world of civilization ever witnessed.

The honorable Senator from Pennsylvania, in the course of his able and plausible speech, pressed me with some inconsistencies of my argument, as he thought them. Certainly, as he construed and collated the arguments, they wore a look of inconsistency; and I felt, and feel, that they will require, before I have done, some effort to reconcile them. In the mean time, will he allow me in turn to ask him whether he and his friends have not fallen, in the warmth doubtless of discussion, into some pretty remarkable inconsistencies themselves? Sir, I have been exceedingly struck while listening to gentlemen, and particularly so perhaps while listening to the Senator from Pennsylvania, with the fact, that while the ends and objects at which they aim are all so pacific, their speeches are strewn and sown thick, broadcast, with so much of the food and nourishment of war. Their *ends* and *objects* are peace; a treaty of peace; but their *means* and their *topics* wear a certain incongruous grimness of aspect. The "bloom is on the rye;" but as you go near, you see bayonet-points sparkling beneath; and are fired upon by a thousand men in ambush! The end they aim at is peace; but the means of attaining it are an offensive and absurd threat. Their ends and their objects are peace; yet how full have they stuffed the speeches we have been hearing with every single topic the best calculated to blow up the passions of kindred races to the fever heat of battle! The honorable Senator from Pennsylvania is for peace, but England is proud, powerful, and greedy; England sends Lord Ashburton here with a red line in his pocket, and a white lie in his mouth; England is pressing on with giant tread to the occupation of Oregon, in which she has no color of title; the English press, high and low, is vilifying, day and night, not our faults or vices, but all that we love and all that we honor! Nay, further, by a most unhappy and remarkable mere lapse of tongue it must have happened, for the honorable Senator never forgets to say that he is for peace, he tells us, that while our cities love England, as I understand him, a little too much, "not wisely, but too well" — a remark by the way, calculated, not *intended*, to destroy altogether the influence of the commercial community on a question of peace or war — so well as to have toasted the Queen and insulted the President — the great unsophisticated and honest masses already hate England with a precious and ancient enmity.

I declare, Sir, that while listening to senators whose sincerity and patriotism I cannot doubt, and to this conflict of topics and objects with which they half bewilder me, I was forcibly reminded of that consummate oration in the streets of Rome, by one who "came to bury Cæsar, not to praise him." He did not wish to stir up anybody to mutiny and rage — oh, no! He would not have a finger lifted against the murderers of his and the people's friend — not he! He feared he wronged them — yet who has not admired the exquisite address and the irresistible effect with which he returns again and again to "sweet Cæsar's wounds, poor, poor dumb mouths," and puts a tongue in each; to the familiar mantle, first worn on the evening of the day his great friend overcame the Nervii, now pierced by the cursed steel of Cassius, of the envious Casca, of the well-beloved Brutus; to his legacy of drachmas, arbors, and orchards, to the people of Rome, whose friend, whose benefactor, he shows to them, all marred by traitors — till the mob break away from his words of more than fire, with —

"We will be revenged: — revenge: about!
Seek — burn — fire — kill — slay! — let not a traitor live."

Antony was insincere; senators are wholly sincere; yet the contrast between their pacific professions and that revelry of belligerent topics and sentiments which rings and flashes in their speeches here, half suggests a doubt to me, sometimes, whether they or I perfectly know what they mean or what they desire. They promise to show you a garden, and you look up to see nothing but a wall, "with dreadful faces thronged, and fiery arms!" They propose to teach you how peace is to be preserved; and they do it so exquisitely that you go away half inclined to issue letters of marque and reprisal to-morrow morning.

The argument runs somewhat thus, (I do not pretend to use the exact words of any one:) "We are for peace, — but flesh and blood can't stand everything; we are wholly for peace, — but our emotions almost choke us to death when we think of their sending Lord Ashburton here with his *suppressio veri*, and *allegatio falsi;* we are for peace by all manner of means, — yet see England laying her mortmain and dishonest grasp on the Oregon, as she had before on the highland passes of Maine, enfolding both to her rapacious breast — and bear it who can! we want peace, — but hear that ribald and all-libelling press, that spares neither age, nor sex, nor the secrets of the grave! we want peace, — not that we love England quite so much as the cities, whose treasures indeed, and whose interests, we hope not *all* their affections, are more abroad than at home; we would have the executive dispositions, if we could, as sweet and peace-making as our own, — but impartiality obliges us to remind him where, when, and how, his health was not drunk, and the Queen's was! We, public men, are all for peace; but how long we shall be able to rein in the great body of the people, stung and maddened by the memory of so many wrongs, Heaven only knows." So runs the argument. The proposition is peace; but the audience rises and goes off with a sort of bewildered and unpleasing sensation, that if there were a thousand men in all America as well disposed as the orator, peace might be preserved; but that, as the case stands, it is just about hopeless! I ascribe it altogether to their anxious and tender concern for peace, that senators have not a word to say about the good she does, but only about the dangers she is in. They have the love of compassion; not the love of desire. Not a word about the countless blessings she scatters from her golden urn; but only "the pity of it, Iago! the pity of it!" to think how soon the dissonant clangor of a thousand brazen throats may chase that bloom from her cheek,

> "And death's pale flag be quick advanced there."

Sir, no one here can say one thing and mean another; yet much may be meant, and nothing directly said.

> "The dial spoke not, but pointed full upon the stroke of murder."

Let me advert now, Sir, to the manner in which another

topic, on which I said something before, has been dealt with by the honorable Senator. I suggested, that if you decide to give this notice, the committee on foreign relations ought at once to be directed to inquire whether any and what measures are necessary now to be adopted in view of the expected annulment of the convention. And my reason was, that if, unhappily, we should not have a treaty within the year, at the end of the year our claims and those of the British government must come into direct and forcible collision on the contested territory. The grounds of that apprehension I had the honor quite in detail to lay before you.

Well, what has been the answer to this? Why, Oh, never fear, we shall certainly have a treaty. Beyond that single and satisfactory ejaculation no one goes an inch.

Now, Mr. President, this is very well. But as no gentleman knows that we shall have a treaty, I press my original question: what is to come to pass, where are we to be, what are we to do at the end of a year, with the convention annulled and no treaty concluded? What is the theory of Senators upon such an hypothesis? Surely, it is no answer at all to say we shall have a treaty. We know nothing at all about it; we do not know, we cannot guess, whether we shall or shall not. Since, then, you would have us assume the responsibility of our deserting our settled and approved policy in this behalf, — since you propose that at the end of a year the convention, which has kept the peace of the countries and slowly developed the probable destinies of Oregon for twenty-six years, shall cease to exist, are you not bound to survey the matter on all sides, and therefore to answer this question: Where is Oregon, and where are the countries, when that state of things arrives and brings, as it may bring, no treaty?

Sir, it did and does seem to me, that the annulment of the convention, unaccompanied by treaty, places the governments in collision. Your notice is a declaration that in a year, if the country is not yielded, you will take it. Great Britain has recorded her declaration, that although she does not propose to colonize, and although, as I gather, she would not concern herself in it, if the Hudson's Bay Company, the hunter, and the game, should slowly retire to the more congenial deserts of the North and North-east, yet, that if you forcibly attempt to dispossess them now, she will oppose force to force. If you execute your threat, and she executes hers, you certainly are in collision. If you do not, you will have to retire not very magnificently from a position up to which you will have very loftily strutted. Besides, if the convention is abrogated, collisions among the settlers, each body of them feeling that they represent and are backed by their own government, will become inevitable; each government will defend its own; and there is a war in the Oregon, whether you designed it or not.

I thought therefore, and now do, that in this view of possible consequences, it is not too soon, if the notice is given, to begin to inquire whether Oregon is to be defended in Oregon, or under the walls of Quebec, or on the sea; and if in the Oregon, how it is to be done; by what floating and what stationary force; at what cost; and on what ways and means? Is there a doubt that England would begin to prepare on the day of the notice? With her habits, with her means, under the apprehensions which the notice would excite, would she not begin to accumulate and concentrate a preparation which would enable her to stoop, beak and talons, upon the contested territory, on the day that the year should expire? Will you sit still, and see and hear her preparing? To give this notice, then, and go home without more, were to light a train to the magazine, and then lie down to sleep upon the deck, which in half a minute will be shattered to atoms.

Yet senators are so sure of having a treaty, they are so sure that this proud and grasping power, this power which "pushes her rights with energy while we sleep on ours," this power which will not treat at all without a menace, will treat under menace; that she will sweetly yield the whole matter in dispute in a year; that red lines, courtly diplomatic tricks, the avarice of territory, the dreams of Gibraltars and Maltas on the north-west coast, the pride of protecting all her subjects from what solitary spot of land or sea soever their cries assail the throne — will all give way; so sure are they of all this, that they will not have a committee so much as inquire what is to be done, if none of these fine things happen to come to pass!

Sir, my friends and myself are willing to go before the

country upon this matter. We oppose the notice; but if you give it, then, we say, prepare with a rational forecast for the consequences. Senators on the other side advise the notice, and resist even inquiry into the expediency of any preparation at all.

I come at last, Sir, to that part of my previous observations on which the Senator from Pennsylvania has chiefly diffused himself.

I said, for the purpose of persuading you not to give this notice now, (for that all along is the whole subject of deliberation, — shall it be given now?) — that over and above the possible inauspicious influence of the notice upon the negotiation, the convention was actually working very well for you in the Oregon itself. I said, therefore, that so far from precipitating an attempt to abrogate it to-day, it was perhaps not certain that you would ever do so, treaty or no treaty. It would be very proper, at least, I suggested, that a committee should inquire what is the actual operation of the convention; and whether time, the convention subsisting, did now, and would hereafter, "fight for you or fight for England?" I said that, in my view of the facts, the actual tendencies of events were giving you the agricultural portions of Oregon; and that there was nothing now in operation in England or Oregon which was at all counteracting those tendencies. Such was the actual operation of the convention. And then I said, that although all this might change; although England or the Hudson's Bay Company might put into activity some new agencies of counteraction to keep our agricultural settlers out; yet I did suggest, that if things could be left as now they are, to succeed one another in their natural course; if time and chance, as now, could be continued in the control of events; if collision is not precipitated, and blood is not shed; if exasperated and mad national will, stimulated to undesigned and unreasonable action, is not substituted for the natural sequence of things; if the whole could remain, as now it is, intrusted to the silent operation of those great laws of business and man, which govern in the moral world as gravitation among the stars; upon this hypothesis, I suggested that your people would spread themselves upon the whole agricultural capacities of Oregon, and the Hudson's Bay Company, the hunter and the game, would retire to a fitter region for that wild pursuit. That this would be so I could not assert, of course. Over and over again, I said the British policy might take some new direction. We may brag her into a change of it. The foolishness of debate may change it. In point of fact, however, now, for the present, the convention works well. Continue it, therefore. But keep a constant and keen lookout upon the Oregon; and in the mean time, you are filling it with its appropriate and its natural defenders.

Such, exactly, Sir, was the poetical and self-deceiving policy which so much amuses the honorable Senator from Pennsylvania. Has he adequately met the view I took? Sir, I think not.

Consider, Sir, first, what is the exact question. It is this: Is the actual working of the convention such, as to afford a reason for abrogating it sufficiently clear and weighty to induce you to disregard and take the hazard of those probable inauspicious influences which the proposed notice would exert upon the pending negotiation? The effect of the notice upon negotiation, I hope I have shown, would be bad. The argument of the Senator from Pennsylvania, that notice would help negotiation, I hope I have shown, is not sound nor specious. Still the question arises, does the actual working of the convention afford a reason, irrespective of the effect of notice upon negotiation, for abrogating, or a reason for continuing it? Does it afford so strong a reason for abrogating it, that you should feel obliged to abrogate it *at the expense* of a treaty? I have said, and repeat, that on the contrary, the convention operates so favorably, that, without the least regard to the unpropitious effect of notice upon negotiation, you should not to-day disturb it. Whether you ever shall, and when you shall, events will reveal to you.

What, then, is the actual working of the convention? Are there tendencies and causes now actually in operation, which would fill Oregon with your people, if not counteracted; and are there counteracting agencies and instrumentalities actually in operation which overcome those tendencies and causes, and thus keep your people out? And this, Sir, is a pure question of fact. It is a question of mere evidence. It is a question of the past and the present of Oregon. Examine it, then, as such, and by itself. Do not let it be confounded with the very different, and not very useful question, what is to be the future of Oregon? Let not the honorable Senator jump aside or jump forward from the fact, and exclaim, England *will* do this; the Hudson's Bay Company *will* do that!

Our business is not to guess about the future; but to discern the duties of the present, and to fulfil them. You urge the abrogation of the convention to-day. See, then, how it works to-day. If it work well, you are refuted. And if then you guess it will work badly next year, I say then we can abrogate it next year.

The first suggestion, Sir, which I made touching the existing state of things was, that causes and tendencies now actually in operation are filling the agricultural parts of Oregon with your people; causes and tendencies which, not counteracted, will fill those parts with agricultural settlers from among yourselves. There is already kindled and diffused something like a passion for agricultural emigration to that country. Springing up and spreading, one knows not how; not prompted, as elsewhere, by hunger, by pauperism, by the want of work or wages; springing rather, perhaps, from a craving of personal independence, and an honest old Anglo-Saxon appetite for land; stimulated by our large liberty, and by the feeling that we have vast tracts of new world to divide and possess, wherein each may get his share: the passion exists, is diffused, is growing, and, in the absence of insuperable counteracting agencies, will cover the whole agricultural opportunities of Oregon, as the waters cover the sea. Such, I said, was the view taken by the friends of the resolution. A vivid paragraph from a speech delivered elsewhere well illustrated this.

"Oregon is our land of promise. Oregon is our land of destination. 'The finger of Nature' — such were once the words of the gentleman from Massachusetts, [Mr. Adams,] in regard to this country — 'points that out.' *Two thousand* American citizens are already indwellers of her valleys. *Five thousand* more — aye, it may be twice that number — will have crossed the mountain passes, before another year rolls round. While you are legislating, they are emigrating; and whether you legislate for them or not, they will emigrate still." — *Speech of Mr. Owen, of Indiana, delivered in the House of Representatives of the United States, January* 23*d and* 24*th*, 1844.

To the same effect was the less fervent language of the

Senator from Illinois himself, in his speech upon introducing this resolution.

"The people of the West have not contented themselves with expressing opinions, — they have acted. For many years our citizens have gone into the country west of the Rocky Mountains, for the purpose of hunting, trapping, and trading with the Indians. They have also more recently gone for the purpose of making permanent settlements. During the last year, more than a thousand brave and hardy pioneers set out from Independence, in Missouri, and, overcoming all obstacles, have arrived safe in the Oregon. Thus the first attempt to cross the extensive prairies and high mountains which intervene between the settlements in the States and the Pacific Ocean has been completely successful. The prairie wilderness and the snowy mountains, which have heretofore been deemed impassable, which were to constitute, in the opinion of some, an impenetrable barrier to the further progress of emigration to the West, are already overcome. The same bold and daring spirits, whose intrepidity has heretofore overcome the Western wilderness in the midst of dangers, can never be checked in their march to the shores of the Pacific. During the next summer I believe thousands will follow. Extensive preparations are now making for a general move towards that country. The complete success of those who have first gone will encourage others; and, as the road is now marked out, I do not think I am at all extravagant when I suppose that ten thousand emigrants will go to Oregon next summer."

Indeed, I added, the one great fact which, first, last, everywhere and always strikes you on a review of our history, is the noiseless, innumerous movement of our nation westward.

Setting off two centuries ago from Jamestown and Plymouth, we have spread to the Alleghanies; we have topped them; we have diffused ourselves over the imperial valley beyond; we have crossed the Father of Rivers; the granite and ponderous gates of the Rocky Mountains have opened, and we stand in sight of the great sea. He whose childhood learned his mother's tongue from her loved lips, in the utmost North and East, speaks it to-day in the tones of a man on the shores of the Pacific; speaks it to teach the truths and consolations of religion and of culture to the wasted native race; speaks it there, and is still at home! unexpatriated, unalienated, his "heart, untravelled," still turning to you! In this fact, recorded and exemplified by all our history, there was revealed a law of growth, which, in the absence of counteracting causes, would fill all that was worth filling of the country in dispute.

Such was the first of the facts I urged which make up the *actual present* of this question of Oregon.

And, now, what does the honorable Senator from Pennsylvania say to this? Does he controvert it, or any part of it? Certainly not. Does he doubt the existence of a formed, diffused passion for emigrating to Oregon? Not he, indeed! Does he doubt the agricultural capacities of the country? I understand him to go the whole length of his friends, the friends of this resolution, in their high estimate of those capacities. Does he deride and disbelieve the law which seems to conduct our star of empire westward? Oh no! Hear him: —

"He believed that the system of law and of social order we enjoyed was destined to be the inheritance of this continent. For this it was that the Almighty had put within this entire nation that spirit of progress, and that disposition to roam abroad and seek out new homes and new fields of enterprise. It could not be repressed; it was idle to talk of it; you might as well arrest the stars in their course through heaven. The same Divine hand gave impulse to both. Stop the American people from crossing the Rocky Mountains! You might as well command Niagara not to flow. We had a destiny, and it would be fulfilled."

Sir, how poor, flat, spiritless, prosaic, was all I said, to this! He talk of my poetry, indeed! Why, compared with these arrow flights, these eagle flights, of the soaring Senator, I crept upon the ground; I abased myself; I lay flat on my face; I hid my head in the humble reeds!

No wonder, indeed, that the topic inspires him. Yet it has its sad and fearful aspects, too, on which we may, and soon, have cause to dwell.

Tendencies and causes then in actual operation are conducting your people to the occupation of the whole agricultural Oregon. The next question is, are there any counteracting agencies actually operating to check and restrain these tendencies and causes, and thus to keep your people out? Is the British government and nation now doing anything, is the Hudson's Bay Company now doing anything, to prevent settlers from among yourselves taking up the entire agricultural capacities of that far West?

Beginning, then, with the British government and nation at home, as distinct from the Hudson's Bay Company, whose policy requires to be separately examined, I said, and say, that upon all the evidence to which I have access, and to which you all and all the world have equal access, there is no proof whatever that that government and nation are doing anything which operates in the slightest degree to keep out or to embarrass our agricultural emigration to Oregon. Do not lose sight of the question. That question is, what is the existing state of things? What is that government doing *now?* Three years, six months, the next packet, may change everything. But what is going on now?

In the first place, then, I said, and repeat, that I see no proof that that government and nation, or any party or association or individual of the British nation at home, are now carrying on the agricultural colonization of Oregon; or do now, or ever did, cherish the purpose of colonizing it, or any part of it, for objects of agriculture.

Some proofs and considerations having a tendency to evince that no such thing is doing, and that no such purpose is cherished, were then adverted to. In 1827 Mr. Gallatin, in a letter to the American Secretary of State, observes, that the British negotiators declared "there was no intention on the part of Great Britain to colonize the country (of the Columbia) or impede the progress of American settlement." And then, through all that series of colonization and emigration enterprise, beginning in Great Britain in 1826, perhaps as far back as 1815, by which the British government under successive administrations, and by which associations of private persons, and by which wise and feeling individual minds, have sought to relieve the over-pressure of population at home by opening new fields of British labor and new markets of British goods abroad — an enterprise which has excited so much interest and caused so much discussion in parliament and by the press —an enterprise which has carried many hundreds of thousands of voluntary emigrants to every spot almost of British earth,— to Australia, New Zealand, the Cape of Good Hope, the Canadas, New Brunswick, Nova Scotia, and all the isles of the sea — in the whole history of this enterprise, nobody has proposed to colonize the Oregon, and nobody has taken a step that way. The necessity of colonization on the largest scale has been admitted. It has been forced upon the British public mind. It is most energetically and successfully acted upon.

Colonies are rising everywhere; new fields and new shops of British labor; new markets of British manufactures; new investments of British capital, benefiting him who emigrates and him who stays at home; stimulating British production; "putting the full breast of youthful exuberance to the mouth of the exhausted parent." Yet no human being has emigrated or meditated emigration, that I can see, to the Oregon. The advantages and disadvantages of all these seats of colonization have been repeatedly and warmly discussed in parliament, and by the whole press, high and low, but not one word that I can find has been spoken or written of the Oregon. I referred to a catalogue of books coming under the general denomination of "Emigrants' Guides," just published in London, in which the roving English reader may find something to induce him to go to almost every other spot on earth or sea, and to show him the way to it, but not a puff and not a direction for Oregon. In no paper put forth by the government, or any association of persons; in no speech, in no book, in no act of any description, or of anybody, do I see a particle of proof of the existence of a design to settle that country for agriculture or for anything. Indeed, when you consider of how vast a colonial territory Great Britain is the admitted exclusive proprietor, —a territory on which her descendants may go on for ages spreading to hundreds of millions; a territory more accessible and towards which the current of emigration is already running; on which the foundations of new States are already traced, and the structures going up,—it is not strange that she has not directed her wandering steps to this last home of man, where she does not pretend to own an acre by an exclusive title, and to which we are known to deny her any title at all.

Well, Sir, how does the Senator meet this? Why, he says Great Britain must colonize. "What!" he exclaims, "not colonize? It is the indispensable condition of her existence; she *must* colonize." Certainly, Sir. So I had the honor to say. But she must not colonize the top of Mont Blanc; and she must not colonize the dome of St. Paul's church, that I am aware of; and whether she is colonizing or meditates colonizing the agricultural parts or any parts of Oregon, is a pure and sheer question of fact, to be settled by the proofs.

Returning, then, to the proofs, the Senator has produced nothing but the renewal of the Hudson's Bay Company's charter, in which is reserved a right to colonize. It was my purpose to have remarked on this before, and to urge, as now I do, that it greatly strengthens the position that the British government has not formed the purpose of attempting agricultural settlement in that country. But the Senator from Missouri, [Mr. Atchison,] to whom I was replying, not having adverted to this document, it at the moment escaped my attention.

Sir, the fact is this: In 1837 the company applied for a renewal of its license to trade and hunt. To obtain it, a good story was to be told, and the Oregon, and all the other almost unbounded territory on both sides of the Rocky Mountains, to which the license extended, certainly was described in the color of the rose. The British government, having such an account of it thrust into their very faces, determined to introduce into the renewal a reservation of the right as against the company to colonize any part of the whole country to which the license extended, if during the twenty years for which they gave the renewal it should wish to do so. And this is all. But does this afford a scrap of evidence that that government had then formed, or has now formed, the design of colonizing the Oregon?

In the first place, there is no proof of any one act evincing such a design. It was a Whig administration which in 1838 renewed the license. That administration held power till 1841, and did nothing on the subject. The Tory administration that succeeded it has done nothing. But I may go further. The senator from Indiana, [Mr. Hannegan,] in his speech the other day, produced and read the "Morning Chronicle" of, I believe, 22d August, 1843, to prove some British opinion about the Oregon. I propose to cross-examine his witness; and will put upon the stand for that purpose the same "Morning Chronicle" of August 28, 1843, six days after the date of the paper from which he read. It is an opposition paper, and certainly utters itself with a commendable wrath and freedom. After glancing at certain easy courses, by which the present ministry might have done themselves honor and the State service, the writer taunts them in the bitterest terms with pursuing a directly opposite policy; with not doing this from fear of Louis Philippe; with not doing that from fear of Russia; and, among other things, with "giving up the Oregon," in consideration of having lost the North-eastern boundary before! Certainly, if the Senator's witness is a credible one, he utterly disproves all ministerial design of colonizing the Oregon.

Take another piece of evidence. Here is an article on "the fur trade between the North-west coast of America and China," in "Fisher's Colonial Magazine," published in London, April, 1843. Very probably it was written by an agent of the Hudson's Bay Company. I read a paragraph from page two: "It is truly mortifying to reflect on the ignorance, imbecility, and negligence, of the British government, which is allowing us to be juggled out of this coast, one of the finest in the world, and unquestionably belonging to us by the right of priority in discovery." The last part of the paragraph contains news; but what does the Senator from Pennsylvania say to the former? He can hardly refuse the tribute of his unwilling admiration to Great Britain, for the energy with which "she pushes her rights," or rather her claims, without right. "She is rushing forward," he says, "to get and keep the country!" Whereas, here is an unhappy Hudson's Bay Company proprietor beating his breast and pulling out his hair, because he cannot move such "a dish of skimmed milk" as the British government "to an honorable action." But which to rely on? I cannot help thinking that this writer has the best means of knowledge, both of Oregon and England; and he calls names with a copiousness and heartiness that shows him to be altogether in earnest.

I add a passage or two from the "British Foreign Review" of January, 1844. In an article "on the Oregon Territory," the writer says, "Upon the whole, therefore, the Oregon Territory holds out no great promise as an agricultural field." "We have seen that Oregon offers, upon the whole, very little inducement to agricultural pursuits." "For ourselves, we do not set any great value upon the country as an emigration field, either for England or America."

I submit, then, Sir, that the British government and nation at home has not formed the design of colonizing the agricultural regions of Oregon. This reservation in the license of the company strengthens the proofs of this fact. But for that, the Senator might say, nay, has said, that the government had no right as against the company to colonize. The right is gained, and yet the government does nothing.

Sir, Great Britain is not in the Oregon at all, except in and by the Hudson's Bay Company. She has no fort, nor farm, nor town, nor trace of footstep there, except in and by the Hudson's Bay Company. I come now in the next place to ask, whether that company opposes the slightest obstacle, in point of fact, to the entrance of our agricultural settlers? And nothing is more indisputably certain than that it does not. In one way only does it seem to be probable that it will do so. In one way it may. Send an armed mounted force to eject those persons; drive them home, maimed and spoiled, upon the sympathies and the pride of a government which has recorded its determination to protect them from violence, and thus indeed they may become an obstacle to the entrance of American agricultural immigration. But if, avoiding such insanity as that, you maintain the existing state of things; if under this convention you continue to enter with ploughshare and pruning-hook, and missionary, twenty years more may see them pass away, as night, to the more congenial desert. At present, I say again, that the company does not, in point of fact, oppose the slightest possible counteracting resistance to those tendencies and causes which are giving to your farmers the good lands of Oregon.

We must distinguish when we speak of the Hudson's Bay Company. As a hunting and trading organization, it is very formidable indeed. It wields a large capital; occupies and owns a vast region on this side of the mountains, drained by the waters of the Hudson's Bay; it has a license of trade exclusive of all British subjects over that region, and over other tracts all but boundless on both sides of the mountains; employs agents of great skill, acquired by long experience, and exerts a decisive control upon many of the native races, in the business of obtaining furs, by hunting, trapping, or trade with Indians. A solitary ship, or a stranger going there once or twice in his life, stands no chance with such a body as this.

But thus far, Sir, the company opposes no obstacle at all to your agricultural settlement. The truth is precisely that it is a hunting corporation exclusively; it gives no attention to agriculture; but it permits its retired servants to take up farms about and near its trading-posts; and, to some extent, perhaps a hundred of these retired servants have done so. These persons are the only cultivators of Oregon, excepting your own countrymen. They are English, French, and half-breeds. With them your settlers mingle peaceably; your missionaries preach to them; and they are at this moment coming within your influence; ready to receive your laws; to be blended with your countrymen; to be enfolded in your protecting arms. Meantime, the Hudson's Bay Company pursues its business of seeking furs; but these are fast disappearing; and as the game goes north, the hunter must follow. The process which is going on, then, in the Oregon, is exactly this. The hunter state is disappearing. The agricultural state is succeeding; and your settlers, the farmer, and the missionary, and the retired servants of the Hudson's Bay Company, its servants no longer — these, of diverse race, but with kindred objects, and soon to be a kindred colony, all sprung from you — these are the instruments who are introducing the agricultural state. And to this process, I repeat, thus far, the Hudson's Bay Company opposes no hindrance at all.

Sir, the proofs of all parts of this statement are conclusive. In the first place, that the company, as such, has no agricultural tastes or employments; and that the discharged servants are the only farmers, except our own, is certain. It is no part of its policy or even of its powers to colonize for agriculture. It is a trading company. Its charter makes it such. Its whole corporate business has been to trade and hunt. West of the mountains it has not a foot of land, by grant even from England. Its title as proprietor is confined exclusively to lands on this side, drained by the waters of the Hudson's Bay. On the west side it has a license to trade, and nothing more. It cannot, even as against England, hold; it cannot grant one acre there for independent agricultural occupation.

The Senator from Pennsylvania has referred to the petition of the company for a renewal of their license, and to the papers attending it, for proof that they meditated agricultural undertakings. Doubtless, there are some large and vague intimations of such a purpose or such a hope. But, on a closer examination, it becomes quite clear that it is through their discharged servants only that anything agricultural is to be done; that the company remains — as from the first it has been — a hunter and trader; and that in neither capacity and in neither employment has it earned, or does it expect to earn, any profits, or any considerable profits, on the west side of the mountains. A paragraph or two will suffice to show this: —

"The principal benefit the company derive from the exclusive license of trade is the *peaceable occupation of their own proper territory*, from which they *draw nearly the whole of the profits of their trade*, and for the protection of which they have a right to look to government, in common with the rest of her Majesty's subjects, as the trade of the country embraced in the royal license is as yet of very little benefit to them, and affords greater advantages to the mother-country, in the employment of shipping, and in the revenue arising from imports and exports, than the company derive from it.

"That the Hudson's Bay Company have the strongest possible claims upon her Majesty's government for a renewal of the exclusive license of trade, without any rent or pecuniary consideration whatsoever, cannot, I should hope, admit of a question, after the explanation I have given; but when it is considered that the greater part of the country to which the license applies is Indian country, opened by treaty to citizens of the United States of America as well as to British subjects and, consequently, the license of exclusive trade does not protect the company from the competition of citizens of the United States, it must appear evident that no substantial benefit is likely to arise from the boon we are soliciting, *beyond the probable means* of affording peace to our own territories, in the tranquillity of which her Majesty's government ought to feel as deep an interest as the stockholders of the Hudson's Bay Company."

"The possession of that country to Great Britain may become an object of very great importance, and we are strengthening that claim to it (independent of the claims of prior discovery and occupation for the purpose of Indian trade), by forming the nucleus of a colony, through the establishment of farms, and the settlement *of some of our retiring officers and servants as agriculturists.*"

This petition, whatsoever purposes of agricultural achievement it held out, was presented in 1837. But that in truth the company has not at all modified its character and objects, or become any less exclusively a hunting and trading company than before, all evidence concurs to prove. Mr. Greenhow, in his excellent Memoir on the subject, published in May, 1840, and since then expanded into the most complete and most authoritative work on the whole Oregon question, in all its aspects, which has ever been written, and for which I hope to unite with the Senator from Pennsylvania, and the whole senate, in remunerating the laborious and trustworthy compiler — Mr. Greenhow says, three years after this petition had been presented, "the only settlement which appears to have been made under the auspices of the company beyond the Rocky Mountains is that on the Wallamette, where a few old Canadian *voyageurs* are permitted to reside with their Indian wives and half-breed families, on condition of remaining faithful to their liege lords of the company. In the neighborhood of each large factory, indeed, a portion of ground is cleared and cultivated, and dwelling-houses, mills, and shops for artisans, are erected; but these improvements are all entirely subservient to the uses and objects of the company, all proceedings not strictly connected with its pursuits being discouraged."

I read now from the "British Foreign Review" of January, 1844: "The interests of the company are of course adverse to colonization." "The fur-trade has been hitherto the only channel for the advantageous investment of capital in those regions."

Indeed it is plain, that such a company, as such, can do nothing in agriculture. It cannot live in or near the agricultural state. It is not fields of grain, or grass, or cattle, or pasture, that it requires, but Indians to trade with, beaver and muskrat to kill, a vast wilderness to range in, one whole region of which it may hunt over this year, leaving it fallow the next, to replenish its growth of savage life. It cannot blend, it cannot contemporaneously conduct, agricultural and hunting occupation. There is a sort of chronological incompatibility in it. These are *successive* states, marking successive ages of man. The company must retire before the agricultural life, not enjoy it.

In the next place, Sir, it is as clear, and it is an interesting and pleasing fact, that these discharged servants of the company possess very friendly dispositions to the government of the United States, that they receive our settlers hospitably, that they listen gladly to the instructions of our missionaries, and that they anticipate with pleasure, not fear, the extension of our laws and the unfolding of our flag upon the shores of their tranquil sea. Among the documents accompanying the President's message of this session, is a letter from Dr. Elijah White, our sub-agent beyond the Rocky Mountains. He is a gentleman, as I learn from information through Mr. Crawford of the office of Indian Affairs, of excellent character, whose appointment to his present office was warmly urged by Mr. Linn, late of this senate. In this letter he says, —

"I think I mentioned the kind and hospitable manner we were received and entertained on the way by the gentlemen of the Hudson's Bay Company, and the cordial and most handsome reception I met with at Fort Vancouver, from Governor McLaughlin, and his worthy associate chief factor, James Douglass, Esq., my appointment giving pleasure rather than pain, — a satisfactory assurance that these worthy gentlemen intend, eventually, to settle in this country, and prefer American to English jurisdiction.

"On my arrival in the colony, sixty miles south of Vancouver, being in advance of the party, and coming unexpectedly to the citizens, bearing the intelligence of the arrival of so large a reinforcement, and giving assurance of the good intentions of our government, the excitement was general; and two days after, we had the largest and happiest public meeting ever convened in this infant colony.

"I found the colony in peace and health, rapidly increasing in numbers, having more than doubled in population during the last two years. English, French, and half-breeds, seem equally with our own people attached to the American cause; hence the bill of Mr. Linn, proffering a section of land to every white man of the territory, has the double advantage of being popular and useful, increasing such attachment, and manifestly acting as a strong incentive to all, of whatever nation or party, to settle in this country.

"A petition started from this country to-day, making bitter complaints against the Hudson's Bay Company and Governor McLaughlin. On reference to it, (as a copy was denied,) I shall only say, had any gentleman disconnected with the Hudson's Bay Company been at half the pains and expense to establish a claim to the Wallamette Falls, very few would have raised an opposition. His half-bushel measure I know to be exact, according to the English imperial standard. The gentlemen of this company have been fathers and fosterers of the colony, ever encouraging peace, industry, and good order, and have sustained a character for hospitality and integrity too well established easily to be shaken."

And this is fully confirmed by those who regard the fact with an unfriendly eye. The writer in the "Colonial Magazine," to whom I have just referred, thus complains: "By a strange and unpardonable oversight of the local officer of the company, missionaries from the United States were allowed to take religious charge of the population; and these artful men lost no time in introducing such a number of their countrymen as reduced the influence of the small number of British settlers into complete insignificance. Unless a speedy remedy be applied, our fellow-subjects in that quarter will soon be excluded from the Columbia River, its tributaries and adjacent countries."

It is certain, also, in the next place, that the Hudson's Bay Company proper, the hunting and trading company, finds already that its game is retiring to the north and north-east; and the hunter must follow his game, or cease to be a hunter. You have seen that in the application for a renewal of the license, it is said that no considerable profits were expected to be gathered on the west side of the mountains; that it was upon their own proper territory on this side, drained by the waters of the Hudson's Bay, that their business was to be, if anywhere, advantageously pursued; and that the license to hunt and trade on the west side was expected to be useful mainly as a means of extending and perpetuating that influence over the Indians, and that monopoly of the entire fur-trade in the North-west, which would insure them the peaceful and exclusive range of their own territory, and enable them, by a prudent husbandry and alternation of crops, hunting in one season on one tract, and the next on another, to prevent or postpone the total destruction of game. In point of fact, there is no doubt that, from causes wholly uncontrollable by them, the fur-bearing animals are deserting the Oregon. South of the Columbia, they are substantially extinct. They are disappearing on the north of that river. The company have bought out the interest of the Russian fur-hunters, above 54° 40′; they are exploring the dim neighborhood of the Arctic Sea. One age and state of man is fading away in the Oregon, and another emerges to light. There is not an acre of good land in the whole valley of the Columbia that is not even now ready for the agriculture of civilization. Sir, let me advert to a few proofs of this. A writer on the subject of furs and the fur-trade, in a paper published in "Silliman's Journal," concludes: —

"From the foregoing statements, it appears that the fur-trade must henceforward decline. The advanced state of geographical science shows that no new countries remain to be explored. In North America, the animals are slowly decreasing, from the persevering efforts and the indiscriminate slaughter practised by the hunters, and by the appropriation to the uses of man of those forests and rivers which have afforded them food and protection. They recede with the aborigines, before the tide of civilization."

In the article from the "British Foreign Review," to which I made reference before, it is remarked, "Even now, the animals yielding furs and skins are said to be disappearing, and the toils of the hunters and trappers are less profitable than formerly. The Americans are not probably displeased to observe this, and would rejoice still more if the company should find it necessary to abandon these regions; but, even if such a result should take place, it would be some time before the United States could be prepared to send forth any large body of settlers to the country." You perceive that he does not suggest a doubt that the American wish will be gratified. Again: "The fur-trade is incompatible with the progress of settlement, and must gradually cease as the occupation of the country proceeds." But I pass to far higher authority upon the subject. In a speech of the late Mr. McRoberts, of Illinois, delivered in this place, at the last session, he says, "The leading inducement to the formation of the convention, which was to facilitate the collection of furs and skins, has almost entirely ceased; and particularly in the country south of the Columbia, which is the country best adapted to agricultural pursuits. The hunter has laid by his rifle and traps, and is cultivating the land for a subsistence. If our people go there, they must pursue the mechanic arts, or be cultivators of the soil, — not hunters." To the same effect, sustaining in the fullest manner my entire view, were the remarks of his colleague, Mr. Young, in the course of the same debate. They bear with decisive effect upon all the positions which I have assumed.

"It struck him that it was a mistake to think that Great Britain will ever look to that territory for agricultural purposes. And herein lay a great difference between her views and ours. They are in fact different, and yet not conflicting. We want the territory for agricultural pursuits, mainly. She looks to it for the main pursuit of the Hudson's Bay Company, which is the trade in furs." "In the Oregon Territory, this company, not having for its primary object agricultural pursuits, never have encouraged more culture of the soil than necessary for the temporary support of its employees. But with our citizens, agriculture must be the primary object. We have already a number of our citizens there, engaged in this pursuit. There is no jealousy towards them on the part of the Hudson's Bay Company, so long as they make agriculture their primary pursuit."

And again: —

"The most friendly feelings are evinced by the employees of the Hudson's Bay Company towards our citizens now there. They give no offence by occupying any portion of the soil they please in agriculture. The Hudson's Bay Company can have no objection, and will make none, to agricultural settlements." "There is nothing like an effort or disposition on the part of the Hudson's Bay Company to make permanent agricultural settlements. Theirs is a mere temporary occupation."

Mr. Linn followed Mr. Young, and said, —

"He felt it unnecessary to consume time in debate, after the very lucid statement of the Senator from Illinois, placing the matter on the plain grounds on which it should be viewed."

I say, then, Sir, that the Hudson's Bay Company, in point of fact, is opposing no obstacle at all to your agricultural enterprise to the Oregon. Neither the hunter, not the discharged servant, who is giving his few last and fatigued years to the cultivation of the land, opposes any obstacle. There is no obstacle of force, or fraud, or of inhospitality. I dare say, little controversies there may be, such as there are everywhere; controversies about titles, first possession, prices, monopolies of grinding grain, sawing timber, and the like; such as the memorial presented by the Senator from Missouri [Mr. Atchison] sets forth; but the weight of evidence from all sources, is most decisive to show, that with the Hudson's Bay Company *proper* our settlers come into no contact; and that from the discharged employees, the British, French, and half-breed farmers, they have experienced generally the most hospitable and the kindest reception. Already we are, in numbers, more than two to their one. The whole number of persons, all told, in the employment of the company in the Oregon, or discharged, and cultivating the soil, does not exceed a thousand. We have, I think, seven missionary stations, from two hundred miles south of the Columbia to Paget's Sound, one hundred and forty miles north of it; we have two thousand persons there; we have, beyond doubt, the best grazing and best wheat country in the whole territory, the valley of the Wallamette, which some visitors liken, for fertility and almost for extent, to New York.

The Senator from Pennsylvania, however, twice or thrice takes care to tell you that "the Hudson's Bay Company had murdered four or five hundred of our citizens, as we had learned from good authority, either directly with their own hands, or indirectly through the agency of the Indians, who were under their exclusive control. They had murdered and expelled all our citizens who had gone there for the purpose of interfering with their hunting and trafficking and trading."

The Senator does not assert that they have murdered or expelled anybody who went there to settle. My proposition, therefore, he has not assailed. But, from the terms of his actual statement, I apprehend the senate would derive an impression, undesigned by him, undesigned, certainly, if it be an erroneous impression, which is utterly unsupported by the facts. Sir, the statement of the Senator has no sort of application to, and composes no part of, and throws no light on, the existing policy or purposes of that company, or on the actual circumstances under which our citizens go to that country to-day. Why, Sir, when were these four or "five hundred" murdered? In whose administration? Where? How? Under what circumstances? Will it not surprise you to learn that all this was more than fifteen years — much, much of it more than thirty years ago? Will it not surprise you still more to learn that the circumstances in which it happened are such as to leave it a matter of utter uncertainty whether the company, directly or indirectly, with intention, caused the death of one of the four or five hundred? While upon the whole proof, it will appear, that within the last fifteen years, probably a much longer period, they certainly have not caused or procured the murder of one man!

Before the year 1821, there were two great companies, the Hudson's Bay Company and the North-west Company, which contended for the furs of the north-west portions of North America. They carried the competition to the extent of an actual civil war. Affairs almost amounting to battles were fought. Blood was shed. The most painful scenes of violence, cruelty, insubordination, and selfish disregard of the rights, interests, and lives of men, were exhibited; and this disgraceful and distressing state of things was continued for years, and over almost all the unbounded wilderness which spreads itself out among and on each side of the Rocky Mountains, is traversed by the waters of the Hudson's Bay, and subsides towards the Arctic Sea. The consequence was, of course, that all control of the Indians was lost. Spirituous liquors were freely introduced among them. Their treacherous and ferocious natures were stimulated by all sorts of appliances; and there is no doubt that many American citizens, hunters, and trappers, among and on each side of the mountains, and about the heads of the upper Mississippi and upper Missouri, lost their lives by the hands of these wild men. It has been estimated, and I do not know that it has not been truly estimated, that between 1808, or a few years earlier, and 1821, or a few years later, but before 1829, five hundred American citizens were thus murdered. They were murdered by Indians, wearing European blankets; armed with European rifles; drunk upon European spirits. So much we know. Perhaps it is all we know.

In 1821, the two companies were united in the Hudson's Bay Company. The scene was changed immediately. The white men no longer quarrelled among themselves. The Indians were subjected to a more perfect and better administered *surveillance*. Spirituous liquors were excluded. The reign of law and order was restored, and has in the main been preserved ever since. And from that time, I compute from 1821, or a few years later, 1826 or 1828, I deny that there is a particle of evidence that the Hudson's Bay Company, or anybody else, civilized or savage, by their procurement, has murdered any American citizen anywhere.

Indian murders since that time there may have been; but what I say is, that I have not seen a scrap of proof that they were instigated, directly or indirectly, by this company. Whether the murders of that earlier period were instigated by any white trader, I have not inquired, and do not know. Let me refer you to the account the company give of this matter themselves, in the petition to which the Senator from Pennsylvania has referred: —

"It is unnecessary to say more of the eager competition into which this association entered with the Hudson's Bay Company for the trade of the Indian districts, or of the scenes of demoralization and destruction of life and property to which it led, than to refer your lordship to the ample details on this revolting subject in the Colonial Department; to the agreements at last entered into between the rival companies to put an end to them by the union of their interests in 1821."

"Great loss of property, and in some cases loss of life, have been incurred by savage and murderous attacks on their hunting-parties and establishments, and order has only been restored, and peace maintained by the employment, at a great expense, of considerable force, and by the exercise, on the part of their servants, of the utmost temper, patience, and perseverance."

"Under that arrangement, his lordship, at a very heavy expense, conveyed several hundred families from Europe to that settlement; but the evils attendant on the competition in the fur-trade extending to this settlement, occasioned serious breaches of the peace, much loss of life, and the breaking up or abandonment of the settlement by the whites on two different occasions."

"By that report it will moreover be seen that the animosities and feuds which kept the Indian country in a state of continued disturbance, extending to the loss of lives and to the destruction of property, have, since 1821, entirely ceased; that the sale or distribution of spirituous liquors to the Indians has, in most parts of the country, been entirely discontinued, and in all other parts so much reduced as to be no longer an evil; and that the moral and religious improvement of the native population has been greatly promoted."

You see then, Sir, that these murders were committed from fifteen to thirty years ago. By whomsoever done, by whomsoever procured, they throw no light on the existing dispositions of the company towards agricultural immigrants from the United States; and they do not impugn or qualify in the slightest degree the universality and the truth of my position, that no obstacle is now actually opposed by anybody to our agricultural occupation of the Oregon. I have given you the proofs of that position, and you will judge of them.

Well, what does the Senator from Pennsylvania reply to all this? Why, Sir, only, and exactly, that it is too good to last. That is all. He does not pretend that Great Britain is now colonizing the country agriculturally. He exhibits no proof that she now meditates such a thing. He exhibits no proof that she now cherishes the purpose of building forts or marts in the Oregon. He exhibits no proof that the Hudson's Bay Company is lifting a finger to keep your farmers, artisans, or missionaries, from it. But this is too good to last! Great

Britain will certainly break out into some new development of policy. The Hudson's Bay Company will kill somebody. It is impossible that this state of things should last.

Well, Sir, perhaps it is. What then? I will tell you what then. Keep your eye always open, like the eye of your own eagle, upon the Oregon. Watch day and night. If any new developments of policy break forth, meet them. If the time changes, do you change. New things in a new world. Eternal vigilance is the condition of empire as well as of liberty.

In the mean time, you see the existing state of things. You see the present. You are sure that you see it. Govern yourselves accordingly. Go on with your negotiation. Go on with your emigration. Are not the rifles and the wheat growing together side by side? Will it not be easy, when the inevitable hour comes, to beat back ploughshare and pruning-hooks into their original forms of instruments of death? Alas! that that trade is so easy to learn, and so hard to forget! Who now living will see the time when nations shall learn war no more; when the wicked shall cease from troubling, and the weary be at rest, on this side the grave?

I do not follow senators, therefore, a step in their speculations on the direction which any new policy of England or the Hudson's Bay Company may take in the Oregon. Where no man knows whether there is to be a new policy at all, it is vain and idle to begin to guess what shape it may take, and what details it may involve. Wait and see. Wait and see.

The Senator wonders at the "inconsistency" with which the Senator from Massachusetts told the senate that Great Britain would go to war for Oregon, and in the next breath that the Hudson's Bay Company would abandon it without a "struggle." What inconsistency? I said that the Hudson's Bay Company were hunters, not farmers; that their game was retiring northward, and inland, and that the hunter had already followed and would follow his game; and that even now he had left your agricultural settlers to lay the foundation of their colony in peace; and seen without a struggle his influence upon his own retired employees, and on your countrymen, annihilated by American missionaries and American predilections. I said that England did not in point of fact interfere with this; but that, if, anticipating and disturbing the natural course of things, you urge on a forcible attack upon the yet lingering company; burn their stockade forts; rob them of their peltries, and shed their blood, England had expressly declared, in the negotiation of 1827, that she would interpose, and that it was probable that she would. Where is the inconsistency of one of my views with the other?

The Senator says, also, "to imagine England was going to give up the right of colonizing in Oregon without a struggle was to imagine what seemed very strange, not to say impossible." Well, Sir, if it is impossible, there is an end of it. We will wait and see. But does not the Senator himself expressly tell us that "England is too wise to risk a war for the possession of that country?" "That it is a moral impossibility at this day, in the nineteenth century of the Christian era?" "That she would not go to war with us, unless upon a question where her honor was concerned?" which I understand him to suppose is not concerned. If it is impossible she should risk a war for the country, and yet also impossible to imagine she will yield it without a struggle, why, she must look to herself. But if the Senator is right in the last opinion which he expressed, which was that she would not fight unless the point of honor became involved, why may she not go on, as now she does, allowing events to take their own course? Why is it not a graceful and obvious way of disengaging herself from connection with a subject for which she is said to be too wise to fight? On one of the Senator's views of the matter, this would seem exactly the sensible and easy policy. But again I say, wait and see!

I observe that the British and Foreign Reviewer advances the suggestion, that we, or our settlers, are welcome to all the agricultural Oregon; but the British government will seek to retain a common use of the rivers and the harbor of Fuca. Well, now, in this I think I see the whole question *collapsing* into a pretty small and very manageable thing. In the first place, the nation that owns the land will be likely, if it chooses, to hold rivers and harbor. In the next place, as the game retires, the use of these becomes of less and less importance to Great Britain. In the third place, I do not know that permission of a temporary and restricted enjoyment of these waters, in general subordination to our right, involves any very terrific consequences. Witness the case of the St. John. And finally, by great bad luck, there is but one harbor; and the rivers are good for nothing! "The rivers of Western America," says Mr. Greenhow, "present in fact few or no facilities for commercial transportation. They nearly all run in their whole course through deep ravines among stony mountains; and they are frequently interrupted by ledges or accumulations of rock, producing falls and rapids, to overcome which all the resources of art would probably be unavailing."

Senators tell us that England maintains Gibraltar and Malta on points about which she owns no agricultural settlements; and therefore infer she will never be easy till she hears that encircling and importunate drum beat on the desert coast of the North-west. Well, Sir, I cannot say. If she begins to build a Gibraltar there, do you begin too. Let your walls ascend with hers. Go up with her story by story; a tier of guns for every new one she plants; and the day when she throws out the red cross flag from the turret of her consummated structure, cast abroad the radiant stainless stars and stripes, to tell her that there "foreign dominion shall not come." In the mean time, let me say that this Gibraltar and Malta analogy does not seem to me very direct. Gibraltar and Malta are men-of-war harbors, where whole armadas may lie afloat, directly on both the old and both the modern routes of commerce from Europe to the East; points from which a British fleet may unmoor, and in ten days strike with thunder the walls of one or more cities of how many of the nations of Europe, Asia, and Africa: Portugal, Spain, France, Italy, Austria, Greece, Russia by the Black Sea, Turkey, Syria, Egypt, Algiers. To argue from her tenacious possession of such places a necessary desire to see new Gibraltars and new Maltas rise under the 49th degree of north latitude upon the North-west coast, does not strike me as extremely cogent.

One event there is, Sir, which may change your policy and hers, which I marvel not to have heard adverted to. If in five or ten years the isthmus of Panama is cut through, and thus a new track of commerce paved out in the sea; if that great triumph of man over the world of matter is achieved; if that marriage of oceans is really celebrated, then new and intense importance may be given to new lands, and new seas; to the Sandwich Islands, to California, to San Francisco, possibly to the harbor of Fuca itself. He who lives to see that new earth, and those new heavens, will have new and appropriate duties to perform, and new and sufficient lights by which to perform them. In the mean time, we are here. We have the present to work in and provide for. Our situation is the teacher and the limit of our duty. Long, long before that day, I hope this question will have been adjusted, and have taken its place among the follies, among the trivialities, of which, a hundred years hence, men shall read with incredulity and astonishment, that, for such things, Christian nations were once near shedding each other's blood.

In the expression of this hope, Mr. President, I believe I speak for my country. It is true that the Senator from Pennsylvania has said, —

> "He admitted with regret that there were some very dangerous symptoms between the two countries. The whole press of Great Britain, for the last two years, had teemed with abuse of America, and all that was American; our institutions, and everything connected with us, had been made the subject of perpetual vituperation.
>
> "All he had read was substantially of the same tenor, — the abuse was unexampled in any former time. And, on the other hand, among ourselves, though there were many, in our large cities especially, who entertained a warmth of feeling towards England — insomuch that on a great public occasion, in one of the largest of those cities, the health of "the President of the United States" had been drunk in silence, while that of "Queen Victoria" had been received with acclamation — yet with the great mass of our people, a very different feeling prevailed. They still remember the wrongs we had endured in days past; they remembered these things perhaps with too deep a sensibility. And although senators might please their ears with the terms "mother" and "daughter," a vast majority of our people were penetrated with the conviction that to us England had ever acted the part of a cruel step-mother. It was this deep-wrought conviction, these associations of former scenes, that lay at the foundation of the national enmity, which too extensively prevailed. Injuries on one side, and their remembrance on the other, kept up this ill blood. Besides, even were it otherwise, the American people, as one man, felt that there was a calamity even greater than that of war, and that was a sacrifice of the national honor."

But is this so? Is it so, that the great mass of the people of this country are pervaded, are "penetrated" by a deep-seated, "deep-wrought" "sentiment of national enmity" towards this particular nation England? Is it so, that our veins are filled with "ill blood" towards that country,—ill blood generated and fed by the "memory of wrongs endured in days past"? This I understand the Senator to allege, and even to regret. I have repeated to you, however, exactly what he says, to be interpreted by yourselves. But thus I understand it. The cherished remembrance of wrongs endured in past days, the conviction that England *had ever* acted the part of a "cruel step-mother;" the "associations of former scenes," these bitter memories, compose the deep foundations of a too extensive national hostility; these things make the great body of the people enemies of England, in a time of profound peace. Thus I interpret the Senator. Is this so?

Being, Sir, through the favor of a kind Providence, one of the people of America myself; and having been born and bred, not in cities, which are said to love England, but in the country, which is said, as I understand the honorable Senator, to hate her; and having been astonished and pained to hear it asserted that such a people, one of as happy, generous, and kind a nature as the sun shines on, were laboring under a sentiment so gloomy and so barbarous as this, I have been revolving the subject with some care and with some feeling. Exhausted as I am, and as you are, I cannot sit down without denouncing, in the first place, the sentiment thus, as I understand the Senator, ascribed by him to my countrymen, as immoral, unchristian, unchivalrous, unworthy of good men, unworthy of "gallant men, and men of honor;" and without, in the second place, expressing my entire and profound conviction that no such sentiment inhabits the bosom of the American people. Sir, I thank the Senators from Kentucky and Virginia [Mr. Crittenden and Mr. Rives] for their notice of this part of the honorable Senator's address. With my last words, if I knew I were about to speak them, would I unite my judgments and feelings on this subject with them.

Mr. President, we must distinguish a little. That there exists in this country an intense sentiment of nationality; a cherished, energetic feeling and consciousness of our independent and separate national existence; a feeling that we have a transcendent destiny to fulfil, which we mean to fulfil; a great work to do, which we know how to do, and are able to do; a career to run, up which we hope to ascend till we stand on the steadfast and glittering summits of the world; a feeling that we are surrounded and attended by a noble, historical group of competitors and rivals, the other nations of the earth, all of whom we hope to overtake and even to distance — such a sentiment as this exists perhaps in the character of this people. And this I do not discourage; I do not condemn. It is easy to ridicule it. But "grand swelling sentiments" of patriotism no wise man will despise. They have their uses. They help to give a great heart to a nation; to animate it for the various conflict of its lot; to assist it to work out for itself a more exceeding weight and to fill a larger measure of glory. But, Sir, that among these useful and beautiful sentiments, predominant among them, there exists a temper of hostility towards this one particular nation, to such a degree as to amount to a habit, a trait, a national passion, to amount to a state of feeling which "is to be regretted," and which really threatens another war — this I earnestly and confidently deny. I would not hear your enemy say this.

Sir, the indulgence of such a sentiment by the people supposes them to have forgotten one of the counsels of Washington. Call to mind the ever seasonable wisdom of the Farewell Address: —

> "The nation which indulges towards another an habitual hatred, or an habitual fondness, is in some degree a slave. It is a slave to its animosity or to its affection, either of which is sufficient to lead it astray from its duty and its interest. Antipathy in one nation against another disposes each more readily to offer insult and injury, to lay hold of slight causes of umbrage, and to be haughty and intractable, when accidental or trifling occasions of dispute occur. Hence frequent collisions, obstinate, envenomed, and bloody contests. The nation prompted by ill-will and resentment sometimes impels to war the government, contrary to the best calculations of policy. The government sometimes participates in the national propensity, and adopts, through passion, what reason would reject; at other times, it makes the animosity of the nation subservient to projects of hostility, instigated by pride, ambition, and other sinister and pernicious motives. The peace often, sometimes perhaps the liberty of nations, has been the victim."

No, Sir. No, Sir. We are above all this. Let the Highland clansman, half naked, half civilized, half blinded by the peat smoke of his cavern, have his hereditary enemy and his hereditary enmity, and keep the keen, deep, and precious hatred, set on fire of hell, alive if he can; let the North American Indian have his, and hand it down from father to son, by Heaven knows what symbols of alligators and rattlesnakes and war-clubs smeared with vermilion and entwined with scarlet; let such a country as Poland, cloven to the earth, the armed heel on the radiant forehead, her body dead, her soul incapable to die, — let her "remember the wrongs of days long past;" let the lost and wandering tribes of Israel remember theirs, — the manliness and the sympathy of the world may allow or pardon this to them; but shall America, young, free, prosperous, just setting out on the highway of heaven, "decorating and cheering the elevated sphere she just begins to move in, glittering like the morning star, full of life and joy," — shall she be supposed to be polluting and corroding her noble and happy heart, by moping over old stories of Stamp Act, and tea tax, and the firing of The Leopard upon The Chesapeake in a time of peace? No, Sir; no, Sir; a thousand times no! Why, I protest I thought all that had been settled. I thought two wars had settled it all. What else was so much good blood shed for on so many more than classical fields of Revolutionary glory? For what was so much good blood more lately shed at Lundy's Lane, at Fort Erie, before and behind the lines at New Orleans, on the deck of The Constitution, on the deck of The Java, on the lakes, on the sea, but to settle exactly these "wrongs of past days"? And have we come back sulky and sullen, from the very field of honor? For my country I deny it. The Senator says that our people still remember these "former scenes of wrong with perhaps too deep" a sensibility; and that, as I interpret him, they nourish a "too extensive" national enmity. How so? If the feeling he attributes to them is moral, manly, creditable, how comes it to be too deep; and if it is immoral, unmanly, and unworthy, why is it charged on them at all? Is there a member of this body, who would stand up in any educated, in any intelligent and right-minded circle which he respected, and avow, that for his part he must acknowledge, that, looking back through the glories and the atonements of two wars, his veins were full of ill blood to England; that in peace he could not help being her enemy; that he could not pluck out the deep-wrought convictions and "the immortal hate" of the old times? Certainly, not one. And then, Sir, that which we feel would do no honor to ourselves, shall we confess for our country?

Mr. President, let me say, that in my judgment this notion of a national enmity of feeling towards Great Britain belongs to a past age of our history. My younger countrymen are unconscious of it. They disavow it. That generation in whose opinions and feelings the actions and the destiny of the next age are enfolded, as the tree in the germ, do not at all comprehend your meaning, nor your fears, nor your regrets. We are born to happier feelings. We look on England as we look on France. We look on them, from our new world, not unrenowned, yet a new world still; and the blood mounts to our cheeks; our eyes swim; our voices are stifled with emulousness of so much glory; their trophies will not let us sleep; but there is no hatred at all; no hatred; all for honor, nothing for hate! We have, we can have no barbarian memory of wrongs, for which brave men have made the last expiation to the brave.

No, Sir; if public men, or any one public man, think it their duty to make a war or cultivate the dispositions of war towards any nation, let them perform the duty, and have done with it. But do not say that there is an unfortunate, morbid, impracticable popular temper on the subject, which you desire to resist, but are afraid you shall not be able to resist. If you will answer for the politicians, I think I will venture to answer for the people.

SPEECH UPON THE SUBJECT OF PROTECTING AMERICAN LABOR BY DUTIES ON IMPORTS.

DELIVERED IN THE SENATE OF THE UNITED STATES, APRIL 12 AND 15, 1844.

[The Senator from South Carolina [Mr. McDuffie] had introduced, on leave, the following bill: —

A BILL to revive the act of the second of March, one thousand eight hundred and thirty-three, usually called the "Compromise Act," and to modify the existing duties upon foreign imports in conformity to its provisions.

Be it enacted by the Senate and House of Representatives of the United States of America in Congress assembled, That so much of the existing law imposing duties upon foreign imports as provides that duties ad valorem on certain commodities shall be assessed upon an assumed *minimum* value, be, and the same is hereby, repealed, and that said duties be hereafter assessed on the true value of such commodities.

SEC. 2. *And be it further enacted,* That in all cases in which the existing duty upon any imported commodity exceeds thirty per centum on the value thereof, such duty shall be hereafter reduced to thirty per centum ad valorem.

SEC. 3. *And be it further enacted,* That from and after the thirty-first day of December next, all duties upon foreign imports shall be reduced to twenty-five per centum; and from and after the thirty-first of December, one thousand eight hundred and forty-four, to twenty per centum ad valorem.

And the committee on finance of the senate had reported resolutions recommending its indefinite postponement. The debate arose upon those resolutions.]

MR. PRESIDENT, —

IT is not my purpose, and never has been, to engage in a general discussion of this subject. In the actual circumstances, no consideration could induce me to do so. Good taste, if nothing else, ought to prevent it. In my hands, such a discussion could retain neither interest nor usefulness. There is literally nothing at all left to be said or to be refuted. Truths, threadbare and worn to tatters, or novelties, empty, false, sounding, and mischievous, are at least all that is left. It has come to be preëminently that case in which "true things are not new things, and new things are not true things."

Besides, Sir, for the maintenance of the doctrines to which I am devoted, and with the steady and constant practice of which the comfort, the prosperity, and the greatness of the American people, are inseparably intertwined, more general discussion is needless. The defence of the system of protection is made. It has been made before and elsewhere, by ten thousand tongues and pens, and by that which is more eloquent and more persuasive than any tongue or pen, — the teachings of experience, — the lapse of time, — the revelations of events, — the past and present of our own country, and of all countries. It has been made, here and now, by the Senators from Maine, Connecticut, Vermont, Rhode Island, and Georgia, and by my friend and colleague, [Messrs. Evans, Huntington, Phelps, Simmons, Berrien, and Bates,] with a fulness and ability that leaves nothing to be desired and nothing to be added. If this Troy of ours can be defended; if these daily and indispensable employments of our people can be preserved to them; if these fields and shops of useful, honest, and respectable labor — labor which at once elevates and blesses the individual operative, by hundreds of thousands, and, in its larger results, contributes to fill the measure of the nation's glory — if these can be defended, their hands will have been sufficient to make the defence. If theirs are not, my feeble efforts can avail nothing.

There is another reason, Mr. President, on which I decline that larger and more elementary discussion that has occupied so much of this debate, on which, without the least disrespect to any one, I desire to say a word: and that is, that, for myself, I cannot consent to regard this matter of protection as at all that open question which it might seem to have been regarded by senators on all sides. Sir, I presume to prescribe no rule of debate to others; nor to criticise, or even to observe upon their course; but I shall not allow myself to treat this question as open to the extent, and for the objects that have been assumed and contended for. No doubt, there is a sense and an extent in which it may, under proper limitations, be said to be always open. Details may be said to be so. Having due regard to the great considerations of stability and constancy; of giving all things, when once adopted, a fair and full trial; and of changing nothing from lightness and caprice and the pursuit of abstractions, — details may be admitted to be always open. When the lights of a full and fair experience prescribe the change of a duty, it is to be changed. It is open to inquiry, whether a given or a proposed duty is needed for protection, or is enough for it. It is an open question whether the rates of 1789 are sufficient to-day, and whether those of 1828 are required to-day. In such a sense as this, this subject, like all law, like all policy, like the steadfast nature of the Constitution itself, is open to the gentle and reforming hand of the great innovator, time.

But whether there ought to be in our industrial code such a thing as a policy of adequate protection of the universal labor of the country; such a thing as a system designed and sufficient to develop and sustain our whole capacity and all our forms of domestic employment, — on the land, on the sea, in the arts, everywhere, and in everything, — by the imposition, among other means, of duties on imports; a system designed and sufficient to guard the American workman, on whatever field, against the irregular irruptions of the redundant capital, low rates of interest money, low wages, under-fed labor and contingent surpluses of foreign States; this is a question which I do not mean, by my example, to acknowledge an open one. To the dispute whether protection shall always be treated as *incidental* to revenue, or may be made a *principal* object itself; to the dispute as to when it is an incident and when a principal object; whether there is such a thing, and what it is, as a revenue *maximum;* to disputes about forms of duties, specific, ad valorem, minimums, and the like, I attach no great importance. I mean by protecting duties, *duties which protect:* and whether these duties should or should not be blended with, and form part of our impost system, I repeat, I do not mean to discuss as an open question.

And why not open? Because, Sir, I find such a system of protection in operation, *de jure* and *de facto*, to-day; because I know perfectly well, — or all our annals are a dream and a lie, — that the American people established the Constitution and the

Union, very much to insure the maintenance of such a system; because it has been slowly maturing for years; because so large a concurrence of patriotism, intelligence, and experience, has helped to build it up; because, whether it was wise or unwise to introduce such a system, by direct legislation, at first, it would be supreme madness now, now when the first stages are passed, when the evil, if any there ever was, is all done, and the compensations of good are just fairly commencing; when capital has taken this direction; when prices are brought down, skill learned, habits formed, machinery accumulated, the whole scheme of things accommodated to it; when its propitious influence is felt palpably upon agriculture, upon the comfort and the standing of labor, upon domestic and foreign trade, upon defence, upon independence — it would be supreme madness, worthy only of a government nodding to its fall, now to overturn it; because, finally, it is the daily labor, and the daily bread of men, women, and children, our countrymen and countrywomen, whom we reckon by millions.

It is for these reasons, Sir, that I cannot regard it as a debatable question, whether it is lawful, under the Constitution, or expedient in point of political economy, that this system should exist.

While, therefore, I appreciate, as highly as any one can do, the ability and energy with which the Senator from South Carolina [Mr. McDuffie] has urged his opinions in this debate, I must, in conformity with these views, consider it as a sufficient notice for me to take of the bill which he has introduced, and still more, of such a bill as should embody the principles of policy and the Constitution which he has so powerfully advocated, — to pronounce it a stupendous novelty, and there to leave it. It is all a novelty, from the beginning to the end. In its principle; in its object; in its details; in the argument which accompanies it, it is not only unlike, but it is adverse to, it is at war with, every law that has been passed under the Constitution; and not so only, but it forgets, it disregards, it disappoints the desires and purposes and wants of that generation of our fathers which called the Constitution into existence, and enriched it with all its vast powers of good. Why, Sir, what is the bill of the honorable Senator; or, rather, what would it be, if it still more exactly expressed his constitutional and economical doctrines? It is a bill which aspires to construct an impost system, from which all purpose of intentional protection shall be carefully weeded out with thumb and finger. It goes for revenue, and nothing else. It does not merely seek to bring into the treasury a certain aggregate of revenue, having regard to the wants of an economical administration of the government — that would be right — but in all its details it looks to revenue alone. Every single duty is to be laid upon the notion of getting, from that one item, the largest possible amount at the lowest possible rate of impost. The bill does not try to protect. It does not inquire whether it protects. It does not care whether it protects. Live or die under it who will, if the aggregate amount of money is obtained, and if each particular duty yields its prescribed quota of supply, its end is answered. Yes, Sir! The capital and labor and experience, which are producing three or four or five hundreds of millions of annual values, may go up or go down; the skill which years have been educating may be dismissed and squandered; fountains of national wealth and civilization may be dried up; machinery and processes and methods, the splendid triumphs of mind over matter, may be cast aside, as an old bow, which none of this generation knows how to bend, or has strength to bend; a million hands may miss their accustomed labor, a million mouths their accustomed food, — yet the bill has done all that it desires, and is perfectly satisfied with itself! I do not speak of, nor allude to, the wishes and dispositions of the honorable mover himself, of course; they, I doubt not, are just and philanthropic; but I speak of the bill. It goes for revenue; and if it obtains it, it disregards all possible intermediate consequences.

Such a bill, Sir, within the views which I take of this whole subject, I cannot consent to discuss. I pass it by, with entire respect to its friends, as an enormous and pernicious novelty. It is enough for me that no such impost system as this was dreamed of by the people who willed the Constitution into being; or by the minds who framed it and adopted it, or by any president, or congress, or party, who ever administered it; and that no precedent and no warrant for such a thing is to be found in all the series of our legislation. Gratified certainly, I have been, with the able and instructive arguments of my friends in this discussion, showing, with resistless force, that all this is not only novel, but impolitic; that our system is not only settled, but rightly settled. To those reasonings I could add nothing if I would; and I would not if I could. If at this time of day, the labor of the country cannot repose upon the policy of protection as an established policy, then indeed is "the pillared firmament rottenness, and earth's base built on stubble."

While, then, I retire from that general discussion of a boundless and exhausted subject to which we have been invited, I admit that a question more practical, and more properly to be regarded as open, is involved in this deliberation; and that is, not whether adequate protection shall or shall not be given to American labor; not whether mechanical and manufacturing arts and industry are worth preserving for their influence upon all industry, and upon individual prosperity and enjoyment, and national wealth and power; but whether a given or a proposed rate of duty affords that adequate protection, and insures the growth of those useful and those imperial arts? In other words, it is this question, — can you make a proposed great change in the existing rates, and still leave enough for the protection which the government and the country have determined to give?

Sir, this is the question which has been moved by the honorable Senator from Missouri, [Mr. Benton,] not now in his place. That distinguished gentleman comes into this deliberation, not as an enemy, but as a friend of a sufficient protective system. He reminded you that he voted for the act of 1824, and voted "cordially" for it; yet that act, beyond all doubt, permanently laid the foundation of what he calls the "new system;" that he voted for the act of 1828 "reluctantly," but that he voted for it; that he voted for that of 1832 "because it reduced duties on many necessaries," although it still left, as I suppose, for most objects, a pretty energetic protecting tariff, against which both the then senators from South Carolina, and six out of nine of her representatives voted; and, finally, that he voted against the Compromise Act, "because he thought the horizontal line wrong in principle, and for other reasons." Retaining his original friendship, as I understood him, for a sufficient protective system, since he expressly declares himself "willing to give manufactures far more protection than they need," he however counsels a vast change of the existing system, — a change which I am profoundly impressed with the conviction that you cannot make without the ultimate, perhaps quick, but at last inevitable destruction of all the interests which it was created to cherish, and all that multiplied variety of individual and general good which illustrates and recommends it. He counsels an abandonment of the existing system, "the new system," the system which began, as he says, in 1816, and has been embodied successively in the acts of 1816, of 1824, of 1828, and of 1842; the last (against which he voted) being in his judgment "the very worst of all." He counsels an abandonment of this system, and a return to the "good old laws," the good old system, the system of our fathers, — the system "which began in 1789, with the beginning of the government," and continued down to the year 1808. He does not advise you to revive any one law, or any one precise rate of duty, that obtained in the happy and peaceful period to which he turns you back. It is the *system* which he would revive. In his terse, forcible, and clear expression, he sketches rapidly its general features, as he would reproduce them. He indicates certain conditions which must be satisfied, and such protection as can be afforded consistently with the satisfaction of those conditions he means to leave. As well as I remember, — and I speak with the most anxious desire, in his absence this morning from his seat, not to misrepresent him, — among these conditions are these: all minimums are to be abolished; ad valorem duties are, as I infer, although I cannot pronounce positively of his views in this particular, to be computed upon the foreign values; luxuries are to be taxed high; necessaries, although coming in competition with what are woven in your own looms, hammered out on your own anvils, cut and stitched on your own shoemakers' or merchant-tailors' seats, are to be taxed low; and no duty, under whatever denomination, is to ascend above thirty-three and one third per cent. "The average on the whole, he fully believes, will not be equal to the twenty per cent. ad valorem of the Compromise Act." Subject to these conditions, satisfying these conditions to this extent, the distinguished Senator would give you protection. This system he advises you to substitute for the existing one. If it should happen to turn out inadequate, the manufacturer and mechanic have this consolation, — that they have mistaken their calling, and that the system, by which they die, is the good old one of their fathers.

Mr. President, upon this counsel of the honorable Senator let me say a few words. Certainly, in the very form of speech in which it is conceived, there is persuasive argument. He, who advises to return to the good old system of our fathers, has half gained his audience already. He supposes you to have wandered, it is true; but not far, since he encourages you that it is practicable and is easy to come back. He touches your pious and filial memories. He appeals to that powerful prepossession towards the past, which influences the best natures the most. He points to the "old paths," and our feet unconsciously turn to take hold on them.

But we must pause, Sir, somewhat, before we legislate on such sentiments as these. We must distinguish a little in this matter of the imitation of our fathers. It is not what they did, exactly as they did it, in the special and transient circumstances of their time, that we are to reproduce with a timid and literal fidelity of resemblance; but it is what their principles, their spirit, the general character of their permanent aims and substantial objects, as exemplified in their actual policy, would lead them to do *now*, in the altered circumstances of our time, — this is what we are to discern and to imitate, if we are to imitate at all, as becomes them, or as becomes ourselves. Always, Sir, it is good to be emulous of the purity, the simplicity, the patriotism, and all the heroic virtues of a great and wise ancestry. Very often is it wise to meditate their legislation. But before we copy the details of such policy, we must take many an anxious observation; we must heave the lead again and again; we must find out on what new seas, along what unexplored coasts of what new continents, the great current is bearing us; we must sweep the field of midnight sky, to see what stars have risen, and what stars have set; and thus we must learn what change of duty the change of situation prescribes, and what the navigators of a former age would do, were they, not we, piloting the ship to-day. To be true to the *principles* of our fathers, we must sometimes wholly desert or substantially modify their *details*.

What, then, are the arguments by which we are to be persuaded to substitute the system which began in 1789, and endured until 1808, for the system which began in 1816, was matured or nearly so in 1824, and exists now?

Well, in the first place, Sir, we are pointed to an alleged diversity, to an alleged "opposition" between the spirit and principles and objects which presided over the establishment of the former of these systems, and those which presided over the establishment of the latter. The former, it is said, was framed and founded in a loftier spirit, for better objects, under higher influences, with "opposite views," on a sounder principle. It was framed and founded not by "millionary capitalists and ambitious politicians," for "political advancement" and "sectional enrichment," but, as I understand the implication, by statesmen and men of business, fairly, in good faith. In that system revenue was the principal; protection, was the incident; duties were moderate, and values were true values. The latter, the existing system, it is said, on the contrary, was framed by, or under the influence of, "millionary capitalists and aspiring politicians;" for "political advancement and sectional enrichment;" "it makes protection principal, and revenue the incident;" its duties are exorbitant, and its valuations fictitious and delusive.

Now, Mr. President, I find myself quite unable to assent to the historical postulate on which this argument proceeds. I do not agree to this allegation, that a spirit presided over the legislation of 1789 so opposite to that which produced the legislation of 1816 and 1824. I maintain, on the contrary, that both generations of statesmen, those of 1789 and those of 1816 and 1824, had exactly the same object in view. Both intended to do one and the same thing; that is, to foster and protect adequately the existing mechanical and manufacturing industry of the country. They lived in different ages of the world; in different epochs of our national history; and this circumstance prescribed some diversity of instrumental details. The impost duties of 1789, sufficient and designed to protect the domestic labor of 1789, would have been insufficient to protect the labor of 1824, and therefore in part they were enlarged. The impost duties of 1824 would have been unnecessary to the protection of the domestic labor of 1789, and therefore they were not then resorted to. But of both systems the objects were the same; the principle was the same; the policy was the same. I cannot denounce one and applaud the other. I cannot strike a blow at the great men of 1824, that does not pass through and light on the reverend and charmed form of the Father of his Country himself. It is all one policy of protection, one identical policy, *mutatis mutandis* — as of the fathers, so of the children! It is I, then, Sir, who claim the lights and teachers of the first and purest age of our political church for our own in this controversy. It is I who would reconcile the living and the dead, and on their consentaneous authority uphold, if I can, the system of this day.

See then, Mr. President, if this is not so. And in the first place, let us be sure that we comprehend perfectly the objects and the policy, the constitutional and economical doctrines, of the founders of our "first system," as the Senator from Missouri has called it, the system of 1789. This is an indispensable first step. It is not enough to know and to say that they laid what you call moderate duties. The question is, on what principles did they lay them; for what object; with what intent; on what interpretation of the Constitution; on what theory of political economy? Details vary. Principles are the same yesterday, to-day, and through the ages of a nation's life.

To know, then, in this just and adequate sense, the principles which lie at the foundation of our first system, as, after the honorable Senator, I shall continue to call it, we will turn, *first*, to the model law of July 4th, 1789. It is entitled "An act for laying a duty on goods, wares, and merchandises, imported into the United States." It sets off with this preamble: "Whereas it is necessary for the support of government, for the discharge of the debts of the United States, and the encouragement and protection of manufactures, that duties be laid on goods, wares, and merchandises imported." It was the second act passed under the new Constitution; the first having simply "regulated the time and manner of administering certain oaths."

Of this model law, then, Mr. President, I assert: 1. That

it was as really and truly, in its principle and intention, a protective tariff, as the act of 1824. 2. That its framers meant so to construct it as adequately to foster the rising but infant manufactures and mechanic arts of America, and thought they had done so. 3. That it was cast and fashioned into the particular form in which we see it, instead of having been left, as at first was contemplated, in a very different form, — it was moulded into this form, expressly and avowedly, for the purpose of protection. 4. That of the whole number of duties which it imposes, more than twenty were made specific duties, — were made and left what they are, instead of being left ad valorem duties, as at first was contemplated; and that this was done, expressly and avowedly, for the purpose of protection. 5. That of the ad valorem duties imposed by it, from fifteen to twenty were enumerated, and placed under a higher rate than the residuary, horizontal, unenumerated level of five per cent. under which it was at first contemplated to leave them; and that this was done, expressly and avowedly, for the purpose of protection. 6. That fifteen or sixteen articles, which on principles of revenue should pay duties, and which it was at first contemplated to subject to duties, are made free, expressly and avowedly for the purpose of encouraging manufactures and the mechanic arts. 7. That the act was under consideration of congress for a period of nearly three months, and was most laboriously debated and constructed; that throughout the whole discussion the constitutional power to impose, vary, increase duties even to the point of prohibition, for the express and declared purpose of protecting, and fostering the agriculture, the tonnage, the navigation, the commerce, and the manufactures of the nation, — the economical expediency, and the social and political justice of doing so, were assumed or asserted by all, and were denied and doubted by no one member of either branch of the legislature. 8. That the choice was, in the progress of business, distinctly presented to that congress, to pass an act in a different form from this, which would produce more revenue in a shorter time than this, but which would not afford so much protection; or to pass this, which would be less immediately productive of revenue, but would afford more protection to general domestic labor; and that this was chosen, expressly and avowedly, because it afforded more adequate protection. 9. That the actual protection afforded by this act proved to be, as its framers designed it to be, entirely adequate.

Sir, if I can maintain these assertions, you may admire, but perhaps not approve, and not imitate that ingenuity of discrimination, which praises the spirit that produced this law, yet denounces the spirit which produced the law of 1824. You will see, and you will respect, and you will cherish, in both, one and the same identical policy of protection, growing with the growth, strengthening with the strength, flexible to the circumstances of one and the same common country. To see, then, if these assertions are true, I must ask you to trace in the debates of that day the history of this law, — its origin, its first form, its changes, its growth, its consummation. Look beyond its preamble, which, however, most exactly and completely unfolds and announces its objects; look beyond that, to its history. This, I am aware, is familiar to many of you. I am afraid it will be tedious to all. Yet to us, to all of us, to all who would know the constitutional doctrines and the economical and political theories and practice of the age of Washington; to all who would know whether the legislation of 1824 was in principle new folly or "ancient prudence" — how far more important is this investigation than the history of many a council of Trent; many a Magna Charta; many a statute of Edward, or Henry, or Charles the First! I will first relate the history of this law, and then prove and illustrate it.

It was on the eighth of April, 1789, that Mr. Madison opened the business of constructing a system of impost duties, by proposing to the house to pass a mere brief and simple revenue bill. He said that there was not time to prepare a more comprehensive and complete measure; that the object of immediate importance was the speediest practicable supply of the federal treasury; that to effect that object it was expedient to pass an act which should intercept the spring importations, by which means more money would be procured, and in shorter time, than by a more elaborate system which would be longer in constructing. In the actual circumstances, despatch, he thought, was everything. He proposed, therefore, "that congress should take, as the basis of the temporary system which he advised to have adopted," the resolution passed by the old congress of 1783. That resolution imposed specific duties on seven enumerated articles, to wit: spirituous liquors, wines, tea, coffee, sugar, cocoa, and pepper, (not one of which, except rum, could be reckoned of the class of protected articles, no other of them coming into competition with anything produced in the United States;) and on all other articles, without enumeration, a horizontal ad valorem of five per cent. This resolution, "with a clause or two respecting tonnage," he proposed to adopt as a temporary measure of revenue, adapted to the actual circumstances of the moment.

You understand, then, Mr. Madison's first plan. If it had been adopted, we should have seen, for the first and last time, that "faultless monster which the world ne'er saw," a pure, sheer, mere revenue tariff. Some unintentional and unhappy *incidental* protection even such a tariff would yield, — with which constitutional and economical purists must have borne as well as they could. But, upon the whole, it would have come as near the notion of an unadulterated "revenue measure" as the lot of humanity will admit. But was it adopted? Nothing like it, Sir.

Upon its being opened, Mr. Fitzsimons, of Pennsylvania, rose and said that he desired to see a more permanent system adopted, and one that should "carry its views much farther;" a system some way adequate to our whole actual situation, "as it respects our agriculture, our manufactures, and our commerce;" a system which "should encourage domestic production, and foster the infant manufactures of America." He proposed, therefore, that instead of adopting the little revenue resolution of the old congress, an extended bill of detail should be framed, proceeding by enumeration of all the subjects of duty, and imposing on each the particular rate which should blend with revenue the requisite amount of protection.

Here, then, you see, two plans, two bills, different in object, different in details, were presented to the choice of congress. And thereupon a short debate arose on the question, which general scheme and frame of impost law should be adopted. In support of Mr. Madison's original proposition, it was urged "that the great object of the moment was revenue; that, for this, despatch was indispensable; and that the brief revenue resolution, adopted at once, would, by intercepting the expected importations of the spring, bring more money into the treasury, in a shorter time, than a law more carefully matured and passed at a later day." To this it was answered, by Mr. Fitzsimons and others, "that it might be admitted, and was probably true, that the plan first proposed would yield a more immediate supply to an exhausted treasury, but that there were objects of even more importance than that, — objects which that plan could not accomplish; that among these were the 'encouragement of domestic productions, and the protection of American manufactures;' and that if time were necessary to frame a bill which should comprehend and accomplish these, time must be taken for it, whether the treasury were immediately filled or remained somewhat longer empty."

After a short debate, Mr. Madison yielded to the suggestion of Mr. Fitzsimons; the basis, which he at first had proposed to proceed on, was abandoned, and the house engaged assiduously in the business of constructing a blended revenue and tariff bill, by enumeration; each member bringing forward such articles as he deemed worthy of being taken out of, and raised above the unenumerated level of five per cent., and moving such duties upon them as he thought proper, whether on considerations of revenue or protection. The bill was matured and became a law on the fourth of July, 1789. Instead of a law of ten lines, laying a half dozen specific duties upon articles not coming in competition with any domestic manufacture, and an ad valorem duty of five per cent. on all other articles, without enumeration; it became a law of six sections; imposing more than twenty specific and more than fifteen ad valorem duties, expressly for protection; admitting sixteen articles free of duty, which a mere revenue tariff should and would tax, — for the sole purpose of encouraging domestic arts; laying tonnage duties for the benefit of American tonnage; distributing, with a comprehensive and parental impartiality, its fostering care over the agriculture of the South and West; the fisheries and navigation of the East; the mechanical trades of the villages and towns; the manufacturing industry of the whole country; over the producer of cotton, indigo, and hemp; the grain grower and grazier; fishermen, and the owners of ships; workmen in leather, clothing, cordage, iron, glass, paper, and wood, — the universal existing labor of the young America, — a law exactly and completely conforming to the announcement of its preamble; laying duties "for the support of government, for the discharge of the debts of the United States, and the encouragement and protection of manufactures."

Such, Sir, is the history of the model tariff, the corner-stone of the Senator's "good old system" of our fathers. I am now to prove this; and I shall do it by a few selections from the speeches of different gentlemen in that debate, reported in the first volume of "Debates and Proceedings in Congress, &c., compiled by Joseph Gales, senior."

I begin with a passage or two indicating Mr. Madison's original plan, and the reasons assigned for adopting it. Upon introducing it, he said, —

"The deficiency *in our treasury* has been too notorious to make it necessary for me to animadvert upon that subject. *Let us content ourselves with endeavoring to remedy the evil.*"

"The second point to be regarded in adjusting import duties relates to *revenue alone; and this is the point* I mean more particularly to bring into the view of the committee."

"The propositions made on this subject by congress in 1783 having received, generally, the approbation of the several States of the Union, in some form or other, seem well calculated to become the basis of the *temporary system which I wish the committee to adopt.* I am well aware that the changes which have taken place in many of the States, and in our public circumstances, since that period, will require, in some degree, a deviation from the scale of duties then affixed: nevertheless, *for the sake of that expedition which is necessary in order to embrace the spring importations*, I should recommend a *general* adherence to the plan.

"This, with the addition of a clause on tonnage, I will now read, and, with leave, submit it to the committee, hoping it may meet their approbation as an *expedient*, rendered eligible by the *urgent occasion there is for the speedy supplies* of the federal treasury, and a speedy rescue of our trade from its present anarchy."

He then read the resolution of 1783, which was in these words: —

Resolved, (as the opinion of this committee,) That the following duties ought to be levied on goods, wares, and merchandise, imported into the United States, viz: On rum, per gallon, — of a dollar; on all other spirituous liquors, —; on molasses, —; on Madeira wine, —; on all other wines, —; on common bohea teas, per lb., —; on all other teas, —; on pepper, —; on brown sugars, —; on loaf sugars, —; on all other sugars, —; on cocoa and coffee, —; on all other articles, — per cent. on their value at the time and place of importation."

And after Mr. Fitzsimons had disclosed his preference for a more comprehensive and protective measure, and Mr. Madison had yielded to the suggestion, he (Mr. Madison) said, —

"From what has been suggested by the gentlemen that have spoken on the subject before us, I am led to apprehend we shall be under the necessity of *travelling further into an investigation of principles than what I supposed would be necessary, or had in contemplation when I offered the propositions before you.*

"It was my view to restrain the first essay on this subject *principally* to the object of revenue, and make this rather *a temporary expedient* than anything permanent. I see, however, that there are strong exceptions against deciding immediately on a part of the plan, which I had the honor to bring forward, as well as against an application to the resources mentioned in the list of articles just proposed by the gentleman from Pennsylvania.

"I presume that, *however much we may be disposed to promote domestic manufactures,* we ought to pay *some* regard to the *present* policy of obtaining revenue. It may be remarked, also, that by fixing *on a temporary expedient for this purpose, we may gain more than we shall lose by suspending the consideration of the other subject until we obtain fuller information of the state of our manufactures.* We have *at this time* the *strongest* motives for turning our attention to the point I have mentioned; every gentleman sees that the *prospect of our harvest from the spring importations is daily vanishing;* and if the committee delay levying and collecting an impost *until a system of protecting duties shall be perfected,* there will *be no importations* of any consequence on which the law is to operate, *because by that time all the spring vessels will have arrived. Therefore, from a pursuit of this policy, we shall suffer a loss equal to the surplus which might be expected from a system of higher duties.*"

See, too, how others understood Mr. Madison's first proposition.

Speaking of it, Mr. Boudinot said, —

"The plan which he has submitted to the committee appears to be simple and sufficiently complete *for the present purpose;* I shall, therefore, for my own part, be content with it."

Mr. Lawrence concurred in this construction of it: —

"If I am not mistaken, the honorable mover of the plan viewed it as a *temporary system,* particularly calculated *to embrace the spring importations;* hence it may be proper to lay a duty at a certain rate per cent. on the value of all articles, without attempting an enumeration of any; because, if we attempt to specify every article, it will expose us to a question which must require *more time* than can be spared, to obtain the object that appears to be in the view of the committee.

"By adopting the plan I have mentioned, *you will embrace the spring importation, and give time for digesting and maturing one upon more perfect principles;* and, as the proposed system is intended to be but a temporary one, *that* I esteem to be best which requires the least time to form it."

And Mr. White, opposing Mr. Fitzsimons's suggestion in favor of substituting a more mature measure in place of Mr. Madison's, observed, —

"I am inclined to think, that entering so minutely into the detail will consume too much of our time, and thereby *lose us a greater sum than the additional impost on the last-mentioned articles will bring in;* because there may be doubts whether many of them are capable of bearing an increased duty.

"This law would continue until mature deliberation, ample discussion, and full information, enabled us to complete a perfect system of revenue; for, in order to charge specified articles of manufacture, so as to encourage our domestic ones, it will be necessary to examine the present state of each throughout the Union. This will certainly be a work of labor and time, and will perhaps require more of each than the committee have now in their power."

I have read more than enough to show you the nature and objects of Mr. Madison's first revenue resolution. Let me now advert to a selection or two which may display the nature and grounds and objects of the plan presented by Mr. Fitzsimons in opposition, and which was approved by congress.

In introducing it, Mr. Fitzsimons said, —

"I observe, Mr. Chairman, by what the gentlemen have said, who have spoken on the subject before you, that the proposed plan of revenue is viewed by them as a temporary system, to be continued only until proper materials are brought forward and arranged in more perfect form. I confess, Sir, that I carry my views on this subject much further; that I earnestly wish such a one which, in its operation, will be some way adequate to our present situation, as it respects our agriculture, our manufactures, and our commerce.

"I have prepared myself with an additional number of enumerated articles, which I wish subjoined to those already mentioned in the motion on your table. Among these are some calculated to encourage the productions of our country, and protect our infant manufactures; besides others tending to operate as sumptuary restrictions upon articles which are often termed those of luxury."

He therefore offered the following resolution: —

"*Resolved,* (as the opinion of this committee,) That the following duties ought to be laid on goods, wares, and merchandise, imported into the United States."

I will not read the entire list of articles enumerated in his resolution, but among them were upwards of thirty coming in competition with those produced or made in the United States, the production and manufacture of which was intended to be encouraged.

He was followed and supported by his colleague, Mr. Hartly, who said, —

"I have observed, Sir, from the conversation of the members, that it is in the contemplation of some to enter on this business in a limited and partial manner, *as it relates to revenue alone;* but, for my own part, I wish to do it on as broad a bottom as is at this time practicable. The observations of the honorable gentleman from South Carolina [Mr. Tucker] may have weight in some future stage of the business, for the article of tonnage will not probably be determined for several days, before which time his colleagues may arrive and be consulted in the manner he wishes; but surely no argument derived from that principle can operate to discourage the committee from taking such measures *as will tend to protect and promote our domestic manufactures.* If we consult the history of the ancient world, we shall see that they have thought proper, for a long time past, to give great encouragement to the establishment of manufactures, by laying such partial duties on the importation of foreign goods as to give the home manufactures *a considerable advantage in the price when brought to market.* It is also well known to this committee, that there are many articles that will bear a higher duty than others, which are to remain in the common mass, and be taxed with a certain impost ad valorem. From this view of the subject, I think it both politic and just that the *fostering hand of the* general government *should extend* to all those manufactures which will tend to national utility. I am therefore sorry that gentlemen seem to fix their mind to so early a period as 1783; for we very well know our circumstances are much changed since that time: we had then but few manufactures among us, and the vast quantities of goods that flowed in upon us from Europe, at the conclusion of the war, rendered those few almost useless; since then we have been forced by necessity, and various other causes, to increase our domestic manufactures to such a degree as to be able to furnish some in sufficient quantity to answer the consumption of the whole Union, while others are daily growing into importance. Our stock of materials, is, in many instances, equal to the greatest demand, and our artisans sufficient to work them up, even for exportation. In these cases, I take it to be the policy of every enlightened nation to give their manufactures that degree of encouragement necessary to perfect them, without oppressing the other parts of the community; and under this encouragement, the industry of the manufacturer will be employed to add to the wealth of the nation. Many of the articles in the list proposed by my worthy colleague will have this tendency; and therefore I wish them to be received and considered by the committee; if sufficient information cannot be obtained as to the circumstances of any particular manufacture, so as to enable the committee to determine a proper degree of encouragement, it may be relinquished; but at present it will, perhaps, be most advisable to receive the whole."

And Mr. Madison, yielding to these and other considerations in favor of a more extended and comprehensive scheme of imposts than his own first plan, proceeded to unfold, in a speech of much clearness and frankness, the principles upon which such a scheme should be constructed. Declaring himself then in favor, as the general rule, of a "very free system of commerce," he said, —

"If my general principle is a good one, that commerce ought to be free, and labor and industry left at large to find its proper object, the only thing which remains will be to discover the exceptions that do not come within the rule I have laid down. I agree with the gentleman from Pennsylvania, that there are exceptions, important in themselves, and which claim the particular attention of the committee. Although the freedom of commerce would be advantageous to the world, yet, in some particulars, one nation might suffer to benefit others, and this ought to be for the general good of society.

"If America were to leave her ports perfectly free, and make no discrimination between vessels owned by her citizens and those owned by foreigners, while other nations make this discrimination, it is obvious that such policy would go to exclude American shipping altogether from foreign ports, and she would be materially affected in one of her most important interests. To this we may add another consideration, that by encouraging the means of transporting our productions with facility, we encourage the raising them: and this object, I apprehend, is likely to be kept in view by the general government.

"Duties laid on imported articles may have an effect which comes within the idea of national prudence. It may happen that materials for manufactures may grow up without any encouragement for this purpose. It has been the case in some of the States; but in others regulations have been provided, and have succeeded in producing some establishments, *which ought not to be allowed to perish, from the alteration which has taken place. It would be cruel to neglect them, and divert their industry to other channels:* for it is not possible for the hand of man to shift from one employment to another, without being injured by the change. There may be some manufactures, which, being once formed, can advance towards perfection, without any *adventitious aid, while others,* for want of the fostering hand of government will be unable *to go on at all.* Legislative attention will therefore be necessary to collect the proper objects for this purpose, *and this will form another exception to my general principle.*

"Upon the whole, as I think, *some of the propositions may be productive of revenue, and some may protect our domestic manufactures,* though the latter subject ought not to be too confusedly blended with the former, I hope the committee will receive them, and let them lie over, in order that we may have time to consider how far they are consistent with justice and policy."

You see, then, that in place of the original mere revenue measure, it was proposed to substitute a law which should reconcile with the purpose and the effect of raising revenue the purpose and effect of an adequate protection of domestic labor. This proposition was adopted, and thereupon the house proceeded to frame a bill of enumerations and of discriminations. After Mr. Madison had intimated his opinion that a more elaborate measure than he at first designed was made necessary, and after Mr. Fitzsimons's motion, and his list of enumerated articles had been received and was pending, Mr. Goodhue said, —

"I think, when the original motion was introduced, it was only intended as a temporary expedient; but, from what has fallen from the gentleman on this subject, *I am led to believe that idea is abandoned, and a permanent system is to be substituted in its place. I do not know that this is the best mode of the two, but perhaps it may take no more time than the other, if we apply ourselves with assiduity to the task.*"

In the same stage of the business, —

"Mr. Clymer submitted it to the consideration of the committee, how far it was best to bring propositions forward in this way. Not that he objected to this mode of *encouraging manufactures and obtaining revenue*, by combining *the two objects in one bill.* He was satisfied that a political necessity existed *for both the one and the other*, and it would not be amiss to do it in this way, but perhaps the business would be more speedily accomplished by entering upon it systematically."

And Mr. Boudinot said, —

"The subject in debate *was originally brought forward as a temporary expedient to obtain revenue to support the exigencies of the Union. It has been changed* by successive motions for amendment; and the idea of a *permanent system, to embrace every object connected with commerce, manufactures, and revenue, is held up in its stead.*

"Let us take, then, the resolution of congress, in 1783, as presented by the honorable gentleman from Virginia, (Mr. Madison,) and make it the basis of our system, *adding only such protecting duties as are necessary to support the manufactures established by the legislatures of the manufacturing States.*"

The house then plunged at once into the details of a revenue and protective tariff. Every member presented such articles as he thought deserving of enumeration for encouragement by a particular duty; and his motion was resisted and supported very much as similar motions are supported and resisted in the tariff debates of our day. It would carry me too far to read this part of the history of the law, but a few passages, which might seem gathered from "Niles's Weekly," Register of 1828, (so little is there new under the sun, so immortal is truth, so immortal is error, so narrow is the circle of identical, recurrent ideas in which these discussions go round and round,) a few passages will not be irrelevant to my purpose.

Hear the debate about the proposed duty on *steel:* —

"Mr. Lee moved to strike out this duty; observing that the consumption of steel was very great, and essentially necessary to agricultural improvements. He did not believe any gentleman would contend that enough of this article to answer consumption *could be fabricated* in any part of the Union; hence it would operate as an oppressive, though an indirect tax upon agriculture; and any tax, whether direct or indirect, upon this interest, at this juncture, would be unwise and impolitic."

"Mr. Tucker joined the gentleman in his opinion, observing that it was impossible for some States to get it but by importation from foreign countries. He conceived it more deserving a bounty to increase the quantity, than an impost which would lessen the consumption and make it dearer also."

"Mr. Clymer replied, that the manufacture of steel in America was rather in its infancy; but as all the materials necessary to make it were the produce of almost every State in the Union, and as the manufacture *was already established, and attended with considerable success,* he deemed it prudent to emancipate our country from the manacles in which she was held by foreign manufacturers. A furnace in Philadelphia, with a very small aid from the legislature of Pennsylvania, made three hundred tons in two years, and now makes at the rate of two hundred and thirty tons annually, and with a little further encouragement would supply enough for the consumption of the Union. He hoped, therefore, gentlemen would be disposed, under these considerations, *to extend a degree of patronage to a manufacture which* a moment's reflection would convince them was highly deserving protection."

"Mr. Madison thought the object of selecting this article *to be solely* the encouragement of the manufacture, and not revenue; for on any other consideration, it would be more proper, as observed by the gentleman from Carolina, (Mr. Tucker,) to give a bounty on the importation. It was so materially connected with the improvement of agriculture and other manufactures, that he questioned its propriety *even on that score.* A duty would tend to depress many mechanic arts in the proportion that it protected this; he thought it best to reserve this article to the non-enumerated ones, where it would be subject to a five per cent. ad valorem."

"Mr. Fitzsimons. Some States were, from local circumstances, better situated to carry on the manufacture than others, and would derive some little advantage on this account in the commencement of the business. But, laying aside local distinctions, what operates to the benefit of one part, in establishing useful institutions, will eventually operate to the advantage of the whole."

"Suppose five shillings per hundred weight was imposed, it might be, as stated, a partial duty, *but would not the evil be soon overbalanced by the establishment of such an important manufacture? — a great and principal manufacture for every agricultural country*, but particularly useful in the United States."

On beer, ale, and porter: —

"Mr. Fitzsimons meant to make an alteration in this article, by distinguishing beer, ale, and porter, imported in casks, from what was imported in bottles. He thought this manufacture one highly deserving of encouragement. If the morals of the people were to be improved by what entered into their diet, it would be prudent in the National Legislature *to encourage* the manufacture of malt liquors. The small protecting duties laid in Pennsylvania had a great effect towards *the establishment of breweries;* they no longer imported this article, but, on the contrary, exported considerable quantities, and, in two or three years, with the fostering aid of government, would be able to furnish enough for the whole consumption of the United States. He moved nine cents per gallon."

"Mr. Lawrence seconded the motion. He would have this duty so high as to give a decided preference to American beer; it would tend also to encourage agriculture, because the malt and hops consumed in the manufacture were the produce of our own grounds."

"Mr. Sinnickson declared himself a friend of this manufacture, and thought if the duty was *laid high enough to effect a prohibition, the manufacture would increase, and of consequence, the price be lessened.* He considered it of importance, inasmuch as the materials were produced in the country, and tended to advance the agricultural interest."

"Mr. Madison moved to lay an impost of eight cents on all beer imported. He did not think this sum would give a monopoly, *but hoped it would be such an encouragement as to induce the manufacture to take deep root in every State in the Union;* in this case, it would produce the collateral good hinted at by the gentleman from New Jersey, which, in his opinion, was an object well worthy of being attended to."

On candles: —

"Mr. Fitzsimons moved to lay a duty of two cents on all candles of tallow, per pound."

"Mr. Tucker observed, that some States were under the necessity of importing considerable quantities of this article also, while others had enough, and more than enough, for their own consumption; therefore the burden would be partially borne by such States."

"Mr. Fitzsimons. The manufacture of candles is an important manufacture, and far advanced towards perfection. I have no doubt but, in a few years, we shall be able to furnish sufficient to supply the consumption for every part of the continent. In Pennsylvania we have a duty of two pence per pound; and under the operation of this small encouragement the manufacture has gained considerable strength. We no longer import candles from Ireland or England, of whom, a few years ago, we took considerable quantities; the necessity of continuing those encouragements which the State legislatures have deemed proper, exist in a considerable degree; therefore it will be politic in the government of the United States to continue such duties till their object is accomplished."

"Mr. Boudinot apprehended that most States imported considerable quantities of this article from Russia and Ireland; he expected they would be made cheaper than they could be imported, if a small encouragement was held out by the government, as the materials were to be had in abundance in our country."

"Mr. Lawrence thought that, if candles were an object of considerable importation, they ought to be taxed for the sake of obtaining revenue; and, if they were not imported in considerable quantities, the burden upon the consumer would be small, while it tended to cherish a valuable manufacture."

On coal: —

"Mr. Bland, of Virginia, informed the committee that there were mines opened in Virginia capable of supplying the whole of the United States; and, if some restraint was laid on the importation of foreign coal, those mines might be worked to advantage. He thought it needless to insist upon the advantages resulting from a colliery, as a supply for culinary and mechanical purposes, and as a nursery to train up seamen for a navy. He moved three cents a bushel."

On hemp: —

"Mr. Moore declared the Southern States were well calculated for the cultivation of hemp, and, from certain circumstances, well inclined thereto. He conceived it the duty of the committee to pay as much respect to the encouragement and protection of husbandry (the most important of all interests in the United States) as they did to manufactures."

"Mr. Scott stated a fact or two; being, perhaps, as well acquainted with the Western country as any member of the committee. The lands along the frontiers, he could assure the committee, were well calculated for the cultivation of this plant; it is a production that will bear carriage by land better than any other, tobacco not excepted. He believed an encouragement of the kind now moved for would bring, in a year or two, vast quantities from that country, at little expense, to Philadelphia, even from the waters of the Ohio; the inhabitants expect some encouragement, and will be grateful for it."

"Mr. White. If the legislature take no notice of this article, the people will be led to believe it is not an object worthy of encouragement, and the spirit of cultivation will be damped; whereas, if a small duty only was laid, it might point out to them that it was desirable, and would induce an increase of the quantity."

"Mr. Moore. By the encouragement given to manufactures you raise them in price, while a competition is destroyed, which tended to the advantage of agriculture. He thought the manufacturing interest ought not to stand in the way of the other; but, as the committee had agreed to give it encouragement, he hoped the other would receive its share of legislative support."

"Mr. Burke thought it proper to suggest to the committee what might be the probable effect of the proposed measure in the State he represented, (South Carolina,) and the adjoining one, (Georgia). The staple products of that part of the Union were hardly worth cultivation, on account of their fall in price; the planters are therefore disposed to pursue some other. The lands are certainly well adapted to the growth of hemp, and he had no doubt but its culture would be practised with attention. Cotton is likewise *in contemplation among them;* and, if good seed could be procured, *he hoped it might succeed.* But the low, strong, rice lands would produce hemp in abundance, — many thousand tons even this year, if it was not so late in the season. He liked the idea of laying a low duty now, *and encouraging it* against the time when a supply might be had from our own cultivation."

On glass: —

"Mr. Carroll moved to insert window and other glass. A manufacture of this article was begun in Maryland, and attended with considerable success; if the legislature were to grant a small encouragement, it would be permanently established; the materials were to be found in the country in sufficient quantities to answer the most extensive demands."

On paper: —

"Mr. Clymer informed the house that the manufacture of paper was an important one; and, *having grown up under legislative encouragement,* it *will be wise to continue it.*"

On wool cards: —

"Mr. Ames introduced wool cards, with observing that they were manufactured to the eastward as good and as cheap as the imported ones."

"Mr. Clymer mentioned that, in the State of Pennsylvania, the manufacture was carried to great perfection, and enough could be furnished to supply the demand. A duty of fifty cents per dozen was imposed on wool cards."

Prohibitory duties were moved, without a word of doubt, from any quarter, of the constitutional power, and, in some cases, the economical expediency, of imposing them. Thus, —

"Mr. Bland, of Virginia, thought that very little revenue was likely to be collected on the article of beef, let the duty be more or less; and, as it was to be had in sufficient quantities within the United States, *perhaps a tax amounting to a prohibition would be proper.*"

It was rejected as totally unnecessary, "nothing being to be apprehended from rivalship."

On manufactured tobacco, —

"Mr. Sherman moved six cents, *as he thought the duty ought to amount to a prohibition.* This was agreed to."

I have detained the senate longer than I could have wished, upon these proofs and illustrations of the constitutional and economical doctrines which compose the foundation of our "old system" of impost duties. They establish conclusively, if I rightly apprehend them, that in every just sense of the language, in principle, aims, and forms, the "model law" was a protective tariff. It was as much so as the law of 1824. It assumed and asserted exactly the same theory of power, of right, of duty, of expediency. It sought to bring such a sum of money into the treasury as the wants of administration exacted; but it sought to effect this by such arrangements of detail, by such discriminations of high and low duties, by prohibition here, by total exemption there, as should secure to the vast and various labor of America, on the land, in the shop, on the sea, a clear and adequate advantage over the labor of the alien nations of the world. The proofs that these opinions and these intentions presided over and controlled the whole law, and every part of it, are everywhere, — in its preamble, in its provisions, in its history, origin, growth, successive changes, and final form. Sir, the very day of its passage, July 4th, 1789, seems to mark the energetic "Americanism" of its nature!

But it has been a hundred times repeated in the debate, that the duties laid by this law are moderate duties. Much arithmetical pains have been wasted in calculating their average per cent. I say wasted; for, in the first place, we cannot reduce the numerous specific duties, in which it abounds, to their equivalent ad valorems, because we do not know the prices of 1789; in the next place, an average, ever so exactly calculated, conveys no idea of the degree of protection secured by a highly discriminating tariff; and, finally, however moderate may be the duties of this law, it is not the less, in principle, in intent, in its constitutional and economical doctrines, and in its effect, a protective tariff. What is such a tariff? What makes it such? Where, and how, do you draw the line between it and a revenue tariff? Of two tariffs, each yielding about the same supply to the treasury, by what standard, by what tests, do you pronounce that one is a measure of finance, the other a measure of protection? Sir, although these two things run very much into each other, although they have a good deal in common, and all definitions are inadequate and are hazardous, yet are they essentially distinct; and I will venture to submit, that, by universal consent, a tariff which looks to the protection of domestic labor against foreign labor, as *one* important, substantial, influencive object and purpose, either jointly with, or in exclusion of, the object and purpose of revenue; a tariff which, in numerous instances, selects a certain form and a certain rate of duties, rather than another and lower, upon the avowed ground that the form and rate chosen are better for protection than the form and rate rejected, though no better and not as good for revenue; which lays some duties of prohibition, and asserts the power to lay others; which lays many duties which, in and by themselves, are expected and designed to check particular kinds of importations, in order to give the domestic producer an advantage in the market over the foreign producer, and thus to diminish the revenue to be drawn from those particular and numerous sources; and which does all this, to a greater degree than an equally or more effective revenue tariff would do it, in consideration and contemplation of prospective ultimate advantages to result from the establishment of certain domestic employments — a tariff which does all this, upon these reasons, is a protecting tariff, or there is no such thing in any legislative code in the world. I do not care whether the duties are high or low; how they average, or what are the extremes. Such a tariff asserts the constitutional power, the social and political right, and the economical expediency of so regulating foreign commerce, of so gathering in revenue, as to bring to life, and to keep alive, the whole or particular forms of domestic labor, as distinct from foreign labor; and it asserts it practically. This covers the whole ground. Such a tariff, exactly, is this of 1789. Such a tariff totally rejects the doctrine which has been maintained in the debate, that of several duties on the same subject, each yielding the same amount of revenue, the lowest is to be preferred. It adopts and exemplifies the directly opposite doctrine, that, even where the highest will yield less revenue, it may wisely, justly, constitutionally be preferred, because it will produce a compensation of other good in another way. It rejects the doctrine asserted in this debate, that under our system protection is merely an accidental incident to revenue, to be endured, not favored; it declares, on the contrary, that the two purposes of revenue and protection, may be harmoniously blended; may be regarded as of equal importance; that one may predominate in this duty, and another in that; that it is a legitimate and a noble enterprise of statesmanship, to transform the very evil and burden of taxation into a means of individual comfort and enjoyment and national greatness and glory. It teaches the lawgiver, that instead of bewildering himself, and wasting his precious time in trying to find the revenue maximum of duty, — more hopeless and more useless than the search after the quadrature of the circle or the perpetual motion, — he should just, sincerely, honestly, and constantly propose this problem to himself: How can I procure that amount of revenue which an economical administration of government demands, in such manner as most impartially and most completely to develop and foster the universal industrial capacities of the country, of whose vast material interests I am honored with the charge?

Whether its duties are high or low, then, this is a protecting tariff. But who knows whether that portion of them which is specific is high or low? We have no prices current, and no other proof of the prices of that day; and without such proof how can you reduce these duties to their equivalent ad valorem? I read a passage from one of the speeches of Mr. Bland, of Virginia, during the debate, from which it would seem that some of the rates would be called high even now: —

"The enumerated articles in this bill are very numerous; they are taxed from fifty per cent. downwards; the general mass pays five per cent."

We are told in this discussion that thirty per cent. and thirty-three and one third per cent. are the maximum of revenue duty. Here were fifty per cent. duties, and in *the specific form*, and therefore certain of collection; while the ad valorem forms, on foreign values, are as certain to be evaded and defrauded.

But, Mr. President, there is another answer to the suggestion that these duties were moderate. Sir, in the actual circumstances of the time, they were entirely sufficient for the protection of the agricultural, navigating, commercial, manufacturing, and mechanical industry, which they were intended to protect. They effected their object perfectly. And when you consider the circumstances, how plain, coarse, hardy, simple, were the existing mechanical manufacturing employments of the country; how unlike the various, refined, and sensitive forms, which in a later age they put on; that they were, very much, manufactures of wood into cabinet-ware, furniture, carriages, and ships; of leather, in tanneries; of iron in blacksmiths' shops; of cloth, from cotton, wool, and flax, chiefly in private families; that they were many of them very far in the interior; that there was not yet a single cotton mill, and perhaps not a single woollen mill, in the country; that thus they exacted no large accumulations of capital, nor high degrees of skill slowly acquired, nor expensive machinery continually changing; and when you consider, too, that England, that all Europe, was just about to rush into the wars of the French revolution, drawing the sword which was never to be sheathed until night should fall on the hushed and drenched field of Waterloo — in view of these circumstances, you will not wonder that even these duties were sufficient. The statesmen of that time, Sir, meant to protect domestic labor; they knew how to do it, and they did it. In point of fact, from 1789 to 1808, the progress of manufactures was slow but sure. Then began a new era, of which I will speak in its place.

I think, Mr. President, that it is scarcely necessary to look beyond this survey of the history of the law of 1789, to discover the spirit, principles, and aims, which presided in and framed it. Let me give you, however, a little supplementary evidence to prove that I have not misconceived its essential structure and nature. Hear, first, in what terms Washington could speak of it, and of the subsequent and kindred legislation upon the same policy. In his last Address, in December, 1796, he says, —

"Congress *have repeatedly, and not without success, directed their atten-*

tion to the encouragement of manufactures. The object is of too much consequence not to insure a continuance of their efforts in every way that shall appear eligible. Ought our country to remain dependent on foreign supply, precarious, because liable to be interrupted? If the necessary article should in this mode *cost more in time of peace,* will not the security and independence thence arising form an ample compensation?"

That great man thought, you perceive, that even if a protective policy should enhance the prices of a time of peace, security and independence were equivalents with which a nation might be content. Sir, we have won the equivalents, and yet we do not pay the compensation. The "necessary article costs" less, not more; yet is our security more absolute, our independence more real, our greatness more steadfast.

See, too, how Mr. Jefferson, in 1802, describes the policy, which, when he wrote, had been pursued from 1789, for thirteen years: —

"To cultivate peace and maintain commerce and navigation in all their lawful enterprises, and *to protect the manufactures adapted to our circumstances, are* (among others) *the landmarks by which to guide ourselves in all our proceedings.* By *continuing* to make these the rule of our action, we shall endear to our countrymen the true principles of the Constitution, and promote an union of sentiment and of action equally auspicious to their happiness and safety."

And Mr. Dallas, Secretary of the Treasury, in 1816, in his very able report to congress upon the subject of a tariff of duties, remarks, —

"There are few if any governments which do not regard the establishment of domestic manufactures as a chief object of public policy. The United States have always so regarded it. In the earliest acts of congress which were passed after the adoption of the present Constitution, the obligation of providing, by duties on imports, for the discharge of the public debts, is expressly connected with the policy of encouraging and protecting manufactures."

And Mr. Madison, looking back, in 1828, to a scene in which his part had been so conspicuous, says, in his letter to Mr. Cabell: "That the encouragement of manufactures was an object of the power to regulate trade, is proved by the use made of the power for that object, in the first session of the first congress under the Constitution; when among the members present were so many who had been members of the federal convention which framed the Constitution, and of the state conventions which ratified it; each of these classes consisting also of members who had opposed and who had espoused the Constitution in its actual form. It does not appear, from the printed proceedings of congress on that occasion that the power was denied by any of them. And it may be remarked, that members from Virginia, in particular, as well of the Anti-federal as the Federal party, the names then distinguishing those who had opposed and those who had approved the Constitution, did not hesitate to propose duties and to suggest even prohibitions in favor of several articles of her productions. By one, a duty was proposed on mineral coal, in favor of the Virginia coal pits; by another, a duty on hemp was proposed, to encourage the growth of that article; and by a third, a prohibition even of foreign beef was suggested, as a measure of sound policy."

And now, Mr. President, let me say, passing strange it would have been, if that congress had not made just such a law; had not founded just such a system! Composed as it was, to so large an extent, of members of the convention which had framed the new Constitution, and of the conventions which had adopted it, — fresh, all of them, from the people, and intimately familiar with the evils, the fears, and the hopes, of which the recent government was born: the excessive importations; the exhausting drain of specie to pay for them; the mountain weight of debt not yet paid to the foreign manufacturer and mechanic; the depression of labor, the derangement of currency, the decline of trade; penetrated profoundly with the certain knowledge that a leading, a paramount object, held universally in view throughout the great effort, just crowned with success, to frame a new Constitution, was to insure the capacity and the will to extend governmental protection to domestic labor, — such a congress, thus admonished, thus enlightened, could not help making such a law and founding such a system. They would not have dared to go home without doing so! I once, Mr. President, in this place, on a former occasion, and with a different purpose, attempted to collect and combine, and to exhibit under a single view, the proofs contained in the writings, such as they are, which appeared in this country between the peace of 1783 and the adoption of the Constitution, tending to show that *a policy of protection by means of duties on the produc-*

tions of foreign labor was most prominent among the beneficial instrumentalities which the new government was expected to possess and exert, and among the controlling inducements to its establishment. Those proofs are very numerous; they are very widely scattered over many hundred pages of newspapers and larger periodical publications, and over a space of six years and more, during which the public mind was in a state of unexampled agitation, anxiety, and activity; they consist of essays, addresses, the proceedings of public meetings, and the like; and they are contributed in almost an equal proportion by every part of the country, although the largest number perhaps come from the central States. Taken altogether, and making every allowance for the fact that a great deal of the writing and speech, in which the opinions, hopes, fears, and intentions of that age were embodied, has perished; and that among the opinions and intentions thus expressed, but of whose existence no contemporary record is left, there may have been some of a different character — taken altogether, they prove as clearly that a leading, main, prominent purpose of that generation of our fathers was to create a government which could and should protect American labor, by regulating the introduction of the products of foreign labor, by prohibiting them, by subjecting them to duties of discrimination, and by such other policy as the accomplishment of the object should prescribe — they prove this as clearly as you can prove out of the Irish newspapers of this day that Catholic Ireland is agitating for repeal. Sir, I shall not trouble the senate with the repetition of all or many of the proofs which I at that time exhibited; but I cannot resist the temptation of reminding you how North Carolina and South Carolina could reason then on the nature and the cure of the evils which bore down the young America to the dust; on the difference between manufacturing abroad and manufacturing at home, — the difference to national wealth, to currency, to true and durable public and private prosperity; on the general policy of the protection of American labor, by a more restrained importation of the productions of foreign labor. I read for that purpose, first, a selection or two from certain letters written in North Carolina in 1787, which I find in the American

Museum for August, 1787. The name of the writer is not given, but he sets out by declaring, —

"That his complaints are not occasioned by personal misfortunes; but he finds himself a member of a great family; he interests himself as a brother in the happiness of his fellow-citizens, and he suffers when they are grieved."

The annunciation of his subject marks his fitness to discuss it.

"We are going to consider whether the administration of government, in these infant States, is to be a system of patchwork and a series of expedients — whether a youthful empire is to be supported, like the walls of a tottering ancient palace, by shores and temporary props, or by measures which may prove effectual and lasting — measures which may improve by use and strengthen by age. We are going to consider whether we shall deserve to be a branch of the most poor, dishonest, and contemptible, or of the most flourishing, independent, and happy nation on the face of the earth."

And what do you think is his "measure which is to improve by use, and strengthen by age"? Why, exactly, the encouragement of domestic manufactures, by taxes on foreign manufactures.

"The more I consider the progress of credit and the increase of wealth in foreign nations, the more fully am I convinced that paper money must prove hurtful to this country; that we *cannot be relieved from our debts except by promoting domestic manufactures.*"

Having adverted to the vast accumulation of our foreign debt since the peace, and to the discreditable and startling fact that it had been contracted for numerous articles of necessity which we could better produce, and numerous articles of luxury which we could better dispense with, he proceeds: —

"Let us turn our attention to manufactures, and the staple of our country will soon rise to its proper value, for we have already glutted every foreign market. By this expedient, instead of using fictitious paper, we shall soon obtain hard money sufficient; instead of toiling in the field, and becoming poor, *that we may enrich the manufactures of other countries*, we shall prosper by our labor, *and enrich our own citizens.*"

"Every domestic manufacture is cheaper than a foreign one, for this plain reason: by the first nothing is lost to the country; by the other, the whole value is lost, — it is carried away, never to return. It is perfectly indifferent to this State or to the United States, *what may be the price of domestic manufactures*, because that price remains in the country."

"All wise governments" (such is his argument, page 124) "have thought it their duty, on special occasions, to offer bounties for the encouragement of domestic manufactures; but an excise on foreign goods must operate as a bounty." "I have said that an excise is more favorable to the poor than a land or poll tax. I will venture an additional sentiment: there never was a government in which an excise could be of so much use as in the United States of America. In all other countries, taxes are considered as grievances. In the United States, an excise on foreign goods would not be a grievance: like medicine to a sick man, it would give us strength; it would close that wasteful drain by which our honor and our wealth are consumed. What though money was not wanted, — though we did not owe a florin to any foreign nation, — though we had no domestic debt, — and though the expenses of civil government could be supported for many years without a tax, still it may be questioned whether an excise would not be desirable. It would certainly be the best expedient *for promoting domestic manufactures;* and the condition in which we now live, our general dependence on a foreign country for arms and clothing, is dishonorable — it is extremely dangerous."

"It is the duty of the statesman either to check or to promote the several streams of commerce by taxes or bounties, so as to render them profitable to the nation. Thus it happened in Massachusetts. A tax of twenty-five per cent. was lately imposed on nails, and the poor of Taunton were immediately returned to life and vigor.

"*If any man has doubts concerning the effect of large taxes on foreign manufactures, he should turn his eyes to the Eastern States.* The mechanic is generally the first who perceives of a pernicious commerce; for the support of his family depends on his daily labor." "Hence it is that the merchant may be profited by a particular branch of commerce, and may promote it diligently, while his country is sinking into a deadly consumption."

Sir, these opinions had spread, still earlier, still farther south. Let me recall to your recollection a few passages from the book of the wisdom of South Carolina. Here is an essay, in two letters, written in Charleston, in that State, in 1786, by some one whose enlarged and wise nationality of spirit and aims is indicated by his signature, — "American." The position which he asserts is, that the "only method, consistent with humanity, by which nations have raised themselves to opulence and power, is the encouraging agriculture, manufactures, and commerce." In proof of this, he glances at the history of Egypt, "which to tilling the land soon joined the mechanic arts," and whose "pyramids and sepulchres, fine linens and purples, attested the degree to which she advanced them;" of Tyre, which "enriched herself by her *manufactures* and commerce;" of Carthage, "which carried with her the mechanic arts and the spirit of commerce;" of Venice, the greatest *entrepôt* in the world, "which imported the raw materials of other nations, manufactured them, and exported them to an immense amount;" of Spain, which "expelled her manufacturers and merchants from the kingdom, — a loss that she has not recovered to this day, and perhaps will not for centuries to come," — a loss which all the mines of America have not compensated; for "*with them went the spirit of manufacturing and commerce, which always gives vigor to agriculture*" — Spain, "which, possessing one of the finest climates and soils of Europe, must remain poor, till manufactures and commerce can convince the haughty Spaniard that they alone are the only true permanent source of wealth;" England, which, "in the reign of Queen Elizabeth, made but a small figure in the political or mercantile scale of Europe, which exported chiefly in foreign bottoms her wheat, which is now consumed by her manufacturers, a little lead, tin, and wool, to Flanders, and, in return received foreign manufactures;" Scotland, "a century ago almost as poor as the satire of Churchill painted it, but which had increased in wealth with a rapidity never exceeded, and by these means: manufacturers were invited thither, — these, with the great number of sailors, and victualling their ships, raised the price of provisions, and gave life to agriculture, — land rose in value, — the barren heaths were manured and tilled, — rents rose, — the tenants grew rich, — the numbers increased, — their cities were improved, — their large villages became cities, — and new towns were built in places that, till lately, seemed to defy human art to improve them. This is," he adds, "the effect, and always will be, of manufactures and commerce in every country."

"It is in vain," he concludes, "for any people to attempt to be rich or have a sufficient circulating specie among them, whose imports exceed their exports; the hand of the manufacturer in a distant land seems to act upon gold and silver as the loadstone does upon the needle."

Commenting on the fact that England once raised annually a revenue of three millions and a half by monopolizing our trade, he says, —

"A great part of this may be saved to these States by our becoming our own merchants and carriers; and a great part of the remaining sum may be saved in a few years *by encouraging our* own manufacturers; and even this encouragement will be of service to our revenues. I mean, laying *a duty on our imports*, and giving a small part in bounties to our own tradesmen."

"I do not wish our planters to turn from planting to manufacturing; I only wish to encourage European tradesmen to come to reside here. I wish to see as much as possible exported and as little imported. The planters that buy the manufactures of America stop so much money in this country, which must return again to the planters' hands as long as traders eat."

Of such as this is the whole political literature of that day. There breathes throughout it all a profound and earnest conviction that, without a government which can, and which will, develop and guard the labor of America by protective tariffs and other kindred instrumentality, independence was not yet achieved; the hopes of liberty were a delusive dream; a barren sceptre only had been grasped, unfruitful of joy, unfruitful of glory.

Sir, the congress of 1789 might have known, by another and shorter process, the public sentiment of that day, — the public sentiment of the age of the Constitution. There were members who had witnessed and united in some one of the processions and assemblies which, in so many towns and villages, had just been celebrating the institution of the new government; and they might have learned there what the people expected of them! Very striking exhibitions they were, Sir; and altogether worthy of the contemplation of him who would truly and adequately know for what the Constitution was created. On an appointed day, men came in from the country, and, mingling themselves with those of the town, were arranged in order by thousands. Beneath bright skies, — the moral and national prospect how much brighter than the natural! — with banners and music, gazed on, sympathized with by wives and mothers and daughters and sisters, thronging at windows, in balconies, and up to the house-tops, the long and serried files, not of war, but of peace, the long and serried files of labor, moved from street to street, and at length composed themselves to unite in thanksgiving to God, and in listening to discourses commemorative of the event, and embodying the gratitude and the expectations with which the new government was welcomed in, — embodying a survey of its powers and objects, and a sketch of the transcendent good of which it was full, for that age, and for all time. Sir, in the banners of various device which marked the long course of those processions; in the mottoes upon their flags; in the machines, and models and figures, with which the pacific and more than triumphal march was enriched and enlivened; in the order of its arrangements; in the organizations of tradesmen and artisans, and all the families of labor which swelled it; in the conversation of individuals of those "grave and anxious multitudes" one with another; in the topics and thoughts of the orators of the day; in the applause of the audience; in all this vast, vivid, and various accumulation and exhibition of the general mind, almost as well as in the journals of the convention, the "Madison Papers," the debates of public bodies or the grave discussions of "The Federalist" itself you may read—the congress of 1789 might read—what kind of government the people thought they had constructed. I could almost say that the Constitution is what the general belief of that age held it to be; and in these great and solemn festal scenes is the expression of that general belief.

Take the Philadelphia procession for an instance, of the fourth of July, 1788, and see what the readers of "Poor Richard's Almanac," the pupils and contemporaries of Franklin, expected of the federal Constitution. It was a column of many thousands of persons, of all trades and callings. The more advanced figures and devices of the procession were intended to represent, in a chronological series, the great events which preceded the adoption of the new government. There was one on horseback, representing Independence, and bearing the staff and cap of liberty; next followed one, riding upon a horse, formerly of Count Rochambeau, and carrying a flag with devices of lilies and stars, commemorative of the French alliance, to which we owed so much; then another, with a staff surmounted with laurel and olive, announcing the treaty of peace; after him, another, bearing aloft the name of Washington; then a herald, proclaiming with sound of trumpet the NEW ERA; then a representation of the convention which framed the Constitution; and then others, of the Constitution itself; "a lofty ornamental car, in the form of an eagle;" and a grand federal edifice, the dome supported by thirteen columns, and surmounted by a "figure of plenty." After these, came an appropriate and golden train, the long line of the various labor of America, for whom the new era had risen, with healing in its wings. First, as it ought to have been, was the agricultural society. Then came the manufacturing society, with spinning and carding machines; looms and apparatus for the printing of muslins and calicoes. This bore three flags. The device on one was a bee-hive, with bees issuing from it, standing in the beams of a rising sun; the field of the flag blue, and the motto, "in its rays we shall feel new vigor." The motto on the next was, "may the Union government protect the manufactures of America;" and, on the next, "may government protect us." On the carriage of the manufacturers, drawn by ten horses, were a carding machine, worked by two persons "carding cotton;" a spinning machine, worked by a woman, and drawing cotton suitable for fine jeans; looms on which laces and jeans were being woven; a man designing and cutting prints for shawls; and "Mrs. Hewson and her four daughters," in cotton dresses of their own manufacture, pencilling a piece of chintz of Mr. Hewson's printing. There followed then great numbers; I believe there may have been more than fifty bodies of tradesmen and mechanics, each with its banner, devices, and motto, expressive of the same hopes and the same convictions, evidencing equally the universal popular mind. But I need pursue the matter no further. Sir, what was seen in this procession was seen, on a larger or smaller scale, everywhere. The pageant is passed. The actors have retired from human view. The awful curtain has dropped on them forever. All the world's a stage, and this part is played! Yet the spirit of philosophical history — that spirit to which the half-obliterated figures of a procession upon a wasting architectural fragment reveal intelligibly and instructively some glory or some sorrow of a past age — will not disdain to gather up and ponder these manifestations of the hopes, desires, and purposes, of that mighty heart now hushed. I do not wish or expect to understand the objects for which the Constitution was framed better than the generation which made it; and of their understanding of them I have referred you to very vivid and very authentic proofs. I cannot forbear to read you a sentence or two, before I take leave of the subject, from "Observations on the Philadelphia Procession," written by an eye-witness, very soon after the celebration: —

"The large stage on which the carding and spinning machines displayed the manufacture of cotton was viewed with astonishment and delight by every spectator. On that stage were carried the emblems of the future wealth and independence of our country. Cotton may be cultivated in the Southern and manufactured in the Eastern and Middle States, in such quantities, in a few years, as to clothe every citizen of the United States. *Hence will arise a bond of Union to the States, more powerful than any article of the new Constitution.* Cotton possesses several advantages over wool as an article of dress and commerce. It is not liable to be moth-eaten, and is proper both for winter and summer garments. It may, moreover, be manufactured in America at a less expense than it can be imported from any nation in Europe. From these circumstances, I cannot help hoping that we shall soon see cotton not only the uniform of the citizens of America, but an article of exportation to foreign countries. Several respectable gentlemen exhibited a prelude of these events by appearing in complete suits of jeans, manufactured by the machines that have been mentioned."

Compare this with the judgment of Mr. Calhoun, in his speech in the house of representatives, April, 1816: —

"Capital employed in manufacturing is calculated to bind together more closely our widely spread Republic. It will greatly increase our mutual dependence and intercourse."

I leave, then, the first period of our policy. The law of 1789 was a protective tariff, in principle, intention, and effect. It was made so in execution of the universal will of the age of the Constitution. In the "good old days," protection, whether "principal" or "incident," was held indispensable, and was made sufficient.

And now we are prepared to compare or to contrast with this the second system, — the existing system, — that which began in 1816, and was matured in 1824 and 1828. Sir, it is exactly the system of 1789, accommodated to the altered circumstances of the nation and the world. The statesmen of the last period followed in the very footsteps of their fathers. It is not enough to say their objects were as honest and as useful, their spirit and aims as high, their principles as sound. They were *the same*, — just the same, — *mutatis mutandis*. The law of 1789 was framed to protect the existing manufacturing and mechanical industry of the country. So was that of 1816 and 1824. The times compelled a change of details, and details were changed. Principles, policy, were unchanged. I cannot discern the hand of "millionary capitalists," or "trading politicians" in the framing of the later, more than in that of the earlier system. I see it in neither. Sir, I defend the lawgivers of 1816 and 1824, first, by the example of their fathers, and then by every consideration of enlightened patriotism which may influence American statesmen.

The congress of 1789 found many manufacturing and mechanical arts starting to life, and soliciting to be protected. The congress of 1816, and that of 1824, found families and groups and classes of manufacturing and mechanical arts, far more numerous, far more valuable, far more sensitive also, and with more urgent claim, soliciting protection. In the interval between 1789 and 1816, this whole enterprise had not only immensely enhanced its value, but it had totally changed its nature. It had increased its annual productions to $120,000,000 in 1810, and to $150,000,000 or perhaps $200,000,000 in 1816. But its nature had become different. Instead of a few plain, hardy, coarse, simple, household employments, it had become a various, refined, sensitive industry, —demanding associated capital, skill, long and highly trained, costly and improving machinery,—more precious, but presenting a far broader mark to the slings and arrows of fortune, to hostility, to change, to the hotter foreign competitions which its growth was sure to provoke. Now, you all praise the husbandry of 1789, which so carefully guarded the few blades, just timidly peeping forth into the rain and sunshine, of that April day, hardly worth the treading down; will you depreciate the husbandry of 1824, which with the same solicitude, but at the expense of a higher wall, guarded the grain, then half-grown, and evincing what the harvest was to be?

The statesmen of 1816 and 1824 then might justify themselves by the example of the age of Washington and the Constitution. But I desire to make their defence upon considerations even higher and broader.

In the first place, Sir, their legislation may not only be justified, but it is entitled to praise, honor, and imitation, on the ground of the transcendent value of manufacturing and mechanical industry to a people. Do not fear that I am about to inflict upon you a commonplace upon this topic. I do not understand that there are two different opinions upon it in the civilized world. Certainly there are not two here. Senators who will not lift a finger to introduce or to foster such industry; who think that neither this government nor the State governments have any power to do so, by the only means that are worth a straw, protective duties — this government having none because the Constitution does not give it, and the State governments having none because the Constitution takes it from them to bestow it on nobody — senators who think that, power or no power, you ought to do nothing directly, openly, and avowedly, to exert it — all vie with one another in glowing and lofty estimates of the uses and value of this industry to our nation — to any nation. Doubtless, Sir, to the higher forms of a complete civilization, a various, extensively developed, intellectual manufacturing and mechanical industry, aiming to multiply the comforts and supply the wants of the great body of the people, is wholly indispensable. Its propitious influence upon the wages and enjoyments of labor; the reasonable rewards which it holds out by means of joint stock, in shares, to all capital, whether the one hundred dollars of the widow and orphan, or the one hundred thousand of their wealthier neighbor; its propitious influence upon all the other employments of society; upon agriculture, by relieving it of over-production and over-competition, and securing it a market at home, without shutting up its market abroad; upon commerce, creating or mainly sustaining its best branch, domestic trade, and giving to its foreign trade variety, flexibility, an enlargement of field, and the means of commanding a needful supply of the productions of other nations, without exhausting drains on our own; its influence upon the comforts of the poor, upon refinement, upon security, defence, independence, power, nationality — all this is conceded by everybody. Senators denounce the means, but they glorify the end. Protective duties make a bill of abominations; but an advanced and diversified mechanical industry is excellent. The harvest is delightful to behold; it is the sowing and fencing only that offend the constitutionalist who denies the power, and the economist who denies the expediency, of reaping anything but spontaneous growths of untilled soils. While, therefore, a general defence of this class of employments, and this species of industry would be wholly out of place, there is, however, an illustration or two of their uses, not quite so commonly adverted to, on which I pause to say a word. And one of them is this: that, in connection with the other tasks of an advanced civilization, with which they are always found associated, they offer to every faculty and talent and taste, in the community, the specific work best suited to it; and thus effect a more universal development and a more complete education of the general intellect than otherwise would be practicable. It is not merely that they keep everybody busy, in the evening and before light as well as in the daytime, in winter as well as in summer, in wet weather as well as in fair, women and children as well as men, but it is that everybody is enabled to be busy on the precise thing the best adapted to his capacity and his inclinations. In a country of few occupations, employments go down by an arbitrary, hereditary, coercive designation, without regard to peculiarities of individual character. The son of a priest is a priest; the son of a barber is a barber; a man raises onions and garlic, because a certain other person did so when the Pyramids were building, centuries ago. But a diversified, advanced, and refined mechanical and manufacturing industry, coöperating with these other numerous employments of civilization which always surround it, offers the widest choice, detects the slightest shade of individuality, quickens into existence and trains to perfection the largest conceivable amount and the utmost possible variety of national mind. It goes abroad with its handmaid labors, not like the elegiac poet into the church-yard, but among the bright tribes of living childhood and manhood, and finds there in more than a figurative sense, some mute, inglorious Milton, to whom it gives a tongue and the opportunity of fame; the dauntless breast of some Hampden still at play, yet born to strive with the tyrant of more than a village; infant hands that may one day sway the rod of empire; hearts already pregnant with celestial fire; future Arkwrights and Watts and Whitneys and Fultons, whom it leads forth to a discipline and a career that may work a revolution in the arts and commerce of the world. Here are five sons in a family. In some communities they would all become hedgers and ditchers; in others, shore fishermen; in others, hired men in fields, or porters or servants in noblemen's families. But see what the diversified employments of civilization may make of them. One has a passion for contention and danger and adventure. There are the gigantic game of the sea; the vast fields of the Pacific; the pursuit even "beneath the frozen serpent of the South," for him. Another has a taste for trade: he plays already at bargains and barter. There are Wall Street and Milk Street, and clerkships and agencies at Manilla and Canton and Rio Janeiro, for him. A third early and seriously inclines to the quiet life, the fixed habits, the hereditary opinions and old ways of his fathers; there is the plough for him. Another develops from infancy extraordinary mechanical and inventive talent; extraordinary in degree, of not yet ascertained direction. You see it in his first *whittling*. There may be a Fulton, or an Arkwright; there may be wrapped up the germs of an idea which, realized, shall change the industry of nations, and give a new name to a new era. Well, there are the machine-shops at Lowell and Providence for him; there are cotton mills and woollen mills for him to superintend; there is stationary and locomotive steam-power for him to guide and study; of a hundred departments and forms of useful art, some one will surely reach and feed the ruling intellectual passion. In the flashing eye, beneath the pale and beaming brow of that other one, you detect the solitary first thoughts of genius. There are the seashore of storm or calm, the waning moon, the stripes of summer evening cloud, traditions, and all the food of the soul, for him. And so all the boys are provided for. Every fragment of mind is gathered up. Nothing is lost. The hazel rod, with unfailing potency, points out, separates, and gives to sight every grain of gold in the water and in the sand. Every taste, every faculty, every peculiarity of mental power, finds its task, does it, and is made the better for it.

Let me say, Sir, that there is another influence of manufacturing and mechanical arts and industry, which should commend them to the favor of American statesmen. In all ages and in all nations they have been the parents and handmaids of popular liberty. If I had said of democratical liberty, I should have expressed myself more accurately. This praise, if not theirs alone, or preëminently, they share perhaps with commerce only. I observe, with surprise, that Mr. Calhoun, in his speech in opposition to Mr. Randolph's motion to strike out the mininum valuation on cotton goods, in the house of representatives, April, 1816, a speech in many respects remarkable and instructive, and to which I shall make frequent reference before I have done — in that speech Mr. Calhoun gives some slight countenance to the suggestion that "capital employed in manufacturing produced a greater dependence on the part of the employed, than in commerce, navigation, or agriculture." Sir, I think this is contradicted by the history of the whole world. "Millionary manufacturing capitalists," like all other persons possessed of large accumulations, are essentially conservative, timorous, disinclined to change, on the side of law, order, and permanence. So are millionary commercial capitalists, and millionary cotton-growing and sugar-growing capitalists, and millionary capitalists of all sorts. But the artisans of towns — mechanics, manufacturing operatives, that whole city and village population, wherever concentrated, by whom the useful arts of a civilized society are performed — are among the freest of the free, the world over. They are no man's slaves; they are "no man's men." Brought together in considerable numbers, and forming part of a still larger urban population in immediate contact; reciprocally acting on, and acted on by, numerous other minds; enjoying every day some time of leisure, and driven by the craving for stimulus which the monotony of their employments, their own mental activity, and all the influences about them, are so well calculated to produce — driven to the search of some external objects of interest, they find these in conversation, in discussion, in reading newspapers and books, in all the topics which agitate the crowded community of which they are part; and thus they become curious, flexible, quick, progressive. Something too in their position and relations, — just starting in the world, their fortunes to seek or to make; something in their half antagonistical, half auxiliary connection with their employers, — free associated labor employed by large associated capital; something, with unfailing certainty, determines them to the side of the largest liberty. So always it has been. So it was in the freest of the Greek republics. So too, in the Middle Age, after her sleep of a thousand years from the battle of Pharsalia, liberty revived and respired among the handicraftsmen and traders of the small commercial and manufacturing towns of Germany, Italy, and England. There, in sight of the open and glorious sea, law, order, self-government, popular liberty, art, taste, and all the fair variety of cultivated things, sprung up together, and set out together on that "radiant round," never to cease but with the close of time. And where do you feel the pulses of democratical England and Scotland beat quickest and hottest to-day? What are the communities that called loudest for parliamentary reform; and call loudest now for those social and political ameliorations, the fear of which perplexes the throne, the church, and the aristocracy? Certainly, the large and small manufacturing towns. "The two great powers," I read from the ablest Tory journal in Great Britain, "operating on human affairs, which are producing this progressive increase of democratical influence, are the extension of manufactures and the influence of the daily press." What British periodical is it, which most zealously advocates the cause, asserts the dignity, appreciates the uses and claims, of manufacturing industry? Precisely the most radical and revolutionary of them all. And whose rhymes are those which convey to the strong, sad heart of English labor "thoughts that wake to perish never," the germs of a culture growing up to everlasting life, the "public and private sense of a man;" the dream, the hope, of social reform; and a better, but not revolutionary liberty? Whose, but Elliot's, the worker in iron, the "artisan poet of the poor"?

The real truth is, Sir, that manufacturing and mechanical, and commercial industry, is "the prolific source of democratic feeling." Of the two great elements, which must be combined in all greatness of national character and national destiny, — permanence and progression, — these employments stimulate the latter; agriculture contributes to the former. They are one of those acting and counteracting, opposing yet not discordant powers, from whose reciprocal struggle is drawn out the harmony of the universe. Agriculture is the other. The country is the home of rest. The town is the theatre of change. Senators are very fond of reminding us that the census shows so large a preponderance of numbers at work on the land. Then,

Sir, over and above all the good you do them, by calling off some who would crowd that employment into other business, and providing a better market for those who remain in it, why should you be afraid, on a larger and deeper reason, to temper and attend this by other occupation? You have provided well for permanence. Be not afraid of the agents of intelligent progress. It is the union of social labors which causes the wealth, develops the mind, prolongs the career, and elevates and adorns the history of nations.

But, Mr. President, there was another consideration, which might well have weight to induce the statesmen of 1816 and 1824 to protect the manufacturing and mechanical arts of their country. It was not merely that they were useful, but that they were *a thing actually existing*, not requiring to be made out of the whole cloth, if I may borrow a figure from the subject, but only requiring to be *saved*, preserved, sheltered. It is one thing to force these arts by main strength, by a violent policy, right out of the ground, out of the mine, out of the waterfall; and quite another, after they have so started, after capital has taken that direction, after the evil is done and the good is beginning, after skill is acquired, machinery accumulated, investments made, habits formed—after all this, not to let them die. The first may be unwise; the other cannot be. The statesmen of 1816 and 1824 were not required to choose between the theory of Adam Smith, and the practice of England. They were not required to choose between Scotch and French philosophy, and that immemorial, steady, daring, and perhaps happy disregard of such philosophy, which has domesticated and naturalized the whole circle of civilized arts on that narrow and stormy isle; which has raised on it the throne of the sea; which has given it the wealth that (poured out on the banks of the Neva, of the Danube, and of the Tagus) may have disappointed the dream of a universal French monarchy. They had no such choice to make. Not at all. There were the arts in existence — *non sine diis animosi infantes!* before them. It no more followed, because they might not have forced them into being, that they were to let them perish, than it follows, because you advise a young friend not to marry till he is older, that you mean, if he disregards your counsel, to have him kill his infant child. In such a case, new and precious elements mingle in the deliberation. The existence of interests, spontaneously, undesignedly arisen, may turn the scale. And so Mr. Calhoun, in the speech from which I have once read, reasoned. He said,—

"Besides, we have already surmounted the greatest difficulty that has ever been found in undertakings of this kind. The cotton and woollen manufactures are not to be *introduced*, — they are *already* introduced to a great extent; freeing us entirely from the hazards, and, in a great measure, the sacrifices experienced in giving the capital of the country a new direction. The restrictive measures and the war, though not intended for that purpose, have, by the necessary operation of things, turned a large amount of capital to this new branch of industry."

"A good patriot and true politician," says Burke, "always considers how he shall make the most of the existing materials of his country." Sir, we are forced to hear it sometimes said, in these tariff discussions, that the precepts of philosophy, the dictates of common sense, and the teachings of experience, appear to come in conflict. I do not know how that is; but this I will say, that if in all that political economy has reasoned or dogmatized or dreamed, in any one page of any one book on the subject, of high authority, or of little authority, there can be found one solitary sentence which asserts, that in the actual circumstances of this country in 1816, 1824, and 1842 — after manufacturing industry had advanced to the state in which then it existed, after so much capital was invested, and skill learned — that it was, at these periods, wise and expedient to have given to that industry less than an adequate protection, and to have suffered it to die, or asserts any principle which fairly applies to and governs such a case, then I will confess that the dictates of common sense and the revelations of experience are a far better guide than such madness and foolishness of science. I have heard no such proposition read, now or formerly.

In this attempt, Mr. President, to show that the statesmen of 1816 and 1824, the framers of the "second system," acted not under the influence of "millionary capitalists," not in the spirit of "ambitious politicians," for "sectional enrichment and political advancement," but upon grounds and considerations worthy of them, and which should even recommend the system itself, I must not forget one influence which I doubt not had its effect. Sir, between the year 1807 and the year 1816, the national character, or at least the national spirit, tone, temper, underwent a great change. A more intense nationality was developed. Everybody felt taller, stronger, more wholly American, prouder of America than he did in 1807. Everybody felt that we had passed through one epoch and stage of our history, and were come to another. We felt that we were emerging from the class of small States, to the class of large States. We had just gone through a war with honor; we had contended not ingloriously with the first power in the world; we had recovered our long lost self-respect. The long wrongs of England for a quarter of a century had been avenged. Our flag floated again, all unstained as on the day when freedom

> "Tore the azure robe of night,
> And set the stars of glory there."

Yes, Sir, everybody felt that that age — never to be remembered without a tear for America — the age of gunboats and torpedoes; of proclamations and philanthropy, falsely so called; when we were knocked down one day by a Berlin or Milan decree, and the next by an order in council; when we retired from all the seas, and hid ourselves under embargoes and acts of non-intercourse — everybody felt that that age was gone forever. The baptism of blood and fire was on our brow, and its influence was on our spirit and our legislation. Sir, I believe it was under the influence of this change of national feeling that the public men of 1816, scarcely conscious of it, perhaps, turned with the instinct of a true and happy civil discretion to a policy which was appropriate to the altered temper, the prouder spirit, the more national sentiments, the new age of their country. They turned to find in her various climate, diversified soil, exhaustless mines, ample water-power, in her frugality and industry, the materials of that self-derived and durable greatness to which they now felt that she was destined. They turned to make her independent in reality as in name. Foul shame they deemed it, that the American soldier at least should not sleep under an American blanket; that the very halyards by which we send up the stars and stripes in the hour of naval battle should be made in a Russian ropewalk; that an American frigate should ride at anchor by a British chain cable!

These, Mr. President, I believe, I hope, these, and such as these, and not the influence of avarice or of personal ambition, were among the sentiments and convictions which produced and which justify our legislation of 1816 and 1824. Wise statesmen, true patriots, admonished by the bitter experience of the war, kindling with the sentiments and carrying out the policy of a new era of our history, not "millionary capitalists" or "trading politicians," were its authors. I claim for it as noble an origin as for the elder system. With what degree of truth and justice I have done so, it is for you to judge.

The tariffs, then, of 1816 and 1824, were framed on the same interpretation of the Constitution, and the same doctrines of political economy, as was the tariff of 1789. You need not ascend from the later to the earlier, to find a better spirit, worthier objects, or sounder policy. The statesmen of 1824 did just what the statesmen of 1789 would have done in the same age, by the same lights, on the same facts. Why, then, I shall be asked, were the duties of 1824 so much higher than those of 1789? Sir, I pause to answer the question, because, in doing so, I make an argument, *valeat tantum*, for the duties of 1842. They were so much higher, because the duties of 1789, sufficient for revenue and protection then, were totally insufficient for either in the altered circumstances of 1824, and would be totally insufficient for either now.

Consider, in the first place, that the manufacturing and mechanical arts and industry of the country, as they existed and were to be provided for in 1816, had not *grown* up to the state in which Congress found them, under the influence of the protecting duties of 1789. They were, on the contrary, the stimulated and joint product of certain artificial and temporary causes of great energy, to wit: the commercial embarrassments which preceded the war, and the war itself. Upon this subject I think I have remarked two erroneous views: one attributes too much influence to the war, and supposes that manufacturing employments had not made much progress before the war; the other correctly appreciates their very prosperous condition as early as 1810, but ascribes it to inadequate causes, — to spontaneous growth, to the natural progress and developments of things, or to the gentle influence of the moderate protection of the legislation of 1789. Both are erroneous. That in 1810 manufacturing industry had been very far advanced is certain. It was then that Mr. Gallatin, while Secretary of the Treasury, surveyed and analyzed it, and arrived at the conclusion that its annual product exceeded one hundred and twenty millions of dollars. He says, —

"From this imperfect sketch of American manufactures it may, with certainty, be inferred that their annual product exceeds *one hundred and twenty millions of dollars.* And it is not improbable that the raw materials used, and the provisions and other articles consumed by the manufacturers, create a home market for agricultural products not very inferior to that which arises from foreign demand — a result more favorable than might have been expected from a view of the natural causes which impede the introduction and retard the progress of manufactures in the United States." — *Mr. Gallatin's report, April* 17, 1810.

But what had caused this? Certainly not the duties of 1789; certainly not those duties coöperating with the natural and spontaneous course and progression and changes of national industry. I do not know that the honorable Senator from Missouri intended to express the opinion that these were the cause of the manufacturing prosperity of 1810. But in the effort to show, what is certainly true, that the war did not produce it, he, unintentionally, doubtless, leaves the implication that it was a purely spontaneous growth under the duties of the "old system." Thus he says, "I must again advert to the date. The modern champions of manufactures say it was the war which gave birth to manufactures; and that we must have high duties now, to protect what the war created. But the work of Mr. Coxe shows this to be a grand mistake; that this great interest had taken deep and wide root before the war, and was going on well even before the year 1810." This is certainly true; but the honorable Senator omits to advert to those other causes which before the war had exerted an influence similar and almost equal to war itself. Sir, the exact historical fact is this. Down to the year 1807, the progress of American manufactures was very slow. Our capital was richly rewarded upon the sea, and upon the sea it remained. In 1807, two new and most powerfully stimulating influences supervened, by which a sudden, new, and vast impulse was communicated to these employments, and which really produced that splendid result which, in 1810, attracted the notice and justified the admiration of Mr. Gallatin. These causes were, first, the violations of our rights of neutrality by the great belligerents, England and France; and, second, our own commercial restrictions. These causes had the double operation of driving our capital from the sea, to seek other investments, and of keeping foreign fabrics out. The instantaneous effect of the two, in conjunction, was, that manufacturing industry started at once, in a hundred new or enlarged forms, to life, and grew, I will not say with a rank and unhealthy, but with a stimulated and hastened luxuriance, down to the war, and through the war. I suppose that nine tenths, perhaps more, of all that Mr. Gallatin surveyed and analyzed and admired, in 1810, had sprung up within the three years before.

The proofs of this are familiar and decisive. Look first at the dates of certain not very agreeable events. The Berlin decree was made in November, 1806; the first order in council, January, 1807; the Milan decree in November, 1807. The embargo was laid in December, 1807; it continued till March, 1809, when it was succeeded by the act of non-intercourse, which continued until the war. Here, therefore, were three years — more than three years — during which one of the causes to which I have adverted was in operation, and more than two years during which they both were so, before Mr. Gallatin made his report. Well, Sir, mark the results. In 1789 there was not a cotton spindle in the United States. In 1805 and 1806 there were only 5,000; in 1810, there were 80,000! an increase of sixteen-fold in four or five years. I gather these facts, in part, from Mr. Gallatin's report itself, and in part from an instructive report upon the subject of cotton, submitted to congress by the Senator from New Hampshire, [Mr. Woodbury,] when Secretary of the Treasury. But let me refer you to the proof a little more largely. I read first a few passages from Mr. Gallatin's report: —

"The first cotton-mill was erected in the State of Rhode Island *in the year* 1791; another in the same State in the year 1795; and two more in the State of Massachusetts in 1803 and 1804. During the three succeeding years, ten more were erected, or commenced, in Rhode Island,

and one in Connecticut — making, altogether, *fifteen* mills erected before the year 1808, working at that time about *eight thousand spindles*, and producing about three hundred thousand pounds of yarn a year.

"Returns have been received of *eighty-seven* mills which were erected at the end of the year 1809, sixty-two of which (forty-eight water and fourteen horse mills) were in operation, and worked at that time thirty-one thousand spindles. The other twenty-five will all be in operation in the course of this year, and, together with the former ones, (almost all of which are increasing their machinery,) will, by the estimate received, work more than *eighty thousand* spindles at the commencement of the year 1811.

"The increase of carding and spinning of cotton by machinery in establishments for that purpose, and exclusively of that done in private families, has, therefore been *fourfold*, during the last two years, and will have been *tenfold* in *three years*.

"But by far the greater part of the goods made of those materials (cotton, flax, and wool) are manufactured in private families, mostly for their own use, and partly for sale. They consist principally of coarse cloth, flannel, cotton stuffs and stripes of every description, linen and mixtures of wool with flax or cotton. The information received from every State, and from more than sixty different places, concurs in establishing the fact of *an extraordinary increase during* THE LAST TWO YEARS, and rendering it probable that about two thirds of the clothing, including hosiery, and of the house and table linen worn and used by the inhabitants of the United States who do not reside in cities, is the product of family manufactures.

"The *demand of last year* was *double of that* of 1808, and is still rapidly increasing.

"The annual importations of foreign hemp amounted to 6,200 tons. *But the interruption of commerce has greatly promoted the cultivation of that article* in Massachusetts, New York, Kentucky, and several other places; and it is believed that a sufficient quantity will, in a short time, be produced in the United States. *The injurious violations of the neutral commerce of the United States, by forcing industry and capital into other channels, have broken inveterate habits, and given a general impulse*, to which *must be ascribed the great increase of manufactures during the last two years.*"

So far Mr. Gallatin.

But listen to the not less weighty evidence of Mr. Jefferson, in his message of 1808: —

"*The suspension of foreign commerce produced by the injustice of the belligerent Powers, and the consequent losses and sacrifices of our citizens, are subjects of just concern. The situation into which we have thus been forced has impelled us to apply a portion of our industry and capital to internal manufactures and improvements.* The extent of this conversion is daily increasing, and little doubt remains that the establishments formed and forming will, under the auspices of cheaper materials and subsistence, the freedom of labor from taxation with us, and of *protecting duties* and *prohibitions*, become *permanent*."

And of Mr. Madison, in his message of 1810: —

"I feel particular satisfaction in remarking that an interior view of our country presents us with grateful proofs of its substantial and increasing prosperity. To a thriving agriculture, and the improvements relating to it, is added a highly interesting extension of useful manufactures, the combined product of professional occupations and of household industry. Such, indeed, is the experience of economy, as well as of policy, in these substitutes for supplies heretofore obtained by foreign commerce, that in a *national* view the change is justly regarded as, of itself, more than a *recompense for those privations and losses resulting from foreign injustice, which furnished the general impulse required for its accomplishment.* How far it may be expedient to guard the infancy of this improvement in the distribution of labor, *by regulations of the commercial tariff*, is a subject which cannot fail to suggest itself to your patriotic reflections."

And in his message of 1811: —

"Although other subjects will press more immediately on your deliberations, a portion of them cannot but be well bestowed on the *just and sound* policy of *securing* to our manufactures the success they have attained, and are still attaining, *under the impulses of causes not permanent, and to our navigation* the fair extent of which is at present abridged by the unequal regulations of foreign governments. Besides the reasonableness of saving our manufactures from sacrifices which a change of circumstances might bring upon them, the national interest requires that, with respect to such articles, at least, as belong to our defence and primary wants, we should not be left in a state of unnecessary dependence on external supplies."

Let me call your attention to a selection from the report of Mr. Dallas, when Secretary of the Treasury, in 1816: —

"It was emphatically during the period of the restrictive system and the war that the importance of domestic manufactures became conspicuous to the nation, and made a lasting impression on the mind of every statesman and every patriot. From 1783 to 1808, the march of domestic manufactures was slow but steady. It has since been bold, rapid, and firm."

Mr. Newton, of Virginia, chairman of the committee on commerce and manufactures, in a liberal and able report, in February, 1816, expressed the same opinion: —

"Prior to 1806 and 1807, establishments for manufactures of cotton had not been attempted, but in a few instances, and on a limited scale. Their rise and progress are attributable to embarrassments to which commerce was subjected."

The impulse thus given was continued and increased by the war; and thus the manufactures of 1816 were, as I have said, the joint and stimulated product of that event, of the interruptions of commerce which for five years preceded it, and of what I may call the national progress and changes of national industry.

Now, Sir, for the protection of manufactures thus called into existence, and which, instead of the plain, hardy, coarse, and household employments of 1789, had grown a refined, complicated, and sensitive industry, the duties of 1789 had become totally inadequate in 1816. It cannot be too often repeated nor too literally understood, that then a new age had opened on the world. With the battle of Waterloo one era ended, and another begun. The thunders of that day of doom —what were they but the great bell of time sounding out another hour? Then arose a new age on the exhausted nations; an age to which "no monarch shall affix his name; the age of industry; the age of comforts to the poor; the age of the people." Immediately they all turned to the development and culture of their own resources; to the contests of peace, more glorious than the contests of war. England, in a preeminent sense and degree, went back, with all her energies, all her capital, and all her numbers, from the Tagus, the Rhine, the Neva, to contend in Birmingham and Manchester and Liverpool for the markets of the United States. On that field, Sir, we were then no match for her. On others, we had won some laurels; there we were not yet her match. It became indispensable that the government should throw its protecting arm around the labor of the country; should guard it against the fierce, new, and hot competition which assailed it; should shelter it from the torrent heat and the sudden blasts of the new world in which it found itself. The duties of 1789 would have been as unavailing as bow and arrow against the bayonet and flying artillery of modern war. Sir, one most striking and decisive proof of this is at hand. The tariff of 1816 was meant to be a protecting tariff. As such, it was assailed and defended. Some things it did protect. Some effects it did produce. It put an end to the importation of cotton fabrics made in the East Indies of East Indian cotton; and to that extent it extended the market of the cotton of America. I have no doubt that, taking it all together, it was a better tariff than this bill of the Senator from South Carolina; better than such a bill as the principles indicated by the Senator from Missouri would construct. But what were its effects? Manufactures were prostrated. From an annual product of two hundred millions in 1816, they had fallen in 1820 to an annual product of thirty-six millions only. This it was which stimulated that great effort in 1820 for a more adequate system. In this, as in 1789, Pennsylvania took the lead. She was powerfully seconded by the eloquence and zeal of Mr. Clay; a better law passed the house, but failed by one vote in this body. We lived along, languishing, until 1824, when government at length recognized the existence and the demands of the new age of the world. We came fairly into line, and entered on that contest of industrial glory with the nations, where the prizes are unstained by tears or blood; where the victory is without guilt, and the triumph without abatement.

I have spoken, Mr. President, of a new age. I hold here a curious and striking proof and product of such an age. It is a pamphlet called "Foreign Tariffs; their injurious effects on British manufactures, especially the woollen manufacture;" and it is a collection of the protecting regulations of different governments, adopted since 1815, with "proposed remedies." It is compiled by Mr. Bischoff, a British manufacturer, no doubt; but who at all events "most potently and powerfully believes" that the world was created solely for the sake of consuming British manufactures. You could get no other idea into his head. If he could see the nations, one and all, coming back to British cottons, woollens, iron, and glass, and all else which makes up the circle of her arts, he would die happy. Read the motto on his title-page. "Encourage those trades most that vend most of *our* manufactures." He takes it from Sir Josiah Childs's discourses on trade; but it embodies the whole sum and substance of the political economy of England. What effect the consummation which he so devoutly wishes might have on the comforts, the population, the wealth, the aggrandizement of the consuming and non-manufacturing nations, he very naturally and very properly leaves them to consider. That is their business. It is his "to vend the manufactures of England." Well, it is quite plain that he feels that his country is a little wronged by the way the world is going. Hear how pathetically he ejaculates: —

"The ink with which the treaties of Vienna were signed was scarce dry, ere Russia, to which an immense trade used to be carried on in woollens, *prohibited the importation of all coarse* cloth by enormous duties, excepting, indeed, what was ordered by her own government for the clothing of the troops. The King of Sardinia, who had his Italian dominions restored to him by British valor, and Genoa with its rich territories and fine seaport added to his kingdom, not only deprived us of the great privileges we formerly enjoyed, but imposed almost prohibitory duties on the importation of British manufactures, not only into his own dominions, but into those territories which were added to his kingdom. The Emperor of Austria prohibited the introduction of our woollens and cottons into his empire, including also his newly acquired Italian States, Lombardy, the Milanese, Venice, &c., which formerly took large quantities of our goods. And other governments acted in a similar manner.

"Such was the policy, *and such has continued to be the policy of the continental powers*, without apparently a single objection, remonstrance, or protest, from England, or any effort made to *preserve our manufactures;* and thus has our trade in the near markets of Europe been almost destroyed.

"The continental States have, moreover, by adopting the mode of imposing duties on *weight instead of, as formerly, on value*, struck an irreparable blow, unless that system be altered, at the old staple manufactures of the country — cloths, coatings, and other woollens of low qualities, which consume British wool, making a pound weight of the coarsest fabrics pay the same amount of duty as a pound of the very best superfine cloth. That system is as injurious to the wool grower as it is to the manufacturer.

"With scarce a single exception, all States have had in view what has been deemed *protection* or stimulus to their own fabrics. This has been the policy of France, Spain, Portugal, Belgium, Prussia, Denmark, Sweden, Russia, Austria, Sardinia, Naples, and even the United States of America. Whether the course so adopted be wise or not — whether the term *shackles* would not be more properly applied to the system than '*protection*' — whether it be just or not, to tax the many for the supposed advantage of the few, is not now the question: they had the example of England, which appears to have been the rule upon which they have acted."

In all Europe, Holland is perhaps the single country which has not adopted such a policy. And she, Sir, is not quite the Holland she was in the times of Charles the Second, when the thunders of her cannon "startled that effeminate tyrant in his own palace, and in the arms of his mistresses;" not what she was in 1688, when she gave a deliverer to England; not what she was when she was the carrier and banker of all the world. All but her are taking care of themselves, with the most total and provoking disregard of all the free-trade preaching by which England would persuade mankind that the methods which have made her rich and great will make all other nations poor and feeble. Turkey improves a little on all, "letting everything come freely into her dominions, but letting nothing go out;" borrowing her policy, it might seem, from her own Mediterranean, into which there ever runs an unreturning flood.

A distinguished friend not long since remarked to me, that the character and topics of the British parliamentary debates, compared with those of a half century ago, very strikingly indicated the existence of that new world which statesmen have to act in. I have thought I could remark the same thing. What could such a leader as the elder Pitt do with such a house of commons and such subjects of debate? What would the exaggerated eloquence of the great war minister find to say about "onion seed"? Sir Robert Peel speaks as well on that important article as he does on Ireland. "The glory of a great minister in the last century was, that he made this country flourish still more by war than by peace. The glory of the present era is, that things have returned to their natural course; and that peace is become, as it ever ought to be, a greater restorer of national force than war."

Yes, Sir, the times have changed. That is the wisest nation which the most adequately comprehends the degree, the permanence, the nature of the change, and first places itself at the head of the great industrial revolution. It is the praise of the statesmen of 1816 and 1824, that they understood and acted upon this truth. It was because they did, that they at once held fast by the principles and deserted the details of the legislation of 1789. If you would restore the dress and the cradle of infancy, you must bring back again its tiny limbs, and its stature of a span long. If the statesmen of the age of Washington were alive to-day, they would not revive the duties of their time, unless you could give back again from the dim dominion of the past the world of their time.

Another consideration urged by the honorable Senator from Missouri, for returning to the good old legislation, for abandoning protective duties, and substituting duties which I think are not protective, was this, — that certain statistical tables which he produced reveal some very unfavorable practical results of the present system, as contrasted with the results of the former system. And I agree at once, that if the clear and unequivocal teachings of a sufficient experience pronounce against the existing policy, it is to be abandoned. But do these tables make out such a case?

I find, Sir, that I shall not have occasion to detain you upon them as long as I at first designed to do, because I think that one general observation applies to and disposes of the matter. If the premises are true, the conclusions do not appear to follow. If the tables are true, and the whole truth, they prove nothing against the policy of protection. If every figure in every column is right, still the great question of the effect of that policy on agriculture, commerce, and revenue, which has been so instructively debated, is left just where it was before. No new argument is afforded against the views which the Senators from Maine, Connecticut, Vermont, Rhode Island, Georgia, and my colleague, have taken; and no additional force or illustration is given to the views of the Senators from South Carolina and New Hampshire. The tables either do not show what the working of the existing system has been, or they show nothing which has not been asserted and conceded before.

Suppose, for example, in the first place, that the tables indicate that the receipts from customs were more regular before 1808 than since 1816; that they went on advancing with a more regular progression, with less of fluctuation from large in one year to small in the next, and the reverse; how can you possibly refer this to the low duties of one period, or the high duties of the other? I can very well understand that sudden and great changes from one rate to another, too many of which have disfigured and disturbed the latter period, will cause fluctuations in all things, in imports, exports, business, hopes, fears, plans, everything. It is for that very reason that I deprecate the proposed great change. But that a fixed, settled policy of high duties, known, promulgated to the world, promulgated to the foreign manufacturer and shipper, such a system as that of England, for instance, should cause more fluctuations in the receipts from customs, than a policy of low duties no better known and no more firmly fixed — this I have not organs to comprehend. Sir, you must show some connection between high duties as such and the fluctuations you complain of. You must not say *post hoc ergo propter hoc.* This would be to attribute the rise of cotton to icebergs or meteors, if I may employ an illustration of the Senator from South Carolina. I think it is Addison's country gentleman who insisted upon it there had been no good weather in England since the revolution of 1688. I cannot speak for the weather; but, good or bad, nobody but the Tory fox-hunter himself threw the blame on the going out of the Stuarts. Sir, no doubt there are far more causes of irregularity in our imports and in our receipts from customs, wholly disconnected with the absence or presence of a protective policy, now, than when we were poorer, fewer, traded less, and had a market for which foreign producers less desperately contended. If you go back to good old colonial times, to 1650 and 1670, I dare say you might find still less irregularity in these particulars. Probably, too, the Indians of the North-west have received their annual supplies of gunpowder, blankets, and the like, from the British colonial government, with a regularity still more severely and beautifully guarded. A thousand causes of this kind of fluctuations there must be, with which the rates of duties have no more to do than the icebergs with the price of cotton, or the revolution with the bad weather. In a country whose numbers have been growing from ten millions to seventeen millions; with a commerce extending as far as winds blow and waters roll; a commerce which trades in everything, with everybody; a country partly supplying its home market, and partly carrying its own productions in its own ships, and yet contending for that market and that navigation with numerous and greedy foreign competitors; passing through more than one great convulsion which has shaken the whole world of trade; agitated by the currents and winds of its own seasons of local speculation; its currency sometimes disordered; its policy too often changing; all things, business, values, wages, the solemn temples of its Constitutions themselves rising and falling on the waters of opinion which know no rest — in such a country I shall neither be surprised nor scared to see, under whatever rates of duty, a great deal of irregularity in imports and in revenue from imports. Whether it be an evil or not, and to whatever extent it be one, I see no connection between it and a known, settled, promulgated, well and widely understood policy of protection.

Perhaps I might not entirely concur with the distinguished Senator from Missouri, in his estimate of the magnitude of the evil. An evil, it no doubt is. Sometimes, in some circumstances, irregularity would be an intolerable one. In the case he puts, of a balloon in the air, now "bursting with distention, now collapsing from depletion," it would be greatly inconvenient. But all greatness is irregular. All irregularity is not defect, is not ruin. Take a different illustration from that of the balloon. Take the New England climate in summer — you would think the world was coming to an end. Certain recent heresies on that subject may have had a natural origin there. Cold to-day, hot to-morrow; mercury at 80° in the morning, with wind at south-west; and in three hours more, a sea turn, wind at east, a thick fog from the very bottom of the ocean, and a fall of 40 degrees of Fahrenheit; now so dry as to kill all the beans in New Hampshire, then floods carrying off the bridges and dams of the Penobscot and Connecticut; snow in Portsmouth in July, and the next day a man and a yoke of oxen killed by lightning in Rhode Island—you would think the world was twenty times coming to an end! But I don't know how it is; we go along; the early and the latter rain falls each in his season; seed-time and harvest do not fail; the sixty days of hot corn weather are pretty sure to be measured out to us; the Indian summer, with its bland south-west and mitigated sunshine brings all up; and on the twenty-fifth of November, or thereabouts, being Thursday, three millions of grateful people, in meeting-houses, or around the family board, give thanks for a year of health, plenty, and happiness. All irregularity, whatever the cause, is not defect, nor ruin.

Suppose, in the next place, that these tables show a diminished consumption of foreign imports, since 1816, in proportion to our numbers, compared with the consumption before 1807? The protective policy is not the cause. This is my first answer. And the evil is over-balanced by the good.

This is my next answer. You may consume less of foreign fabrics, in proportion to your numbers, than before 1808, for the reason that the decline of agricultural prices, the diminished agricultural exportation, the loss of the profits and freights of the golden age of commerce and navigation, may really have made you less able than before to exchange your labor for foreign labor. Is the policy of protection to blame for this? Is it not, on the other hand, its office, its aim, to counteract this very evil which it does not produce, by enabling you to exchange that labor for domestic fabrics, which you cannot pass for foreign fabrics? You may consume less of some imported fabrics than before, for the reason, that while your general ability is greater, your demand is supplied by the domestic manufacturer. And is there anything very dreadful in this? Suppose that, by this means, that useful foreign commerce which binds the nations together may not grow quite in proportion to our increasing numbers; or rather, that its outward and homeward cargoes somewhat change their nature; still enough of it is left, enough for philanthropy, for civilization, for national wealth, for diversified social employment, while that far more useful domestic commerce which binds together associated States, and kindred hearts and tribes, has expanded till it carries a value of a thousand millions of dollars in a year.

Suppose, finally, the honorable Senator's tables announce a diminished export of agricultural productions since the year 1816, — diminished since the time when Europe forgot agriculture, to pursue war, — how is the tariff of protection responsible for this? Does anybody believe that we should sell one pound or one peck the more, if we imported from England the very shoes which we put upon our horses' feet? No, Sir; you sell all which the necessities of foreigners oblige them to buy at remunerating prices; so you would, tariff or no tariff; and you would do no more. Sir, to hold our protective legislation responsible for this falling off of these exports, is to hold it responsible for the very evils whose existence compelled you to resort to it, in order to break their force; evils which, but for this, you could not bear at all. You lay the fault, not on the ferocious assailant, but on the defensive armor, and the manly resistance, without which the attack would have been fatal.

Yes, Sir, it is far nearer the truth to say this: that it was because foreign tariffs, discriminating for colonial agriculture and against yours; the increased agricultural production of Europe; the great bulk of that class of commodities compared with the value — it was because these and other causes had deprived your farmers of their foreign market, that your statesmen turned to find them one at home, and have already to an encouraging extent succeeded; it was because the wings of our ancient golden foreign commerce had been clipped, that they turned to find a substitute in domestic commerce; it was because the old world had unexpectedly developed new and extraordinary resources and powers and productiveness, that they sought, in another sense than Mr. Canning used the lofty boast, "to restore the balance," by bringing a new world into existence *in the new world*. This is far nearer the truth than to describe the protective policy as the author of the evils which it seeks to mitigate.

I have done, then, Sir, with the argument drawn from the tables. As I said, I do not think they affect at all the great question which we have had so long and ably discussed, of the operation of protective duties on commerce, agriculture, and revenue. They leave that where they find it. I do not mean to repeat a word of that discussion. Neither these tables, nor any quantity of tables, nor any amount of reasoning, nor any public opinion of one region, or of all regions of the country, nor all the polemical political economy of manufacturing England, will bring me to doubt that I do good service to agriculture by lessening the numbers that pursue it, and giving them a nearer and better market; that even the foreign trade of a nation, which manufactures as well as tills the earth, will be richer, wider, steadier, better prepared to spread its sails to every breeze, than the foreign trade of a nation which only tills the earth; and, finally, that domestic commerce among such States as ours is better than an exclusive foreign commerce. These truths, at last, are above all cavil. I will not confess that they require vindication, by attempting to vindicate them.

It has been urged, Sir, as another consideration to induce or to reconcile us to a return to the old system, that manufacturing and mechanical industry is in a highly prosperous general condition. Its products are said to be vast. Its profits are said to be great.

I admit, undoubtedly, that an immense amount of capital is invested in it. I admit that it employs and feeds millions — men, women, and children — of our own household. I admit that it has spread over the whole country; that it is inseparably intertwined with the labor and the prosperity of the whole; that it benefits all; that it harms none. I admit that, with the general business of the nation, it is just now prosperous.

But what then? Does the Senator from Missouri say, that because these employments are so numerous, so widespread, so interwoven with all the nerves of business, and so flourishing, that therefore he would destroy or lessen or impoverish them? The direct reverse. He desires to see them prosper. He is willing to leave them more protection than they need. So I understood his speech; and so I understood him to say in reply to my friend from Rhode Island, [Mr. Simmons,] whom he supposed to have suspected him of unfriendliness to protection. I mean to treat, then, this argument from the prosperous condition of this industry, as the argument of a friend of adequate protection, who will maintain the existing degree and mode of protection, if it is necessary; who would, however, be desirous to reduce that degree, and depart from that mode, if manufacturing employments can bear the reduction and the change, and who infers from their present prosperity that they can bear it.

To him, then, Sir, who, being a friend of sufficient protection, and of a diffused, multiform, advanced manufacturing and mechanical industry, tells us, that a reduction of one half or one third of the existing protection will leave enough, I answer by asking, how do you know this? How do you make me, how do you make the senate, know it? How do you prove it? Where is your evidence? I respect your opinions highly. But I must see the grounds of this opinion.

The burden is on you. The presumption in the first instance is, that the existing rates of duty cause, and are necessary to, the existing prosperity. *Prima fronte* it is so. Here is the apparent cause. There is the apparent effect. Here is the law of 1842. Side by side, contemporaneous, coexistent, is the acknowledged prosperity. Here are the fruits: figs and grapes; they *seem* to grow, not on that thorn, or that thistle, but on the kindred tree and vine.

Well, this presumption is heightened by looking back a little. Duties ran down, in 1841, into the neighborhood of those which you say will give ample protection now. Manufacturing labor ran down too, and *pari passu.* You raised the duties, by the present law, to their present height. These employments sprung up, too, with an instantaneous and marvellous sympathy. The revival followed so close upon the passage of the law of 1842, it followed so naturally, it was so exactly what was predicted, so exactly what was expected, it was so entirely conformable to all our experience and to all analogy, that we can hardly in the first instance resist the conviction that the law was cause, the revival effect.

Then, I repeat it, the burden is heavy on you, who say that half or any other proportion of the duties of 1842 will give adequate protection, to prove it. This law of 1842 is no *new* law; it has no new, inflamed, untried rates of protection in it. It is for substance the law of 1828 — the law of 1824. It has been twenty years in maturing. It has been constructed with great care; with much labor and much thought; by the aid of much investigation and much evidence. The system which it embodies has been long and thoroughly tried. You have tried it as in 1825, 1829, 1843, by keeping it in force; and you have tried it as in 1820 and 1841, by suffering it to fall. If now you say it is a great blunder, and that it lays duties in any proportion larger than its own objects require, you must prove it.

Well, what are the proofs? Have you any evidence of experienced persons, collected by a committee? Have any witnesses been examined, any opinions taken, any parliamentary inquisition holden? Nothing at all of the sort.

You say, manufactures flourished on the low duties of 1789 and 1807. Why, we might as well be told that antediluvians lived a thousand years. Where is the period from 1789 to 1807? With the days beyond the flood. Why reason from the experience of a world, which neither you nor I shall ever see again? Why not consult the experience of the actual world for which you legislate? You tried low duties in 1816, since the present age began, and you failed. You tried them in 1841, and you failed again. Is not this experience, decisive and stern, to dispel the delusive dreams, whispered by the irrevocable and inapplicable past? To go back to the protection of 1789, for the prosperity of 1789, is to go back in old age to the place of our birth, to seek for the singing-birds of childhood which now sing no more.

You say some branches of manufactures are earning enormous profits. Well, what then? What does the bill of the Senator from South Carolina thereupon propose? What do the principles of the Senator from Missouri provide for such a case? Do you institute an investigation into the appalling phenomenon, to ascertain whether the fact is so; how long it has been so; what are the temporary and accidental causes; whether the laws of business hydrostatics are not already bringing such profits down to the general level of all employments? Not at all. Do you proceed to reduce the duties on these unreasonably prosperous branches? No such thing. You seize the scythe, and just swing it at large over the whole field of labor, prosperous or unprosperous. Worse than Procrustes, who only pared down the too tall one, you, because one man is longer than the standard, cut the whole regiment in two in the middle. Cottons thrive, say the free-trade newspapers,—and down go the duties on hats! Fustians are lively, — and off comes the shoemaker's protection! Great stories are credibly and anonymously told of large salaries at Lowell; dividends which they are afraid to divide; and calico printing which is making all their fortunes; whereupon, in our zeal, we propose to take off about one third, more or less, of the duties on ready-made clothing! I do not understand the logic of the operation. Here is a building, some seven or ten stories high, with a thousand tenants. You propose to put your hands on the top of it, and press it down, bodily, into the ground about one half way. I humbly suggest the question, whether it is altogether safe for the persons in it? Perfectly so, say you, perfectly so; why do these people want to live seven, eight, ten stories in the air? Well, for them it may be safe, but what becomes of those who inhabit the basement and the ground rooms? They will be stifled to death!

Sir, let me respectfully recommend cautious and delicate handling of these interests. Vast, various, prosperous, as they are, a breath can unmake them, as a breath has made. This bill strikes a blow, the extent, degree, and nature of whose injurious effect no man can foresee or limit or cure. That which you certainly mean to do, involves consequences which you certainly do not mean. You begin by saying profits are too high. Then you propose to reduce profits. You begin by saying more foreign manufactures must be imported, because you propose to increase revenue by reducing duties. This demands, of course, enlarged importations. To that extent, to a new and undefined extent, you displace, disturb, diminish the domestic market of your own manufacturers. But can you really strike down the general profits and break up the actual market of American labor, and yet leave it prosperous, rewarded, and contented?

I intended, Sir, to have said something on the fallacy of the argument, that when manufactures are so firmly established as to have reduced prices, and made them reasonable, stable, and proportional to other prices, that then you may abolish protecting duties. But this topic has been so well handled by others, and particularly by my colleague, and I have already detained you so long, that I forbear. Let me read a single passage from the same speech of Mr. Calhoun, to which I have referred so much: —

"But it will no doubt be said, if they are so far established, and if the situation of the country is so favorable to their growth, where is the necessity of affording them protection? It is to put them beyond the reach of contingency."

I may say, however, in a more general way, that, in the universal judgment of the world, stability, steadiness, the lapse of considerable periods of time, years, years of adequate protection, are required to build up manufacturing and mechanical arts to a consummated and durable prosperity. The policy of caprice will not do it; the policy of high duties to-day and low ones to-morrow; of inflation and collapse, jumping back fifty years, to rock grown men in the cradles of infants — this never will do it. Let me call to your notice a few extracts from the "Monthly Review," London, March, 1844, which convey, I think, a certain and important truth: —

"It is to be hoped free trade sophistry will not go so far as to exclaim: England having once brought her manufactures — no matter by what means — to the utmost degree of perfection, free trade can only prove her advantage, since foreign competition in her market is out of question in most articles, while her own will be brought to foreign markets free of duty.

"They (the continental statesmen) well know that, as soon as the system of free trade is adopted, all idea must be abandoned of ever establishing manufactories in the present agricultural countries, even for home consumption alone; since it lies in the nature of a manufacturing country to have at command a mass of knowledge, expertness, practice, implements, and machinery, wholesome public institutions and regulations, vast connections and wealth, in all of which agricultural countries are deficient, as they can only be acquired slowly and gradually, *through an uninterrupted series of ages*, and the possession of which is manifest in the comparative *cheapness of the manufactures.* It is the principle of stability, continuation, and perseverance, that constitutes the basis of all the great works and institutions realized by the hands of men.

"The history of dynasties, nations, countries, and towns, as well as of the arts and sciences, corroborate the power of that principle. The latter (arts and sciences) have arrived at their present state of development, as the former did at power, riches, and authority, only through the exertions of a series of generations, striving and working to one and the same end, the succeeding generation always taking up the thread where the preceding had left off. By this principle alone was it possible to erect monuments, the stupendousness of which we now admire, even in their decay. To bring their principle more home, inquire of every master mechanic or manufacturer, and he will tell you to how many difficulties and expenses the outset of a contrivance is subject, and how comparatively easy and profitable the more advanced progress is. In looking more attentively into the history of the useful arts, and the various departments of industry, which are now brought to so flourishing a condition, we find that one branch has sprung out of the other, and that the success of one depended on that of the others; in short, that they all mutually influence each other, and that the elements hostile to the principle of stability and continuation — such as civil disturbances, critical periods in trade, and *fluctuations in prices* — have destroyed in a very short time the labor of ages."

Germany is attempting, as we are, to develop her industrial capacities, and is annoyed, as we are, by the selfish and senseless prattle of free trade. I like the good sense and the firmness with which a writer in the "Augsburg Journal" remarks on the honeyed and gilded plausibilities of Dr. Bowring: —

"Dr. Bowring deceives himself very much, if it be his belief that Germany desires no better fortune than to be allowed exportation of her corn and wood to England, receiving in return English manufactures. Some few landholders on the Lower Elbe, and some few possessors of forests on the Baltic, may cherish the same hopes, and have expressed the same wishes, as the Doctor.

"*Manufactures are plants of slow growth; and in a few years is easily destroyed that which took ages to build. Now or never is the time to found durably German industrial independence and the greatness of Germany.* To this end, it is before all things necessary that the Germans themselves should feel full confidence *in the solidity of German industry.*

"The more Germany advances on the path of industry which she has adopted, the more decidedly appears the necessity of *a determined and changeless duty* system, having for its aim *the regular advancement of German industry.*"

Let me say, Mr. President, that it would seem to me no matter of rejoicing or pride to see the absolutism of the European continent attracting and retaining about its steadfast thrones these useful and manly arts, denied to us, yet so much more appropriately and more naturally forming the ornament, strength, and enrichment of popular liberty. Other arts I could give those governments up. I could resign, without a sigh, all the beauty and all the grace that live on canvas. They may have the breathing and speaking marble, for me. I could give them up all the poetry and all the music that ever consoled a nation for the loss of freedom. But I cannot so far divest myself of the prejudices, if they are such, instilled by the study of the history of the Constitution and of its earlier administration; I cannot so far forget the counsels of so many presidents and great men, the living and the dead; I cannot so far overlook the mighty causes of the wealth and power of nations, as not to feel a profound anxiety that these nobler and manlier arts, these arts which, as Washington thought, guard our independence, insure our security, and clothe and feed our masses; these arts, whose only regulator, whose only patron, whose only reward, is the wants of the people — that these arts should be all our own. Whether they shall be or not, depends on the stability and energy of our policy. It depends on you. It depends on the deliberations of this day.

You see, then, Mr. President, that I concur with the distinguished Senator from Missouri in the importance of stability and of harmony,—harmony in the country; stability in the law. They are worth something. They are worth a great deal. But, Sir, without an adequate protection to these forms of labor, you can have no harmony and no stability; and they would not be worth having, if you could. Our seasons of inadequate protection have not been seasons of harmony, because they have not been seasons of prosperity. Such was the period from 1783 to 1789. Such that from 1816 to 1824. Bad legislation; bad systems; systems inadequate to the demands, the hopes, the glory, of a free, busy, and aspiring people, will not be stable. They ought not to be. They will not be so till the pulses of liberty are dead, and the cold, bitter, unfruitful, and calm sea of despotism shall cover us over. Stable protecting legislation, not an unprotecting stability, and not a fluctuating protection, is the one grand desideratum for American harmony and prosperity.

I have done, Sir, with the discussion of the general subject, and will soon resume my seat. The honorable Senator from Missouri thinks that the present is an unpropitious moment for the adjustment of the tariff; referring, as I understand him, to the approaching presidential election. The Senator from Georgia [Mr. Berrien] concurs in this opinion. I go further, Sir, than either, and for reasons somewhat different. I should be quite willing, for my part, if for the six months preceding such an election, such a subject as this should be *tabooed* ground. It should be interdicted. The time should be *dies non juridicus* — the time of stump speaking, if you please, not of congressional legislation. I distrust my own ability to come with the requisite care and calmness to such a deliberation. I distrust myself; almost I distrust you. We are within a few months of an election which is to determine who is to wield the vast executive powers of this government for the next four years; who are to administer the executive departments; who to represent you at all the courts of the world, who to fill all the national offices; what will, what spirit, what dispositions, are to preside in the administration, for all good or evil which administration can accomplish. We are surrounded by many millions of people, whose hearts are throbbing, as the heart of one man, with anxiety for the result. Among these all, are we sure that we are quite cool ourselves? Are we sure that we are quite in a condition to adjust this vast system, to settle these infinite and delicate details? Is there no danger that disturbing elements may enter into the deliberation? Is there no danger that we shall be thinking how this rate of duty or how that may *affect votes*, instead of inquiring exclusively how it will affect labor, prices, revenue? Do you think the master of a steamboat is quite so good a judge how much his boilers will bear while he is running a race with a new rival on a ten thousand dollar wager?

I declare, Sir, that it has more than once crossed my mind, barely crossed it, that this circumstance of our legislating under the pernicious heat of this dog-star may help to explain the extraordinary attention that has been paid to Massachusetts in the debate. It is her profits for which newspapers have been ransacked. It is her advocacy of the tariff to which senators have supposed themselves replying. If a sneer could be insinuated against her opinions about the last war, or, better still, about abolition, it seems to have passed for some sort of argument against a protecting policy. The silence which has been observed towards Pennsylvania has been quite as remarkable as the eloquence which has been expended on Massachusetts. I deceive myself, if there has been the slightest allusion to her, or her iron duties, in the whole winter's debate. I perceive that, in the report of the committee of ways and means of the house, very affectionate and patriotic things are even said about iron. Now, Sir, when you consider that Massachusetts never made a protecting tariff; that she took no leading or influencive part in 1816; that she opposed that of 1824 with almost her entire vote, and with great zeal and ability; that she voted against that of 1828; that she has done nothing but just to stay where you placed her; that Pennsylvania, on the other hand, has been the founder, the steadfast support and stay of the whole system; that she made the protecting parts of the act of 1789; that in 1816, 1820, 1824, 1828, always, always her numerous vote, and her powerful and cultivated talents, have been prominent and controlling in maintaining and giving energy and completeness to the policy; and when you consider, too, what are the interests which it protects for her — considering all this, is it strange that the question has passed through my mind, whether the extraordinary notice of Massachusetts, and the extraordinary reserve towards Pennsylvania, may not possibly be attributable to her having a large electoral vote which is thought to be somewhat doubtful; while ours is a small one, *not at all* doubtful? Whatever the cause, the fact is certain. I amused myself the other evening with imagining what sort of history of the tariff a writer two thousand years hence might make up, from materials derived exclusively from one side of this debate. The Senator from New Hampshire once wrote a very good discourse on the uncertainties of history; he will not wonder, therefore, to find this sketch pretty full of blunders. It might run nearly thus: "In the year 1824, the State of Massachusetts somewhat abruptly ejaculated, Go to, now! let us make a protecting tariff. And thereupon that State, having, as it would appear, by some means not clearly explained, acquired a large majority of votes in both houses of congress, did actually proceed to force such a thing down the throats of the other astounded and reluctant States. What renders this the more remarkable is, that the Constitution evidently contemplated no such thing, that celebrated compact having been a mere great free-trade league, entered into mainly with a view to promoting the culture of a certain beautiful vegetable wool, called cotton. However, she made a tariff. And thenceforward the domestic history of the States seems to have consisted very much of a series of the most desperate and most chivalrous struggles, on the part of all the others, to get rid of a system which at once debauched their understandings and picked their pockets. In this contest, though all did well, South Carolina and New Hampshire particularly distinguished themselves; one being the great cotton-growing, and the other the great navigating State of the Union. Well might they take the lead; they were most ably represented, (there the historian is right;) and it appears to have been an indisputable and melancholy fact, that the tariff had killed all the cotton in the fields of South Carolina, and had rotted down the ten thousand masts of the merchant navy of New Hampshire, piecemeal, — so that in 1842 the whole number of human beings who sailed from her ports, in her vessels, were only fifty-six men and three boys!" Here the manuscript terminates; and it is about as true as the first five books of Livy, nine tenths of Plutarch, and a considerable part of Hume's history of the Puritans and the Stuarts!

Certainly, Sir, we are very much in these employments. You may thank yourselves for that. And is it not an excellent thing for you that we are? Are we not a very much more useful member of the partnership, more useful to the other partners, than we could be without? Is it not a good, honest, genial, social, "live and let live" sort of business you have driven us into? Suppose, Sir, you could drive us out of it again, as you may; suppose you should send us back to ice and granite, to sawing boards, raising beans and corn, drying nets and making fish on the rocks of our iron-bound and stern coast, or to roaming the ocean for freights, in competition with the black-bread sailors of Bremen and Hamburg; suppose that thus you could drive three quarters of our people away, to return no more, — what good would it do you? Now, if we had a Chinese wall around Massachusetts; if our work was done two thousand feet under ground; if it was the digging of gold or quicksilver, to be sent abroad in our vessels or foreign vessels; if all that you saw of us was when, once a year, we came here with the soot of the furnace on our faces, to beg for bounties and prohibitory duties, — why, that would be one thing. But is it nothing that we take and consume within that single State an annual amount of more than forty millions of dollars of your productions; an amount out of all manner of proportion to any other State, except Rhode Island; an amount equal to about one half of the whole exports of the whole Union, exclusive of manufactures? Is it nothing that we take these productions, not only from all the great regions, East, Central, South, and West, but from every State something, — cotton, grain, rice, sugar from the South, and South-west; naval stores from North Carolina; grain and meats from the Central regions; lead and corn from Missouri; buffalo robes from the Rocky Mountains? I hold here the enumeration of these productions, in an excellent speech of Mr. Hudson, of Massachusetts, delivered at the session of 1842, in the other house, to which senators may have access. — [See Note, p. 245.] And is this nothing? Is it not a truly national business which we pursue; national in the surface it spreads over; national in the good it does; national in the affections it generates? Well said Mr. Calhoun, in 1816, —

"It produces an interest strictly American, as much so as agriculture, in which it had the decided advantage of commerce or navigation. The country will from this derive much advantage. Again: it is calculated to bind together more closely our widely spread Republic. It will greatly increase our mutual dependence and intercourse; and will, as a necessary consequence, excite an increased attention to internal improvements — a subject every way so intimately connected with the ultimate attainment of national strength and the perfection of our political institutions."

Yes, Sir, manufacturers and mechanics are Unionists by profession; Unionists by necessity; Unionists always. Learn to know your friends. The time may come you will need them!

I have been pained inexpressibly, Sir, by some things which have been insinuated, not very distinctly said, in this debate. In a discussion of the tariff, I have heard allusions to the course of Massachusetts in 1812, and to the abolition sentiments which she cherishes to-day. How am I to understand them? Does any one dare to propose, or dare to intimate, that speculative opinions on one subject are to be punished by unkind, deleterious, practical legislation on other subjects? For our opinions on the last war, or on the institution of slavery, do you propose to drive our artisans and mechanics from their livings and their homes? God forbid. Do not think of such a thing. Banish it. Disdain it. Despise it. Despise, I am sure you do, a retaliation so absurd, so mean, so unjust, so profligate. Permit me to say, that you must take the States of America as you find them. All of them have their peculiarities. All have their traits. All have their history; traditions; characters. They had them before they came into the Union. They will have them after

——" Rome in Tiber melts, and the wide arch
Of the ranged empire falls."

South Carolina has hers — Massachusetts has hers. She will continue to think, speak, print, just what she pleases, on every subject that may interest the patriot, the moralist, the Christian. But she will be true to the Constitution. She sat among the most affectionate at its cradle; she will follow, the saddest of the procession of sorrow, its hearse! She sometimes has stood for twenty years together in opposition to the general government. She cannot promise the implicit politics of some of her neighbors. I trust, however, that she will not be found in opposition to the next administration. I have heard that once her senate refused to vote thanks for a victory for which her people had shed their blood. Sir, you must take the States as you find them! You must take her as you find her! Be just to her, and she will be a blessing to you. She will sell to you at fair prices, and on liberal credits; she will buy of you when England and Canada and the West Indies and Ireland will not; she will buy your staples, and mould them into shapes of beauty and use, and send them abroad, to represent your taste and your genius in the great fairs of civilization. Something thus she may do, to set upon your brow that crown of industrial glory, to which "the laurels that a Cæsar reaps are weeds." More, Sir, more. Although she loves not war, nor any of its works; although her interests, her morals, her intelligence, are all against it; although she is with South Carolina, with all the South, on that ground; yet, Sir, at the call of honor, at the call of liberty, if I have read her annals true, she will be found standing, where once she stood, side by side with you, on the darkened and perilous ridges of battle.

Be just to her, coldly, severely, Constitutionally just, and she will be a blessing to you.

NOTE TO PAGE 215.

EXTRACT OF A NOTE ON ADAM SMITH'S WEALTH OF NATIONS, BY M'CULLOCH, VOL. I. PP. 211, 212, EDIN. EDITION, 1828.

They [manufacturing operatives] are thus driven to seek for recreation in mental excitement; and the circumstances under which they are placed afford them every possible facility for gratifying themselves in this manner. By working together in considerable numbers, they have constant opportunities of discussing every topic of interest or importance. They are thus gradually trained to habits of thinking and reflection; their intellects are sharpened by the collision of conflicting opinions; and a small contribution from each individual enables them to obtain a large supply of newspapers, and of the cheaper class of periodical publications. But whatever difference of opinion may exist respecting the *cause*, there can be no doubt of the fact, that the intelligence of the workmen employed in manufactures and commerce has increased according as their numbers have increased, and as their employments have been more and more subdivided. I do not think that there are any good grounds for supposing that they were ever less intelligent than the agriculturists; though, whatever may have been the case a century since, no one will now venture to affirm that they are inferior to them in intellectual acquirements, or that they are mere machines, without sentiment or reason.

NOTE TO PAGE 243.

EXTRACT FROM MR. HUDSON'S SPEECH.

I have taken great pains to ascertain as near as possible the amount of articles consumed in Massachusetts annually, which are the growth or product of other States in the Union. I have written to intelligent gentlemen connected with almost every branch of business in my own State, and have consulted all the statistics which have fallen into my hands; and I confess that our consumption is greater than I had supposed. Probably some of the estimates may be too high, and others I am confident are too low. As a whole, I believe them to be a fair estimate. In fixing the prices, I have endeavored to take the average for the last three or four years. I speak of these articles as *consumed* in Massachusetts. They are consumed in the sense in which such articles are capable of consumption. Cotton and wool are consumed, in the sense in which I use the term, by being converted into cloth; and the same is true of all other articles which go into our manufactures. The result I will now present for the consideration of the committee.

An Estimate of the Products of the Soil, &c., of other States consumed or manufactured annually in Massachusetts.

Cotton	185,000 bales	$7,200,000
Flour	620,000 bbls.	4,100,000
Corn and other grain	3,730,000 bush.	2,790,000
Coal	175,000 tons	1,300,000
Wood	188,600 cords	1,300,000
Wool	8,000,000 lbs.	3,200,000
Lumber of all kinds		3,690,000
Leather and hides		7,600,000
Beef, pork, hams, and lard		2,800,000
Butter and cheese		1,000,000
Horses, cattle, sheep, and swine		600,000
Potatoes		300,000
Poultry of all kinds		70,000
Pig lead		1,450,000
Furs, buffalo robes, &c.		45,000
Rags, junk, &c., for paper		965,000
Lime	82,800 casks	72,000
Pot and pearl ashes	500 tons	58,000
Tobacco	960 hhds.	68,000
Rice		325,000
Tar, pitch, and turpentine		1,200,000
Iron		800,000
Sugar and molasses		47,000
Staves, casks, boxes, &c.		360,000
Domestic spirits and beer		100,000
Feathers, hair, and bristles		185,000
Oysters, venison, sand, sweet potatoes, summer fruits, such as peaches, melons, &c.		210,000
Hay, grass-seed, flaxseed, flax, linseed oil, castor oil, beans, bees-wax, tallow, onions, and nuts		175,000
		$42,010,000

Here we have the round sum of $42,000,000 of domestic products consumed in the State of Massachusetts — a State of 737,000 inhabitants — in a single year. The importance of such a home market will appear when we consider that the average of our entire export from the United States for the last ten years, exclusive of the manufactured articles, amounts to only $82,200,000. So that the State of Massachusetts consumes annually, of the products of other States, more than half the amount of our whole foreign export, less the manufactured articles; and the articles thus consumed in my own State are the product of every State in this Union.

Maine supplies lumber, wood, lime, leather, and potatoes; New Hampshire, wool, butter, cheese, beef, and pork; Vermont, wool, iron, beef, pork, butter, cheese, and potash; Rhode Island, lime; Connecticut, iron; New York, flour, wool, leather, butter, cheese, and grain; New Jersey, grain, grass-seed, and fruit; Pennsylvania, iron, coal, wool, leather, and potash; Delaware, grain; Maryland, corn, tobacco, and leather; Virginia, corn, flour, tobacco, and coal; North Carolina, tar, pitch, and turpentine; South Carolina, Georgia, Alabama, and Mississippi, cotton and rice; Louisiana, cotton, sugar, and molasses; Arkansas, cotton, beef, and pork; Tennessee, cotton, wool, tobacco, and corn; Kentucky, tobacco, wool, flour, and whiskey; Missouri, lead and corn; Indiana, flour, corn, wool, beef, and pork; Illinois, lead, flour, corn, and pork; Michigan, flour; Ohio, flour, corn, beef, pork, wool, and potash.

This is a specimen of some of the leading articles which the different States furnish to the Massachusetts market. Besides these, there are other articles, which are produced by the whole valley of the Mississippi, such as hides, fur, beans, castor oil, flax-seed, &c.

SPEECH ON THE BILL FOR THE ESTABLISHMENT OF THE SMITHSONIAN INSTITUTION.

DELIVERED IN THE SENATE OF THE UNITED STATES, JANUARY 8, 1845.

I AM sure that, whatever opinion may be at last formed on this bill, its principles, or its details, all will concur in expressing thanks to the Senator from Ohio, [Mr. Tappan,] for introducing it. We shall differ more perhaps than could be wished, or than can be reconciled, about the mode of administering this noble fund; but we cannot differ about our duty to enter at once on some mode of administering it. A large sum of money has been given to us, to hold and to apply, in trust, "for the increase and diffusion of knowledge among men." We have accepted the trust. "To this application" — such is the language of our act of the first of July, 1836 — "to this application of the money the faith of the United States is hereby pledged." The donor is in his grave. There is no chancellor to compel us to redeem our pledge; and there needs none. Our own sense of duty to the dead, and the living, and the unborn who shall live, — our justice, our patriotism, our policy, common honesty, common decorum, urge us, and are enough to urge us, to go on, without the delay of an hour, to appropriate the bounty according to the form of the gift. I thank the Senator, therefore, for introducing a bill with which, to my own knowledge, he has taken much — and, so far as I can see or conceive — disinterested pains, and which affords us an opportunity to discharge a plain duty, perhaps too long delayed.

I think, too, Sir, that the Senator has, in the first section of the bill, declared the true fundamental law according to which this fund ought to be permanently administered. He lends to the United States the whole sum of $508,318 actually received out of the English chancery, from the third of December, 1838, when it was received, at an interest of six per cent. per annum. He leaves the sum of $209,103, which is so much of the interest as will have accrued on the first day of July next, to be applied at once to the construction of buildings, the preparation of grounds, the purchase of books, instruments, and the like; and then appropriates the interest, and the interest only, of the original principal sum, for the perpetual maintenance of the institution, leaving the principal itself unimpaired forever. This all, is exactly as it should be.

But when you examine the bill a little further, to discern what it is exactly which this considerable expenditure of money is to accomplish,—when you look to see how and how much it is going "to increase and diffuse knowledge among men," I am afraid that we shall have reason to be a little less satisfied. I do not now refer to the constitution of the board of management, of which, let me say, under some important modifications, I incline to approve; although on that I reserve myself. I speak of what the fund, however managed, is to be made to do. The bill assumes, as it ought, to apply it, "to increase and diffuse knowledge among men." Well, how does it accomplish this object?

It proposes to do so, for substance, by establishing in this city a school, a college, for the purpose of instructing its pupils in the application of certain physical sciences to certain arts of life. The plan, if adopted, founds a college in Washington to teach the scientific principles of certain useful arts. That is the whole of it. It appoints, on permanent salaries, a professor of agriculture, horticulture, and rural economy; a professor of natural history; a professor of chemistry; a professor of geology; a professor of astronomy; a professor of architecture and domestic science; together with a fluctuating force of occasional auxiliary lecturers; and all these professors and lecturers are enjoined "to have special reference, in all their illustrations and instructions, to the productive and liberal arts of life,—to improvements in agriculture, manufactures, trades, and domestic economy." Thus, the professor of chemistry is to analyze different kinds of soils, and to learn and teach how to enrich them; the professor of natural history is to deal with noxious or useful animals and insects; the professor of geology is to illustrate the working of mines; the professor of astronomy is to teach navigation; the professor of architecture and domestic science is charged with the theory and practice of building, lighting, and ventilating all manner of edifices; and the professor of agriculture, horticulture, and domestic economy is to make experiments to see what exotics will grow and what will not, all over the United States. And, in pursuance of the same theory of administration of the fund, it is provided that not a book is to be purchased for the institution except "works on science and the arts, especially such as relate to the ordinary business of life, and to the various mechanical and other improvements and discoveries which may be made."

Now, I say, that this creates a college or school — such as it is — on the basis of a somewhat narrow utilitarianism — to be sure, erroneously so called — but a college or academical institution. Who is to be taught agriculture, architecture, domestic science, rural economy, and navigation? Not you, Mr. President, I suppose; not congress; not the government; not men at all. Students, pupils, youths, are to be brought hither, if you can find them; "rules and regulations," (so runs the eighth section of the bill,) are to be made "for the admission into the various departments of the institution, and their conduct and deportment while they remain therein," and instruction is to be given them by professors and lecturers. This, surely, is a school, a college, an academical institute of education — such as it is — or nothing.

Well, Sir, in reviewing, as I have had occasion to do, the proceedings of congress upon this subject heretofore, I have received the impression that it had become quite your settled judgment, — settled on the most decisive reasons, — that no school, college, or academical establishment, should be constituted. It seems that, in the session of 1838, a joint committee of the two branches was charged with this deliberation. The chairman of the committee from this body was Mr. Robbins, and the chairman, on the appointment of the house, was Mr. Adams, — both of them, I may pause to say, persons of the most profound and elegant acquisition, — both of them of that happy, rare class who "grow old still learning." The two committees differed on this very question, whether a school or college should be established. The opinion of the committee of the house is expressed in the fourth section of the bill (No. 293, Senate,) which they desired to report, and which is in these words : —

"Sec. 4. And be it further enacted, That no part of the said Smithsonian fund, principal or interest, shall be applied to any school, college, university, institute of education, or ecclesiastical establishment."

That of the committee of the senate is distinctly enough intimated in the beautiful speech with which Mr. Robbins introduced the subject in January, 1839. I find it in the appendix to the "Congressional Globe:" —

"I could wish, if all were agreed in it, that this institution should make one of a number of colleges, to constitute a university to be established here, and to be endowed in a manner worthy of this great nation and their immense resources. But as opinions are divided upon this subject, — not, I should hope, as to the great desirableness of such an establishment, but as to the constitutional competency of congress to undertake it, — I will not embarrass my present object by involving it with that subject. This, as an independent institution, may hereafter be made a part of such a university, should one be established; but it is now to be looked at only as an independent institution."

It was to embody and execute this conception that Mr. Robbins drew the senate bill, No. 292.

Finding themselves unable to agree, it was determined that each committee should report both of these bills to their respective houses. On the twenty-fifth February, 1839, the bill drawn by Mr. Robbins was taken up in this body, and, after an animated discussion, was laid on the table by a vote of twenty to fifteen. This vote is regarded, I perceive, by Mr. Adams in his subsequent reports of 1840 and 1842, as expressing the judgment of the senate against the establishment of such academical institute of learning. He says, —

"It is, then, to be considered as a circumstance propitious to the final disposal of this fund, by the organization of an institution the best adapted to accomplish the design of the testator, that this first but erroneous impression of that design — an institute of learning, a university, upon the foundation of which the whole fund should be lavished, and yet prove inadequate to its purpose, without large appropriations of public moneys in its aid — should have been presented to the consideration of congress, referred to a numerous joint committee of both houses, there discussed, reported for the deliberation of both houses, fully debated in the house where it originated, and then decisively rejected."

If such may be inferred to have been the judgment of the senate, it may be defended on the most decisive reasons. It is hardly worth while to move the question, whether it would be expedient to apply the fund as far as it would go to the founding of a great university deserving of the name, — a national university, in which all the branches of a thorough education should be taught; which should fill the space between the college and professional schools, which should guide the maturer American mind to the highest places of knowledge; for such should be the functions of such a university. It is not worth while to move this question; because no such proposition is before us. I am afraid, with Mr. Adams, that to found such a university would consume the whole fund, interest and principal, almost at once, and reduce you to the alternative of a signal failure, or of occasional and frequent application to the government for aid which could never be granted. But the Senator from Ohio contemplates no such thing. He constructs his college on a far more moderate model; and of this college of his I am constrained to say, that I think it, in the actual state of academical education, wholly unnecessary, and in a great degree useless. Why, Sir, there are in the country more than a hundred colleges; I have seen them estimated at one hundred and seventy-three. These are distributed all over the United States; two are in this District. They are at the doors of the people. I suspect that every one of them has a professor for every department provided for in this bill, except architecture and domestic science, and agriculture and rural economy. In every one, without any difficulty, that special attention here recommended to the application of science "to the ordinary business of life," may be, if it is not now, secured, if in the judgment of those who are intrusted with their management it is thought expedient. Why, Sir, I recollect that navigation was taught in one at least of our common, free district-schools of Massachusetts thirty years ago. I cannot concur with the honorable framer of the bill, therefore, that his school is to "furnish facilities for the acquisition of such branches of knowledge as are not taught in the various universities." It will do no such thing. It will injure those universities, rather, if it has any effect, by withdrawing from them some portion of the patronage for which they are all struggling, and of which so few get a full meal.

Such a school, then, I think, is scarcely now necessary. In this city it would be, to say no more, very far from generally useful. It would hardly appear to be an instrumentality coming up to the sonorous promise of "increasing and diffusing knowledge among men." Who would its pupils be? Who could afford to come all the way to Washington from the South, West, and North, to learn architecture, navigation, and domestic science? Certainly only the sons of the wealthy, who would hardly come, if they could, to learn any such branch of homely knowledge. You might collect some few students in the District and the borders of the adjacent States; but for any purpose of wide utility the school would be no more felt than so much sunshine on the poles. Meantime, here would be your professors, their salaries running on, your books and apparatus and edifices, — a show of things, — a pretty energetic diffusing of the fund, not much diffusion of knowledge.

I shall venture, then, to move to strike out all those parts of the bill which indicate the particular mode in which the bequest is to be applied to the increase and diffusion of knowledge. I except the provision for experiments in seeds and plants, on which I will say a word hereafter. If this motion prevails, the whole question will recur, What shall we do with the fund?

It has seemed to me that there are two applications of it which may just now meet with favor.

In the first place, to begin with the least important, — I adopt, with some modifications, the suggestion in the bill that lectures be delivered in this city for two or three months during every session of congress. These lectures should be delivered not by professors permanently fixed here, upon annual salaries, to do nothing in the recess of congress, or to do nothing that cannot be as well done at one hundred and fifty other places; but by gentlemen eminent in science and literature, holding situations elsewhere, and coming hither under the stimulations and with the ambition of a special and conspicuous retainer. They might be professors of colleges, men of letters, persons distinguished in the professions, or otherwise. Names will occur to you all which I need not mention; and their lectures should be adapted to their audiences. Who would their audiences be? Members of congress with their families, members of the government with theirs, some inhabitants of this city, some few strangers who occasionally honor us with visits of curiosity or business. They would be public men, of mature years and minds; educated, disciplined to some degree, of liberal curiosity, and appreciation of generous and various knowledge. Such would be the audience. The lectures should be framed accordingly. I do not think they should be confined to three or four physical sciences in their applications to the arts of life,—navigation, useful or hurtful insects and animals, the ventilation of rooms, or the smoking of chimneys.

This is knowledge, to be sure; but it is not all knowledge, nor the half of it, nor the best of it. Why should not such an audience hear something of the philosophy of history, of classical and of South American antiquities, of international law, of the grandeur and decline of States, of the progress and eras of freedom, of ethics, of intellectual philosophy, of art, taste, and literature in its most comprehensive and noblest forms? Why should they not hear such lectures as Sir James Mackintosh delivered when a young man to audiences among whom were Canning, and such as he? Would it not be as instructive to hear a first-rate scholar and thinker demonstrate out of a chapter of Greek or Italian history how dreadful a thing it is for a cluster of young and fervid democracies to dwell side by side, *independent and disunited*, as it would to hear a chemist maintain that to raise wheat you must have some certain proportion of lime in the soil? But the subjects of lectures would of course be adapted to time, place, and circumstances, and varied with them. Whatever they should treat of, they would be useful. They would recreate and refresh and instruct you. They would relieve the monotony and soften the austerity, and correct all the influences of this kind of public service.

But, Mr. President, all this is no administration of the fund; all this ought to cost less than $5,000 a year. We could not sustain more than one lecture in a week, nor that for more than three months of any session. Here is an accumulated interest of $200,000; and here is an annual interest of $30,000, of which thus far I have provided for an expenditure of some $5000 only. What will you do with the rest?

It is easy to waste this money; it is easy to squander it in jobs, salaries, quackeries; it is easy, even under the forms of utility, to disperse and dissipate it in little rills and drops, imperceptible to all human sense, carrying it off by an insensible and ineffectual evaporation. But, Sir, I take it that we all earnestly desire — I am sure the Senator from Ohio does so — so to dispense it as to make it tell. I am sure we all desire to see it, instead of being carried off invisibly and wastefully, embody itself in some form, some exponent of civilization, permanent, palpable, conspicuous, useful. And to this end it has seemed to me, upon the most mature reflection, that we cannot do a safer, surer, more unexceptionable thing with the income, or with a portion of the income, — perhaps $20,000 a year for a few years, — than to expend it in accumulating a grand and noble public library, — one which, for variety, extent, and wealth, shall be, and be confessed to be, equal to any now in the world.

I say for a few years; twenty thousand dollars a year, for twenty-five years, are five hundred thousand dollars; and five hundred thousand dollars discreetly expended, not by a bibliomaniac, but by a man of sense and reading, thoroughly instructed in bibliography, would go far, very far, towards the purchase of nearly as good a library as Europe can boast. I mean a library of printed books, as distinct from manuscripts. Of course such a sum would not purchase the number of books which some old libraries are reported to contain. It would not buy the seven hundred thousand of the Royal Library at Paris, the largest in the world; not the five hundred thousand or six hundred thousand of that of Munich, the largest in Germany; not the three hundred thousand, four hundred thousand, or five hundred thousand of those of Vienna and St. Petersburg, and the Vatican at Rome, and Copenhagen, and the Bodleian at Oxford. But mere numbers of volumes afford a very imperfect criterion of value. Those old libraries have been so long in collecting, accident and donation, which could not be rejected, have contributed so much to them, a general and indiscriminate system of accumulation gathers up, necessarily, so much trash; there are so many duplicates and quadruplicates, and so many books and editions which become superseded, that mere bulk and mere original cost must not terrify us. *Ponderantur non numerantur.* Accordingly the library of the University at Gottingen, consisting of perhaps two hundred thousand volumes, but well chosen, selected for the most part, within a century, and to a considerable extent by a single great scholar [Heyne], is perhaps today as valuable a collection of printed books as any in the world. Towards the accumulation of such a library, the expenditure of two thirds of this income for a quarter of a century would make, let me say, a magnificent advance. And such a step taken, we should never leave the work unfinished; yet when it should be finished, and your library should rival anything which civilization has ever had to show, there would still be the whole principal of your fund unexpended, yielding its income forever, for new and varying application for increasing and diffusing knowledge in the world.

[Mr. Choate here read a letter of Professor Torry of Burlington, showing at what reduced prices valuable books may now be purchased.]

I hesitate, from an apprehension of being accused of entering too far into a kind of dissertation unsuited to this assembly of men of business, to suggest and press one half the considerations which satisfy my mind of the propriety of this mode of expenditure. Nobody can doubt, I think, that it comes within the terms and spirit of the trust. That directs us to "increase and diffuse knowledge among men." And do not the judgments of all the wise, does not the experience of all enlightened, States, — does not the whole history of civilization, concur to declare that a various and ample library is one of the surest, most constant, most permanent, and most economical instrumentalities to increase and diffuse knowledge? There, it would be durable as liberty, durable as the Union, — a vast storehouse, a vast treasury, of all the facts which make up the history of man and of nature, so far as that history has been written; of all the truths which the inquiries and experiences of all the races and ages have found out; of all the opinions that have been promulgated; of all the emotions, images, sentiments, examples of all the richest and most instructive literatures; the whole past speaking to the present and the future; a silent yet wise and eloquent teacher, dead, yet speaking; not dead! for Milton has told us that a "good book is not absolutely a dead thing, — the precious life-blood rather of a master-spirit; a seasoned life of man embalmed and treasured up on purpose to a life beyond life." Is not that an admirable instrumentality to increase and diffuse knowledge among men? It would place within the reach of our mind, of our thinkers and investigators and scholars, all, or the chief, intellectual and literary materials and food and instruments now within the reach of the cultivated foreign mind; and the effect would be to increase the amount of individual acquisition, and multiply the number of the learned. It would raise the standard of our scholarship, improve our style of investigation, and communicate an impulse to our educated and to the general mind. There is no library now in this country, I suppose, containing over fifty thousand volumes. Many there are containing less. But, from the nature of the case, all have the same works; so that I do not know, that of all the printed books in the world, we have in this country more than fifty thousand different works. The consequence has been felt and lamented by all our authors and all our scholars. It has been often said that Gibbon's history could not have been written here for want of books. I suppose that Hallam's "Middle Ages" and his "Introduction to the Literature of Europe" could not. Irving's "Columbus" was written in Spain. Wheaton's "Northmen" was prepared to be written in Copenhagen. See how this inadequate supply operates. An American mind kindles with a subject; it enters on an investigation with a spirit and with an ability worthy of the most splendid achievement; goes a little way, finds that a dozen books, one book perhaps, is indispensable, which cannot be found this side of Gottingen or Oxford; it tires of the pursuit, or abandons it altogether, or substitutes some shallow conjecture for a deep and accurate research, — and there an end. Let me refer to a passage or two of the complaints of studious men on this subject: —

"An extensive library, answering to the wants of literary men who are to use it, is essential to the public and effectual promotion of learning. In this country the want of large libraries is a serious discouragement of superior attainments and accurate researches in almost every walk of study. The time necessary for reading or examining a particular book is often consumed in attempts to discover or obtain it; and frequently, after every effort, it cannot be procured. We are obliged to give over our inquiries on subjects where we would arrive at fulness and exactness in our knowledge, because destitute of the assistance which the learned, in the same track of study, have furnished, or to continue them under the disadvantage of ignorance respecting what has been done by others. Thus, we are liable to be occupied in solving difficulties which have been already cleared, discussing questions which have been already decided, and digging in mines of literature which former ages have exhausted. Every one who has been in the way of pursuing any branch of study in our country beyond the mere elements, or the polite and popular literature of the time, knows how soon the progress is often arrested for want of books. This is not the case merely with persons of moderate means, who are unable to purchase a library of their own; but it is a want felt under the most favorable circumstances.

"It is also of great importance that the library of a university should not only be good, but very good, — ample, munificent; a deposit of the world's knowledge. It is a grievous thing to be stopped short in the midst of an inquiry for perhaps the very book that throws most light upon it; and the progress of learning must be small indeed among us, so long as the student must send across the Atlantic at every turn for the necessary aids to his pursuits. It is not with us as it is in Europe, where very many large libraries exist, and where what is not contained in one may be found in another; and the learned are able to aid each other's labors, by furnishing mutually, as desired, extracts and references to such books as may exist at one place and fail at another. To say nothing of our two best libraries being remote from each other and from many parts of the country, they are themselves, of course, inadequate. In making one tolerably complete department expressly chosen for that, and entirely devoted to it, we might easily comprise the amount of books in our largest collection. When it is added that the libraries mentioned are miscellaneous, their number of books small, as the sum total is scattered over all the parts of knowledge, and many introduced by separate contributions without mutual reference to each other, it is obvious that, comparatively speaking, the best must be extremely defective." — *North American Review*, vol. viii. p. 192.

"What public library in this country contains the materials for an accurate history of any one department of science? Take even the most limited, or rather one of the most recent of all, — the science of political economy. Here, our researches are confined to one definite period. We have no dusty archives to explore, no time-worn manuscripts to decipher. The origin of the science is within the memory of our fathers, and we ourselves have witnessed its sudden growth and rapid development. Yet how much is to be done, how many authorities to be weighed, how many different treatises to be analyzed and compared, before we can venture to say, Here is the history; for such was the rise, such the progress, such the changes of opinions, such the received and such the rejected theories of political economy! The writers of the first French school, of the Scotch school (and if we wish for history, we must go beyond the publication of Adam Smith's great work), the Italian, the new French, and the new English schools, all have not merely a claim upon our attention, but are entitled to a full and accurate examination. And even then our task would be incomplete; for literary justice would require us to trace, through the works of general political writers, the hints and remarks which have contributed to the progress of the branch we are studying, by the discovery of truth or by the exposition of error. If such be the obligation of the student whose researches are confined to a subject so new, what must be the necessities of the historian who attempts to throw light upon those periods for which the testimony of printed authorities is to be confronted with that of manuscripts and public documents, and where ignorance and prejudice have combined with the more powerful incentives of interest to perplex his path by contradictory statements and conflicting opinions!

"Books are needed, not confined to any single branch, but embracing the whole range of science and of literature, which shall supply the means of every species of research and inquiry, and which, placed within reach of all, shall leave idleness no excuse for the lightness of its labors, and poverty no obstacles which industry may not surmount.

"Whoever reflects, though but for a moment, upon the numerous branches into which modern literature runs, and remembers that the literary glory of a nation can only be secured by a certain degree of success in each of them — whoever considers the immense mass of varied materials without which no historical work of importance can be composed, or the extensive learning which is required of even the most gifted genius of an age like ours, and adds to these considerations the general and undeniable fact that of those who would gladly devote themselves to literature, but a few can ever hope to obtain by their own resources the command of the works that are essential to the successful prosecution of their studies, will be ready to acknowledge that we have, as yet, done but a small part of what may be justly claimed from a nation which aspires to the first rank for the liberality and politeness, and high moral tone of its civilization. Late, however, as we are to begin, scarce anything in this department has been accomplished in Europe which might not be done with equal success in America. And so numerous and manifest are our advantages in some important particulars, that a prompt will and sound judgment in the execution of it might, in the course of a very few years, render the American student nearly independent of those vast collections which, in Europe have required centuries for their formation. The undertaking, however, in order to be successful, should be a national one. Without arguing that no State is fully equal to it, or that in the bounds of any single State it would not answer the same purpose, we may be permitted to say that the enlargement of the library of congress upon those broad principles, the application of which to the collection of books has become a difficult and important art, would reflect an honor upon the country equal to the permanent advantages which it would secure to every member of the community." — *North American Review, vol.* xlv. p. 137.

Yet these writers had access to the best library in this country.

Now, there are very many among us, and every day we shall have more, who would feelingly adopt this language. Place within their reach the helps that guide the genius and labors of Germany and England; and let the genius and labors of Germany and England look to themselves! Our learned men would grow more learned and more able; our studies deeper and wider; our mind itself exercised and sharpened; the whole culture of the community raised and enriched. This is, indeed, to increase and diffuse knowledge among men.

If the terms of the trust, then, authorize this expenditure, why not make it? Not among the principal, nor yet the least of reasons for doing so, is, that all the while that you are laying out your money, and when you have laid it out, you have the money's worth, the value received, the property purchased, on hand, to show for itself and to speak for itself. Suppose the professors provided for in the bill should gather a little circle of pupils, each of whom should carry off with him some small quotient of navigation, or horticulture, or rural economy, and the fund should thus glide away and evaporate in such insensible, inappreciable appropriations, how little would there be to testify of it! Whereas here, all the while, are the books; here is the value; here is the visible property; here is the oil, and here is the light. There is something to point to, if you should be asked to account for it unexpectedly, and something to point to, if a traveller should taunt you with the collections which he has seen abroad, and which gild and recommend the absolutisms of Vienna or St. Petersburg.

Another reason, not of the strongest to be sure, for this mode of expenditure is, that it creates so few jobs and sinecures; so little salaried laziness. There is no room for abuses in it. All that you need is a plain, spacious, fire-proof building; a librarian and assistants; an agent to buy your books, and a fire to sit by. For all the rest, he who wants to read goes and ministers to himself. It is an application of money that almost excludes the chances of abuses altogether.

But the decisive argument is, after all, that it is an application the most exactly adapted to the actual literary and scientific wants of the States and the country. I have said that another college is not needed here, because there are enough now; and another might do harm as much as good. But that which is wanted for every college, for the whole country, for every studious person, is a well-chosen library, somewhere among us, of three or four hundred thousand books. Where is such a one to be collected? How is it to be done? Who is to do it? Of the hundred and fifty colleges, more or less, distributed over the country, one has a library of perhaps fifty thousand volumes; others have good ones, though less; others smaller, and smaller, down to scarcely anything. With one voice they unite, teacher and pupil, with every scholar and thinker, in proclaiming the want of more. But where are they to come from? No State is likely to lay a tax to create a college library, or a city library. No death-bed gift of the rich can be expected to do it. How, then, is this one grand want of learning to be relieved? It can be done by you, and by you only. By a providential occurrence, it is not only placed within your constitutional power, but it has become your duty; you have pledged your faith; you have engaged to the dead and living that, without the charge of one dollar on the people, you will meet the universal and urgent demand by the precise and adequate supply. By such a library as you can collect here something will be done, much will be done, to help every college, every school, every studious man, every writer and thinker in the country to just what is wanted most. Inquirers after truth may come here and search for it. It will do no harm at all to pass a few studious weeks among these scenes. Having pushed their investigations as far as they may at home, and ascertained just what, and how much more, of helps they require, let them come hither and find it. Let them replenish themselves, and then go back and make distribution among their pupils; ay, through the thousand channels, and by the thousand voices of the press, let them make distribution among the people! Let it be so that —

> "Hither as to their fountains other stars
> Repairing, in their golden urns, draw light."

I have no objection at all — I should rejoice rather — to see the literary representatives of an instructed people come hither, not merely for the larger legislation and jurisprudence, but for the rarer and higher knowledge. I am quite willing, not only that our "Amphictyonic Council" should sit here, but that it should find itself among some such scenes and influences as surrounded that old, renowned assembly; the fountain of purer waters than those of Castalia; the temple and the oracle of our Apollo! It will do good to have your educated men come to Washington for what has heretofore cost voyages to Germany. They will be of all the parts of the country. They will become acquainted with each other. They will contract friendships and mutual regards. They will go away not only better scholars, but better Unionists. Some one has said that a great library moulds all minds into one republic. It might, in a sense of which he little dreamed, help to keep ours together.

I have intimated, Mr. President, a doubt whether a college or university of any description, even the highest, should be at present established here. But let it be considered by the enlightened friends of that object, if such there are, that even if your single purpose were to create such a university, you could possibly begin in no way so judiciously as by collecting a great library. Useful in the other modes which I have indicated, to a university it is everything. It is as needful as the soul to the body. While you are doubting, then, what to do, what you will have, you can do nothing so properly as to begin to be accumulating the books which you will require, on whatever permanent plan of application you at last determine.

I do not expect to hear it said in this assembly that this expenditure for a library will benefit a few only, not the mass; that it is exclusive, and of the nature of monopoly. It is to be remembered that this fund is a gift; that we take it just as it is given; and that by its terms it must be disbursed here. Any possible administration of it, therefore, is exposed to the cavil that all cannot directly and literally and equally partake of it. How many and of what classes of youth from Louisiana, or Illinois, or New England, for example, can attend the lectures of your professor of astronomy? But I say it is a positive and important argument for the mode of application which I urge, that it is so diffusive. Think of the large absolute numbers of those who in the succession of years, will come and partake directly of these stores of truth and knowledge! Think of the numbers without number who through them, who by them indirectly, will partake of the same stores! Studious men will come to learn to speak and write to and for the growing millions of a generally educated community. They will learn that they may communicate. They cannot hoard if they would, and they would not if they could. They take in trust to distribute; and every motive of ambition, of interest, of duty, will compel them to distribute. They buy in gross, to sell by retail. The lights which they kindle here will not be set under a bushel, but will burn on a thousand hills. No, Sir; a rich and public library is no anti-republican monopoly. Who was the old Egyptian king that inscribed on his library the words: the dispensary of the soul? You might quite as well inscribe on it, armory and light and fountain of liberty!

It may possibly be inquired what account I make of the library of congress. I answer, that I think it already quite good, and improving; but that its existence constitutes no sort of argument against the formation of such a one as I recommend. In the theory of it, that library is collected merely to furnish congress and the government with the means of doing their official business. In its theory it must be, in some sort, a professional library; and the expenditure we now make — five thousand dollars in a year, or, as last year, two thousand and five hundred — can never carry it up to the rank and enable it to fulfil the functions of a truly great and general public library of science, literature, and art. The value of books which could be added under the appropriations of the last year, cannot greatly exceed twenty-two hundred dollars. Doubtless, however, in the course of forming the two, it would be expedient and inevitable to procure to a great extent different books for each.

I do not think, Mr. President, that I am more inclined than another to covet enviously anything which the older civilization of Europe possesses which we do not. I do not suppose that I desire, any more than you, or than any of you, to introduce here those vast inequalities of fortune, that elaborate luxury, that fantastic and extreme refinement. But I acknowledge a pang of envy and grief that there should be one drop or one morsel more of the bread or water of intellectual life tasted by the European than by the American mind. Why should not the soul of this country eat as good food and as much of it as the soul of Europe? Why should a German or an Englishman sit down to a repast of five hundred thousand books, and an American scholar, who loves truth as well as he, be put on something less than half allowance? Can we not trust ourselves with so much of so good a thing? Will our digestion be impaired by it? Are we afraid that the stimulated and fervid faculties of this young nation will be oppressed and overlaid? Because we have liberty which other nations have not, shall we reject the knowledge which they have and which we have not? Or will you not rather say, that, because we are free, therefore will we add to our freedom that deep learning and that diffused culture which are its grace and its defence?

[Mr. Choate then moved certain amendments in conformity with the views of his speech.]

MISCELLANEOUS SPEECHES.

MISCELLANEOUS SPEECHES.

SPEECH BEFORE THE YOUNG MEN'S WHIG CLUB OF BOSTON, ON THE ANNEXATION OF TEXAS.

DELIVERED IN THE TREMONT TEMPLE, AUGUST 19, 1844.

[The meeting having been called to order by Charles Francis Adams, President of the Club, Mr. Choate was introduced. He came forward and spoke as follows:]

MR. PRESIDENT AND GENTLEMEN, —

I REGARD the approaching election as one of more interest to the whole country, and to the States of the North in a preëminent degree, than any which has preceded it. The peculiarity of this election is, that while it involves all the questions of mere policy, which are ever suspended on the choice of a president, — questions of the currency, of the lands, of internal improvements, of protection, of foreign policy, and all else; while it involves in its broadest extent the question, *how shall the nation be governed?* — it involves — the first presidential election that has done so — the further, more fundamental, and more startling question, *what shall the nation be; who shall the nation be; where shall the nation be;* who, what, and where, is, and is to be, our country itself? Is it to be any longer the Union which we have known; which we have loved, to which we have been accustomed? — or is it to be dissolved altogether? or is it to be a new one, enlarged by the annexation of a territory out of which forty States of the size of Massachusetts might be constructed; a territory not appended equally to the East, the West, the Centre, and the South; not appended equally to the slave States and the free States; to the agricultural and the planting; to the localities of free trade and the localities of protection; not so appended as to work an equal and impartial enlargement and assistance to each one of those various and heterogeneous elements of interest and sentiment and position out of whose struggle comes the peace, out of whose dissonance comes the harmony, of our system; — not so, but appended in one vast accession to one side, one region, one interest, of the many which compose the State; so appended as to disturb the relations of the parts; to change the seat of the centre; to counteract the natural tendencies of things; to substitute a revolution of violent and morbid policy in place of the slow and safe action of nature, habit, and business, under a permanent law; so appended, in short, as not merely to make a small globe into a larger one, but to alter the whole figure of the body; to vary the shape and the range of its orbit; to launch it forth on a new highway of the heavens; to change its day and night, its seed-time and harvest, its solar year, the great cycle of its duration itself.

This it is that gives to this election an interest peculiar and transcendent. It is a question, not what the policy of the nation shall be, — but what, who, where, *shall the nation be!* It is not a question of national politics, but of national identity. For even if the Union shall survive the annexation of Texas, and the discussions of annexation, it will be a new, a changed, another Union, — not this. It will be changed, not by time, which changes all things, — man, monuments, states, the great globe itself; not by time, but by power; not by imperceptible degrees, but in a day; not by a successive growth, unfolded and urged forward by an organic law, an implanted force, a noiseless and invisible nutrition from beneath and from without, of which every region, every State, takes the risk; but by the direct action of government — arbitrary, violent, and unjust — of which no part has ever agreed to take the risk. It is to this element in the present election, the annexation of Texas, that I wish to-night, passing over all the rest, to direct your attention.

I shall consume but little of the time of such an assembly as this, in attempting to prove that the success or failure of this enterprise of annexation is suspended — for the present — perhaps for our day — on the result of the pending election. You, at least, have no doubt on this point. Is there one man now before me, in the first place, who does not believe, or who does not greatly and rationally fear, that if Mr. Polk is the next president, Texas will come in — under the unostentatious, and not so very terrible form of *a territory*, of course, in the first instance — in twelve months, unless some great and extraordinary interposition of the people should prevent it? Does any one — if such an one may be supposed among you to-night — who, opposed to Texas, as you are, has yet a hankering for Mr. Polk, and means to vote for him, if he can obtain the consent of his conscience — who wants to vote for Mr. Polk, but shrinks from the idea of promoting annexation — does any such one say, Oh, it doesn't follow that if he is chosen, Texas will be annexed? Be it so; but does it not increase the chances of annexation? Does it not tremendously enhance the difficulties of resistance? Does it not at least, expose you to the terrible hazard of being compelled, hereafter, to encounter, by memorial, by convention, by remonstrance, by extreme and extraordinary action, that which you can now, peaceably, innocently, seasonably anticipate and prevent at the polls? Does not every stock-jobber, and land-jobber, and flesh-jobber, who clamors for annexation, understand perfectly, that he aids his objects by choosing Mr. Polk? Are not those honest gentlemen all on his side, and do they not well know what they are about? Does not Mr. Polk come in — if he comes — pledged to annex if he can, and determined to do it if he can? Does he not come in pledged and determined to put in requisition the whole vast power of the Executive — the whole vast power of the flushed party that elects him, and to effect annexation? Is any man foolish enough to deny, that Mr. Van Buren was cast overboard, and Mr. Polk nominated, expressly and solely that the candidate might be, as they exquisitely express it, "Texas to the backbone?" — And how can you suppose that, nominated for this very purpose, elected for this very purpose, he will do nothing to accomplish it? Why, if he should be disposed to do nothing, do you think that a party or a faction, strong enough to go into a National Convention, and there trample instructions under foot; strong enough to force upon the body an audacious, not very democratic rule of proceeding, which put it out of the power of a majority to nominate the choice of a majority; strong enough to laugh Colonel Benton and Mr. Wright in the face; strong enough, not merely to divide Mr. Butler's last crust with him, but to snatch the whole of it; strong enough to ejaculate Mr. Van Buren out of the window — under whom they had once triumphed — on whom they rallied again in six months after the defeat of 1840, and who had been their candidate as notoriously and avowedly as Mr. Clay had been ours — and of whom no man of any party will deny, that in point of accomplishment and talent and experience of public affairs, he is immeasurably Mr. Polk's superior; strong enough to have dissolved that convention in a half an hour, had it not conceded their utmost demands — ruining if they could not rule; — if Mr. Polk should be disposed to do nothing, do you believe such a party, or such a faction as this, would permit him to do nothing? No. No. Desperately, weakly, fatally, does he deceive himself who will not see, that everything which an Executive, elected expressly to do this deed, can do, will be done, and done at once! He will put it forward in his very first message. He will put it forward as the one, grand measure of his party, and of his administration. Nothing will be left unstirred to effect it. The farewell words of General Jackson will be rung in admiring and subservient ears. Aye, that drum shall be beaten, which might call the dead of all his battles to the "midnight review," in shadowy files! The measure will not be attempted again, in the first instance, in the form of a treaty, requiring two thirds of the senate, but in the form of a law, requiring a majority of only one. Do you say such a majority cannot be commanded? Do not be too sure of that. I pray you, give no vote, withhold no vote, on such a speculation as that. Do not, because President Tyler has not been able to command a majority — President Tyler, without a party, with one whole division of the Democratic party, with Colonel Benton and Mr. Wright at its head, against him; with the Southern Whigs, under the seasonable and important lead of Mr. Clay, against him to a man—do not, because under these special and temporary circumstances, he has not been able to obtain a majority, therefore, lay the flattering unction to your soul, that when a president who has a party, and that party a majority of the people, flushed with a recent victory won on this precise issue, shall try his hand at the business; when Colonel Benton — the temporary and special circumstances of his recent resistance having subsided — shall resume his natural and earlier position; and "La Salle" and "Americanus" shall be himself again; when Southern Whigs, no longer rallying to the lead of Mr. Clay, shall resume their natural position, or shall divide on the question; when the whole tactics of party, the united or general strength of the South, the vast and multiform influence of a strong Executive shall be combined; when the measure comes to be pressed, under every specious name, by aid of every specious topic of patriotism and aggrandizement; when, if any one, or two, or ten, or twenty members of congress should manifest symptoms of recusancy, or should try the effect of a little "sweet, reluctant, amorous delay," the weird sisters of ambitious hearts shall play before their eyes images of foreign missions, and departments, and benches of justice — do not deceive yourselves into the belief, that the majority of one will not be secured. I speak now of the admission of Texas as a mere territory. The erection of that territory into States will be a very different undertaking — later, less promising, a far more dreadful trial of the ties of Union. Of that I have something to say hereafter; but I have no doubt whatever, and I feel it to be an urgent duty to declare it, that the territory, *as territory*, will be admitted in twelve months after Mr. Polk's election, unless some extraordinary interposition of the people, on which I dare not speculate, shall prevent it.

[Mr. Choate then proceeded to observe upon a letter, which he had read in the "National Intelligencer," signed by seven prominent members of the Democratic party in New York, including the accomplished editor of the "Evening Post," in which the writers declare their purpose of supporting Mr. Polk, but recommend the election of members of congress "who will reject the unwarrantable scheme now pressed on the country." He remarked on the concessions of the letter, to wit: "that the Baltimore convention had placed the Democratic party at the North in a position of great difficulty;" that it exposed the party to the constant taunt "*that the convention rejected Mr. Van Buren and nominated Mr. Polk*, for reasons connected with the *immediate annexation of Texas;*" "that it went still further and interpolated into the party creed a *new doctrine*, hitherto unknown among us, — at war with some of our established principles, and abhorrent to the opinions and feelings of a great majority of Northern freemen!" And he doubted whether a State which should give its vote for a president nominated solely for the very purpose of annexing Texas, would or could, in the same breath, elect members of congress to go and defeat the "scheme," — "*unwarrantable*" enough, no doubt, but yet the precise and single "scheme" which Mr. Polk was brought forward to accomplish, — and whether they, or such as they, who surrendered to the candidate at Baltimore, would be very likely to beard and baffle the incumbent at Washington. He then resumed :]

The election of Mr. Polk, then, will, or may probably annex Texas as a territory. The election of Mr. Clay defeats or postpones it indefinitely. Some persons pretend to doubt, or at least seem to deny this. But do they do him, themselves, and the great subject, justice? Read his letter upon this subject; observe the broad and permanent grounds of exclusion which he there sketches; advert to the well-weighed declaration, that so long as any considerable opposition to the measure shall be manifested, he will resist it; and you cannot fail to see that unless you yourselves, — unless Massachusetts and Vermont and Ohio, — should withdraw their opposition, for his term at least, you are safe, and all are safe. That letter, in my judgment, makes him a title to every anti-Texas vote in America. The circumstances under which it was given to the world, I happened well to know. It was before either convention had assembled at Baltimore. It was as yet, to me at least, uncertain what ground Mr. Van Buren would take. Warm friends of Mr. Clay in congress would have dissuaded him from immediate publication. They feared its effect even on the Whig convention itself; they feared its wider and more permanent effect. Wait a little, they said. Feel the pulse of the delegates as they come to Washington. Attend for a few days the rising voice of the general press of the South. He rejected these counsels of indecision, and directed it to be given to the country. In my judgment, that act saved the country. It fixed and rallied the universal Whig opinion upon this subject instantly, and everywhere. It suspended the warm feelings of the South, until its sober second thought could discern, as now it has begun to discern, that fair and tempting as this forbidden fruit shows to the sense, it brings with it death, and all woe, with loss of Eden. The position which Mr. Clay held, — the inhabitant of a slave State; his birth-place Virginia; the part he transacted in the Missouri controversy; his known and intense Americanism of feeling, eager enough, eager in the man as in the boy, to lay hold of every occasion to carry up his country to the loftiest summit of a durable and just glory, and therefore not disinclined to mere enlargement of territory, if the acquisition had been just, prudent, equitable, honorable — this felicity of position enabled him to do what few other men of even equal capacity and patriotism could do; enabled him to quench in the spark, if now the people sustain him, this stupendous conception of madness and of guilt.

If the election of Mr. Polk, then, may annex Texas, and that of Mr. Clay defeat or indefinitely postpone it, what are the *moral* duties of the opponents of annexation, of *all parties?* You are a Democrat, for example, and you would, on every other account than this of Texas, desire the success of the Democratic ticket. You are an Abolitionist, and without expecting the success of your ticket, you would desire to give it the utmost practicable appearance of growth and strength. But can you, in sense and fairness, say, that all the other good which, even on your principles, the election of Mr. Polk, or the exhibition of a growing vote for Mr. Birney, would accomplish, or all the other evils which either of these results would prevent, would compensate for the various and the transcendent evil of annexation? Can you doubt, when you calmly weigh all the other good which you achieve by effecting your object against the mischief you do by annexation, — can you doubt that the least thing which you owe your conscience, your country, the utmost which pride and consistency have a right to exact of you, is *neutrality?* You will not say, for instance, that you believe, that a mere postponement of Democratic ascendency for five years will permanently and irreparably impair the Constitution, and the prosperity of our country, or bereave her of a ray of her glory? She can endure so long, even you do not doubt, the evil of the politics which you disapprove. She can afford to wait so long, even you will admit, for the politics which you prefer. But the evil of annexation is as immediate as irretrievable, and as eternal as it is enormous! Time, terms of presidential office, ages, instead of healing, will but display, will but exasperate, the immedicable wound! Yes, yes! He who, some space hereafter — how long, how brief that space, you may not all taste of death until you know — he who — another Thucydides, another Sismondi — shall observe and shall paint a Union dissolved, the silver cord loosed, the golden bowl broken at the fountain; he who shall observe and shall paint the nation's flag folded mournfully, and laid aside in the silent chamber where the memorials of renown and grace, now dead, are gathered together; who shall record the ferocious factions, the profligate ambition, the hot rivalry, the wars of hate, the truces of treachery, — which shall furnish the matter of the history of alienated States, till one after another burns out and falls from its place on high, — he shall entitle this stained and mournful chapter, the Consequences of Annexation.

But look at this business a little more in its details.

I will not move the question of its effect on American slavery. Whether it will transplant the stricken race from old States to new; whether it will concentrate it on a different, larger or smaller area than it now covers, whether the result of this again would be to increase or diminish its numbers, its sufferings, and its chances of ultimate emancipation — this is a speculation from which I retire. I repeat what I had the honor to say in the debate on the treaty, that the avowed and the direct object of annexation certainly is, to prevent the abolition of slavery on a vast region which would else become free. The immediate effect intended and secured in the first instance, therefore, certainly is the diffusion and increase of slavery. So far we see. So much we know. More than that, no man can be certain that he sees or knows. Whether this is to work an amelioration of the *status* of slavery while it lasts, or to shorten its duration, is in His counsels, "who out of evil still educes good in infinite progression." The means we see are evil. The first effect is evil. The end is uncertain. But, if it were certain and were good, we may not do evil that good may come. While, therefore, I feel it to be my duty distinctly to say, that I would leave to the masters of slaves every guaranty of the Constitution and the Union — the Constitution as it is, the Union as it is, — without which there is no security for you or for them — no, not for a day, — I still controvert the power, I deny the morality, I tremble for the consequences, of annexing an acre of new territory, *for the mere purpose* of diffusing this great evil, this great curse, over a wider surface of American earth. Still less would I, *for such a purpose merely*, lay hold on such a territory as Texas, larger than France, and almost as fair; least of all now, just when the spirit of liberty is hovering over it, in act to descend.

But trace the consequences of annexation on ourselves. First, chief, most comprehensive, and most irretrievable of its evils, *will be its disastrous aspect on the durability of the Union.* Texas, let us suppose, the territory, as territory, is annexed. The war with Mexico is at an end. The valor of the West has triumphed. The debt of the war, the debt of Texas is funded. Time passes. New States carved out of its ample fields knock for admission into the Union. Do you consider that it may cut up into forty as large as Massachusetts? But suppose twenty, fifteen, ten, five, only — apply one after another. Is there a man, out of a mad-house, who does not see that five, three, *one*, such application could not be acted on, and either rejected or granted, without shaking this government to its foundation? Is there a man who does not see that if all the malice and all the ingenuity of Hell were appealed to, to devise one fiery and final trial of the strength of our American feeling, of our fraternal love, of our appreciation of the uses of union, of all our bonds of political brotherhood, it could contrive no ordeal half so dreadful as this? To me this seems so palpable, that I have doubted whether Colonel Benton is not right in his conjecture that *disunion* is the exact object aimed at by some of the movers of annexation. Certainly, in looking over that grim beadroll of South Carolina toasts and dinner-speeches which covers a broadside of the last "Intelligencer," it is quite impossible to resist the conclusion that, as regards some individuals of this body of annexationists, either they are laboring under very treasonable politics, or that their madeira has quite too much brandy in it. I will say, too, of any annexationist, who thinks that because we survived the Missouri question, it would be a pretty thing to move a half-dozen more such questions, that he means to sever the States, or is profoundly ignorant of the way by which they are to be kept together. Does he consider under what totally different circumstances these new Missouri questions would break out, from those which attended the old! Does he consider that the territory of Missouri was already parcel of the United States, and had been so for near twenty years; that, unlike Texas, it had been annexed as part of Louisiana, with no view at all to the diffusion and perpetuation of slavery; but on grounds of policy which the severest moralist, the strictest expounder of the Constitution, the most passionate lover of liberty, might approve; and, therefore, that having been received as a territory *diverso intuitu*, the public sensibility was less shocked by its emergence into a slave State than now it would be, when the end and aim of the original acquisition is slavery, wholly slavery, and nothing but slavery? Does he reflect how vast a change the sentiments of civilization have undergone on that whole subject since eighteen hundred and twenty? Does he remember that in that learning the world is five hundred years older than it was then? Can he not read the gathering signs of the times? Does he not mark the blazing characters traced by the bodiless hand, as in the unfinished picture? Does he not remember what the nations have done, and especially what England has done, within twenty years? Does he not see and feel that in that interval, a public opinion has been generated, has been organized, wholly new, aggressive, intolerant of the sight, intolerant of the cry, of man in chains? Does he not see and feel with what electrical force and speed it strikes from one quarter of the globe to another, and is spreading to enfold the whole civilized world like an atmosphere? Does he think it wise to blow such an atmosphere into a hurricane of flame? Does he really expect to bring his five States into the Union? Is he not sure of failing, and is he not seeking a pretext for flying in a passion; for complaining that territory constitutionally entitled to admission is excluded, and thereupon for retiring from the Union, if he can, himself? However this may be, I say that he means to sever the States, or he is profoundly ignorant, or criminally reckless, of the temper and the policy by which they are to be holden together.

I would have him, who desires adequately to comprehend the probable influence of annexation on the durability of the Union, and its influence on the temper and feelings of the States composing the Union, one towards another, to consider also, whether, over and above these eternal antipathies of liberty and slavery, which it must kindle into inextinguishable flame—whether over and above these, this measure will not appear, and ought not to appear, to be a mere attempt to retain, or to give, to one region and one interest of the republic, an ascendancy, to which, as against the others, it is not entitled? Is there not vast danger, that in this way, it will array States, and regions of States, against each other, on a contest of interest, of business, of relative local power? Will it not be regarded as affrontive to the pride, as a usurpation on the constitutional rights, as menacing to the pockets, of portions of the people of America, as well as an outrage on the sentiment of liberty and the spirit of the age? How can it be defended, on the principles of our political association? The generation of our fathers, who framed the Union, saw as well as we do the great natural regional divisions of the country. They foresaw, as well as we now see, that one of these regions might come to prefer one system of industrial governmental policy, and another to prefer another; that one might incline to free trade, and another to protection; that one might a little more solicitously favor the interests of cotton-planting; another, those of navigation; another, those of general agriculture; another, those of the mechanical and manufacturing arts. They foresaw that in this way, there might grow to be such a thing as a Southern, or a Western, or a Central, or an Eastern administration, — each of which should be a constitutional administration, — and yet, the policy of each might take a tincture from the locality which predominated in its origin and composition. They foresaw, too, that there would come to be, what you would call Southern influence and Western influence and Central influence and Eastern influence; that these would strive together, without rest, for amicable mastery; and they fondly dreamed, or rationally hoped, that out of this opposition and counteraction, "this reciprocal struggle of discordant powers," might flow a harmony that should never end. They foresaw, too, that in the progress of time, the operation of natural causes might change, and change often, all those relations which marked the era of 1789. The young cotton-plant of the South, scarcely known to art or commerce then, might place or might keep the fair and fertile region that alone produced it, for ages, at the head of the confederacy. The exhaustless soil and temperate climate of the West might attract and seat the centre of power there, — on the impurpled prairie, — by the shores of inland oceans. Labor and liberty and culture might sometimes win it back to the rock of Plymouth, to the battle-fields of Bunker Hill and Bennington, to the summits of our granite mountains, to the side of our bridal sea. Of all these alternations, they intended that the people of America, the people of each region of America, should take the risk. Of all these, we are ready to take the risk. Of all these, we always have run the risk. But there is one thing, of which the framers of the Constitution never meant that we or any region should take the risk; and that is, that any region, any interest, should call in *foreign allies to prolong and augment an ascendancy, which, under the action of natural causes, might be imagined to be passing away!* They never meant that the North should call in the Canadas, or Newfoundland, or Greenland, for the sole purpose of giving us more votes in congress for lumber duties, or potash duties, or peltry duties, or fishing bounties, or the protection of wool. They never meant that the South should bring in Mexico, or Cuba, for the sole purpose of voting down the tariff, or maintaining any dominion or any institution, merely because the broad, deep, and resistless stream of time was threatening to bear it silently away. No! No! That is not the Union we came into. That is not the race we set out to run. We agreed to love, honor, and cherish, a certain national identity. We agreed to place ourselves in the power of a certain national identity. We agreed to take our chance, of any constitutional administration of government; any fashion of politics; any predominance of interests, opinions, and institutions, to which that might constitutionally subject us. But we did not agree to love — we did not agree to be governed by — *all creation!* We did not agree that the merchants of Matanzas, the gold miners of Mexico, the logwood cutters of Honduras, the Indian traders of Santa Fe, Coahuila, or Chihuahua, whose "barbarous appellations" we can neither pronounce nor spell, should make our laws. *Non hæc in fœdera veni!* Take care lest the people of all regions, but one, should give the translation, — "We made no such bargain, and we stand no such nonsense."

With these impressions of the evils of annexation, it is difficult to suppress a sentiment of indignation at what would otherwise deserve nothing but ridicule, — the reasons which men give for this measure, who are ashamed or afraid to give the true one. "Texas is so fair and fertile," they say; as if this were not just as good an argument for annexing France — a better one, since France, though not so large, is fairer and more fertile. "It will increase our exportations of cotton and sugar so much" — as if we should not grasp Egypt and Brazil and Hindostan on that reason; as if Colonel Holmes's letter, just published, did not tell us that the consumption of cotton is already stationary in England and France, and that the thing aimed at by South Carolina is not to increase the supply against that demand, but to increase the demand, by increasing English ability to consume; and to do that *by giving to the English manufacturers the market of America.* "The waters of Texas flow into our Mississippi, and therefore it would be *impious* not to reunite what nature had joined." Impious! — as if there would not be exactly the same clamor for it, if its waters flowed into I know not what lake, of fire or of death! "It will consume such unknown quantities of northern manufactures." Unknown, indeed! as if we were quite so verdant as not to be perfectly aware that the precise object of some of the more prominent movers of this business is to get Texan votes to stop your mills, not Texan customers to buy your cloth; that some of those men would be glad to-day, to see you send your children or your horses to England to be shod; that what they notoriously aim at, is not at all an increased ability to consume your *manufactures*, but an increased vote against your tariff, and an easier victory over your labor. "Texas will admit British goods, duty free, or under low duties, and they will be smuggled in such quantities into the United States, as to diminish our revenue, and evade our law of protection!" — a reason which I am sorry to see receive the sanction of a convention of Massachusetts men, of whatever politics, — scarcely satisfactory, I venture to conjecture, to any manly-minded and intelligent member of that body of our Democratic fellow-citizens, who have just made their nomination of governor; as if Texas, starved to death, crushed, paralyzed, for want of money — Texas, almost compelled to let go the sweet and proud boon of national independence, because she has not the financial ability to assert her title to it —

as if she can afford to admit English goods free of duty, or under duties so far below our own as to warrant such an absurd apprehension; as if all Louisiana and Arkansas and Missouri were going to form a great copartnership of smuggling with Yorkshire and Liverpool; as if, on this hypothesis, you must not have Mexico too, for she is under English influence, and will lend a hand to this hopeful scheme of turning the flank of the tariff; and Canada, — which is England herself, — in direct contact with more States than Texas touches; — nay, as if you must not, as a good Alabama Whig said, make up your minds to have "no outside row at all, for the squirrels to eat;" and so strike dead to the water all round, at once, not forgetting your right to a marine league, of say a couple of thousand miles long, to prevent hovering on your coasts.

No, Fellow-citizens, there is no case made for annexation at all. Let him who is making his mind up on that subject, and who desires to do so, not in the small spirit of a narrow and local selfishness, but as a patriot, a Unionist, a statesman, a Christian, a lover of his kind; let him unroll the map of our territory as now we hold it, broad, boundless as an ocean; let him, on that map, observe how that territory spreads itself out from the St. John to the Sabine, eight and twenty hundred miles of coast, and inland to the Rocky Mountains, aye, to the great tranquil sea, more than thirty-five hundred miles — wider than the vast Atlantic, let him mark how it extends through twenty parallels of latitude and thirty of longitude, through all climates and all soils; let him observe, as he descends from North to South, how it successively displays a sample and a rival of all the great productions and all the great productive regions of the globe, — pine forests, like those of Norway; wheat fields outmeasuring those of Poland; pastures ampler and fairer than the shepherds of England and Spain ever saw; cotton, rice, for the world, though Egypt and India were smitten with instant and perpetual sterility; let him reflect that there are limits of a nation's territorial extent, which the laws of nature and of man do not permit them to transcend, beyond which the warm tides of the national heart cannot be propelled, or cannot flow back,— beyond which, unity, identity, nationality, are dissolved and dissipated; and then let him bear in mind that our territory is already three times larger than England, Spain, France, and Italy, all put together, — larger than the Roman Empire in its zenith; and he will be prepared to say whether, with or without the cost of a war; with or without the violation of treaties; with or without the approval of the moral judgments of the world; irrespective of all influence upon his own State, or region of States, he thinks it well to add to this vast region another, forty times larger than Massachusetts, — larger than France, for the purpose of perpetuating slavery, on a soil, certain otherwise, and speedily, to be free. How far wiser, more innocent, more glorious, to improve what we have; to fell our forests; to construct our railroads; to reclaim our earth; to fit it all up to be the spacious and beautiful abode of one harmonious family of Man!

And, now, Fellow-citizens, if these are the evils of annexation; and if the election of Mr. Polk will, or probably may, effect annexation, and that of Mr. Clay will defeat, or postpone it indefinitely, — what, I ask, once more, are the duties of the opponents of this measure, of all parties? What are your moral duties? If the mischiefs of Mr. Polk's administration would agree to take any shape but this; if they were certain not to go beyond four years of disordered currency; interrupted improvements; indiscreet disposition of the lands; unstable and insufficient protection of labor — if this were all, — I would not ask a man — I would not thank a man, to change or to withhold a vote. I know there are Whigs enough, Whigs from their mothers' arms — now and always such, who, without the stimulus of uncompromising hostility to Texas, — without that, — on a calm, habitual estimate of the general politics involved, — could turn Mr. Polk back again upon the convention that discovered him, and win anew the victory of 1840. But I acknowledge an earnest desire to see "this unwarrantable scheme," — as the New York Democrats have pronounced it, — encountered by an opposition approaching to unanimity. I should like to see it shamed out of sight, for at least our day. Why, the wisdom and patriotism of the better South disowns it! See how the old glorious North Carolina has gone into action, and how she has come out of it! Hark to the thunder that announces the risen and triumphant Kentucky! Is this a day for New England to be inactive, or to be distracted? Do you need to be told, what I love not to dwell or touch upon, that if the designs of some of those who would annex Texas could be accomplished; if they could succeed in turning Texas to the account which they dream of; if, by that aid, they could subvert your industrial policy; could retransfer your workshops to Europe; could prevent the industry of America from doing the work of America; could suspend these diversified employments, which develop, discipline, occupy, and reward the universal faculties of this community; which give to every taste and talent the task best suited to it; which give occupation to the strong and weak; the bright and the dull; to both sexes and to all ages, and at all times, — in winter and summer; in wet weather and in dry weather; by daylight and lamplight; to all and each, — "a fair day's wages for a fair day's work;" — if they could strike down the giant arm of Labor helpless to his side — if the politics which you are this day in the field to resist could triumph, — do you not know — that even if the Union were preserved, New England would be cast into provincial, into parochial insignificance? aye, that this New England, the New England that we love; the New England of our fathers and of history — that the places which once knew *this* New England, would know her no more? Having a form to live, she would be dead. Having a form of constitutional life, the strong, soaring, and beautiful spirit would have departed. If the Union were preserved; if the great constellation still held on its journey in the sky, these once jubilant stars of the morning would be silent and dim.

But I would rather show you a loftier motive than any impulse of local interest, or local affection, or local pride. I tell you, Fellow-citizens of all parties, here and everywhere, that if you love the Union as once you did, out of a pure heart, fervently; if neither the small gasconades of nullifiers, nor the gloomy ravings of fanatics have chilled that sweet, cherished and hereditary sentiment; if you yet love to turn away from the croaker who predicts, the hypocrite who desires, the bully who threatens, the arithmetician who computes, the traitor who plots, dissolution of the Union; if you love, turning from these, to go and erect and refresh your spirits by pondering the farewell counsels of Washington, by drawing from that capacious national heart, by retracing that illustrious life, — if you, whoever you are, wherever you are, whatever you are, are for the Union against everybody, for the Union with anybody, for the Union first, last, and always, — then stand by us, and we will stand by you — this once! This once! Another time, on other subjects, we can quarrel, but not now — not now, when the legions throng up to the very walls of the city of David, and the engines thunder at its gate. Another time we can sleep on and take our rest, but not now:

Awake, arise, or be forever fallen!

SPEECH ON THE JUDICIAL TENURE.

DELIVERED IN THE MASSACHUSETTS STATE CONVENTION, JULY 14, 1853.

It is not my purpose to enter at large on the discussion of this important subject. That discussion is exhausted; and if it is not, your patience is; and if not quite so, you have arrived, I apprehend, each to his own conclusion. But as I had the honor to serve on the committee to whom the department of the judiciary was referred, I desire to be indulged in the statement of my opinions, abstaining from any attempt elaborately to enforce them.

I feel no apprehension that this body is about to recommend an election of judges by the people. All appearances; the votes taken; the views disclosed in debate; the demonstrations of important men here, indicate the contrary. I do not mean to say that such a proposition has not been strenuously pressed, and in good faith; yet, for reasons which I will not consume my prescribed hour in detailing, there is no danger of it. Whether members are ready for such a thing or not, they avow, themselves, that they do not think the people are ready.

What I most fear is, that the deliberation may end in limiting the tenure of judicial office to a term of years, seven or ten; that in the result we shall hear it urged, "as we are good enough not to stand out for an election by the people, you ought to be capable of an equal magnanimity, and not stand out for the present term of good behavior;" and thus we shall be forced into a compromise in favor of periodical and frequent appointment, — which shall please everybody a little.

I have the honor to submit to the convention that neither change is needed. Both of them, if experience may in the least degree be relied on, are fraught with evils unnumbered.

To hazard either, would be, not to realize the boast that we found the capitol, in this behalf, brick, and left it marble; but contrarywise, to change its marble to brick.

Sir, in this inquiry what mode of judicial appointment, and what tenure of judicial office, you will recommend to the people, I think that there is but one safe or sensible mode of proceeding, and that is to ascertain what mode of appointment, and what length and condition of tenure, will be most certain, in the long run, guiding ourselves by the lights of all the experience, and all the observation to which we can resort, to bring and keep the best judge upon the bench—the best judge for the ends of his great office. There is no other test. That an election by the people, once a year, or an appointment by the governor once a year, or once in five, or seven, or ten years, will operate to give to an ambitious young lawyer (I refer to no one in this body) a better chance to be made a judge — as the wheel turns round — is no recommendation, and is nothing to the purpose. That this consideration has changed, or framed, the constitutions of some of the States whose example has been pressed on us, I have no doubt. Let it have no weight here. We, at least, hold that offices, and most of all the judicial office, are not made for incumbents or candidates, but for the people; to establish justice; to guarantee security among them. Let us constitute the office in reference to its ends.

I go for that system, if I can find it or help find it, which gives me the highest degree of assurance, taking man as he is, at his strongest and at his weakest, and in the average of the lot of humanity, that there shall be the best judge on every bench of justice in the commonwealth, through its successive generations. That we may safely adopt such a system; that is to say, that we may do so and yet not abridge or impair or endanger our popular polity in the least particular; that we may secure the best possible judge, and yet retain, aye, help to perpetuate and keep in health, the utmost affluence of liberty with which civil life can be maintained, I will attempt to show hereafter. For the present, I ask, how shall we get and keep the best judge for the work of the judge?

Well, Sir, before I can go to that inquiry, I must pause at the outset, and, inverting a little what has been the order of investigation here, ask first, who and what is such a judge; who is that best judge? what is he? how shall we know him? On this point it is impossible that there should be the slightest difference of opinion among us. On some things we differ. Some of you are dissatisfied with this decision or with that. Some of you take exception to this judge or to that. Some of you, more loftily, hold that one way of appointing to the office, or one way of limiting the tenure, is a little more or less monarchical, or a little more or less democratic than another — and so we differ; but I do not believe there is a single member of the convention who will not agree with me in the description I am about to give of the good judge; who will not agree with me that the system which is surest to put and to keep him on the bench, is the true system for Massachusetts.

In the first place, he should be profoundly learned in all the learning of the law, and he must know how to use that learning. Will any one stand up here to deny this? In this day, boastful, glorious for its advancing popular, professional, scientific, and all education, will any one disgrace himself by doubting the necessity of deep and continued studies, and various and thorough attainments, to the bench? He is to know, not merely the law which you make, and the legislature makes, not constitutional and statute law alone, but that other ampler, that boundless jurisprudence, the common law, which the successive generations of the State have silently built up; that old code of freedom which we brought with us in the Mayflower and Arabella, but which in the progress of centuries we have ameliorated and enriched, and adapted wisely to the necessities of a busy, prosperous, and wealthy community, — that he must know. And where to find it? In volumes which you must count by hundreds, by thousands; filling libraries; exacting long labors,—the labors of a life-time, abstracted from business, from politics; but assisted by taking part in an active judicial administration; such labors as produced the wisdom and won the fame of Parsons and Marshall, and Kent and Story, and Holt and Mansfield. If your system of appointment and tenure does not present a motive, a help for such labors and such learning; if it discourages, if it disparages them, in so far it is a failure.

In the next place, he must be a man, not merely upright, not merely honest and well-intentioned, — this of course, — but a man who will not respect persons in judgment. And does not every one here agree to this also? Dismissing, for a moment, all theories about the mode of appointing him, or the time for which he shall hold office, sure I am, we all demand, that as far as human virtue, assisted by the best contrivances of human wisdom, can attain to it, he shall not respect persons in judgment. He shall know nothing about the parties, everything about the case. He shall do everything for justice; nothing for himself; nothing for his friend; nothing for his patron; nothing for his sovereign. If on one side is the executive power and the legislature and the people, — the sources of his honors, the givers of his daily bread, — and on the other an individual nameless and odious, his eye is to see neither, great nor small; attending only to the "trepidations of the balance." If a law is passed by a unanimous legislature, clamored for by the general voice of the public, and a cause is before him on it, in which the whole community is on one side and an individual nameless or odious on the other, and he believes it to be against the Constitution, he must so declare it, — or there is no judge. If Athens comes there to demand that the cup of hemlock be put to the lips of the wisest of men; and he believes that he has not *corrupted the youth, nor omitted to worship the gods of the city, nor introduced new divinities of his own,* he must deliver him, although the thunder light on the unterrified brow.

This, Sir, expresses, by very general illustration, what I mean when I say I would have him no respecter of persons in judgment. How we are to find, and to keep such an one; by what motives; by what helps; whether by popular and frequent election, or by executive designation, and permanence dependent on good conduct in office alone — we are hereafter to inquire; but that we must have him, — that his price is above rubies, — that he is necessary, if justice, if security, if right are necessary for man, — all of you, from the East or West, are, I am sure, unanimous.

And finally, he must possess the perfect confidence of the community, that he bear not the sword in vain. To be honest, to be no respecter of persons, is not yet enough. He must be believed such. I should be glad so far to indulge an old fashioned and cherished professional sentiment as to say, that I would have something of venerable and illustrious attach to his character and function, in the judgment and feelings of the commonwealth. But if this should be thought a little above, or behind the time, I do not fear that I subject myself to the ridicule of any one, when I claim that he be a man towards whom the love and trust and affectionate admiration of the people should flow; not a man perching for a winter and summer in our court-houses, and then gone forever; but one to whose benevolent face, and bland and dignified manners, and firm administration of the whole learning of the law, we become accustomed; whom our eyes anxiously, not in vain, explore when we enter the temple of justice; towards whom our attachment and trust grow even with the growth of his own eminent reputation. I would have him one who might look back from the venerable last years of Mansfield, or Marshall, and recall such testimonies as these to the great and good Judge: —

"The young men saw me, and hid themselves; and the aged arose and stood up.

"The princes refrained talking, and laid their hand upon their mouth.

"When the ear heard me, then it blessed me, and when the eye saw me, it gave witness to me.

"Because I delivered the poor that cried, and the fatherless, and him that had none to help him.

"The blessing of him that was ready to perish came upon me, and I caused the widow's heart to sing for joy.

"I put on righteousness and it clothed me. My judgment was as a robe and a diadem. I was eyes to the blind, and feet was I to the lame.

"I was a father to the poor, and the cause which I knew not, I searched out.

"And I brake the jaws of the wicked, and plucked the spoil out of his teeth."

Give to the community such a judge, and I care little who makes the rest of the constitution, or what party administers it. It will be a free government, I know. Let us repose, secure, under the shade of a learned, impartial, and trusted magistracy, and we need no more.

And now, what system of promotion to office and what tenure of office is surest to produce such a judge? Is it executive appointment during good behavior, with liability, however, to be impeached for good cause, and to be removed by address of the legislature? or is it election by the people, or appointment by the executive for a limited term of years?

To every system there are objections. To every system there are sound, or there are specious objections; objections of theory; objections of fact. Any man's ability is equal to finding, and exaggerating them. What is demanded of us is to compare the good and evil of the different systems, and select the best. Compare them by the test which I have proposed. See which will most certainly give you the judge you need, and adopt that. It may be cavilled at; even as freedom, as religion, as wholesome restraint, as liberty of speech, as the institution and the rights of property, may be cavilled at; but in its fruits, in its product, judged by a long succession of seasons, is its justification and its glory.

Applying then, Sir, this test, I think the existing system is, out of all comparison, the best one. At the hazard of repeating and weakening the views presented yesterday in the impressive and admirable address of my friend for Manchester, [Mr. Dana,] and in the instructive and able arguments of the two gentlemen, [Mr. Greenleaf and Mr. Parker,] whose established professional reputations give to them such just weight with you, I beg to submit, briefly, why I think so.

In the first place, then, it seems to me most clear that the weight of sound general opinion and of the evidence of a trustworthy experience vastly preponderates in favor of it. How the system of popular elections, or of short terms, is actually working now in any one of the States which have recently introduced it; how, still more, it is likely to work there after the influences of the earlier system, the judges which it bred, the habits which it formed, the bars which it trained, have passed away, there is no proof before this Convention deserving one moment's notice. We do not know what is the predominant conviction on this subject, to-day, of those fittest to judge, in any one State. We do know that they cannot yet possibly pronounce on the matter, however close or sagacious their observation. What they have not yet seen, they cannot yet tell.

Certainly the result of all that I have been able to gather is a general and strong opinion against the new system; and in favor of a return, if to return were possible, to that which we are yet proud and privileged to call our own. But the evidence is too loose for the slightest consideration. My friend for Manchester read letters yesterday from persons of high character, as he assured us, in New York, deploring the working of her new system; and I have no doubt that the witnesses are respectable, and the opinions perfectly sound. But other gentlemen guess that very different letters might be obtained, by applying to the right quarters; and the gentleman from New Bedford, [Mr. French,] is quite confident that the people of that great State — the two or three millions — are in favor of the change, because one, if not two, or even three individuals have personally told him so. And, therefore, I say, we have not here now so much evidence of the practical working of their recent systems anywhere, even as far as it has gone, that any honest lawyer would advise his client to risk a hundred dollars on it.

But, on the other hand, are there not most weighty opinions; is there not the testimony of the widest, and longest, and most satisfactory experience, that executive appointment for good behavior yields the best judge?

What is British opinion and British experience to the point? On the question what tenure of office promises the best judge, that opinion and that experience may well be adverted to. Whether a particular mode, or a particular tenure, is consonant to the republican polity of government, we must settle for ourselves. That is another question. Monarchical and aristocratical principles we will not go for to England or elsewhere, nor buy even learning, impartiality, and titles to trust, at the cost of an anti-republican system. But to know how it practically operates to have the judge dependent on the power that appoints him; dependent for his continuance in office; dependent for his restoration to it; dependent on anything or on anybody but his own official good behavior, and that general responsibility to the legislature and public opinion, "that spirit of observation and censure which modifies and controls the whole government" — we may very well consult British or any other experience. The establishment of the tenure of good behavior was a triumph of liberty. It was a triumph of popular liberty against the crown. Before the revolution of 1688, or certainly during the worst years of the Stuart dynasty, the judge held office at the pleasure of the king who appointed him. What was the consequence? He was the tool of the hand that made and unmade him. Scroggs and Jeffreys were but representatives and exemplifications of a system. A whole bench sometimes was packed for the enforcement of some new and more flagrant royal usurpation. Outraged and in mourning by judicial subserviency and judicial murder, England discerned at the revolution that her liberty was incompletely recovered and imperfectly guarded, unless she had judges by whom the boast that an Englishman's house is his castle, should be elevated from a phrase to a fact; from an abstract right to a secure enjoyment, so that, although that house were "a cottage with a thatched roof which all the winds might enter, the king could not." To that end the Act of Settlement made the tenure of good behavior a part of the British Constitution; and a later amendment kept the judicial commission alive, as my friend for Manchester yesterday reminded us, notwithstanding the demise of the sovereign, and perfected the system. Sir, the origin of the tenure of good behavior — marking thus an epoch in the progress of liberty; a victory, so to say, of individuality, of private right, of the household hearth of the cottager, of the "swink'd hedger," over the crown, — and still more, its practical workings in the judicial character and function, may well entitle it to thoughtful treatment. Compare the series of British judges since 1688 with that before, and draw your own conclusions. Not that all this improvement, in impartiality, in character, in titles to confidence and affection is due to the change of tenure; but the soundest historians of that Constitution recognize that that is one element of transcendent importance. With its introduction she began to have a government of laws and not of men.

I come to other testimony, other opinions — the lights of a different experience. There is a certain transaction and document called the Federal Constitution. Consult that. In 1787, that Convention, — assisted by the thoughts and discussions of the five years of peace preceding it, upon the subject of national government, — to be constructed on the republican form of polity — into which were gathered all, or almost all, of our great men, in our age of greatness; men of deep studies, ripe wisdom, illustrious reputation, a high spirit of liberty; that Convention, upon a careful survey of the institutions of the States of America, and of those of other countries, and times past and present; upon, I think we cannot doubt, a profound appreciation of the true functions of a judicial department; of the qualities of a good judge; of the best system of appointment and tenure to obtain them — of the true nature of republican government — and how far, consistently with all its characteristic principles and aims, the people may well determine to appoint to office indirectly, rather than directly, and for good behavior, rather than for a limited term, when the great ends of the stability of justice, and the security of private right prescribe it — incorporated into the great organic law of the Union the principle that judges shall be appointed by the executive power, to hold their office during good behavior.

The gentleman from Lowell [Mr. Butler] last evening observed, referring, I believe, to the time when our Constitution was adopted, that it was long before the age of the steamboat and railroad and magnetic telegraph. It is true; but do we know better than they knew, the nature of man; the nature of the judicial man; what he ought to be to discharge his specific functions aright; how motives, motives of ambition, of fear, of true fame, of high principle, affect him; whether dependence on another power is favorable to independence of the wishes and the will of that other power? Do we know more of republican government and true liberty, and the reconciliations of personal security under due course of law with the loftiest spirit of freedom, than they? Has the advancement of this kind of knowledge quite kept pace with that of the science of the material world?

I wish, Sir, the time of the Convention would allow me to read entire that paper of "The Federalist," the seventy-eighth I believe, in which the principle of the independence of the judiciary is vindicated, and executive appointment, during good behavior, as the means of attaining such independence, is vindicated also. But read it for yourselves. Hear Hamilton and Madison and Jay; for we know from all sources that on this subject that paper expressed the opinions of all, — on the independence of the judiciary, and the means of securing it, — a vast subject adequately illustrated by the highest human intelligence and learning and purity of principle and of public life.

Sir, it is quite a striking reminiscence, that this very paper of "The Federalist," which thus maintains the independence of the judiciary, is among the earliest, perhaps the earliest, enunciation and vindication, in this country, of that great truth, that in the American politics, the written Constitution — which is the record of the popular will — is above the law which is the will of the legislature merely; that if the two are in conflict, the law must yield and the Constitution must rule; and that to determine whether such a conflict exists, and if so, to pronounce the law invalid, is, from the nature of the judicial office, the plain duty of the judge. In that paper this fundamental proposition of our system was first presented, or first elaborately presented, to the American mind; its solidity and its value were established by unanswerable reasoning; and the conclusion that a bench, which was charged with a trust so vast and so delicate, should be as independent as the lot of humanity would admit — of the legislature, of the executive, of the temporary popular majority, whose will it might be required thus to subject to the higher will of the Constitution, was deduced by a moral demonstration. Beware, Sir, lest truths so indissolubly connected — presented together, at first; — adopted together — should die together. Consider whether, when the judge ceases to be independent, the Constitution will not cease to be supreme. If the Constitution does not maintain the judge against the legislature, and the executive, will the judge maintain the Constitution against the legislature and the executive?

What the working of this principle in the national government has been, practically, there is no need to remind you. Recall the series of names, the dead and living, who have illustrated that Bench; advert to the prolonged terms of service of which the country has had the enjoyment; trace the growth of the national jurisprudence; compare it with any other production of American mind or liberty; then trace the progress and tendencies of political opinions, and say if it has not given us stability and security, and yet left our liberties unabridged.

I find a third argument for the principle of executive appointment during good behavior, in this: that it is the existing system of Massachusetts, and it has operated with admirable success. It is not that it exists; it is that it works well. Does it not? Sir, is it for me, or any man, any member of the profession of the law most of all, to rise here, and now, and because our feelings may have sometimes been ruffled or wounded by a passage with the Bench; because we have been dissatisfied by a ruling or a verdict; because our own over-wrought brain may have caused us, in some moment, to become forgetful of ourselves; or because a judge may have misunderstood us, and done us an unintentional injury — is it for us to disclaim the praise, so grateful, so just, which the two eminent gentlemen, one of them formerly of New-Hampshire [Mr. Parker], one of them formerly of Maine [Mr. Greenleaf], speaking without the partiality of native sons, and from observations made by them from a point of view outside of us, and distant from us — have bestowed on our Bench and our law? Theirs are lips from which even flattery were sweet; but when they concur in reminding you with what respect the decisions of this court are consulted by other courts of learning and character; how far their reputation has extended; how familiar is the profession of law with the great names of our judicial history; how important a contribution to American jurisprudence, and even to the general products of American thought, our local code composes — do we not believe that they utter their personal convictions, and that the high compliment is as deserved as it is pleasing?

If it has worked well, it is good. Do men gather grapes of thorns, or figs of thistles? If it has continued to us a long succession of men, deeply learned, wholly impartial, deserving, and clothed with the trust, love, and affectionate admiration of all parties of the community, does it not afford a reasonable ground of inference that there is something in such a mode of appointment, and in such a tenure, *intrinsically*, *philosophically* adapted to insure such a result?

Some criticism has been made on the practical administration of our law, which deserves a passing notice. It requires the less because it has already been replied to.

The gentleman from New-Bedford [Mr. French] told a story of some one, as I understood him, who was about to lose, or had lost, or dared not sue, a note of a hundred dollars, because it would cost him one hundred and fifty dollars to collect it. A very sensible explanation was suggested by the gentleman from Cambridge [Mr. Parker] just now; and I will venture to advise the gentleman from New-Bedford in addition, the very first time he sees his friend, to recommend to him to change his lawyer as quick as he possibly can. As a reason for a change of the Constitution, and the tenure of the judicial office, it seems to me not particularly cogent.

The same gentleman remembers that your Supreme Court decided that the fugitive-slave law is constitutional; and what makes it the more provoking is, he knows the decision was wrong. Well, Sir, so said the gentleman from Manchester [Mr. Dana.] His sentiments concerning that law and its kindred topics do not differ, I suppose, greatly from those of the member from New-Bedford; but what did he add? "I thank God," he said, "that I have the consolation of knowing the decision was made by men as impartial as the lot of humanity would admit; and that if judges were elected by the people of Massachusetts it would hold out no hope of a different decision." He sees in this, therefore, no cause for altering our judicial system on any view of the decision; and I believe — though I have never heard him say or suggest such a thing — that my friend's learning and self-distrust — that "that learned and modest ignorance" which Gibbon recognizes as the last and ripest result of the profound knowledge of a large mind — will lead him to agree with me, that it is *barely possible*, considering how strongly that law excites the feelings, and thus tends to disturb the judgment, considering the vast weight of judicial opinion, and of the opinions of public persons in its favor; recalling the first law on that subject, and the decision in Prigg and Pennsylvania — and who gave the opinion of that Court in that case — that it is *just barely possible* that the gentleman from New-Bedford does not certainly know that the decision was wrong. That he thinks it so, and would lay his life down upon it, the energy and the sentiments of his speech sufficiently indicate. My difficulty, like my friend's for Manchester, is to gather out of all this indignation the least particle of cause for a change of the judicial tenure.

The gentleman from Lowell, [Mr. Butler,] animadverted somewhat, last evening, on the delays attending the publication of the reports of decisions. I had made some inquiry concerning the facts; but have been completely anticipated in all I would have said by the gentleman from Cambridge [Mr. Parker]. To me his explanation seems perfectly satisfactory; and in no view of such a question would the good sense of the gentleman from Lowell, I think, deem it a reason for so vast an innovation as this, on the existing and ancient system.

To another portion of that learned gentleman's speech, I have a word to say, in all frankness and all candor. Placing his hand on his heart, he appealed, with great emphasis of manner, to the honor of the bar, as represented in this Convention, whether we had not heard complaints of particular acts of some of our judges? Sir, that appeal is entitled to a frank and honorable response. I have known and loved many; many men; many women — of the living and the dead — of the purest and noblest of earth or skies — but I never knew one — I never heard of one — if conspicuous enough to attract a considerable observation, whom the breath of calumny, or of sarcasm, always wholly spared. Did the learned gentleman ever know one? "Be thou as chaste as ice, as pure as snow, thou shalt not escape calumny."

And does he expect that in a profession like ours; overtasked; disappointed in the results of causes; eager for victory; mortified by unexpected defeat; misunderstanding or failing to appreciate the evidence; the court sometimes itself jaded and mistaken — that we shall not often hear, and often say, hasty and harsh things of a judge? I have heard such of every judge I ever saw — however revered in his general character. Did Mansfield escape? Did Marshall? Did Parsons? Did Story? What does it come to as an argument against the particular judge; still more as an argument against a judicial system? Are we to go on altering the mode of appointment, and the tenure, till you get a *corps* of judges, against no one of which, no one ever hears anybody say anything?

But, Sir, I am to answer the learned gentleman's appeal a little farther; and I say upon my honor, that I believe it the general opinion of the bar to-day, its general opinion ever since I entered the profession, that our system of appointment and tenure, has operated perfectly well; that the benches and courts have been, and are, learned, impartial, entitled to trust; and that there is not one member of either who, taking his judicial character and life as a whole is not eminently, or adequately, qualified for his place.

Turn, now, from the existing system to the substitute which is offered; and see, if you can, how that will work.

It is not enough to take little objections to that system, in its general working so satisfactory. He who would change it is bound to show that what he proposes in place of it will do better. To this, I say, it is all a sheer conjectural speculation, yet we see and know enough to warrant the most gloomy apprehensions.

Consider first, for a moment, the motion immediately pending; which proposes the election of judges by the people. I said in the outset, I have no fear of your sustaining it; but for the development of a full view of the general subject, it will justify some attention.

Gentlemen begin by asking if we are afraid to trust the people. Well, Sir, that is a very cunning question; very cunning indeed. Answer it as you will, they think they have you. If you answer, Yes, — that you are afraid to trust the people, — then they cry out, He blasphemeth. If you answer, No,— that you are not afraid to trust them, — then they reply, Why not permit them to choose their judges?

Sir, this dilemma creates no difficulty. I might evade it by saying that however ready and however habituated to trust the people, it does not follow that we should desert a system which has succeeded eminently, to see if another will not succeed as well. If the indirect appointment by the people; appointment through the governor whom they choose, has supplied a succession of excellent judges, why should I trouble them with the direct appointment — however well they might conduct it — which they have not solicited; which they have not expected; about which you dared not open your mouths during the discussion concerning the call of a Convention; in regard to which you gave them — it is more correct to say — every reason to believe you should make no change whatever? Get a Convention by a pledge to the people not to make judges elective — and then tell us we shall make them elective, on pain of being denounced afraid to trust the people! Will such flattery be accepted in atonement for such deception?

But I prefer meeting this dilemma in another way. It is a question certainly of some nicety to determine what offices the public good prescribes should be filled by a direct election of the people; and what should be filled by the appointment of others, as the governor and council, chosen by the people. On the best reflection I have been able to give it, this seems to me a safe general proposition. If the nature of the office be such, the qualifications which it demands, and the stage on which they are to be displayed be such, that the people can judge of those qualifications as well as their agents; and if, still farther, the nature of the office be such that the tremendous ordeal of a severely contested popular election will not in any degree do it injury, — will not deter learned men, if the office needs learning, from aspiring to it; will not tend to make the successful candidate a respecter of persons, if the office requires that he should not be; will not tend to weaken the confidence and trust, and affectionate admiration of the community towards him, if the office requires that such be the sentiments with which he should be regarded, — then the people should choose by direct election. If, on the other hand, from the kind of qualifications demanded, and the place where their display is to be made, an agent of the people, chosen by them for that purpose, can judge of the qualifications better than they can; or if from its nature it demands learning, and the terrors of a party canvass drive learning from the field; or if it demands impartiality and general confidence, and the successful candidate of a party is less likely to possess either, — then the indirect appointment by the people, that is, appointment by their agent, is wisest.

Let me illustrate this test by reference to some proceedings of the Convention. You have already made certain offices elective, which heretofore were filled by executive appointment — such as those of sheriffs; the attorney-general; district-attorneys, and others.

Now, within the test just indicated, I do not know why these offices may not be filled by election, if anybody has a fancy for it. Take the case of the sheriff, for instance. He requires energy, courtesy, promptness, — qualities pertaining to character rather, and manner, displayed, so to speak, in the open air; palpable, capable of easy and public appreciation. Besides, his is an office which the freedom and violence of popular elections do not greatly harm. There are certain specific duties to do for a compensation, and if these are well done, it does not much signify what a minority or what anybody thinks of him.

Totally unlike this in all things is the case of the judge. In the first place, the qualities which fit him for the office are quite peculiar; less palpable, less salient, so to speak, less easily and accurately appreciated by cursory and general notice. They are an uncommon, recondite, and difficult learning, and they are a certain power and turn of mind and cast of character, which, until they come actually, and for a considerable length of time, and in many varieties of circumstances, to be displayed upon the bench itself, may be almost unremarked but by near and professional observers. What the public chiefly see is the effective advocate; him their first thought would be perhaps to make their candidate for judge; yet experience has proved that the best advocate is not necessarily the best judge, — that the two functions exact diverse qualifications, and that brilliant success in one holds out no certain promise of success in the other. A popular election would have been very likely to raise Erskine or Curran to the bench, if they had selected the situation; but it seems quite certain that one failed as Lord Chancellor, and the other as Master of the Rolls, and pretty remarkably, too, considering their extraordinary abilities in the conduct of causes of fact at the bar. I have supposed that Lord Abinger, who, as Mr. Scarlett, won more verdicts than any man in England, did not conspicuously succeed in the exchequer; and that, on the other hand, Lord Tenterden, to name no more, raised to the bench from no practice at all, or none of which the public had seen anything, became, by the fortunate possession of the specific judicial nature, among the most eminent who have presided on it. The truth is, the selection of a judge is a little like that of a professor of the higher mathematics or of intellectual philosophy. Intimate knowledge of the candidate will detect the presence or the absence of the *specialty* demanded; the kind of knowledge of him which the community may be expected to gain, will not. On this point I submit to the honor and candor of the bar in this body an illustration which is worth considering. It often happens that our clients propose, or that we propose, to associate other counsel with us to aid in presenting the cause to the jury. In such cases we expect and desire them to select their man, and almost always we think the selection a good one. But it sometimes happens, too, that it is decided to submit the cause to a lawyer as a referee. And then do we expect or wish our client to select the referee? Certainly never. That we know we can do better than he, because better than he we appreciate the legal aspects of the case, and the kind of mind which is required to meet them; and we should betray the client, sacrifice the cause, and shamefully neglect a clear duty, if we did not insist on his permitting us, for the protection of his interests intrusted to our care, to appoint his judge. Always he also desires us for his sake to do it. And now, that which we would not advise the single client to do for himself, shall we advise the whole body of our clients to do for themselves?

But this is, by no means, the principal objection to making this kind of office elective. Consider, beyond all this, how the office itself is to be affected; its dignity; its just weight; the kind of men who will fill it; their learning; their firmness; their hold on the general confidence — how will these be affected? Who will make the judge? At present he is appointed by a governor, his council concurring, in whom a majority of the whole people have expressed their trust by electing him, and to whom the minority have no objection but his politics; acting under a direct personal responsibility to public opinion; possessing the best conceivable means to ascertain, if he does not know, by inquiry at the right sources, who does, and who does not possess the character of mind and qualities demanded. By such a governor he is appointed; and then afterward he is perfectly independent of him. And how well the appointing power in all hands has done its work, let our judicial annals tell. But, under an elective system, who will make the judge? The young lawyer leaders in the caucus of the prevailing party will make him. Will they not? Each party is to nominate for the office, if the people are to vote for it, is it not? You know it must be so. How will they nominate? In the great State caucus, of course, as they nominate for governor. On whom will the judicial nominations be devolved? On the professional members of the caucus, of course. Who will they be? Young, ambitious lawyers, very able, possibly, and very deserving; but not selected by a majority of the whole people, nor by a majority, perhaps, of their own towns, to do anything so important and responsible as to make a judge, — these will nominate him. The party, unless the case is very scandalous indeed, will sustain its regular nominations; and thus practically a handful of caucus leaders, under this system, will appoint the judges of Massachusetts. This is bad enough; because we ought to know who it is that elevates men to an office so important — we ought to have some control over the nominating power — and of these caucus leaders we know nothing; and because, also, they will have motives to nominate altogether irrespective of the fitness of the nominee for the place, on which no governor of this Commonwealth, of any party, has ever acted. This is bad enough. But it is not all, nor the worst. Trace it onwards. So nominated, the candidate is put through a violent election; abused by the press, abused on the stump, charged ten thousand times over with being very little of a lawyer, and a good deal of a knave or boor; and after being tossed on this kind of blanket for some uneasy months, is chosen by a majority of ten votes out of a hundred thousand, and comes into court, breathless, terrified, with perspiration in drops on his brow, wondering how he ever got there, to take his seat on the bench. And in the very first cause he tries, he sees on one side the counsel who procured his nomination in caucus, and has defended him by pen and tongue before the people, and on the other, the most prominent of his assailants; one who has been denying his talents, denying his learning, denying his integrity, denying him every judicial quality, and every quality that may define a good man, before half the counties in the State. Is not this about as infallible a recipe as you could wish to make a judge a respecter of persons? Will it not inevitably load him with the suspicion of partiality, whether he deserves it or not? Is it happily calculated altogether to fix on him the love, trust, and affectionate admiration of the general community with which you agree he ought to be clothed, as with a robe, or he fills his great office in vain? Who does not shrink from such temptation to be partial? Who does not shrink from the suspicion of being thought so? What studious and learned man, of a true self-respect, fitted the most preëminently for the magistracy by these very qualities and tastes, would subject himself to an ordeal so coarse, and so inappropriate, for the chance of getting to a position where no human purity or ability could assure him a trial by his merits?

But you will not make judges elective. What is to be feared is, that instead of attempting a larger mischief, in which you must fail, you will attempt a smaller, in which you may succeed. You will not change the system which has worked so well, very much, you say, but you will change it some; and therefore you will continue to appoint by the governor. But instead of appointing during good behavior, subject to impeachment, and subject to removal by the legislature, you will appoint him for a term of years — five years, seven years, ten years.

Well, Sir, without repeating that no reason for any change is shown, and that no manner of evidence has been produced to prove that this project of executive appointment, for limited terms, has ever succeeded anywhere — pretty important considerations for thoughtful persons, likely to weigh much with the people — there are two objections to this system, which ought, in my judgment, to put it out of every head. And in the first place, it will assuredly operate to keep the ablest men from the bench. You all agree that you would have there the ablest man whom three thousand dollars or twenty-one hundred dollars per annum, will command. The problem is, one part of the problem is, how shall we get the best judge for that money?

And now, if my opinion is worth anything, I desire to express it with all possible confidence, that this change of tenure will infallibly reduce the rate of men whom you will have on the bench. Not every one, in all respects equal to it, can afford it now. It has been said, and is notorious, that it is offered and rejected. The consideration of its permanence is the decisive one in its favor, whoever accepts it. The salary is inadequate, but if it is certain, certain as good judicial behavior — it ought not to be more so — it may be thought enough. Deprive it of that moral makeweight, and it is nothing. Why should a lawyer, accumulating, or living, by his practice, look at a judgeship of ten years? What does he see and fear? At the end of that time he is to descend from the bench, a man forty-five or fifty, or sixty years of age, without a dollar, or certainly requiring some means of increasing his income. Every old client is lost by this time, and he is to begin life as he began it twenty or thirty years before. Not quite so, even. Then he was young, energetic, and sanguine. He is older now, and is less disposed to the contentious efforts of the law. More than that, he is less equal to them for another reason than the want of youth. If he has, during the full term of ten years, been good for anything; if he has been "a judge, altogether a judge, and nothing but a judge," then his whole intellectual character and habits will have undergone a change, itself incapable of change. He will have grown out of the lawyer into the magistrate. He will have put off the gown of the bar, and have assumed the more graceful and reverend ermine of the bench. The mental habits, the mental faults of the advocate, the faults ascribed by satire to the advocate, the faults or habits of his character, the zeal, the constant energy bestowed on all causes alike; the tendencies, and the power to aggravate and intensify one side of a thesis, and forget or allow inadequate importance to the other — these, if he has been a good judge, or tried his best to be a good judge for ten years, he has lost, he has conquered, and has acquired in their place that calmer and that fairer capacity to see the thing, fact, or law, just as it is. Thus changed, it will be painful to attempt to recover the advocate again; it will be impracticable, if it is attempted. To regain business, he must find new clients; to find or keep them, he must make himself over again. Accordingly, how rare are the cases where any man above the age of forty, after having served ten years on the bench, seeking to cultivate judicial habits, and win a true judicial fame, has returned to a full business at the bar. I never heard of one. Such a retired judge may act as a referee. He may engage somewhat in chamber practice, as it is called, though the result of all my observation has been, that unless he *can attend his opinions through court;* can there explain and defend them; *unless he can keep his hand so much in that he feels and knows at all times which way the judicial mind is tending on the open questions of the law* — his chamber practice holds out a pretty slender promise for the decline of a life unprovided for. He who would be a lawyer, must unite the study of the books and the daily practice of the courts, or his very learning will lead him astray.

I have been amused at the excellent reasons given to show why an able man, at the head of the bar, in full practice, forty years of age, a growing family and no property, should just as soon accept a judgeship for ten years as during good behavior. Some say a judge never lives but ten years on the bench — or thirteen at the outside — anyhow. They show statistics for it. They propose, therefore, to go to such a man and tender him the situation. He will inconsiderately answer that he should like the bench; thinks he could do something for the law; should rejoice to give his life to it; but that the prospect of coming off at fifty, and going back to begin battling it again with "these younger strengths," is too dreary, and he must decline. "Bless you," say the gentlemen, "don't trouble yourself about that, if that is all. You can't live but thirteen years, the best way you can fix it. Here is the secretary's report — with a printed list as long as a Harvard College catalogue — putting that out of all question!" Do you think this will persuade him? Does he expect to die in ten years? Who does so? Did the names on these statistics?

Others guess that the ten-years judge will be reappointed, if he behaves well. But unless he is a very weak man indeed, will he rely on that? Who will assure it to him? Does he not know enough of life to know how easy it will be, after he has served the State, the law, his conscience and his God for the stipulated term; after the performance of his duty has made this ambitious young lawyer or that powerful client his enemy for life; after having thus stood in the way of a greedy competitor too long — how easy it will be to bring influences to bear on a new governor, just come in at the head of a flushed and eager party, to allow the old judge's commission to expire, and appoint the right sort of a man in his place? Does he not know how easy it will be to say, "Yes, he is a good judge enough, but no better than a dozen others who have just put you in power; there are advantages in seating a man on the bench who is fresh from the bar; there is no injustice to the incumbent—didn't he know that he ran this risk?" Too well he knows it, Sir, to be tickled by the chance of "finding the doom of man reversed for him," and he will reject the offer.

Herein is great and certain evil. How you can disregard it—how you can fail to appreciate what an obvious piece of good economy it is; economy worthy of statesmen—binding on your conscience; to so construct your system as to gain for the bench the best man whom three thousand dollars per annum can be made to command, passes all comprehension. Surely you will not reply that there "will be enough others to take it." If the tendency of what you propose is appreciably to lessen the chances of obtaining the best, is it any excuse to say that fools will rush in where others will not tread?

But there is still another difficulty. He who does accept it, and performs as an hireling his day, will not only be an ordinary man comparatively, at the start, but he holds a place, and is subjected to influences, under which it will be impossible to maintain impartiality, and the reputation of impartiality; impossible to earn and keep that trust, and confidence, and affectionate and respectful regard, which the judge must have, or he is but half a judge.

I have sometimes thought that the tenure of good behavior has one effect a little like that which is produced by making the marriage tie indissoluble. If the "contract which renovates the world" were at the pleasure of both parties, they would sometimes, often, quarrel and bring about a dissolution in a month. But they know they have embarked for life—for good and ill—for better and worse; and they bear with one another; they excuse one another—they help one another—they make each other to be that which their eyes and their hearts desire. A little so in the relation of the judge to the bar, and the community. You want to invest him with honor, love, and confidence. If every time when he rules on a piece of evidence, or charges the jury, a young lawyer can say, half aloud in the bar, or his disappointed client can go to the next tavern to say, "My good fellow, we will have you down here in a year or two—you shall answer for this—make the most of your time" — and so forth; is it favorable to the culture of such sentiments? Does it tend to beget that state of mind towards him in the community which prompts "the ear to bless him, and the eye to give witness to him?" Does it tend in him to "ripen that dignity of disposition which grows with the growth of an illustrious reputation; and becomes a sort of pledge to the public for security?" Show to the bar, and to the people, a judge by whom justice is to be dispensed for a life-time, and all become mutually coöperative, respectful, and attached.

And still further. This ten-years judge of yours is placed in a situation where he is in extreme danger of feeling, and of being suspected of feeling so anxious a desire to secure his re-appointment, as to detract, justly or unjustly, somewhat from that confidence in him without which there is no judge. It is easy for the gentleman from Abington [Mr. Keyes] to feel and express with his habitual energy, indignation at the craven spirit which could stoop to do anything to prolong his term of office. It is easy, but is it to the purpose? All systems of judicial appointment and tenure suppose the judge to be a mortal man, after all; and all of them that are wise, and well tried, aim to fortify, guard, and help that which his Maker has left fallible and infirm. To inveigh against the lot of humanity is idle. Our business is to make the best of it; to assist its weakness; make the most of its virtue; by no means, by no means to lead it into any manner of temptation. He censures God, I have heard, who quarrels with the imperfections of man. Do you not, however, tempt the judge, as his last years are coming, to cast about for re-appointment; to favor a little more this important party, or this important counsel, by whom the patronage of the future is to be dispensed? He will desire to keep his place, will he not? You have disqualified him for the more active practice of his profession. He needs its remuneration. Those whom he loves depend on it. The man who can give it, or withhold it, is before him for what he calls justice; on the other side is a stranger without a name. Have you placed him in no peril? Have you so framed your system, as to do all that human wisdom can do — to "secure a trial as impartial as the lot of humanity will admit?" If not, are we quite equal to the great work we have taken in hand?

There are two or three more general observations with which I leave the subject, which the pressure on your time, and my own state of health, unfit me for thoroughly discussing.

In constructing our judicial system, it seems to me not unwise so to do it, that it shall rather operate, if possible, to induce young lawyers to aspire to the honors of the bench, not by means of party politics, but by devoting themselves to the still and deep studies of this glorious science of the law. A republic, it is said, is one great scramble for office, from the highest to the lowest in the State. The tendencies certainly are to make every place a spoil for the victor, and to present to abilities and ambition *active service in the ranks of party*, *victory under the banner*, *and by the warfare of party*, as the quickest and easiest means of winning every one. How full of danger to justice, and to security, and to liberty, are such tendencies, I cannot here and now pause to consider. These very changes of the judicial system, facilitating the chances of getting on the bench by party merits and party titles, will give strength incalculable to such tendencies. How much wiser to leave it as now, were it only to present motives to the better youth of the profession to withdraw from a too active and vehement political life; to conceive, in the solitude of their libraries, the idea of a great judicial fame and usefulness; and by profound study and the manly practice of the profession alone seek to realize it; to so prepare themselves, in mind, attainments, character, to become judges by being lawyers only, that when the ermine should rest on them, it should find, as was said of Jay — as might be said of more than one on the bench of both our Courts, of one trained by our system for the bench of the Supreme National Court — it should find "nothing that was not whiter than itself."

I do not know how far it is needful to take notice of an objection by the gentleman from Fall River [Mr. Hooper,] and less or more by others, to the existing system on the ground that it is monarchical, or anti-republican, or somehow inconsistent with our general theories of liberty. He has dwelt a good deal on it; he says we might just as well appoint a governor or a representative for life, or good behavior, as a judge; that it is fatally incompatible with our frame of government, and the great principles on which it reposes. One word to this.

It seems to me that such an argument forgets that our political system, while it is purely and intensely republican, within all theories, aims to accomplish a twofold object, to wit: liberty and security. To accomplish this twofold object we have established a twofold set of institutions and instrumentalities; some of them designed to develop and give utterance to one; some of them designed to provide permanently and constantly for the other; some of them designed to bring out the popular will in its utmost intensity of utterance; some of them designed to secure life, and liberty, and character, and happiness, and property, and equal and exact justice, against all will, and against all power. These institutions and instrumentalities in their immediate mechanism and workings, are as distinct and diverse, one from the other, as they are in their offices, and in their ends. But each one is the more perfect for the separation; and the aggregate result is our own Massachusetts.

Thus, in the law-making department, and in the whole department of elections to office of those who make and those who execute the law, you give the utmost assistance to the expression of liberty. You give the choice to the people. You make it an annual choice; you give it to the majority; you make, moreover, a free press; you privilege debate; you give freedom to worship God according only to the dictates of the individual conscience. These are the mansions of liberty; here are her arms, and here her chariot. In these institutions we provide for her; we testify our devotion to her; we show forth how good and how gracious she is — what energies she kindles; what happiness she scatters; what virtues, what talents wait on her — vivifying every atom, living in every nerve, beating in every pulsation.

But to the end that one man, that the majority, may not deprive any of life, liberty, property, the opportunity of seeking happiness, there are institutions of security. There is a Constitution to control the government. There is a separation of departments of government. There is a judiciary to interpret and administer the laws, "that every man may find his *security* therein." And in constituting these provisions for security, you may have regard mainly to the specific and separate objects which they have in view. You may very fitly appoint few judges only. You may very fitly so appoint them as to secure learning, impartiality, the love and confidence of the State; because thus best they will accomplish the sole ends for which they are created at all. If to those ends, too, it has been found, in the long run, as human nature is, that it is better to give them a tenure of good behavior, you may do so without departing in the least degree from either of the two great objects of our political system. You promote one of them directly by doing so. You do it without outrage on the other. Your security is greater; your liberty is not less. You assign to liberty her place, her stage, her emotions, her ceremonies; you assign to law and justice theirs. The stage, the emotions, the visible presence of liberty, are in the mass meeting; the procession by torchlight; at the polls; in the halls of legislation; in the voices of the press; in the freedom of political speech; in the energy, intelligence and hope, which pervade the mass; in the silent, unreturning tide of progression. But there is another apartment, smaller, humbler, more quiet, down in the basement story of our capitol — appropriated to justice, to security, to reason, to restraint; where there is no respect of persons; where there is no high nor low, no strong nor weak; where will is nothing, and power is nothing, and numbers are nothing — and all are equal, and all secure, before the law. Is it a sound objection to your system, that in that apartment you do not find the symbols, the cap, the flag of freedom? Is it any objection to a court-room that you cannot hold a mass meeting in it, while a trial is proceeding? Is liberty abridged, because the procession returning by torchlight, from celebrating anticipated or actual party victory, cannot pull down a half-dozen houses of the opposition with impunity; and because its leaders awake from the intoxications of her *saturnalia* to find themselves in jail for a riot? *Is it any objection that every object of the political system is not equally provided for in every part of it?* No, Sir. "Everything in its place, and a place for everything!" *If the result is an aggregate of social and political perfection, absolute security combined with as much liberty as you can live in*, that is the state for you! Thank God for that; let the flag wave over it; die for it!

One word only, further, and I leave this subject. It has been maintained, with great force of argument, by my friend for Manchester, that there is no call by the people for any change of the judicial system. Certainly there is no proof of such a call. The documentary history of the Convention utterly disproves it. But that topic is exhausted. I wished to add only, that my own observation, as far as it has gone, disproves it too. I have lost a good many causes, first and last; and I hope to try, and expect to lose, a good many more; but I never heard a client in my life, however dissatisfied with the verdict, or the charge, say a word about changing the tenure of the judicial office. I greatly doubt, if I have heard as many as three express themselves dissatisfied with the judge; though times without number they have regretted that he found himself compelled to go against them. My own tenure I have often thought in danger — but I am yet to see the first client who expressed a thought of meddling with that of the Court. What is true of those clients, is true of the whole people of Massachusetts. Sir, that people have two traits of character — just as our political system in which that character is shown forth, has two great ends. They love liberty; that is one trait. They love it, and they possess it to their hearts' content. Free as storms to-day do they not know it, and feel it — every one of them, from the sea to the Green Mountains? But there is another side to their character; and that is the old Anglo-Saxon instinct of property; the rational, and the creditable desire to be secure in life, in reputation, in the earnings of daily labor, in the little all which makes up the treasures, and the dear charities of the humblest home; the desire to feel certain when they come to die that the last will shall be kept, the smallest legacy of affection shall reach its object, although the giver is in his grave; this desire, and the sound sense to know that a learned, impartial, and honored judiciary is the only means of having it indulged. They have nothing timorous in them, as touching the largest liberty. They rather like the exhilaration of crowding sail on the noble old ship, and giving her to scud away before a fourteen-knot breeze; but they know, too, that if the storm comes on to blow; and the masts go overboard; and the gun-deck is rolled under water; and the lee shore, edged with foam, thunders under her stern, that the sheet-anchor and best bower then are everything! Give them good ground-tackle, and they will carry her round the world, and back again, till there shall be no more sea.

SPEECH DELIVERED AT THE CONSTITUTIONAL MEETING IN FANEUIL HALL.

NOVEMBER 26, 1850.

["The Citizens of Boston and its vicinity, who reverence the Constitution of the United States; who wish to discountenance a spirit of disobedience to the laws of the land, and refer all questions arising under those laws to the proper tribunals; who would regard with disfavor all further popular agitation of subjects which endanger the peace and harmony of the Union, and who deem the preservation of the Union the paramount duty of every citizen, are requested to meet and express their sentiments on the present posture of public affairs, in Faneuil Hall, Nov. 26, 1850, at 4 o'clock, P. M."

The above call having been published in the newspapers, and posted up in the "Merchants' Reading Room" for some days, received the signatures of about five thousand citizens of Massachusetts, and the meeting was convened agreeably to the request therein expressed.

At a few minutes before four o'clock, the Committee of Arrangements came in, and were received with loud cheers. At four o'clock, precisely, Thomas B. Curtis, Esq., mounted the rostrum, and nominated for President John C. Warren.

A series of resolutions having been read, the meeting was addressed by B. R. Curtis, B. F. Hallett, and S. D. Bradford; after which Mr. Choate spoke as follows:]

I FEEL it, fellow-citizens, to be quite needless, for any purpose of affecting your votes now, or your judgment and acts for the future, that I should add a word to the resolutions before you, and to the very able addresses by which they have been explained and enforced. All that I would have said has been better said. In all that I would have suggested, this great assembly, so true and ample a representation of the sobriety, and principle, and business, and patriotism of this city and its vicinity, — if I may judge from the manner in which you have responded to the sentiments of preceding speakers, — has far outrun me. In all that I had felt and reflected on the supreme importance of this deliberation, on the reality and urgency of the peril, on the indispensable necessity which exists, that an effort be made, and made at once, combining the best counsels, and the wisest and most decisive action of the community — an effort to turn away men's thoughts from those things which concern this part or that part, to those which concern the whole of our America — to turn away men's solicitude about the small politics that shall give a State administration this year to one set, and the next year to another set, and fix it on the grander politics by which a nation is to be held together — to turn away men's hearts from loving one brother of the national household, and hating and reviling another, to that larger, juster and wiser affection which folds the whole household to its bosom — to turn away men's conscience and sense of moral obligation from the morbid and mad pursuit of a single duty, and indulgence of a single sentiment, to the practical ethics in which all duties are recognized, by which all duties are reconciled, and adjusted, and subordinated, according to their rank, by which the sacredness of compacts is holden to be as real as the virtue of compassion, and the supremacy of the law declared as absolute as the luxury of a tear is felt to be sweet — to turn away men's eyes from the glare of the lights of a philanthropy — they call it philanthropy — some of whose ends may be specious, but whose means are bad faith, abusive speech, ferocity of temper, and resistance to law; and whose fruit, if it ripens to fruit, will be woes unnumbered to bond and free, — to turn all eyes from the glitter of such light to the steady and unalterable glory of that wisdom, that justice, and that best philanthropy under which the States of America have been enabled and may still be enabled to live together in peace, and grow together into the nature of one people, — in all that I had felt and reflected on these things, you have outrun my warmest feelings and my best thoughts. What remains, then, but that I congratulate you on at least this auspicious indication, and take my leave? One or two suggestions, however, you will pardon to the peculiarity of the times.

I concur then, *first*, Fellow-citizens, with one of the resolutions, in expressing my sincerest conviction that the Union is in extreme peril this day. Some good and wise men, I know, do not see this; and some not quite so good or wise, deny that they see it. I know very well that to sound a false alarm is a shallow and contemptible thing. But I know, also, that too much precaution is safer than too little, and I believe that less than the utmost is too little now. Better, it is said, to be ridiculed for too much care, than to be ruined by too confident a security. I have then a profound conviction, that the Union is yet in danger. It is true that it has passed through one peril within the last few months, — such a peril, that the future historian of America will pause with astonishment and terror when he comes to record it. The sobriety of the historic style will rise to eloquence, — to pious ejaculation, — to thanksgivings to Almighty God, — as he sketches that scene and the virtues that triumphed in it. "Honor and praise," will he exclaim, "to the eminent men of all parties — to Clay, to Cass, to Foote, to Dickinson, to Webster — who rose that day to the measure of a true greatness, — who remembered that they had a country to preserve as well as a local constituency to gratify, — who laid all the wealth, and all the hopes of illustrious lives on the altar of a hazardous patriotism, — who reckoned all the sweets of a present popularity for nothing in comparison of that more exceeding weight of glory which follows him who seeks to compose an agitated and save a sinking land."

That night is passed, and that peril; and yet it is still night, and there is peril still. And what do I mean by this? I believe, and rejoice to believe, that the general judgment of the people is yet sound on this transcendent subject. But I will tell you where I think the danger lies. It is, that while the people sleep, politicians and philanthropists of the legislative hall—the stump, and the press—will talk and write us out of our Union. Yes — while you sleep, while the merchant is loading his ships, and the farmer is gathering his harvests, and the music of the hammer and shuttle wake around, and we are all steeped in the enjoyment of that vast and various good which a common government places within our reach—there are influences that never sleep, and which are creating and diffusing a PUBLIC OPINION, in whose hot and poisoned breath, before we yet perceive our evil plight, this Union may melt as frost-work in the sun. Do we sufficiently appreciate how omnipotent is opinion in the matter of all government? Do we consider especially in how true a sense it is the creator, must be the upholder, and may be the destroyer of our united government? Do we often enough advert to the distinction, that while our State governments *must* exist almost of necessity, and with no effort from within or without, the UNION of the States is a totally different creation — more delicate, more artificial, more recent, far more truly a mere production of the reason and the will — standing in far more need of an ever-surrounding care, to preserve and repair it, and urge it along its highway? Do we reflect that while the people of Massachusetts, for example, are in all senses one — not *E Pluribus Unum* — but one single and uncompounded substance, so to speak — and while every influence that can possibly help to hold a social existence together — identity of interest; closeness of kindred; contiguity of place; old habit; the ten thousand opportunities of daily intercourse; everything — is operating to hold such a State together, so that it must exist whether we will or not, and "cannot, but by annihilating, die"—the people of America compose a totally different community — a community miscellaneous and widely scattered; that they are many States, not one State, or if one, made up of many which still coexist; that numerous influences of vast energy, influences of situation, of political creeds, of employments, of supposed or real diversities of material interest, tend evermore to draw them asunder; and that is not, as in a single State, that instinct, custom, a long antiquity, closeness of kindred, immediate contiguity, the personal intercourse of daily life and the like, come in to make and consolidate the grand incorporation, whether we will or not; but that is to be accomplished by carefully cultivated and acquired habits and states of feeling; by an enlightened discernment of great interests, embracing a continent and a future age; by a voluntary determination to love, honor, and cherish, by mutual tolerance, by mutual indulgence of one another's peculiarities, by the most politic and careful withdrawal of our attention from the offensive particulars in which we differ, and by the most assiduous development and appreciation, and contemplation of those things wherein we are alike — do we reflect as we ought, that it is only thus — by varieties of expedients, by a prolonged and voluntary educational process, that the fine and strong spirit of NATIONALITY may be made to penetrate and animate the scarcely congruous mass — and the full tide of American feeling to fill the mighty heart?

I have sometimes thought that the States in our system may be compared to the primordial particles of matter, indivisible, indestructible, impenetrable, whose natural condition is to repel each other, or, at least, to exist, in their own independent identity, — while the Union is an artificial aggregation of such particles; a sort of *forced state*, as some have said, of life; a complex structure made with hands, which gravity, attrition, time, rain, dew, frost, not less than tempest and earthquake, coöperate to waste away, and which the anger of a fool — or the laughter of a fool — may bring down in an hour; a system of bodies advancing slowly through a *resisting medium*, operating at all times to retard, and at any moment liable to arrest its motion; a beautiful, yet fragile creation, which a breath can unmake, as a breath has made it.

And now, charged with the trust of holding together such a nation as this, what have we seen? What do we see to-day? Exactly this. It has been, for many months, — years, I may say; but, assuredly for a long season, — the peculiar infelicity, say, rather, terrible misfortune of this country, that the attention of the people has been fixed without the respite of a moment, exclusively on one of those subjects — the only one — on which we disagree precisely according to geographical lines. And not so only, but this subject has been one — unlike tariff, or internal improvements, or the disbursement of the public money, on which the dispute cannot be maintained, for an hour, without heat of blood, mutual loss of respect, alienation of regard — menacing to end in hate, strong and cruel as the grave.

I call this only a terrible misfortune. I blame here and now, no man, and no policy for it. Circumstances have forced it upon us all; and down to the hour that the series of compromise measures was completed and presented to the country, or certainly to congress, I will not here and now say, that it was the fault of one man, or one region of country, or one party more than another.

"But the pity of it, Iago — the pity of it."

How appalling have been its effects; and how deep and damning will be his guilt who rejects the opportunity of reconcilement, and continues this accursed agitation, without necessity, for another hour!

Why, is there any man so bold or blind as to say he believes that the scenes through which we have been passing, for a year, have left the American heart where they found it? Does any man believe that those affectionate and respectful regards, that attachment and that trust, those "cords of love and bands of a man" — which knit this people together as one, in an earlier and better time, — are as strong to-day as they were a year ago? Do you believe that there can have been so tremendous an apparatus of influences at work so long, some designed, some undesigned, but all at work in one way, that is, to make the two great divisions of the national family hate each other, and yet have no effect? Recall what we have seen in that time, and weigh it well! Consider how many hundreds of speeches were made in congress — all to show how extreme and intrepid an advocate the speaker could be of the extreme Northern sentiment, or the extreme Southern sentiment. Consider how many scores of thousands of every one of those speeches were printed and circulated among the honorable member's constituents, — not much elsewhere, — the great mass of whom agreed with him perfectly, and was only made the more angry and more unreasonable by them. Consider what caballings and conspirings were going forward during that session in committee rooms and members' chambers, and think of their private correspondence with enterprising waiters on events. Turn to the American newspaper press, secular and religious — every editor — or how vast a proportion! transformed into a manufacturer of mere local opinion — local opinion — local opinion — working away at his battery — big or little — as if it were the most beautiful operation in the world to persuade one half of the people how unreasonable and how odious were the other half. Think of conventions sitting for secession and dismemberment, by the very tomb of Jackson — the "buried majesty" not rising to scatter and blast them. Call to mind how many elections have been holden — stirring the wave of the people to its profoundest depths — all turning on this topic. Remember how few of all who help to give direction to general sentiment, how few in either house of congress, what a handful only of editors and preachers and talkers have ventured anywhere to breathe a word above a whisper to hush or divert the pelting of this pitiless storm; and then consider how delicate and sensitive a thing is public opinion, — how easy it is to mould and color and kindle it, and yet that when moulded and colored and fired, not all the bayonets and artillery of Borodino can maintain the government which it decrees to perish; and say if you have not been encompassed, and are not now, by a peril, awful indeed! Say if you believe it possible that a whole people can go on — a reading and excitable people — hearing nothing, reading nothing, talking of nothing, thinking of nothing, sleeping and waking on nothing, for a year, but one incessant and vehement appeal to the strongest of their passions, — to the pride, anger, and fear of the South, to the philanthropy, humanity, and conscience of the North, — one half of it aimed to persuade you that they were cruel, ambitious, indolent, and licentious, and therefore hateful; and the other half of it to persuade them that you were desperately and hypocritically fanatical and aggressive, and therefore hateful — say, if an excitable people can go through all this, and not be the worse for it! I tell you nay. Such a year has sowed the seed of a harvest, which, if not nipped in the bud, will grow to armed men, hating with the hate of the brothers of Thebes.

It seems to me as if our hearts were changing. Ties the strongest, influences the sweetest, seem falling asunder as smoking flax. I took up, the day before yesterday, a religious newspaper, published in this city, a leading Orthodox paper, I may describe it, to avoid misapprehension. The first thing which met my eye was what purported to be an extract from a Southern religious newspaper, denouncing the Boston editor, or one of his contributors, as an infidel — in just so many words — on the ground that one of his anti-slavery arguments implied a doctrine inconsistent with a certain text of the New Testament. Surely, I said to myself, the Christian thus denounced will be deeply wounded by such misconstruction; and as he lives a thousand miles away from slavery, as it really does not seem to be his business, as it neither picks his pocket nor breaks his leg, and he may, therefore, afford to be cool, while his Southern brother lives in the very heart of it, and may, naturally enough, be a little more sensitive, he will try to soothe him, and win him, if he can, to reconsider and retract so grievous an objurgation. No such thing! To be called an infidel, says he, by this Southern Presbyterian, I count a real honor! He thereupon proceeds to denounce the slave-holding South as a downright Sodom, — leaves a pretty violent implication that his Presbyterian antagonist is not one of its few righteous, whoever else is — and without more ado sends him adrift. Yes, Fellow-citizens, more than the Methodist Episcopal Church is rent in twain. But if these things are done in the green tree, what shall be done in the dry? If the spirit of Christianity is not of power sufficient to enable its avowed professors to conduct this disputation of hatred with temper and decorum, — to say nothing of charity, — what may we expect from the hot blood of men who own not, nor comprehend the law of love?

I have spoken what I think of the danger that threatens the Union. I have done so more at length than I could have wished, because I know that upon the depth of our convictions and the sincerity of our apprehensions upon this subject, the views we shall take of our duties and responsibilities, must all depend.

If you concur with me that there is danger, you will concur with me in the *second place*, that thoughtful men have something to do to avert it; and what is that? It is not, in my judgment, Fellow-citizens, by stereotyped declamation on the utilities of the Union to South or North that we can avert the danger. It is not by shutting our eyes and ears to it that we can avert it. It is not by the foolish prattle of "Oh, those people off there need the Union more than we, and will not dare to quit." It is not by putting arms a-kimbo here or there and swearing that we will stand no more bullying; and if any body has a mind to dissolve the Union, let him go ahead. Not thus, not thus, felt and acted that generation of our fathers, who, out of distracted counsels, the keen jealousies of States, and a decaying nationality, by patience and temper as admirable as their wisdom, constructed the noble and proportioned fabric of our federal system. "Oh, rise some other such!"

No, Fellow-citizens — there is something more and other for us to do. And what is that? Among other things, chiefly this: to accept that whole body of measures of compromise, as they are called, by which the government has sought to compose the country, in the spirit of 1787, — and then, that henceforward every man, according to his measure, and in his place, in his party, in his social, or his literary, or his religious circle, in whatever may be his sphere of influence, set himself to suppress the further political agitation of this whole subject.

Of these measures of compromise I may say, in general, that they give the whole victory to neither of the great divisions of the country, and are therefore the fitter to form the basis of a permanent adjustment. I think that under their operation and by the concurrence of other agencies it will assuredly come to pass, that on all that vast accession of territory beyond and above Texas, no slave will ever breathe the air, and I rejoice at that. They abolish the slave-trade in the District of Columbia, and I rejoice at that. They restore the fugitive to the master, — and while I mourn that there is a slave who needs to run, or a master who desires to pursue, I should be unworthy of the privilege of addressing this assembly, if I did not declare that I have not a shadow of doubt that congress has the constitutional power to pass this law just as it is, and had no doubt, before I listened to the clear and powerful argument of Mr. Curtis to-night, that it was out of all question their duty to pass some effectual law on the subject, and that it is incumbent on every man who recognizes a single obligation of citizenship, to assist, in his spheres, in its execution.

Accepting, then, these measures of constitutional compromise, in the spirit of Union, let us set ourselves to suppress or mitigate the political agitation of slavery.

And in the first place, I submit that the two great political parties of the North are called upon by every consideration of patriotism and duty to strike this whole subject from their respective issues. I go for no amalgamation of parties, and for the forming of no new party. But I admit the deepest solicitude that those which now exist, preserving their actual organization and general principles and aims, — if so it must be, — should to this extent coalesce. Neither can act in this behalf effectually alone. Honorable concert is indispensable, and they owe it to the country. Have not the eminent men of both these great organizations united on this adjustment? Are they not both primarily national parties? Is it not one of their most important and beautiful uses that they extend the whole length and breadth of our land, and that they help or ought to help to hold the extreme North to the extreme South by a tie stronger almost than that of mere patriotism, by that surest cement of friendship, — common opinions on the great concerns of the Republic? You are a Democrat; and have you not for thirty-two years in fifty united with the universal Democratic party in the choice of Southern presidents? Has it not been your function for even a larger part of the last half century to rally with the South for the support of the general administration? Has it not ever been your boast, your merit as a party, that you are in an intense, and even characteristic degree, national and Unionist in your spirit and politics, although you had your origin in the assertion of State rights; that you have contributed in a thousand ways to the extension of our territory and the establishment of our martial fame; and that you follow the flag on whatever field or deck it waves? — and will you for the sake of a temporary victory in a State, or for any other cause, insert an article in your creed and give a direction to your tactics which shall detach you from such companionship and unfit you for such service in all time to come?

You are a Whig — I give you my hand on that — and is not your party national too? Do you not find your fastest allies at the South? Do you not need the vote of Louisiana, of North Carolina, of Tennessee, of Kentucky, to defend you from the redundant capital, matured skill, and pauper labor of Europe? Did you not just now, with a wise contempt of sectional issues and sectional noises, unite to call that brave, firm and good OLD MAN from his plantation, and seat him with all the honors in the place of Washington? Circumstances have forced both of these parties — the Northern and the Southern divisions of both — to suspend for a space the legitimate objects of their institution. For a space, laying them aside, and resolving ourselves into our individual capacities, we have thought and felt on nothing but slavery. Those circumstances exist no longer, — and shall we not instantly revive the old creeds, renew the old ties, and by manly and honorable concert, resolve to spare America that last calamity, — the formation of parties according to geographical lines?

I maintain, in the *second place*, that the CONSCIENCE of this community has a duty to do, not yet adequately performed; and that is, on grounds of moral obligation, not merely to call up men to the obedience of law, but on the same grounds to discourage and modify the further agitation of this topic of slavery, *in the spirit in which, thus far, that agitation has been conducted.* I mean to say, that our moral duties, not at all less than our political interests, demand that we accept this compromise, and that we promote the peace it is designed to restore.

Fellow-citizens, was there ever a development of sheer fanaticism more uninstructed, or more dangerous than that which teaches that conscience prescribes the continued political, or other exasperating agitation of this subject? That it will help, in the least degree, to ameliorate the condition of one slave, or to hasten the day of his emancipation, I do not believe, and no man can be certain that he knows. But the philanthropist, so he qualifies himself, will say that slavery is a relation of wrong, and whatever becomes of the effort, conscience impels him to keep up the agitation till the wrong, somehow, is ended. Is he, I answer, quite sure that a conscience enlightened to a comprehension and comparison of all its duties impels him to do any such thing? Is he quite sure that that which an English or French or German philanthropist might in conscience counsel or do, touching this matter of Southern slavery, that that also he, the American philanthropist, may, in conscience, counsel or do? Does it go for nothing in his ethics, that he stands, that the whole morality of the North stands, in a totally different relation to the community of the South from that of the foreign propagandist, and that this relation may possibly somewhat — aye, to a vast extent — modify all our duties? Instead of hastily inferring that, because those States are *sister States*, you are bound to meddle and agitate, and drive pitch-pine knots into their flesh and set them on fire, may not the fact that they are *sister States*, be the very reason why, though others may do so, you may not? In whomsoever else these enterprises of an offensive and aggressive morality are graceful or safe or right, are you quite sure that in you they are either graceful or safe or right?

I have heard that a great statesman, living in the North, but living and thinking for the country, has been complained of for saying that we have no more to do with slavery in the South, than with slavery in Cuba. Are you quite sure that the sentiment went far enough? Have we quite as much to do — I mean can we wisely or morally assume to do quite as much — with Southern as with Cuban slavery? To all the rest of the world we are united only by the tie of philanthropy, or universal benevolence, and our duties to that extent flow from that tie. All that such philanthropy prompts us to print or say or do, touching slavery in Cuba, we may print, say, or do, for what I know or care, subject, I would recommend, to the restraints of common sense, and taking reasonable thought for our personal security. But to America — *to our America*, we are united by another tie, and may not a principled patriotism, on the clearest grounds of moral obligation, limit the sphere and control the aspirations and prescribe the flights of philanthropy itself?

In the first place, remember, I entreat you, that on considerations of policy and wisdom — truest policy, profoundest wisdom, for the greater good and the higher glory of America — for the good of the master and slave, now and for all generations — you have entered with the Southern States into the most sacred and awful and tender of all the relations, — the relation of country; and therefore, that you have, expressly and by implication, laid yourselves under certain restraints; you have pledged yourselves to a certain measure, and a certain spirit of forbearance; you have shut yourselves out from certain fields and highways of philanthropic enterprise — open to you before, open to the rest of the world now; — but from which, *in order to bestow larger and mightier blessings on man, in another way*, you have agreed to retire.

Yes, we have entered with them into the most sacred, salutary, and permanent of the relations of social man. We have united with them in that great master performance of human beings, that one work on which the moralists whom I love concur in supposing that the Supreme Governor looks down with peculiar complacency, the building of a Commonwealth. Finding themselves side by side with those States some sixty years ago in this new world, thirteen States of us then in all! thirty-one to-day,—touching one another on a thousand points, — discerning perfectly that unless the doom of man was to be reversed for them, there was no alternative but to become dearest friends or bitterest enemies,—so much Thucydides and the historians of the beautiful and miserable Italian republics of the Middle Age had taught them,—drawn together, also felicitously, by a common speech and blood, and the memory of their recent labor of glory,—our fathers adopted the conclusion that the best interests of humanity, in all her forms, demanded that we should enter into the grand, sacred, and tender relations of country. All things demanded it,—the love of man, the hopes of liberty,—all things. Hereby, only, can America bless herself, and bless the world.

Consider, in the *next place*, that to secure that largest good, to create and preserve a country, and thus to contribute to the happiness of man as far as that grand and vast instrumentality may be made to contribute to happiness, it became indispensable to take upon themselves, for themselves, and for all the generations who should follow, certain engagements with those to whom we became united. Some of these engagements were express. Such is that for the restoration of persons owing service according to the law of a State, and flying from it. That is express. It is written in this Constitution in terms. It was inserted in it, by what passed, sixty years ago, for the morality and religion of Massachusetts and New England. Yes; it was written there by men who knew their Bible, Old Testament and New, as thoroughly, and reverenced it and its Divine Author and his Son, the Saviour and Redeemer, as profoundly as we. Others of those engagements, and those how vast and sacred, were implied. It is not enough to say that the Constitution did not give to the new nation a particle of power to intermeddle by law with slavery within its States, and therefore it has no such power. This is true, but not all the truth. No man pretends we have power to intermeddle by law. But how much more than this is implied in the sacred relation of country. It is a marriage of more than two, for more than a fleeting natural life. "It is to be looked on with other reverence." It is an engagement, as between the real parties to it, an engagement the most solemn, to love, honor, cherish, and keep through all the ages of a nation. It is an engagement the most solemn, to cultivate those affections that shall lighten and perpetuate a tie which ought to last so long. It is an engagement then, which limits the sphere, and controls the enterprises of philanthropy itself. If you discern that by violating the express pledge of the Constitution, and refusing to permit the fugitive to be restored; by violating the implied pledges; by denying the Christianity of the holder of slaves; by proclaiming him impure, cruel, undeserving of affection, trust, and regard; that by this passionate and vehement aggression upon the prejudices, institutions, and investments of a whole region — that by all this you are dissolving the ties of country; endangering its disruption; frustrating the policy on which our fathers created it; and bringing into jeopardy the multiform and incalculable good which it was designed to secure, and would secure, — then, whatever foreign philanthropy might do, in such a prospect, — *your* philanthropy is arrested and rebuked by a "higher law." In this competition of affections, Country, — "*omnes omnium charitates complectens*," the expression, the sum total of all things most dearly loved, surely holds the first place.

Will anybody say, that these engagements thus taken, for these ends, are but "covenants with hell," which there is no morality and no dignity in keeping? From such desperate and shameless fanaticism — if such there is — I turn to the moral sentiments of this assembly. It is not here — it is not in this hall — the blood of Warren in the chair — the form of Washington before you — that I will defend the Constitution from the charge of being a compact of guilt. I will not here defend the Convention which framed it, and the Conventions and people which adopted it, from the charge of having bought this great blessing of country, by immoral promises, more honored in the breach than the observance. Thank God, we yet hold that that transaction was honest, that work beautiful and pure; and those engagements, in all their length and breadth and height and depth, sacred.

Yet, I will say that, if to the formation of such a Union, it was indispensable, as we know it was, to contract these engagements expressed and implied, no covenant made by man ever rested on the basis of a sounder morality. They tell us that although you have the strict right, according to the writers on public law, to whom Mr. Curtis has referred, to restore the fugitive slave to his master, yet that the virtue of compassion commands you not to do so. But in order to enable ourselves to do all that good, and avert all that evil—boundless and inappreciable both — which we do and avert by the instrumentality of a Union under a common government, may we not, on the clearest moral principles, agree not to exercise compassion in that particular way? The mere virtue of compassion would command you to rescue any prisoner. But the citizen, to the end that he may be enabled, and others be enabled, to indulge a more various and useful compassion in other modes, agrees not to indulge it practically in that mode. Is such a stipulation immoral? No more so is this of the Constitution.

They tell us that slavery is so wicked a thing, that they must pursue it, by agitation, to its home in the States; and that if there is an implied engagement to abstain from doing so, it is an engagement to neglect an opportunity of doing good, and void in the forum of conscience. But was it ever heard of, that one may not morally bind himself to abstain from what he thinks a particular opportunity of doing good? A contract in general restraint of philanthropy, or any other useful calling, is void; but a contract to abstain from a specific sphere of exertion, is not void, and may be wise and right. To entitle himself to instruct heathen children on week days, might not a pious missionary engage not to attempt to preach to their parents on Sunday? To win the opportunity of achieving the mighty good summed up in the pregnant language of the preamble to the Constitution, such good as man has not on this earth been many times permitted to do or dream of, we might well surrender the privilege of reviling the masters of slaves with whom we must "either live or bear no life."

Will the philanthropist tell you that there is nothing conspicuous enough, and glorious enough for him, in thus refraining from this agitation, just because our relations to the South, under the Constitution, seem to forbid it? Aye, indeed! Is it even so? Is his morality of so ambitious and mounting a type that an effort, by the exercise of love or kindness or tolerance, to knit still closer the hearts of a great people, and thus to insure ages of peace — of progress, of enjoyment — to so vast a mass of the family of man, seems too trivial a feat? Oh, how stupendous a mistake! What achievement of philanthropy bears any proportion to the pure and permanent glory of that achievement whereby clusters of contiguous States, perfectly organized governments in themselves every one, full of energy, conscious of strength, full of valor, fond of war, — instead of growing first jealous, then hostile, — like the tribes of Greece after the Persian had retired, — like the cities of Italy at the dawn of the modern world, — are melted into one, so that for centuries of internal peace, the grand agencies of amelioration and advancement shall operate unimpeded; the rain and dew of Heaven descending on ground better and still better prepared to admit them; the course of time — the Providence of God — leading on that noiseless progress whose wheels shall turn not back, whose consummation shall be in the brightness of the latter day. What achievement of man may be compared with this achievement? For the slave, alone, what promises half so much? And this is not glorious enough for the ambition of philanthropy!

No, Fellow-citizens — first of men are the builders of empires! Here it is, my friends, here — right here — in doing something in our day and generation towards "forming a more perfect Union" — in doing something by literature, by public speech, by sound industrial policy, by the careful culture of fraternal love and regard, by the intercourse of business and friendship, by all the means within our command — in doing something to leave the Union, when we die, stronger than we found it, — here — here is the field of our grandest duties and highest rewards. Let the grandeur of such duties, let the splendor of such rewards, suffice us. Let them reconcile and constrain us to turn from that equivocal philanthropy which violates contracts, which tramples on law, which confounds the whole subordination of virtues, which counts it a light thing that a nation is rent asunder, and the swords of brothers sheathed in the bosoms of brothers, if thus the chains of one slave may be violently and prematurely broken.

SPEECH DELIVERED IN FANEUIL HALL.

OCTOBER 31, 1855.

I AM gratified, beyond the power of language to express, by your kindness. By this thronging audience I am even more gratified. In this alone I hope I see the doom of the geographical party. It would have been a thing portentous and mournful, if commercial Boston had not thus poured itself into this Hall, to declare, by its ten thousand voices, against the first measure tending practically and with a real menace to a separation of the States ever yet presented, or certainly in our time presented, to the judgment or the passions of the people of America. Who should be of the earliest to discern and of the wisest to decide the true great question of the day? Did anybody suppose that your intelligence could not see what a proposition to organize the people of this country into two great geographical parties must come to if successful? Did anybody suppose that, seeing this, you would help it on, or fall asleep upon it? You, the children of the merchant princes,—you, whose profession of commerce and arts give you to know and feel, with a sort of professional consciousness and intensity, our republic to be one,—one and undivided; one and indivisible, let us say,—you, whose hearts, abroad, yet untravelled, have sometimes leaped up when you have seen the radiant flag, burning on the waste sea, along the desolate and distant coast, beneath unfamiliar constellations;—and when you have felt your country's great arm around you, were you expected to be indifferent upon a proposition to rend her into two great rabid factions, or to be cheated into a belief that there was no such proposition before the country at all?

Thank God, this sight dispels both branches of this misapprehension. The city is here, all right and straight out! Commerce is here! Commerce, in whose wants, on whose call, the Union, this Union, under this Constitution, began to be; Commerce that rocked the cradle is here, — not to follow the hearse, but to keep off the murderer; or, if they prefer it, to keep off the doctor!

The arts, the industry, of civilization, of intellect, and of the people, are here; they to which the mines and wheat-fields and cotton-grounds of a bountiful and common country supply that raw material which they give back in shapes of use and taste and beauty — they are here; — they who celebrated the establishment of the government by long processions of the trades, by music and banners, and thanksgiving to God, — singing together as morning stars over the rising ball, for the hope of a future of rewarded labor — they are here to bear witness, that the prayers of the fathers have been graciously heard, and to remember and to guard that instrumentality of constitutional union, to which, under his goodness, they owe all these things. Aye, and the charities, the philanthropy, the humanity, that dwell in these homes and hearts, are here to make their protest against the first step to moral treason — charities that love all human kind; yet are comprehended all and enfolded in the dear name of country, — philanthropy and humanity — not spasmodic, not savage, not the cold phrase of the politician, not hypocritical, not impatient, but just, wise, combining, working with — not in spite of — the will of the Highest, sowing the seed with tears, with trust, and committing the harvest to the eternal years of God — these are here. Yes, we are all here. We come to ratify the ratification. We come to say to our excellent representatives in the late Convention, again and again, Well done, good and faithful! We come to engage our hearty support and our warmest good wishes for the success of the candidates they have nominated, every man of them. We come to declare that upon trying ourselves by all the approved tests, we are perfectly satisfied that we are alive; that we are glad we are alive, since there is work to do worthy of us; that we prefer to remain for the present, Whigs! Constitutional Whigs! Massachusetts Whigs! Faneuil Hall Whigs! Daniel Webster and Henry Clay Whigs! — that we have no new party to choose to-night; that, when we have, we shall choose any other, aye, any other, than that which draws the black line of physical and social geography across the charmed surface of our native land, and finds a republic on one side to love, and nothing but an aristocracy to be "abhorred" and "avoided" on the other! Take any shape but that! We come to protest, with all possible emphasis and solemnity, against the inauguration, as they call it, of the party of the sections. We say that for any object which constitutional patriotism can approve, such a party is useless. We say, that for its own avowed objects, if it has any specific and definite objects which are constitutional and just, it is useless. We say, that if defeated in its attempt to get possession of the national government, the mere struggle will insure the triumph of that very administration on which it seems to make war; will make the fortune of certain local dealers in politics; will agitate and alienate and tend to put asunder whom God hath joined. We hold that if it should succeed in that attempt, it would be the most terrible of public calamities. I, for one, do not believe that this nation could bear it. I am not, it is true, quite of the mind of the Senator from Ohio, who dared to tell an assembly in Maine, not many days since, that there is now no union between us and the South; that the pretended Union is all meretricious; that there is no heart in it; that Russia does not hate England, nor England Russia, more than the men of the North and the men of the South hate each other. The allegation is, I think, yet untrue; the pleasure, the apparent pleasure and exultation with which he uttered it, is nothing less than awful! But yet, when we keep in view, as ever we must, the grand and unalterable conditions and peculiarities of the American national life; the capital fact lying underneath that we are historically, by constitutional law, and to a vast practical extent, a mere neighborhood of separate and sovereign States, united practically by a written league, or more accurately, by a government holding only a few great powers, and touching a few large objects; united better, perhaps, so far as united at all, by the moral ties of blood and race, a common flag, the memory of common dangers, the heritage of a common glory; — united thus, partially by that subtile essence of nationality, the consciousness of unity, the pride of unity, — itself a spirit of recent creation, requiring still to be solicited, to be reinforced, to be diffused; having regard to those instrumentalities and influences, moral and physical, which encompass us ever and endanger us, and especially to the consideration that besides the centrifugal tendencies of sovereign States, impelling them ever apart, there is a line, — a dark, dark line, — almost a fissure in the granite, whose imperfect cohesion can scarcely resist the vast weight on either side; — recollecting these things, and recollecting, too, how much more than by reason or public virtue or their true interests, men are moved by anger, pride, and force, in great civil crises, — in any way we can survey it, we cannot possibly fail to see that the process of forming such an organization, and its influence, if completely formed and fully in action, would compose a new and disturbing element in our system, which it is scarcely able to encounter, and to which no wise man and genuine Unionist would not shudder to see it exposed.

Why, look at it. Here is a stupendous fabric of architecture; a castle; a capitol; suppose the capitol at Washington. It is a fortress at once, and a temple. The great central dome swells to heaven. It rests grandly on its hill by its own weight kept steadfast, and seemingly immovable; Titan hands might have built it; it may stand to see the age of a nation pass by. But one imperfection there is; a seam in the marble; a flaw in the iron; a break scarcely visible, yet a real vertical fissure, parting by an imperceptible opening from top to foundation the whole in two. The builder saw it, and guarded against it as well as he might; those who followed, to repair, with pious and skilful hands, tried by underpinning, by lateral support, by buttress and buttress alternately, to hold the disjointed sides in contact. Practically, it was becoming less formidable; the moss was beginning to conceal it, even; and here comes a workman who proposes to knock out the well-planned lateral supports, loosen the underpinning of the ends, dig a yawning excavation under both of them, and then set on each the mountain weight of a frowning and defiant dome of its own. Down the huge pile topples in an hour. Small compensation it is that the architect of ruin finds his grave, too, beneath it!

It is to do what we may to scatter this organization in its beginnings that we are here to-night. It is for this opportunity, chiefly, that the Whigs of Massachusetts are absolutely glad that they are alive. True, we seek also to redeem Massachusetts. That last legislative year of all sorts of ignorance, and all sorts of folly, and all sorts of corruption; not dignified, but made hateful and shameful by a small and mean mimicry of treason, withal — we would blot it all out from our proud annals forever. The year which deserted Washburn, slighted the counsels of Clifford, struck a feeble but malignant blow at the judicial tenure, nullified a law of the Union, constitutional, if the Constitution is constitutional, — we would forget. Let it not come into the number of our months. In fact, let us talk of something else.

Yes, Whigs of Boston and Massachusetts! We strike at higher game. It is because the experiment is now making, whether a sectional party, merging and overriding all others, is possible; whether candidates for the presidency shall openly electioneer for that office, by advocating the formation of such a party, and not see the mantling cup of honors, to which they are reaching, dashed to their feet by the indignation of the whole country — it is because this experiment is making today, that we feel that we have a duty to do. Who of us knows that it is not his last civil labor? Who of us does not feel that if it were so, our noblest labor were our last? Were it even so, what signifies it whether we personally and politically sink or swim — live or die — survive or perish! Would not that be a bright page wherein the historian, after having recorded in the former chapters of his book the long antecedents of the Whigs, — that they held the government of this good old State, with small exception, for a quarter of a century; that they held it long enough to embody their politics in official state papers; on the statute book; in public speech; through their accredited press; in the prevailing tone and maxims of public life; long enough to see those politics bear rich, practical autumnal fruits; that while they held power, popular education was improved; the instrumentalities of intercourse of all parts of the State with each other, and with the States beyond, were multiplied and perfected, and the universal industrial prosperity of the people advanced by the reforming hand, reforming wisely; that the sentiment of obedience to law, popular or unpopular, while law, of observance of order, of the supremacy of the national Constitution, within its limits over the State, and of the State constitution over the legislature; of the practicability and the necessity of reconciling and performing all political duties, not one, nor half, but *all*,—that this sentiment was taught and was practised; that liberty of conscience was held sacred; that the right to be represented equally in the government of the State was recognized, and sought to be retained in the Constitution as belonging to every human being, because such, inhabiting her soil; that they held even good laws powerless, and a government of laws impossible, if not interpreted and administered by judges as impartial as the lot of humanity will admit, and helped to be so by the tenure of independence of the ebb and flow of party; that although ever they boasted to be a branch of a national Whig connection, and as such, held a creed of national politics, combining a policy of peace with honor, industry protected by wise discrimination, improvement of the great natural agencies of intercourse, a provident and liberal and statesmanlike administration of the public domain,—a creed on which wise and good men of every State, in large numbers, sometimes by large majorities, were with them; although they held this creed of union, they yet left themselves wholly free to cherish and act on the local sentiment of slavery; that they opposed its extension by their press, by their vote, by public debate—its extension by annexation of Texas and Cuba, and by repeal of the compromise, and that their greatest and best, all who represented them, did so ever up to the limits of the Constitution and an honest statesmanship, and paused reverentially there;—would it not be a glorious page on which, after concluding this detail, he should record that their last organic act was to meet the dark wave of this tide of sectionalism on the strand, breast high, and roll it back upon its depths; aye, or to be buried under it! Would not that be higher than to follow the advice of one, once of us, who counsels the Whigs to march out of the field with all the honors? Yes, we reject the word of command. We will not march out of the field at all. We will stand just where we are, and defend those honors and add to them. Perhaps we may fall. That were better than the flight he advises; to fall, and let our recorded honors thicken on our graves. That were better than flight;

but who can tell that there are not others higher to be won yet? Laurels farther up; more precious—less perishing; to be won by more heroic civil duty, and the austerer glory of more self-sacrifice. Be these ungathered laurels ours to reap!

But it occurs to me, that I have been a little too fast in assuming that your minds are already all made up not to join this geographical party. Let us then pause, and inspect the thing a little. Let us do it under a threefold dissection. See then, first, exactly what it is to be; what, if completely formed, it is to be. Second, what good it will do. And, third, what evil it will do; what evil the process of forming it will do; what evil it will do after it is formed. First, what is it to be, when formed? Exactly an organization of all the people of the free States, if they can get all, if not, majorities of all, into a political party proper, to oppose the whole people of all the slave States, organized into just such another association upon the single, but broad and fertile topic of slavery. Into this organization, on one side and the other, every other party is, if possible, to be merged; certainly by this one, every other is to be out-voted and vanquished. This promising and happy consummation, mark you, is to be a *political party proper.* It is not to be a public opinion on slavery. It is not to be a public opinion against slavery. It is not to be a mere universal personal conviction of every man which he may carry with him into all his political duties and relations, and bind up with his Democratic opinions, or Whig opinions, or Native American opinions; — that is not it, at all. It is to be, and act, as a political party properly, technically, and with tremendous emphasis so called. It is to fill office, make laws, govern great States, govern the nation; and to do this by the one single test of what is called opposition to slavery; on the one single impulse of hate and dread of the aristocracy of the South, by which slavery is maintained. To carry out this opposition, to breathe forth this hate, and this dread in action, it lives; it holds its conventions, supports its press, selects its candidates, prescribes their creed, conducts its electioneering, and directs every act that it does and every word that it speaks. And now, when you consider how prodigious an agency in a republic a flushed and powerful party is at the best; when you remember what it has done to shame and scare away liberty from her loved haunts and home by the blue Ægean, or beneath the sunny skies of Italy; when you consider how party, as the general fact, is sure to form and guide that public opinion which rules the world; how it grows to be "the madness of the many for the benefit of the few;" when you consider that to win or retain the general voice, all the ability this organization can possibly command will be enlisted and paid; that it will offer office to the ambitious, spoils to the greedy, the dear, delicious indulgence of his one single idea to the zealot, strong in faith, fierce and narrow in his creed; to the sentimentalist and *littérateur*, the corrupting praise of a foreign press; to a distempered and unmeaning philanthropy, the cure of one evil by the creation of ten thousand;—meditating on these things, you attain to some conception of what this party is to be.

And now, what good is it to do? And first, what on earth is it going to do, anyhow? It is formed, we will say. It has triumphed. It has got power in the free States. It has got the general government. It has chosen its president. It has got a majority in both houses of congress. The minority are a body of representatives of slaveholders. And they have met in the great chambers. What to do? Now, it is agreed, on all hands, that in regard to what they are to do as a party, on any subject, human or divine, *outside of slavery*, we know no more than if they were so many men let down in so many baskets from the clouds. As a party,—and they gained power as a party, they are to rule us as a party;—but as a party they solemnly adjure that they hold no opinion on anything whatever, on anything but slavery. They spread their arms wide open to every humor of the human mind; to all the forms of sense and nonsense; to more irreconcilable and belligerent tempers and politics than ever quarrelled in a menagerie; to men of war and men of peace; to the friend of annexation, if he can find free soil to annex, as you may, in Canada, and the enemy of any more area; to protectionists and free traders; men of strict, and men of large construction, and men of no construction at all; temperance men and anti-temperance men; the advocate of ten hours of labor, the advocate of twelve,—in short, they make a general bid for every opinion on everything, with the pledge of the party to each and all, that if they will roar with a common consent, and make a satisfactory *hullaba-*

loo on slavery, every man of them shall have a fair chance, and no privilege, and everybody may enact everything, if he can.

And now, in the name of all common sense, in the whole history of elective government, was a free people ever called on to commit power, the whole vast enginery, the whole thunder of the State, to such a ruler as this! Slavery, they do say, they will oppose, right and left; but what other one maxim of government they will adopt, state or national; what one law, on what one subject, they will pass; what one institution, or one policy of the fathers they will spare; what one sentiment they will inculcate; what one glory they will prize; what of all that government can cause or cure, they will cause or cure or try to — we have no more to guide us than if they were an encampment of a race never seen before, poured by some populous and unknown North, from her frozen loins! How mad, how contemptible to deliver ourselves over to such a veiled enthusiast as this! Better the urn and the lot of Solon — better the fantastic chances of hereditary descent, a thousand fold.

Well, on their one single *specialty* of slavery, what are they going to do? And I say that we have not one particle more of evidence, what specific thing, or what thing in general they mean to do on slavery, than on anything else. I do say this, however, that those honest men, who, in the simplicity of their hearts, have sympathized with this new party in the hope of having the Missouri Compromise restored, have not one particle of assurance that they would do it if they could; or that if they could, they would rest there, or within half the globe of it. Loud they are in their reprobation of the repeal. So are we all! But is it a restoration they seek? No, nothing so little. When, a few days ago, a respectable Whig gentleman presented himself at one of their meetings, and being invited to speak, began by saying that they were all there to unite for the repeal of the repeal, they hissed him incontinently. Less discourteously in the manner of it, quite as unequivocally they have set forth in terms the most explicit, in the address of their convention, that the restoration of the Compromise of 1820 is not what they desire. What are they to do, then, if they win power? Either nothing at all which Whigs could not do, and would not do, if a wise and large statesmanship permit it; or they bring on a conflict which separates the States. Nothing at all which we would not do, if our fidelity to the Constitution would allow us, or that which under the Constitution cannot be done. Nothing at all, or just what their agitation from 1835 to this hour, has accomplished, — rivet the iron chains of the slave, loose the golden bands of the Union. So much for the good it will do.

But now survey the evil it would do. We cannot, of course, foreknow exactly what it would do, if it could, nor how much, exactly, it could do, if it would. We cannot know, in other words, exactly where or when or how, if it attained the whole power that it seeks, it would bring on the final strife. But one thing we know, that they cannot, by possibility, go through the process of merely and completely organizing such a party but by elaborately and carefully training the men on this side of their line to "abhor" and "avoid" the men on the other. The basis of the organization is reciprocal sectional hate. This is the sentiment at bottom. This, and nothing else. To form and heighten this; to fortify and justify it; to show that it is moral and necessary and brave, the whole vast enginery of party tactics is to be put in request. If the ingenuity of hell were tasked for a device to alienate and rend asunder our immature and artificial nationality, it could devise nothing so effectual!

I take my stand here! I resist and deprecate the mere attempt to form the party. I don't expect to live to see it succeed in its grasp at power. I am sure I hope I shall not, but I see the attempt making. I think I see the dreadful influence of such an attempt. That influence I would expose. Woe! woe! to the sower of such seed as this! It may perish where it falls. The God of our fathers may withhold the early and latter rain and the dew, and the grain may die; but woe to the hand that dares to scatter it.

Painful it is to see some of whom a higher hope might have been cherished, on motives and with views I dare say satisfactory to themselves, giving aid and comfort to such a thing. In looking anxiously out of my own absolute retirement from every form of public life, to observe how the movers of this new party mean to urge it upon the people, what topics they mean to employ, what aims they mean to propose, and, above all, what tone and spirit they mean to breathe and spread, and what influence to exert on the sectional passions or the national sentiments of our country — I have had occasion to read something of their spoken and written exhortations — this inauguration eloquence of sectionalism — and think I comprehend it. And what work do they make of it? Yes — what? With what impression of your country, your whole country — that is the true test of a party platform and a party appeal — do you rise from listening to the preachers of this new faith? What lesson of duty to all, and of the claims of all, and of love to all, has it taught you? Does not our America seem to lose her form, her color, her vesture, as you read? Does not the magic of the metamorphosis come on her?

> "Her spirits faint,
> Her blooming cheeks assume a pallid teint,
> And scarce her form remains."

Does it not seem as if one half of the map were blotted out or rolled up forever from your eye? Are you not looking with perplexity and pain, your spirits as in a dream all bound up, upon a different, another, and a smaller native land? Where do you find in this body of discourse one single recollection that North and South compose a common country, to which our most pious affections are due, and our whole service engaged? Where, beneath this logic and this rhetoric of sectionalism, do you feel one throb of a heart capacious of our whole America? The deep, full, burning tide of American feeling, so hard to counterfeit, so hard to chill, does it once gladden and glorify this inauguration oratory and these inauguration ceremonies? Is not the key-note of it all, that the slaveholders of the South are an aristocracy to be "abhorred" and "avoided;" that they are insidious and dangerous; that they are undermining our republic, and are at all hazards to be resisted? Do they not inaugurate the new party on the basis of reciprocal hate and reciprocal fear of section to section? Hear the sharp and stern logic of one of these orators: — "Aristocracy, through all hazards is to be abhorred and avoided. But a privileged class are sure to become, nay, are an aristocracy already. The local Southern law, and the national Constitution, make the slaveholders a privileged class. They are, therefore, an aristocracy to be abhorred and avoided." Such is the piercing key-note of his speech. To this he sets his whole music of discord. To this he would set the whole music of the next presidential canvass. To this, the tens of thousands of the free States are to march. "Abhor" and "avoid" the aristocracy of the South! Organize to do it the better! They are insidious and dangerous. They are undermining republican liberty. March to defend it! Aye, march, were it over the burning marl, or by the light which the tossing wave of the lake casts pale and dreadful.

"I might show," the same orator proceeds, "that the Constitution is wrong in thus conceding to a privileged class. I might show, *a priori*, that such a class would be dangerous. I choose rather to teach you so to read the history of America, that you shall find its one great lesson will be hatred and dread of the aristocracy of the South, for its conduct even more than for its privileges." And so he unrolls the map, and opens the record. He traces the miraculous story; he traces the miraculous growth from the birthday of the Constitution, and from the straitened margin of the old thirteen States, through all the series of expansion, — the acquisition of Louisiana, and the adoption of that State into the Union; the successive adoption, also, of Kentucky, Tennessee, Mississippi, Alabama and Missouri; the annexation of Florida and Texas, and California, — a growth in fifty years, from a narrow heritage between the Atlantic and Alleghany, and the spring-heads of the Connecticut and the mouth of the St. Mary's in Georgia, to the dimensions of Roman, of Russian, of Asiatic boundlessness — this he traces across the Alleghanies, across the imperial valley and the Father of Rivers, through the opened portals of the Rocky Mountains to the shores of the great tranquil sea — aye, and beyond these shores to richer dominion over the commerce of the East, to which it opens a new and nearer way — this majestic series, our glory, our shame, he runs over; and the one single lesson he gathers and preaches from it is, that the aristocracy of the South is as insidious and dangerous and undermining in practice as it is threatening *a priori;* that we should "abhor" and "avoid" it, for what it has done, as well as for what the Constitution and the laws secure to it. This is the lesson of the History of America. As he studies the map and reads the history, so is the new party to do it; so are the fathers, and so are the children of the free States all to read it; it is to teach them all one dull lesson, and to sound in their ears one single, dreary, and monotonous warning. The annexation of Louisiana, the master-work of Jefferson, unless you say the Declaration of Independence is his master-work; the annexation of Florida, by treaty, for which John Quincy Adams acquired so just a fame, and which stipulates for the incorporation of its inhabitants into the Union; the victories of Palo Alto, Monterey, Buena Vista, and Contreras, which crowned the arms of America with a lustre imperishable, although they could not vindicate to justice and history, the administration or the politics which brought on the war, nor the Free Soilers of New York, whose tactics caused the election of that administration; this expansion, so stupendous — this motion, silent and resistless, of all the currents of national being towards the setting sun—like that of our astronomical system itself, towards the distant constellation; this all is to kindle no emotion, to inspire no duty, to inculcate no truth, but to "abhor" and "avoid" the aristocracy, whose rapacious use or insidious fabrication of opportunity, so strikingly illustrates the folly of the Constitution.

Oh! how soothing and elevating to turn from this to the meridian brightness, the descending orb, the whole clear day, of our immortal Webster! How sweet, how instructive to hang again on the lips now mute, still speaking, whose eloquence, whose wisdom, were all given ever to his whole America! How grand to feel again the beat of the great heart which could enfold us all! He saw, too, and he deplored the spread of slavery. He marked, and he resisted the frenzy of the politics by which the then administration gave it so vast an impulse by annexing Texas and making war with Mexico. He had surveyed—no man had so deeply done it—the growth of his country from the rock of Plymouth and the peninsula of Jameston to the western sea. But did he think it just to trace it all to the aggressive spirit of the aristocracy who hold slaves? Could his balanced and gigantic intelligence and his genuine patriotism have been brought to believe and to teach that the single desire to find a new field for slavery to till, has in fifty years transformed a strip of sea coast into a national domain larger than Europe?

Is nothing to be ascribed to the necessities of national situation and the opportunities of national glory; nothing to the sober, collective judgment of the people of all the sections; nothing to the foresight of some great men — like Jefferson and John Quincy Adams — who loved not slavery, nor the expansion of the area of slavery, but who did love their country dearly and wisely, and knew that that evil would be more than compensated by the exceeding good; nothing to a diffused, vehement nationality, brave, ambitious, conscious of a mighty strength, burning to try itself against the resistance of foreign contact, and finding on its West and South-west border no equal force to hold it back; nothing to the blindness of mere party tactics and the power of a popular administration; nothing to the love of glory, and contention, and danger which flames and revels in the adolescent national heart? Is it all mere and sheer negro-breeding and negro-selling that has done this? More. Is nothing to be ascribed to the influence of Northern aggression against slavery, provoking by an eternal law a Southern rally for its defence and propagation? Have these great readers of our history forgotten that as far back as 1805, as 1801, the press, some influential portions of the press of a large political party at the North, began to denounce the election and reëlection of Jefferson as a triumph of the slave power; the acquisition of Louisiana, that absolute necessity of our peace, how much more of our greatness, as another triumph of the slave power; that this form of sectionalism already assailed the slave representation of the Constitution, and tried to strike it out; that it bore its part, a large part, in inflaming New England to the measure of the Hartford Convention; that, hushed to silence by the fervid flood of nationality which swept the country at the close of a war, breathing into us the full first inspiration of American life, it awoke again on the application of Missouri for admission; that, silenced once more by that adjustment, a few years later it took on the more virulent type of abolitionism; and from that moment, helped on by the general progress of the age, it has never ceased for an hour to make war on the institutions of the South, to assail the motives, and arraign the conscience of the slave-holder; to teach to "abhor" and to "avoid" him, and denounce the Union as a compact with hell? Is it not possible that a part of what they call the aggressive spirit of slavery may be reäction against our own aggression? May it not be, that in this recrimination of the sections, and in the judgment of history, there may be blows to take as well as blows to give? That great man whose name I have spoken, could see, and he dared to admit, the errors of both sections. In those errors, in this very hate and this very dread which the new party would organize, he saw the supreme danger of his country. To correct those errors, to allay that dread, to turn that hate to love, was the sublime aim of his last and noblest labor. "I am looking out," he said, "not for my own security or safety, for I am looking out for no fragment on which to float away from the wreck, if wreck there must be, but for the good of the whole, and the preservation of all. I speak to-day for the Union! Hear me, for my cause!" He could not have abandoned himself, he never saw an hour in which he could have any more abandoned himself to this gloomy enterprise of sectionalism, than Washington could have done it, stooping from the pathos and grandeur and parental love of the Farewell Address; than the leader of Israel could have done it, as he stood in that last hour on Pisgah and surveyed in vision, the wide-spread tents of the kindred tribes, rejoicing together in the peace and in the light of their nation's God. O, for an hour of such a life, and all were not yet lost.

ARGUMENT ON THE REMOVAL OF JUDGE DAVIS.

[THE following history of the case is taken mainly from the "Monthly Law Reporter": —

At a *nisi prius* term of the Supreme Court of Maine, held within and for the county of Cumberland, in January, 1856, by the Hon. Woodbury Davis, a question arose which of two persons claiming the office was the lawful sheriff of the county. Mr. Seward M. Baker was in occupation of the office under an old commission, which, by its terms, had not expired, and did the duties of sheriff during the first week of the term. At the end of the week, Mr. Daniel C. Emery and his counsel called upon Judge Davis at his chambers, and informed him that Mr. Emery had received a commission and qualified under it, and should claim the right to perform the duties of sheriff, on Monday. Judge Davis expressed his wish that the case should be presented to the full bench, and his reluctance to pass upon it at *nisi prius;* but Mr. Emery and his counsel thought proper to present the question to the judge, and it was understood that it would be so presented on Monday morning. Accordingly, on Monday, January 21st, Mr. Emery appeared in court, presented his commission, and his claim to this office was argued by Judge Howard and the Hon. Nathan Clifford in his behalf. They contended that the executive had the right to remove the incumbent and appoint a new sheriff, and that the judge must, from the necessity of the case, pass upon the question. At the close of their arguments, no argument being made in behalf of the incumbent, Judge Davis, alluding to the newness of his own position on the bench, and the longer professional experience of several members of the bar present, invited suggestions from the bar. His invitation was responded to by Hon. Samuel Fessenden, who controverted the positions of Mr. Emery's counsel, and contended that the governor had no power, under the amended constitution, to make the removal and appointment in question. The doubt arose upon the effect of an amendment of the constitution, recently adopted by the people. Before the amendment, sheriffs were appointed and removed by the governor. The amendment made them elective, and expressly took away the power of appointment from the governor, except in case of vacancies. The time for an election had not arrived. It was urged on behalf of Mr. Emery, that the amendment, though adopted by the people, and passed upon by the governor and council, had not become a part of the constitution when the governor issued the commission. And, if it had become a part of the constitution, yet, as the time for an election had not arrived, and no officer had been elected, the effect of the adoption of the amendment was either to create a vacancy at once, or to leave the officers under the power of the executive as before, until the election. It was replied that the amendment was in full operation when the governor issued the new commission, and that he could not, under that amendment, create "a vacancy" within the meaning of the amendment, by merely issuing a new commission; and that the adoption of the amendment did not of itself create vacancies in the offices it affected, but left the old commissions alive until the new officers should be elected, and in terms took from him the appointing power, except in those cases. There was no question of fact in issue between the parties, and Judge Davis, after expressing his regret that the question came before him suddenly, at *nisi prius*, and not in *banc*, admitted the necessity he was under, from the nature of the case, to determine which of the two claimants he should recognize as sheriff, and gave his decision in favor of the incumbent, Mr. Baker. He limited his decision within the closest possible bounds, deciding only that he should, under the present circumstances, as at present advised, recognize and employ the incumbent as the lawful sheriff for the purposes of the court, and expressly refusing to pass upon the general question of title and the validity of the commission, beyond that. No opposition was offered to this decision, no appeal taken, and no steps to bring the question before the full bench, by *mandamus*, *quo warranto*, or otherwise.

The March term of the court for the same county, for criminal trials, was held by Judge Davis. In the interval, Mr. Emery obtained possession of the jail by force, and appointed a keeper of the prisoners. When it became necessary for the prisoners to be produced, on motion of the county attorney, the judge, in the usual manner, sent an officer in attendance, with verbal orders to have the prisoners produced. The keeper refused to obey the order, and the judge then issued a *capias* to an officer, commanding him to bring the prisoners, and directing the keeper of the jail to deliver them to him. This precept the keeper complied with, and no further difficulty arose during the term.

The legislature of Maine assembled soon after; and on the 19th day of March, the senate passed substantially the following resolves:—

Resolved, That the senate will proceed to consider the adoption of an address to the governor, for the removal of Woodbury Davis, one of the justices of the Supreme Judicial Court, for the causes following:

Because the said Davis has refused to recognize Daniel C. Emery as the sheriff of Cumberland County:

Because the said Davis, in his capacity of judge, denied the validity of the commission issued to Daniel C. Emery:

Because the said Davis removed by unlawful proceeding certain prisoners from jail then in the custody of Emery:

Because the said Davis has recognized as the sheriff of said county another person who had before been lawfully removed from that office, and has undertaken to issue the orders of the said court, to be executed by the person who has been so removed from office:

Because the continuance of such acts, proceedings, and assumptions of the said Woodbury Davis tends to produce insubordination, confusion, and violence; is of dangerous and pernicious example; confounds the distribution of the powers of government; and tends to the subversion of the actual, constituted, and lawful authority of the State.

The constitution of Maine contains the following provision, (Art. ix. sec. 5,) under which these proceedings were had:

"Every person holding any civil office under this State, may be removed, by impeachment, for misdemeanor in office; and every person holding any office may be removed by the governor, with the advice of the council, on the address of both branches of the legislature. But, before any such address shall pass either house, the causes of removal shall be entered on the journal of the house in which it originated, and a copy thereof served on the person in office, that he may be admitted to a hearing in his defence."

The above constitute, it is believed, all the facts necessary to a full understanding of Mr. Choate's argument in this case, which was pronounced by very eminent authority as "a valuable addition to the constitutional literature of America, and one that will fully sustain Mr. Choate's great reputation as a jurist, orator, and scholar."

After the close of Mr. Choate's argument the Convention dissolved.

The address on the subject was carried in the senate by a vote of twenty-five to three; and in the house by a vote of eighty-one to sixty, nearly or quite a party vote, as we have been informed, in both places. Fifty-nine members of the house offered a protest against the address, which the house refused to receive.

It is proper to add, that the legislature which removed Judge Davis also abolished his office, probably for the purpose of clinching the removal. It had this effect for a time, for the Supreme Court, finding that there was no question between different claimants for the office, did not think it necessary to pass upon the general questions involved in the action of the other branches of the government. But it also left an easy way of redress; for the legislature of 1857 happening to differ in politics from their predecessors, renewed the office; and Judge Davis was appointed to fill it.]

Mr. President, —

I cannot permit myself to proceed a step in this discussion, until I have relieved my heart, by the warmest expression of thanks to you and to the Convention, for your kindness to me personally. That kindness has not restored me to perfect health, but it has impressed me with a sense of gratitude and obligation, which neither sickness nor health will ever efface or abate.

It will at the same time occur to you that I am placed under some peculiar embarrassment, from not having had the pleasure and help of listening to the arguments of my associated counsel, which are represented from all sources to have been powerful and instructive. I incur the double hazard of seeming, by the omission of topics which they have treated, to disallow their importance; and by the repetition of arguments which they have advanced, to impair their strength. Prudence, therefore, and good taste, prescribe that I confine myself to a few supplementary suggestions, abstaining from that elaborate and complete discussion which the stage of the debate and personal considerations alike discourage.

If the case of Judge Davis had seemed to depend in any considerable degree, on any question of local law or local policy, of this great State, I should have thought it presumptuous in me to appear for him, and would not have assumed to do so. In every view, it may be matter of regret to him, as well as to me, that my place is not held by some one of this full and able bar, whose learning and eloquence have been already so admirably represented here; and by some one of a recognized personal authority in the counsels of the people of Maine. But, Sir, it is impossible not to see, that the deliberation in which you are engaged, turns, in one of its aspects at least, on a deep and general question, in regard to which there can scarcely be, under the written constitutions of our country, such a thing as a local law or a local policy at all, and for the discussion of which no specific and local training or studies, are demanded or furnished anywhere. It is true the cause is here. The high forum is here. The judge whose official life, hopes, and honor are menaced; the judge, through whom the independence of all judges — through whom the power of a coördinate department — supreme within its sphere, under your constitution, and all written constitutions, and all unwritten constitutions, pretending to be free and wise — through whom that power is menaced — he is here. It is your fundamental law, and your amendments of that law, and your statutes, and your legislative practice, that are immediately to be interpreted and applied. The topics, the responsibilities, the first results, are here. This is true, certainly.

But yet the great first question on which this whole deliberation turns, or one which in one decisive aspect it turns, is an American question, and not a question of local law at all. It is one on which the presumption is absolutely conclusive in advance, that the doctrines of every State — preëminently so of such a State as this — will be found to be in conformity with a general and a grand American doctrine of law and liberty, old as any of our written constitutions, recognized by the terms and by the practical interpretations of every one of them in all periods — a doctrine, not one thing in Maine and another in Massachusetts; one thing in New York and another in South Carolina, and another in Ohio; not so — nor one to-day and another to-morrow; but a doctrine of American law and liberty, properly and exactly so denominated — combining and reconciling security with liberty — maintained through all our history; pervading our whole system; held sacred in all transports of popular excitement; adopted and cherished in every commonwealth which under its local symbol owns the Union flag — the boast, and the safety of all alike. On such a question we ought all to feel ourselves at home, before any judicial forum, and at the higher bar of any legislature — even this.

And what is this larger, first question? I state it thus: — With what specific purpose, and under what limitations have the people of Maine given to the legislature the power to remove, or to cause and coöperate in the removal, by address, of a judge of their highest judicial tribunal; and are you now about to use that power as they intended and expected it to be used when they gave it? Did they mean to authorize their agents and servants of *one department* — the legislature, or the legislature and governor — to remove their agents and servants of another department — a judge or a bench of judges — admitted to be honest — admitted to be competent — *for the single reason that in a case regularly before him or them, he or they formed and expressed an opinion on the interpretation of the constitution and a statute*, (the interpretation of which belongs exclusively to the judge,) *differing from the opinion entertained by you?* Did the people give you the power to remove for such difference of opinion on the sense of the written law? Did they mean by this power of removal, after having distributed the functions of government among three classes of servants, and ordained for the well-being of the State, that one of these, the judiciary, shall, and the two others, legislative and executive, shall not, conclusively construe the constitution and the statute — did they mean, by the grant of this power, to say that you and the governor may punish, by deprivation of office, the judge for doing exactly what he is authorized to do, and you are not authorized to do — simply because you dislike the construction he makes? Did they mean to say that under this power, the legislature and the governor — for the sole and palpable purpose of making the judge utter *your* judgments and not his own, on a question which the people, by this same constitution, commits exclusively to *his judgment*, for this precise and only purpose — may remove him? Did they mean to authorize you to supersede and absorb the practical functions of a whole department, which they have carefully established under the conviction that its existence and its independence of you, and its free and full action, were just as needful as your own? Was this their meaning; or did they intend that this power should be held and used in harmony with, and *in trust for* the whole constitution; that is to say, for the removal of the corrupt and incapable judge, found such after trial, upon written charges, and a hearing in his defence? This is the question, the ends, the purpose and limitations intended by the people of Maine. And I believe I only do this State the justice she may demand of all men, and pay her the respect which all ought to feel, when I assume that in framing this clause, she just intended to stand where all our States have stood; to stand where Massachusetts stood when she was of her, — to so large a degree her ornament, pride, and strength. How the people of America have answered this question, in other words, for what exact objects, and with what precise limitations they have given this power of removal, is hereafter to be examined. Thus far I have said only that it is one of general constitutional jurisprudence, and not of local law; and I find in this my apology for presuming to discuss it here.

Mr. President, have I not stated the question before you exactly as it arises? Am I not warranted in saying that the precise and the single reason on which you are moved to displace this judge, is that — admitted to be honest, and admitted to be competent — he has put a judicial interpretation on a statute and on the constitution, which you think erroneous? And if so, is it not the true and sole inquiry, did the people mean to give you the power to do such an act, for such a cause? Sir, who comes to accuse Judge Davis of anything else? The causes of the proposed removal, your constitution requires to be stated of record, that he may defend to them. Here they are. And do they allege dishonesty or incompetency? Do they allege any one dishonest act? Do they allege any one act as evidencing dishonesty or incompetency? Do they ascribe his act as being or as proving corruption or unfitness? Nothing like it. No, Sir. These charges, these causes, whatever they are, tacitly admit him to be upright, capable, of pure intentions; in this very judgment conscientious; in this very judgment honestly in error only. If they intended, if they dared to breathe or inspire a doubt or suspicion of his integrity, his learning, his capacity, they were bound by the constitution to do so clearly, certainly, and boldly, that he might have given the scandal to the winds. There is no such charge, and there is no such insinuation. Honest error of opinion, that is the whole. "The head and front of his offending hath this extent, no more." Does this record say he did not take pains enough — all the pains he could — to find the truth? No. Does it say the question was not a difficult one? No. Does it say that it was so clear and easy that his alleged mistake proves bad faith, or weakness, or ignorance? Not a word of it. Is it even pretended that he had seen the opinion of the Massachusetts judges, although in that opinion there is nothing whatever that should have changed his own? No. The charge is, that he did a certain act in direct course of judicial duties; a duty he would gladly have postponed; a duty forced on him; founded on a judicial opinion of the constitution and the statute; right, if that opinion was right: wrong, if that opinion was erroneous; but if a mistake, the mistake of a learned and able mind, after a conscientious search for truth, concerning the sense of a written law.

"I should be ashamed of myself," a great judge somewhere says, "if to a question of common law I could not answer without taking time to reflect. I should be equally ashamed of myself if to a question of statute law I did not take time to answer."

Time to answer was not given to Judge Davis. He was coerced into an immediate decision; and because some of you, and some elsewhere, think it erroneous, they demand his removal. That his decision was right, I entirely believe; that it was conscientious, and that in no man's judgment it proves unfitness, his accusers on this record and these proofs admit.

Two or three allegations, or intimations, there are among the charges, which may require a remark; and which the facts now before you completely dispose of. He assumes, it is suggested, without any legal issue raised, and without judicial trial, to pronounce upon the comparative validity of these two competing sheriffs' commissions. Sir, if this means merely that the question was not before him on a *quo warranto*, or mandamus, or an action on a sheriff's bond, it is true, although it is nothing to the purpose. But if it means to deny that without procurement or connivance by him, against his wishes, against his recommendation, an issue was practically and regularly made up, and pending before him, and forced upon him, which it was indispensable for him to try at once, for the purpose of securing due and orderly proceeding in court, — as much so as if a person should present himself at this moment and claim to preside over this Convention, — if this record means to deny this, it is not true, and it is completely disproved by the evidence now before you. By that evidence you now know, that when the counsel of the last-commissioned sheriff gave him notice that he should appear with his client in court, and claim that he be declared and recognized as sheriff by the judge, he urged, as far as decorum and judicial self-respect would permit him to do it, or permit any honest, prudent, and firm judge to do it, that a question so delicate, possibly difficult, to his reflections as yet wholly new, should be presented at once to the whole court. He expressed his desire to facilitate this, and indicated the way to do it legally and promptly. You know that this suggestion was wholly disregarded; and that the determination to press the issue on him, had been, for some reason and on some policy, deliberately adopted, and was strenuously persisted in. You know that thereupon two persons came in open court, before the judge, and each then and there unrolled his commission, and made public claim, and demanded instant possession of an office in its nature indivisible. One only could have it. One must have it. One was entitled to it, and was entitled to it at once. For the preservation of order in court; for the due, accustomed, and decent conduct of its business; to protect its justice from obstruction, and itself from contempt; it became necessary to decide at once in some way, on some ground, and to some extent, which one should be deemed the sheriff. To say upon these facts now established conclusively, that an issue, in a strict sense, was not raised, — so raised and so presented that the judge not only legally might try it, but could not possibly escape trying it, — is to speak unintelligibly, or to speak absurdly. That he must decide, for the term, and for the place, who was to be deemed sheriff, you all agree. But by what principle must he decide it? Was he to do it piously by lot? Was he cunningly to take the highest on the alphabet? Was he to enact judicial corruption, or judicial cowardice, and to mask them under maxims of the law, arbitrary and inapplicable, and resorted to insincerely to enable himself to evade his duty? Was he to say, first in time is first in right, and therefore I continue the old sheriff; or to say, the last will is ever the true will, and therefore I admit the new one? Or was he to decide like an honest man, and a conscientious and courageous judge, that *he was the true sheriff in his court whom the law of the land declared to be the true sheriff;* and thereupon address himself, in the fear of God, to learn what was that law in that behalf? How can two opinions be held on such a subject? Each party was before him, asserting his legal rights. Each opened and pleaded his own commission. The last one had the *prima facie* advantage of being the last; but when the holder of the first alleged against this, that the people of Maine had, by an amendment of their constitution, withdrawn from their governor the legal authority to issue it, and to prove the allegation, cited to the judge the amendment and the statute under which the people had voted on it, and urged as a conclusion of law, on that statute and that amendment, that the executive authority was withdrawn upon a day certain, and that before the date of the last commission — could the judge refuse to hear the allegation, and to try its soundness? Could he say, — this court, especially at *nisi prius*, knows nothing of the people; it knows nothing of the constitution; it only knows who is governor, and what he wills; and what he wills the court obeys, constitution or no constitution? Could he say this? But if not, then the question of constitutional and statute law was cast directly on him. He must decide it to restore order to his court; and woe unto him, or any judge, if he had not decided the question according to his conscience. So much to the suggestion that no issue was before him. On the peculiar position and duties of a single judge at *nisi prius*, I have more to say hereafter.

I find in these charges an allegation or a suggestion that certain consequences of disorder and insubordination have followed his decision. But, Sir, the character and quality of his official act in making the decision, are not in the least degree dependent upon these consequences, whatever they have been. The act is not to be judged by the consequences. Does this accusation assert that he foresaw them? Certainly not. Does it assert that he ought, in the exercise of a sound discretion, to have foreseen them? Certainly not. Does it assert that not to have foreseen them evinces incompetency? Nothing like it. With what justice, then, are they paraded and aggravated, as if he had been intentionally or rashly and responsibly their author! If a party to a suit, urged to madness by an unanticipated and unfavorable decision, conscientiously pronounced, goes out and hangs himself, is the judge his murderer? That some acts of irregularity and even violence have occurred may be admitted. You know better than I can presume to do, how that is. By whom they have been done, under what counsels, with what policy, you know or you can learn. Who is to answer for them, the people of Maine will decide as becomes their wisdom and their justice. That Judge Davis has set an example of insubordination, even undesignedly, it is idle to pretend. That any part of his conduct in this whole business has had, in the least degree, a tendency to weaken in the breast of such a community as this, that accustomed, fond, and rational sentiment of obedience to law, and honor to magistrates and magistracy, which is the characteristic and pride of New England, there is no proof and no probability. Whoever is responsible, he is not. Who believes — who so slanders this people as to say he believes — that the spectacle of a judge, representing the judiciary of Maine in that act, and for that time, — as always does the judge at *nisi prius*, in the performance of every official work regularly devolved on him, — the spectacle of such a judge, anxiously inquiring for the truth, and calmly and decorously declaring it; of a judge, who in a sharp and sudden trial — such he felt it, — in a crisis, for himself, certainly, —

under much temptation to falter and turn aside, — remembered that by his solemn oath, and by his high place, he was bound to be no respecter of persons in judgment; that he was the minister and interpreter of that higher law of the constitution which the people had set over the highest executive magistrate as well as the humblest citizen; that he had a duty to do, and a God to serve by duty, rather than a man or a party to please; that such a spectacle as this breeds riot, and contempt of law, and the denial of its just powers to any department of government? To me it seems rather a sight "soothing and beautiful to the moral eye;" an act which irrespective of its mere legal correctness, "is a lesson too;" not unfitted to lift up, and succor, and animate all forms, and all service of public life. How far prouder for him; how much more nobly useful in its mere influences on others, than a politic cowardice!

On this record of charges, then, Mr. President, no cause of removal is stated, but this: — an alleged mistake in the interpretation of a statute and of the constitution. It is not incompetency; it is not corruption; it is not bad behavior; it is not the absence of good behavior, in any sense which any lawyer, or any writer, has ever yet attached to that expression. It is only and exactly an alleged mistake, in the hurry of *nisi prius*, of an honest and a competent judge, upon the meaning of a written law.

I need not say, that by this record he is to be tried. Upon this record, you and all will be so too. Yet let me add, that I have heard from no quarter a suggestion of anything else to his disadvantage. Let me go further, and bear witness, that in my interviews with him, — absolute strangers before, — his clearness of thought and expression, his good sense, his calmness and self-control — judicial qualities all of them — have created an impression very strongly in his favor. It seemed to me that I recognized the judicial character and habit of mind. It is the universal evidence that he has a true fondness for his profession; that he aspires, and with no unreasonable ambition and hope, to the fame of an eminent judge; and that in his short, but in an unusual degree laborious, official life, he has won the entire respect and the affectionate regard of his learned associates, and of the bar who have practised before him. Well may he be proud to hold a seat on that bench which the Mellens, and Westons, and Shepleys have illustrated; and to preside over a bar which reared your Wilde, and King, and Holmes, and Sprague, and Orr, and Greenleaf, and Rogers, — for time would fail me to rehearse the names of its living ornaments. God grant that that bench may preserve its fame by vindicating its independence; and that it may find in this legislature, what in all the past time of Maine it has found here, a constitutional auxiliary, and not an unconstitutional master!

Yes, Mr. President, I submit to you upon this record of charges, and upon these proofs, all comes back to this. A judge, upright, competent, rising in the professional and public esteem, by circumstances which he could not control becomes charged with the immediate performance of an official duty. The performance of that duty involved and demanded the construction, in the first instance, of a statute and the constitution, — the specific function for which the judge and the judiciary exist; and in respect of which the ultimate judicial decision is conclusive on everybody, and every department. Representing the judiciary, as the judge at *nisi prius* always does, presiding over the proceedings of his own court, with a power absolute, — that is, for which he was responsible only to the law of the land, — it became his duty to make this construction, so far at least as to decide the issue presented, and thus preserve the order, and direct the course of the term. Cautiously, and with pains-taking; availing himself of all attainable opportunities of light; requesting further, but denied them, he made his construction; and, just so far as necessary to dispose of the practical question before him, he announced it and acted on it. You think his construction erroneous; and that is his crime! The judges, sitting as a whole court, have not yet reversed or revised it; it is a question purely judicial by concession of everybody; many easy, usual and constitutional modes exist for submitting it to their review; you reject them all: you differ from him; and that is his crime! For that exactly, and only, they move you to withdraw these honors, and cast down these hopes, and show him forth as a warning of what a judge of your supreme court has to fear, who dares to regard his oath as binding on his conscience, and the will of the people, spoken and recorded in their constitution, as the supreme law of the land.

Mr. President, I hope, I expect, that Maine by her legislature will set no such example. For a thousand years to come — nor yet — till we have reached the downward age of our institutions and our liberty, may the sun see that sight here, or in any State! Looking to your own proud motto — looking for you to direct — lead us not yet that way!

The empire State of New England; larger than the whole territory beside; the democratic State — by eminence so; full of hearts to love liberty, and hands to defend; you to whom Providence has assigned the frontier of our Greece, to guard it against the Persian, against the Macedonian; do not you forget that it is American liberty you watch, — liberty, whose essence, whose end, whose boast, whose fruit is, security.

And now I am ready to resume the examination of the first and larger question, as I have stated it, the question of the object for which, and the limitations under which, the people placed this power of removal in the constitution; and I maintain with the most perfect conviction, that they never intended by it to authorize you to remove a judge, admitted to be honest, and admitted to be competent, for the single reason that you think he mistook the meaning of a written law. What they did intend, it is, as a general proposition, easy to discern, and easy to state. They meant to establish an able, impartial, and independent judiciary, whose function it should be, according to the general American idea, conclusively and finally to declare and administer the law; and of course to interpret conclusively and finally the constitution and statutes. This was the kind of department they meant to establish; and they established it to the end that the constitution itself should at all times be enforced as the permanent and supreme rule, and that all departments of government, all magistrates, high or humble, and all citizens, should obey it; and that all men should find security for their rights under the law.

To attain this great end by these means, they introduce three classes of provisions into the constitution. The object of the *first* was to obtain the original appointment of just and competent judges; and therefore the appointing power is intrusted to the governor and council. The object of the *second* was to insure that while these incumbents continued just and competent, they should be absolutely independent of the other branches of the government; responsible to God, to conscience; in a real and effectual sense to the public judgment; and responsible to no other department and to no combination of departments. And to this end, the tenure of good behavior during the prescribed official term was provided; so that while he continues to be of good behavior; so long as you cannot charge on the record, and establish by proof, after hearing, some act of bad behavior — something which, in the received and the proper sense of the language, may be so charged and so established — no other department, during his prescribed official term, can touch a hair of his head.

The object of the *third* class of provisions was, that when he ceased, in the received and the proper sense of that language, to be of good behavior, and that fact could be charged and proved on trial, he may be removed, by impeachment, if it amounted to misdemeanor in office; and by address, if it did not.

In a general way, then, of stating it, the intention of the people by the grant of this power was to enable and secure the removal of a judge for bad behavior, not being a misdemeanor, in office, — a judge who in some way, by crime, by intemperance, by mental imbecility, by manifested ignorance and incompetency, by incurable indolence, by cruelty, by corruption, by loss of character, — should come to dishonor or cumber the bench, and to bear the sword of justice in vain. But if he is honest, competent, a conscientious seeker of truth, of character unspotted, of gentle and dignified manner; if his official life hitherto has been such as to win the approval and love of his associates, and the regard of the bar; if all that his accusers dare put on the record against him; all that they dare summon him to defend is an alleged single instance of mistake in the interpreting of a written law, confessedly not so clear, and in the absence of all evidence showing the least degree of incompetence, or any other failing unbecoming a good judge, — in such case the people did not intend to authorize you to remove him. In their sense of the language, there is no bad behavior. And without that, they declare him independent of you.

This, then, is my general statement of the objects and the limitations of this power. Let it be examined.

On a question of the objects and the limitations of a power

contained in almost all of our American constitutions, and on a question whether for one decision of a good judge at *nisi prius*, thought by the legislature to be erroneous, they may declare him of bad behavior, and that he thenceforth holds office, not by the tenure of independence, but at their will, — on these questions, the general sense of our country affords high evidence of the people of Maine. And permit me therefore to remind you, *first*, that you can find no case, — no, not one! — in the whole history of constitutional liberty, in which a legislature has used this power, and construed this language, as you must use and construe it, if on this record and these proofs you remove this judge. I doubt if you can find a case of an attempt to do it. Courts have been sometimes abolished, by a repeal of the law creating them. Judges have been removed for mental imbecility. The legislature of Maine once displaced a justice of the peace who had counterfeited money. Incumbents of inferior and semi-judicial jurisdictions, county commissioners and the like, have been displaced, too. But for the removal of a judge of the highest judicial tribunal in the State, for the single cause that he declared his own opinion, instead of the opinion of a governor or a legislature, on the interpretation of a law, — for this, thus far, in the maddest and briefest hour of party excitement, there has never yet been found one precedent under the written constitutions of America. If gentlemen have such a precedent, will they produce it? If your memories or your studies supply one, will you refer me to it here and now? No, Sir, it is a portentous novelty, and this alone may well give us pause. On this point I do not rely exclusively on my own researches. I am able to avail myself of the far more exact and thorough examination of this branch of the question, by which Mr. Dana, of the Massachusetts bar, prepared himself at the last session of her legislature, to resist the attempt to remove Judge Loring. In that memorable exigency, elevating himself above the claims of his political connections; submitting even his personal sympathies and personal antipathies to his love of truth and sense of duty; standing alone against his friends, he produced an argument and an appeal against that folly and madness, of which any man might be proud; skilfully reasoned and eloquently urged in all parts, but particularly instructive in its treatment of the history and the practical interpretation of this power. With the results of his inquiries I am attended, and I repeat, that for such a proceeding as here is threatened, the file affords no precedent. Why, he tells us that even the leaders in the attempt against Judge Loring — or the more prudent and better taught of these leaders — did not venture to maintain a doctrine so novel and so outrageous, as that the legislature could remove an honest and competent judge for the reason that they thought he had erred conscientiously in the interpretation of a statute. Even in the madness of that hour; even in the presence of that flushed and frantic majority, they shrank from this extravagance. In his argument on that occasion, Mr. Dana remarks, —

"The grounds upon which Mr. Phillips puts the case are, that though guilty of no impeachable conduct in office, Judge Loring has shown himself unfit to hold the office; that he has wilfully disregarded the will of the people, as expressed by the legislature; that he has shown such a want of the judicial qualities, such inhumanity, such corruptness of mind, and so forfeited the confidence of the community, and so incurred its permanent and just abhorrence, that the retaining him in office is a public scandal, and the public interests in the probate-office demand his removal."

That was the case on which they pretended to press his removal. If such a case had been proved, it might have constituted the "bad behavior" of the constitution, and might have come within the power. Such a case that fanatical majority was brought to feel had been proved, and therefore, not so much in violation of law, as under the blindest and wildest misapprehension of facts, they voted the address. You know the rest. The governor refused to remove. The sober second thought of Massachusetts, although she has "conquered none of her prejudices" against the fugitive slave law, and those who administer it, sustained him, and has pronounced the courage, the sobriety of mind, the correct appreciation of facts, and sound exposition of the constitution, which he then and thus displayed, the true honor of his public life.

Sir, this long and uniform practical interpretation of this power by the States, is high evidence of the meaning of their constitutions. It is high evidence of the meaning of your own. The recorded debates in the several conventions which framed or adopted these constitutions, throw some light, though less than could be wished, on the objects and limitations of this power, and on what is really meant by continuing or ceasing to be of good behavior. But the contemporaneous and subsequent usage, so uniform and so emphatic, more than supplies the deficiency, and more than completes the *a priori* demonstration. Taken in connection with the actual structures of the constitutions themselves, to which I shall in a few moments address myself, it places the meaning of the people beyond all doubt. It proves that they never intended nor imagined, by this power, to impair the true independence of the judiciary, as a separate and coequal department of government, supreme in its sphere over both the others, — no, nor of any single judge, in the least degree. It proves that they never intended to establish the tenure of good behavior *in terms*, and yet to establish the tenure of mere legislative will, *in effect*. It proves that they never intended that the legislature, or the governor, or both together, should have power to compel the supreme court to utter their opinions, instead of its own, on a matter of judicial cognizance, on peril of deprivation of office under the scandalous charge of bad behavior. It prepares us to find when we come critically to inspect the constitutions themselves, that they are harmonized and consistent systems; every part co-working with every other; each and all capable of complete and reasonable execution; demanding only to be administered in the spirit and from the point of view in which they were constructed.

In this connection it may not be undeserving of notice, that the source from which we perhaps adopted this provision for the removal by address, and the history of its origin there, afford some additional ground of presumption, *a priori*, that we did not design it as a means of impairing judicial independence, and help to explain perhaps, to some extent, the sparing and special use we have always made of it. The framers of our constitutions found it existing in that of England. They knew how it came there, and why it came there. They knew, therefore, that it had its origin in no intention to make the judge dependent on the mere pleasure of any body; in no intention to enable king or parliament, or both, to compel a court, *in banc* or *nisi prius*, to accept the executive, or the legislative exposition of statutes, in place of its own; in no intention to nullify the fundamental maxim of liberty which prescribes the separation of executive, legislative, and judicial powers. They knew on the contrary, that the parliament which first incorporated this provision into the public law of England, at that very moment, and by a system of provisions of which this very one was part, was designing and accomplishing that last and not the least grand and beneficent result of the revolution, to which even William yielded late and reluctantly, a true, practical, and safe judicial independence.

It was one of a scheme of measures, not aiming to make the judge dependent on parliament, but to make him independent of the king. Its precise object was to secure him in office while his official behavior was good; to make known that the simple and conscientious refusal to interpret a statute, or do anything else, against his own convictions, and for the pleasure of the king, was not bad official behavior, *per se;* and to guaranty to him that until the justice and honor of both houses of parliament should authorize it, no power in the constitution might remove him from his place. Its object was not to enable parliament, but to restrain the king. Always the two houses could petition for anything. This clause acquired no new rights for them. It was not intended to do so. It was *diverso intuitu.* It was to give to the people of England what before they had never had, or had by happy accident only, a judge who knew no master but the law, and no distinctions but of rights. Before the Revolution of 1688, judges held office at the pleasure of the crown. They had been therefore, with glorious and rare exceptions, the instruments, say rather more plainly, if you do not think too concisely, the tools of the crown. Such, under such tenures, the British statesmen of the revolution foresaw they must ever continue; and while they should continue such, they discerned that they had achieved the revolution in vain. In the year 1700, therefore, in the final act of settlement, entitled "An act for the further limitation of the crown, and better securing the rights and liberties of the subject," they consummated their work by substituting the tenure of good behavior, for the tenure of the pleasure of the king; thus giving to the people of England, through all their generations, that indispensable and that vast security of right and liberty, an independent judiciary. This exactly, and merely, was the object of the seventh clause of the act of settlement. So the framers of our constitution understood that precedent; and so they interpreted its lessons. No wonder that a provision having such an historical origin, aiming at and marking so brilliant and beneficent a trial of judicial independence, should have been administered uniformly thus far in the spirit of that origin. No wonder that, designed to assure the judges of England that mere disobedience of the king's will shall not forfeit their commissions, it has been uniformly interpreted here to assure our judges that mere disobedience of the governor's will shall not forfeit theirs. No wonder that, introduced there to encourage and to compel the judge to form and utter his own opinions of the law, under his responsibility to conscience and the people, instead of echoing and registering the opinions of others, it has never yet been understood here to make an honest and careful judicial opinion a crime. Before so vast an innovation is hazarded, let us be quite certain that there is something in the constitution of Maine to distinguish it from the general American model, and to warrant a departure from the uniform American practice.

And this conducts me to that instrument itself. In what terms is your power given? In the following: —

> "Sec. 5. Every person holding any civil office under the State, may be removed by impeachment, for misdemeanor in office; and every person holding any office, may be removed by the governor with the advice of the council, on the address of both branches of the legislature. But before such address shall pass either House, the causes of removal shall be stated and entered on the journal of the House in which it originated, and a copy thereof served on the person in office, that he may be admitted to a hearing in his defence."

This language you say is quite general. Certainly. Taken by itself, and without attention to the whole well-considered and consistent writing of which it is part, it is so. He may remove on address. But for what cause did the people of Maine intend that you should address? Some *causes* there must be; some causes that may be stated and entered of record, and against which he must be heard in his defence. For *what* causes then? It does not enumerate them in terms, nor define in terms either the general object, or the particular limitations. But will any man therefore venture to say that they authorize a removal without cause? Certainly not. If, then, there must be cause, capable of statement on the record, and to which the incumbent must be allowed to defend, it must be good cause. And how shall we know what the people meant should be deemed a good cause? Shall we say they meant that anything which the legislature of the hour might bring themselves to vote a good cause, is, and becomes a good cause? Why, this would be to give you in this behalf arbitrary power. It would be to give to one branch of government arbitrary power over another branch of government. It would be to authorize two branches to extinguish a third, or turn it into an echo and a shadow of themselves, at their mere pleasure. It would be to place the honor of the judge — his sensibilities, his reasonable expectations, his right to his office guaranteed during good behavior in his turn — at the disposal of whim, passion, pride, partisanship — the humor of the "elective despotism" of the moment. Sir, such power cannot be given, and cannot be taken, by mere implication. It must be given in clear and peremptory terms, or it is not given at all. Do you find it so given? No. Do you find it said, "and the legislature may so address, and the governor may so remove, at their mere pleasure"? No. Then the power is not arbitrary. It is not unlimited. It is limited to the existence of *good cause* proved on trial. Well, to determine whether any particular cause alleged is what the people meant should be deemed good cause; to determine whether in any particular case they meant you should exercise this power, you are to take the whole constitution together, and to see, upon a careful collation of all its parts, whether so to exercise it, and for such cause, is or is not incompatible with other provisions, whose meaning you cannot misunderstand; whose objects and whose spirit you cannot and would not deny that you perfectly knew. If it is so incompatible, it is not authorized. If it is so incompatible, it is forbidden. And I assert of the proposed removal of this judge for this cause — an honest and able man — for an interpretation of the constitution and the statute, which you think mistaken, it is a use of this power absolutely incompatible with the rest of the constitution, with its whole structure and pervading spirit and general idea, and with numerous particular provisions whose sense and end no man can help seeing. For that reason, I say it is unauthorized and is forbidden. So to exercise the power were to abuse and pervert it. If there is no other department of government to revise and reverse such a proceeding, as I believe there is, there would still be some responsibility to character, to conscience, and to the great popular law-giver behind, which no servant of the public can disregard if he would, or would if he could.

It need not be argued to such an assembly as this, that the true rule of interpreting the constitution requires that every provision of it, however general in terms, be so construed as to be made consistent with every other. Each is to be deemed a part of a careful and skilful whole. Every power is to be deemed given, and is to be used in trust for *all* the constitution. And therefore, if of two constructions of a power like this — of removing a judge — one construction reconciles it with all the residue of the instrument, and especially its more fundamental provisions and principles, while the other construction brings it directly in conflict with them, and would annul or essentially defeat their ends and embarrass their administration — of these two constructions, that which harmonizes and executes all, is the true construction. Surely, this is too clear for argument. You construe every writing, however hasty, and however unskilful, by this rule. You presume an intention to make harmonious and consistent work; and you give effect, if you can, to every stipulation and to every word; although to do so you depart here and there from the ordinary use, and here and there limit and restrict the apparent generality. So you would deal with the most inartificial instrument, touching the most trivial concern. But with how much more reason should you so interpret a written constitution of free government? Is there any production of human art, of human will, so prodigious and so grand? Is there any to which more reason, thought, virtue, deeper studies, more fervent prayer to God, have been invoked? Is there any writing of man's hands, in which we may be more certain to find harmony of parts; coöperation of all with each and each with all; the easy and sure play of the auxiliary machinery of order and adjustment; not a conflict of antagonisms? Think how many of our greatest minds have coöperated in this kind of work; how much discussion among the people has preceded and attended and assisted it; in how true a sense it has been the master-work of American reason and virtue, — and say if you do not expect to find such a document true to itself? Do you expect to find, that in such a constitution as yours — in which are embodied, not only the thoughts of the Kings, and Holmeses, and Thatchers, and Emerys, and Whitmans, but the thoughts of all who have set their hands to our American public law, from the Declaration of Independence — that in such a constitution the latter end of the commonwealth will be found to have forgot the beginning? Surely here, if anywhere, you will look for consistency and harmony.

And therefore, if of two interpretations, each satisfying the mere words of a clause like this, one is found to execute the whole, and the other to defeat half; one found to carry out certain grand ideas, as separation of departments, and independence of each of the other two; and the other to erase or stifle them — if one makes the constitution a system of coöperation, and the other a chaos of conflict, you will not hesitate which to adopt.

And now I submit that there are parts of this constitution, with which such an interpretation of this power, as would authorize the removal of an honest and competent judge for what you are pleased to call a mistake of written law — an honest mistake — is totally incompatible. There are parts of it whose clear sense and acknowledged ends are totally defeated by such an interpretation. If so, it is demonstrated to be false. What are they?

In the first place, there is that provision which, according to the universal doctrine of American liberty under written constitutions, ordains that there shall be a distribution of all the powers of government among three departments — legislative, judicial, and executive; that each shall possess its own; each, as the general principle, within its sphere, be supreme, coördinate with, and independent of, both the rest; and ordains, more precisely, that of the powers thus assigned to the judiciary, shall be that of interpreting and administering the constitution and statutes; and that in that function of interpretation, the judiciary is not only independent of the legislative and executive, but is the supreme power in the last resort, whose determinations are conclusive on all other branches and all other men.

That there is such a provision in your constitution is certain. It forms the matter of article third: —

"Sec. 1. The powers of this government shall be divided into three distinct departments — the *legislative*, *executive*, and *judicial*.

"Sec. 2. No person or persons, belonging to one of these departments, shall exercise any of the powers properly belonging to either of the others, except in the cases herein expressly directed or permitted."

So then, there are three "distinct departments;" each with its own powers; each, and every member of each, forbidden to exercise those of another; each with its own work to do; each to do it all; and neither to usurp; neither to share.

Such is the principle. From what great constitutional examples you borrowed it; by what great masters it comes recommended; how universally it has been adopted into our constitutions; how indispensable it is to liberty and the government of law — you all know. You all know that the American doctrine in this behalf is, that without it there is no liberty. For want of it, the beautiful but headlong and passionate republics of Greece and Italy burned out and fell, successively, from their thrones on high. In the sublime and fine language of Harrington, adopted into the constitution of Massachusetts, we established this separation of departments "to the end it may be a government of laws and not of men." And now, to accomplish such separation, what does the theory, what does the practice of American constitutional liberty demand? Not, certainly, that each department should be totally disconnected from each; for that were impossible and useless, and even calculated to defeat the practical enforcement of the principle itself. But these things are of its essence — that "neither department ought to possess, directly or indirectly, an overruling influence in the administration of the powers of another;" "that all be so constituted, as far as is practicable, as to keep each in its proper place;" "that each department have a will of its own;" "that each be independent of the others, as far as may be, for its continuance in office as well as the emoluments of office;" and that "each be armed with the necessary constitutional means and personal motives to resist the encroachments of the others."

I have set these forth in the very terms of that masterly examination of this principle of liberty contained in "The Federralist," Nos. 47 to 51 inclusive; and as you find them, for substance, embodied in your own constitution.

And now, under this distribution of powers, what is assigned to the judiciary? What are the powers which it is appointed to perform; which it alone can perform; on which, therefore, it is made the supreme arbiter in the last resort? Sir, not to enumerate them all, let me say, that by concession of everybody, among them are these: — to interpret the constitution; to interpret statutes; to try all legislative action assuming the form of law, and all executive action affecting individual right, by the standard of the constitution, and if it find it unauthorized by that fundamental rule, to declare it void. So much is conceded by everybody. The people establish the constitution, and they declare therein, that the judiciary shall in the last resort determine its meaning, and that that determination shall bind all other branches of government. They provide for the enactment of statutes by the legislature, but they declare that the judiciary shall determine their meaning, and that that also shall bind all other branches. Creating the constitution as the supreme law, and intending, therefore, that no act of magistrates high or humble, and no statute, passed by any majority, repugnant to that supreme law, shall have force or effect, they devolve on the judiciary the duty of ascertaining if such repugnance exists; and if so, to uphold their will against their servants, by annulling what they have attempted. This you all concede. The constitution of Maine does not, no constitution in terms does, define the extent and particulars, or declare the nature of judicial power, or the effect of judicial action. To learn these, it sends us to political science, to American political science, to the systems and language of writers, to the practice of governments under written constitutions, to the judgments of courts, to the acquiescence of the people. And these demonstrate that such, in our system, are the character and functions of the judiciary. Since the 78th paper of "The Federalist" was written, indeed, such has been the universal opinion. So your own courts have holden. So does the majority of your own committee, appointed to inquire how far your constitution has been amended, and when the amendments took effect. In terms they say that this, in the last resort, must be decided by the judiciary, and to that extent they agree with everybody else.

Now, Sir, my proposition is, that to these provisions of your constitution, that interpretation of this power, which would remove this judge for the cause alleged on this record, is absolutely repugnant, and must therefore be rejected. If it be admitted, as it must be, that the people have distributed among the three classes of their servants the three descriptions of power, assigning to each its own, and making each within its sphere supreme; and if it be admitted, as it must be, that in this distribution they have assigned the power of interpreting the constitution and the law, and of deciding whether acts of magistrates and statutes of the legislature are or are not void, to the judiciary; and if it be finally admitted, as it must be, that this power of removal is to be so construed as to reconcile it with the residue of the instrument, and make of it a harmonious whole, — then surely it cannot be supposed to have intended to authorize the legislature and the governor to punish the court or the judge for doing just what they were created to do, and what the governor and the legislature were not created to do; that is to say, honestly to interpret and administer the constitution and law in questions of conflicts of right. Would not such a construction cover the whole instrument with contempt? Can you imagine its framers, can you imagine the people of Maine, to set forth in this master-work, that whereas the examples and the teachings of the past, the warnings of history, the necessities of free constitutions, inculcate a division of the powers of government, we therefore adopt it, we commit the office of interpretation to the judge, and we declare that as against his interpretation the opinions of the executive and the legislature shall be absolutely inoperative and void; can you imagine them, after saying this, within two pages onward falling into such ridiculous and incredible inconsistency as to say, "but the executive and legislature may punish him by deprivation of office for exercising honestly, and according to his judgment, this very power of interpretation which we commit exclusively to him, and deny to them? He shall interpret, and they shall not. His interpretation shall bind them, and theirs shall not bind him; but, if they disapprove his interpretation, they may turn him out; if they fear the interpretation he is about to make, they may terrify him, by the threat of removal, into the adoption of theirs. They shall not exercise judicial power, and he shall; their opinions shall not give the law, and his shall; but they may constitutionally put in and put out, until he shall echo and record exactly what they would have him to do!" Such inconsistency is inconceivable. It would be so if the distribution of power among three departments were a mere matter of convenience or form. But when you recall the grand reasons on which that doctrine and practice depend; when you consider that the framers of this instrument were deeply learned in these reasons; that history, examples old and new, the concurrent expression of all great political thinkers, the universal American judgment and habit, all were familiar, and all taught that without this separation there was an end of liberty; that without it they were establishing a government, not of laws, but of men; that without an independent judicial department — independent of the law-making power, neither private right nor the constitution itself was secure, — you feel how impossible it is that they should laboriously and carefully provide for it on one page, and on another forget it, and give it to the winds! They solemnly record their attestation to the truth, importance, and grandeur of this maxim of political liberty. They formally construct their constitution according to it. They expressly forbid each to exercise the powers of another, except in the precise cases provided in the constitution itself. The interpretation of statutes and the constitution is not one of these cases. Such interpretation, as against the judiciary, the executive and the legislature are therefore expressly forbidden to make, — because that is an accumulation of powers in the same hands, and is the very definition of tyranny; and yet they are intentionally authorized to accomplish the very same thing without disguise, by punishing the judge for doing the very work, in his own way, assigned him and forbidden them!

Run it out, Sir, in its application to this case. The governor of Maine can appoint a sheriff, if the constitution in force at the time he assumes to appoint one authorizes him to do so. If it does not, he cannot. All agree to this. Whether the constitution then in force does so authorize him is a question which the instrument itself commits exclusively to the judiciary. It ordains that his opinion shall not decide it; that the legislative opinion shall not decide it; but that the judicial opinion shall decide it, whether he like the opinion, or the legislature like it, or not. So far all agree. "We ordain this," say the people, "to the end that ours may be a government of laws, and not of men; and that no governor shall usurp a power of appointment which our constitution does not give him; because under that, and of that, an independent judiciary is a calmer, more learned, safer, and more competent arbiter than he, or the legislature of his party." So far, you agree, the people speak; so far wisely, so far worthily; but then comes "provided, and nevertheless, and notwithstanding, that if the governor and legislature think the judiciary decide erroneously against his authority, they may remove the old judges and he may appoint new ones, until the bench shall agree in an opinion with his excellency, and the two houses approve; and then he may appoint his sheriff!" That is the proviso which they who would remove this judge have to find in the constitution. Sir, it is not there, the text is a forgery, and the doctrine it is interpolated to support is an error of the deadliest type.

Mr. President, this article providing for separation of departments, is not the only one in the constitution to which this construction of the power of removal is utterly repugnant. To other particular provisions, to its whole structure, and its whole spirit, it is so equally.

This constitution means to make the judge independent of other branches; your interpretation totally defeats it. When the convention which formed it, had nearly completed their work, and were about to vote on its final acceptance, Mr. Holmes, who had borne so conspicuous a part in its deliberations, could rise, and in a brief and glowing speech, congratulate them "that among other great results, they had established an *independent judiciary*, responsible to the people." But how could he have made that boast, if on a mere difference of opinion upon the law, the other branches might displace the court? Where and what was that pretence, and that dream of independence, if a party leader, plaintiff or defendant, dissatisfied with a ruling at *nisi prius* on a charter party or a deed with warranty, without waiting for an opportunity of appealing to the whole bench, could run to the legislature and turn out the judge on an allegation of mistake of law?

See how this conception of independence pervades the constitution, and what a fancy, and what a mockery it is, if this interpretation of the power of removal is indulged. Its declaration of rights begins by proclaiming that all men "have certain natural inherent and inalienable rights, among which are those of enjoying and defending life and liberty, acquiring, possessing, and protecting property, and of pursuing and obtaining safety and happiness."

But what are all these sounding abstractions worth, if the studies, and the firmness, and the virtues of the judge are not engaged to ascertain those rights and administer them; and how and where are you to find the possessor, if his very first decision is to forfeit his office? It declares all men "equally under the protection of the laws." And what does this avail, if the commission of the governor of a day and a party, goes for conclusive evidence of the law? It guarantees "impartial trial." And who can give such a trial, but an independent judge? It guarantees to "all men their legal rights; a due course of law; justice administered freely and without sale, completely and without denial, promptly and without delay." But at whose hands shall they have them, if the supreme dictator is but a pensioner on the bounty of an hour? It engages to the judge for his seven years of official life, a tenure as certain as his good behavior! But how empty a name is good behavior, if to differ on the law from the governor or legislature, is bad behavior! It entitles him to a statement of the causes of removal, before he can be removed, and a chance to defend against them. But how can he defend against your mere good pleasure? How can he stand against the unanswerable and stern recital, "*Licet hoc* DE JURE *non possumus volumus tamen de* PLENITUDINE POTESTATIS."

It is framed in all its parts to meet and supply that twofold demand of the Anglo-Saxon nature, liberty and security; liberty with security, liberty for the sake of security. To provide for the perpetuity of freedom was an easy undertaking. But to unite with that the inviolate sacredness of rights; to bless and temper it with peace, order, trust, contentment; to give to every man his own; to guard the earnings of labor from injustice, fraud, and force, while he lives, and transmit them to those nearest to his blood and heart when he dies; to make freedom yield with certainty and in abundance those fruits, was a harder, nor less noble achievement. For this it has ordained the administration of law, whose power constrains the greatest, and whose care compasses the least about. But how can it have this, without the studies, virtues, courage, and impartiality of a bench that owns no master but the law, and no duty but justice?

It has been suggested, I hear, that the limitations on this power for which we contend, may be admitted to be sound, in so far as they apply to the whole bench of judges of the Supreme Court, and to the whole judicial department; but that they have no application to a single judge holding a legal term alone. You cannot remove the judges, it is said, for the law they lay down when all together; but for the law any one lays down at *nisi prius*, you may. He may be able and he may be conscientious; it may be just as clearly his official duty to form and express an opinion in one case as the other; he may give the same reasons and come to the same results; but for what he does in company he is safe; for what he does alone, you may forfeit his commission.

Mr. President, a distinction like this it seems scarcely possible seriously to maintain, or seriously to deny. It all proceeds of course, upon this enormous supposition; that a judge sitting alone, is officially bound to receive and administer as law that which his learning and reason inform him is not law; and which, sitting with the whole court the next week, he will be bound by his conscience to declare not to be law. This, without phrases, is the whole of it. At *nisi prius* he must obey the governor; as one of the whole court, he may obey the constitution. In one place he is the servant of the executive. In the other he is servant only of the people. In one place he is nothing but a citizen. In the other he is altogether a judge. In one place he is bound to pronounce the commission of a sheriff valid, although clear and certain in his convictions that the people, by an amendment of their constitution, have withdrawn from the governor the authority to make it. In the other, on the very same day, he is bound, under the same conviction, by his oath, by his responsibility to God, the people and the constitution, to pronounce it invalid. That conduct which in one place would be virtue, conscientiousness, judicial independence, the upholding of the powers and the performance of the duties of a coördinate department, made supreme within its sphere, "to the end that it may be a government of laws and not of men," that same conduct, on exactly the same evidence, and exactly the same opinions, is in the other place, insubordination, ignorance, and bad temper, so gross as to forfeit his office!

Where is the evidence of any such distinction as this? Does the constitution make it? Nowhere. Does his commission? No, certainly. That commission, reciting the confidence of the appointing power in his learning, fidelity, and ability, appoints him a judge of the Supreme Court of Maine — nor less nor more. By that act it clothes him with the entire judicial character, and charges him with the whole judicial duty; and whatsoever, anywhere by the constitution and statutes and common law of Maine, one judge may do, he is authorized to do. Is it by statute, then, that the single judge at *nisi prius* is forbidden to administer the law, according to his lights: saving to parties aggrieved their right, by exceptions, or otherwise, according to the subject-matter, to subject his determinations to review by the whole court? Sir, you know, and I cannot be presumed to know, the statutes of Maine, and its practice in this behalf; but I am instructed, and I submit to your learning, that in your system, as in that of Massachusetts, the single judge is bound to find, declare, and enforce the law at *nisi prius*, by the same obligation, to the same extent exactly, with the firmness and the same impartiality, as when he sits *in banc*, — subject, only, of course, to the ultimate reversal of his decisions at the law term of the court. Certain classes of causes, by statute, he may not try alone, — capital causes, for example, and others perhaps, — because the statute restrains it; but others again, — all others arising before him, he is required to try, and required to decide in the first instance; and for the rule of trial, and the rule of decision, — in all cases, without any exception on which the judgment of the Supreme Court, as a whole court, has not already been authoritatively uttered, — for the rule of trial, and the rule of decision, he is bound to have resort to the law, as his studies and his reason teach him the law.

Yes, Sir. For the determination of all matters before him, in the first instance, he is the judiciary of Maine. For all such matters, and in the first instance, he represents, he is, that whole department, clothed with all its constitutional immunities, affected by all its constitutional responsibilities, to the people, to the law, to conscience, to honor.

True, the decision of the court at *nisi prius* may be revised and reversed by the whole court. But he is authorized to make them. He is required to make them as a judge. He is required to make them. He is required to make them, then, according to law. It is as a court of law he makes them. That which is law for him anywhere, is law for him there. That which is evidence of the law for him anywhere, is evidence of the law for him there. Some questions indeed, he must, from their nature, decide at once. From their nature they must, for the present, be irreversibly decided. Such, exactly, was the one, whether A. or B. was the sheriff of his court for his term. Was he to allow them to fight it out in his presence? Was he to allow that fight to proceed till the law term of the court? Then he must decide it on the spot, and he must decide it by law, or he is no judge. Think, Sir, how absurd, and how sad would be the consequences, if the judge at *nisi prius* is to be held above or below the law of the land for his rule of decision! When you consider that he tries, in the first instance, all cases, civil and criminal, under the degree of capital; that in a vast proportion, from the necessities of parties, or the circumstances of the case, his decisions are practically final; that in his quickness, firmness, memory, learning, sagacity, the whole value of the trial by jury so largely depends, you will pause before you sanction this whim that he is *legibus solutus;* that he is at liberty to substitute a fancy of expediency; to substitute fear, favor, affection; the hope of reward, or the respect of persons, for that established law, in whose learning he is instructed, and in whose presence magistrates and people stand on an absolute equality.

But there is another view in which the attempted distinction appears quite as inadmissible. It leads directly to the confusion of the departments of government; to the annihilation of judicial independence, and the accumulation of power in the hands of the executive and legislature. You cannot remove the judge for an honest, judicial decision at a law term. That, you agree, is not within the scope and objects of this power. Every other part of the constitution, you have seen, forbids it. But if a judge can be removed for his decision at *nisi prius* just as honestly made, does it not come to exactly the same thing? If you can remove one, can you not another, and another? The whole bench is safe, but every member may be picked off in detail! If a judge concurs with his brethren *in banc*, in a question on a charter-party, or a bill of exchange, or policy of insurance against fire, he is beyond your reach; but if he had ruled the same point the same way in a jury trial the week before, he might have been removed for it! Who does not see that on such a distinction the boast of judicial independence is idle and deceptive?

You will not understand me as denying or undervaluing the expediency and the duty of the single judge, and of all judges, paying true and constant respect to the action and opinions of the other departments of government. My client does not deny or undervalue it. He has never failed, in any just sense, in that duty and that policy. Our system is a system, not of antagonisms, but of coöperation. Each department, in the first instance, must form its own opinions and order its own conduct for itself. The governor of Maine, in the first instance, had the clear, constitutional right to adopt and act on the conviction that the recent amendments had not bereaved him of his power to appoint a sheriff. He adopted that conviction, and under it made this appointment. When this fact became judicially known to Judge Davis, or to the whole court, they were bound to receive it as an opinion of a coördinate branch of government, and as such to treat it with entire respect. So he did receive it. So he did treat it. But when, on that appointment, a question arose before him, in his own court, in the direct course of judicial duty, — a question of legal right to office,—a question whether in that court-house, for that term, the old or the new one was the sheriff, and this depended on a proposition of law; when the incumbent cited the existing constitution, and the statute for amending, and the amendment itself, and claimed that the governor had mistaken the law, — then, Sir, the smaller morals of deference and assentation were displaced in a moment by the requirements of duty. That moment the judge was bound to remember that he was a judge. That moment he was bound to remember that he was one of that department by whom the legal opinions of governors and legislatures are intended by the constitution to be conclusively revised and corrected; and that subserviency and cowardice then would be crime against the State and against conscience, and injustice to the party before him, who had established his title to his perfect conviction.

And does not this put the doctrine of the reciprocal respect of departments on its true ground? Does it not secure decorum, courtesy, honor, to and from whom they are due? Would you carry it farther, and train your public servants to meanness and to servility, — train them to stifle their sense of duty and character, and to seek thrift by fawning?

The argument thus far has aimed to prove, from the historical origin of this power, from its practical uniform administration, and from the general structure and particular provisions of the constitution itself, and especially from the relations and functions of the several departments, and the nature and conditions of a true judicial independence, that you are not authorized to remove a judge for this cause; that the power of removal is given for objects and under limitations which forbid such an exercise of it.

There is a narrower view of the subject, perhaps even more decisive, to which I advert rather for the purpose of expressing my full concurrence with the elaborate argument of my associates, than of taxing my own strength to restate and enforce it. And that is, that if the act here complained of has any character of delinquency at all, for which you can punish,—as I have attempted to show it has not, — it is a misdemeanor in office; and that there you are restricted to the mode of impeachment. If there is bad behavior at all, it is bad behavior in office. It was an act done on the bench; it was an act giving direction to the immediate course of proceedings in court; and it was an execution, for the time, of an opinion on a point of law. It was behavior in office; and if bad behavior, it was misdemeanor in office; that or nothing. It is not charged as evidencing incompetency or dishonesty. It is one act, and that act is a misdemeanor, if it is anything. It follows by the express terms of the constitution, that if you believe it bad behavior at all, and of course believe it, as you must, a misdemeanor in office, you may proceed by the mode of impeachment. But is not that the only mode? If the official misdemeanor prove or include the additional ingredient of unfitness, of dishonesty, of incompetency, it might with some plausibility, but not with soundness, be argued that you might remove by address, for this included an additional element, dropping the misdemeanor, as such, out of view. But where, as here, this is not so; where the misdemeanor, such as it is, does not prove or include any disqualifying or objectionable trait or defect, and consists in one single alleged mistake of an honest and able man, — there is only the act itself to proceed for, and that is a naked and mere misdemeanor, or nothing. Must you not deal with it then by impeachment? Is not the rule of law quite general, and does it not directly apply, that when a statute creates or declares an offence, and provides a mode of trying and punishing it, all other modes are, *prima facie*, excluded? Is it not another rule of law, that if a statute bestow a power or franchise, and prescribe a mode of exerting it, it can, *prima facie*, be exerted in no other? And does not your power to remove for official misdemeanor by impeachment come within this rule? Other modes, in both classes of cases, may, in words or necessary construction, be permitted, no doubt. But here are no words to say, that for official misdemeanor merely an officer may be removed by address. Nor is that a necessary construction; for all the other language of the article may be satisfied by applying it to causes *other than* official misdemeanor. And when you consider the improbability that double and totally diverse, nay, incompatible proceedings, should be provided for the very same act; that a misdemeanor being a species of criminal offence, — though certainly not necessarily an indictable offence, — it seems fit, and according to all analogy, that a real, well-guarded, and cautious trial should be allowed for it; the presentment by one branch; the hearing on oath by the other; all the forms and all the substance of trial for crime,—it seems difficult to resist the conclusion, that this great statute is to be construed like every other, and the mode prescribed be held the only mode intended. Reflect that protection to judges is protection to suitors. The judge must feel safe, that parties may have justice. You secure yourselves fair trial when you secure him fair trial.

But this topic I have not strength to pursue; — and I leave it with great pleasure upon the powerful reasonings you have heard already. It is due to frankness in taking leave of it to say, that I do not suppose that there is one member of this Convention, or one man out of it, who believes that there has been committed a misdemeanor in office. No man believes, anywhere, that an impeachment could command one vote in either branch. But why? Because the act is not indictable? No, indeed; for that is universally admitted not to be necessary to support an impeachment. Why then? Exactly because Judge Davis's intent was honest; and his error, if he erred, innocent. And if so, and if it does not prove incompetency, ignorance, or any other quality or deficiency disqualifying or unbecoming a judge, — as the record of charges admits, and all the proofs demonstrate, — pray, Sir, for what do you remove him? The act is mere misdemeanor, if it is anything; and as misdemeanor, they dare not impeach it.

Thus far, Sir, the argument has assumed that Judge Davis mistook the law. But there is another side of the question. That he made no mistake at all; or that no man can be so far certain that he made it, as to find in his entire conduct in this matter a colorable pretext for imputation on his learning, ability, uprightness, and discretion, will now be very briefly submitted. It involves in part a point of local law, and in part a more flexible inquiry of official ethics and proprieties; and in neither aspect does it ask or warrant very elaborate consideration. And in the first place, is it not rather *premature* to proceed to such extreme action as this, on such cause as this? You are moved to displace him for mistaking a point of law. But under the constitution, who is the ultimate judge of this? Certainly the Supreme Court. So much the report of your own committee concedes. So much all men concede. This Convention, abounding doubtless in ability, learning, and weight of character, is not the judge. Until that tribunal shall determine his opinion erroneous, can it be constitutionally known, and safely or prudently pronounced to be erroneous? To punish for it, before it can be known such, is that discreet? What if the supreme power of the constitution should declare his decision to be good law? What then were his position, and what yours? Certainly the executive and legislative branches of government may in the first instance, and for the guidance of their proper departmental duties, provisionally decide a question of interpretation. But before they try and punish a member of another branch for misinterpretation, is it not wise to have the highest evidence that this offence has really been committed?

But to your judgment, is the misinterpretation established? The people of Maine, it is now conceded by all, have so amended their constitution as to withdraw from the executive the power to appoint sheriffs, and resumed it to themselves. The general question which came before Judge Davis was, — had they so withdrawn the power and so resumed it at the time when the new sheriff received his commission? And this question divided itself into two: first, had their amendments become part of the constitution before he had his commission; and if so, secondly, did they at once withdraw the executive power to create a vacancy and to appoint to it; or did they leave it as it stood before, until some future day and event?

The determination of both these questions depended upon the true intent of the fourth section of the tenth article of the existing constitution, and the true intent of certain resolves of the legislature of Maine, adopted on the 17th of March, 1855. By a just construction of that article and those resolves, did the amendments become part of the constitution in November, 1855, upon its being made to appear to the governor and council that a majority of votes given were in favor of them; or did they not become so until the next legislature should so declare?

The article of the constitution is this: —

"The legislature, whenever two thirds of both houses shall deem it necessary, may propose amendments to this constitution; and when any amendment shall be so agreed upon, a resolution shall be passed and sent to the selectmen of the several towns, and the assessors of the several plantations, empowering and directing them to notify the inhabitants of their respective towns and plantations, in the manner prescribed by law, at their next annual meeting in the month of September, to give in their votes on the question, whether such amendment shall be made; and if it shall appear that a majority of the inhabitants voting on the question are in favor of such amendment, it shall become a part of this constitution."

The resolves are these: —

RESOLVES PROVIDING FOR AN AMENDMENT OF THE CONSTITUTION RELATING TO THE ELECTIVE FRANCHISE.

Resolved, Two thrids of both branches of the legislature concurring, that the constitution of this State shall be amended in the eighth section of the first part of the fifth article, by inserting after the words "judicial officers," in the second line of said section, the words "except Judges of Probate and Municipal and Police Courts," and by striking out the words "Attorney-General, the Sheriffs, Registers of Probate," in second and third lines thereof, and by inserting after the words "provided for," in the seventh line of said section, the words "except the Land Agent."

The sixth article shall be amended by inserting the following sections at the end of said article: —

"SECTION 7. Judges and Registers of Probate shall be elected by the people of their respective counties, by a plurality of the votes given in, at the annual election on the second Monday of September, and shall hold their offices for four years, commencing on the first day of January next after their election. Vacancies occurring in said offices by death, resignation, or otherwise, shall be filled by election in manner aforesaid, at the September election next after their occurrence; — and in the mean time, the Governor, with the advice and consent of the Council, may fill said vacancies by appointment; and the persons so appointed shall hold their offices until the first day of January thereafter.

"SEC. 8. Judges of Municipal and Police Courts shall be elected by the people of their respective cities and towns, by a plurality of the votes given in, at the annual meeting in March or April, and shall hold their offices for four years from the Monday following the day of their election. Vacancies in said offices shall be filled by elections at the next annual meeting in March or April; and in the mean time, the Governor, with the advice and consent of the Council, may fill said vacancies by appointment until the Monday following said annual meeting."

The third section of the seventh article shall be amended by striking out the words "appointed by the Governor and Council," and inserting instead thereof the words "chosen annually by joint ballot of the Senators and Representatives in convention."

The ninth article shall be amended by inserting at the end thereof the following sections: —

"SEC. 9. Sheriffs shall be elected by the people of their respective counties, by a plurality of the votes given in, on the second Monday of September, and shall hold their offices for two years from the first day of January next after their election. Vacancies shall be filled in the same manner as is provided in the cases of Judges and Registers of Probate.

"SEC. 10. The Land Agent and Attorney-General shall be chosen annually, by joint ballot of the Senators and Representatives in convention. Vacancies in said offices occurring when the Legislature is not in session may be filled by appointment by the Governor, with the advice and consent of the Council."

And in all cases of elections provided for in this resolve, the first elections shall take place on the days and times herein prescribed, occurring next after the amendment providing for such elections shall have been declared by the Legislature to have been adopted as a part of the Constitution.

Resolved, That the Aldermen of cities, and Selectmen of the several towns, and Assessors of the several plantations in the State, are hereby empowered and directed to notify the inhabitants of their respective cities, towns, and plantations, in the manner prescribed by law at the annual meeting in September next, to give in their votes upon the amendments proposed in the foregoing resolve; and the question shall be, Shall the Constitution be amended as proposed by a resolve of the Legislature providing that the Judges of Probate, Registers of Probate, Sheriffs, and Municipal and Police Judges shall be chosen by the people; and also providing that the Land Agent, Attorney-General, and Adjutant-General shall be chosen by the Legislature, as the Secretary of State, State Treasurer and Councillors now are; and the inhabitants of said cities, towns, and plantations shall vote by ballot on said questions of electing said officers, separately, those in favor of said amendments, respectively expressing it by the word "Yes," upon their ballots; and those opposed to the amendments respectively expressing it by the word "No," upon their ballots; and the ballots shall be received, sorted, counted, and declared in open ward, town, and plantation meetings; and lists shall be made out of the votes by the Aldermen, Selectmen, and Assessors and Clerks of the several cities, towns, and plantations, and returned to the office of Secretary of State, in the same manner as votes for senators; and the Governor and Council shall count the same and make returns thereof to the next Legislature; and if a majority of the votes are in favor of any of said amendments, the constitution shall be amended accordingly.

Resolved, That the Secretary of State shall prepare and furnish the several cities, towns, and plantations, blank returns, in conformity to the foregoing resolves, accompanied with a copy thereof.

[Approved March 17, 1855.]

In coming to consider the question, it was quite fit that Judge Davis should begin by adopting some rule, according to which he might decide between two interpretations, either of which should satisfy the language which he had to interpret, and neither of which was clearly and unequivocally demanded by the language. Accordingly he would seem to have adopted this: that of two such interpretations, both satisfying the language, that one is to be preferred which gives the earliest possible effect to the popular will, after that will has been certainly and regularly proved. And therefore, finding that by the count of the governor and council in November, 1856, it had been clearly and regularly made to appear to a body authorized to ascertain it, that the popular will had declared itself in favor of the amendments, he reasoned, that since the language to be construed was as fairly susceptible of a construction which should hold them out of it for some longer time and some more distant event, he ruled in their favor for the earliest time, and executed their declared will, "completely and without denial, promptly and without delay."

And is that not a sound rule of interpretation for a case of equivocal language, on such a subject? If each satisfies the words, and each provides perfectly for a sure ascertainment of the fact of a majority vote, — is not that a true one which gives the speediest effect to that vote? Why? Because that which the people have voted to have for their constitution, it is a fair presumption they mean to have at once. If they want it at all, and it is certainly known that they do, it is a fair presumption that they want it now. If they have declared that there is a good which they would possess, it is a fair presumption that they would possess it now. If they have declared that there is an evil which they would correct, it is a fair presumption that they would correct it now. If they have discovered that on reasons of state, reasons of liberty, reasons of policy, it is expedient to render the executive power and patronage safer, by rendering it less, and so to abridge it of a class of appointments, and have decided to do so, it is a fair presumption that they do not mean to wait for more abuse or more danger, but to have safety now. Consider that they are sovereign; that their right is to have instant obedience, and instant indulgence. They are not to be dealt with in such a matter as so many spendthrift young heirs approaching one-and-twenty, and to be kept out of their property by shifts of prudence or selfishness, until their wild oats are sown. We are not to regard them as incoming tenants whom we may forcibly or fraudulently resist till we can compensate ourselves by strip and waste for the unexpected refusal of the landlord to renew our lease. They are the good men of the house, asking entrance into their own; and whether they come at evening, or midnight, or earliest dawn of day, we are to rise and admit them. *Prima fronte*, on the very day they voted, they would be held to have changed the constitution. But security against fraud, security against revolution, requires some formal and authentic ascertainment of the result of their day's voting. The article and the resolves which I have read prescribe such ascertainment;—and now I repeat, that of two interpretations, each warrranted by the words, and each securing an authentic and formal ascertainment of the fact that a majority desire a change, that interpretation which accomplishes it soonest is the true one.

Let the rule be applied to this language. Recurring to the article of the constitution, you find it declaring, — after providing for the vote, — "if it shall appear that a majority of the inhabitants voting on the question are in favor of the amendment, it shall become part of the constitution." What does this condition, "if it shall appear," call for? Exactly and merely that it shall be *shown; proved*, to somebody authorized to ascertain the fact. Then come the resolves which authorize a body to ascertain the fact. They authorize the governor and council to ascertain it by a count. The moment they have done, "it appears," that is, it is shown; proved; made known, to a tribunal authorized to find it. The moment "it appears," the fourth section of the tenth article itself attaches on it, and ordains that it is part of the constitution. Certainly it so attaches and so ordains, unless the resolves, in clear terms, go on to provide that some further counting is to be had, and some further postponement or suspension is to be allowed. In the absence of some such clear and certain provisions, the old constitution adopts instantly the new amendments into its bosom.

Well, turning to the resolves, there is nothing to require a further count; there is nothing in terms to suspend or postpone the will of the people, already made to appear, for another moment. On the contrary, they simply require a return of the count to the legislature; they prescribe no duty of recounting to the legislature; they declare only that if a majority of the votes are in favor of the amendment, — that is, if on the count by the governor and council, they are so, — the fact regularly appears, and the constitution is instantly amended. They expect, no doubt, in conformity with all your usage, that the legislature will then make declaration of the fact that the constitution has been amended. But it is to be a declaration of a fact as already accomplished; by the will of the people, authentically made to appear to the governor and council.

It cannot therefore be maintained that the construction of this article and these resolves, which hold, first, that on its being made to appear that a majority have voted for amendments, the amendment is adopted; second, that it is so made to appear, when it is ascertained by the count of a body legally authorized to ascertain it; third, that the governor and council are so legally authorized; and, fourth, that no other count is commanded, and no postponement of the time of taking effect is unequivocally and certainly provided for, and therefore, that the popular will takes immediate effect, — it cannot be maintained that this construction does not satisfy all the language, and provide completely for the ascertainment of the all-important fact. It follows, that it is the true construction, because it soonest gives to the people what they have resolved to have.

On these reasons, the judge would seem to have rightly held that the amendments were adopted as soon as the state of the vote appeared to the governor and council, and was notified by return to the legislature. On these reasons the first question would therefore seem satisfactorily disposed of. That his conclusion is fortified by the uniform practical interpretation of Maine, and that it is fortified by a consideration of the consequences of the opposite doctrine, seems clear; but of this, a stranger to your legislative history and local politics may hardly presume to hazard an opinion.

It has been suggested, however, that even if the amendments had become part of the constitution before the governor issued this commission, they had not yet deprived him of his prerogative to create a vacancy, and then to fill it. They left him the power to do so, it has been suggested, until an actual election by the people themselves. This I have called the second question on which Justice Davis had to pass. But is it any question at all? What has the opinion of the judges of Massachusetts to do with it? In the case submitted to them, the amendments did not, in terms, from the moment of their adoption, strike out from the constitution the power of the governor to create a vacancy, and then to fill it. They only ordained generally, that certain classes of officers enumerated should be elected by the people. How the law should stand until an election was actually made, they left in terms unexpressed. But of your amendments, one, in terms, strikes out the old power from the constitution. The adoption of the amendments, then, instantly withdrew it, and there is no case, and there is no room for conjectural interpretation at all. Who can say, against terms so clear and so peremptory as these, that the people meant to endure for a year, or a month, or a day, the exercise of a prerogative of removal and appointment, which they had declared unsafe or inexpedient? They had abridged that prerogative on general considerations of liberty and policy; and why suppose they did not do at once, what they had determined for their security to do at last?

That the respondent, then, has not mistaken the law in this behalf, seems a conclusion reasonably certain. That fair, learned, able judgments might differ on it, is past all doubt. That you differ from him, therefore, no more proves his unfitness, his ignorance, his dishonesty, his partisanship, than it proves your own. If he erred at all, he erred on the side of the people; and to them, when your judgment is rendered, he must stand or fall.

In taking leave of the cause, Mr. President, the very strong professional and personal interest which I feel for my client, will be my excuse for adverting to two or three considerations on his behalf, to which the justice and candor of this tribunal will not be inattentive. They have been anticipated, perhaps, already, but the repetition may be indulged.

Let it be recollected, first, that the sense of justice and fairness, which is in all men, demands that liberal and generous allowances be made for him, who in any trust, and on any field, and in any exigency of duty, is called on suddenly, and without lights, and without helps, to resolve a problem of difficulty, and to act out at once. Of such a man, so tried, good faith alone is exacted by the universal sentiment of justice and kindness. The sailor on the deck, in a mutiny, or upon a lee shore; the soldier in the extreme crisis of battle; the surgeon by the side of the unconscious and crushed patient, — all who are forced on instant and exigent action, — *inopes consilii* — are so judged in the long run, and by the sober, manly, second thought. In such a position, and entitled to such indulgence, the respondent was placed by circumstances he could not control. He sought delay; he proposed a mode of invoking the assistance of his brethren; he foresaw but too distinctly the personal crisis in which he was involved. They compelled him to act, and he acted in the spirit of a man "who has endeavored well."

Consider, next, that his failing, if he failed, leaned to the side of public virtue. Between the people and the executive; between the master and the servant; between the constitution and those who forgot it, he declared for liberty and for the supreme law. Subserviency, cowardice, meanness, falsehood to himself, all counselled other action. These you may have for nothing. But will you discourage the nobler and the rarer qualities of public and official life?

Acknowledge, further, that if the question before him had been thought to be a question of doubt, as it was not, he but followed the universal habit and doctrine of the courts, — that the actual *possession* is to stand for title, till it is clearly shown to be unlawful. There was an existing possession. The old officer was there. The old officer claimed, and pleaded the constitution and the law. That title he was obliged to examine. That title he was obliged to compare with the new and competing title. He did compare; his judgment was convinced that the old was best. But if he had doubted, should not the possession be maintained till the doubt was resolved? Is not this the doctrine of law, and the practice of the bench? What business was it of his, that a governor's commission was waved in his face? It was a conflict of right and demand between two private parties, one in possession, and the other out. Could he displace the possession till he found a better title? Is not possession title, as a general proposition of law?

Consider finally, that he conformed to the established and approved judicial habit and doctrine, and that he followed *the precedents* of Maine, from her first amendments of her constitution to this day. I do not say that these precedents conclusively construe these resolves. But I say that the judge who respects them as *nisi prius;* who accepts them as *primâ facie* evidence of the law; who pauses before he sets up his own judgment, or the judgment of the executive of the day against them, has given some proof of the possession of the qualities and character, of which our highest judicial tribunals are or ought to be composed. With these precedents you are all familiar. They go back to 1834, now twenty years; and they seem to demonstrate that heretofore no legislature has assumed to call itself "a party" to "a change of the constitution;" that every one instead, has simply designated a *counting* body, to whom the state of the vote was to be proved; that every one has regarded the count of the body so designated, as a "making to appear," and regarded itself as having nothing at all to do but to declare what had already been made to appear, and what amendment had already been completely and certainly adopted. To have followed these precedents evinces the possession of judicial qualities, and exemplifies a judicial character, which entitle the respondent, if he stood in need of it, to the candor and indulgence of an assembly of honorable minds.

And now, Mr. President, the discussion is closed. It is an infelicity of the judicial office, that the judge does not, and can never come to his own day of trial attended and assisted by a demonstrative and sustaining popularity. The necessities of the great trust he stands in prescribes seclusion, and thought, and the study of books. They prescribe the duty, and they form the habit of looking less to the party than to the cause; the habit of meditations on rights more than of intercourse with men. He grows formal, therefore, and reserved, if not austere. In old age he becomes venerable by the establishment of an illustrious reputation, — we rise up and bless him; we follow his footsteps and attend him to his grave, with tears, and reverence, and gratitude. But the earlier and middle life of the good judge, of the best judge, has won little of the popularity which follows; none at all of that which is run after. The respondent, thus, is here almost alone. I am told, and I believe, that if his self-respect and good taste would have permitted it, if the nature of the charge, if the necessities of the hour had allowed it, we might have shown you by the testimony of the bar over whom he has had opportunity to preside, by the testimony of all who have observed his brief, but studious and most busy official life, that already an ornament of the bench, he has a future of distinction and usefulness, which may justify any degree of hope of his friends and of the public. But here and now he seems alone, — upheld by consciousness of his own innocence, and by trust in his judges, of this convention, and of the people. The soul's calm sunshine, and the heart-felt joy are his. Some circumstances invest him and his position with extraordinary interest. He represents a grand doctrine of constitutional freedom, dear to Maine as are the ruddy drops that visit her large heart. He represents that transcendent idea of a separation of departments of government, without which tyranny is begun already. He represents that element of security, without which liberty itself is an empty and dreary thing, and its worship a vain oblation, — a security of right under an equal law, and a learned and incorrupt judge. He commands and he has that respect of God and man, which is yielded ever to him who strives to protect himself, and those he loves, from oppression and dishonor. Your kindness thus far he has experienced, and his counsel have experienced, in bountiful measure. This you might give or might withhold; but justice he has a right to demand; and justice even this high tribunal is bound to render.

SPEECH "ON THE POLITICAL TOPICS NOW PROMINENT BEFORE THE COUNTRY."

DELIVERED AT LOWELL, MASS., OCTOBER 28, 1856.

I HAVE accepted your invitation to this hall with pleasure — although it is pleasure not unattended by pain.

To meet you, Fellow-citizens of Lowell and of Middlesex, between whom, the larger number of whom, and myself, I may hope from the terms of the call under which you assemble, there is some sympathy of opinion and feeling on the "political topics now prominent before the community;" to meet and confer, however briefly and imperfectly, on the condition of our country, and the duties of those who aspire only to be good citizens, and are inquiring anxiously what in that humble yet responsible character they have to do — to meet thus, and here — not as politicians, not as partisans, not as time-servers, not as office-seekers, not as followers of a multitude because it is a multitude, not as sectionalists, but as sons and daughters of our united and inherited America; who love her, filially and fervently for herself; our own — the beautiful, the endeared, the bounteous; the imperial and general Parent! — and whose hearts' desire and prayer to God is only to know how we shall serve her best, — this is a pleasure and a privilege for which I shall be very long and very deeply in your debt.

And this pleasure, there is here and now nothing to alloy. Differing as we have done, some of us, through half our lives; differing as now we do, and shall hereafter do, on means, on details, on causes of the evil, on men, on non-essentials — non-essentials I would say in so far as the demands of these most rugged and eventful times are concerned — I think that on the question, what is the true issue before us and the capital danger we have to meet ; on this, and on all the larger ideas, in all the nobler emotions which ought to swell the heart and guide the votes of true men to-day — through this one sharp and dark hour we shall stand together, shoulder to shoulder, though we have never done so before, and may never do so again.

I infer this from the language of your invitation. The welcome with which you have met me, allows me to expect so much. The place we meet in gives assurance of it.

If there is one spot of New England earth rather than another, on whose ear that strange music of discords to which they are rallying the files — a little scattered and a little flinching, thank God! — of their Geographical party — must fall like a fire-bell in the night, it is here ; it is in Middlesex ; it is in Lowell!

If this attempt at combining States against States for the possession of the government has no danger in it for anybody, well and good. Let all then sleep on, and take their rest. If it has danger for anybody, for you, Fellow-citizens of Lowell, more than for any of New England or as much, it has that danger. Who needs the Union, if you do not? Who should have brain and heart enough to comprehend and employ the means of keeping it, if not you? Others may be Unionists by chance ; by fits and starts ; on the lips ; Unionists when nothing more exciting, or more showy, or more profitable, casts up. You are Unionists by profession ; Unionists by necessity ; Unionists always. Others may find Vermont, or Massachusetts, or New Hampshire, or Rhode Island, large enough for them. You need the whole United Continent over which the flag waves to-day, and you need it governed, within the limits of the actual Constitution, by one supreme will. To secure that vast, and that indispensable market at home ; to command in the least degree a steady, uniform, or even occasional protection against the redundant capital, matured skill, pauper labor, and ebbing and falling prices of the Old World at peace ; to enable the looms of America to clothe the teeming millions of America ; — you need a regulation of commerce, uniform, one, the work of one united mind, which shall draw along our illimitable coast of sea and lake, between the universal American race on one side, and all the rest of mankind on the other, a line, not of seclusion, not of prohibition, but a line of security, and discrimination — discrimination between the raw material at least and the competing product — a line of social and industrial boundary behind which our infancy may grow to manhood; our weakness to strength; our "prentice hand" to that skill which shall hang out the lamp of beauty on the high places of our wealth, and our power, and our liberty!

Yes, this you need; and you know how, and where, you can have it.

How perfectly our springing and yet immature manufacturing and mechanical interests in 1788 discerned this need, and with what deep, reasonable, passionate enthusiasm they celebrated the adoption of the Constitution which held out the promise of meeting it! I know very well that all good men; all far-seeing men; all large-brained and large-hearted men were glad that day. I recall that grand and exultant exclamation of one of them: "It is done; we have become a nation." But even then it seemed to some, more than to others, the dawn of a day of good things to come. If you turn to that procession and that pageant of industry, in Philadelphia, on the 4th of July, 1788, — that grand and affecting dramatic action through which, on that magnificent stage as in a theatre, there were represented the sublime joy, and the sublime hopes with which the bosom of Pennsylvania was throbbing, — then and thus I think you seem to see, that while the Constitution promised glory and happiness to all our America, it was to the labor of America the very breath of life. We hear it said that it was for trade — foreign and domestic, largely — that the new and more perfect union was formed, and that is true. Very fit it was that in that gorgeous day of national emblems, the silver Delaware should have shown forth prominently — decorated and festive — to announce and welcome from all her mast-heads the rising orb of American commerce. Yet was there one piece in the performance opening a still wider glimpse of its immense utilities and touching the heart with a finer emotion. That large "stage borne on the carriage of the Manufacturing Society, thirty feet in length, on which carding machines, and spinning machines, and weaving machines were displaying the various manufacture of cotton, was viewed," says an eye-witness, "with astonishment and delight by every spectator." "On that stage was carried the emblem of the future wealth and independence of our country." In that precious form of industry in which the harvest of Southern suns and the labor of Northern hands and brains may meet to produce a fabric for all nations to put on, — the industry of reason, and of the people, — "in that," says he, "is a bond of union more powerful than any one clause of the Constitution." In the motto on that carriage, "May the Union government protect the manufactures of America," read the hopes and the necessities of this labor. Such still is your prayer; such your right; as with the fathers so with the children! May that same Pennsylvania which so celebrated the adoption of the Constitution perpetuate it to-day! Wheresoever else the earth may shake, and the keepers and pillars of the house may tremble and bow themselves, let the keystone of the national arch, intrusted to hold it against the sky, stand fast in its place of strength and beauty forever!

Pardon me if I have seemed to find in the *mere interests* of Lowell a reason why, if there is a danger, you should be the first to discern and first to meet it. I turn from the interests of Lowell to the *memories* of Middlesex; and I find in them at least assurance that if there is a danger, your eye will see it and your ear catch it as far and as quick as the old Minutemen saw the midnight signals in the belfrys, and caught the low midnight drum-beat. Surely, surely, that immortal boast of Webster will be yours, "Where American liberty raised its first voice, and where its youth was nurtured and sustained, there it still lives, in the strength of its manhood and full of its original spirit. If discord and disunion shall wound it, if party strife and blind ambition shall hawk at and tear it, if folly and madness, if uneasiness under salutary and necessary restraint, shall succeed in separating it from the Union — by which alone its existence is made sure — it will stand, in the end, by the side of that cradle in which its infancy was rocked; it will stretch forth its arm with whatever of vigor it may still retain over the friends who gather around it; and it will fall at last, if fall it must, amidst the proudest monuments of its own glory, and on the very spot of its origin." Yes, it was here, that the American people began to be, and the American nation was born in a day. There, on the 19th of April; there, on the 17th of June; on that narrow green; beyond that little bridge; on those heights of glory; there, — even as the cloud of battle parted and the blood of your fathers was sinking into the ground — the form and faces of the old thirteen colonies passed away, and the young Republic lifted his forehead from the "baptism of fire;" the old provincial flags were rolled up and disappeared as a scroll, and the radiant banner by which the united America is known, and shall be, for a thousand years of history, known to all the world as one, was handed down from the sky. Here at least shall not the dismemberment of that nation begin. Here at least the first star shall not be erased from that banner!

No, Fellow-citizens of Middlesex. They may persuade you that there is no danger in what they are doing; they may persuade you that a combination of sixteen States to wrest the possession of the government from the other fifteen, is all right, all safe, and all necessary. But if they fail in this; if they fail to show that whatever they wish or mean to do, they are not subjecting the Union of America, and the peace and honor of America, to a trial which may exceed its strength, then tell them they had better try that case in *some other county*. Tell them that while the summit of that monument catches the rays of the rising and descending sun, and the returning or departing sailor greets it from his mast-head, it shall stand the *colossal image of a whole country;* and the flag that floats from it to-day shall float there while the earth bears a plant, or the sea rolls a wave!

I meet you for these reasons with pleasure. But I said and feel that that pleasure is attended close by pain. Some of you will partake of that with me also. All will comprehend it. I do not disguise that I look on the occasion with too anxious an interest, with too many fond memories of the past, with too keen a sense of the contrast of the present with the past, with too much thought of the possible future, for unmixed pleasure even here. I will not call this presidential election in advance a peril or a crisis, for that might be to beg the question, but I will venture in advance to say, that the best wish a patriot could make for his country is that she may never undergo such another. The first desire of my heart, at least, is that I may never see such another. To this desire, personal considerations do not at all contribute. I should be ashamed of myself if they did, although I cannot but wonder at that discriminating injustice and insolence of dictation which claims freedom of thought and purity of motive for itself, and allows them to others, and denies them to me. But this is nothing. Is there no one here who shares with me the wish, that his country, that himself, might never see another such a crisis as this? Is there no one here, — are there not hundreds here, — who, recalling the presidential elections they have assisted in, and contrasting their safe and their noble stimulations; their sublime moments; their admirable influences, as a training to a closer union, and a truer and intenser American feeling and life, with this one; does not confess some anxiety, some bewilderment, some loathing, some fear? Those generous, animated, fraternal contendings of the American people for a choice of the successor of Washington; conducted in the name and under the control of two great parties; running, both of them, through and through the Union, into every State and every vicinage, every congressional district, and every school district, and every parish; and binding Texas to Maine, Georgia to New Hampshire, Missouri to Massachusetts, by a new, artificial, and vehement cohesion, — a tie, not mystic, by which you greeted, every man greeted, a brother and an ally, "*idem sentientem de republica*"; everywhere that careful, just, and constitutional recognition on every party banner; by every party creed and code; in every party speech, and song, and procession of torchlight, — the recognition of an equal title to love, regard, honor, equality, in each and every state and region; that studious and that admirable exclusion of all things sectional; all things which supposed the existence of a conflict of sections; all opinions, all theories of policy, all enterprises of philanthropy, all aims of all sorts in which his geographical and social position could prevent any one American from sharing alike; those platforms broad as our continent; equal as our Constitution; comprehensive as our liberty; those mighty minglings of minds and hearts, in which Webster could address Virginians in the Capitol Square at Richmond, and Berrien and Bell and Leigh and Johnson could feel and heighten the inspiration of Faneuil Hall and Bunker Hill,—all everywhere at home; — those presidential contests which left our Union stronger, our mutual acquaintance and respect closer and deeper, our country a dearer and fairer and grander ideal, hastening forward the growth of our nationality almost as much as a foreign war, without its blood, its crime, and its cost, — is there no one, are there not hundreds here, who recall and regret them? Contrasted with them and their day, does not this one, and this time, seem more a dream than a reality? Can we avoid the vain wish that it was only and all a dream? Does this attempt to weave and plait the two North wings of the old national parties into a single Northern one, and cut the Southern wing off altogether, strike you to be quite as far-sighted and safe as it is new and bold? In the temporary and local success which seemed a little while ago to attend it here, and which led certain small editors, little speakers on low stumps, writers of bad novels and forgotten poems, preachers of Pantheism and revilers of Jefferson, and excellent gentlemen, so moral and religious that they could not rejoice at their country's victories over England, — led these people to suppose they had all at once become your masters and mine; in that temporary and local success did you see nothing but rose colors and the dawn of the Millennium? To combine States against States, in such a system as ours, has it been generally held a very happy device towards forming a more perfect union and insuring domestic tranquillity? To combine them thus against each other geographically, to take the whole vast range of the free States, lying together, sixteen out of thirty-one, seventeen millions out of five or six and twenty millions, — the most populous, the strongest, the most advancing, — and form them in battalion against the fewer numbers and slower growth, and waning relative power on the other side; to bring this sectional majority under party drill and stimulus of pay and rations; to offer to it as a party the government of our country, its most coveted honors, its largest salaries, all its sweets of patronage and place; to penetrate and fire so mighty and so compact a mass with the still more delicious idea that they are moving for human rights and the equality of man; to call out their clergy from the pulpit, the library, the bedside of the dying, the chair of the anxious inquirer, the hearth of the bereaved, to bless such a crusade; to put in requisition every species of rhetoric and sophistry, to impress on the general mind that the end justifies the means; that the end here to be attained is to give Kansas to freedom; to stanch her blood and put out her fires; and then to execute the sublime and impressive dogma that all men are born free and equal; and that such a Geographical party is a well-adapted means to that end, — does this strike you as altogether in the spirit of Washington, and Franklin, and the Preamble to the Constitution, and the Farewell Address? Does it strike you that if carried out it will prove to be a mere summer excursion to Moscow? Will there be no bivouac in the snow; no avenging winter hanging on retreat? No Leipsic; no Waterloo?

Fellow-citizens, if the formation and growth of this faction of Northern States against the South has impressed us at all alike, you appreciate why I said that I meet you with pain. It was the pain of anxiety; the pain of fear. Relieved as I am from that in a great degree by the late decisive demonstrations from Pennsylvania and Indiana, we yet feel together that we have a duty to perform or to attempt still. That which we cannot hinder here, we may at least deplore and expose. That which we cannot do for ourselves, New Hampshire, Connecticut, the great, calm, central mass of States may do for us. Against that which locally and temporarily is too strong for our strength here, we may at least protest.

With courtesy then; with justice to those from whom we differ; in the fear of God; in the love of our whole America; in all singleness of heart; appealing from the new men to the old; to the sober second thought of Massachusetts and New England; to their judgment; to their patriotism, — after some generations, perhaps some days, have passed, — let us put on record our reasons for deliberate and inextinguishable opposition to this Geographical party.

You see, Fellow-citizens, already what I regard as the issue we have to try. In their mode of stating that issue, I take leave totally to differ from some of the organs of this movement here. The question to-day is not as they would frame it and force it on us, whether we would have Kansas free soil or slave soil, any more than whether we worship an "anti-slavery God and believe in an anti-slavery Bible." The question is this: Shall slavery be permitted, through the agency of extreme Northern or extreme Southern opinions, to combine and array the sixteen States in which it does not exist, and the fifteen States in which it does exist, into two political parties, separated by a physical and social boundary, for the election of president, for the constituting of the two houses of congress, and the possession of the government? Much trouble it has caused us; much evil it has done. It is the one stupendous trial and peril of our national life. But shall it bear this, the deadliest fruit of all?

I say, Not so; never; but certainly not yet. This is the issue.

And now addressing myself to this issue, the first thing I have to say is, such a party is absolutely useless for every one of its own objects which it dares avow. For every one which it avows it is useless. Every one of them it is certain to endanger or to postpone.

But here let me submit a preliminary thought or two.

In trying the question whether the exigencies of the times demand such a tremendous organization as this, or whether we are bound to oppose it, I hold it to be time worse than wasted to get up a disputation in advance as to what party, or what section is most to blame for the occurrences of the last two years. This is all well enough for politicians. To you and to me it is trifling and it is criminal. If a resort to this stupendous innovation is necessary and is safe; if it will work great, certain, and needful good, and will not formidably and probably endanger the domestic tranquillity and the more perfect union of the States, — form it, and triumph in it. If such a resort is unnecessary; if it will work no certain and great good; if it will disturb our peace and endanger our existence, let it be condemned and punished as moral treason, and there an end. Try it, and judge it by itself.

What is it to you or me; what is it to the vast, innocent, and quiet body of our countrymen, North or South, whose folly, whose violence, whose distrust, whose fanaticism for slavery or against slavery, whose ambition low or high, is responsible for the past or present? Leave this to them whose trade is politics, whose trade is agitation, and let us meet the practical measure they present us, and pass on that. I know very well there are faults on both sides; faults South, faults North, faults of parties, faults of administration. We should not have voted for the repeal of the Compromise. We would have voted, when that thing was done and its restoration was seen to be impossible, to secure to Kansas the opportunity, uninvaded, unawed, uninfluenced, to grow to the measure of a State, to choose her own institutions, and then come to join the "Grand Equality." As she is to-day, at rest, at peace, — in some fair measure so, — revived, respiring, so ought she ever to have been, if freedom and slavery were to be allowed to meet breast to breast upon her surface at all. Herein is fault. Herein is wrong. Beyond, far back of all this, years before that Compromise, years before that repeal, the historian of sectional antagonisms might gather up more matter of reciprocal crimination. Either region might draw out a specious manifesto enough on which to appeal to the reason and justice of the world and to the God of nations, and to the God of battle for that matter, if that were all.

But to this great question, thus forced on us, Shall the States of the North be organized for the purpose of *possessing the government* upon the basis of this party, what are all these things to the purpose? Because there has been violence and blame, are you therefore to fly on a remedy ten thousand times worse than the disease? We should like to see slavery cease from the earth; but should we like to see black regiments from the West Indies landing at Charleston or New Orleans to help on emancipation? We would like to see Kansas grow up to freedom; but should we like to see the bayonets that stormed the Redan and the Malakoff glittering there to effect it? This glorifying him who does his own work, and this denunciation of him who holds a slave; this singing of noisy songs, and this preaching of Sharpe's rifle sermons; these lingering lamentations about the spread of the cotton plant, about the annexing of Louisiana by Jefferson, and of Florida by John Quincy Adams, do not touch the question before the nation. That question is about the new party. That question is on combining the North against the South on slavery to win the government. Shall that party, shall that attempt triumph, or shall it perish under the condemnation of your patriotism?

Is that needful? Is that just? Is that prudent? That is

the question; and to that hold up its orators, and poets, and preachers; and let the sound and calm judgment of America decide it.

Something else when that is decided, as it seems now likely to be, we shall have to do. Some changes of administrative politics must be and will be had. But in the mean time, and in the first place, the question is, Shall your Geographical party live or die?

I have said, then, for my first reason of opposition, that for any and every one of the objects this new party dares to avow, it is absolutely useless. It is no more needed for any object it dares to avow, than thirty thousand of Marshal Pelissier's Zouaves are needed in Kansas to-day.

And on this question of necessity is not the burden of proof on him who undertakes to introduce into our political order and experience so tremendous a novelty as this? Is not the presumption in the *first* instance altogether against getting up a Geographical party on slavery for possession of the government? Considering that such a thing, if not necessarily and inevitably poison, is, however, extreme medicine at the best; that it has been down to this hour admitted to be and proclaimed to be the one great peril of our system by all who have loved it best and studied it most deeply; that every first-class intelligence and character in our history of whatever type of politics, and what is quite as important, the sound and sober general mind and heart, has held and taught this, is it too much to say that he whose act outrages our oldest, and most fixed, and most implicit habits of thought and most cherished traditions on this subject; who mocks at what we have supposed our most salutary and most reasonable fears; who laughs at a danger to the American confederacy, at which the firmness of Washington, the courage of Hamilton, and the hopeful and trusting philanthropy and philosophy of Jefferson, confident always of his countrymen, at which these men trembled, — is it too much to tell the propounder of this project that he shall make out its necessity, or he shall be nonsuited on his own case? I say to him, then, Pray confine yourself in the first instance to the point of *necessity*. Do not evade that question. Don't mix others with it. Tell us exactly what you really propose to do about slavery, without phrases, and then show us that if it ought to be done it is necessary to combine the Northern States against the South on a presidential election in order to do it. Speak to this. Don't tell us how provoked you are, or how provoked the Rev. Mr. This, or the Hon. Mr. That, has come to be against the South; how passionately one Southern member spoke, or another Southern member acted; how wicked it was in Washington to hold slaves, and what a covenant with hell a Constitution is which returns the fugitive to the master. Don't exasperate yourself irrelevantly. Don't mystify or trick us with figures to prove that the seventeen millions of people in the Northern States contribute three fourths of the whole aggregate of $4,500,000,000 of annual industrial production. This, if it were true, or were not true, might beget vanity, and the lust of sectional dominion, and contempt; but it is nothing at all to the purpose. Don't say you want to teach the South this thing or that thing. Don't say you want to avenge on a section to-day the annexation of Louisiana or Florida or Texas. Don't keep coming down on the South; just condescend to come down on the question. What are your objects precisely; and how comes this new and dangerous combination of States necessary to accomplish them?

What, then, first, are the objects of the Geographical party, and is such a party necessary for such objects? I ask now for *its measures*. What would it do if it could?

To find out these to reasonable perfection, for me, at least, has not been easy. It is not easy to know where to look for the authentic evidence of them. The Philadelphia platform and Colonel Fremont's letter of acceptance are part of that evidence. They are not all — they are not the most important part. You must go elsewhere for it. The actual creed and the real objects must be sought in the tone and spirit of their electioneering; in the topics of their leaders; in the aggregate of the impression their whole appeal is calculated to make on the public mind and the collective feelings of the North. These speak the aims, these make up the life, these accomplish the mission of a party. By these together judge it.

Much meditating on this evidence, I arrive at two results. I find one object distinctly propounded; one of great interest to the Northern sentiment, and one which you and I and all should rejoice to see constitutionally and safely accomplished at the right time and in the right way, — and that is the accession of Kansas as a free State to the Union. This is one. Beyond, behind this, more or less dim, more or less frowning, more or less glittering, more or less constitutional, there looms another range or another show of objects, swelling and subsiding and changing as you look, — "in many a frozen, many a fiery Alp," — cloud-land, to dazzle one man's eye, to disappear altogether before the gaze of another, as the showman pleases. These are their other objects.

Turn first, then, to that one single practical and specific measure which they present to the North, and on which they boast themselves by eminence and excellence the friends of Kansas, — the admission of that territory as a free State.

And now if this is all, will any sane and honest man, uncommitted, tell you that there is a necessity for this tremendous experiment of an organization and precipitation of North on South to achieve it? Have you, has one of you, has one human being north of the line of geographical separation, a particle of doubt that if Kansas has peace under the reign of law for two years, for twelve months, the energies of liberty, acting through unforced, unchecked, and normal free-soil immigration, would fill her with freedom, and the institutions of freedom, as the waters fill the sea? What more than such peace under such rule of law do you want? What more does Mr. Speaker Banks think you want? Legislation of anybody? No. Interference by anybody? No. Hear him: —

"Now for this (the repeal of the Compromise) we have a remedy. It is not that we shall legislate against the South on the subject of slavery. It is not that we shall raise the question whether in future territories slavery shall be permitted or not. We lay aside all these questions, and stand distinctly and simply on the proposition that that which gave peace to the country in 1820, that which consummated the peace of the country in 1850, ought to be made good by the government of the United States, and with the consent of the American people. (Applause.) That is all. No more, no less — no better, no worse. That is all we ask — that the acts of 1820 and 1850 shall be made good, in the place of conflagration, and murder, and civil war for the year 1856 — by the voice of the American people, South, let me say, as well as North. (Applause.) Now, to do that no legislation is required. It is not necessary that the halls of congress should be opened again to agitation. We desire the election of a man to the presidency of the United States of simple views and of determined will,— a man who will exert the influence of this government in that portion of the territory of the United States, so as to allow its people to settle the question for themselves there."

What is this but to say, Put out the conflagration, stop the reign of violence, give peace, law, and order to rule, and Kansas will have freedom, if she does not prefer slavery, as certainly she will not. And such, I take it, is the all but universal judgment of the North.

Well; but do they answer, Oh, very true; but we cannot have this peace unless the North gets possession of the government. Mr. Buchanan's administration will not insure it. Mr. Fillmore's administration will not insure it.

I might content myself with replying that the condition of Kansas at this hour gives this extravagance to the winds. I will not say that terrritory to-day is as quiet as Middlesex; but I will say that before the next President takes his seat it will be as free as Middlesex. It has a majority for freedom, and it is increasing. Of a population of about thirty thousand, some five thousand only are from the slave States.

I will not leave it on that reply. With what color of justice, I choose to add, do the leaders of this party assume to tell you that they alone desire to give or are able to insure Kansas her only chance to be free? With what justice do they tell you that the Democratic party, or the Fillmore party, refuse to give her peace, and all the practical opportunities of liberty? Do they suppose that we have not read the record of the last two months of the last congress? We, whose sons and brothers are on that disturbed and sad soil; we, who deplore the repeal of the Compromise quite as much as they do; we, who should see with exultation and thanksgiving to God the peaceful victories of freedom in that frontier; we, who hate and dread the gamblings of politicians, and the selfish and low tactics of party, but should rejoice unspeakably to see the statesmanship of our country securing the government of that territory to its own free will, — do they suppose that we did not read, or could not understand, or cannot remember how the leaders and the members of every party in congress dealt with this great subject? Republicans the only helpers of Kansas to freedom, indeed! How did they propose to reach the object? By making some twenty-five thousand people into a sovereign State, and bringing it, just as it was, into the Union under the Topeka constitution! Yes, you would have made them a State *extempore*. You would have given to these twenty-five thousand people, organized as absolutely without law and against law as if two thousand should get together on Boston Common and make a government, the same voice in the Senate of the United States which the Constitution gives to New York, to Pennsylvania, to Virginia, to Massachusetts; the power to turn the scale and decide the vote on a debate of war and peace, or a treaty of boundary, or of commerce, or a nomination to the highest judicial or diplomatic office in the Constitution.

This they would have done — a measure of passion; an act for which the file affords no precedent; revolutionary almost; almost a crime in the name of liberty.

Defeated in this, they would do nothing. They would allow nobody else to do anything. They passed Mr. Dunn's bill to be sure, — the first one in the history of this government which legislated human beings directly into a state of slavery; but as they engrafted the restoration of the Missouri Compromise into it, they knew it could not become a law, and that goes for nothing. There they stuck; and had they not repeatedly an opportunity to unite in putting out the fires, and stanching the blood, and hushing the shrieks of Kansas; in giving her a chance to revive and respire; in giving her a chance to choose herself of the fruit of the tree of liberty and live? Yes; repeatedly. Did they avail themselves of it? No. Did they allow others to do so? No. No! Did not Mr. Toombs present a bill, and did not the Senate pass it and send it to the House? Did not this bill propose an early admission of Kansas, — in so far just what the Republicans wanted? Did it not annul the more obnoxious part of the obnoxious laws of the territorial legislature? Did it not provide for registration of voters, commissioners to take census of inhabitants, and an interval of ample sufficiency for those whom violence had expelled to return and assert their rights? Did not Mr. Hale of New Hampshire say of this: —

"I take this occasion to say that the bill, as a whole, does great credit to the magnanimity, to the patriotism, and to the sense of justice of the honorable Senator who introduced it. It is a much fairer bill than I expected from that latitude. I say so because I am always willing and determined, when I have occasion to speak anything, to do ample justice. I THINK THE BILL IS ALMOST UNEXCEPTIONABLE."

Did the Republicans — when they found that the Missouri Compromise could not be restored, nor Kansas be admitted instantly under the Topeka constitution — in order to stanch the blood, and to silence the cry of the territory, the crime against which they assumed to prosecute and avenge — give ground *an inch?* Would they take a single step towards temporary truce even, or a time to breathe? Not one, — Mr. Clayton, Mr. Crittenden in the Senate, and Mr. Haven in the House, held up successively the olive-branch, tempted and entreated them, by eloquence, and reason, and feeling, to do something, if they could not do all, or what they wished, to close the feast of horrors! — but not a finger would they lift. Cold and motionless as the marble columns about them — the 25,000 men and the Topeka constitution should come in a State — as they knew it would not — or murder, arson, and rapine might waste Kansas, and electioneer for the Geographical party.

I do not say they intended that the reign of terror should continue in Kansas; all of them could not have so intended, I do not say that any of them did. I say that if it had continued, a full share of the responsibility had been theirs. I say that it is no thanks to them that it has ceased. I say that it does not lie in their mouths to tell the calm, just, and reasonable men of the North that they are the only party, and a combination of States against States the only means, of giving to Kansas the freedom we all desire for her.

Easy it were in my judgment to demonstrate or afford the highest degree of probability that their triumph would defeat, or postpone, or impair and profane the consummation which they seek. But I am confined to the question of the necessity of their measures, for the attainment of our ends.

So much for this function of the new party, the admission of Kansas as a free State. To this end it is no more needed than sixteen black regiments from the Leeward Islands.

Beyond this, what are its objects? With anxious and curious desire to comprehend the whole of this extraordinary phenomenon, I have extreme difficulty in making these ulterior objects out. Some of them are unavowed, I suppose — some of them are avowed in one place and denied in another; some of the speakers have one — some have another. If you tell them their aims are dangerous, unconstitutional, revolutionary, Mr. Banks shall reply, "Not a bit of it; we don't mean to legislate against the South on slavery at all; we don't mean to say that future territories shall not have slavery if they like it, to their heart's content. We want nothing and nobody but a President of 'simple views and determined will,' who will allow the 'people of Kansas to settle the question for themselves there.'" If thereupon you answer, Well, if this is all, there really seems to be no great need of evoking such a tremendous spirit as the combination of North against South to reach it; less force, less fire, less steam, less wear and tear of machinery would do the business one would think; up rises another, more fervid, more gloomy, better informed, or not so cunning, and exclaims, "No, that is not all! that is hardly the beginning. We sing and hear a strain of far higher mood than that; we have the tide of slavery to roll back; the annexation of Louisiana and Texas to avenge or compensate; we too would taste the sweets of power, and we will have power; it is a new order of the ages we bring on; our place of worship (such is Governor Seward's expression) is neither in this mountain, nor yet in Jerusalem; our mission is equality and freedom to all men."

To seek, through all this Babel of contradictory and irresponsible declarations, what they really design to do, were vain and idle. To maintain the necessity of organizing a party like this, to accomplish no mortal can tell us what, seems pretty bold dealing with the intelligence of the country. That which it is impossible to state, it is not apparently needful to try to do. If there is no perplexity of plot to be unravelled, why is such a divinity invoked? If there is one, will they show us what it is?

I must not forget in this search for their objects, outside of Kansas, that they have been much in the habit of sending us to the Declaration of Independence to find them. Their platform does so; their orators are said to do so. If I understand Governor Seward, in his first speech in Detroit, he does so. Reverend teachers of Republicanism do so. They are the party of the Declaration of Independence, and not a Geographical party. Here are two of their resolutions: —

> "*Resolved,* That the maintenance of the principles promulgated *in the Declaration of Independence, and embodied* in the Federal Constitution, are essential to the preservation of our republican institutions; and that the Federal Constitution, the rights of the States, and the union of the States, shall be preserved.
>
> "*Resolved,* That, with our republican fathers, we hold it to be self-evident truth that all men are endowed with inalienable right to 'life, liberty, and the pursuit of happiness,' and that the *primary object* and *ulterior design* of our Federal Government were to secure these rights *to all persons* within its exclusive jurisdiction; that as our republican fathers, when they had abolished slavery in all our national territory, ordained that no *person* should be deprived of 'life, liberty, or property,' without due process of law, it becomes our duty to maintain this provision of the Constitution against all attempts to violate it, for the purpose of establishing slavery in the territories of the United States, by positive legislation prohibiting its existence or extension therein. That we deny the authority of congress, of a territorial legislature, or any individual or *association of individuals,* to give legal assistance to slavery in any territory of the United States, while the present Constitution *shall be maintained.*"

And yet what information does this afford about the object of the new party? How do we know what they mean to do, and whether it ought to be done, and whether a combination of free States to do it is fit and is necessary any the more for this? It is a thing so extraordinary for a political party to put forward the Declaration of Independence as its platform, or as a prominent and distinguishing part of its platform, and to solicit the votes of a section of the States of this Union by the boast that it claims some special and characteristic relation to that immortal act and composition; that it means to put it to some use, and derive from it some power, or some rule of interpretation, or some motive to governmental action which are new and peculiar to itself, — that we pause on it with wonder, and perplexity, and alarm.

If a newly organized political party should announce that its principles were the principles of the Bible, and its spirit and aims the spirit and aims of the Bible; should put this ostentatiously in its platform, write it on its flags, carry it about by torchlight, thunder it from its pulpits and from the stands of its mass-meeting speakers, lay or clerical; should you not feel some small or some considerable confusion, perplexity, misgiving, mirth, and fear in view of such demonstration? If you did not, or if you did, think it a poor, arrogant, impious, and hypocritical method of electioneering, would you not wish to know with a trifle more of precision and fulness what were these principles, and that spirit, and those aims of the Bible thus suddenly adopted into the creed of a party? If they told you they meant those principles and that spirit "promulgated in the Bible" and "embodied in the Constitution," should you feel that you knew much more than you did before? So here. What do these mean by this adoption of the Declaration of Independence into their creed? What are "*those principles promulgated*" *in it, and* "*embodied in the Constitution?*" The Declaration announces all men to be born free and equal, and to have certain inalienable rights, among which is the right to liberty. The Constitution sends back the fugitive slave to his master. Is this a case of a principle *promulgated* in one, and *embodied* in the other? If not, how does their platform deal with it? What are the "principles so *embodied?*" In what article, in what word, are they so? Which do they go for, the "promulgation," or the "embodiment?" What practical legislation, or administration, are they supposed to prescribe or warrant? Nay — come a little closer; what do they intend to say they get from the Declaration, or do by means of the Declaration, more than anybody else gets from it, and does by means of it? Would they venture the proposition that the Federal Government derives any powers, any one power from that source? Certainly not; or if so, it is the most dangerous and most revolutionary heresy ever yet promulgated. Would they say that they call in the Declaration to interpret the *language* of the Constitution? I suppose not; for, that the meaning of those who constructed that consummate frame of government, and weighed, measured, and stamped its words of gold, and drew, or sought to draw, with so much precision and certainty, the delicate line which parts the powers given to the Union from those retained to the States or the people, and therein ordained that all powers not delegated to the United States, or prohibited to the States, are reserved respectively to the States or the people, — that this language, in this instrument of 1787, can be *interpreted*, enlarged or narrowed, darkened or illustrated by the language of that other instrument, not less renowned, penned in 1776, in a time and for a purpose so different,—that thrilling appeal to the reason and justice of nations, in which a people assume to vindicate upon grounds of natural right their claim to take their place in the great equality of States, and then announce their sublime decision to make their claim good by revolution and battle — composed to engage the sympathies of mankind for the new nation, and to lift up its own spirit to the demands of the great crisis, — that the latter of these papers, in point of time, is to be interpreted by the former in any sense, of which any jurist, or any reader of his mother-tongue, can form conception, is a proposition too extravagant to be imputed to the author of the platform.

Well, then, if they do not use the Declaration as a source of power, nor as a help to construction, what do they mean to do with, or do by it? How profiteth it them any more than others? than us? Why, they would say they were going to execute their constitutional powers "in the *spirit* of the Declaration." That is it, is it? They are to take the constitutional powers as they exist — to find them as you find them, and as all find them, by just and legitimate interpretation. But the difference between you and them is, they "are going to *execute* them in the spirit of the Declaration." Well, now, what does even this mean? What sort of execution is this to insure? How do you apply your rule? Nay — what is the rule? What is the spirit of the Declaration in this behalf? Is it anything more than its meaning? It is what the framers of it, the congress of 1776, then *meant*, by their language, is it not? Did they mean then to assert that slaves had an inalienable right to liberty? Did they mean to make any assertion at all upon the subject of master and slave? Was that application of this generality of natural right in their contemplation in any, the least degree? Were they consciously and intentionally conceding and proclaiming that it was a sin to hold a slave and a duty to emancipate?

How the student of the history of that act may answer this inquiry is not now to the purpose. The question is not now on the actual principles of the Declaration as its framers understood and limited and applied them. It is on the meaning of the framers of the Republican platform. What is *their* "spirit of the Declaration," and how do they mean to use it; and what do they mean to draw from it in executing the Constitution? If they will point out one single object they can or design to accomplish through it, which other parties have not accomplished and cannot accomplish, by administering the government upon these principles of equal and exact justice to all the States and all the sections, in the purpose of promoting internal tranquillity and a more perfect Union, which have heretofore constituted the recognized creed of American statesmanship, we can then judge whether this parade of that instrument and that act in their platform has any meaning at all, and if so whether what is meant is needful or safe. We can then judge whether they have used a form of language intended to lead the passionate and unthinking to believe they intended something, and yet to leave themselves at liberty to protest when examined on it that they intended nothing. We can then judge whether this language of their creed is revolutionary and dangerous, or whether it merely

> "Palters with us in a double sense;
> That keeps the word of promise to our ear,
> And breaks it to our hope."

Holding then, Fellow-citizens, the clear and settled conviction that this combination of Northern States against the South is totally unnecessary for any purpose, I record my protest against the attempt to form it and give it power. No interest of freedom requires or will be helped by it. No aspects of slavery justify it. It will not give liberty to an acre, or to a man, one hour sooner than they will have it without. It will not shorten or lighten the rule or limit the spread of slavery in the least degree.

And is not this enough to deter you from an innovation so vast, an experiment so untried, an agency of influences so incapable to be calculated?

But what if, more than novel and more than needless, it proves only an enormous evil? What if it proves, of all the fruits that slavery has borne yet, the deadliest?

To many I know the bare imagination of such fear is matter of mirth. Seeing farther than I can see, or more sanguine, or more bold, for them it seems without terror; or promises only good, or a preponderance of good, or to be a necessary evil and a risk worth taking at the worst. Let me dare to avow that which I assuredly believe and deeply feel. To me, to many thoughtful men whose opinions are far more important than mine, there is occasion for the wisdom of fear.

The grounds and the particulars of the apprehension with which such men may regard this party, there is no need here and now to open at large.

We have come so near to the time when practical consequences are to take the place of our conjectures, — or to be scattered to the winds forever or for a space, if this party is defeated, — that I may forbear to display them in detail. I compress my convictions upon the whole subject of the proposed organization in a brief, articulate enumeration, and deliver them to your judgment.

They are: —

That in the exact sense in which the language has been used, and the thing been held out for warning in the Farewell Address, and by all the illustrious men of both schools of our politics, of Washington and of Jefferson, whom heretofore the American people has regarded as its safest and most sagacious councillors, — but on a scale more gigantic and swayed by passions far more incapable of control or measure than they have any of them feared, — it is a *Geographical party*, — confined exclusively in fact and in the nature of things to one of the two great regions into which the American States are distributed; seeking objects, resting on principles, cultivating dispositions, and exerting an aggregate of influence and impressions calculated to unite all on one side of the line which parts the two regions against all on the other, upon the single subject on which, without the utmost exercise of forbearance, sense, and virtue, they cannot live at peace; but for which they could not fail to be one people forever; by reason of which their disruption is possible at all times.

That in the sense of the language heretofore employed in American politics and history to describe this kind of thing there is not now and there never has been another Geographical party; that both the other two which now divide or now unite the people, — extending through every State North and South, professing political and industrial creeds, seeking objects, breathing a spirit and presenting candidates which every region may own alike, exerting each an aggregate of influence and impression calculated to foster an American feeling and not a sectional animosity; — that both these — whatever else may be alleged against them — are national parties.

That the Geographical party, in its nature and spirit and immediate object of taking possession of the government, is founded in essential injustice to the section which it excludes; that in ethics and reason these States are partners, and stockholders, and contractors each with all, — a partnership, an incorporation for all the good and glory and progress to which national life may aspire; that therefore, although the will of the majority is the law of the mighty concern, yet that that requires a will obedient to justice; and it is not just that a section, or a class of partners should associate among themselves by that organization called a party, to appropriate, to the practical exclusion of the rest, the government, and all the honor, profit, and power which belongs to its possession and administration, for an indefinite period, or for a presidential term, forasmuch as it violates or deserts the great implied agreement of the society — implied in the act of coming into the federal tie — that a property, a privilege, a power, a glory so large, so desirable, as the possession and administration of the government, shall pass about by a just and equitable rotation, and every section shall at all times have its share:

That if the manner in which the South has performed its duties to the Union and to the Northern section of States be regarded as a whole, from the adoption of the Constitution to this day, it affords no justification of the attempt to take possession of the government, to the exclusion of that section of States; that her federal obligations, as such, have been discharged as the general fact; that she has set no example of such sectional exclusion as this; that her federal life and activities have been exerted in and through national parties, and as a branch or wing thereof; that she has supplied her proportionate share of capacity and valor to the service of the whole country, and that the bad language, and violent acts, and treasonable devices of her bad men create no case for the injustice here meditated:

That the repeal of the Missouri Compromise, and the disposition of the South to form Kansas into a slave State, while we condemn and deplore the former, and demand that the free-will of all its people shall be permitted to disappoint the latter, creating no necessity for the Geographical party, afford no excuse for the injustice meditated:

That such a party is dangerous to the internal tranquillity and general welfare of the United States, and that it tends by probable and natural consequence less or more remote to their separation.

Such was once, was ever, until to-day, the universal judgment of wise and honest men and true patriots; and by their counsels it is safe, moral, and respectable to abide.

That such a party, militant or triumphant, electioneering for the administration or in possession of it, must exert influences of wide and various evil, even whether they do or do not reach to the overthrow of our system; that it accustoms the people of each section to turn from contemplating that fair and grand ideal, the whole America, and to find their country in one of its fragments; a revolution of the public affections, and a substitution of a new public life; that it accustoms them to exaggerate, intensify, and put forward into everything the one element of discord and diversity, and to neglect the cultivation of the less energetic elements of resemblance and union; that, in fixing their attention on a single subject, and that one appealing simply to passion and emotion, to pride, to fear, to moral sensibilities, it exasperates and embitters the general temper, and sows the seeds of sentiments which we did not inherit, but which we may transmit, — sentiments of the vehement and energetic class which form and unform nations; that it has to an extraordinary degree changed the tone of political discussion in this its own section, and made it intolerant, immoral, abusive and insolent to those who differ, to an extent to which our party disputes have before afforded no example; that it tends to place moderate men and national men, North and South, in a false position, by presenting to them the alternative of treason to the whole or treason to the section,— thus putting moderate counsels to shame, and destroying the influence which might help to restore the good temper and generous affection of the parts and the whole.

That while it is organized on the single basis of resistance to what it calls the slave power, it misconceives or disregards the true duties of the patriotism, philanthropy, and Christianity of the Free States in the matter of slavery; that it excites hatred of the master, but no prudent, nor reasonable, nor useful love of the slave; that to hinder the mere extension of that relation over more area, although one good thing, is not the only one demanded; that even that may be rendered worse than useless by the mode of seeking to effect it; that whatsoever else we do or attempt, in whatsoever else our power comes short of our wishes in this regard, we are bound to know that discords and animosity on this subject between North and South, however promoted, do but retard the training for freedom and postpone the day of its gradual and peaceful attainment. If ye so hate the master, or so fear him, or so contend with him, that ye rivet the fetters of the slave or lengthen the term of his slavery, what reward have ye or has he?

With these opinions, Fellow-citizens, I aim, in this election, at one single object; I feel but one single hope, and one single fear. To me, all of you, all men who aim at that object and share that hope and that fear, seem allies, brothers, partners of a great toil, a great duty, and a common fate. For the hour, opinions upon other things, old party creeds adapted for quiet times, old party names and symbols and squabbles and differences about details of administration, seem to me hushed, suspended, irrelevant, trifling, — the small cares of a master of ceremonies in the palace on the morning of the revolution, about red heels, small-clothes, and buckles in the shoe, within an hour of the final storm. I care no more now whether my co-worker is a Democrat, or an American, or an old Whig, a Northern man or a California man, than you should care if a fire fell on your city in winter and was devouring your workshops and streets one after another, and houseless women and children and old men and sick were seen hovering on the side of the river in the snow, whether he who passed or received your buckets was rocked in his cradle on this side of the sea or the other; whether he was an Arminian or Calvinist; a ten-hours' labor man or a twenty-four hours' labor man. The election once over, we are our several selves again. "If we get well," the sick man said, when with difficulty reconciled to his enemy, both being supposed dying, "if we get well, it all goes for nothing."

Certainly somewhat there is in the position of all of us a

little trying, — ties of years, which knit some of us together, are broken; cold regards are turned on us, and bitter language and slander, cruel as the grave, is ours.

> "I cannot but remember such things were,
> That were most precious to me."

You have decided, Fellow Whigs, that you can best contribute to the grand end we all seek, by a vote for Mr. Fillmore. I, a Whig all my life, a Whig in all things, and, as regards all other names, a Whig to-day, have thought I could discharge my duty most effectually by voting for Mr. Buchanan and Mr. Breckenridge; and I shall do it. The justice I am but too happy in rendering you, will you deny to me? In doing this, I neither join the Democratic party, nor retract any opinion on the details of its policy, nor acquit it of its share of blame in bringing on the agitations of the hour. But there are traits, there are sentiments, there are specialties of capacity and of function, that make a party as they make a man, which fit it in an extraordinary degree for special service in special crises, —to meet particular forms of danger by exactly adapted resistance—to fight fire with fire—to encounter by a sharper, more energetic, and more pronounced antagonism the precise type of evil which assails the State. In this way every great party successively becomes the saviour of the Constitution. There was never an election contest that in denouncing the particulars of its policy I did not admit that the characteristic of the Democratic party was this: that it had burned ever with that great master-passion this hour demands—a youthful, vehement, exultant, and progressive nationality. Through some errors, into some perils, it has been led by it; it may be so again; we may require to temper and restrain it, but to-day we need it all, we need it all! — the hopes — the boasts — the pride — the universal tolerance — the gay and festive defiance of foreign dictation — the flag — the music — all the emotions — all the traits — all the energies, that have won their victories of war, and their miracles of national advancement,— the country needs them all now to win a victory of peace. That done, I will pass again, happy and content, into that minority of conservatism in which I have passed my life.

To some, no doubt, the purport and tone of much that I have said may seem to be the utterance and the spirit of fear. Professors among their classes, preachers to implicit congregations, the men and women of emotion and sentiment, will mock at such apprehensions. I wish them joy of their discernment; of the depth of their readings of history; of the soundness of their nerves. Let me excuse myself in the words of an English statesman, then and ever conspicuous for spirit and courage, the present prime minister of England, in a crisis of England far less urgent than this. "Tell me not that this is the language of intimidation; tell me not that I am appealing to the fears instead of to the reason of the House. In matters of such high concern, which involve not personal and individual considerations, but the welfare of one's country, no man ought to be ashamed of being counselled by his fears. But the fears to which I appeal are the fears which the brave may acknowledge, and the wise need not blush to own. The fear to which I appeal is that early and provident fear which Mr. Burke so beautifully describes as being the mother of safety. 'Early and provident fear,' says Mr. Burke, 'is the mother of safety, for in that state of things the mind is firm and collected, and the judgment unembarrassed; but when fear and the thing feared come on together and press upon us at once, even deliberation, which at other times saves us, becomes our ruin, because it delays decision; and when the peril is instant, decision should be instant too.' To this fear I am not ashamed of appealing; by this fear legislators and statesmen ought ever to be ruled; and he who will not listen to this fear, and refuses to be guided by its counsel, may go and break his lances against windmills, but the court of chancery should enjoin him to abstain from meddling with public affairs."

They taunt you with being "Union-savers." I never thought that a sarcasm of the first magnitude, but as men can but do their best, let it go for what they think it worth. I take for granted, Fellow-citizens, that you, that all of us, despise cant and hypocrisy in all things,—the feigning a fear not felt, the cry of peril not believed to exist, all meanness and all wickedness of falsehood in our dealings with the mind of the people. But I take it for granted, too, that we are above the cowardice and immorality of suppressing our sense of a danger, threatening precious interests and possible to be averted, from the dread of jokers of jokes; and that we are above the folly of yielding that vast advantage which deep convictions give to earnest men in the dissensions of the Republic. Think what a thing it were to win the proud and sounding name in reality which they bestow in derision! Suppose, only suppose it so for the argument, that there is danger, over-estimated perhaps by the solicitude of filial love, but real or probable and less or more remote, — suppose, merely for the supposition, that Washington had reason to leave that warning against this kind of geographical combinations, *under all pretexts*, and that this one comes within the spirit and the terms of that warning, — suppose it to be so that we are right; that vehement passions, eager philanthropy, moral emotions not patient nor comprehensive of the indispensable limitations of political duty; that anger, pride, ambition, the lust of sectional power, the jealousy of sectional aggression, the pursuit even of ends just and desirable by means disproportioned and needless and exasperating — the excess and outbreak of virtues, by which more surely than by vices a country may be undone, — that these all working in an unusual conjuncture of affairs and state of public temper, have exposed and are exposing this Union to danger less or more remote, — and then suppose that by some word seasonably uttered, some vote openly and courageously given, some sincere conviction plainly expressed, we could do something to earn the reality of the praise which they give us in jest, — something for the safety, something for the peace, of this holy and beautiful house of our fathers, — something, were it ever so little, — would not this be compensation for the laughter of fools; aye! for alienated friendships, averted faces, and the serpent tooth of slander, — a thing worth dying for, and even worth having lived for?

AMERICAN NATIONALITY.

AN ORATION DELIVERED IN BOSTON ON THE EIGHTY-SECOND ANNIVERSARY OF AMERICAN INDEPENDENCE, JULY 5, 1858.

It is well that in our year, so busy, so secular, so discordant, there comes one day when the word is, and when the emotion is, "Our country, our whole country, and nothing but our country." It is well that law, our only sovereign on earth; duty, not less the daughter of God, not less within her sphere supreme; custom, not old alone, but honored and useful; memories; our hearts, — have set a time in which, — scythe, loom, and anvil stilled, shops shut, wharves silent, the flag, — our flag unrent, — the flag of our glory and commemoration waving on mast-head, steeple, and highland, we may come together and walk hand in hand, thoughtful, admiring, through these galleries of civil greatness; when we may own together the spell of one hour of our history upon us all; when faults may be forgotten, kindnesses revived, virtues remembered and sketched unblamed; when the arrogance of reform, the excesses of reform, the strifes of parties, the rivalries of regions, shall give place to a wider, warmer, and juster sentiment; when turning from the corners and dark places of offensiveness, if such the candle lighted by malignity, or envy, or censoriousness, or truth, has revealed anywhere, — when, turning from these, we may go up together to the serene and secret mountain-top and there pause, and there unite in the reverent exclamation, and in the exultant prayer, "How beautiful at last are thy tabernacles! What people at last is like unto thee! Peace be within thy palaces, and joy within thy gates! The high places are thine, and there shalt thou stand proudly, and innocently, and securely."

Happy, if such a day shall not be desecrated by our service! Happy, if for us that descending sun shall look out on a more loving, more elevated, more united America! These, no less, no narrower, be the aims of our celebration. These always were the true aims of this celebration. In its origin, a recital or defence of the grounds and principles of the Revolution, now demanding and permitting no defence, all taken for granted, and all had by heart; then sometimes wasted in a parade of vainglory, cheap and vulgar, sometimes profaned by the attack and repulse of partisan and local rhetoricians; its great work, its distinctive character, and its chief lessons remain and vindicate themselves, and will do so while the eye of the fighting or the dying shall yet read on the stainless, ample folds the superscription blazing still in light, "Liberty and Union, now and forever, one and inseparable."

I have wished, therefore, as it was my duty, in doing myself the honor to join you in this act, to give some direction to your thoughts and feelings, suited at once to the nation's holiday, and seasonable and useful in itself. How difficult this may be, I know. To try, however, to try to do anything, is easy, and it is American also. Your candor will make it doubly easy, and to your candor I commit myself.

The birthday of a nation, old or young, and certainly if young, is a time to think of the means of keeping alive the nation. I do not mean to say, however, because I do not believe, that there is but one way to this, the direct and the didactic. For at last it is the spirit of the day which we would cherish. It is our great annual national love-feast which we keep; and if we rise from it with hearts larger, beating fuller, with feeling purer and warmer for America, what signifies it how frugally, or how richly, or how it was spread; or whether it was a strain on the organ, the trumpet tones of the Declaration, the prayer of the good man, the sympathy of the hour, or what it was, which wrought to that end?

I do not, therefore, say that such an anniversary is not a time for thanksgiving to God, for gratitude to men, the living and the dead, for tears and thoughts too deep for tears, for eulogy, for exultation, for all the memories and for all the contrasts which soften and lift up the general mind. I do not say, for example, that to dwell on that one image of progress which is our history; that image so grand, so dazzling, so constant; that stream now flowing so far and swelling into so immense a flood, but which burst out a small, choked, uncertain spring from the ground at first; that transition from the Rock at Plymouth, from the unfortified peninsula at Jamestown, to this America which lays a hand on both the oceans, — from that heroic yet feeble folk whose allowance to a man by the day was five kernels of corn, for three months no corn, or a piece of fish, or a moulded remainder biscuit, or a limb of a wild bird; to whom a drought in spring was a fear and a judgment, and a call for humiliation before God; who held their breath when a flight of arrows or a war-cry broke the innocent sleep or startled the brave watching, — from that handful, and that want, to these millions, whose area is a continent, whose harvests might load the board of famishing nations, for whom a world in arms has no terror; — to trace the long series of causes which connected these two contrasted conditions, the Providences which ordained and guided a growth so stupendous; the dominant race, sober, earnest, constructive, — changed, but not degenerate here; the influx of other races, assimilating, eloquent, and brave; the fusion of all into a new one; the sweet stimulations of liberty; the removal by the whole width of oceans from the establishments of Europe, shaken, tyrannical, or burdened; the healthful virgin world; the universal progress of reason and art, — universal as civilization; the aspect of revolutions on the human mind; the expansion of discovery and trade; the developing sentiment of independence; the needful baptism of wars; the brave men, the wise men; the Constitution, the Union; the national life and the feeling of union which have grown with our growth and strengthened with our strength, — I do not say that meditations such as these might not teach or deepen the lesson of the day. All these things, so holy and beautiful, all things American, may afford certainly the means to keep America alive. That vast panorama unrolled by our general history, or unrolling; that eulogy, so just, so fervent, so splendid, so approved; that electric, seasonable memory of Washington; that purchase and that dedication of the dwelling and the tomb, the work of woman and of the orator of the age;

that record of his generals; that visit to battle-fields; that reverent wiping away of dust from great urns; that speculation, that dream of her past, present, and future; every ship builded on lake or ocean; every treaty concluded; every acre of territory annexed; every cannon cast; every machine invented; every mile of new railroad and telegraph undertaken; every dollar added to the aggregate of national or individual wealth, — these all as subjects of thought, as motives to pride and care, as teachers of wisdom, as agencies for probable good, may work, may insure, that earthly immortality of love and glory for which this celebration was ordained.

My way, however, shall be less ambitious and less indirect. Think, then, for a moment, on AMERICAN NATIONALITY itself; the outward national life, and the inward national sentiment; think on this; *its nature, and some of its conditions and some of its ethics* — I would say, too, some of its dangers, but there shall be no expression of evil omen in this stage of the discourse, and to-day, at least, the word is safety, or hope.

To know the nature of American nationality, examine it first by contrast, and then examine it in itself.

In some of the elemental characteristics of political opinion, the American people are one. These they can no more renounce for substance than the highest summit of the highest of the White Hills, than the peak of the Alleghanies, than the Rocky Mountains can bow and cast themselves into the sea. Through all their history, from the dawn of the colonial life to the brightness of this rising, they have spoken them, they have written them, they have acted them, they have run over with them. In all stages, in all agonies, through all report, good and evil, — some learning from the golden times of ancient and mediæval freedom, Greece and Italy and Geneva, from Aristotle, from Cicero and Bodinus, and Machiavel and Calvin; or later, from Harrington and Sidney and Rousseau; some learning, all reinforcing it directly from nature and nature's God, — all have held and felt that every man was equal to every other man; that every man had a right to life, liberty, and the pursuit of happiness, and a conscience unfettered; that the people were the source of power, and the good of the people was the political object of society itself. This creed, so grand, so broad, — in its general and duly qualified, so true, —

planted the colonies, led them through the desert and the sea of ante-revolutionary life, rallied them all together to resist the attacks of a king and a minister, sharpened and pointed the bayonets of all their battles, burst forth from a million lips, beamed in a million eyes, burned in a million bosoms, sounded out in their revolutionary eloquence of fire and in the Declaration, awoke the thunders and gleamed in the lightning of the deathless words of Otis, Henry, and Adams, was graved forever on the general mind by the pen of Jefferson and Paine, survived the excitements of war and the necessities of order, penetrated and tinged all our constitutional composition and policy, and all our party organizations and nomenclature, and stands to-day, radiant, defiant, jocund, tiptoe, on the summits of our greatness, one authoritative and louder proclamation to humanity by Freedom, the guardian and the avenger.

But in some traits of our politics we are not one. In some traits we differ from one another, and we change from ourselves. You may say these are subordinate, executory, instrumental traits. Let us not cavil about names, but find the essences of things. Our object is to know the nature of American nationality, and we are attempting to do so, first, by contrasting it with its antagonisms.

There are two great existences, then, in our civil life, which have this in common, though they have nothing else in common, that they may come in conflict with the nationality which I describe; one of them constant in its operation, constitutional, healthful, auxiliary, even; the other rarer, illegitimate, abnormal, terrible; one of them a force under law; the other a violence and a phenomenon above law and against law.

It is first the capital peculiarity of our system, now a commonplace in our politics, that the affections which we give to country we give to a divided object, the States in which we live and the Union by which we are enfolded. We serve two masters. Our hearts own two loves. We live in two countries at once, and are commanded to be capacious of both. How easy it is to reconcile these duties in theory; how reciprocally, more than compatible, how helpful and independent they are in theory; how in this respect our system's difference makes our system's peace, and from these blended colors, and this action and counteraction, how marvellous a beauty, and how grand a harmony we draw out, you all know. Practically you know, too, the adjustment has not been quite so simple. How the Constitution attempts it is plain enough. There it is; *litera scripta manet*, and heaven and earth shall pass before one jot or one tittle of that Scripture shall fail of fulfilment. So we all say, and yet how men have divided on it. How they divided in the great convention itself, and in the very presence of Washington. How the people divided on it. How it has created parties, lost and given power, bestowed great reputations and taken them away, and colored and shaken the universal course of our public life! But have you ever considered that in the nature of things this must be so? Have you ever considered that it was a federative system we had to adopt, and that in such a system a conflict of head and members is in some form and to some extent a result of course? There the States were when we became a nation. There they had been for one hundred and fifty years — for one hundred and seventy years. Some power, it was agreed on all hands, we must delegate to the new government. Of some thunder, some insignia, some beams, some means of kindling pride, winning gratitude, attracting honor, love, obedience, friends, all men knew they must be bereaved, and they were so. But when this was done, there were the States still. In the scheme of every statesman they remained a component part, unannihilated, indestructible. In the scheme of the Constitution, of compromise itself, they remained a component part, indestructible. In the theories of all publicists and all speculators they were retained, and they were valued for it, to hinder and to disarm that centralization which had been found to be the danger and the weakness of federal liberty. And then when you bear in mind that they are sovereignties, *quasi*, but sovereignties still; that one of the most dread and transcendent prerogatives of sovereignties, the prerogative to take life and liberty for crime, is theirs without dispute; that in the theories of some schools they may claim to be parties to the great compact, and as such may, and that any of them may, secede from that compact when by their corporate judgment they deem it to be broken fundamentally by the others, and that from such a judgment there is no appeal to a common peaceful umpire; that in the theories of some schools they may call out their young men and their old men under the pains of death to defy the sword point of the federal arm; that they can pour around even the gallows and the tomb of him who died for treason to the Union, honor, opinion, tears, and thus sustain the last untimely hour, and soothe the disembodied, complaining shade; that every one, by name, by line of boundary, by jurisdiction, is distinct from every other, and every one from the nation; that within their inviolate borders lie our farms, our homes, our meeting-houses, our graves; that their laws, their courts, their militia, their police, to so vast an extent protect our persons from violence, and our houses from plunder; that their heaven ripens our harvests; their schools form our children's mental and moral nature; their charities or their taxes feed our poor; their hospitals cure or shelter our insane; that their image, their opinions, their literature, their morality are around us ever, a presence, a monument, an atmosphere — when you consider this you feel how practical and how inevitable is that antagonism to a single national life, and how true it is that we "buy all our blessings at a price."

But there is another antagonism to such a national life, less constant, less legitimate, less compensated, more terrible, to which I must refer, — not for reprobation, not for warning, not even for grief, but that we may know by contrast, nationality itself, — and that is, the element of sections. This, too, is old; older than the States, old as the Colonies, old as the churches that planted them, old as Jamestown, old as Plymouth. A thousand forms disguise and express it, and in all of them it is hideous. *Candidum seu nigrum hoc tu Romane caveto.* Black or white, as you are Americans, dread it, shun it! Springing from many causes and fed by many stimulations; springing from that diversity of climate, business, institutions, accomplishment, and morality, which comes of our greatness, and compels and should constitute our order and our agreement, but which only makes their difficulty and their merit; from that self-love and self-preference which are their own standard, exclusive, intolerant, and censorious of what is wise and holy; from the fear of ignorance, the jealousy of ignorance, the narrowness of ignorance; from incapacity to abstract, combine, and grasp a complex and various object, and thus rise to the dignity of concession and forbearance and compromise; from the frame of our civil polity, the necessities of our public life and the nature of our ambition, which forces all men not great men, — the minister in his parish, the politician on the stump on election day, the editor of the party newspaper, — to take his rise or his patronage from an intense local opinion, and therefore to do his best to create or reinforce it; from our federative government; from our good traits, bad traits, and foolish traits; from that vain and vulgar hankering for European reputation and respect for European opinion, which forgets that one may know Aristophanes, and Geography, and the Cosmical Unity and Telluric influences, and the smaller morals of life, and all the sounding pretensions of philanthropy, and yet not know America; from that philosophy, falsely so called, which boasts emptily of progress, renounces traditions, denies God and worships itself; from an arrogant and flashy literature which mistakes a new phrase for a new thought, and old nonsense for new truth, and is glad to exchange for the fame of drawing-rooms and parlor windows, and the side-lights of a car in motion, the approval of time and the world; from philanthropy which is short-sighted, impatient and spasmodic, and cannot be made to appreciate that its grandest and surest agent, in His eye whose lifetime is Eternity, and whose periods are ages, is a nation and a sober public opinion, and a safe and silent advancement, reforming by time; from that spirit which would rule or ruin, and would reign in hell rather than serve in heaven; springing from these causes and stimulated thus, there is an element of regions antagonistic to nationality. Always I have said, there was one; always there will be. It lifted its shriek sometimes even above the silver clarion tone that called millions to unite for independence. It resisted the nomination of Washington to command our armies; made his new levies hate one another; assisted the caballings of Gates and Conway; mocked his retreats, and threw its damp passing cloud for a moment over his exceeding glory; opposed the adoption of any constitution; and perverted by construction and denounced as a covenant with hell the actual Constitution when it was adopted; brought into our vocabulary and discussions the hateful and ill-omened words North and South, Atlantic and Western, which the grave warnings of the Farewell Address expose and rebuke; transformed the floor of congress into a battle field of contending local policy; convened its conventions at Abbeville and Hartford; rent asunder conferences and synods; turned stated assemblies of grave clergymen and grave laymen into shows of gladiators or of the beasts of gladiators; checked the holy effort of missions, and set back the shadow on the dial-plate of a certain amelioration and ultimate probable emancipation, many degrees. Some might say it culminated later in an enterprise even more daring still; but others might deny it. The ashes upon that fire are not yet cold, and we will not tread upon them. But all will unite in prayer to Almighty God that we may never see, nor our children, nor their children to the thousandth generation may ever see it culminate in a Geographical party, banded to elect a Geographical President, and inaugurate a Geographical policy.

"Take any shape but that, and thou art welcome!"

But now, by the side of this and all antagonisms, higher than they, stronger than they, there rises colossal the fine sweet spirit of nationality, the nationality of America! See there the pillar of fire which God has kindled and lifted and moved for our hosts and our ages. Gaze on that, worship that, worship the highest in that. Between that light and our eyes a cloud for a time may seem to gather; chariots, armed men on foot, the troops of kings may march on us, and our fears may make us for a moment turn from it; a sea may spread before us, and waves seem to hedge us up; dark idolatries may alienate some hearts for a season from that worship; revolt, rebellion, may break out in the camp, and the waters of our springs may run bitter to the taste and mock it; between us and that Canaan a great river may seem to be rolling; but beneath that high guidance our way is onward, ever onward; those waters shall part, and stand on either hand in heaps; that idolatry shall repent; that rebellion shall be crushed; that stream shall be sweetened; that overflowing river shall be passed on foot dry shod, in harvest time; and from that promised land of flocks, fields, tents, mountains, coasts and ships, from North and South, and East and West, there shall swell one cry yet, of victory, peace, and thanksgiving!

But we were seeking the nature of the spirit of nationality, and we pass in this inquiry from contrast to analysis. You may call it, subjectively regarded, a mode of contemplating the nation in its essence, and so far it is an intellectual conception, and you may call it a feeling, towards the nation thus contemplated, and so far it is an emotion. In the intellectual exercise it contemplates the nation as it is one, and as it is distinguished from all other nations, and in the emotional exercise it loves it, and is proud of it as thus it is contemplated. This you may call its ultimate analysis. But how much more is included in it! How much flows from it! How cold and inadequate is such a description, if we leave it there! Think of it first as a state of consciousness, as a spring of feeling, as a motive to exertion, as blessing your country, and as reacting on you. Think of it as it fills your mind and quickens your heart, and as it fills the mind and quickens the heart of millions around you. Instantly, under such an influence, you ascend above the smoke and stir of this small local strife; you tread upon the high places of the earth and of history; you think and feel as an American for America; her power, her eminence, her consideration, her honor, are yours; your competitors, like hers, are kings; your home, like hers, is the world; your path, like hers, is on the highway of empires; our charge, her charge, is of generations and ages; your record, her record, is of treaties, battles, voyages, beneath all the constellations; her image, one, immortal, golden, rises on your eye as our western star at evening rises on the traveller from his home; no lowering cloud, no angry river, no lingering spring, no broken crevasse, no inundated city or plantation, no tracts of sand, arid and burning, on that surface, but all blended and softened into one beam of kindred rays, the image, harbinger, and promise of love, hope, and a brighter day!

Think of it next, as an active virtue. Is not all history a recital of the achievements of nationality, and an exponent of its historical and imperial nature? Even under systems far less perfect, and influences far less auspicious than ours, has it not lifted itself up for a time above all things meaner, vindicating itself by action, by the sublimity of a brave daring, successful or unsuccessful, by the sublimity of a working hope? How loose, for example, and how perfidious, was that union of the States of Greece in all times! How distinct were the nations of Attica, of Laconia, of Thessaly, of Bœotia, and how utterly insufficient the oracle, the Amphyctionic Assembly, the games, the great first epic, to restrain Athens and Sparta and Thebes from contending, by diplomacy, by fraud, by battle, for the mastery! And yet even in the historical age, when the storm of Eastern invasion swept that blue sea, and those laughing islands, and iron-bound coast, over, above, grander and more useful than the fear and policy which counselled temporary union, — were there not some, were there not many, on whose perturbed and towering motives came the thought of that great, common, Greek name; that race, kindred at last, though policy, though mines of marble, though ages had parted them, — that golden, ancient, polished speech, that inherited ancestral glory, that national Olympus, that inviolated, sterile and separate earth, that fame of camps, that fire of camps which put out the ancient life of the Troy of Asia; and was it not such memories as these that burn and revel in the pages of Herodotus? Did not Sparta and Athens hate one another and fight one another habitually, and yet when those Lacedæmonian levies gazed so steadfastly on the faces of the fallen at Marathon, did they not give Greek tears to Athens and Greek curses to Persia, and in the hour of Platæa did they not stand together against the barbarian?

What else formed the secret of the brief spell of Rienzi's power, and burned and sparkled in the poetry and rhetoric of his friend Petrarch, and soothed the dark hour of the grander soul of Machiavel, loathing that Italy, and recalling that other day when "eight hundred thousand men sprang to arms at the rumor of a Gallic invasion?"

Is not Prussia afraid of Austria, and Saxony of Bavaria, and Frankfort jealous of Dresden, and so through the twenty-seven or eight or thirty States, great and small; and yet the dear, common fatherland, the old German tongue, the legend of Hermann, the native and titular Rhine flowing rapid, deep, and majestic, like the life of a hero of antiquity — do not these spectacles and these traditions sometimes wake the nationality of Germany to action, as well as to life and hope?

But if you would contemplate nationality as an active virtue, look around you. Is not our own history one witness and one record of what it can do? This day and all which it stands for, — did it not give us these? This glory of the fields of that war, this eloquence of that revolution, this wide one sheet of flame which wrapped tyrant and tyranny and swept all that escaped from it away, forever and forever; the courage to fight, to retreat, to rally, to advance, to guard the young flag by the young arm and the young heart's blood, to hold up and hold on till the magnificent consummation crowned the work — were not all these imparted as inspired by this imperial sentiment? Has it not here begun the master-work of man, the creation of a national life? Did it not call out that prodigious development of wisdom, the wisdom of constructiveness which illustrated the years after the war, and the framing and adopting of the Constitution? Has it not, in the general, contributed to the administering of that government wisely and well since? Look at it! It has kindled us to no aims of conquest. It has involved us in no entangling alliances. It has kept our neutrality dignified and just. The victories of peace have been our prized victories. But the larger and truer grandeur of the nations, for which they are created and for which they must one day, before some tribunal give account, what a measure of these it has enabled us already to fulfil! It has lifted us to the throne and has set on our brow the name of the great Republic. It has taught us to demand nothing wrong, and to submit to nothing wrong; it has made our diplomacy sagacious, wary, and accomplished; it has opened the iron gate of the mountain, and planted our ensign on the great, tranquil sea; it has made the desert to bud and blossom as the rose; it has quickened to life the giant brood of useful arts; it has whitened lake and ocean with the sails of a daring, new and lawful trade; it has extended to exiles, flying as clouds, the asylum of our better liberty; it has kept us at rest within all our borders; it has repressed without blood the intemperance of local insubordination; it has scattered the seeds of liberty, under law and under order, broadcast; it has seen and helped American feeling to swell into a fuller flood; from many a field and many a deck, though it seeks not war, makes not war, and fears not war, it has borne the radiant flag all unstained; it has opened our age of lettered glory; it has opened and honored the age of the industry of the people!

We have done with the nature of American nationality, with its contrasts, analysis and fruits. I have less pleasure to remind you that it has conditions also, and ethics. And what are some of these? This is our next consideration.

And the first of these is that this national existence is, to an extraordinary degree, not a growth, but a production; that it has origin in the will and the reason, and that the will and the reason must keep it alive, or it can bear no life. I do not forget that a power above man's power, a wisdom above man's wisdom, a reason above man's reason, may be traced without the presumptuousness of fanaticism in the fortunes of America. I do not forget that God has been in our history. Beyond that dazzling progress of art, society, thought, which is of His ordaining, although it may seem to a false philosophy a fatal and inevitable flow under law — beyond this I do not forget that there have been, and there may be again interpositions, providential, exceptional, and direct, of that Supreme Agency without which no sparrow falleth. That condition of mind and of opinion in Europe, and more than anywhere else, in England, which marked the period of emigration, and bore flower, fruit and seed after its kind in the new world; that conflict and upheaval and fermenting in the age of Charles the First, and the Long Parliament, and Cromwell, and Milton — violated nature asserting herself; that disappearance of the old races here, wasting so mysteriously and so seasonably — that drear death giving place as in nature to a better life; that long colonial growth in shade and storm and neglect, sheltered imperfectly by our relations to the mother country, and not yet exposed to the tempest and lightning of the high places of political independence; burdened and poor, but yet evolving, germinant, prophetic; that insane common attack of one tyranny on so many charters; that succession of incompetent English commanders and English tactics against us in the war; that one soul breathed in a moment into a continent; the Declaration so timely, and so full of tone; the name, the services, the influence of Washington — these are "parts of His ways," and we may understand and adore them.

I do not forget either that in the great first step we had to take — that difficulty so stupendous, of beginning to mould the colonies into a nation, to overcome the prejudices of habit and ignorance, the petty cavils of the petty, the envy, the jealousy, the ambition, the fears of great men and little men; to take away partition walls, roll away provincial flags and hush provincial drums, and give to the young Republic *E Pluribus Unum*, to set out onward and upward on her Zodiac path,— I do not forget that in this, too, there were helps of circumstances for which no philosophy and no pride can make us unthankful.

Take one. Have you ever considered, speculating on the mysteries of our national being, how providentially the colonial life itself, in one respect, qualified for Union, and how providentially it came to pass that independence and nationality were born in one day? Suppose that from the times when they were planted respectively, these colonies had been independent of one another, and of every one — suppose this had been so for one hundred and fifty years, for one hundred and seventy years; that in the eye of public law they had through all that time ranked with England, with France; that through all that time they had made war, concluded peace, negotiated treaties of commerce and of alliance, received and sent ministers, coined money, superintended trade, "done all other things which independent States of right may do;" and then that a single foreign power had sought to reduce them. I do not say that that power would have reduced them. I do not say that necessity, that prudence, which is civil necessity, would not have taught them to assist one another, and that in one sense, and that a just one, they would have fought and triumphed together. But when that victory was won and the cloud rolled off seaward, would these victors have flown quite so easily into a common embrace and become a single people? This long antecedent several independence; this long antecedent national life — would it not have indurated them and separated them? These old high actions and high passions flowing diverse; these opposed banners of old fields; this music of hostile marches; these memories of an unshared past; this history of a glory in which one only had part, — do you think they could have been melted, softened, and beaten quite so easily into the unity of a common life? Might not the world have seen here, instead, another Attica, and Achaia and Lacedæmonia, and Messina, and Naples and Florence and Saxony? Did not that colonial life, in its nature — that long winter and lingering spring — discipline and prepare men for the future of their civil life, as an April snow enriches the earth it seems to bury? Did it not keep back the growths which might otherwise have shot up into impracticable ranknesses and diversities? Did it not divert men from themselves to one another — from Massachusetts and Virginia and New York, to the forming or the possible America? Instead of stunting and enfeebling, did it not enlarge and strengthen? And when all that host flocked together, to taste together the first waters of independent life, and one high, common, proud feeling pervaded their ranks, lifted up all hearts, softened all hearts at once — and a Rhode Island General was seen to fight at the Eutaws; and a New Yorker, or one well beloved of Massachusetts, at Saratoga; and a Virginian to guide the common war, and a united army to win the victory for all — was not the transition, in a moment so sublime, more natural, less violent, more easy to the transcendent conception of nationality itself?

I do not deny, too, that some things subordinate and executory are a little easier than at first; that the friction of the machine is less somewhat; that mere administration has grown simpler; that organizations have been effected which may move of themselves; that departments have been created and set going, which can go alone; that the Constitution has been construed authoritatively; that a course, a routine has been established in which things — some things — may go on as now, without your thought or mind. Bold he is, moreover, I admit, not wise, who would undertake to determine what chance, or what Providence may do, and what man may do in the sustentation of national life. But remember, that is a false philosophy and that is no religion which absolves from duty. That is impiety which boasts of a will of God, and forgets the business of man. Will and reason created, will and reason must keep. Every day, still, we are in committee of the whole on the question of the Constitution or no Constitution. Eternal vigilance is the condition of union, as they say it is of liberty. I have heard that if the same Omnipotence which formed the universe at first should suspend its care for a day, primeval chaos were come again. Dare we risk such a speculation in politics and act on it? Consider how new is this America of yours! Some there are yet alive who saw this infant rocked in the cradle. Some there are yet alive who beheld the first inauguration of Washington; many that felt how the tidings of his death smote on the general heart. Some now alive saw the deep broad trench first excavated, the stone drawn from the mountain-side, the mortar mingled, the Cyclopean foundation laid, the tears, the anthems, the thanksgiving of the dedication day. That unknown, therefore magnified, therefore magnificent original; that august tradition of a mixed human and Divine; that hidden fountain; the long, half-hidden flow glancing uncertain and infrequent through the opening of the old forest, spreading out, at last, after leagues, after centuries, into the clear daylight of history; the authoritative prescription; the legend, the fable, the tones of uncertain harps, the acquiescence of generations, rising in a long line to life as to a gift, — where for us are they? On all this architecture of utility and reason, where has Time laid a finger? What angularity has it rounded; what stone has it covered with moss; on what salient or what pendant coigne of vantage has it built its nest; on what deformity has its moonlight and twilight fallen? What enables us then to withhold for a moment the sustaining hand? The counsel of philosophy and history, of Cicero, of Machiavel, of Montesquieu, to turn to the first principles, to reproduce and reconstruct the ancient freedom, the masculine virtues, the plain wisdom of the original — is it not seasonable counsel eminently for you? Remember, your reason, your will, may keep, must keep what reason and will builded. Yours is the responsibility, yours, to country, to man, unshared, unconcealed.

I do not know that I need to say next that such a spirit of nationality reposing on will and reason, or, however produced, not spontaneous, and therefore to some extent artificial, demands a specific culture to develop it and to make it intense, sure and constant. I need not say this, because it is so plain; but it is important as well as plain. There is a love of country which comes uncalled for, one knows not how. It comes in with the very air, the eye, the ear, the instincts, the first taste of the mother's milk, the first beatings of the heart. The faces of brothers and sisters, and the loved father and mother, — the laugh of playmates, the old willow-tree, and well, and school-house, the bees at work in the spring, the note of the robin at evening, the lullaby, the cows coming home, the singing-book, the catechism, the visits of neighbors, the general training, — all things which make childhood happy, begin it; and then as the age of the passions and the age of the reason draw on, and love and the sense of home and security and of property under law, come to life; — and as the story goes round, and as the book or the newspaper relates the less favored lots of other lands, and the public and the private sense of a man is forming and formed, there is a type of patriotism already. Thus they had imbibed it who stood that charge at Concord, and they who hung deadly on the retreat, and they who threw up the hasty and imperfect redoubt on Bunker Hill by night, set on it the blood-red provincial flag, and passed so calmly with Prescott and Putnam and Warren through the experiences of the first fire.

But now to direct this spontaneous sentiment of hearts to the Union, to raise it high, to make it broad and deep, to instruct it, to educate it, is in some things harder, some things easier; but it may be done; it must be done. She, too, has her spectacles; she, too, has her great names; she, too, has her food for patriotism, for childhood, for man. "Americans," said an orator of France, "begin with the infant in the cradle. Let the first word he lisps be Washington." Hang on his neck on that birth-day, and that day of his death at Mount Vernon, the Medal of Congress, by its dark ribbon; tell him the story of the flag, as it passes glittering along the road; bid him listen to that plain, old-fashioned, stirring music of the Union; lead him when school is out at evening to the grave of his great-grandfather, the old soldier of the war; bid him, like Hannibal, at nine years old, lay the little hand on that Constitution and swear reverently to observe it; lift him up and lift yourselves up to the height of American feeling; open to him, and think for yourselves, on the relation of America to the States; show him upon the map the area to which she has extended herself; the climates that come into the number of her months; the silver paths of her trade, wide as the world; tell him of her contributions to humanity, and her protests for free government; keep with him the glad and solemn feasts of her appointment; bury her great names in his heart, and into your hearts; contemplate habitually, lovingly, intelligently, this grand abstraction, this vast reality of good; and such an institution may do somewhat to transform this surpassing beauty into a national life, which shall last while sun and moon endure.

But there is another condition of our nationality of which I must say something, and that is that it rests on compromise. America, the Constitution, practicable policy, all of it, are a compromise. Our public is possible — it can draw its breath for a day — only by compromise.

There is a cant of shallowness and fanaticism which misunderstands and denies this. There is a distempered and ambitious morality which says civil prudence is no virtue. There is a philanthropy, — so it calls itself, — pedantry, arrogance, folly, cruelty, impiousness, I call it, fit enough for a pulpit, totally unfit for a people; fit enough for a preacher, totally unfit for a statesman; — which, confounding large things with little things, ends with means, subordinate ends with chief ends, one man's sphere of responsibility with another man's sphere of responsibility, seed-time with harvest, one science with another science, one truth with another truth, one jurisdiction with another jurisdiction, the span-long day of life with the duration of States, generals with universals, the principle with the practice, the Anglo-Celtic-Saxon of America with the pavers of Paris, cutting down the half-grown tree to snatch the unripe fruit — there is a philanthropy which scolds at this even, and calls it names.

To such a spirit I have nothing to say, but I have something to say to you. It is remarked by a very leading writer of our times, Lord Macaulay — ennobled less by title than by genius and fame, — "that compromise is the essence of politics." That which every man of sense admits to be so true, as to have become a common-place of all politics, is peculiarly true of our national politics. Our history is a record of compromises; and this freedom and this glory attest their wisdom and bear their fruits. But can these compromises stand the higher test of morality? Concessions for the sake of the nation; concessions for what the general opinion of America has pronounced concessions for America; concessions in measures; concessions in spirit for such an end; — are they a virtue?

I hope it is worth something, in the first place, that the judgment of civilization, collected from all its expression and all its exponents, has ranked concession for the keeping and well-being of the nation, among the whiter virtues. Starting with the grand central sentiment that patriotism is the noblest practical limitation of universal philanthropy, and reserving its enthusiasm, its tears, for the martyred patriot, and deeming his death the most glorious of deaths, it has given ever the first place to him whose firmness, wisdom, and moderation have built the State, and whose firmness, wisdom, and moderation keep the State. These traits it has stamped as virtues. These traits it has stamped as great virtues. Poetry, art, history, biography, the funeral discourse, the utterance of that judgment, how universally have they so stamped them! He whose harp, they said, attracted and fused savage natures; he who gave to his people, not the best government, but the best that they would bear; he who by timely adaptations elevated an inferior class to equality with a superior class, and made two nations into one; he whose tolerance and comprehension put out the fires of persecution, and placed all opinions and religions on one plane before the law; he whose healing counsels composed the distractions of a various empire, — he is the great good man of civilization. Ambition might have been his aim to some extent, but the result is a country, a power, a law. On that single title, it raised his statue, hung on it the garland that cannot die, kept his birthday by the firing of cannons, and ringing of bells, and processions, and thanks to God Almighty. He may not have been fortunate in war; he may not have been foremost among men of genius; but what Luxembourg, what Eugene, what Marlborough heaped on his ashes such a monument, as the wise, just, cold, Dutch deliverer of England? What Gates, what Lee, what Alexander, what Napoleon, won such honor, such love, such sacred and warm-felt approval as our civil father, Washington? Does that judgment, the judgment of civilization, condemn Demosthenes, who would have invited Persia to help against Macedon; or Cicero, who praised and soothed the young Octavius, to win him from Anthony; or the Calvinist William, who invited the papal Austria to fight with him against Louis XIV.? Does it dream of branding such an act as hypocrisy, or apostacy? Does it not recognize it rather as wisdom, patriotism, and virtue, masculine and intelligent? Does it not rather give him all honor and thanks, who could forego the sweets of revenge, rise above the cowardice of selfishness and the narrow memory of personal inapplicable antecedents, and for the love of Athens, of Rome, of England, of liberty, could magnanimously grasp the solid glory of great souls?

But this judgment of civilization, I maintain next, is a sound moral judgment. It is founded on a theory of duty which makes the highest utility to man the grandest achievement of man. It thinks that it discerns that the national life is the true useful human life. It thinks that it discerns that the greater includes the less; that beneath that order, that government, that law, that power, reform is easy and reform is safe — reform of the man, reform of the nation. It ventures to hold that a nation is the grandest of the instrumentalities of morals and religion. It holds that under that wing, beneath that lightning, there is room, there is capacity, for humbly imitating His plan who sits in the circle of eternity, and with whom a thousand years are as one day; room, motive, capacity for labor, for culture, for preparation, for the preaching of the gospel of peace to all, for elevating by slow, sure, and quiet gradations down to its depths, down to its chains, society itself. Concession to keep such an agent is concession to promote such ends.

Do you remember what a great moralist and a great man, Archbishop Whately, said on this subject in the House of Lords? He was advocating concession to Catholics; and see how much stronger was truth than the hatred of theologians. The biographer of Peel calls the speech a splendid piece of reasoning; and it decided the vote: —

"So great is the outcry which it has been the fashion among some persons for several years past to raise against *expediency*, that the very word has become almost an ill-omened sound. It seems to be thought by many a sufficient ground of condemnation of any legislator to say that he is guided by views of expediency. And some seem even to be ashamed of acknowledging that they are, in any degree, so guided. I, for one, however, am content to submit to the imputation of being a votary of expediency. And what is more, I do not see what right any one who is not so has to sit in Parliament, or to take any part in public affairs. Any one who may choose to acknowledge that the measures he opposes are expedient, or that those he recommends are inexpedient, ought manifestly to have no seat in a deliberative assembly, which is constituted for the express and sole purpose of considering what measures are *conducive to the public good;*— in other words, 'expedient.' I say, the '*public* good,' because, of course, by 'expediency' we mean, not that which may benefit some individual, or some party or class of men, at the expense of the public, but what conduces to the good of the nation. Now this, it is evident, is the very object for which deliberative assemblies are constituted. And so far is this from being regarded, by our Church at least, as something at variance with religious duty, that we have a prayer specially appointed to be offered up during the sitting of the Houses of Parliament, that their consultations may be 'directed and prospered for the *safety*, *honor*, and *welfare* of our sovereign and her dominions.' Now, if this be not the very definition of political expediency, let any one say what is."

I have no doubt, however, that this judgment of civilization rests in part on the difficulty and the rarity of the virtue which it praises. We prize the difficult and the rare because they are difficult and rare; and when you consider how easy and how tempting it is to fall in with and float with the stream on which so many swim; how easy is that broad road and how sweet that approved strain; how easy and how tempting it is to please an assenting congregation, or circle of readers, or local public; how easy and how tempting to compound for sins which an influential man "is not inclined to, by damning those he has no mind to;" how easy to please those we see, and forget those out of sight; what courage, what love of truth are demanded to dissent; how hard it is to rise to the vast and varied conception, and to the one idea, which grasps and adjusts all the ideas; how easy it is for the little man to become great, the shallow man to become profound; the coward out of danger to be brave; the free-state man to be an anti-slavery man, and to write tracts which his friends alone read; when you think that even the laughter of fools and children and madmen, little ministers, little editors, and little politicians, can inflict the mosquito bite, not deep, but stinging; — who wonders that the serener and the calmer judgment allots "to patient continuance in well doing," to resistance of the parts, to contention for the whole, to counsels of moderation and concession, "glory, honor, and immortality?"

> What nothing earthly gives or can destroy,
> The soul's calm sunshine, and the heartfelt joy.

But this judgment of civilization is the judgment of religion too. You believe with the Bible, with Cicero, with the teachings of history, that God wills the national life. He wills civilization, therefore society, therefore law, therefore government, therefore nations. How do we know this? Always, from the birth of the historical time, civilized man led the national life. Therein always the nature God has given him has swelled to all its perfection, and has rendered the worthiest praise to the Giver of the gift. He who wills the end wills the indispensable means; he wills the means which his teachers, nature and experience, have ascertained to be indispensable. Then he wills these means, concession, compromise, love, forbearance, help, because his teachers, nature and experience, have revealed them to be indispensable. Then he wills our national life. Then he wills the spirit which made it and which keeps it. Do you dare to say, with President Davies, that you believe that Providence raised up that young man, Washington, for some great public service, — with the spectator of that first inauguration, that you believe the Supreme Being looked down with complacency on that act, — with that Senate which thanked God that he had conducted to the tomb a fame whiter than it was brilliant; and yet dare to say that the spirit of Washington ought not to be your spirit, his counsels your guide, his Farewell Address your scripture of political religion? But what does he say? I need not repeat it, for you have it by heart; but what said a greater than he? "Render unto Cæsar the things which are Cæsar's." Render under Cæsar the things that are Cæsar's, and thus, to that extent, you "render unto God the things which are God's." Be these words our answer and our defence. When they press us with the common-places of anti-slavery, be these words of wisdom our answer. Say to them, "Yes, I thank God I keep no slaves. I am sorry there is one on earth; I am sorry even that there is need of law, of subordination, of order, of government, of the discipline of the schools, of prisons, of the gallows; I wonder at such a system of things; piously I would reform it; but beneath that same system I am an American citizen; beneath that system, this country it is my post to keep; while I keep her there is hope for all men, for the evil man, for the intemperate man, for slaves, for free, for all; that hope your rash and hasty hand would prostrate; that hope my patience would advance." Have they done? Are they answered?

There are other conditions and other laws of our nationality on which there needs to be said something if there were time. That it is not and that it cannot come to good, that it cannot achieve its destiny, that it cannot live even, unless it rests on the understanding of the State, you know. How gloriously this is anticipated by our own Constitution, you remember. How well said Washington — who said all things as he did all things, well — "that in proportion as governments rest on public opinion, that opinion must be enlightened." There must then be intelligence at the foundation. But what intelligence? Not that which puffeth up, I fancy, not flippancy, not smartness, not sciolism, whose fruits, whose expression are vanity, restlessness, insubordination, hate, irreverence, unbelief, incapacity to combine ideas, and great capacity to overwork a single one. Not quite this. This is that little intelligence and little learning which are dangerous. These are the characteristics, I have read, which pave the way for the downfall of States; not those on which a long glory and a long strength have towered. These, more than the general of Macedon, gave the poison to Demosthenes in the Island Temple. These, not the triumvirate alone, closed the eloquent lips of Cicero. These, before the populous North had done it, spread beneath Gibraltar to the Lybian sands in the downward age. These, not Christianity, not Goth, not Lombard, nor Norman, rent that fair one Italy asunder, and turned the garden and the mistress of the earth into a school, into a hiding place, of assassins — of spies from Austria, of spies from France, with gold to buy and ears to catch and punish the dreams of liberty whispered in sleep, and shamed the memories and hopes of Machiavel and Mazzini, and gave for that joy and that beauty, mourning and heaviness. This is not the intelligence our Constitution means, Washington meant, and our country needs. It is intelligence which, however it begins, ends with belief, with humility, with obedience, with veneration, with admiration, with truth; which recognizes and then learns and then teaches the duties of a comprehensive citizenship; which hopes for a future on earth and beyond earth, but turns habitually, reverently, thoughtfully to the old paths, the great men, the hallowed graves of the fathers; which binds in one bundle of love the kindred and mighty legend of revolution and liberty, the life of Christ in the Evangelists, and the Constitution in its plain text; which can read with Lord Chatham, Thucydides and the stories of master States of antiquity, yet holds with him that the papers of the Congress of 1776 were better; whose patriotism grows warm at Marathon, but warmer at Monmouth, at Yorktown, at Bunker Hill, at Saratoga; which reforms by preserving, serves by standing and waiting, fears God and honors America.

I had something to say more directly still on the ethics of nationality, on the duty of instructing the conscience; on the crimes of treason, and slander, and fraud, that are committed around us in its name; on the shallowness and stupidity of the doctrine that the mere moral sentiments, trained by a mere moral discipline, may safely guide the complex civil life; of the teachers and studies which they need to fit them for so precious, difficult, and delicate a dominion; of the high place in the scale of duties, which, thus fitted, they assign to nationality; of the judgment which, thus fitted they would apply to one or two of the common-places and practices of the time. But I pass it all to say only that these ethics teach the true subordination, and the true reconciliation of apparently incompatible duties. These only are the casuists, or the safest casuists for us. Learn from them how to adjust this conflict between patriotism and philanthropy. To us, indeed, there seems to be no such conflict, for we are philanthropists in proportion as we are unionists. Our philanthropy, we venture to say, is a just philanthropy. That is all. It loves all men, it helps all men, it respects all rights, keeps all compacts, recognizes all dangers, pities all suffering, ignores no fact, master and slave it enfolds alike. It happens thus that it contracts the sphere of our duty somewhat, and changes not the nature, but the time, the place, the mode of performing it. It does not make our love cold, but it makes it safe; it naturalizes it, it baptizes it into our life; it circumscribes it within our capacities and our necessities; it sets on it the great national public seal. If you say that thus our patriotism limits our philanthropy, I answer that ours is American philanthropy. Be this the virtue we boast, and this the name by which we know it. In this name, in this quality, find the standard and the utterance of the virtue itself. By this, not by broad phylacteries and chief seats, the keener hate, the gloomier fanaticism, the louder cry, judge, compare, subordinate. Do they think that nobody is a philanthropist but themselves? We, too, look up the long vista and gaze, rapt, at the dazzling ascent; we, too, see towers rising, crowned, imperial, and the tribes coming to bend in the opening of a latter day. But we see peace, order, reconciliation of rights along that brightening future. We trace all along that succession of reform, the presiding instrumentalities of national life. We see our morality working itself clearer and clearer; one historical and conventional right or wrong, after another, falling peacefully and still; we hear the chain breaking, but there is no blood on it, none of his whom it bound, none of his who put it on him; we hear the swelling chorus of the free, but master and slave unite in that chorus, and there is no discordant shriek above the harmony; we see and we hail the blending of our own glory with the eternal light of God, but we see, too, shapes of love and beauty ascending and descending there as in the old vision!

Hold fast this hope; distrust the philanthropy, distrust the ethics which would, which must, turn it into shame. Do no evil that good may come. Perform your share, for you have a share, in the abolition of slavery; perform your share, for you have a share, in the noble and generous strife of the sections — but perform it by keeping, by transmitting, a UNITED, LOVING AND CHRISTIAN AMERICA.

But why, at last, do I exhort, and why do I seem to fear, on such a day as this? Is it not the nation's birthday? Is it not this country of our love and hopes, which celebrates it?

This music of the glad march, these banners of pride and beauty, these memories so fragrant, these resolutions of patriotism so thoughtful, these hands pressed, these congratulations and huzzaings and tears, this great heart throbbing audibly, — are they not hers, and do they not assure us? These forests of masts, these singing workshops of labor, these fields and plantations whitening for the harvest, this peace and plenty, this sleeping thunder, these bolts in the closed, strong talon, do not they tell us of her health, her strength, and her future? This shadow that flits across our grasses and is gone, this shallow ripple that darkens the surface of our broad and widening stream, and passes away, this little perturbation which our telescopes cannot find, and which our science can hardly find, but which we know cannot change the course or hasten the doom of one star; have these any terror for us? And He who slumbers not, nor sleeps, who keeps watchfully the city of his love, on whose will the life of nations is suspended, and to whom all the shields of the earth belong, our fathers' God, is he not our God, and of whom, then, and of what shall we be afraid?

SPEECH ON THE BIRTHDAY OF DANIEL WEBSTER, JANUARY 21, 1859.

[THE seventy-seventh anniversary of the birthday of Daniel Webster was commemorated by a banquet at the Revere House. At the conclusion of the feast, and after the opening address by the president of the day, Hon. Caleb Cushing, Mr. Choate, being called upon, spoke as follows:]

I WOULD not have it supposed for a moment that I design to make any eulogy, or any speech, concerning the great man whose birthday we have met to observe. I hasten to assure you that I shall attempt to do no such thing. There is no longer need of it, or fitness for it, for any purpose. Times have been when such a thing might have been done with propriety. While he was yet personally among us, — while he was yet walking in his strength in the paths or ascending the heights of active public life, or standing upon them, — and so many of the good and wise, so many of the wisest and best of our country, from all parts of it, thought he had title to the great office of our system, and would have had him formally presented for it, it was fit that those who loved and honored him should publicly, — with effort, with passion, with argument, with contention, — recall the series of his services, his life of elevated labors, finished and unfinished, display his large qualities of character and mind, and compare him, somewhat, in all these things, with the great men, his competitors for the great prize. Then was there a battle to be fought, and it was needful to fight it.

And so, again, in a later day, while our hearts were yet bleeding with the sense of recent loss, and he lay newly dead in his chamber, and the bells were tolling, and his grave was open, and the sunlight of an autumn day was falling on that long funeral train, I do not say it was fit only, it was unavoidable, that we all, in some choked utterance and some imperfect, sincere expression, should, if we could not praise the patriot, lament the man.

But these times have gone by. The race of honor and duty is for him all run. The high endeavor is made, and it is finished. The monument is builded. He is entered into his glory. The day of hope, of pride, of grief, has been followed by the long rest; and the sentiments of grief, pride, and hope, are all merged in the sentiment of calm and implicit veneration. We have buried him in our hearts. That is enough to say. Our estimation of him is part of our creed. We have no argument to make or hear upon it. We enter into no dispute about him. We permit no longer any man to question us as to what he was, what he had done, how much we loved him, how much the country loved him, and how well he deserved it. We admire, we love, and we are still. Be this enough for us to say.

Is it not enough that we just stand silent on the deck of the bark fast flying from the shore, and turn and see, as the line of coast disappears, and the headlands and hills and all the land go down, and the islands are swallowed up, the great mountain standing there in its strength and majesty, supreme and still — to see how it swells away up from the subject and fading vale? to see that, though clouds and tempests, and the noise of waves, and the yelping of curs, may be at its feet, eternal sunshine has settled upon its head?

There is another reason why I should not trust myself to say much more of him to-night. It does so happen that you cannot praise Mr. Webster for that which really characterized and identified him as a public man, but that you seem to be composing *a tract for the times.*

It does so happen that the influence of his whole public life and position was so *pronounced* — so to speak — so defined, sharp, salient; the spirit of his mind, the tone of his mind, was so unmistakable and so peculiar; the nature of the public man was so transparent and so recognized everywhere, — that you cannot speak of him without seeming to grow polemical, without seeming to make an attack upon other men, upon organizations, upon policy, upon tendencies. You cannot say of him what is true, and what you know to be true, but you are thought to be disparaging or refuting somebody else.

In this way there comes to be mingled with our service of the heart something of the discordant, incongruous, and temporary. So it is everywhere. They could not keep the birthday of Charles James Fox, but they were supposed to attack the grave of Pitt, and aim at a Whig administration and a reform bill. An historian can hardly admire the architecture of the age of Pericles, or find some palliation of the trial of Socrates, but they say he is a Democrat, a Chartist, or a friend of the secret ballot. The marvellous eloquence, and noble, patriotic enterprise of our Everett, can scarcely escape such misconstruction of small jealousy.

Yes; sad it is, but true, that you cannot say here to-night what you think, what you know, what you thank God for, about the Union-loving heart, the Constitution-defending brain, the moderation-breathing spirit, the American nature of the great man, — our friend, — but they call out you are thinking of them! So powerful is the suggestion of contrast, and such cowards does conscience make of all bad men!

I feel the effect of this embarrassment. I protest against such an application of anything I say. But I feel, also, that it will be better, than such a protest, to sum up in the briefest and plainest and soberest expression, what I deem will be the record of history, — let me hope, with the immunities of history, — concerning this man, as a public man.

He was, then, let me say, of the very foremost of great American Statesmen. This is the class of greatness in which he is to be ranked. As such, always, he is to be judged. What he would have been in another department of thought; how high he would have risen under other institutions; what he could have done if politics had not turned him from calm philosophy aside; whether he were really made for mankind, and to America gave up what was meant for mankind; how his mere naked intellectual ability compared with this man's or that, — is a needless and vain speculation.

I may, however, be allowed to say that, although I have

seen him act, and heard him speak, and give counsel, in very high and very sharp and difficult crises, I always felt that if more had been needed more would have been done, and that half his strength or all his strength he put not forth. I never saw him make what is called an effort without feeling that, let the occasion be what it would, he would have swelled out to its limits. There was always a reservoir of power of which you never sounded the depths, certainly never saw the bottom; and I cannot well imagine any great historical and civil occasion to which he would not have brought, and to which he would not be acknowledged to have brought, an adequate ability. He had wisdom to have guided the counsels of Austria as Metternich did, if he had loved absolutism as well; skill enough and eloquence enough to have saved the life of Louis the Sixteenth, if skill and eloquence could have done it; learning, services, character, and dignity enough for a Lord Chancellor of England, if wisdom in counsel and eloquence in debate would have been titles to so proud a distinction.

But his class is that of American Statesmen. In that class he is to find his true magnitude. As he stood there he is to take his place forever in our system. To that constellation he has gone up, to that our telescopes or our naked eye are to be directed, and there I think he shines with a large and unalterable glory.

In every work regard the writer's end. In every life regard the actor's end.

In saying this I do not mean to ignore or disparage his rank, also, in the profession of the law. In that profession he labored, by that he lived, of that he was proud, to that he brought vast ability and exquisite judgment, and in that he rose at last to the leadership of the bar. But I regard that, rather, as a superinduced, collateral, accessional fame, a necessity of greatness, — a transcendent greatness, certainly; but it was not the labor he most loved, it was not the fame which attracts so many pilgrims to his tomb, and stirs so many hearts when his name is sounded. There have been Bacons, and Clarendons, and one Cicero, and one Demosthenes, who were lawyers. But they are not the Bacons, the Clarendons, they are not the Cicero and the Demosthenes of historical fame.

It is a noble and a useful profession; but it was not large enough for the whole of Webster.

In that class, then, let me say next,—which is the class of American statesmen,—of foremost American statesmen,—it happened to him to be thrown on our third American age. This ever must be regarded when we would do him justice, or understand him, or compare him with others.

It is easy to say and to see that if his lot had made him a member of the Revolutionary Congress, he would have stood by the side of Washington and Jefferson, Adams and Chase, and that from his tongue, too, Independence would have thundered. It is easy to say and see that it would not have been that his lips were frozen and his arm palsied; that the cabals of Gates, of Conway, could have gone undetected there; that a foolish fear of long enlistments would have delayed the great strife; that so many retreats, pinched winter-quarters, blood traced on the snow by the naked feet of bleeding men, would have proved that the want of funds and the fear of unpopularity were too strong for the sentiment of Liberty!

It is easy to say, too, and to see that if he had been thrown on the constitutional age he would have been found with Hamilton, Jay, and Madison; that his pen, too, and his tongue would have leaped to impress that generation with the nature and necessity of that great work; that he would have risen to the utmost height of the great argument, and that on the pillars, on the foundation-stones of that Constitution which he first read on the little pocket-handkerchief, his name, his wisdom, too, would now be found chiselled deeply. But he was cast on the third age of our history, and how was his part acted there?

In this class, then, let me say further, of the foremost of great American statesmen, I say there was never one, of any one of our periods,—I shall not except the highest of the first period,—of a more ardent love of our *America, and of the whole of it;* of a truer, deeper, broader sense of what the Farewell Address calls the Unity of Government,—its nature, spring, necessity,—and the means of securing it; or who said more, and did more to sink it deep in the American heart. Of the relations of the States to our system,—of their powers, their rights, their quasi sovereignty,—he said less, not because he thought less or knew less, but because he saw there was less necessity for it. But the Union, the Constitution, the national federal life, the American name,—*E Pluribus Unum*,—these filled his heart, these dwelt in his habitual speech.

This, I think, exactly, was his specialty. To this master passion and master sentiment his whole life was subordinated carefully. He was *totus in illis*. He began his public course in opposition to the party which had the general government; and he dearly loved New England; but he "had nothing to do with the Hartford Convention." He drew his first breath in a Northern State and a Northern region; his opinions were shaped and colored by that birth-place and by that place of residence; the local interests he powerfully advocated; for that advocacy he has even been taunted and distrusted. But it was because he thought he saw, and just so far as he saw, that the local interest was identical with the national interest, and that that advocacy was advocacy for the whole, and that policy was American policy, that he espoused it.

Some aged clergyman has been reported to have said, that the sermon — whatever the theology, whatever the ability — was essentially defective, if it did not leave on the hearer the impression that the preacher loved his soul, and that God and the Saviour loved it. I never heard him make a speech, — a great speech, — whatever were the topic, or the time, that did not leave the impression that he loved nothing, desired nothing, so much as the good and glory of America; that he knew no North and no South; that he did not seem to summon around him the whole brotherhood of States and men, and hold them all to his heart! This gave freshness and energy to all his speech. This set the tune to the universal harmony. Even his studies revealed this passion. He knew American history by heart, as a statesman, not as an antiquary, should know it; the plain, noble men, the high aims, and hard fortunes of the colonial time; the agony and the glory of the Revolutionary War, and of the age of the Constitution, were all familiar to him; but chiefly he loved to mark how the spirit of national life was evolving itself all the while; how the colonies grew to regard one another as the children of the same mother, and therefore, fraternally; how the common danger, the common oppression, of the ante-revolutionary and revolutionary period served to fuse them into one; how the Constitution made them formally one; and how the grand and sweet and imperial sentiment of a united national life came at last to penetrate and warm that whole vast and various mass, and move it as a soul.

> "Spiritus intus alit, totamque infusa per artus
> Mens agitat molem, et magno se corpore miscet."

In this master sentiment I *find the key* to all his earlier and all his later policy and opinions. Through his whole lifetime, this is the central principle that runs through all, accounts for all, reconciles all.

In the department of a mere adventurous and originating policy, I do not think he desired to distinguish himself. In the department of a restless and arrogant and clamorous reform, I know he did not wish to distinguish himself. The general tendency of his mind, the general scope of his politics, were towards conservation.

This rested on a deep conviction that, if the government continued to exist, and this national life continued to be kept, and if these States were held in peace together, the growth of it, the splendid future of it, were as certain as the courses of the seasons. He thought it wiser, therefore, always, that we should grow great under the Union, than that we should be forced to grow great by legislation. He thought it wiser, therefore, at first, — local opinion may have, or may not have, a little influenced this, — to let America grow into a manufacturing people, than that she should be forced to become so. But when that policy was adopted, and millions had been invested under it, and a vast, delicate, and precious interest had grown up, then it seemed to him that just so much had been added to our American life, that for so much we had gone forward in our giant course, and he would guard it and keep it.

He did not favor a premature and unprincipled expansion of territory; though he saw and rejoiced to see, if America continued just, and continued brave, and the Union lasted, how widely — to what Pacific and tropic seas — she must spread, — and how conspicuous a fame of extent was spread out before her. But when the annexation was made and the line drawn and the treaty signed, then he went for her, however "butted and bounded;" then he kept steady to the compact of annexation; then there was no date so small, no line so remote, that he would not plant on it the ensign all radiant, that no foreign aggression might come! *Here you have the Websterianism of Webster.*

I cannot trace this great central principle and this master sentiment and trait which is the characteristic of his whole politics, through the last years of his life, without awakening feelings, some feelings unsuited to the time. I believe, you believe, the country and history will believe, that all he said and all he did, he said and did out of a "full heart for the Constitution," and that the "austere glory" of that crisis of his America and of himself will shine his brightest glory. When some years have passed away, if not yet, that civil courage, that wisdom which combines, constructs, and reconciles; which discerns that in the political world, in our political world especially, no theory and no idea may be pressed to its extreme, and that common sense, good temper, good nature, and not the pedantry of logical abstraction, and the clamor of intemperate sectional partisanships, are the true guides of life; and that deemed a gloomy foolishness, refuted by our whole history, that because in this cluster of States there are different institutions, a different type of industry, different moral estimates, they cannot live together and grow together to a common nationality by forbearance and reason; that an honest, just, and well-principled patriotism is a higher moral virtue than a virulent and noisy philanthropy; and that to build and keep this nation is the true way to serve God and serve man — these traits and these opinions will be remembered as the noblest specimen of the genius and wisdom of Webster. Better than any other passage, or any other catastrophe, these will be thought most happily to have "concluded the great epic of his life." I refer you for them all to his immortal volumes; lasting as the granite of our mountains, lasting as the pillars of our capitol and our Constitution.

They say he was ambitious! Yes; as Ames said of Hamilton, "there is no doubt that he desired glory; and that, feeling his own force, he longed to deck his brow with the wreath of immortality." But I believe he would have yielded his arm, his frame to be burned, before he would have sought to grasp the highest prize of earth by any means, by any organization, by any tactics, by any speech, which in the least degree endangered the harmony of the system.

They say, too, he loved New England! He loved New Hampshire — that old granite world — the crystal hills, gray and cloud-topped; the river, whose murmur lulled his cradle; the old hearth-stone; the grave of father and mother. He loved Massachusetts, which adopted and honored him — that sounding sea-shore, that charmed elm-tree seat, that reclaimed farm, that choice herd, that smell of earth, that dear library, those dearer friends; but the "sphere of his duties was his true country." Dearly he loved you, for he was grateful for the open arms with which you welcomed the stranger and sent him onwards and upwards.

But when the crisis came, and the winds were all let loose, and that sea of March "wrought and was tempestuous," then you saw that he knew even you only as you were, American citizens; then you saw him rise to the true nature and stature of American citizenship; then you read on his brow only what he thought of the whole Republic; then you saw him fold the robes of his habitual patriotism around him, and counsel for all — for all.

So then he served you — "to be pleased with his service was your affair, not his."

And now what would he do, what would he be if he were here to-day? I do not presume to know. But what a loss we have in him.

I have read that in some hard battle, when the tide was running against him, and his ranks were breaking, some one in the agony of a need of generalship exclaimed, "Oh for an hour of Dundee!"

So say I, Oh for an hour of Webster now!

Oh for one more roll of that thunder inimitable!

One more peal of that clarion!

One more grave and bold counsel of moderation!

One more throb of American feeling!

One more Farewell Address! And then might he ascend unhindered to the bosom of his Father and his God.

But this is a vain wish, and I can only offer you this sentiment —

The birth-day of Webster — Then best, then only well celebrated — when it is given as he gave that marvellous brain, that large heart, and that glorious life, to our country, our whole country, our united country.

APPENDIX.

TRANSLATIONS.

HORÆ THUCYDIDIANÆ.

1 *August*, 1845.

[I BEGIN to-day the *study* of Thucydides. I have read him before and read of him, but I propose now to *translate*, meditate, and retain him. I have Arnold's, Bloomfield's, and Haack's editions, with Smith's translations and the best Greek histories. My great want is a good Greek Lexicon. The prefatory chapters I must stop occasionally to verify, fill out, and correct; but I shall hasten forward to his history itself. The period, however, from the Persian to the Peloponnesian War will demand careful attention.

Even in the introduction, you mark the unity of design which distinguishes all Grecian art. He has composed the history of the war of the Peloponnesians and Athenians. All the earlier history of Greece is excluded from his subject. Yet a rapid and general sketch of that history would usefully, and should naturally, precede and introduce the immediate great work. He presents such a sketch, therefore, but he, *in form,* appears to do it solely for the purpose of justifying his actual choice of a subject, by displaying the superior importance of his period and his scenes to all which had gone before. You set out, then, with a useful review of other facts, but you advert to them mainly and immediately as having for various reasons less interest or certainty or consequence than the facts of the Peloponnesian War.]

(TRANSLATION.)

THUCYDIDES.

BOOK I.

I. THUCYDIDES, an Athenian, has composed the history of the war of the Peloponnesians and Athenians, as the belligerents conducted it, having commenced the undertaking immediately upon the breaking out of the war, and having even then anticipated that it would be one of great importance, and more worthy of record than any that had preceded it; a belief to which he was conducted by observing that the two contending States were in an extraordinary degree and by every form of resource prepared for it, and that the entire Greek race was to range itself on the side of one or the other of those States, — some cities instantly doing so, — others meditating it. 2. For this civil commotion constituted the most considerable war that ever befell the Greeks, or that ever befell a large part of the nations not Greek, or, as I may say, the great body of the race of man itself; since of those which immediately preceded it, and those still more ancient, it is in the first place impossible, from remoteness of time, surely to discern the historical truth; and then, in so far as I may judge from all the evidence on which, after the widest and farthest view, I can rely, I do not think that they were really great transactions, either as wars or in any other aspects.[1]

II. It is certain that the region now called Greece was anciently not inhabited in a permanent or settled and secure manner, but that in the earliest time there was a continual practice of transmigration from one spot to another, and every one was

[1] The point on which the reader of history craves assurance is its trustworthiness. In this particular, I do not know that any affords higher promise than this of Thucydides. He was born B. C. 471. The war began 431 B. C. He was therefore forty years of age at its commencement; and he declares that, foreseeing its importance beforehand, he determined to write its history, and began the great task with the breaking out of the war. What means had he to be accurate? He was an Athenian, and I think at Athens at that precise point of time; his faculties at their best, his intellect deep, capacious, full, intimate with the great scientific and practical minds of the day, — intensely stimulated by the stormy scene beginning to open. There he staid, acting and observing, till the seventh year of the war, when he was assigned the command of a naval and military force for the coast of Thrace. This presupposes character, experience, and activity at Athens, as well as ties, relatives and property in Thrace itself. He was sent to encounter Brasidas, among the most energetic of the Peloponnesian generals; he conducted a single enterprise, that for the defence of Amphipolis, with vigor and skill; he was unsuccessful, was banished by a demagogue, and retired to Scapte Hyle in Thrace, at the age of forty-eight, calm, firm, passionless, to observe, to study, and to write. In all historical literature, I know no combination of circumstances giving such assurance of certainty of knowledge. During his banishment, he is said to have availed himself of Peloponnesian sources of information. Treason to Athens, infidelity, revenge, never have been imputed to him. Perhaps we have gained impartiality, judicial calmness and indifference, truth and use, by the campaign and the condemnation which withdrew Thucydides from participation in one side, and gave back to mankind, to posterity, and to history the mind which belonged to them.

How can Thucydides say of the Persian War that it was not intrinsically and absolutely *great*, both as a war and in all aspects? Is this true? Could he have thought so? I think the παλαιότερα alone were in his mind, or chiefly; for he blends the difficulty of discerning the truth and the far view from which his researches had set out with the want of greatness, as applicable all to the same events or times.

Yet, — ch. 23, — he speaks of the brief duration of the Persian War and the fewness of its battles as showing its comparative insignificance. Therefore does not Thucydides rhetorically depreciate the past and exaggerate the present?

accustomed easily to abandon his place and possessions, whenever compelled to do so by an invasion of a greater number. 2. For since there was no trade by sea, and no man mingled without fear and without hazard with other men, on land or water; since no one appropriated to himself or used what he had, farther or more than to sustain his daily life, accumulating nothing, nor so much as planting a tree or a vine, uncertain when another might invade and snatch the product of his toil away,— the cities too all unwalled; and since moreover it was universally thought that the needful supply of daily sustenance might be found anywhere, men habitually and perpetually migrated, without difficulty, without resistance, without regret. For this reason, too, the nations or tribes of these times did not grow to strength by the magnitude of their cities, or by any other form of military preparation.[1] 3. These changes of inhabitants were most frequent in the more fertile regions of Greece, — in what is now Thessaly, for example, in Bœotia, in the greater part of the Peloponnesus, except Arcadia. 4. For by means of the fertility of the soil, inequalities of fortune were produced, some citizens acquiring more wealth than others, and thus dissensions and revolutions were brought on, by which they perished. Such, too, were more exposed to the incursion of foreign or distinct tribes. 5. Attica, on the other hand, exempted from internal dissension and revolution, from the remotest period, by the lightness or thinness of its soil, untempting, the same men had inhabited immemorially.[2] 6. And in this instance of Attica, its history and its comparatively more rapid growth, I remark a proof of the statement which I before advanced, that it was

[1] The historical fact here asserted may well be presumed to be true and to have been true from the time the first Pelasgic or ante-Pelasgic hunter set foot in Greece, for ages of barbarism. The great feature in the sketch is the practice of migration. There was no fixed individual or social or political state, residence, and existence. All intercourse was hostile and fearful. No one made accumulations of property, or sought from property more than support of daily life, the means of which he could find anywhere. He walled no cities, he planted no vine or tree. He expected to be driven out by a greater number and a greater strength. His habits and sentiments were formed to it; he offered slight resistance, and he suffered little regret. What epoch is described in these sections? The ante-Hellenic? The age subsequent to the diffusion upon Greece of the Pelasgi, — that in which foreign settlers are beginning to approach Greece? Or is it true of many periods, the original occupation by the Pelasgi, that of the accession of foreigners, that of the development of the Hellenes, — all the time down to the dawn of the historic period?

[2] The fact of infrequency of change rests on Thucydides. His disposition to speculation you discern in his explanation of the fact. Inequalities of fortune, larger accumulations side by side with smaller, induce revolution, dissension, and invite hostility; and these inequalities and accumulations you find only — while as yet trade has no existence — on rich soils.

attributable to this practice of incessant migration that other parts of Greece did not thrive. The truth is, that of those who by faction or by invasion were driven from other parts, the more wealthy and more considerable retired on Athens, as a place of security; and being admitted to the privilege of citizenship, they even in the earliest ages so filled the city with inhabitants, that at length, Attica becoming insufficient to contain them, colonies were sent forth to Ionia.[1]

III. I discern the political weakness and insignificance of these old times in these things also, that before the Trojan war Greece had accomplished no united and national undertaking, nor had its cities and tribes so much as the common name of Greece. Before the age of Hellen, the son of Deucalion, this designation, Hellas, appears not to have existed at all; and

[1] This passage is thought to be and is obscure. I interpret thus: Thucydides opens his second chapter by the statement that anciently migrations were incessant from place to place in Greece, and that nowhere were secure and permanent settlements. He exposes the causes; and declares that by reason of it the strength of cities and the preparations of war were not attained. He then adverts to the fact that these migrations were most frequent in the most fertile parts; and gives the reason that there the acquisition of inequalities of wealth generated faction and tempted invasion, he instances Thessaly and Bœotia as examples of fertile regions torn by faction and wasted by invasion, and Attica as an example of a country whose light soil exempted it from both, and enabled it at all times to retain its original inhabitants at home. With this, he dismisses this incidental or parenthetical remark about the effect of fertility and barrenness, and returns to his original statement that migrations were frequent and hindered the growth of strong cities and the accumulations of preparations for war. The instance of Attica — the facts of its history and the causes of its more rapid growth than the rest of Greece, afford me a proof of what I have said, to wit, that migrations prevented the thriving of old Greece. Attica was a place of security. Her old population could and did live ever safely at home. When war or faction banished the more wealthy and powerful of other cities, they fled to this asylum. Thus, in the earliest times she became so overstocked as to be compelled to colonize Ionia. Comparing this case with the rest of Greece, you see the influence of migration on prosperity. This case of Attica — its greater growth — proves my position that these other places were checked by migration. To them none resorted. From them many fled. She held her own. She welcomed new. These *facts*, introduced by ἐκ γὰρ &c., are the τόδε preceding.

The real question, however, is, — is διὰ τὰς μετοικίας a repetition and explanation of what λόγος is, or is it the proof of the λόγος? Is it this, — and the fact that other parts of Greece did not grow equally with Attica, proves what I said above, and leaving the reader to go back for what he said? I rather incline to this; for this assertion, διὰ &c., is an assertion not made before. He had not said that others had not *grown* or thriven as much as Athens. He had said migrations were common, and checked growth. He said where they were most frequent, where least, and why; *i.e.*, from qualities of soil. But he had not yet said that those where fewest were most prosperous. He now says that. The case of Athens suggests it. Here, said he, *in this fact*, to wit, that other parts flourished less, I find proof of disastrous effects of migration.

every tribe, the Pelasgic more extensively than any other, gave its own name to its own habitation. 2. After Hellen and his children had come to be chiefs of power in Phthiotis, they were called in by other tribes to contribute succor from time to time, and thus one tribe after another, by continuance of intercourse with them, came to be called Hellenes; yet was it long before that spread to be the prevalent national name.[1] 3. And of this assertion Homer affords the strongest proof; for although writing long after the Trojan war, he does not bestow this name as a common appellation on all the Greeks, nor does he apply it at all except to the followers of Achilles from Phthiotis, who were the first Hellenes, as I have before said; but when he speaks of the Greeks collectively, he calls them Argives, Danai, and Achæans. 4. Neither does he employ the term *βάρβαροι* as a general designation of all not Greeks, apparently because the Greeks themselves were not yet set apart and gathered together by that or any one national name, distinguishing them from all others. 5. This people, I repeat, whose various cities and communities thus came gradually and successively to be called Hellenes, by adopting a common Hellenic language, and to which, as a whole, that appellation came at last to be applied, although, as we have seen, subsequently to Homer, — this people, before the Trojan war, in no stage of progress in the ante-Hellenic or post-Hellenic period, effected any great common enterprise, through weakness and the want of alliance and coöperation with each other. And for even that war they were able and inclined to unite, only because they had then become more familiar with the life *of the sea.*

IV. The first who constructed a navy, of whom we hear, was Minos, who acquired the command of the greater part of the Hellenic Sea, conquered the Cyclades, and first colonized the larger number of them, having expelled some of their Carian inhabitants and established his own sons in the government. Piracy, too, he swept from the sea, as he naturally would do, as far as he was able, for the sake of securing larger returns of revenue to himself.

V. Now, anciently, the Greeks and such of the barbarians as dwelt either on the coasts of the mainland or on islands, after they had begun more frequently to traverse the sea in vessels,

[1] The general fact that the earliest inhabitants of the after Greece were disunited tribes, and that before the Trojan war they associated for no common enterprise, and bore no common name, is received. That these tribes gave each its own name to its own region, may be. The wider extension of the Pelasgic, and its priority to the time and name of Hellen, is also generally received. Thessaly, where is Phthiotis, produced the race and name by which Greece became called and created.

devoted themselves to the practice of piracy. Setting forth under the command of leaders of consideration and power, to enrich themselves and to procure food for those in want, they would fall upon unwalled towns and on the scattered inhabitants of villages, and plunder them, and thence they derived the chief of their subsistence. And this way of life was marked by no disgrace, but rather conferred something of glory. 2. You may see a proof of this in certain inhabitants of the continent at this day, who esteem it creditable to conduct a piratical expedition adroitly and bravely; and in the old poets, who everywhere introduce persons inquiring of those who came into port whether they were pirates, and who neither represent him to whom the inquiry is addressed as denying, ashamed of such a calling, nor him who makes the inquiry as designing it for matter of reproach. 3. On land, too, this life of reciprocal plunder was led. To this very day many parts of Greece retain this old condition of society and manners. As the Locri-Ozolæ and Ætolians and Acarnanians, and the continent nearest to them. Their custom of going armed while engaged in their ordinary occupations has descended to these people from the usages of the old piracy.

VI. For in that earlier and unquiet day all Greece wore arms, for the reason that settlements were unfortified, travel was unsafe, and all habitually lived with weapon in hand, like the barbarians. 2. Those parts of Greece in which this practice survives, prove and exemplify what then was the universal condition of society. 3. Of all the Greeks the Athenians first disused the wearing of arms, and then relaxing the severity of ancient customs, passed into a more refined and luxurious mode of life. It is even now only a short time since the more elderly of the wealthier class of Athenians ceased to wear, — so luxurious had their habits of dress become, — linen embroidered garments, and to wreathe their hair into a topping clasped around by golden grasshoppers; whence also among the elderly men of their kindred Ionians, a similar fashion prevailed. 4. A plain and simple dress, of the style of the present day, was first adopted by the Lacedæmonians and worn by all classes. In all things else, too, or in most things as well as in dress, the rich and the many of Lacedæmon lived in equality. 5. They were the first who appeared naked publicly, and stripping themselves for all to see, anointed themselves for the games. For anciently the athletes in the Olympic contests strove with broad girdles about them, for decency, and it is but recently that this practice [upon which the Lacedæmonians first innovated,] has wholly ceased. So among some of the barbarians at this day, especially the Asiatics, contests of boxing and wrestling are observed, and the competitors wear similar broad girdles. 6. Many other points of resemblance might we indicate between the customs of the ancient Greece and those of modern barbarism.

VII. Cities built subsequent to the most ancient period, and after navigation had been rendered more safe and practicable, and with larger accumulation of wealth, were constructed with walls at the very sea-coast, and were made to command isthmuses for the sake of trade, and for strength against neighbors. But those founded in that earlier period, by the reason of the prevalent piracy, were built far inland, both those of the continent and of the islands; for those who dwelt near the sea, though not following the sea, plundered one another; and to this day they are built far inland.

VIII. Of all pirates, the islanders, who were both Carians and Phœnicians, were not the least active and famous. These Carians and Phœnicians colonized [successively, however,] most of the islands. An illustration of which was recently afforded; for when the Athenians undertook the purification of Delos, and removed the graves of those who had died therein, above half were discovered to be Carians, recognized by the fashion of their arms which were buried with them, and by the mode of interment, the same now practised by them. 2. After Minos had constructed his navy, navigation became more practicable and safe and common; for the old robbers of the islands were removed by him, and at the same time he planted on many of them new colonists; 3. and those who lived on the sea-coast becoming more wealthy, adopted a more settled and civilized mode of life, and some of the wealthiest encircled themselves with walls. The poorer, for gain, submitted to serve others, and the richer and more powerful subjected the weaker and less wealthy. 4. And thus having advanced to a greater degree of power, at length, in an after time, they united in the war on Troy.

IX. And with regard to that expedition, it seems to me that Agamemnon was able to assemble the armament which was destined to it, rather by reason of his being the most powerful prince of his time, than by reason of the oaths exacted by Tyndarus of the suitors of Helen. 2. The more clear traditions of the Peloponnesus assert that Pelops first acquired power therein by the wealth which he brought from Asia to a people who were poor, and thus, although a foreigner, gave his name to the country, and afterwards became still more renowned in his posterity. Atreus was his son. Having slain Chrysippus, his half brother, the son of Pelops, he fled to the court of Eurystheus his nephew; and he, when he set out on his expedition to Attica, for this relationship, committed to him Mycenæ and his whole government to administer in his absence. In that expedition Eurystheus died by the hands of the Heracleidæ in Attica; and thereupon Atreus — the Mycenæans through fear of the Heracleidæ desiring it, holding, too, a high estimation of his ability, and won by his cultivation of the favor of the masses — acquired the throne of Eurystheus, and made the line of Pelops greater than that of the Perseidæ.[1] 3. To this throne and this power Agamemnon succeeded, and thus, I think, and by the acquisition of a larger naval force than elsewhere existed, was enabled, more by the terror he inspired than by the favor which he attracted, to compel the enterprise against Troy. 4. I say by the acquisition of a superior naval force; for he appears to have come attended by more ships than any other, and furnishing vessels too for the soldiers of Arcadia, — as indeed Homer establishes, — if we may rely on such testimony, — who, in the passage wherein he traces the transmission of his sceptre, declares him "to be king over many isles and all Argos." Of many isles he could not have been king, — dwelling on the Continent, — nor of any but those few immediately adjacent to it, unless he had possessed supremacy at sea. 5. From the extent and character of this expedition to Troy, we may form a conjecture of those which preceded it.

X. That Mycenæ was small — as indeed what city of that far remote period seems for its magnitude worthy of notice — affords no satisfactory proof that this armament was not as considerable as the poets have sung, and as the received opinion deems. 2. For if the city of the Lacedæmonians were wasted and deserted to-day, and its temples and the foundations of its great structures only were left, there would be cherished in the course of time, I think, with those of after ages, a general disbelief that its power ever justified its renown. Yet do the Lacedæmonians possess two of the five divisions of the Peloponnesus, and command it all, and many allies beyond it; but their city not being compactly built, nor containing in it any considerable variety of temples and other great structures, — distributed rather into separate villages, in the old fashion of Greece,

[1] Arrived at the age of Agamemnon, let us sum up and complete the sketch of the historical facts and dates of the times before. The Hellenes issuing from Phthiotis in Thessaly, gave their name successively to each city, — at last to all Greece. This is after Homer. Still, before the Trojan war, no united enterprise is undertaken. For that even they were fitted at last only by becoming naval powers. Minos first created a navy, expelled the Carians from the Cyclades, colonized them, and swept the old piracy from the sea. The age and customs of piracy sketched. Its suppression paved the way for permanent settlements. The accumulation of wealth and the advancement of civilization, fitting at last for the expedition to Troy. The Asiatic origin of Pelops, the bestowment of his name on the Peninsula, — the accession of Atreus to his throne and that of Eurystheus, prefacing a grand and strong succession for the son and grandson Agamemnon, and blending the lines of Perseus and of Pelops.

— it would appear inferior to the reality. If, on the other hand, a similar calamity should befall Athens, we might infer from her ruins that she had been double her actual dimensions. 3. Hasty incredulity, therefore, we are not to indulge, nor to advert rather to the looks than the actual power of cities; and we may rationally hold that the army of the siege of Troy was larger than any which preceded it from Greece, yet inferior to those of this time, relying so far upon Homer, who, while as a poet he would amplify and aggrandize it, yet leaves it smaller than those of the present day. 4. Homer makes the expedition to consist of twelve hundred ships. Those of the Bœotians he makes to contain one hundred and twenty men, — those of Philoctetes fifty, — expressing, I think, only the largest and the smallest numbers; for in his catalogue of the ships he mentions the numbers in no other vessels. That all on board were at once rowers and soldiers, is probable. With regard to the ships of Philoctetes, he expressly declares all who rowed to have been archers also; and that there should have been many supernumeraries on board, except the kings and chiefs, is unlikely, as the ships were full of warlike equipments and without decks, like the pirate vessels of an earlier day. 5. Making an average, then, of the numbers in each of the twelve hundred ships, the whole armament, when you consider that all Greece united to send it forth, will not appear to have been very considerable.

XI. The cause of this I do not find so much in the fewness of the inhabitants of Greece, as in their want of the ways and means of war. For want of provisions they led forth a smaller force than otherwise they might and would, and such an one only as they thought might by force subsist itself. Arrived at the seat of war, they defeated the enemy in battle. This is proved by their having been able to fortify their camp with a wall, which else they could not have done. It is quite plain, too, that they did not subsequently bring their whole force into action, but for want of provisions they were obliged to be diverted towards the cultivation of the Chersonesus and to piracy, whereby the Trojans were enabled to hold out by force for ten years, being at all times equal to that part of the scattered forces of the Greeks which remained to prosecute the war. 2. But had they carried with them an adequate supply of the means of the service, and could they with united forces, undiverted by agriculture or piracy, have pressed the siege uninterruptedly, they could easily have taken it by battle; since a detachment of them alone were able always to oppose the Trojans. Sitting down regularly to besiege it, in less time, with less effort, they could have effected the object in view. 3. Through want of means of war it was that all military expeditions before this were inconsiderable; and this, more renowned than any of them, appears to have been inferior to the fame with which poetry has invested it.

XII. And after the Trojan war, too, Greece still presented the same form of life, migrating from place to place, unsettled, so that it might not yet rest and grow. 2. The return of the Greeks, so long deferred, produced many changes, and revolutions or seditions followed in many cities, I may say everywhere, which expelled portions of the inhabitants, who then set forth and planted colonies elsewhere. 3. For example, the nation now called Bœotians, in the sixtieth year after the taking of Troy, being expelled from Arne by the Thessalians, settled as a colony in the State now called Bœotia, before that called Cadmeïs, although there had been a detachment from them in that State before, of whom were those of that name who shared in the Trojan war. And in the eightieth year after the taking of Troy, the Dorians, with the Heracleidæ, took possession of and held Peloponnesus. 4. So that through a long series of difficulties it was, and after a long time, that Greece became settled and at rest. When it did so, it began to send forth colonies, and the Athenians planted Ionia and many of the islands, and the Peloponnesians planted the greater part of Sicily and of Southern Italy, and some portions of other parts of Greece. All this era of colonization was subsequent to the Trojan war.

XIII. And now Greece having grown more powerful and more rich, there were in almost all her cities tyrannies established, individual accumulation of wealth having greatly increased. The earlier form of government had been monarchic, hereditary, and with defined prerogatives. Now also the Greeks began to build navies, and to attach themselves more closely to the sea. 2. And the Corinthians are related to have first attained to a naval architecture very closely resembling that which now obtains, and to have constructed triremes first at Corinth. 3. It is quite certain that Ameinocles, a Corinthian ship-builder, constructed four vessels for the Samians, about three hundred years before the close of the war whose history I have undertaken, and that the earliest naval battle of which we know, was one between the Corinthians and Corcyræans, two hundred and sixty years prior to the close of that war. 5. This early naval superiority of Corinth in war was attributable to its situation on the Isthmus, by means of which felicity of position it became a mart of trade for all the Greeks; since from the earliest times the tribes, both within and without the Peloponnesus, holding intercourse more by land than sea, mingled with each other through the Corinthian territory. Hence, the city became rich, as is indicated by the old poets, who call the place "the wealthy." And after general Greece had turned itself somewhat more to naval life, Corinth by its own more considerable fleets, of which I made mention before, contributed prominently to clear the sea of piracy, and thus making itself an enlarged mart, both for the trade of the water and the land, grew still more powerful by a still larger accession of wealth. 6. Next to Corinth the Ionians acquired a considerable navy in the time of Cyrus the first king of the Persians, and of Cambyses, his son; and during the war with Cyrus, in which they were involved, they for some time asserted the mastery of the sea which washes their coast. Polycrates, who was king of Samos during the reign of Cambyses, having a predominant naval force, subjected other islands, and having taken Rhenea, annexed it to the Delos of Apollo. The Phocæans, too, who engaged in founding Massilia, vanquished the Carthaginians in a battle on sea.

XIV. These were the more important of the ancient naval forces and states. And these navies, it is quite certain, for many generations after the Trojan war, contained very few *triremes*, but were composed mainly of long sharp ships, single banked and of fifty oars, according to the model of the time of the Trojan war. 2. And it was only just before the Persian war and the death of Darius, who succeeded Cambyses on the throne of Persia, that the tyrants of Sicily, and the Corcyræans, possessed any considerable number of triremes; and these last were the only navies worth mentioning which existed in Greece before the expedition of Xerxes. 3. For the Æginetans and the Athenians, and any others possessing any fleets, had inconsiderable fleets, chiefly of the class of single-banked fifty-oars. And it is now quite recently that Themistocles persuaded the Athenians, then engaged in war with the Æginetans, and expecting daily an incursion of the barbarians, to construct the ships in which they fought, and these were not completely decked.

XV. And these were the earlier and the later navies of Greece. Yet those chiefly rose to power who possessed them, acquiring by that means revenues and dominion over others. For they reduced and annexed the islands. Such especially did so whose territory had before been insufficient. 2. On land there was no war whence dominion could be won. All such hostilities were directed only against the adjoining neighbor. Armies of foreign invasion Greece sent not forth. 3. For her States did not project and execute expeditions of invasion, by entering into leagues either of subordination to some large State or of equality among themselves, but confined themselves to strifes with their neighbors. The only considerable exception was the case of the war of the Chalcidians and Eretrians, in which the rest of Greece, on one side or the other, generally participated.

XVI. The growth of all parts of Greece was slow. Some obstacle hindered one, some another. To the Ionians it befell, that when their affairs had advanced to a very prosperous condition, Cyrus, the prince of Persia, having conquered Crœsus, and all within the Halys, advanced to the sea, and reduced the cities of the main land to slavery; and that Darius subsequently, by aid of a Phœnician fleet, subjected the adjacent islands.

XVII. And with regard to the tyrants of the Greek cities, having an eye only to their own private interests, looking only to their own personal security and pleasure, and the aggrandizement of their own families, their policy was to govern as quietly and as securely as possible; and nothing worthy of notice was achieved by them, unless it were against their several neighbors. The Sicilian tyrants, it is true, advanced to a large measure of power. 2. And thus, by these various influences, it came to pass that universal Greece was for a long period crippled and held down, so that it neither achieved any splendid united enterprise, and no one city dared attempt anything.

XVIII. And after the tyrant of Athens and of those other parts of Greece, which, quite universally and even before it happened to Athens, had become subjected to tyrants, had been deposed, except those of Sicily, by the Lacedæmonians, (for Lacedæmon, although, from the time of its settlement by the Dorians, it was torn by factions for a longer season than any other State whose history we know, yet from a very ancient time has been under the administration of good laws, and has never been governed by tyrants; for it is more than four hundred years, reaching backward from the end of the Peloponnesian war, that it has maintained the same polity, and has thus become powerful itself, and able to assist in settling the affairs of other States), after this expulsion, I say, of the tyrants by Lacedæmon, it was but a few years before the battle of Marathon was fought by the Medes and Athenians. 2. Ten years after that battle the barbarian again invaded Greece with a large army, for the purpose of reducing it to slavery. In that great crisis the Lacedæmonians took the lead of the united Grecian States, being the first in power, and the Athenians upon the approach of the Medes, having determined to leave their city, broke up their homes, and embarking in ships, became an armed fleet. Having by a common effort repulsed the barbarians, it soon happened that all, both those who had revolted from the king, and those who, independent before, had associated to repel him, divided into two classes, and attached themselves, some to the Athenians, others to the Lacedæmonians, the two far most powerful States, and which decidedly took the lead both by land and sea. 3. And after the common anti-Persian league had subsisted a brief space, the Athenians and Lacedæmonians quarrelled, went to war, each accompanied by their respective allies; and throughout Greece, if any States fell into hostilities with each other, they attached themselves to one or the other of the two great belligerents. So that from the close of the Persian war to the beginning of this, by being continually occupied either in concluding truces or prosecuting hostilities against each other or their allies, these two States came to have thoroughly trained themselves to the practice of war, and became the more skilful, as their place of exercise was not the parade but the field of battle.

XIX. And to speak of the comparative policy of the two great States, the Lacedæmonians did not subject their allies to the payment of tribute, but took care only that their form of government should be oligarchical, and that they should consult under that form their own interests only. The Athenians on the contrary acquired in time possession of the fleets of all their subject cities except those of Chios and Lesbos, and levied a stated contribution on them all; and their own individual preparation for this war was greater, and their own resources and strength more formidable, and their dominion more extended, than when formerly they had been in their most prosperous state as a leading member of the as yet unbroken alliance against Persia.

XX. Such, in fine, I have thought I discover to be the general outline of our ancient history. I am aware that it is not easy to command a confident belief of its truth, or certainly a confident reliance on every particular proof, and on the exact series of deduction, on which I have insisted. For narratives of remote ages are distrusted by sound minds, with reason. For they observe that men habitually receive from one another the hearsay of the past, even of their own country, without inquiry and without accuracy. 2. The generality of Athens, for instance, suppose that Hipparchus was slain by Harmodius and Aristogeiton while tyrant, unaware that Hippias was the eldest son of Pisistratus, and succeeded to his father's power, and that Hipparchus and Thessalus were his younger brothers; and that Harmodius and Aristogeiton, suspecting, on the very hour of the consummation of their conspiracy against the actual tyrant, that somewhat had been betrayed to Hippias by some one of those in the plot, spared him as forewarned; and yet, determined before they should be arrested to achieve something worthy of the inevitable peril in which they stood, happening to meet Hipparchus near the temple of the daughters of Leos, superintending the Panathenaic celebration, put him to death. 3. Other erroneous opinions, touching the actual present, not the forgotten past, are holden by other Greeks also. For example, they think the kings of the Lacedæmonians do not give their votes each with one stone, but with two; and that there is a Pitanatan *lochus* in their army, which never existed. So little of painful effort with the many is there in the search for truth, and so naturally do they turn to the received, in fact, opinion.

XXI. Rationally, therefore, as sound minds distrust those narratives of the past, yet I think that he who from the proofs I have displayed, shall adopt the conclusions I have formed, and shall not credit what poets have hymned about the old time, aggravating and decorating it, and what annalists have constructed for attractiveness, not for truth, — stories incapable of proof or confutation, utterly unworthy of trust from lapse of time, — and which has won its way to the domain and name of fable — he, I say, who shall accept the conclusion that what I have thus sketched is, for its extreme antiquity, ascertained with satisfactory certainty on the best proof which can be employed, will not err. 2. And now is it my judgment of the present war, that although men habitually regard that which actually rages, and in which they actually serve, to be the greatest, and when it is over, ever return with larger wonder to those more ancient still, yet that this war, to those who will measure it by its events, will show itself the greatest of all.

XXII. With regard to the several speeches of those about to engage in it or already embarked, it was difficult to retain in memory the exact terms of all that was said, difficult to me for what I heard, and to others who reported to me; but that which it appeared to me every one might have, with most propriety, said on each successive occasion, adhering always as closely as possible to the general sense of what actually was said, this I have recorded as spoken. 2. With regard again to the facts of the war, I have not deemed it fit to set down what I gathered from any random report, but those things only which I personally knew, or those which I have collected by the most careful and scrupulous examination of the testimony of others. 3. Difficult and laborious has been this search of truth, since even the eye-witnesses of any particular event did not concur in their relation of it . . . . , but testified, every one as his memory might serve or his prepossessions might sway him. 4. A narrative thus divested of all the attractions of fable may be found less pleasing to read; but if those who read to learn the exact truth of the past, and to form a rational conjecture of that future, which, after the course of human things, will be as or like the past, — if such judge my history useful, it shall suffice me; since it is composed, not as a prize performance for a single reading, or a single hearing, but for an everlasting possession.

XXIII. Of all the previous wars of Greece the Persian was greatest; yet was it quickly decided by two battles on sea and two on land; but this, of which I am to write, was prolonged to a great duration, and was marked by evils to Greece such as never befell her in an equal period of time. 2. Never before were so many cities taken and wasted, some by barbarians, others by the discordant armies of Greece, some even witnessing a total change of their inhabitants; never so many slain and driven into exile, some by war and some by civil strife. 3. Events too, the relations of which are found indeed in the old traditions, but whose actual occurrence was deemed doubtful, became no longer unworthy of belief; earthquakes, which were experienced over the greater part of Greece, and of the most terrific description; eclipses of the sun, which were beheld more frequently than in all the memory of the past; in some regions great droughts, from which proceeded famine; and, not least, wasting pestilence, which consumed a large part of the whole Grecian nation. All these portents and calamities came in the train of this war. 4. It was a war of the Athenians and the Peloponnesians, begun by dissolving the truce of thirty years which they concluded after the conquest of Eubœa. 5. The causes which led to it I have recorded, that no one might have to inquire the origin of a war so great. 6. The real cause, speaking in the most exact sense, though least in the mutual avowals of the parties, I judge to have been this, — that Athens, grown great, and inspiring alarm to the Lacedæmonians, forced them to fight; but the pretexts more formally assigned on the one side and the other, upon which they dissolved the truce and set themselves in array of war, were those which follow.[1]

XXIV. Epidamnus is a city on his right hand who sails into the Ionian Gulf; and next it dwell the Taulantii, bar-

[1] Let me in a brief note survey the Greece and the historical world of this moment. The truce, made for thirty years, was concluded B. C. 445. The security of Greece against Persia had been attained B. C. 466, by Cimon, at the Eurymedon. The age of Pericles may date from the death of Cimon, or from the making of the truce, or from the expulsion of Thucydides, B. C. 444. In the ninth year after the truce was made, B. C. 436, began the events with which Thucydides opens his regular narrative. The power of Athens was then at its highest. It was the era of the Athenian empire, composed of Athens the mistress and her thousand subject cities, commanded by her fleet, reflecting her image, moulded by her polity, contributing to her treasury, pampering her vanity.

barians of the Illyrian race. 2. It was planted by a colony from Corcyra, led out by Phalius, the son of Eratocleides, a Corinthian, and of the family of the descendants of Hercules, who, according to the ancient custom, had been summoned to that command from the mother city. He was attended by other Corinthians, and by some of the rest of the Doric race. 3. With the course of years, Epidamnus became a large and populous city. 4. Becoming, then, for a long season, the prey of internal factions, having their origin from a war with the neighboring barbarians, it was greatly reduced, and spoiled of power. 5. And at last, and before the present war, the people expelled the aristocracy, who, departing, united with the barbarian enemy, and carried on a war of plunder on the city by land and sea. 6. Thus pressed upon, the Epidamnians sent an embassy to Corcyra, as their mother state, entreating her not to neglect them, thus perishing away, but to effect a reconciliation with the aristocratic exiles, and to terminate the barbarian war. 7. The ambassadors of this entreaty seated themselves in the temple of Juno, and preferred their prayer; but the Corcyræans did not grant it, and sent them away with an unaccomplished mission.

XXV. The Epidamnians, ascertaining that they could receive no aid from Corcyra, were held for a time in a state of uncertainty how to act; and they sent to Delphi, to consult the god whether they should cast themselves upon Corinth as the planter of their colony, and attempt to obtain aid from her. He counselled them to submit to her protection, and to acknowledge her sovereignty. 2. Proceeding, then, to Corinth, according to the advice of the oracle, they tendered the state to her; and, having proved that the leader of their original colony was a Corinthian, and having announced the response of Delphos, they besought her not to neglect them in their extremity, but to interfere for their succor.[1] 3. The Corinthians undertook to assist them, and this with justice, for they considered Epidamnus as not less

[1] The leading idea of Thucydides is, that the sources of the antagonisms of this war were: I. Tribal; Doric against Ionian; II. Constitutional.

I. Sparta led the Doric, Athens the Ionian sentiment. Yet, 1. Athens, regardless of tribal ties, asserted her empire on the sea everywhere; 2. States, neither Doric nor Ionian, acted in the war; 3. Ionian States sometimes resisted Athens — Doric States, as Argos and Naupactus, aided her.

II. Oligarchy was the Spartan, Democracy the Athenian Constitution. Oligarchs everywhere favored Sparta — Democrats everywhere Athens.

III. Add to this any possible view of policy by which each city might from time to time be actuated, and you have reasons of race, of government, politics, and policy, to incline each to one or the other of the great rivals. Hatred of its own imperial chief by each dependent city is an element. The particular constitutional or other opinions of each ascendant party, another.

their colony than it was the colony of the Corcyræans; and they, at the same time, hated Corcyra for treating with neglect her mother country, Corinth, and disregarding what was due to the relation of colonial child and colonial parent. 4. For the Corcyræans did not accustom themselves to accord to Corinthians at the public assemblies the recognized ceremonies of deference, privileges and points of honor, nor to select a Corinthian to perform the first part at sacrifices, as was the wont of other colonies towards their parent states. Indeed, they assumed to treat Corinth with contempt; having themselves become among the wealthiest of the Greek states of the time, and for war more completely prepared than Corinth. Sometimes, too, they boasted of their naval prominence, or preëminence, such as became the successors of the Phæacians, who once possessed Corcyra, and had risen to a high maritime supremacy and fame. Emulous of such example, they bestowed the greater attention on their navy, and acquired one of no inconsiderable character, for they began the war with a hundred and twenty triremes.[1]

XXVI. Having these grounds of complaint against Corcyra, therefore, the Corinthians with pleasure proceeded to send succor to Epidamnus, authorizing any who desired to become its inhabitants to go thither, and detaching troops of Ambracians and Leucadians and Corinthians to garrison the city. 2. The expedition advanced on foot to Apollonia, itself a colony of Corinth, adopting this route and mode from an apprehension that the Corcyræans would intercept their passage by sea. 3. The Corcyræans were enraged when they heard that this body of settlers and of troops for garrison had gone to Epidamnus, and that the colony had been yielded up to the Corinthians; and having sailed thither with twenty-five ships, and subsequently with another armament, they haughtily and for insult commanded them to receive back the aristocratic exiles, (for they had come to Epidamnus, and there had pointed to the graves of their own ancestors, and there had vindicated their kindred blood, and by this appeal had solicited their restoration,) and to dismiss the settlers and the troops which the Corinthians had sent to them. All this the Epidamnians disregarded and disobeyed. 4. The Corcyræans then began the war on them with forty ships, and with the aid of the exiles, whose restoration they thus appeared to be attempting, and with that of the Illyrians, whom they had added to their own forces. 5. Sitting down before the city, they proclaimed that any Epidamnian or stranger who desired

[1] How came Corinth by these allies? *What were their relations to her?* Megara was settled in some age by a colony of Corinth, and was Peloponnesian, — Doric; Trœzene, Doric, of Argolis; Epidaurus also; Hermione also; Leucadia, colony of Corinth; Ambracia, colony of Corinth.

to depart might do so unsuffering, but that they should deal with those who remained as enemies. No one appearing to be influenced by this annunciation, the Corcyræans proceeded to lay siege to the city, which is situated upon an isthmus.

XXVII. As soon as messengers from Epidamnus announced to them that the city was besieged, the Corinthians prepared an armed expedition, and at the same time proclaimed the planting of a colony at Epidamnus, upon the basis of an equality of rights of the settlers, one with another, and with those who should remain in the parent state. It was farther proclaimed, that if any one were not prepared immediately to set forth with the new settlers, and yet wished to secure to himself the privilege of a colonist, he might, by the payment of fifty drachmas, remain at Corinth. Under this proclamation many sailed at once, and many deposited the money. 2. The Corinthians applied also to the Megareans to convey them forward by ships, if their passage should be threatened to be intercepted by the Corcyræans, and they accordingly equipped eight ships for the purpose. Pale added four of thè Cephallenians. They applied to the Epidaurians also, who contributed five; Hermione gave one; the Trœzenians two; the Leucadians ten; and the Ambracians eight. Of the Thebans and Phliasians they solicited money, and of the Eleans unarmed ships and money. Of their own ships they equipped and sent thirty, and three thousand heavy armed soldiers.

XXVIII. Obtaining information of this expedition, the Corcyræans sent ambassadors to Corinth, attended by ambassadors from Lacedæmon and Sicyon, whom they took with them, to demand that the troops and the colonists who had gone to Epidamnus should be withdrawn, upon the ground that Corinth had no just cause to interpose in the affairs of Epidamnus, and no rightful concern with it. 2. They further proposed that if Corinth persisted in urging such a pretence, the controversy should be submitted to the arbitration of such cities of the Peloponnesus as should be mutually agreed on; and that she to whom the colony should be awarded should hold it. 3. From war they dissuaded; but announced that, if it were resolved on, they, too, should be compelled by the hostilities of Corinth to engage friends whom they should not desire, and of very different character from those, the Epidamnian exiles, with whom then they were acting. 4. The Corinthians answered, that, if the Corcyræans would withdraw their fleet and the barbarians from Epidamnus, they would accede to this proposition of reference; but that it was not fit that Epidamnus should be sustaining a siege, while Corinth and Corcyra were litigating their title to it. 5. To this the Corcyræans rejoined, that if they, too, would withdraw their forces from Epidamnus, they would do likewise; or, that they were willing that both should remain quiet and where they were, and to enter into convention to do nothing until the litigation should be determined.

XXIX. The Corinthians acceded to none of these propositions; but as soon as their ships were manned and their allies had arrived, having first sent forward a herald to declare war against the Corcyræans, getting under weigh, with seventy-five ships and two thousand hoplitæ, they sailed towards Epidamnus for the purpose of beginning the war. 2. The fleet was commanded by Aristeus, the son of Pellichas, and Callicrates, the son of Callias, and Timanor, the son of Timanthes; and the army by Archetimus, the son of Eurytimus, and Isarchidas the son of Isarchus. 3. Upon their arrival at Actium, a promontory of Anactorium, where is the temple of Apollo, at the mouth of the Ambracian Gulf, the Corcyræans sent a herald in a light boat to forbid their approach towards them; and they at the same time manned their ships, repairing the old and equipping the rest. 4. The herald reporting no answer of peace from the Corinthians, and the ships of the Corcyræans, to the number of eighty, having been manned, (for forty sail were besieging Epidamnus,) they set forth in order of naval battle, engaged with their enemies, gained a clear victory, and destroyed fifteen ships. On the same day, it happened to their forces employed in the siege of Epidamnus, to reduce it to surrender, upon the terms that the new comers should be sold into slavery, and the Corinthians held in chains to await the further pleasure of the victor.

XXX. After this battle, the Corcyræans, having first erected a trophy on Leucimne, a promontory of Corcyra, put to death all their other prisoners, but held the Corinthians in chains; 2. and subsequently, when the Corinthians and their allies, having been defeated, had retired homeward, they rode triumphant over all that region of the sea, and sailing to Leucas, a colony of Corinth, they laid waste a portion of its country, and burned Cyllene, the seaport of the Eleans, because they had contributed ships and money to Corinth. 3. And this mastery over those seas they asserted for the greater part of the time after the battle, and ravaged the cities and country of the allies of Corinth, until she, as the season was drawing to a close, moved by their exposure and sufferings, placed an army in station at Actium and around Chimerium of Thesprotis, to protect Leucadia and her other friends. 4. Over against this force the Corcyræans anchored a fleet, and encamped an army at Leucimne. 5. Neither having advanced against the other, but having thus sat over against each other till the season ended, with the approach of winter each returned home.

XXXI. During the entire year after the battle, and during the next year, the Corinthians, exasperated by the course of the war of Corcyra, were engaged in building ships and in equipping fleets of the most approved character, procuring, by the temptation of pay, rowers from Peloponnesus and the rest of Greece. 2. Hearing of these preparations, the Corcyræans became alarmed; and being in alliance with no Greek state, nor inscribed among the confederates of either Athens or Lacedæmon, they determined to apply to the Athenians to receive them into alliance, and to attempt to derive assistance from them. 3. This coming to the knowledge of the Corinthians, they also sent ambassadors to Athens, lest an Attic fleet, added to a Corcyræan, might present an insuperable obstacle to such termination of the war as they desired. 4. There, an assembly having been convoked, the parties came before it for the discussion of their subjects of difference, and the Corcyræans spoke to this effect: —

XXXII. "It is fit, Athenians, that those who approach others as we now approach you, about to solicit assistance, by whom no right to any considerable active kindness or alliance has been already earned, should make it evidently appear first, if possible, that what is sought will be useful to those of whom it is sought, but at least that it will not be prejudicial, and next that it will be received with a constant gratitude; and if they do not make any of these points clear, they ought not to be angry if they wholly fail to obtain what they seek. 2. The Corcyræans have sent us to you in the confidence that in urging our solicitation of alliance we shall be able to make these points clear. 3. And yet it happens to us, that that very peculiarity in our policy by which we have been distinguished, must appear to you inconsistent with our present request, and is found prejudicial to our interests in the existing crisis. 4. We, who never would become the allies of any State, now approach to ask alliance of others: that practice and those counsels of which we formerly boasted as wisdom and as strength, by which we shunned exposure to hazards at the will and pleasure of foreign connections, now leave us destitute and alone for the war with Corinth, and turn to folly and weakness. 5. It is true that in the naval battle which has been fought, we did alone repulse the Corinthians; but since they are rushing upon us with more formidable preparation from Peloponnesus and from the rest of Greece, since we perceive ourselves to be unable successfully to contend with them by our own power, and since it will involve a great common danger, if we are overcome by them, we are under a necessity to ask aid of you and of others, and we hope we shall be excused for adopting a policy in this particular opposed to that former neutrality, which we practised not from evil intention, but from error of judgment.

XXXIII. "And yet the happening of this our necessity of aid, if you are persuaded to aid us, will prove in many respects useful to yourselves;—in the first place, because you will carry succor to those who are assailed by injury, themselves unoffending; and next, because by extending the hand of kindness to those whose largest interests are at hazard, you will have treasured up a benefit, with a certainty, as far as such a thing may be, that it will be eternally remembered and restored with enlargement, since we have a navy more powerful than any other except your own. 2. Consider, then, what contingency of good fortune there could be, less likely to occur, or more distressing to your enemies, than that an accession of power, which you would have prized beyond great sums of money, and for which you would have incurred the most burdensome obligations of gratitude, should spontaneously come to you without peril and without cost, and should bear with it fame to the people, the duty of gratitude from those you succor, and strength to the State. To few, indeed, in all the past time, has such a combination of utilities happened; and few there have been, who, soliciting alliance, have conferred on those by whom they have been succored, security and honor equalling what they have received. 3. If now any one of you holds the opinion that that war, in the event of which we may aspire to be useful, will not come, he errs in judgment, and does not perceive that the Lacedæmonians are thirsting for hostilities through fear of you, and that the Corinthians, who have influence with them, and are inimical to yourselves, have attempted to strike a blow at you by aiming at us beforehand, to the end that we may not mutually withstand a common foe, and that they may not fail through want of promptness of exertion to accomplish either an injury to us or an addition to their own power. 4. Our business, therefore, it should be to anticipate them, and by alliance offered by us, accepted by you, to concert offensive rather than defensive operation.

XXXIV. "If the Corinthians should say that it is not just that you should admit their colonists to alliance of friendship, let them learn that every colony which experiences kindness from the mother city, cherishes it; and every one which suffers an injury is alienated; for they are not sent forth to be the slaves, but the equals of those who stay behind. 2. That they have done us injury, is palpable; for when we solicited them to submit our controversy concerning Epidamnus to arbitration of a third party, they chose rather to prosecute their accusations by war than in a just and equitable manner. 3. Let the example of their treatment of us, their kinsmen, admonish you neither to be deceived by sophistry, nor persuaded by open solicitation into rendering them assistance. For he who has the fewest services to his enemy to repent of, leads the safest life.

XXXV. "Nor will you break your truce with the Lacedæmonians by admitting us to alliance, since now we are allies of neither of the parties to that truce. 2. Indeed, in its terms it is provided that any Greek city, not now the ally of either, may attach itself to which it pleases; 3. and it would be most hard if they, the Corinthians, may man their fleets from States bound by the truce, from all other parts of Greece, and not least from your subject allies, and yet prohibit us from the alliance which we seek, and from aid from any other quarter, and even have the effrontery to pretend that it would be unjust in you to grant our prayer. 4. Far juster ground of complaint will your denial of our request afford to us. For you will have thrust us away, — us who are in peril and are not your enemies; and you will not only have failed to restrain those who are your enemies and our assailants, but you will suffer them to derive accessions of strength from your own empire. This is unjust. You ought instead, either to put under and restrain such of their forces as are hired from your territory, or to send us secret and small aid, or admitting us openly to alliance, effectually assist us. 5. We present to you, as we prefaced at first, many inducements of advantage to admit us to the alliance which we seek; among the greatest of which is that we have the same enemies with yourselves, — that surest of all pledges of fidelity, — and those not inconsiderable, but of strength severely to injure those who desert their connection. It is the alliance of a naval, not of an interior power, too, that is offered you, and therefore its rejection involves far other and more important losses of advantage. The first attempt of your policy should be to permit no one but yourselves to possess a fleet at all; but if you cannot effect this, to have the strongest naval state for your friend.

XXXVI. "And if there be any one to whom these shall seem to be advantageous issues of the proffered alliance, but who yet fears, lest if he act upon them, he shall break the existing treaty, let him assure himself that even under the influence of such fears, if strengthened by alliance, he will become more really formidable; while, unstrengthened by such alliance, despite all the bold security with the delusive sense of which the observance of the treaty would soothe him, he will become only weaker. Better the power acquired by breaking, than the security hoped for from keeping such a treaty. Let him consider, too, that he now consults not more on the welfare of Corcyra than on that of Athens; and that he does not discern her true interest, if he hesitates, from a too narrow attention to the passing moment to attach to her against that war so close at hand, a city on whose hostility or friendship the largest consequences of good or evil turn. 2. For it lies in the very path of the voyage to and from Italy and Sicily, so that it can prevent a fleet from those regions assailing the Peloponnesus, and can facilitate the passage of your fleets destined to assail them; and in other respects presents a most advantageous connection. 3. And now, to comprise the substance of the matter,—the parts and the whole into the briefest possible summary,—let this single view admonish you not to reject our appeal. In all Greece there are but three considerable navies—yours, ours, and that of Corinth. If you suffer two of these to become united, and Corinth seizes upon ours, you will have single-handed to fight with Peloponnesus and with Corcyra too; but if you accept our alliance, you will be able to meet the Peloponnesians with a fleet outnumbering theirs by the whole accession of our own." Thus spake the Corcyræans; and then the Corinthians thus:—

XXXVII. "It seems necessary, since the Corcyræans have not only addressed themselves to the subject of admission to alliance, but have been pleased to accuse us of having done them wrong and of pressing them even now with an unreasonable war, that we should call to mind some things pertaining to both these subjects, before advancing to the other and main consideration; to the end that you may the more clearly perceive the ground of our request, and may with surer intelligence decline to satisfy their needs. 2. They say, then, that upon a prudential policy they have never contracted an alliance. But we say they have pursued this system on a motive, and for an end, not creditable but disgraceful to them, for evil and not for good;—since we say they have shunned an ally because they neither wished to have a witness of their crimes, nor to experience the shame of invoking help to commit them. 3. Their city too, made self-sufficing by its position, enables them, when they have done an injury to judge it for themselves, instead of submitting it to the determination of others. Since while they may seldom have occasion to sail to the ports of their neighbors, necessity so often drives others to take refuge in theirs. 4. And herein lies the secret of that abstinence from foreign connection which they so speciously boast; not that they fear that they should thus be drawn in to aid in the infliction of injustice, but that they want to have the doing of all the injustice to themselves; to take by force when strongest, by fraud when weakest; and be spared the blush of shame which the eye of a witness might enkindle. 5. Needless is it to say that if they were the virtuous men they pretend to be, the less they are in the power of others, the more signally might they manifest their virtue, by doing and submitting to justice uncompelled.

XXXVIII. "Virtuous men however they are not, neither in their intercourse with us nor with others. Colonies of our planting, they have ever stood coldly aloof; and now they make war on us, alleging that they were not sent forth for the purpose of being subjected to ill-treatment from the mother-city. 2. To which we reply, that we too did not send them forth for the purpose of being subjected to insolence at their hands, but that we might retain imperial relation to them, and receive the accustomed and suitable honors of that relation. 3. Our other colonies honor us, and love us with a strong filial love. 4. It is plain, then, if we give satisfaction to the greater number, the discontent of this single colony must be unreasonable; nor do we make a discreditable war upon it, since our moderation has been extreme. 5. Nay, had we failed in some point of right, it would have been honorable to them to yield to our irritation, while it would have been disgraceful for us to have violently pressed upon their moderation. 6. But puffed up with pride and wealth they have in many other respects done us injuries; and more recently, Epidamnus, which, while it was torn by dissensions, they did not seek to possess, the moment we set forth to assist it, they seized and held by force.

XXXIX. "They say, too, they were willing that this controversy should have been determined by fair judicial trial before they occupied Epidamnus. We answer that he who has won the cause already, and is secure, means nothing and says nothing, who then talks of trying it; he only is sincere, who, before he begins to fight, is willing to subject his claim and his acts to an equal, fair arbitrament. 2. But no pretence of this specious readiness to submit this controversy to the determination of justice did these Corcyræans parade, until after they had blockaded the island and after they knew we could not overlook the wrong. Hither now they come, not content with being guilty of wrong themselves, but having the assurance to demand that you shall become, not their allies, but their accessories; shall become our enemies to become their friends. 3. Surely they ought rather to have been here when in a condition of safety, not after they had wronged us and involved themselves; not to beg you for aid to whom they never contributed; not to make you responsible to us by adoption of injustice in which you had at first no share. To entitle themselves to help in their weakness they should long since have imparted to you of their strength.

XL. "That we lay before you, then, well-grounded charges, and that these Corcyræans are violent and grasping, is proved. 2. That you cannot justly accept their alliance, it remains for you to learn. It is certain that it is ordained in our articles of truce that an unregistered state may ally itself to whom it will. But this does not embrace the case of a city allying itself to the injury of others, but only of such as, without withdrawing from any one the aid they owe, seek safety for themselves in good faith, and such as do not bring war instead of peace by their alliance, as Corcyra will not to those who are wise; as you will find she will, if we do not persuade you to reject her. 3. For you would become not merely helpers of her, but enemies of us, now at truce with you; since, of necessity, if you espouse their part, we must avenge ourselves on them not separately from you. 4. And now justice demands of you that you hold yourselves aloof from both belligerents; but if not so, that you take part with us and against them, (since you are united by treaty with us, but with them not so much as by truce,) and not that you sanction the principle of law that he who deserts his allies may be admitted to new alliance. 5. When the Samians revolted from you, and other Peloponnesians were divided on the question of assisting them, we gave no vote against you, but distinctly maintained that every state should be permitted to chastise its own allies. 6. If you receive and help those who are guilty of injustice, as many of your allies will be found coming to us as of ours to you. So that you will have introduced a doctrine of law rather against yourselves than against us.

XLI. "Such are the claims of right which we may prefer to you, which are decisive by the law of Greece. We think, too, leaving the matter of right, we may solicit and persuade you to a favor, with which you ought in this crisis to requite us, — us who have been neither your enemies to do you harm, nor your friends to interchange, habitually and of course, mutual offices of kindness. 2. For when, before the Median times, you were destitute of long ships for the prosecution of your war against the Æginetans, you procured twenty of Corinth. And this friendly service, and that we rendered in the case of the Samians, enabled you to conquer Ægina and to punish Samos. 3. These services, too, were rendered at one of those moments when men, going out to battle with their enemies, hold all things else as nought in comparison with victory; when they hold him who helps them to be their friend, though before their foe, and him who hinders them their foe, though before their friend; for they will even incur the evils of a bad administration of their domestic affairs under the strong excitement of present conflict.

XLII. "Bearing these things in mind, — the young among you learning them from the elder, — deem it just to requite us by similar offices; and do not be satisfied to hold that this would be right in theory and in words, but that utility, in time of war, prescribes a different course. 2. For, ever, utility follows the closest approximation to the right, and the issue of the war by the dread of which these Corcyræans would persuade you to injustice, is as yet all uncertain. Scarcely worth while would it be, under the influence of that cause, to incur the immediate and open hostility of Corinth. It were wiser rather, to do somewhat to remove the distrust formerly excited by the proceedings of Megara, and still cherished. 3. For the last favor rendered, though smaller, if seasonable, has power to atone for a greater previous cause of complaint. 4. Do not, either, suffer yourselves to be drawn into this connection by this offer to give you the alliance of a powerful fleet, for not to injure one's equals is a source of more strength than are the perilous acquisitions prompted by the mere temptation of a present palpable advantage.

XLIII. "And now, having ourselves come-to require the application of the principle which we avowed at Lacedæmon, that every State should be permitted the uncontrolled coercion of its own allies, we have to ask to receive the benefit of its application from you; and that you, to whom we gave our vote, shall not give yours against us. 2. Requite us, then, as we treated you, since you cannot fail to know that this is an exigency when he who aids is a friend indeed, and he who opposes is an enemy indeed. 3. Admit not these Corcyræans to alliance against our will, or help them in the wrong they perpetrate. 4. Thus will you do at once what is right in itself and what is expedient to you."[1]

XLIV. Having heard both parties, the Athenian assembly was twice holden to deliberate. In the first, the reasons urged by the Corinthians were thought not less weighty than those of the Corcyræans; but in the second, a change of opinion manifested itself, and it was determined, not indeed to enter into general alliance with Corcyra to such extent as to regard the

[1] The interposition of Corinth for Epidamnus in the first instance seems to have been rightful and even praiseworthy. Epidamnus was engaged in a war with the barbarians of the neighboring Continent, who found allies in her own aristocracy expelled by herself. I must suppose that for that war she had a right to seek alliance, as she certainly needed it. As between her and the barbarian enemy, she seems to have been admitted by Corcyra and Corinth to be in a just war, in which another State might properly assist her.

She applies to Corcyra for that assistance, and is peremptorily refused it.

enemies and friends of each the enemies and friends of the other, and to be engaged to offensive as well as defensive operations, (for if the Corcyræans should please to require them to sail with them against Corinth, it would involve a breach of the truce with the Peloponnesians,) but to form a league strictly defensive, by which they engaged mutually to assist each other, if any one should assail Corcyra or Athens, or their allies. 2. For they judged that war with the Peloponnesians there must be, whether they violated the truce or not; and they felt unwilling to see Corcyra, with so considerable a fleet, become a dependency of Corinth, but desired rather to have them wear each other out by mutual contention, so that if hostilities must come between Athens and Corinth, and other cities possessing fleets, she might find a feebler enemy. 3. It was not overlooked, too, that this island lay most on the coasting route to Italy and Sicily.

XLV. Upon this policy, and to this extent, the Athenians received the Corcyræans to alliance. They sent ten ships to assist them, accordingly, soon after the Corinthians left the city. 2. They were commanded by Lacedæmonius, the son of Cimon, and Diotimus, the son of Strombichus, and Proteas, the son of Epiclees. They were instructed not to engage in naval battle with the Corinthians, unless they should sail to Corcyra, or some of the places belonging to them, and should threaten to land; 3. in which case, they were to use every exertion to prevent them. These instructions were given to avoid the breaking of the truce. The ships proceeded to Corcyra.

XLVI. The Corinthians, when their preparations had been completed, set sail towards Corcyra, with a hundred and fifty ships. Of these the Eleans contributed ten, the Megareans twelve, the Leucadians ten, the Ambracians twenty-seven, the Anactorians one. Corinth herself sent ninety. 2. The ships of each city had a leader appointed by itself; and the Corinthian commander was Xenocleides, the son of Euthycles, with whom four were associated, — four colleagues, — himself the first. 3. Departing from Leucadia, they approached the main-land, opposite Corcyra, and arrived to seek anchorage at Chimerium, in Thesprotis. 4. There opens a harbor, and above it, at a distance from the sea, in Eleatis of Thesprotis, is the city Ephyre. Near this city, the lake Acherusia moves towards the sea, and into this lake the river Acheron, which flows through Thesprotis, empties itself, and communicates to it its own name. The river Thyamis, by its course, divides Thesprotis from Cestrine, and between it and the Acheron the Chimerian point advances into the waves. 5. At this part of the main-land, the Corinthians anchored and pitched their camp.

XLVII. Ascertaining this hostile advance, the Corcyræans filled one hundred and ten ships with troops, under command of Meiciades and Æsimides and Eurybatus, and stationed themselves at one of the small islands which are called Sybota. Ten Athenian ships were also with them. 2. Their foot-soldiers were posted on the promontory of Leucimne, with ten thousand heavy-armed Zacynthian allies. 3. The Corinthians, too, on the main-land, had many barbarian allies; for the inhabitants of that region were always their friends.

XLVIII. When the Corinthians had completed their preparations, they took provisions for three days, and set sail by night from Chimerium, for the purpose of naval battle, and, at daybreak, while continuing their course, they observed the Corcyræan fleet on the main sea, sailing toward them. 2. Upon discovering each other, both sides formed their order of battle. Upon the Corcyræan right were stationed the Athenian ships; the rest of the line they composed themselves, having distributed their ships in three divisions, each of which was led by one of their three commanders. 3. Such was the Corcyræan order of battle. The right wing of the Corinthians was held by the Megareans and Ambraciots; the centre by the other allies, each by himself; the left wing, opposite the Athenians and the Corcyræan right, by the Corinthians themselves, with their fleetest ships.

XLIX. Upon the signals being hung out on both sides, mingling, they engaged in battle, each fleet having numerous heavy-armed troops with archers and throwers of javelins upon their decks, being in this particular equipped in the old and less improved mode. 2. The battle was severe, but not in an equal degree marked by naval science, and rather resembling a battle on land. 3. For whenever they happened to run on board one another, they could not easily disengage themselves, by reason of the number and disorder of the ships; and, therefore, trusting for victory to the heavy-armed soldiers on board, they remained facing and fighting while the vessel lay still. There was no breaking of lines, but on both sides they fought with courage and strength rather than skill. The battle was disorderly, and attended by a wild and general uproar. In the progress of it, the Athenian vessels came to the assistance of such of the Corcyræans as happened to be most sorely pressed upon, and thus intimidated the enemy, but did not actually commence battle, their commanders being deterred by the previous instructions. 5. The right wing of the Corinthians chiefly suffered; for the Corcyræans, with twenty ships, put it to flight, pursued the scattered ships to the shore, and, sailing to the enemy's encampment, disembarked and burnt and plundered the deserted tents.

6. On this wing, thus the Corinthians and their allies were beaten, and the Corcyræans had advantage. But on the left wing of the Corinthians, where they themselves fought, they were decidedly victorious, the twenty ships of the Corcyræan fleet, itself the smallest before, not having returned from their pursuit. 7. Perceiving that the Corcyræans were hard pressed, the Athenians began more openly to contribute their assistance, having hitherto abstained from coming directly in contact with any one of the enemy. And as the flight became more marked, and the Corinthians began to be on both sides intermingled among them, then every one put his hand to the work, and there was no longer any discrimination of friends from foes, and so urgent a necessity arose, that Corinthians and Athenians engaged with each other in direct conflict.

L. After the rout had become complete, the Corinthians did not attempt, by lashing to the hulks of the enemy which they had partially sunk, to draw them off, but they aimed rather at mere cutting through and through the wrecks to slay rather than take alive; and in doing this they slew their own friends unawares, not having perceived that their right wing had been beaten. 2. For, as there were many ships on both sides, and covering a great extent of sea, after they became intermixed with each other, it was not easy to discriminate between victor and vanquished. Indeed, in regard of the number of vessels in action, this was the most considerable battle in which Greeks had ever engaged Greeks. 3. After the Corinthians had pursued the Corcyræans to land, they turned their attention to their own disabled ships and their own dead, and recovered the greater number and conveyed them to the Sybota, whither the land army of their barbarian allies had marched to coöperate with them. The Sybota is a port of Thesprotis, without a town. 4. Having accomplished this, they formed again in order of battle and sailed toward the Corcyræans, who, with such of their own ships as the action had left fit for the sea, and with those which had not partaken in the engagement, and with their Athenian allies, advanced at once to meet the Corinthians, fearing lest they might attempt to force a descent upon their territory. 5. It was now late, and the Pæan for the assault had been sung, when the Corinthians discerned that twenty Athenian ships were approaching them, and suddenly retired, keeping their bows to the enemy. These twenty ships the Athenians had sent to render aid, after their first ten, fearing, what actually happened, lest the Corcyræans should be defeated, and the ten ships inadequate to support them.

LI. Discerning them, therefore, and suspecting that more

than they could see had arrived from Athens, the Corinthians slowly retired. 2. By the Corcyræans they were not immediately discerned, for they were approaching from behind, and were out of their view, and they were wondering to see the Corinthians retire, when the cry was given, — "There are ships coming down to us." Upon this, they, too, retired, for it was growing dark, and the Corinthians, by turning away, caused the suspension of hostilities. 3. So the combatants separated, and the battle ended with the approach of night. 4. When the Corcyræans had resumed their station off Leucimne, these twenty Athenian ships, under command of Glaucon, son of Leager, and Andocides, son of Leogoras, borne through floating bodies of the slain and through floating wrecks, arrived at the station soon after they had been first discovered. 5. At first, for it was night, they were thought to be enemies, and great alarm was excited; but after they were recognized, they, too, came to anchor.

LII. The next day, the thirty Athenian ships, and such of the Corcyræans as were in condition to sail, put to sea and proceeded towards the port in the Sybota, where the Corinthians lay at anchor, for the purpose of ascertaining if they would fight. 2. And they, heaving their ships afloat, and arranging them in line out from the shore, lay still, not being inclined voluntarily to begin an action, for they perceived that fresh ships had arrived from Athens, and they were incommoded by certain embarrassments also, having numerous prisoners to guard on board ship, and having no means of refitting on that uninhabited coast. 3. Indeed, they began to contemplate returning homeward, fearing that the Athenians might be induced to regard the truce as terminated by the battle, and might endeavor to intercept them.

LIII. To make trial of their intentions in this respect, they determined to send messengers in a light boat, without the rod of truce, to ascertain by inquiry. And these messengers addressed them. 2. "You have been guilty of injustice already, Athenians, by commencing war in violation of the truce; for while we sought to punish our own enemies, you interposed to prevent us, sword in hand. And if, now, it is your purpose to oppose our sailing to Corcyra, or whithersoever we wish, and thus complete the breach of the truce, seize our persons first, and treat us as enemies." 3. Thus they. Such of the Corcyræans as heard them shouted, — "Let them be seized at once and slain." But the Athenians replied; 4. "We do not, men of Peloponnesus, begin war nor dissolve the truce. We only come to assist the Corcyræans, our allies. If, therefore, you desire to go elsewhere, we do not interpose. But if you sail towards Corcyra, or any of its territories, we shall, to the utmost of our power, prevent it."

LIV. Such was the answer of the Athenians. Upon this, the Corinthians began to prepare for the voyage homeward, and erected a trophy on the Sybota of the mainland. On the other hand, the Corcyræans raised and took up the wrecks and the dead bodies as they floated towards them, borne by the tide and the wind, which during the night had scattered them far and wide; and erected a trophy on the insular Sybota, as if they too had conquered. 2. The grounds on which each claimed the victory were these. The Corinthians, because they had the advantage in the action until night, so as to have brought to their station at Sybota the greater part of the wrecks and bodies of the dead, and because they had taken not less than a thousand prisoners, and had sunk about seventy ships. The Corcyræans, because they had destroyed near thirty ships, and, after the arrival of the Athenians, had carried off their wrecks and dead, and because the Corinthians had first retired upon discovery of the Athenian ships, and to their offer of battle had not met them from Sybota.

LV. Proceeding homeward the Corinthians took Anactorium, at the mouth of the Ambracian Gulf, by stratagem. It had belonged in common to Corcyra and Corinth. Placing a Corinthian garrison therein, they returned home. Of the Corcyræan prisoners, eight hundred, who were slaves, they sold; two hundred and fifty they, after putting them in bonds, placed under the guard of persons appointed to watch them, and treated with a studied attention, in the view that on their return to Corcyra they might gain it over to Corinth; for the greater number of them happened to be of the first in point of consideration in the city. 2. Thus, then, Corcyra had success in this war with Corinth, and the ships of Athens retired from the island. But the aid thus rendered by her to Corcyra during the existence of the truce was the first occasion of hostilities between her and Corinth.

LVI. Immediately after the transactions which I have now related, the occurrence which I am now to relate fell out, tending to war between Athens and the Peloponnesians. 2. While the Corinthians were concerting measures to punish them, the Athenians, suspecting their hostile mind, commanded the Potidæans, who dwelt on the isthmus of Pallene, colonists of Corinth, and tributary allies of themselves, to demolish the wall towards Pallene, to give hostages, to expel the magistrates sent them from Corinth, and thenceforward to decline receiving such as the mother country annually deputed. The fear was that they might revolt and bring off the rest of Thrace to revolt with them.

LVII. These designs against the Potidæans the Athenians set on foot immediately after the naval action with Corinth; 2. for the Corinthians were now openly on terms of hostility, and Perdiccas, the son of Alexander the King of Macedonia, who had been the friend and ally of Athens, had become its enemy. 3. He became such by reason that the Athenians had become allies of his brother Philip and Derdas, who were concerned in a common war with him. 4. Dreading the consequences of this, he projected a mission to Sparta, for the purpose of fomenting a war between Peloponnesus and Athens, and was attempting to bring over the Corinthians to his connection, with a view to cause the Potidæans to revolt. 5. He was making proposals also to the Chalcidians and Bottiæans of Thrace to revolt with Potidæa, deeming that if he could acquire those countries, his neighbors, as allies, he could with more hope of success prosecute his war on Athens. 6. Becoming apprised of these movements, and anxious to anticipate the defection of these cities, the Athenians, who had before sent thirty ships and one thousand heavy-armed troops to that region, under command of Archestratus and ten colleagues, issued orders, as I have related, to the commanders of their ships, to exact hostages of the Potidæans, and to demolish the wall, and to maintain a strict watch over the other cities to anticipate and prevent their revolt.

LVIII. While these events were in progress, the Potidæans, who had sent ambassadors to the Athenians to attempt to persuade them to force on them no change of policy, sent also to Lacedæmon ambassadors, accompanied by others from Corinth, to procure assistance, if need there should be, after they perceived that their utmost efforts would effect nothing useful at Athens, since her fleet, which had sailed towards Macedonia, was destined against them too; and they so far succeeded that the magistrates of the Lacedæmonians engaged that, if Athens should assail Potidæa, they would invade Attica. Thereupon, at the same time with the Chalcidians and Bottiæans, they revolted and pledged themselves by the same oath. 2. Perdiccas also sought to induce the Chalcidians, who dwelt by the sea, to leave and destroy their cities, and to remove up to Olynthus, and make that single city one of great strength; and he gave to them part of his territory of Mygdonia to occupy and enjoy while the war with Athens should continue. They did so remove accordingly, destroyed their cities and prepared for war.

LIX. The thirty ships of the Athenians arrived on the coasts of Thrace, colonized by the Greeks, and found Potidæa and the other cities in revolt. 2. Their commanders, deeming it impracticable to contend against Perdiccas and the entire revolted region successfully with their actual force, turned towards Macedonia, — the original object indeed of the expedition, — and assuming a station and forming a junction with Philip and the brothers of Derdas, who had descended from the interior with an army, they prosecuted the war.

LX. At the same time the Corinthians, Potidæa having revolted, and the Athenian fleet hanging on the coast of Macedonia, apprehensive for the safety of the place, and deeming the peril as their own, sent forward a force of sixteen hundred heavy-armed and four hundred light-armed soldiers, — in part their own troops serving gratuitously, and in part Peloponnesians whom they had hired. 2. This army was commanded by Aristeus, the son of Adeimantus, always well affected to Potidæa, a friendly regard towards whom was not the least of the motives which induced the greater number of the Corinthian troops to attend him gratuitously. 3. They arrived in Thrace on the fortieth day after the revolt of Potidæa.

LXI. News reached the Athenians of the revolt of the cities, and as soon as they heard that the forces under the command of Aristeus had reinforced the garrison, they sent to this disaffected region two thousand of their own heavy-armed troops, and forty ships, with Callias, the son of Calliades, for general, with four others. 2. Immediately on their arrival, they effected a junction with the one thousand men who had preceded them, who had just taken Therma, and were besieging Pydna. 3. Halting then themselves, they laid siege to Pydna, but very soon became obliged, by the defection of Potidæa and the arrival of Aristeus, to conclude an accommodation and the best practicable terms of alliance with Perdiccas, and to retire from Macedonia. 4. They proceeded, therefore, along the coast toward Potidæa, but diverged, before arriving thither, from their line of march to the left to attack Berœa, and failing in their attempt on it, resumed their original route. This force consisted of three thousand heavy-armed Athenian troops, besides a numerous body of allies, and six hundred Macedonians in the service and attached to the cause of Philip and Pausanias. Seventy ships accompanied the march of the army. Advancing very leisurely, on the third day they arrived at Gigonus, and encamped.

LXII. Awaiting the approach of the Athenians, the Potidæans, with their Peloponnesian allies, took a station upon the isthmus over against Olynthus, and established a market of supplies without the city. 2. They appointed Aristeus commander of the whole foot, and Perdiccas of the horse; for he had again abruptly deserted the cause of Athens, and attached himself to that of Potidæa, having designated Iolaus to succeed him in the post which he left. 3. The plan of Aristeus was to keep the force under his command upon the isthmus to watch the approach of the Athenians, if they should seek to enter it, and that the Chalcidians and their allies without the isthmus and the two hundred horse of Perdiccas should remain in Olynthus; and that when the Athenians should advance against him, these coming to his assistance in rear should place the enemy between two assaults. 4. But Callias and his associate commanders detached their Macedonian horse and a few of their allies to Olynthus, in order to shut in those there posted, and so prevent their coöperation; and then breaking up their encampment, they advanced directly towards Potidæa. 5. Approaching near the isthmus, they saw that the enemy had made his preparation for action, whereupon they set themselves also in order of battle, and soon engaged. The wing under immediate command of Aristeus and the Corinthians, and other picked troops around him, put to flight the wing opposed to them, and pursued it a considerable distance; but the other part of the army, composed of Potidæans and Peloponnesians, was beaten by the Athenians, and fled within the city wall.

LXIII. Returning from his pursuit, Aristeus discerned the defeat of this part of his army, and for a space was at a loss whether he should run the hazard of retreating to Olynthus or to Potidæa. The more expedient course, however, seemed to him to contract his troops to the smallest possible space, and to force his way by running at full speed to Potidæa. Accordingly, he marched along through the water around the projecting end of the mole, exposed to a severe discharge of missiles, by which he lost a few men, although he brought off the greater number. 2. When the battle began, and its signals were lifted up, the troops stationed to aid the Potidæans at Olynthus, which is about sixty stadia distant, and conspicuously situated, advanced a little way, as with a view to assist; and the Macedonian horse were drawn out and arranged to prevent them; but victory declaring speedily for the Athenians, and the signals of battle being lowered, they retired again within the walls, and the Macedonians fell back on the Athenians; so that the cavalry of neither army assisted the infantry in the engagement. 3. The Athenians then erected a trophy, and gave up the slain under truce to the Potidæans. Of these and their allies died a little less than three hundred; of the Athenians one hundred and fifty, of whom was Callias, their commander.

LXIV. In pursuance of the plan of war, the Athenians next proceeded to construct a wall of circumvallation around that wall of Potidæa, which looked forth upon the main land, and therein to place a garrison. The wall looking towards Pallene, they did not immediately so inclose; for they deemed themselves unable to maintain a garrison upon the isthmus, and also to pass through and construct a line of circumvallation towards Pallene, apprehending that this separation of their army into two disconnected divisions might induce an attack of the Potidæans and their allies. 2. Hearing in Athens that no wall of circumvallation was built towards Pallene, the government, some time afterwards, sent sixteen hundred heavy-armed native troops, under Phormio, the son of Asopius, to the seat of war. Arriving in the peninsula, and establishing his head-quarters at Aphytis, he led his army towards Potidæa, advancing slowly and wasting the country before him. No one sallying out to fight him, he built a wall of circumvallation on the side of Pallene; 3. and thus Potidæa became closely besieged on both sides, and was assailed also by the fleet from the sea.

LXV. Thus walled in, and retaining no hope of safety, unless something from the Lacedæmonians or some other accidental circumstance should supervene, Aristeus advised that all but five hundred, waiting fair winds, should escape by sea, so that their provisions might hold out the longer, he himself preferring to be one to remain. This advice not being followed, as the next best step to be taken, and with a view of giving the most favorable direction to operations elsewhere, he caused his whole force, secretly and unobserved by the Athenian garrison of blockade, to put to sea. 2. For some time he remained in Chalcidice, and, besides other military operations, he cut off great numbers of the Sermylians, by planting an ambuscade about the city. He took measures, also, by communicating with the Peloponnesus, to obtain assistance from that quarter. Phormio, after accomplishing the circumvallation of Potidæa, at the head of sixteen hundred men, visited Chalcidice and Bottice, and took several towns.

LXVI. Thus, therefore, were these additional grounds of reciprocal accusation induced upon the other difference between the Peloponnesians and Athenians. The Corinthians had to complain that the Athenians had besieged Potidæa, their colony, and Corinthians and other Peloponnesians within it. The Athenians, that the Peloponnesians had moved an ally and tributary to revolt, and had openly sent thither an expedition and fought for the Potidæans. Still war had not broken out, and the truce subsisted, for thus far the Corinthians had acted alone.

LXVII. The siege of Potidæa, however, determined the Corinthians to remain inactive no longer, both because their own troops were shut up within it, and because they feared for its safety. Forthwith, therefore, they invited their allies to Lacedæmon, and going thither themselves, they vehemently inveighed against the Athenians for breaking the truce, and for doing injury to Peloponnesus. 2. The Æginetans, too, although they openly sent no delegation, from fear of Athens, yet in secret not less strenuously urged Lacedæmon to war, alleging that they were not permitted to be independent according to the spirit of the truce. 3. Whereupon the Lacedæmonians, having summoned their confederates, and all such others as had aught of wrong to complain of against Athens, and having convoked their accustomed assembly, called upon them to speak. 4. Others thereupon preferred, each in succession, their accusations against Athens, and among them the Megareans, who displayed numerous matters of grievance, and particularly that they were restrained from all intercourse of trade, both by sea and land. 5. Last of all the Corinthians, having permitted those who preceded them to exasperate the Lacedæmonians, thus addressed them.

LXVIII. "The good faith, Lacedæmonians, which marks your own system and your own private life, inclines you to disbelieve a charge of bad faith, when made against others. It is thus that you are distinguished by moderation and sobriety of mind and policy, and yet labor always under a corresponding misconception of the affairs of other States. 2. When we have forewarned you, as frequently we have done, of injuries Athens was about to inflict on us, you did not always derive the instruction which you might have done from our representations, but rather suspected us of speaking from private interests. The consequence has been, that not in anticipation but under the actual pressure of suffering have you assembled the allies. Among these it is not unfit that we should have most to say, since we have the weightiest charges to prefer, — charges of outrage against Athens, of neglect against you. 3. If she had prosecuted her policy of injury to Greece in a secret manner, it would be necessary to apprise you of it, as if ignorant of its existence. But now, why consume time in enumerating those whom you yourselves see, some reduced to servitude, others plotted against, and of these, among the most prominent, our own allies, herself all the while prepared beforehand for the war which possibly you may resolve to hazard? 4. For what else but a design against the liberties of Greece, could have prompted them secretly to withdraw and hold Corcyra from us, and to lay siege to Potidæa — Potidæa, that post so eminently important to secure you the use of your Thracian dominion, — Corcyra, which could give Peloponnesus the largest navy?

LXIX. "Of all this the blame rests on you, in that you suffered them, after the Persian war, first to strengthen their city, and then to construct the long walls; and in that also you have down to this moment bereaved of liberty, not those alone whom they have reduced to servitude, but your own allies. For not he whose direct act reduces to servitude, but he who, able to prevent it, does nothing, is author of the deed; especially is he so, who arrogates the praise of being hailed liberator of Greece. 2. Even now we have met tardily to act we see not on what. For no longer ought we to be pondering whether we are sustaining injury or not, but rather how to repel it. This moment they are advancing, active, resolved, and undallying, upon you, all undetermined what to do. 3. In what manner indeed, by what gradual advance they assail others, we know. While they suppose themselves unobserved through your inattentiveness, they are less audacious; but when they discover that you know and permit what they do, they will press on you vehemently. Ye alone of all the Hellenes are quiet, repelling your enemy, not by force but by being evermore about to resort to force,—alone of all ye prefer to break down his doubled strength rather than his incipient growth. 5. And yet ye used to be reckoned worthy of all reliance,—a reputation which outwent the fact. For it is within our own knowledge that the Mede advanced from the very ends of the earth into Peloponnesus, before you went out to meet him as became you. And now you look supinely upon the Athenians, not distant as he was, but at your door, and instead of marching upon them, you prefer awaiting to repel their attack on you, casting yourselves on the doubtful chances of a war with an adversary grown far stronger than you. And all this, although you are well aware that the barbarian overthrew himself more than he was overthrown, and that any advantages which we have gained over the Athenian, these we have gained more by their blunders than by your help. Indeed the hope of help from you has wrought the ruin of some, unprepared because they trusted it. Let no one deem this the reproach of enmity, but rather the remonstrance of friendship, for remonstrance we address to a friend who mistakes, reproach to an enemy who wrongs.

LXX. "Yet do we think that, if any ever might, we may complain of our neighbors, especially since subjects of controversy so vast have arisen, which you seem to us very inadequately to appreciate, and since you seem not to comprehend who, what, how totally in all things unlike yourselves, are these Athenians with whom you may have to contend. 2. They are ever projectors of some novelty, quick to plan and to execute; you guard what you have, devise nothing new, and fail to accomplish even that which is absolutely necessary. 3. They, again, dare beyond their ability, incur risks unwarranted by a sound judgment, are full of hope in the midst of perils. Your acts fall below your ability; you trust not in the safest determinations of judgment; from peril you despair of ever being extricated. 4. It is the strife of the ever-ready with the ever-procrastinating, of the roamer abroad with the dweller at home. To leave their possessions, they think the way to enlarge them. You think to invade others, the way to lose what you have. Victorious, they press on farther, and beaten, they despond less than all other men. 5. Their bodies they squander for the state, as if they were the bodies of other persons; their best thoughts they cultivate, as somewhat most cherished and personal, for her. 6. If they fail to accomplish their whole plan of conquest, they deem themselves robbed of their own; if they succeed, they consider that they have had the fortune to do little compared with what is left to do. Defeated in one enterprise, they substitute for success, hope; and to them alone, so promptly do they put their plans into execution, are fruition and expectation the same. 7. Thus ever in labors and perils, do they wear out life. Less than all others do they enjoy what they have, because they are ever striving to acquire. For them to do what ought to be done, is the only festival of life, and in their mind repose, accomplishing nothing, is as great an evil as occupation the most laborious. 8. So that one might, in a word, justly characterise them as a race born neither to rest themselves, nor to permit it to others.

LXXI. "And yet, Lacedæmonians, with such a State in array against you, you hesitate. You do not consider that peace is sure to be longest theirs who, while they practise what is right, yet announce their determination to submit to nothing wrong; but you do what is right with the policy and upon the principle of neither inflicting injury on others, nor of being subjected to injury in resorting to self-defence. 2. This you could scarcely effect, even if your next neighbor were guided by a policy exactly the same; but now your system, as against such as they, is obsolete. It is a law of human life that new policy, like a last innovation in art, should ever triumph. 3. For a State wholly still, unchanging customs are best; but for one which is impelled to much and various novelty of enterprise, new arts of policy are indispensable. Hence, in Athens, practised in a larger variety of national experience, all is newer than with you. 4. Of all this procrastination, let this be the end. Succor at once us and the Potidæans by invading Attica; them, lest you abandon friends and kindred to the enemy; us, lest you compel us in despair to seek other alliance. 5. In such a measure we should be guilty of no crime, neither in the sight of the gods who enforce oaths, nor in that of men who appreciate them; for it is not they who, deserted by their allies, seek new ones, but they who withhold assistance from those to whom they have sworn it, that are the breakers of truce. 6. But if you will be prompt to help us, we remain with you. It were unjust to change our connection, nor elsewhere could we find those more congenial to us. 7. Judge wisely, then, on these things, and see to it that that supremacy in Peloponnesus which you have inherited, you preserve unimpaired."

LXXII. Such was the discourse of the Corinthians. It happened that there was at that moment an embassy of the Athenians in Sparta, which had been sent thither before for other objects. Having ascertained what had been said, they judged it expedient to wait on the assembly of the Lacedæmonians, not for the purpose of answering to the accusations which the cities had preferred, but to intimate in relation to the general subject a caution not to decide rashly, but to weigh maturely. They desired too to set forth the power of Athens, to remind the old of what they knew, and to inform the young of what they did not, supposing that this would turn their hearts rather to peace than to war. 2. Going, therefore, to the Lacedæmonians, they declared a wish to say somewhat to the assembly, unless it should be forbidden. 3. They directed them to enter; whereupon, having done so, they said, —

LXXIII. "The object of our embassy was not to make defence against your allies, but different and more general. Learning, however, that a very vehement outcry has been here raised against us, we present ourselves, not to repel the accusation of the parties, for this were to try a cause before those neither our judges nor their judges; but lest, persuaded by your allies, you should adopt unwise counsels upon a subject of vast importance. We have desired, too, in reference to the entire discourse which has arraigned us, to demonstrate that what we possess we have not unfairly acquired, and that Athens may challenge a just glory. 2. Of the remote past, of which tradition, not your own eyes, is the witness, why need we speak? But of the Persian war, and of the events which have passed under your own observation, irksome though it is to us so often to display them, we must say something. For what we then did was an achievement of peril, effected for the general good. You shared that good; let us be indulged, — whatever its value, — in a share of the glory. We shall recall these things, too, not so much for excuse and deprecation, as to remind you with what manner of city, if unwise counsels guide you, the contest must be. 4. We aver, then, that at Marathon we foremost and alone encountered the peril of barbarian war. Invaded a second time, unable to resist on land, we embarked with our whole people on the sea, and fought his fleet at Salamis. The effect of that victory was to hinder his ships from successively attacking and destroying the cities of the Peloponnesus, since against a naval force so overwhelming, they could not have defended themselves. 5. Of the great results of that victory, he himself offered a proof the most signal; for his fleet being defeated, appreciating the great diminution and comparative inferiority of his force, at once, with most of his army, he retreated.

LXXIV. "To this great achievement, demonstrating that Greece existed but in her navy, we contributed in three particulars most effectively, — the largest number of ships, a commander the most consummate in capacity, and zeal the most untiring. We furnished towards the whole fleet of four hundred sail a little less than two parts in three; we furnished for commander, Themistocles, who, more than all others, was instrumental in bringing on the battle of Salamis, whose wisdom saved Greece, whom you yourselves, for a service so transcendent, honored as you never honored a stranger guest before. 2. We displayed a zeal the most daring, since on land, no one helping us, every State as far as Athens submitting, we resolved not to desert the cause of those allies who still remained to us, to take no offence that you had not extended a prompter aid, not to render ourselves useless by dispersing; but to embark and dare the perils of naval war. 3. We boast, therefore, to have conferred on you as much benefit as we have received. You, fearing rather for yourselves than for us, — for before we were attacked, you came not near us, — issued forth at length to aid, from cities unwasted, — your cities, — to preserve them for yourselves. We, sallying out from a city that had ceased to exist, and perilling ourselves on a chance, only not desperate, at once, in some real sense and measure, saved you and ourselves. But had we, in the first instance, from fear yielded, like others, to the Persian, or had we not dared, as already ruined, to embark, you could have fought no naval battle, for you had no ships; and all things would have quietly fallen into the exact course which he desired.

LXXV. "Say, then, Lacedæmonians, considering the zeal and the wisdom of the counsels with which we met that day, ought the empire we have won to subject us to such a burden of the envy of Greece? 2. That empire we did not grasp by violence, but acquired it by your declining the prosecution of the war against the barbarian to its close, and by the allies coming to us and entreating us to permit them to elevate us to the command. 3. Once acquired, from the nature of supremacy, we were forced, in the first instance, to elevate it to its present height, chiefly by reason of the jealousy of others; in part, too, for our glory, in part for our profit. 4. It seemed unsafe that we, odious to the greater number, (some of them actually reduced from open revolt — yourselves no longer friendly as at first, but distrustful and at variance with us,) should risk the hazards of resigning command; for the revolters from us would have gone to you. 5. Surely, it is no cause of reproach to any to meet with prudence the great crises of their affairs.

LXXVI. "Yourselves, Lacedæmonians, having imposed upon the States of Peloponnesus a polity to subserve your own interests, rule them; and had you continued, as we did, to exercise command, always odious, through and since the war, you, too, would have become equally the object of hatred with the allies, and would have been, as we are, obliged to govern with a firm hand, or to subject yourselves to great peril. 2. We say, then, we have done nothing so wonderful or so totally out of the course of human action, in just accepting a supremacy which was proffered to us, and in so far yielding to the transcendent considerations of glory, fear, and advantage, as not to give it away. Nor are we the originators of such a precedent, since ever it was the decree that the weaker should be commanded by the stronger. Let us say, too, that we hold ourselves worthy of this rule; nor did you deem us not so, until now, when interest prompts you to begin to discourse of justice, — justice, no love of which ever yet restrained the acquisitions of power."

* * * * * * *

TRANSLATION FROM TACITUS.

October, 1845.

I AM reading, meditating, and translating the first of Greek historians, Thucydides. I study the Greek critically in Passow, (Liddell and Scott,) Bloomfield, Arnold, and Duker; and the history in Mitford, Thirlwall, Wachsmuth, Hermann, &c., &c., and translate faithfully, yet with some attention to English words and construction; and my purpose is to study deeply the Greece of the age of Pericles, and all its warnings to the liberty and the anti-unionisms of my own country and time.

For purposes more purely rhetorical, I would translate and study Tacitus, too; and (somewhat abruptly, for I am a little way advanced in the study of his immortal work) begin with the death of Germanicus. My helps are Ernesti, Lipsius, Ruperti, and the common historians, Leverett's Dictionary, and Murphy; and my object is an elegant, yet true and resembling version, and a collection of rhetorical sentiments and phrases, and of general wisdom. I begin October 9, 1845.

ANNALS. BOOK II.—CHAPTER 70.

THESE proceedings of Piso exasperated Germanicus as much as they alarmed him. "If my threshold," he said, "is to be beseiged, if my blood is to be poured out under the eye of my enemies, what will befall my most wretched wife; what my children, yet infants? Piso thinks poison too slow! He hastens; he presses eagerly onward that he may grasp the province and the legions in his single hand. But he shall learn that Germanicus is not yet wholly vanquished; nor shall the murderer earn the reward of his crime of blood." He composed letters to Piso, in which he renounced his friendship. According to the relation of most writers, he added a command that he should depart from the province. Without more delay Piso set sail, yet proceeded slowly on his voyage that he might have the less distance to return if the death of Germanicus should open to him the gates of Syria.

Ch. 71. Germanicus at first, for a brief space, was elevated to the hope of recovery, but soon perceived that his end was approaching; and with wearied frame, thus addressed the friends who stood around him: — "If I were yielding to a decree of nature, I might yet justly grieve for the ordination even of the gods who snatch me away from parents, children, country, by a premature departure in my season of youth. But now, intercepted violently and suddenly by the crime of Piso and Plancina, I leave my last prayers in your hearts. Tell my father and my brother by what afflictions torn asunder, by what treachery circumvented, I closed my most unhappy life, and by the most inglorious death. If there are those in whom my earlier hopes, my kindred blood awakened an interest; if there are any in whom, while living, I moved an emotion of envy, they will weep that he, once shining the survivor of so many wars, has fallen by the fraud of woman. There will be allowed you opportunity of preferring a complaint to the senate, and of invoking the laws. It is not the chief office of friendship to stand looking after the departed with listless sorrow, but to remember his wishes and to perform his injunctions. Even strangers will weep for Germanicus. You will vindicate him, if it were himself rather than his conspicuous fortune, which you loved and cherished. Show to the people of Rome the granddaughter of Augustus, my wife; enumerate my six children. Sympathy will enlist itself with the accusers; and they who may only pretend that their crimes were commanded by a higher will shall not be believed, or shall not be held guiltless." Taking the right hand of the dying man his friends swore that they would sooner lose life than revenge.

Ch. 72. Then turning to his wife he entreated her by his memory, by their common children, to suppress all vehemence of resentment, to resign her spirit to her cruel fortune when she should return to the city, to avoid by emulation of power exasperating those above her in the State.

These dying injunctions Germanicus openly communicated. Other things he confidentially said, by which he was believed to have conveyed a suspicion of Tiberius. Within a brief space afterwards he died, to the profound sorrow of the province and of the countries around it. Foreign nations and kings mourned for him. Such had been his courtesy to his subjects of the province; such his clemency towards enemies; such reverence did his countenance and his speech alike conciliate, that while he preserved and displayed the grandeur and dignity of the highest estate, he escaped envy and the accusation of arrogance.

Ch. 73. His funeral was celebrated not with statues nor

with pomp, but by praises, and by the memory and rehearsal of his virtues. Some there were who drew a parallel between him in respect of form and of age, the kind of his death, the general region in which he died, and the traits and fortune of Alexander the Great. Each of them it was called to mind was of dignified and graceful person and illustrious family, and each, not much past the thirtieth year of life, died by the treachery of his countrymen in foreign lands. But Germanicus was gentle towards his friends, temperate in his pleasures, the husband of one wife, the father of legitimate children only. Nor was he, they urged, less a warrior, although characterized by less rashness; and although he had been hindered from forcing the Germans, stunned by so many victories, into entire subjection. But had he been the sole disposer of affairs; if that field of war had belonged to him in name and of right, he would have won the glory of arms with a promptness and energy as much more conspicuous as was his superiority in clemency, temperance, and all other moral traits. His body, before it was burned, was exposed naked in the forum of Antioch, which was the place assigned for funeral ceremonies. Whether it revealed indications of poison may not certainly be known, for observers drew opposite conclusions, accordingly as they were influenced by sorrow for Germanicus and by suspicions previously taken up, or by partiality towards Piso.

Ch. 74. It then became the subject of consultation among the commanders of legions and such senators as were present, who should be designated to the Government of Syria; the claims of others not having been importunately urged, the competition came to be between Vibius Marsus and Cneius Sentius; it was long debated which should obtain the post. Ultimately, Marsus yielded to Sentius, who was elder, and who contended for it with the more persevering energy. At the request of Vitellius, Veranius, and others who were now engaged in framing the accusation and collecting the proofs of guilt as if against a party whose name was already presented to the Prætor for criminal proceedings, the new governor sent to Rome a female of the name of Martina, infamous in that province for her practices of poisoning, and with whom Plancina had maintained a very marked intimacy.

Ch. 75. But Agrippina, although faint from sorrow and sickness, yet unable to endure the delay of revenge, ascended the fleet with the ashes of Germanicus and with her children, attended by universal commiseration that a woman, the highest in nobility, but yesterday the wife of a most illustrious marriage, accustomed to be seen, surrounded, thronged, admired, and congratulated, should now be bearing away the ashes of the dead in her bosom; uncertain of revenge; anxious for herself; her exposure to fortune multiplied and heightened by the sad possession of so many children.

Meantime, tidings of the death of Germanicus overtook Piso at the Island of Cos. In the transports of intemperate delight, he sacrificed victims, and went for thanksgivings to the temple of the gods. He made no effort to disguise or restrain his joy; and his wife, still more elated, then first changed her dress of mourning for a lost sister, to garments of praise and gladness.

Ch. 76. Already were the centurions flowing in around him and reminding him that the preferences of the legions were decisive for him, and counselling that he should reacquire the province now without a chief, which had been unjustly wrested away. Proceeding then to consult them what he should do, his son Marcus Piso declared his opinion to be that he should hasten to the city; that no inexpiable offence had yet been committed; that groundless suspicions, and the empty things of report were not to be feared; that the quarrel between him and Germanicus might perhaps expose him to odium but was not a subject of punishment; that he had made expiation to his enemies by the deprivation of his province. But that if he returned to Syria and Sentius should oppose him, a civil war is instantly begun, nor would the centurions and soldiers remain faithful to his cause, since with them the fresh memory of their late commander and the profound attachment to the Cæsars with which they were penetrated would prove a more powerful influence.

Ch. 77. In opposition to this, Domitius Celer, who shared his most intimate friendship, argued that he should grasp the contingency. "It is Piso," said he, "not Sentius, who is intrusted with Syria. To him are committed the fasces and the pretorian jurisdiction; to him the legions. If anything of war should violently assail him, with how much more justice could he resist, who had received the authority, and the appropriate orders of a governor of the province? Besides, time should be given to reports, that they may grow old. With a recent odium, the contest of our innocence is unequal. If he should retain the army and increase his power chance might be relied on for unexpected aid. Shall we rush to Rome, attending the very ashes of Germanicus, that the passionate grief of Agrippina, the violence of an ignorant mob, may hurry you, in the first excitation of slanderous report to death, unheard, undefended? With you is Augusta privy, accessorial to the deed; with you is the favor of Cæsar, but secretly both. And none will more ostentatiously mourn that Germanicus is dead, than those who most rejoice."

Ch. 78. Piso, ever inclined to daring action, was with no

great difficulty drawn into this opinion, and addressed letters to Tiberius accusing Germanicus of arrogance and luxuriousness, and setting forth that himself, who had been expelled from the province the moment an opportunity of rebellion had opened, had resumed the command of the army under the influence of the same sentiments of loyalty with which he had originally held it. At the same time, he placed Domitius in command of a trireme; and gave him orders to sail for Syria, keeping clear of the coasts on the outside of the Islands. He formed the deserters, who flocked to him, into corps, he armed the sutlers, and crossing to the continent with his fleet, he intercepted and retained a body of recruits marching to Syria. He wrote to the petty chiefs of Cilicia to assist him. His son Piso, although he had dissuaded from undertaking the war, approved himself full of energy for its service.

Ch. 79. Setting out for Syria they met, as they passed the coast of Lycia and Pamphilia, the ships which bore Agrippina; and kindled with hostile sentiments, both sides prepared their weapons for battle; but restrained by reciprocal fear they did not pass the limit of reproaches. Vibius Marsus gave notice to Piso to come to Rome to stand his trial, to which Piso replied with a sneer, that he would be sure to do so the moment the Prætor, who holds pleas of poisonings, should assign a day for accuser and accused. Meantime, Domitius having arrived at Laodicea, proceeded to the winter quarters of the sixth legion, which he supposed would be, more than any other, particularly well disposed to new policy and action, but found himself anticipated and baffled by Pacuvius. This attempt and its result, Sentius exposed by letters to Piso, and admonished not to assail the camp by corruption, nor the province by war. He proceeded to draw together those whom he had observed to love the memory of Germanicus, or to be the enemies of his enemies, all the while throwing out intimations of the power of the emperor, and that the State was assailed by arms, and at length placed himself at the head of a powerful body of troops prepared for battle.

Ch. 80. Nor did Piso, although his enterprise was beginning to approach a result other than he had hoped, fail to adopt measures — the safest in the actual exigency. He took military occupation of a castle in Cilicia, strongly fortified, of the name of Celendris, for he had mixed together deserters, the new recruits which he had recently intercepted, his own and Plancina's servants, and the levies sent by the chiefs of Cilicia, and had disposed them into the organized forms and numbers of a legion. He asseverated that he, the deputy of Cæsar, was expelled from the province which the emperor had given to him, not by the legions, for upon their call he had come, but by Sentius, cloaking private malice under false accusation of public crime. He asked them only to form and stand in array of battle; for the soldiers would not fight, he urged, when they should perceive that Piso, whom once they had held as parent, in a contest of right was the stronger, and in a contest of arms was not weak. He then displayed his companies in front of the fortified points of the castle, upon a steep and broken hill — for all places were girt by the sea. Against these stood the veterans, drawn up in ranks and with reserves. On one side was the courage and discipline of soldiers, on the other advantage of position — but without bravery, without hope, with no weapons even but rustic instruments of annoyance snatched up on a sudden emergency. When forces so imperfectly matched came to blows, the contest was doubtful only while the Roman cohorts were struggling to ascend to the equal and level ground on which the enemy was posted. The instant that was accomplished the Cilicians turned their backs and shut themselves up in the castle.

BOOK III.

Ch. 1. UNDELAYED by a winter's sea, Agrippina pursues her voyage, and is borne to the island of Corcyra, opposite to the Calabrian shore. There, violent by grief, and untaught and unknowing how to endure, she passed a few days in a struggle to compose herself. Meantime the news of her approach having preceded her, the more intimate of the friends of Germanicus and the greater number of those who had borne military office under him, and crowds of persons unknown, some of whom supposed they were performing acceptable duty to the prince, while the larger part implicitly followed them, rushed to Brundusium, the nearest port and the safest harbor to which she might come. And now that the fleet is first dimly discerned far at sea, the harbor, and all the adjacent shore nearest the water, and not these alone but walls, and roofs of houses, even the remotest, from which a glimpse could be gained, are thronged by a vast and sorrowing multitude. They inquire often, one of another, whether they shall receive her as she descends from her ship, with silence, or with any uttered expression of feeling? Nor had they determined which would most befit the time, when the fleet slowly entered the port, not gliding to that joyful stroke of the oar with which the sailor, his voyage ending, comes to land, but with the manner in all things and with the aspects of a procession of mourning. And when Agrippina with her two children, bearing the urn of the dead, had descended from the ship and fixed her eyes sadly on the ground, one general equal sob burst forth from all that vast multitude, nor could you distinguish by the degree or the form of sorrow, strangers from near friends, nor man from woman; except that those in the train of Agrippina, exhausted by long-indulged grief, were less passionate and vehement than those more recent in their expression of it who thus came forth to meet them.

Ch. 2. The Emperor had sent two Prætorian cohorts to attend the arrival and approach of Agrippina, and had also issued a decree that the Apulians, the Campanians, and the magistrates of Calabria should perform the last offices to the memory of his son. The ashes therefore were borne forward upon the shoulders of tribunes and centurions; before them there moved along standards undecorated, and fasces inverted; and as the procession passed through successive colonies, the people clad in black, and the Equites in their robes of state, as the means of the region might supply, burned garments, odors, and such things else as use to honor the burial of the dead. Even they whose cities the procession did not pass through, came out to meet it, and offering sacrifices, and erecting altars to the gods of the dead, attested their sorrow by tears and united wailing.

Drusus had advanced as far as Terracina with his brother Claudius, and with those children of Germanicus who had remained at Rome. The consuls Marcus Valerius and Caius Aurelius (for they now exercised that magistracy), the Senate and the great body of the people thronged the way; without order of procession or arrangement, each man by himself weeping unrestrained — the sorrow of the heart — not the service of adulation — since all knew well that the joy of the Emperor for the death of Germanicus was scarcely veiled by the decencies of dissimulation.

Ch. 3. Tiberius and Augusta secluded themselves from the public eye; either deeming it beneath the imperial majesty openly to mourn; or fearing that the universal gaze might discern in their countenances the insincerity of their hearts. I do not find in any historian, nor in the public journals of daily events, that the mother of Germanicus performed any conspicuous part in the service of the day; while besides Agrippina, Drusus and Claudius, the names of many other kinsmen of the deceased are recorded. Whether she were prevented by ill health, or, overcome by grief, could not endure to look upon that spectacle of so great calamity, we may not know. I should more easily believe, that she was detained at home by Tiberius and Augusta, who went not forth themselves, to the end that each might seem overwhelmed with a similar sorrow, and that they might seem to have been kept within by her example.

Ch. 4. On the day on which the remains were borne to the tomb of Augustus, there reigned at times a desolate silence, and at times it was disturbed by sounds of sorrow. The streets were filled; funereal torches gleamed in the Campus Martius; and there were soldiers in arms; there were magistrates without the badges of office; the people by tribes; and from all lips there burst forth the frequent cry so unrestrained, and loud, that they might seem to have forgotten that they had a master — "the Republic is fallen — there is no more hope." Nothing however more deeply penetrated Tiberius, than the enthusiastic sentiments which appeared kindled towards Agrippina. All saluted her as the grace of the State; the one in whose veins alone ran the blood of Augustus; the sole surviving specimen of the old, noble, Roman matronage; and lifting their eyes towards heaven they prayed that her children might be happy, and might be spared the malice of their enemies.

Ch. 5. Some there were who demanded the pomp of a public funeral, and contrasted with these services, the honors and the magnificence with which Augustus had observed the burial of Drusus, the father of Germanicus, remembering how the Emperor himself in the severest of winter, had advanced as far as the Ticinus, and never leaving the dead, had entered the city with it; how the statues of the Claudii and Livii encompassed the bier; how the dead was wept in the Forum, and praised before the rostra; how all the ancient and all the late funeral honors were accumulated upon him. But Germanicus has not received the common ceremonies of burial, and such as were due to every noble Roman. Properly enough perhaps by reason of the distance of his place of death from Rome, his body was burned in some manner, in a foreign land. But so much the more splendid and careful ought the later observances to be, since fortune had denied him the earlier. Instead, not his own brothers advanced more than a day's journey to meet the dead; nor his uncle even as far as the gate! Where were the customs of their fathers; the image of the dead exposed upon the bier; verse composed in memory of his virtues; eulogy and tears, or at least the shows of sorrow?

Ch. 6. The general feeling was discerned by Tiberius, and in order to silence the speech of people, he put forth an admonitory edict. "Many illustrious Romans," it bore, "had died for the Republic; but the funeral of no one had been solemnized by so passionate a public sorrow. This was creditable to the Emperor and to all, if it were submitted to some degree of moderation, for that excess of sorrow which might become an humble house or an inconsiderable city, were unsuitable to Princes and an imperial people. For recent affliction, sorrow, and the solaces of grief indulged, were fit; but now, at length, the mind ought to be brought back to firmness again; as once Julius, bereaved of his only daughter; as Augustus, his grandsons torn from him, suppressed all signs of gloom. Nor is there need of remembering earlier examples; how often, with constancy, has the Roman people borne the slaughter of armies; the death of generals. Noble families, from their foundations, overthrown and perished. Great men die. The Republic is eternal. Let Rome then return to its duties, and referring to the spectacle of the Megalesian games just now at hand, resume its pleasures."

Ch. 7. The vacation of mourning having been closed, Rome returned to its labors: Drusus proceeded to resume the command of the Illyrian army, followed by the universal hope that expiation would be exacted from Piso, and by a general or frequent complaint that "lounging at his leisure through the beautiful Asia and Achaia, by an arrogant and fraudulent delay he was gradually suppressing the proofs of his guilt." For it was a current rumor that Martina, infamous for her poisons, who had been sent towards Rome, as I have related, by Cneius Sentius, had died suddenly at Brundusium, that poison had been found hidden in a ringlet of her hair, and that no other appearance of self-implicated death was detected on her.

Ch. 8. But Piso, having just sent forward his son to Rome, with messages by which he might soften the Prince, himself goes to Drusus, whom he hoped to find less exasperated by a brother's death, than reconciled or kinder by the removal of a competitor. Tiberius, that he might give assurance of an impartial and undisturbed judgment, received the young man kindly, and enriched him by the liberality which he usually displayed to the sons of the noble. To Piso Drusus said, that if those things were true which rumor spread abroad, he should occupy the chief place in the sorrow of the time. But he added that he would prefer that they should prove false and vain, and that the death of Germanicus should involve fatal results to no one. This he said openly, shunning with care all concealment; and there is no doubt that he, who on other occasions had seemed an artless facile youth, had now been counselled beforehand by Tiberius to employ these arts of age.

Ch. 9. Piso having crossed the Dalmatian sea, and left his fleet at Ancona, passing through Picenum and then over the Flaminian way, came up with the legion, which was then on its march from Pannonia to the city, thence to be sent to garrison in Africa; and it became the subject of rumor that, on the march and among the troops, he took much pains to present himself frequently before the eyes of the soldiers. From Narnia, either to avoid the suspicion of designs on the troops, or because the plans of the fearful are wont to be undecided and changing, he descended on the Nar, and on the Tiber. Even so he heightened the exasperation of the populace by landing at the tomb of the Cæsars in the daytime, a multitude looking on, and by walking towards the city, himself and Plancina, their countenances full of cheerfulness; he surrounded by a throng of clients, she by a train of women. To all other stimulants of the popular hatred was added this, — that his house which overlooked the Forum, stood wreathed with laurel, and illuminated; a banquet spread in it, and full of guests, the conspicuousness of the place exposing all things to view.

Ch. 10. The next day Fulcinius Trio accused Piso to the Consuls. Against this proceeding Vitellius and Veranius and others, who had attended Germanicus, insisted that no part of the function of prosecution belonged to Trio; that they themselves did not appear as accusers, but that in obedience to the injunction of Germanicus they had come to disclose and to bear witness. Resigning all participation in that cause, Trio obtained the right of arraigning the former life of Piso, and a request was preferred to the Prince that he would himself assume jurisdiction of that matter. To this not even the accused made objection, for he feared the anxious desires of the people and Senate to convict him; and, on the other hand, he believed Tiberius to be firm to despise rumor, and to be also, to some extent, a sharer of his mother's knowledge of the deed; that a single judge could more surely discriminate between the true and the false exaggerated; while hatred and envy would sway a numerous tribunal. Tiberius did not misconceive the great responsibilities of such a trial, nor the unfavorable suspicions by which he was assailed. Calling together therefore a few friends for witnesses, he just heard the threats of the accusers and the appeal of the accused, and then remitted the whole cause untried, to the Senate.

Ch. 11. Meantime Drusus returning from Illyricum, although the Senate had decreed him an ovation for recapturing Maroboduus, and for his achievements of the former summer, postponed that honor and entered the city. For counsel, after Titus, Arruntius, Fulcinius, Asinius Gallus, Æserninus Marcellus, and Sextus Pompeius, whom he had solicited to defend him, had on various grounds excused themselves, the accused was attended by Lepidus, Piso, and Regulus. The whole city was kindled with expectation, wondering what trust there might be in the friends of Germanicus; what degree of confidence Piso cherished; whether Tiberius would completely suppress and hide his thoughts. Engrossed, more than even before, with these subjects of anxious interest and speculation, the universal people indulged themselves more than ever before, in confidential speech, or ominous silence against the Prince.

Ch. 12. On the assembling of the Senate, Cæsar pronounced a discourse of studied moderation. Piso, he said, had been a friend and one of the lieutenants of his father, and had by him, with approbation of the Senate, been given to Germanicus, to assist in the administration of the East. Whether there he had wounded the sensibilities of the young man by insolence and contentious rivalry, and had rejoiced at his death, or whether he had murdered him, the Senate, with impartial mind, was to discriminate. "For if, in his capacity of lieutenant, he has gone beyond the proper limit of official duty; if he has manifested want of respectful devotedness to his commander; if he has been found rejoicing at his death, and at my grief — I should loathe him indeed; I should banish him from my house; and thus — and not by an exertion of the high power of the Prince — should I punish these quarrels of individuals. But if a crime is developed, deserving to be avenged by the death of any human being, I exhort you to soothe the children of Germanicus, and us his parents, by the consolations to which we are entitled. You will consider, too," he continued, "whether Piso did exercise his military trust in a mutinous and seditious manner; whether he took armed occupation of a province, and from motives of ambition cultivated the attachment of the troops; or whether exaggerations and falsehoods in relation to these matters have been spread abroad by his accusers, with whose excess of unfriendly zeal I am justly incensed. For, what proper purpose could it subserve to lay bare that body of the dead; to give it to be gazed on by vulgar eyes; to send out the rumor, even through foreign nations, that he had been slain by poison, if all were yet unascertained and requiring to be investigated? I mourn, and shall ever mourn my son; but I neither prohibit the accused from producing all proofs by which his innocence may be raised to light; nor any evidence by which the crime of Germanicus, if such there were, may be established; and, I entreat you, not to receive accusation for crime merely because the inquiry is involved with my personal griefs. If kindred blood, or if friendship have induced these to become his advocates, let them aid the accused in his peril by the utmost exertion of fidelity and eloquence. To the same effort and the same fidelity let me urge the prosecutors also. This only we have granted to Germanicus beyond the law; that in the Curia instead of the Forum; by the Senate instead of the judge, the question of his death shall be tried. In all things else let there be as absolute a deference to the general law, as if the case of a private citizen were on trial. Let no one regard the tears of Drusus; let no one regard my grief; let no one regard those other sentiments which false rumors have imputed to me."

Ch. 13. Two days were then assigned for presenting and proving the charges; and then it was ordered that after an interval of six days, three should be conceded to the defence. At the time ordained, Fulcinius began by accusing him that he had displayed ambition and avarice in his administration of Spain — a stale and unimportant charge — on which conviction would not harm him if he answered the new one; from which, acquittal would not save him if he were convicted of the graver crimes. After him, Servæus, Veranius, and Vitellius, with equal earnestness of effort, but Vitellius, with far superior eloquence, maintained that through hatred of Germanicus and purpose of revolution, he had by license and wrong of the allies, so debauched the common soldiers, that the worst of them bestowed on him the appellation of father of the legion; that, on the other hand, he had shown great cruelty against every one of the best, and particularly against the attendants and friends of Germanicus; that he had at length destroyed him by poison and by sorcery; that for this purpose were designed those accursed sacrificial rites and preparations of Piso and Plancina; that he had assailed the Republic by arms; and that before the criminal could be subjected to prosecution, it had been necessary first to conquer him in battle.

Ch. 14. The defence, against all charges but that of poison, was timorous and incomplete; for his military ambition, and his exposures of the Prince to the plunder of the most rapacious of his force, and his insolence to his commander, could not be denied. The charge of poisoning alone, he seems to have rejected. Indeed, his accusers scarcely in the first instance made it sufficiently probable; for they assumed the ground that at an entertainment given him by Germanicus, as Piso reclined above Germanicus, he with his own hands poisoned the meats; whereas, it seemed absurd, that, surrounded by another's servants, under the eye of so many standing near, in the very presence of Germanicus, he should have attempted such an act. Besides this improbability, the accused offered to subject his own servants to the question by torture, and demanded that those of Germanicus should be so too. For various reasons his judges were inexorable: Cæsar, for the war made upon the province; the senate, from the belief that Germanicus could not have died without unfair means. All the time, too, the cries of the people in front of the Curia were heard, exclaiming, "that their hands should not spare him if he escaped conviction by the senate." Already they had dragged the statues of Piso to the Gemonian stairs, and would have dashed them in pieces had they not been by command of the Prince, protected and restored to their places. The prisoner was therefore put upon a litter, and conveyed forth by a tribune of the Prætorian cohort — a murmur of doubt and of divided opinion running through the multitude, whether it were a guard or an executioner who attended him.

Ch. 15. Towards Plancina there was the same popular odium, but greater favor of the court; so that it was felt to be uncertain to what extremity the Prince would permit the proceedings against her to go. She herself, while Piso's prospects were yet doubtful, with an equal chance of acquittal or conviction, would promise that she would share his fortune whatever it were; and if such were the issue, would be partaker of his death. As soon, however, as through the secret intercession of Augusta she had obtained pardon, she began by degrees to separate herself from her husband, and to conduct her defence upon a distinct policy. The accused perceived that this inferred his ruin, and doubted whether he should struggle further. Urged by his sons, however, he nerved himself, and again entered the senate, and although he encountered renewed accusation, the hostile speeches of Senators, and all things adverse and stern, he was alarmed by nothing so much as to see Tiberius without pity, without anger, unmoved and close; so that no species of emotion might break forth. Having been borne again to his house, as if for the purpose of meditating his defence for the next day, he wrote a few lines, sealed them, and delivered them to his freedman. He then bathed, and bestowed the other accustomed cares upon his person. When his wife, at a late hour, left his chamber, he ordered the doors to be closed; and at daylight was found with his throat pierced through, his sword lying on the ground.

Ch. 16. I remember to have heard, from ancient men, that there was more than once seen in the hands of Piso, a little volume, which he himself did not make public; but that his friends ever persisted in repeating that it contained letters of Tiberius, and instructions against Germanicus; and that he had determined to produce it in the senate, and arraign the Prince on it if he had not been overreached by the deceitful assurances of Sejanus; and further, that he did not die by his own hand but was slain by an assassin, who was sent in for that purpose. The truth of either of these representations I may not assert; yet ought I not to conceal that they were made by old men, who were still alive down to the age of my youth. Composing his features to an expression of sorrow, Tiberius complained that odium was sought to be cast on himself by such a mode of death, and endeavored to learn, by numerous inquiries, how Piso had passed his last day and night of life. To some of these inquiries his son answered discreetly, to others less so. Tiberius took and read aloud the last letter of Piso, composed in nearly these terms:—

"Borne down by a conspiracy of enemies, and the odium of a false charge — truth and innocence no longer availing me — I call the immortal gods to witness, Cæsar, that my whole life has been marked by my fidelity towards you, and an equal piety towards your mother. I beseech you, protect my children. Cneius had no share in my fortunes, whatever they were, since his whole time was passed in the city, and Marcus urgently dissuaded me from reacquiring Syria. Oh, had I yielded to my young son — not he to his aged father! For this I the more earnestly entreat, lest he, who is innocent, shall be doomed to expiate my guilt. By my long series of loyal services, extending through five-and-forty years; by our united consular office; I, once the cherished friend of Augustus, your father — once yours also; I, who shall never ask you more — ask the safety of my unhappy son." Of Plancina, he said nothing.

Ch. 17. After listening to this, Tiberius absolved the young man from the crime of the civil war. A son, he said, could not disobey the orders of a father; nor could he himself refuse a sentiment of compassionate regard for the dignity of the house, and for the fate of Piso himself, however deserved. On behalf of Plancina, he discoursed too; but with an air as of shame and self-disgrace — pleading the prayers of his mother in her behalf. Against her, however, the secret complainings of all the best of men were increasing every moment. "Was it just," they said, "that a grandmother should favor — should hold intercourse of speech with — should snatch from the jurisdiction of the senate the murderess of her grandson? Should that which the laws exact for all Romans be denied to Germanicus? Behold a Cæsar wept by Vitellius and Veranius, and Plancina defended by the Prince and by Augusta! What hinders that she turn her poisons and all her arts of death, so felicitously tested, upon Agrippina and her children, and glut so excellent a grandmother, and glut the uncle, with the blood of a whole most unhappy house"?

Upon the whole cause two days were consumed in the *forms* of judicial trial, the Prince urging the children of Piso to save their mother. And when the prosecutor and the witnesses had summed up the accusation with their most emulous exertion of ability, and no one replied a word, compassion, rather than hate, was heightened. Aurelius Cotta, the consul, being first asked his opinion — for, upon the proposition of Cæsar, magistrates performed that function also — thus declared it; "that the name of Piso be erased from the public chronicles; that part of his estates be confiscated; that part should be bestowed on his son Cneius Piso; and that he should change his prænomen; that Marcus Piso should be unclothed of his senatorial dignity, and, with a provision of fifty thousand great sesterces, sent into exile for ten years; that Plancina should be spared to the prayers of Augusta."

Ch. 18. The severity of this judgment was in many particulars mitigated by the Emperor. Let not, he said, the name of Piso be erased from the public registers, since that of Marcus Antonius, who had borne arms against his country, and that of Julius Antonius, who had violated the house of Augustus, had been permitted to remain. Marcus Piso, too, he spared the degradation which had been advised, and gave him the whole of his father's estate. Ever, as I have often related, he was sufficiently unmoved by the temptation of wealth, and he was now the more inclined to mercy from the sense of shame that Plancina had been absolved. When, also, Valerius Messalinus proposed that a golden statue of Mars, the avenger, should be set up in the Temple of Mars, and Cæcina Severus, that an altar should be built to revenge, the Prince prohibited it, and said that for victory over a foreign foe such offerings might appropriately be dedicated; that internal evils should be covered over with a silent grief.

Messalinus had added advice that to Tiberius and Augusta, and to Antonia, Agrippina, and Drusus, should be decreed thanks for the revenging of Germanicus, and had omitted the mention of Claudius. Lucius Asprenas, in presence of the senate, inquired of Messalinus if it were prudent to pass by that name? Then, at length, it was added to this proposition.

To me, the wider the survey which I take of the events of older or more recent times, the more do the jests of human life, turning its solemn things to derision and laughter, display themselves; for, surely, all men might seem to have been destined by fame, by hope, by veneration, to the throne, rather than he whom fortune was secretly cherishing for the future Prince.

Ch. 19. A few days afterwards, Cæsar procured a decree of the senate, bestowing the office of priest upon Vitellius, Veranius, and Servæus. To Fulcinius he promised his vote for public honors; yet gave him a hint that he should hold the impetuosity of his eloquence under more restraint. And thus ended the proceedings which sought to punish the death of Germanicus. That event is a subject on which a great diversity of conjecture existed both among the actors in that time and subsequently. All things are shaded in uncertainty, since some believe and report all which they hear, others record falsely, and the original error enlarges with the course of time.

Drusus, who had lost his military command by entering the city, now retired to entitle himself to resume it, and then returned with the honors of ovation. A few days afterwards died Vipsania, his mother. She alone, of all the children of Agrippa, enjoyed the blessing of a peaceful death. Of the rest, some are known to have perished by the sword, and others are believed to have perished by poison or want.

Ch. 20. In the same year, Tacfarinas, who, during the summer before, as I have related, had been expelled from the country by Camillus, recommenced war in Africa. He began by predatory incursions, now here, now there, which his celerity of movement made it impracticable to punish. Soon he advanced to the sack and destruction of whole villages; he began to carry off large and valuable booty; and at length, not far from the river Pagida, he inclosed a Roman legion. Decrius commanded in the camp; a prompt and experienced officer; and he regarded this siege itself a disgrace. Exhorting his soldiers, therefore, to court an opportunity of battle in the open fields, he formed his line in front of the camp. In the first shock the legion gave way. With great gallantry, he threw himself in the way of his flying troops, amid a shower of arrows; he reproached the standard-bearers that a Roman soldier should show his back to a rabble of undisciplined barbarians and deserters. Wounded, his eye pierced through, he still sternly turned his face on the enemy, and continued to fight until, deserted by his soldiers, he fell, slain, upon the field.

Ch. 21. When these events became known to Apronius, who succeeded to Camillus, alarmed rather by the disgrace attached to his own troops than by the fame won by the enemy, he resorted to that extreme measure of the old times, then become almost disused, a decimation; causing every tenth man in the dishonored legion, drawn by lot, to be beaten to death. Such was the effect of this severity, that when the same force of Tacfarinas attacked the post called Thala, a single banner of Roman soldiers, not exceeding five hundred in number, repulsed and routed them. In this action a common soldier, Rufus Helvius, won the glory of saving the life of a citizen, and was presented by Apronius with chains and a spear. Cæsar added the civic crown, gently complaining, but not offended, that Apronius had not given that also, by virtue of his authority as proconsul. Discerning that his Numidians were smitten with terror, and refused to try again the hazards of attempting a siege, Tacfarinas broke up the war into sudden and dispersed attacks, retiring when pursued, and then coming back upon the enemies' rear;

and while the barbarians adhered to this policy, he kept mocking with impunity the baffled and wearied Roman army. After, however, he had directed his incursions towards places on the sea, becoming incumbered with plunder, he risked a more permanent encampment; and then Apronius Cesianus, detached by his father with a force of cavalry and auxiliary cohorts, and a selection of the fleetest troops from the legions, defeated him and drove him into the desert.

Ch. 22. During these events in Africa, Lepida, among whose ancestry, over and above the glory of Æmilian descent, were Pompey and Sylla, was accused of crime at Rome. She was accused of having feigned to have borne a child to her husband, Publius Quirinus, a rich and childless man; of adultery; of poisonings; of having consulted soothsayers concerning the house of the Prince. Manius Lepidus, her brother, conducted her defence. Publius Quirinus, by his vindictiveness, uninterrupted after he had declared his divorce, excited compassion for her, however infamous and guilty. In that trial one could with difficulty divine the great will of the Prince, so did he vary and confound all signs of anger and of clemency. First, he besought the senate not to try the treasonable ingredients of the charge at all, but presently himself drew out some of consular rank, and other witnesses, to reveal the very matter which he had seemed to wish to suppress. The servants of Lepida, who were held in military custody, he transferred to the charge of the consuls; and he would not permit them to be examined by the torture, respecting the accusations of design against his house. He excused, too, his son Drusus, the designated consul of the next year, from the duty of first declaring his opinion. This was attributed by some to kindness towards the accused; that those who should subsequently declare their opinions might be spared the necessity of assentation, and thus inferred from it a sentiment and purpose of unkindness — for why should he, they reasoned, yield the first place unless it were to be first in the work of condemnation?

Ch. 23. On the days of the games which intervened during the trial, Lepida entered the theatre attended by noble women, and there with the most passionate sorrow invoked her ancestors — invoked Pompey himself — whose monuments and whose statues rise around in view. Moved by compassion, all who beheld her melted into tears, and began to denounce Quirinus in terms most bitter and contemptuous — the cruel and detestable conduct of him to whose old age, and childlessness, and obscurity of family, had been sacrificed the destined wife of Lucius Cæsar, the destined wife of the grandson of Augustus."

Subsequently, however, crime was revealed against her by

the torture of servants; and upon the motion of Rubellius Blandus she was sentenced to prohibition of fire and water. To this motion Drusus assented; although many others had voted for one less extreme. Eventually, the indulgence was extended to Scaurus, her former husband, and to whom she had borne a daughter, that her estates should not be confiscated. When the proceedings were closed, Tiberius made it known that he had detected, by examination of the servants of Quirinus, that she had by poison sought his own life.

Ch. 24. These reiterated misfortunes of illustrious houses, — for within a brief space the Calpurnian had lost Piso, and the Æmilian, Lepida, — were alleviated by the restoration of Decius Silanus to the Julian family. Let me in few words relate his case from the beginning.

The public fortunes of Augustus were felicitous; but his domestic life was darkened by the licentiousness of his daughter and granddaughter. He banished them from the city, and punished their paramours with exile or death; for by bestowing on a crime, itself frequent, the grave denomination of dishonor to religion, and of violated majesty, of sacrilege and treason, he enabled himself to go beyond the clemency of the old law, and even of his own. The fate of others, and yet more of the history of that time, I shall relate, — if, after my immediate undertaking shall be accomplished, my life should be prolonged to other exertions. Decius Silanus, to whom I now confine myself, detected in adultery with the granddaughter of Augustus, although he was proceeded against in form no further than to be declared to have lost the friendship of Cæsar, yet well understood that this consigned him to exile. It was not until the accession of Tiberius to the empire, that, resting on the influence of Silanus, his brother, a person conspicuous for his high rank and his eloquence, he presumed to deprecate the anger of the senate and the Prince. When that brother, in open senate, came to give thanks for the successful issue of this appeal, Tiberius replied, that he, too, rejoiced at his brother's return from so long an exile, and that this might be permitted to him without departure from the fundamental jurisprudence, because he had not been expelled by a decree of the senate, or an adjudication pursuant to law. None the less, he added, I cherish against him entire all my father's sentiments of resentment; nor must he assume that his return is to frustrate in any point the will of Augustus. Ever afterwards he remained in the city, but achieved none of its honors.

Ch. 25. Subsequently to this event, a proposition was introduced to mitigate the law Papia Poppæa, which Augustus in the last year of his life had sanctioned, after the passage of the

Julian ordinances upon the subject, for the punishment of celibacy, and for replenishing the finances of the State. It had not operated to multiply marriages, or to promote the rearing of offspring. Such were the privileges of childlessness.

And now, day by day, increased the multitude of those who were brought in peril of prosecution for offences; for there was not a house which the presence of the informer did not threaten to undermine, and the community which once suffered from the frequency of crime, now suffered from the uncertainty of law.

I am admonished by this fact somewhat more deeply to consider and deduce the origin of civil justice, and the successive progress by which this infinite multitude and variety of laws has been accumulated.

Ch. 26. The most ancient of men, in whom as yet there dwelt no passion of evil, lived without disgrace and without guilt, and therefore without punishment and without restraint. Of rewards there was no need, since virtue was sought for love of itself, and desiring nothing forbidden by morality, they were debarred from nothing through fear. But when the equality of nature became destroyed, and ambition and violence took the place of moderation and the dread of dishonor, then came the epoch of tyranny. In many nations this government has continued without change. Some, in their origin, or after they grew weary of kings, declared their preference for laws. They were at first simple, as befitted the childhood of the human mind. Of these the most celebrated were those of Crete, prescribed by Minos; those of Sparta, by Lycurgus; and those more refined and in greater number, of Athens, by Solon. Ourselves Romulus had ruled with uncontrolled absolutism. After him, Numa imposed on the State the restraints of religion and a code of divine law; some further improvements of polity were made by Tullus Hostilius and Ancus Martius, but Servius Tullus was the true founder of a legal constitution which kings themselves should obey.

Ch. 27. Upon the expulsion of the Tarquins, the people of Rome contrived many regulations for the purpose of guarding liberty and consolidating an union, — both endangered by the functions of the senate.

Decemvirs were created; and they, having gathered the best laws from every source, digested them into the twelve tables, with which closes the justice and reason of our legislation; for the laws of later date, although in some instances directed against criminals, and suggested by their crimes, were oftener the fruit of violence and the strife of contending orders in the State, and had for their motive and end the attainment of prohibited honors, the expulsion of illustrious citizens, or some other kindred end or motive of evil. In this disordered age of the State figured the Gracchi and the Saturnini, inflamers of the people; and Drusus, not less enormous in his bribery, but giving in the name of the senate. That age, too, saw our allies debauched by the promises of one faction; mocked by the interference and opposition of another. Even in the Italian war, and subsequently in the civil, numerous and contradictory laws continued to be made, until Sylla the Dictator, abolishing or changing all which existed before, and adding many new, secured to the constitution and to jurisprudence an interval of repose. But it was brief. Immediately after his administration were passed the laws of Lepidus, so productive of disturbance; and a little later was restored to the tribunes their whole vast license of agitating the people at their will. And now acts began to be passed, not for the whole community, but for individual cases; and the more corrupt the State the more numerous grew the laws.

Ch. 28. Then came the age and fortunes of Cneius Pompeius. Chosen a third time consul, to cure the corruption of the time, his remedies were more terrible than the disease; he passed laws to trample on them; the institutions he had guarded by the sword, he subverted by the sword. Twenty continuous years of discord succeeded. There was neither observance of ancient custom, nor settled system of law. Great crimes were committed with impunity. The possession and display of virtues were fatal. At length Augustus, now in his sixth consulship, and firmly seated in power, abolished by a single decree all the ordinances of his triumvirate, and prescribed a body of law adapted to internal peace, and to the government of a prince and to absolutism.

Heavier fetters were now forged. Informers were called into life, and were incited by rewards to expose such as declined to acquire the privilege of parents by marriage, to the end that the people might intercept the legacies bequeathed to them, on the ground of escheat to the general parent. Once recognized by the State, they vastly transcended the functions assigned them. From the letter of the law, they penetrated to what they were pleased to call its spirit. The city, Italy, the universal Roman race everywhere, they enfolded in their grasp. The entire social and civil position of multitudes was overturned. Terror was spreading among all; when Tiberius, for the purpose of achieving a remedy, constituted a commission composed of noble persons, — five who had been consuls, five who had been prætors, with as many from the senate. Those persons, by relaxing the severer and the greater number of the exactions of the law, effected a temporary and small alleviation of the evils brought forward.

Ch. 29. About the same time the Prince commended Nero, a son of Germanicus, just then entering upon the age of youth, to the notice of the senate; and, in the phrase of petition, requested that he might be excused from passing through the official duties of vigintivirate, and might become candidate for the prætorship five years before the legal period. This sort of a request excited in them who heard it an emotion of derision. He alleged, as a precedent, that upon the petition of Augustus the same dispensation had been extended to himself and his brother. I doubt not that there were those who even then silently smiled at the idea of a petition from their master; although at that time the grandeur of the Cæsars was but just in its origin. Old custom was more vividly in view, and the relationship of step-father and step-son formed a far lighter tie than that of grandfather and grandchild. Besides granting the request of the Prince for Nero, the senate, without solicitation, added the pontificate; and on the day of his first entrance to the forum, largesses were bestowed on the multitude, who were overjoyed at beholding a son of Germanicus advanced to the class of young men. Soon the public joy was augmented by the marriage of Nero to Julia, the daughter of Drusus. But while these tidings delighted the general mind, far other sentiments were inspired by rumors that Sejanus was destined by the Prince to become the father-in-law of the son of Claudius. To the people this seemed to stain the nobility of that house, and to lift Sejanus even beyond the daring hopes which he was suspected to have conceived.

Ch. 30. At the close of that year died the celebrated persons, Lucius Volusius and Sallustius Crispus. The family of Volusius was ancient, although it had been illustrated by no honor beyond the prætorship. He raised it to consular rank; he added the self-censorial office of designating the class of knights, and he first acquired that unbounded wealth in which it flourished. Crispus Sallustius was of equestrian rank by birth; was the nephew of the sister of Caius Sallustius, the most celebrated of Roman historians; was by him adopted and named with his name. The way to highest honors was open to him; but, emulating the example of Mæcenas, he declined the senatorial dignity, yet in the reality of power rose far above many a person who could boast his consulships and his triumphs. His splendid and tasteful style of life was in strong contrast with the manners of old times, and his profuseness and gorgeousness of expenditure approached luxury; yet beneath this lay energy of character equal to the weightiest affairs, and which revealed itself with more vigor and more effect at a moment when he seemed most profoundly steeped in sleep and sloth. While, therefore, Mæcenas lived he was second, after his death first, in the confidence of Augustus and Tiberius, and he shared in the knowledge of the murder of Agrippa Posthumus. Later in life, he retained the form rather than the reality of the favor of his prince. This had happened to Mæcenas also. Such seems ever the fate of power. Rarely it lasts a lifetime,—perhaps because satiety seizes the giver or the receiver: the giver, when he has no more to bestow; the receiver, when he has nothing more to ask.

Ch. 31. The fourth consulship of Tiberius and the second of Drusus followed, memorable for the spectacle of father and son bearing office as colleagues. Germanicus, two years before, had stood in the same relation of honor; but was less a cause of joy to the Prince, and less endeared by ties of blood. In the commencement of the same year Tiberius, assigning for the cause the restoration of his health, went into Campania,—perhaps for the purpose of tasting beforehand and by gradual experience a long and permanent removal from Rome; perhaps to permit Drusus, in the absence of his father, to perform the duties of the consulship alone. In his absence a trivial matter, swelling to a serious difficulty, afforded to the young consul an accidental means of acquiring popular favor. Domitius Corbuso, formerly prætor, complained to the senate of Lucius Sylla, a noble youth, that, at the spectacle of gladiators, he had not yielded him precedence of place. . . . .

INDEX.

www.ingramcontent.com/pod-product-compliance
Lightning Source LLC
LaVergne TN
LVHW021310110826
845150LV00003B/541

* 9 7 8 1 4 2 5 5 5 8 9 9 4 *